OFFICE PROCEDURES

for Administrative Professionals

FIRST CANADIAN EDITION

Patsy Fulton-Calkins

Ph.D., CPS
Adjunct Professor, Educational Consultant
Grand Rapids, MI

Diane Blaney

M. Ed., CPS
Capilano College

NELSON / EDUCATION

NELSON / EDUCATION

Office Procedures for Administrative Professionals
First Canadian Edition

Patsy Fulton-Calkins and Diane Blaney

Vice-President,
Editorial Director:
Evelyn Veitch

Senior Acquisitions Editor:
Anthony Rezek

Executive Marketing Manager:
Kevin Smulan

Senior Developmental Editor:
Joanne Sutherland

Permissions Coordinator and
Photo Researcher:
Mary-Rose MacLachlan

Production Editor:
Tammy Scherer

Copy Editor:
Rodney Rawlings

Proofreader:
Erin Moore

Indexer:
Edwin Durbin

Senior Production Coordinator:
Kathrine Pummell

Creative Director:
Angela Cluer

Interior Design:
Sarah Battersby

Cover Design:
Brian Cartwright, Rocket Design

Cover Image:
Digital Vision/Getty Images

Compositor:
Carol Magee

Printer:
Transcontinental

Library and Archives Canada
Cataloguing in Publication

Fulton-Calkins, Patsy, 1934-
   Office procedures for administrative professionals / Patsy
Fulton-Calkins, Diane Blaney.—
1st Canadian ed.

ISBN: 0-17-641572-6

   1. Office management—
Textbooks. 2. Administrative
assistants—Handbooks, manuals,
etc. I. Blaney, Diane, 1944-
II. Title.

HF5547.F84 2004   651
C2004-906280-8

To my wonderful husband Roy for his patience,
understanding, and support in all that I do

Contents

Part 2

COMMUNICATION: SKILLS FOR A DIVERSE WORKING ENVIRONMENT   86

Preface

The administrative professional's role in the workplace today is challenging and ever-changing. Why? A major part of the answer is that we live in an age with a continuous explosion of knowledge. Advances in technology provide us with expanding communication capabilities and equipment that allow us to perform our tasks with greater speed and sophistication than in the past. Administrative professionals can produce complex reports containing graphics and tables with relative speed and efficiency. However, the explosion of knowledge, with the technological advancements it has brought, is only a partial answer to why the workplace is consistently challenging. We also live in a world that is more international in scope, with numerous organizations in Canada having worldwide operations. Additionally, the population of Canada is more diverse than ever before—diverse in race, ethnicity, gender, and age. This world demands that the Canadian administrative professional have not only technology skills but also a broad range of human relations skills (including verbal and written communication) and critical-thinking skills. To keep up with the rate of change in the Canadian workplace, the administrative professional must also commit to continual learning. This textbook will help you be better equipped to meet the demands of that world.

Text Features

To assist you in the learning process, a variety of features are included in *Office Procedures for Administrative Professionals*:

- Administrative professionals presently working in the field share their stories in the *Success Profiles* that open each of the four parts of the text. The stories are of job-related situations in which these persons have been involved and how they solved those situations. You are invited (before you look at their solutions, which come at the end of the last chapter of each part) to determine how you would solve the situations.
- *Learning Objectives*, provided at the beginning of each chapter, reveal expected outcomes from studying each chapter.
- *Self-Checks* in each chapter allow you to test your understanding of the content. Appropriate responses to some of these are included at the end of the chapter.
- *Technology, Human Relations, Health, and Communication Tips* give pointers for professional growth.
- *Key Terms* are highlighted in **boldface** within each chapter, listed at the end, and then defined in the *Glossary* at the end of the text for ease of reference.
- *Chapter Summaries* reinforce the major points in each chapter.
- *Discussion Items* give you the opportunity for further review of key topics.
- The *Critical-Thinking Activities* provide cases based on real-life situations that demand the use of critical-thinking skills.
- *Projects* help you apply the key concepts you've learned in each chapter and are directly tied to the chapter Learning Objectives. Some projects are collaborative and provide opportunities to work with classmates in developing team-building skills. Others ask you to use the Student CD-ROM or require online research.

Soft Skills

Soft skills (such as critical thinking, teamwork, interpersonal skills, and leadership) are consistently identified by organizations as critical skills that all employees must possess. Because of the importance of soft skills to the administrative professional, the related learning objectives appear in *italics* in the Learning Objectives at the start of each chapter. You will also develop a Professional Growth Plan throughout the course that focuses on soft skills.

You'll find the following *Soft Skills* boxed features in the text as follows:

Part 1: The Workplace: Succeeding in a Changing Workplace
Chapter 1 Critical-Thinking (Problem-Solving) Skills
Chapter 2 Self-Management
Chapter 3 Conflict Resolution
Chapter 4 Business Ethics

Part 2: Communication: Skills for a Diverse Working Environment
Chapter 5 Value Clarification
Chapter 6 Ethical and Legal Considerations
Chapter 7 How Creativity Works
Chapter 8 E-mail Ethics

Part 3: Office Administration: Providing Administrative Support
Chapter 9 Continual Learning
Chapter 10 Teamwork
Chapter 11 Committed to the Community
Chapter 12 Effective Decision Making
Chapter 15 Maintain a Positive Attitude

Part 4: Your Career: Planning for the Future
Chapter 16 Live Your Values
Chapter 17 The Right to Lead

Supplements

For Instructors

A comprehensive Instructor's Resource CD-ROM is available that includes

- An Examview® Computerized Test Bank, which offers the instructor the opportunity to create printed tests and choose questions in rank order
- PowerPoint® presentation software, emphasizing key concepts in each chapter
- An Instructor's Manual with teaching suggestions, additional resource suggestions, an optional student project, and responses to the discussion questions, critical-thinking activities, and projects from the text
- Electronic files for many of the forms and figures from the text that can be printed and duplicated for use in the classroom

For Students

A Student CD-ROM is packaged with each text that contains

- Additional projects and worksheets for each chapter
- A Reference Guide that serves as a review of grammar and punctuation rules

- A Business Document Formatting Guide that provides instructions and illustrations on how to correctly format memos, letters, and reports
- Electronic files for many of the sample forms from the text that can be opened in Adobe Acrobat® and printed for easy reference
- Lecture notes in PowerPoint presentation format
- An In-basket Simulation, involving realistic tasks designed to allow students to experience a real-life office situation

Website (www.officeprocedures.nelson.com)

The *Office Procedures for Administrative Professionals* website contains the following additional resources for both instructors and students:

- Relevant weblinks for each chapter
- Interactive quiz questions for each chapter
- Downloadable instructor resources including the Instructor's Manual, PowerPoint slides, and a records management simulation

The Authors

Dr. Patsy J. Fulton-Calkins' experience in the field is extensive. Her past experience in the workplace includes working as an administrative professional for large corporations for six years. Early in her career, she completed the CPS certification. Her teaching experience includes over 13 years at the university, community college, and high school levels.

In addition to her teaching experience, she has worked as an administrator in the following positions:

- Chancellor of Oakland Community College (the chief executive officer), Oakland County, Michigan
- President of Brookhaven College, Dallas, Texas
- Vice-President of Instruction at El Centro College and Cedar Valley College, Dallas, Texas
- Division Chairperson of Business and Social Science, Cedar Valley College, Dallas, Texas

Her present position includes working with Tom Monaghan Associates, Inc. as a senior consultant in institutional advancement work with clients across the United States. Additionally, she is an adjunct professor at the university level.

Her educational credentials include a B.B.A., an M.B.Ed., and a Ph.D. Honors include Outstanding Alumnus, University of North Texas; Transformational Leader in Community Colleges; Who's Who in America, Outstanding Woman in Management; Paul Harris Fellow of Rotary International; Beta Gamma Sigma, National Honorary Business Fraternity; and Piper Professor.

Diane Blaney began her career as an administrative assistant in the Music Department of the Edmonton Public School Board. From there she travelled north to Inuvik, east to Ottawa, and south to Bermuda before finally settling in Vancouver, British Columbia. In every location her administrative skills ensured that she would find challenging and rewarding employment opportunities.

After working for ten years as an administrative professional, she completed the CPS certification, and soon after began teaching at Capilano College. She has taught a variety of technology courses in the Applied Business Technology department as well as the Administrative Procedures course, a course she feels is one of the most important aspects of any administrative professional program.

In addition to her teaching experience, she has been department chair for Applied Business Technology and Coordinator of the Legal Secretarial Program, and is currently the coordinator of the Applied Business Technology Online program at Capilano College. She has been the chair of various college committees and President of the Capilano College Faculty Association, and is currently a governor representing faculty on the College Board. Her work in the community includes a term as President of an internationally renowned private recreational facility.

Diane obtained her M.Ed. in Administrative Leadership from Simon Fraser University in Vancouver, British Columbia and her Instructor's Diploma from the University of British Columbia.

Acknowledgments

Thanks to the staff at Nelson: Anthony Rezek, Senior Acquisitions Editor, Tammy Scherer, Production Editor, Rodney Rawlings, Copy Editor, Erin Moore, Proofreader, and especially to my Senior Developmental Editor, Joanne Sutherland, for all her support, for her forgiveness when I missed a deadline, and for gently keeping me on track throughout the whole process.

Thanks also go to the following reviewers, whose thoughtful comments helped shape this First Canadian Edition:

Jane Brooks, *Sheridan College*
Lynn Burton, *Seneca College*
Carolyn Clark, *Lethbridge Community College*
Patti Collins, *Kwantlen University College*
Faye Desjardins, *Saskatchewan Institute of Applied Science and Technology (SIAST)*
Cherie Hall, *Fanshawe College*
Jacqueline Hingley, *Georgian College*
Linda Lauzon, *Fanshawe College*
Eileen Matthews, *Grant MacEwan College*
Cynthia A. Nolan, *College of the North Atlantic*
Nancy Russell, *Lethbridge Community College*

PART 1

THE WORKPLACE: SUCCEEDING IN A CHANGING WORKPLACE

A Success Profile

Nerissa McNaughton
Executive Secretary and In-House Move Coordinator
The Brick Warehouse LP
Edmonton, Alberta

When I was young, I wanted to be everything from a journalist to a gymnast. With so many aspirations, I still had not settled on a career by graduation. I knew it was important to be certified in *something*, so I enrolled in the Northern Alberta Institute of Technology (NAIT) Office Administration program. Within a few weeks, I realized that I had found my calling. I know that "exciting" is not a word used to typically describe office administration, but when I saw the list of classes—such as accounting, business law, project management, and business communication—I was very impressed. Two years later, I embarked on a rewarding, satisfying, and, yes, very exciting career.

I love challenges, and this is part of why I am successful in my field. You must learn from each challenge and take away something positive. You need to constantly redefine your ideas of what success is. You have to seize opportunities, fail, get up when you fall, and be gracious when you trump someone. I have had to do all these things—sometimes on a daily basis. I have been everything from a one-woman-office receptionist to a printing-shop clerk. I have been fired; I have quit. I have spent many nights lying in bed wondering if I had set my sights too high, but each morning I had a fresh start and a goal within my reach. In February 2003, I reached a personal goal when I was hired at The Brick Warehouse LP.

Although I have held a variety of positions since graduation, I have enjoyed and appreciated each one. My experiences have taught me three things about success:

1. Training and obtaining necessary skills are fundamental regardless of job description, so I encourage you to be serious about your studies. I have relied heavily on the skills I learned at NAIT throughout my professional life.
2. Watching people helps define success. The workplace is filled with both positive and negative people—be thankful for them all. Watch employees and decide which traits you want to emulate. These people provide a spectrum of attitudes that you get to see in action.
3. Attitude is another fundamental key. It is common for a person with a more positive attitude to be hired over someone with better job skills. Additional skills can be learned, but attitude tends to be ingrained. Make sure that you are positive, open-minded, and willing to learn.

The Brick is the largest organization of its kind in Canada. Corporation headquarters, located in Edmonton, controls all operations. As an executive secretary, I assist the vice-president of the real estate division. At first, my job description was very general; it boiled down to "make his busy life easier." I employed my keyboarding, filing, and organizational skills, and when my manager saw my enthusiasm and competence, he gave me more tasks. My responsibilities have grown to the point where I now work with leases, handle landlord/tenant issues, and sit on various corporate projects, including the planning and development of Home Show II (a retail concept under way in Toronto). Currently, The Brick's corporate offices are under renovation, and I have been appointed In-House Move Coordinator.

This position was also, initially, vague. I was to be the liaison between contractors and staff, ensuring that everything would go smoothly. Soon, the position was expanded. There are over 400 people in the corporate office, and when dust is flying, hammers are pounding, and people have to pack up and move to alternative locations, tempers flare. This position was the ideal challenge! When I started at The Brick, I used what we at NAIT called "hard" skills—keyboarding, filing, producing business documents, etc. Now, I rely very heavily on "soft" skills—working with people, dealing tactfully with situations, and not getting stressed in the process.

I love my job and helping with the renovation, but I have to admit that it has its stressful moments. In the past, stress has completely overwhelmed me, to the point where I quit a job. I cannot recommend this course of action for everyone, but in that case, I encountered an extremely stressful situation and was determined not to allow it to drag me down. After making the necessary arrangements that permitted me to end the working relationship positively and on good terms with all involved, I walked away. Knowing that stress was an issue for me, I decided to deal with it. Good nutrition, exercise, sleep, relaxing, and indulging in hobbies are essential for a healthy life balance—there is nothing glorious about burning yourself out. When work gets tense, I know that a healthy mind, body, and spirit help me deal with the situation effectively.

With good job opportunities, excellent instructors at NAIT, and plenty of hard work, I have realized a major goal, but there is still much to learn. New technology and challenges come up every day, so it is vital to continually maintain my skills. For personal development, I am taking part-time classes through Athabasca University, studying art, history, literature, and other things of interest. I am also pursuing physical challenges such as belly dancing and boxing. I enjoy learning new things, and cannot wait to discover a new passion.

I feel honoured to be considered a "success" worthy of being profiled in this textbook, and I know that you too can and will be successful. Success comes in many different forms. Define and pursue it. Get the training you need. Realize that you will have to work hard. Know that disappointments and frustrations are just opportunities in disguise. Remember that your idea of success will change as your career grows, but know that you can earn and deserve it. I am cheering for you every step of the way.

Nerissa McNaughton's Case

Due to renovations at corporate headquarters, whole departments needed to be moved. Some, such as Accounting, were restricted by month-end deadlines. Many people did not want to move; others felt that packing their belongings was not their responsibility. There were also other factors to consider. Did we have enough boxes for forty people at a time to pack? How would these boxes stay organized in the move? Who would switch the phone extensions? Who would do heavy lifting? How would we meet deadlines? Where could I put people if their new spaces were not ready, but existing space was being torn down? How would I deal with complaints?

How did I handle it? Think about what you would do, then turn to the end of Chapter 4 to see my solution.

Chapter 1

Succeeding in the Work Environment

LEARNING OBJECTIVES

1. Describe the changing work environment.
2. Identify the role and responsibilities of the administrative professional.
3. Determine 21st-century traits necessary for the administrative professional.
4. *Develop critical-thinking skills.*
5. Begin the development of a Professional Growth Plan.

Will we ever live on Mars? This question is one that would not have entered the minds of our grandparents and may not have entered the minds of our parents. The possibility of such a happening was too remote to have entered their consciousness. Today such a question is not even unique, and the answer to this question is a possible "yes." With the successful landings in 2004 of the two unmanned rovers *Spirit* and *Opportunity*, we have to wonder—can mankind's first settlement on another world be far behind?

Additionally, here are several less dramatic but nevertheless amazing changes projected to have an impact on our everyday life:

- Intelligent rooms in our homes with walls that can "see" us by the use of sensors and recognize our voices, allowing us to speak our requests and see the results promptly
- The ability in an emergency to call into the air "Call an ambulance!" and get an immediate response
- Clothing and household linens made of smart fabrics that clean and press themselves, making washing machines and ironing boards oddities of the past
- Electronic image spots that display Van Goghs or any other art you dial up
- Homes you can enter and exit by using voice commands, making keys, and locks antiques
- Human gene therapy to revitalize damaged brain cells
- Vehicles that run on magnetized tracks on the highways, travelling bumper to bumper at about 300 kilometres per hour, with no real driving involved
- Onboard computers that monitor the workings of your auto and diagnose incipient or actual failures, automatically informing the shop of spare parts you need
- Aircraft that take off vertically, reducing noise and the size of airports[1]
- Smart cards that contain such information as website passwords and addresses, driver's licence information, medical insurance data, commuter passes, to name some of the possibilities[2]

Just as our world is changing dramatically, so is the workplace and workforce. These are some of the changes you are encountering if you are presently working or you will encounter as you enter the workforce:

- A workforce that is more diverse than ever before, with diversity present in ethnicities and cultures, gender, and age
- A business environment where **multinational corporations** (corporations that operate both within and outside Canada) are the norm rather than the exception
- Large corporations with **merger mania** (mergers occurring nationally and internationally at rates never heard of previously) existing throughout the world

Workplaces with **state-of-the-art technology** (the latest available), including wireless communications and voice-activated technology

- **E-commerce** (businesses that operate on the Internet) expanding rapidly
- More people engaged in **telework** (work that can be performed anywhere and at any time using technology)
- The probability of more than one career in a lifetime (unlike the previous generation for whom working at one job was the norm)

To survive and thrive in this workplace, you need to acquire the knowledge, skills, and qualities that allow you to become a valued part of the organization. A summary of which will eventually be incorporated into your résumé. Throughout this course, be aware of how these elements will eventually be presented in the résumé you will prepare when you begin your job search.

Take a moment now to reread the Learning Objectives given at the beginning of this chapter. It is very important for you to begin each chapter understanding exactly what you are expected to achieve. The Learning Objectives will help you focus your study and use your time efficiently.

The Information Age

Why is the workplace constantly changing? A major part of the answer to that question is that we live in the **information age**—a time of tremendous explosion of knowledge. In the introduction to this chapter, you were reminded of the changes that are projected in our world in the next few years, changes that our grandparents never imagined. Driving these changes is the technology that is an integral part of this information age.

Consider for a moment the tremendous changes that have taken place in the workplace in a few short years. The microcomputer did not exist; the mainframe computer performed all computer applications. The telephone was the standard piece of telecommunications equipment. The conference call was one of the most sophisticated techniques available when communicating with several people. Now workers use computers, voice mail, e-mail, fax machines, and printers/copiers. Cell phones now include text messaging and are used by many people; instant communication with the workplace and our homes is important. **Personal digital assistants (PDAs)** (small handheld computers)

allow us to make frequent changes and additions to our calendar from any location, pick up our e-mail, store our phone numbers, download information from the Web, check our stock portfolios, and perform a number of other functions. People may work from their homes or other locations outside the traditional workplace in a telework environment.

When you add to these technological changes the additional trends such as an increasingly diverse population and the globalization of our economy, you begin to understand why we live in a world of constant change.

A Diverse Labour Force

In the decade immediately preceding the last Canadian census in 2001, the number of people in the Canadian labour force had increased by 1 million or approximately 9.5 percent, most of this increase occurring between 1996 and 2001.[3] This workforce is becoming increasingly diverse, with minorities and immigrants constituting a larger share of the workforce than they have in the past. By the year 2010 it is predicted that over 1.75 million immigrants will have arrived in Canada. This increased diversity will challenge us to find better ways to integrate these newcomers and provide opportunities for them to work to their potential.[4]

Women in the Workforce

More women are in the workforce today than in the past, and that number is projected to grow. During the period 1991 to 2001, the number of women in the workforce grew at twice the pace of that for men, increasing 13.8 percent to 7.3 million while the number of men increased by only 6.0 percent to 8.3 million.[5] Women, both single and married, continue to enter the workforce in greater numbers than in the past. Women who have children are returning to the workforce today while their children are still preschool age. This is particularly true for families maintained by single women, a group that is growing significantly. Women accounted for fully two-thirds, or 884 400, of the overall 1.3 million gain in the labour force during the 1990s. As a result, their share of the workforce increased to 46.7 percent.[6] A recent survey of 700 working men and women found the number one career-related concern for employees of the changing workplace is the ability to balance work and family demands.[7]

Comstock Images

Forty-seven percent of today's workforce are women.

Gender Roles in the Workplace

More than ever, women are assuming positions of authority and responsibility, and positions traditionally filled exclusively by men are becoming more open to women. For example, the assumption that only males would hold supervisory positions is no longer valid as more and more females are taking on such positions. As women assume higher-level functions, we must examine our preconceptions about the way both men and women react in the workforce. One has been that women are more emotional than men. Can we say this is categorically true? No, we cannot. People with different backgrounds and from different cultures react differently to situations, but it is not because they are male or female. The socialization process in various cultures often encourages men and women to develop different traits. For example, if you are from North America and are female, you may have been encouraged to express your feelings openly, while males may have been taught to keep their feelings to themselves.

Notice that "may have" is used in both sentences here. We cannot say that all females born in North America have been socialized in this manner; neither can we say that all males have been. The point of this entire section is to remind you that we cannot **stereotype** (hold a perception or an image of people or things that may be favourable or unfavourable) individuals. We cannot assume that individuals have certain characteristics because of their gender. Your role in the workplace is to be aware that stereotyping can occur and not to let your attitudes or decisions be based on these stereotypes. *Your focus must be on understanding and accepting differences.*

Senior Workers

An aging workforce is not unique to Canada. The number of workers 45 and older is expected to increase due to the aging baby-boom generation. As medical technology continues to make advances that allow people to live longer, we can expect people to stay in the workforce beyond the traditional retirement age of 65. In fact, "boomers," those aged 37 to 55 in 2001, made up 47 percent of the workforce. By 2010 half of them will be 55 or over, and 18 percent of them will be over the age of 60.[8] British Columbia's Laurier Institution states in a recent report that by the year 2010 the working-age population (15 years and over) will have increased by 13.3 percent with the number of people between the age of 15 and 29 increasing by only 5 percent. As a result, by the year 2010 there will be more older workers than young working-age people in the labour force.[9] A similar report by the U.S. Committee for Economic Development shows that in 1950 there were five people working for every person over 65 and retired. Today there are only three workers for every retiree, and in 30 years it is projected that there will be approximately two workers for every person over 65.[10] Such demographic changes in Canada as well will leave businesses scrambling to find workers unless traditional attitudes about retirement change. It will therefore be important for older workers to stay in the workforce.

Thus, you will probably work with people aged 18 to well over 60. Certainly, each generation of our population grows up with differing national and local influences in their lives. For example, the generation of Americans and Canadians who served in World War II are now in their mid-80s. Writers have characterized them as a generation that was extremely patriotic and pragmatic, putting personal goals aside in order to serve the needs of the nation. That generation views the world through a very different lens than people who have never served in a war. Consider yet another example of differences. Those in their teens today have grown up in an age of technology. They are the digital generation. They have probably played video games all their lives; technology has become a part of their daily existence. The Internet is not a mystery, but a way of researching, shopping, sending messages, chatting with people around the world, and exchanging digital photographs. Whereas people in their 50s had to acquire technology skills as adults; these skills were not something they mastered as young children or teenagers.

...hese age differences in the workplace mean that ...may view the world from different perspectives. In ...rder to work together successfully, we have to listen ...closely to each other and tolerate each other's views. Our task is to accept the individual for whom he or she is.

Cultural Diversity

Canada is a nation of immigrants—one that has welcomed and accepted people from countries all over the world. And it is becoming more and more diverse. Prior to the 1970s the bulk of Canada's immigrants came from Europe. More recently, however, the majority of immigrants have come from Asia, the Caribbean region, and Central/South America.[11] At work you will deal with people who are very diverse ethnically. In fact, if you are now working in Ontario or British Columbia, you are probably already experiencing this diverse workforce.

Multiculturalism by definition means "relating to or including several cultures." **Culture** is defined as "the ideas, customs, values, skills, and arts of a specific group of people." As you work in this diverse workplace, you need to be aware of and sensitive to the various cultural differences and backgrounds. You must understand that individuals, because of their different backgrounds, may view situations differently than you do. Your openness to different ideas and perspectives is essential. It may not always be easy to remain open to differences, but the results will be well worth the effort. Only through awareness, understanding, and acceptance of different cultures can we expect to work in a harmonious, productive business world.

Communication Tip

Canada is composed of a mosaic of different cultures, races, and ethnicities. Our openness to each other will help build a more harmonious world.

Increased Education

Due to our ever-increasing technological world, the level of education required for jobs is higher than in the past. Numerous employers require an associate degree, while others require a bachelor's degree. Education is essential in getting a job, and ongoing education is a must in keeping a job.

This education may take a formal route through attendance at a technical/community college or a university. If this is the option you choose, it does not mean you must quit your job to return to school. Many universities and colleges across Canada offer degree and other programs in a distance education format. Courses are delivered via the Internet and students have the flexibility to plan an individual study schedule based on personal needs and availability. The University of Athabasca in northern Alberta has an extensive list of graduate certificate, associate degree and degree programs available to students anywhere in Canada. Check out their website at www.athabascau.ca to see the variety of opportunities available. Additionally, colleges and universities across Canada also offer many onsite or face-to-face programs of study available on a part-time basis where classes are held in the evenings and/or weekends.

Although a formal education may be necessary, informal education through reading, attending seminars and conferences, and being active in professional organizations is essential for maintaining and improving the knowledge and skills needed as work responsibilities change.

Learning is a lifelong process. In addition to formal and informal learning, we learn through experience and through the mistakes we make along the way. Lifelong learning is necessary for all individuals who expect to remain productive citizens of the world.

A Changing Work Environment

Our work environment is constantly changing in numerous ways. Increasingly, there is a globalization of our economy. Mergers, both national and international, are commonplace today. Telework is growing, with the expectation that it will continue to grow rapidly in the future. Companies are putting more emphasis on the use of teams to deliver quality products and services. The traditional workweek is changing, and temporary employees are more and more becoming part of the workforce environment.

Globalization of the Economy

You merely have to pick up a newspaper, read a business magazine, or listen to the news on television to see and hear the many references to our global economy. If you follow the stock market, you hear references to downturns and upturns in the market in Europe and Asia and the interrelatedness of the markets to the North American market. Go into a local electronic store and you notice the number of products manufactured in Asia. Look at the labels on your clothes and shoes, and you become aware of the number of articles that are made outside the country. Observe the cars we drive and you will notice they are made by international firms. We also have a huge number of foreign investors in Canada. In fact, when the stock market takes a downward turn, you hear financial experts expressing concern that foreign investors may take their money out of the country, impacting the stock market even more. Virtually everyone is affected by the rapid globalization of the world economy. It is estimated that 73 million people in today's global workforce work for foreign owners. This continued movement toward a global workforce merely increases the need to not only understand but also effectively handle cultural differences in the workforce.

Merger Mania

Although corporate mergers are not new, they have grown enormously since the late 1970s. These mergers are both national and international. One of the large international mergers was Chrysler (one of the big three of the U.S. automobile industry) with Daimler-Benz in 1998. In early 2001, America Online merged with Time Warner (a $165-billion transaction) for the largest merger in the United States to that point. The combined valuation of the two companies at the time of the merger was approximately $290 billion. All indications are that these kinds of mergers will continue in the foreseeable future. Many industries, both national and international, remain highly fragmented. It is anticipated that the increasing pressure to globalize markets will result in increased multinational mergers and larger and larger multinational corporations. These international mergers demand an in-depth understanding of global issues and cultures.

Quality Focus

Whether the organization is national or international, its effectiveness and long life depends on the production of a quality product or service. Workforce teams have become an important part of producing quality work based on the concepts of Dr. W. Edwards Deming, an American statistician who developed the quality concept. He first introduced his ideas to businesses in the United States but failed to receive support. In the 1950s, he took them to Japan, where industrialists received him and his ideas enthusiastically. Significant productivity results began to emerge in Japanese industries. In fact, Japan began to surpass the United States and Canada in certain areas of production, for example technology and cars. As a result, North American businesses began to pay attention to the processes being used in Japan and began to apply

Deming's principles in their firms. Deming's concepts, as valid today as the day they were written, stressed the principle of continued improvement through **total quality management (TQM)**. This approach is also referred to as **continuous quality improvement (CQI)**. Deming's 14 principles are listed in Figure 1-1 on page 10.

How does TQM affect the administrative professional? How does it change your work? Here are some possibilities. You may find that you are

- More involved in decisions that affect the direction of the organization
- Part of a workforce team (perhaps even leading a team) that is responsible for improving a service or product
- Expected to be a productive member of a team, making unique contributions that assist the company in improving the quality of its goods and services
- More involved in helping to solve the problems of the organization

Downsizing

Downsizing, reducing the number of full-time employees in an organization, has become a large corporate movement. You merely have to be aware of newspaper headlines to notice this trend. Local newspapers carry stories about the downsizing of the area's corporations, and *The Globe and Mail*® or the *National Post*® carry stories reflecting the national movement. Many major companies (such as General Motors®, Xerox®, and IBM®) have downsized their companies in the past few years. There are two major reasons for downsizing—streamlining an organization so that it is more manageable and cutting **overhead costs** (salary and benefit costs). An employee can no longer assume that an organization is committed to providing lifetime employment.

Outsourcing

Outsourcing, getting an outside company or a consultant to take over the performance of a part of an organization's business or to complete a project, is a cost-cutting measure used extensively today. For example, an outside computer firm might be hired to perform the computer operations of a company. This approach can often save the organization the money spent in salaries and employee benefits such as health insurance and retirement options.

A number of organizations use temporary agencies, which supply the business with various types of workers, including accounting assistants, administrative

Figure 1-1

PRINCIPLES FOR AMERICAN MANAGEMENT

W. Edwards Deming

1. Create constancy of purpose toward improvement of product and service, with the aim to become competitive and to stay in business and to provide jobs.

2. Adopt a new philosophy. We are in a new economic age. Western management must awaken to the challenge, must learn their responsibilities and take on leadership for change.

3. Cease dependence on inspection to achieve quality. Eliminate a need for inspection on a mass basis by building quality into the product in the first place.

4. End the practice of awarding business on the basis of price tag. Instead minimize the total cost. Move toward a single supplier for any one item, on a long term relationship of loyalty and trust.

5. Improve constantly and forever the system of production and service, to improve quality and productivity, and thus constantly decrease costs.

6. Institute training on the job.

7. Institute leadership. The aim of leadership should be to help people and machines and gadgets to do a better job. Leadership of management is in need of overhaul, as well as leadership of production workers.

8. Drive out fear so that everyone may work effectively for the company.

9. Break down barriers between departments. People in research, design, sales, and production must work as a team, to foresee problems of production and use that may be encountered with the product or service.

10. Eliminate slogans, exhortations, and targets for the workforce, asking for zero defects and new levels of productivity.

11. Eliminate work standards on the factory floor. Substitute leadership. Eliminate management by objective. Eliminate management by numbers, numerical goals, substitute leadership.

12. Remove barriers that rob the hourly worker of his pride of workmanship. The responsibility of the supervisor must be changed from sheer numbers to quality. Remove barriers that rob people in management and engineering of their right to pride of workmanship. This means, among other things, abolishment of the annual or merit rating and of management by objective, management by numbers.

13. Institute a vigorous program of education and self-improvement.

14. Put everyone in the company to work to accomplish the transformation. The transformation is everyone's job.

Source: Excerpted from W. Edwards Deming, *Out of the Crisis* (Massachusetts: Massachusetts Institute of Technology, 1993).

assistants, and human resources assistants. Statistics show that twice as many temporary workers are employed by organizations today as in the past.

Telework

Today many workers have traded in the traditional work environment for telework, work that can be performed at any place and at any time using technology. There were approximately 137 million teleworkers worldwide in the year 2003.[12] The telecommuting-to-work lifestyle appears to be here to stay.

The concept started several years ago, and was known as **telecommuting**—working from home or another established location via computer hookup. Today, work can be performed using wireless technology or cell phones, fax machines, modems, cable, voice mail, e-mail, laptop and handheld computers, and so on. Job interviews can even be performed through telecommuting centres, with the interviewer being in, say, Australia and the interviewee in Newfoundland. Today "telework" is the word most frequently used. It is a broad term that means using telecommunications to work from a home office, a client's office, or a multitude of other locations. "Telecommuting" today refers to those individuals who are full- or part-time employees of an organization and work from home for part or all of the workweek. Also, **remote employment** (any working arrangement in which the worker performs a significant portion of work at some fixed location other than the traditional workplace) and

> ### Technology Tip
>
> To keep current on telework trends, browse the Web for recent information and read periodicals such as *PC Magazine* and *Home Office Computing*.

the **virtual office** (the operational domain of any organization that includes remote workers) are terms used in describing the concept of work done through technology in which an individual is physically present in one location and virtually present in another. You will learn more about telework in Chapter 2.

Corbis/Magma Photo

Telework can be performed from virtually anywhere at any time using technology.

The Workweek

As you have already learned, the workplace may be the traditional office, the home office, or any of a number of other locations. Just as the workplace has changed, so has the workday, which may either be 9-to-5 or involve flexible hours. In addition to the flexible workday, the workweek may be compressed, may involve flextime, or may involve job sharing with another individual.

With a **compressed workweek,** employees work the usual number of hours (35 to 40); however, the hours are compressed into four days. For example, a 35-hour week consists of three days of nine hours each and a fourth day of eight hours.

Another departure from the workday is the **flextime** approach (the staggering of working hours to enable an employee to work the full quota of time but at periods defined by the company and the individual). Flextime helps to reduce traffic congestion at the traditional peak hours and allows employees needed flexibility in their schedules.

Still another departure from the traditional workday is **job sharing**. Under this arrangement, two part-time employees perform a job that otherwise would be held by one full-time employee. Such a plan may be suitable for a mother or father with small children or workers who want to ease into retirement.

The Administrative Professional's Role and Responsibilities

With the availability of technology and the emphasis on greater efficiency and productivity through **flattened organizational structures** (fewer management levels than the traditional structures of the past) and teams, administrative professionals of today and tomorrow will find that their role is continually shifting. With this shifting role generally comes greater responsibility.

The Shifting Role

For years the administrative professional's title was confined to *secretary, receptionist,* and such specialized titles as *legal* and *medical secretaries.* Although the titles mentioned here are still used to a limited extent, the emerging titles today reflect the shifting role of the administrative professional. A few of these titles are *administrative assistant, executive assistant, marketing assistant, payroll assistant, human resources assistant,* and *office manager.* The shifting role is reflected in the duties of the administrative professional, which include:

- Researching and preparing reports (using the Web as well as traditional research methods) complete with graphics and spreadsheets
- Assisting with the planning and direction of the company by leading TQM teams and serving on organizational teams
- Supervising support staff
- Administering computer networks

Keith Brofsky/Photodisc Green/Photodisc Collection

The administrative professional today may have the responsibility of managing a website.

...ping to upgrade and recommend office software
...oviding computer and software training
Maintaining websites
• Working with outsourcing companies such as accounting and staffing firms

Although job roles and responsibilities differ between the various positions, certain skills and knowledge sets are essential in all administrative professional roles; these will be emphasized throughout this course. The term **administrative professional** will be used consistently throughout this text to denote the workplace support person.

Job Responsibilities

As was mentioned in the previous section, the job responsibilities of the administrative professional have increased in complexity and accountability as compared to several years ago. With technology, many executives now answer their own voice mail and e-mail, key certain correspondence directly on the computer, and handle much of their own scheduling using electronic calendars provided with computer software. This change frees him

or her to get more involved in creating correspondence and become a valued member of the office team.

Job responsibilities of the administrative professional vary depending on educational level, work experience, and even employee initiative. Figure 1-2 lists some of the basic responsibilities that are fairly generic to administrative professional positions.

21st-Century Skills and Qualities

If the administrative professional is to succeed in a world of technology and rapid change, he or she needs certain skills and qualities. You should begin now to develop these skills and qualities.

Employability Skills

In 2000, the Conference Board of Canada identified a number of critical skills that are needed in the workplace

■ Figure 1-2

BASIC JOB RESPONSIBILITIES OF THE ADMINISTRATIVE PROFESSIONAL

- Composing and keying various types of correspondence, including letters, memorandums, and reports
- Researching report information within the defined parameters set by the employer
- Participating in quality teams, with the more experienced administrative professional serving as team leader
- Administering computer networks
- Helping to upgrade and recommend office software
- Providing computer and software training
- Managing websites
- Working with outsourcing companies such as accounting and staff firms
- Solving day-to-day problems within the role of the administrative professional
- Communicating both verbally and in writing with individuals both within and outside the office
- Scheduling appointments

- Setting up meetings and conferences
- Organizing time and work
- Maintaining correspondence and records in both electronic and manual files
- Making travel arrangements for the executive
- Using telecommunications technology, including the telephone, voice mail, and fax
- Interviewing and making recommendations on the employment of office support personnel
- Supervising office support personnel
- Taking and transcribing minutes from various types of meetings
- Making recommendations on equipment purchases
- Purchasing office supplies
- Handling incoming and outgoing mail
- Processing paperwork that involves mathematical calculations (expense reports, budgets, invoices, purchase orders, petty cash, and so on)

whether you work on your own or as part of a team. These skills are grouped into three broad categories:

- *Fundamental skills.* The skills needed as a base for further development. They include communication, information management, numeracy, and problem-solving (critical thinking) skills.
- *Personal management skills.* The personal skills, attitudes, and behaviours that drive one's potential for growth. They include time, stress and workload management, and interpersonal skills.
- *Teamwork skills.* The skills and attributes needed to contribute productively. They include leadership skills and the ability to work with others.

The next section covers these skills in detail.

Fundamental Skills

Communication Skills

Verbal Communication. If you are to be an effective verbal communicator, you must be able to express yourself accurately, concisely, and tactfully. Additionally, you must be a good listener. Although most of us think we spend an inordinate amount of time listening, research studies show that we only listen with 25 to 50 percent efficiency. In other words, 50 to 75 percent of what we hear is never processed. Moreover, even when we do process what we hear, we may not grasp the full implications of what has been said. As you have already discovered, the office continues to become more diverse in the ethnicity, gender, and age of the workforce. This diversity demands your constant improvement in verbal communication so you can effectively interact with co-workers. You will learn more about verbal communication in Chapter 5.

Written Communication. Administrative professionals spend most of their time communicating with others, often in written form through letters, memorandums, reports, e-mail, and faxes. This requires mastery of the English language, an ability to apply the rules of grammar, punctuation, and capitalization. The administrative professional is often expected to be the English expert who corrects any grammatical errors the employer may make.

Software packages today identify incorrectly spelled words and grammar errors as you are keying, by underscoring the words and phrases in red for spelling errors and green for grammar errors. Although this function is extremely helpful, you should recheck the entire document using the spell and grammar check program once you have finished keying.

The spell checker does have limitations. For example, if you key *off* when you actually mean *of,* the spell checker will not catch the error, because the word *of* does exist and it is not spelled incorrectly. This means that you must be an extremely good proofreader even with the tools that are provided on your computer software. Take the time to proofread thoroughly and carefully each document you produce.

Also included in your software package "tools" are readability statistics that give you the following information on the document you have keyed:

- Number of paragraphs
- Sentences per paragraph
- Words per sentence
- Readability statistics, including passive sentences and the Flesch-Kincaid readability level of the document

These statistics are helpful in knowing how easy or difficult your document will be to read. For a general audience, you usually need to write at the 8th-to-10th-grade level. However, if you are writing technical material for a highly educated audience, you may write at the 12th-grade level or above. You will learn more about written communication skills in Chapter 6.

Verbal Presentation Skills. Administrative professionals today serve on project teams and may even chair a team. Project teams often make presentations of their findings and recommendations to peer groups or to executives within the workplace. You may also have occasion to speak at professional organizations to which you belong. If your presentations are to be successful, you must develop verbal presentation skills. Chapter 7 will help you develop these skills.

Information Management

Success today demands that you be technologically competent. You must be

- Proficient on a computer
- Knowledgeable about the most current software packages, including word processing, spreadsheets, databases, and graphics, presentation, and accounting software

> **Communication Tip**
>
> Always proofread all documents you key using your spell and grammar check program.

> **Human Relations Tip**
>
> Commit to learning something new every day. Constantly set new goals for yourself.

Soft Skills: Critical-Thinking (Problem-Solving) Skills

Critical thinking can be defined as "a unique kind of purposeful thinking in which the thinker systematically chooses conscious and deliberate inquiry." *Critical* comes from the Greek word **krinein**, which means "to separate, to choose." When we think critically about a subject, we try to see it from all sides before coming to a conclusion. Critical thinking requires us to see things from perspectives other than our own and to consider the possible consequences of the positions we take. Critical thinking is considered a **soft skill** (a business-related nontechnical skill). Other soft skills you have been introduced to in this section are verbal communication, human relations, and time, stress, and organizational management skills. You will continue to learn about soft skills in other chapters of this book.

Although these skills are known as soft skills because they are nontechnical, do not make the mistake of assuming they are nonessential. In fact, job studies show that people are fired more because of their lack of understanding of soft skills and their inability to produce on soft skills than their lack of ability to produce in the technical area. Just as you must constantly learn new technical skills due to changes in technology, so must you continue to improve your soft skills. Commit yourself now to improving your soft skills in this course and continuing to work on them throughout your career.

Soft skills will be emphasized throughout this course. In this book they are highlighted in two ways. In the Learning Objectives at the beginning of a chapter, if a soft skill is included, it will be italicized. Did you notice that "Develop critical-thinking skills" is italicized in the Learning Objectives for this chapter? Also, within that chapter, the soft skill will be found in a feature box, to remind you of the importance of such skills and the need to develop them.

If you are to succeed in the complex world of the 21st century, you must be able to think critically about the day-to-day decisions you make in the workplace. The Critical-Thinking Activities and the Projects here require that you demonstrate your continual growth in critical thinking. At the end of each chapter, a workplace situation is given in the Critical-Thinking Activity feature. You will be asked to critically analyze an activity and determine how it should be handled.

To help you understand more about how critical thinking is approached, read the list of questions in Figure 1-3. You should ask yourself these questions when you are attempting to critically analyze an issue.

- Competent in using telecommunications equipment
- Competent in using printers/copiers
- Willing to continually learn new workforce technology

Chapters 8, 9, and 10 will help you continue to develop these important skills.

Numeracy and Problem-Solving

Numeracy skills can be defined as the ability to decide what needs to be measured or calculated, to observe and record data using appropriate methods, tools, and technology, and to make estimates and verify calculations. These skills are important not only in our working but also in our personal lives. Chapter 11 will introduce you to these skills.

Personal Management Skills

Time, Stress, and Workload. As an efficient administrative professional, you must be able to organize your time, your workload, and your stress. You must be able to establish priorities, determining what needs to be done first. You must organize your workstation and files, whether they are paper or electronic. You must

■ **Figure 1-3**

CRITICAL-THINKING QUESTIONS

- What is the purpose of my thinking?
- What problem or question am I trying to answer?
- What facts do I need to address this problem or question?
- How do I interpret the facts or information I receive?
- What conclusions can I make from the information I received?
- Are my conclusions defensible?
- Have I dealt with the complexity of the situation?
- Have I avoided thinking in simple stereotypes?
- What will be the consequences if I put my conclusions into practice?

organize your time so your work flows smoothly and tasks are finished as needed. Chapter 3 will help you understand more about these important skills and give you a chance to practise them.

Interpersonal Skills. For years, surveys have shown that more employees lose their jobs due to poor interpersonal skills than poor technology skills. As an administrative professional, you come into contact with a number of people. Within the company, you work with co-workers, your immediate supervisor, and other executives. Contacts outside the company include customers and other visitors to your office, all with different backgrounds and experiences. If you are to be effective, you need to understand and accept them and be able to work with them. Interpersonal skills are like most of our other skills. We must constantly develop and improve these skills if we are to grow in our abilities.

Take the interpersonal skills Self-Check presented here and compare your answers to the suggested responses at the end of this chapter. Where do you need to improve? Commit now to improving these areas during this course. You will have an opportunity to learn more about the importance of interpersonal skills and to continue to develop your skills throughout this course.

Teamwork Skills

You have learned in this chapter that organizations are using teams more and more in producing work. The word **team** can be traced back to the Indo-European word *deuk*, meaning "to pull"; and obviously, if teams are to be successful, individual team members must "pull together." Successful teams in the work environment include groups of people who need each other to accomplish a given task. Teamwork skills are very similar to interpersonal skills in that they demand that you understand, accept, and respect the differences among your team members. Teamwork also demands that you

- Behave courteously to all team members
- Build strong relationships with your team members so the team's goals can be accomplished
- Learn collectively with your team; start with self-knowledge and self-mastery, but then look outward to develop knowledge and alignment with your team members
- Take responsibility for producing high-quality work as an individual team member and encouraging a high-quality team project

Leadership skills are developed over time. They are not something that we have at birth. You begin to develop your leadership skills by seeking out and/or accepting leadership opportunities. For example, accepting the chairperson position of a committee helps you develop leadership skills. Leadership skills do not necessarily come only with advancement in your job; they can also be acquired informally, through other activities in which you participate. Accepting an office in one of your college organizations or in a professional organization to which you belong helps you develop leadership skills. The essential strategy for you to remember is to look for leadership opportunities and take advantage of each one. As you pursue and are granted certain leadership opportunities, learn from each one. Evaluate yourself or ask a close friend to evaluate your performance. What mistakes did you make and how can you correct them?

As you are promoted to higher-level positions, you may also have the responsibility of supervising one or more employees. Being an effective supervisor, able to inspire people to produce at their maximum, demands that you understand and apply effective leadership and management principles. Chapter 17 will help you learn and apply these skills.

SELF-CHECK ✔

Respond to the following comments with a yes or no answer.

1. I understand that differences exist in culture, race, and ethnicity.
   Yes ☑ **No** ☐

2. I respect others' differences in culture, race, and ethnicity.
   Yes ☑ **No** ☐

3. I expect all individuals to react to situations just as I do.
   Yes ☐ **No** ☑

4. I listen carefully when others are talking.
   Yes ☐ **No** ☑ — *WORK ON*

5. I ignore body language when others are talking.
   Yes ☐ **No** ☑

6. I am conscious of the words I use in my written communications.
   Yes ☑ **No** ☐

7. I avoid dealing with conflict.
   Yes ☑ **No** ☐ — *WORK ON*

8. I evaluate individuals when they are talking to me.
   Yes ☑ **No** ☐ — *WORK ON*

9. I trust people who are older than I am.
   Yes ☐ **No** ☑

10. Men are better supervisors than women.
    Yes ☐ **No** ☑

Success Qualities

In addition to the skills that have been identified, certain qualities are essential for the success of the administrative professional: openness to change, dependability, confidentiality, integrity/honesty, initiative/motivation, and flexibility/adaptability.

Openness to Change

Since change will continue to play such an important role in the workplace, you must learn to cope with it—even embrace it. Embracing change means accepting and preparing for change and being creative and flexible. Try to predict the changes you will face, and prepare yourself for them. For example, since you know technology will continue to play an important role in the workplace, keep current on the latest technological changes that might impact your job environment.

Be creative when dealing with change. **Creativity** is the ability to approach existing ideas or things in new ways. When a change occurs, you can usually connect that change to some already-existing idea or way of doing something. Review the steps listed in Figure 1-4 to help you understand how to deal with change.

Dependability

Dependability means being trustworthy. It means being at work on time if you are working at an established location. If you are engaged in telework, it means being productive in performing your job. Dependability is the

■ Figure 1-4

DEALING WITH CHANGE

To deal effectively with change,

- Understand why change is necessary. Determine what circumstances have occurred that have necessitated change.
- Determine what objectives will be achieved by the changes proposed.
- Establish guidelines for achieving those objectives.
- Determine the benefits or rewards that will occur as a result of the change.
- Once the change has occurred, evaluate the effectiveness of the change and your effectiveness in working through the change.

willingness to put in additional time on important assignments. It also means doing what you say you will do, and when you say you will do it.

Confidentiality

As an administrative professional, you have access to information that is extremely confidential. For example, if you are working in the personnel department, you have access to information about employees—their work history, performance evaluations, salaries, ages, and so on. If you work for a criminal attorney, you may have access to information about a client's case. If you work for an M.D., you may have access to patients' files containing highly personal and confidential information about health issues. Your employer may occasionally talk with you about information that is highly confidential—perhaps a pending merger with another company. You may also overhear confidential conversations between executives. You must always maintain the **confidentiality** (secrecy) of the information received or the confidences shared. To let any confidential information leak outside your office may cause irreparable damage to your employer, to others within your organization, to customers, and to your organization. In fact, many firms will actually require employees to sign a confidentiality agreement. In so doing, they highlight the importance of this aspect of the job to new employees and there is less likelihood they might inadvertently breach confidentiality requirements.

Integrity/Honesty

Integrity is defined as "the adherence to a code of behaviour." In the workplace environment, the code of behaviour means in part that you must be honest. It means you do not take equipment or supplies that belong to the company for your personal use. It means you spend your time on the job performing your job duties—not making and receiving personal phone calls or writing personal e-mails. It means you uphold high standards of ethical behaviour. You do not engage in activities in which your morals or values may be questioned.

Initiative/Motivation

Initiative is defined as "the ability to begin and follow through on a plan or task." Initiative is taking the tasks you are given and completing them in an appropriate manner. It means having the ability to set appropriate work goals for yourself. The most highly valued administrative professional has the ability to analyze a task, establish priorities, and see the work through to completion. The professional takes the initiative to make suggestions to the employer about needed changes or revisions and is truly worth his or her weight in gold.

Motivation is closely related to initiative. Motivation means that someone is provided with an incentive to act—a move to action. In taking the initiative to begin a task, you may be motivated **extrinsically** (from outside) or **intrinsically** (from within). For example, you may be motivated to perform a task because it provides a monetary reward for you or external recognition from your supervisor. Additionally, you may be motivated to perform a task because you are committed to learning and growing. You understand that each task you perform provides you the opportunity to learn something new.

Flexibility/Adaptability

Flexibility is being responsive to change. **Adaptability** is being capable of adjusting. As you can readily determine, the two terms are closely related. In our fast-paced global and technology-driven world, we must respond and adjust to the changes that are constantly occurring not only in our work world but also in our personal life. You learned earlier in this chapter about the importance of being able to work with a diverse workforce. You also learned that mergers, downsizing, outsourcing, and telework can and often do make our work environment very different from that of the past. All these changes demand your flexibility and adaptability.

A Professional Image

The administrative professional with a professional image constantly presents to the public the essential skills and success qualities discussed in the previous sections. In addition, he or she must present a positive personal appearance, dressing in appropriate business attire and being well groomed. The administrative professional pays attention to hairstyle, personal hygiene, appropriate jewellery and accessories, physical condition, good posture, and proper eating habits. Depending on the office, appropriate business attire may include a suit and tie for males and a suit or dress for females. Some workplaces may be more relaxed, allowing shirts without a tie for males and skirts or slacks and blouses or sweaters for females. A number of workplaces have a day once a month or even once a week when casual dress is appropriate, even if the remaining days are considered standard business attire. Some organizations allow employees to dress in business casual on a daily basis. Many organizations are

Photodisc Blue/Photodisc Collection

The administrative professional dresses in appropriate business attire and is always well groomed.

becoming more casual in their dress considerations than in the past. If you are uncertain about the appropriate style in your organization, notice how respected co-workers dress and generally follow their lead.

A professional image is more than dressing appropriately, however. A positive personal appearance without the necessary skills and qualities is meaningless. If the administrative professional expects to succeed, he or she must combine an appropriate personal appearance with the necessary skills and qualities. A professional image is a combination of all of these areas.

Professional Growth

In our constantly changing world, you must be willing to continue your professional growth, for example by

- Attending classes at a college or university (either on site or online)
- Attending seminars and workshops provided by your company or outside firms
- Reading business periodicals
- Participating in professional organizations
- Volunteering your time and expertise to organizations in your community

Periodicals

Numerous periodicals are available with articles to assist you in enhancing your knowledge and skills. Several are listed in Figure 1-5 on page 18. Begin now to become familiar with them by reading selected articles. Visit your school or local library to see which ones on this list are available.

IAAP

■ Figure 1-5

PROFESSIONAL PERIODICALS

OfficePro (published by International Association of Administrative Professionals)

The Information Management Journal (published by the Association of Records Managers and Administrators)

Business Week

Fortune

Office Ours (published by the Association of Professional Office Managers)

Time

The Globe and Mail (a newspaper)

PC Magazine

PC World

Home Office Computing

Professional Organizations

Here are several professional organizations that provide growth opportunities for the administrative professional:

- *IAAP (International Association of Administrative Professionals).* This organization is the world's largest association for administrative support staff, with nearly 600 chapters and 40 000 members and affiliates worldwide. IAAP administers two certification programs for administrative professionals. The CPS (Certified Professional Secretary) rating is achieved by successful completion of the exam plus the required work experience. "CPS" after an administrative professional's name indicates the achievement of an internationally recognized standard of proficiency as an administrative professional.
- *The CAP (Certified Administrative Professional) rating.* This goes a step further. The advanced CAP certification, introduced by IAAP in 2001, is achieved when an administrative professional has met educational and work experience requirements similar to the CPS and has passed a four-part, one-and-a-half-day examination. Figure 1-6 on page 19 gives more details about these certifications. IAAP

publishes a magazine called *OfficePro.* The Web address for IAAP is www.iaap-hq.org.

- *ARMA (Association of Records Managers and Administrators).* International, the association for information management professionals. This association serves over 10 000 information management professionals in the United States, Canada, and over 30 other nations. The association sponsors the Certified Records Manager (CRM) designation, whose attainment is based on educational background, professional work experience, and successful completion of a two-day, six-part examination. The exams are offered twice a year, in May and November, and may be taken at any location at which a qualified invigilator can be identified. The Association publishes *The Information Management Journal.* Their Web address is www.arma.org with a link to the Canadian regional address, www.armacanada.org.
- *The International Virtual Assistants Association.* This is an association of virtual assistants—independent entrepreneurs who offer business support services in a virtual environment. The members of this volunteer organization elected their first board of directors in March 2000. The Association is dedicated to supporting the members of the virtual assistants profession, and to educating the public on the role and function of the virtual assistant.

The following U.S. professional associations may also be of interest:

- *National Association of Legal Secretaries (NALS) and Legal Secretaries International.* NALS sponsors an Accredited Legal Secretary (ALS) examination and certification program administered by the Certifying Board of the National Association of Legal Secretaries. This organization also administers an examination to certify a legal secretary with three years of experience as a Professional Legal Secretary (PLS). Legal Secretaries International confers the designation Board Certified Civil Trial Legal Secretary in specialized areas such as litigation, real estate, probate, and corporation to individuals who have five years of law-related experience and pass the exam. The Web address for NALS is www.nals.org; the Web address for Legal Secretaries International is www.legalsecretaries.org.

- *American Association for Medical Transcription (AAMT).* This organization is for office staff, assistants, and technicians employed by physicians or hospitals. It sponsors a certification program, Certified Medical Transcriptionist (CMT), and publishes the *Journal of the American Association for Medical Transcription.* The Web address for the American Association for Medical Transcription is www.aamt.org.

- *National Association of Education Office Professionals (NAEOP).* NAEOP (at www.naeop.org) sponsors a program that issues certificates on the basis of education, experience, and professional activity. It also publishes *National Educational Secretary.*

■ Figure 1-6

PROFESSIONAL CERTIFICATIONS—CPS/CAP

WHY CERTIFICATION?

Job advancement. The CPS or CAP rating gives you a competitive edge for promotion and hiring.

Professional skills. You will learn more about office operations and build your skills by studying for and taking the CPS or CAP exam.

Salary. An IAAP Membership Profile study shows that certificate holders earn an average of $2228 more per year than those who do not have certification.

Esteem. Attaining the CPS or CAP certification demonstrates to your employer and yourself that you are committed as a professional.

College credit. Many colleges and universities offer course credit for passing the CPS or CAP exam.

WHO IS ELIGIBLE?

You may take the CPS or CAP exam if you are employed as an administrative professional or have at least two years of work experience as an administrative professional which could vary depending on your level of college education. Students or teachers in a college business education program also may qualify.

WHEN AND WHERE IS THE EXAM GIVEN?

The CPS examination is a three-part one-day exam. The CAP examination is a four-part one-and-a-half-day exam. CPS holders need only take the Organizational Planning exam to achieve the CAP designation. Both exams are administered each May and November at over 250 locations across the United States, Canada, and other countries.

WHAT ARE THE PARTS OF THE EXAM?

The CPS exam has three parts:

- Finance and Business Law
- Office Systems and Administration
- Management

The CAP exam has four parts:

- Finance and Business Law
- Office Systems and Administration
- Management
- Organizational Planning

Source: International Association of Administrative Professionals site, Columbus, OH, www.iaap-cols.com/certifications.html, accessed June 10, 2004.

Company Scene

While completing activities throughout this course, you will be working for CanAsian Airlines, 2300—888 3rd Street SW, Calgary, AB T2P 4C4. CanAsian is the result of a merger in March 2002 between CanAir, founded in 1980 in Calgary, Alberta, with only 30 employees, and China Airlines, founded in 1985 in Beijing, China, with 40 employees. Figure 1-7 on page 20 presents the organizational chart of CanAsian Airlines. Presently China is the

■ Figure 1-7

ORGANIZATIONAL CHART OF CANASIAN AIRLINES

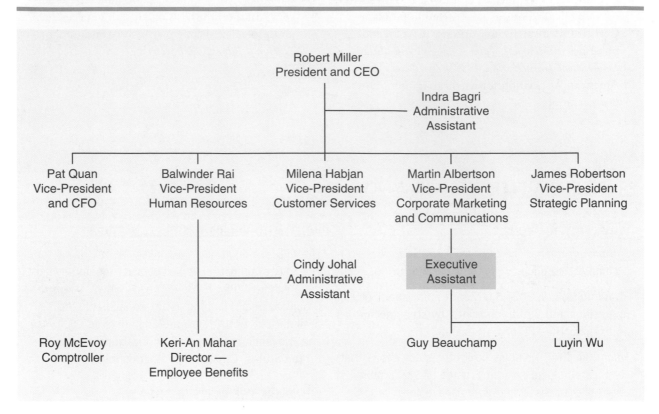

world's third-largest aviation market with airline traffic growing by 20 percent per year (see Figure 1-8 on page 21). Before their merger, CanAir had grown to be the fourth-largest airline in the Canada, garnering 11.7 percent of the market. China Airlines had grown to be the second-largest airline in China, with 30 percent of the market. CanAsian Airlines now employs over 39 000 people. The Canadian head office is located in Calgary at the address just given. The China head office is in Beijing.

Net earnings this past year for the combined company were $5.6 billion, a slight drop from the combined net earnings of the two companies before the merger. CanAsian is listed on the Toronto Stock Exchange and currently lists for $62 per share of common stock. The company is presently developing strategies to increase its overall market share by decreasing labour costs, increasing its on-time performance, lowering ground-handling costs, and providing certain incentives. It is looking at adding a frequent flyer program for the China operation and improved in-flight customer service for the total company.

Your job title is executive assistant. You report directly to Martin Albertson, vice-president of corporate marketing and communications in Calgary. Since the merger, executives in both companies have been discussing how they might assume more social responsibility in the head office cities. They intend to take an active role in the educational, environmental, and social concerns of the community, in both Canada and China. Before the merger, each community saw the airline as a good corporate citizen, and the executives want to ensure things stay that way. Although their profitability picture has been good since the merger, there has been a slight downturn. As a result, the Calgary head office has laid off 50 employees in the corporate office. The result has been a slight morale problem. However, steps have been taken to make the employees feel more a part of the decision making through TQM.

Your duties are extremely varied. They include assisting Martin Albertson set up meetings with government and educational leaders within the local communities to determine issues of common concern. At one point, you travelled to China with your employer and two other support staff to help set up a community conference there. This is the only time you have travelled outside the company; however, you do communicate frequently with China through fax, e-mail, and computer conferencing. Your other duties include

■ Figure 1-8

CANASIAN FLIGHT CENTRES AND FLIGHT PATTERNS

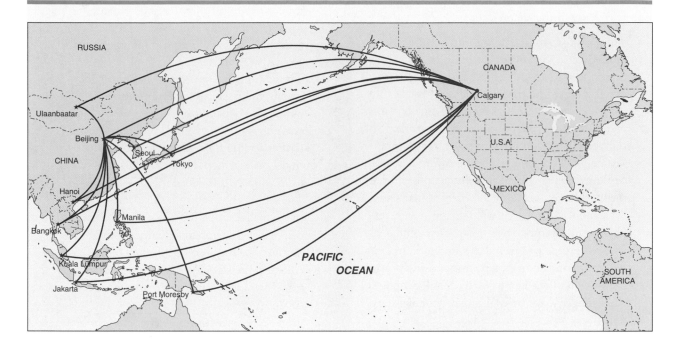

- Researching and preparing all types of correspondence
- Participating in TQM teams
- Organizing your employer's schedule
- Scheduling meetings
- Making travel arrangements
- Handling the mail
- Filing correspondence
- Supervising two assistants

You have two assistants who report to you—Guy Beauchamp (who has been working for CanAsian Airlines for slightly over a year) and Luyin Wu (who has been working for CanAsian Airlines for six months).

Chapter Summary

The summary will help you remember the important points covered in the chapter.

- The workforce of the 21st century will (1) be more diverse than ever before, (2) be more global than in the past, with both national and international mergers continuing at a rapid pace, (3) have state-of-the-art technology, with e-commerce expanding rapidly, and (4) have a large percentage of the workforce engaged in telework.
- Women will continue to be a growing part of the workforce; they will occupy diverse positions in the workforce, including all levels of management.
- We cannot assume that women and men react differently to situations because of their gender.
- The workforce will be older, with workers 45 and older expected to make up an increasingly larger proportion of the labour force. Many people will work longer than the traditional retirement age of 65.
- As you work in the diverse office, you need to be aware of and sensitive to the various cultural differences and backgrounds.
- Age differences may mean that we view the world from different perspectives.
- The level of education for jobs is increasing, with the requirement for an associate degree growing faster than all other levels of education.
- The quality concept developed by W. Edwards Deming is now used by numerous American businesses in an effort to improve quality and productivity. As a result of this emphasis, employees now operate in teams more often than in the past.
- Downsizing and outsourcing are two methods used to cut organizational costs.
- Temporary employees are used extensively to get the work of the organization done as economically as possible in an extremely competitive world.
- Today a number of workers have traded in the traditional office environment for a telework environment—one in which work may be done at any time and in any place.
- Workweeks today may be flexible, with hours varying from the traditional 8- or 9-to-5 workday. The compressed workweek, flextime, and job sharing are all examples of flexible workweeks.
- The administrative professional's role is shifting due to technology, with duties that include researching and preparing reports complete with graphics and spreadsheets, assisting with the planning and direction of the company through TQM teams (and even leading these teams), supervising support staff, administering computer networks, helping to upgrade and recommend office software, providing computer and software training, managing websites, and working in a liaison capacity with outsourcing companies such as accounting and staffing firms.
- The administrative professional needs these employability skills: communication skills—written, verbal and presentation; technology/computer numeracy skills; problem-solving (critical-thinking) skills; time, stress, and organizational management skills; interpersonal skills; teamwork skills; leadership skills.
- The administrative professional must develop these qualities: openness to change, dependability, confidentiality, integrity/honesty, initiative/motivation, and flexibility/adaptability.
- A total professional image (including knowledge, skills, qualities and personal appearance) is essential for success.
- Professional growth can occur through attending classes or seminars/workshops, reading business periodicals, and participating in professional organizations.

Key Terms

The following terms were introduced in this chapter. The page on which the term was introduced is provided to help you locate the new term. Definitions are compiled in the Glossary at the end of the text.

- **multinational corporations** 5
- **merger mania** 5
- **state-of-the-art technology** 6
- **e-commerce** 6
- **telework** 6
- **information age** 6
- **personal digital assistant** (PDA) 6
- **stereotype** 7
- **multiculturalism** 8
- **culture** 8
- **total quality management** (TQM) or **continuous quality improvement** (CQI) 9
- **downsizing** 9
- **overhead costs** 9
- **outsourcing** 9
- **telecommuting** 10
- **remote employment** 10
- **virtual office** 11
- **compressed workweek** 11

- **flextime** 11
- **job sharing** 11
- **flattened organizational structures** 11
- **administrative professional** 12
- **numeracy skills** 14
- **critical thinking** 14
- **krinein** 14
- **soft skill** 14
- **team** 15
- **leadership skills** 15
- **creativity** 16
- **dependability** 16
- **confidentiality** 16
- **integrity** 16
- **initiative** 16
- **motivation** 17
- **extrinsically motivated** 17
- **intrinsically motivated** 17
- **flexibility** 17
- **adaptability** 17

Responses to Self-Check

The most appropriate answers are as follows:

1. Yes	3. No	5. No	7. No	9. Yes
2. Yes	4. Yes	6. Yes	8. No	10. No

Discussion Items

These discussion items provide an opportunity to test your understanding of the chapter through written responses and/or discussion with your classmates and your instructor.

1. Explain how the work environment of the future will be more diverse. What does this diversity suggest for you as a future employee?
2. How is our work environment changing?
3. Where is the workplace of the 21st century? In your response, explain what is meant by telework.
4. How is the administrative professional's role changing?
5. What skills are needed in the 21st century? In your response, explain the meaning of each skill.

Critical-Thinking Activity

CanAsian Airlines has introduced TQM in an effort to improve quality and productivity. You were asked to be part of a team that looks at the improvement of internal communication, and you took the assignment seriously. Before the first meeting, you had identified several communication problems that seem to be ongoing in the organization. You brought these up at the meeting: failure to respond to e-mail (electronic mail) promptly, failure to respond to voice mail, and airline ticket customers who have long waits when attempting to buy tickets by phone. Two of the individuals who work in your department became upset with you. They assumed that your statements referred to situations you had encountered with them. They exploded in the meeting, making these comments:

I can't answer the e-mail you send me within the hour. Get off my back.

The next time you have a complaint about me, talk with me personally.

The manager in charge of the airline ticket sales department asked exactly what you meant by "long waits" with airline customers attempting to buy tickets. He did not seem upset but was merely asking for clarification of your comment.

You let the two individuals in your department know that you were not talking about individual cases. You were attempting to identify problems that needed to be addressed so the customer might be better served. You answered the manager's question with "I don't know the exact length of time; I have just heard complaints." Since the meeting did not get off to a good start, you feel responsible. You want to be a contributor to the process. What should you do? Think through the following items and prepare responses.

- What is the problem?
- Do the upset employees have cause to be concerned about your behaviour?
- Should you talk to these employees before the next meeting? If so, what should you say?
- Did you have enough information about the customer ticket issue to bring it up? How should you handle this type of issue in the future?
- How should you identify problems/issues that are negatively affecting office communication?
- How can you present problems/issues at the next meeting without causing the volatility of the last meeting?

Remember, your task is to critically analyze the situation given here. Before you attempt to answer the questions, review Figure 1-4. Additionally, study the Soft Skills section on thinking and analyzing situations critically.

Critical Thinking

Critical thinking is a unique kind of purposeful thinking in which the thinker systematically and habitually

- Imposes criteria and intellectual standards upon the thinking
- Takes charge of the construction of thinking
- Guides the construction of the thinking according to the standards
- Assesses the effectiveness of the thinking according to the purpose, the criteria, and the standards

Questions to Ask

- Is this belief defensible or indefensible? What is the basis for it?
- Is my position on this issue reasonable and rational?
- Am I willing to deal with complexity, or do I retreat into simple stereotypes to avoid it?
- Is it appropriate and wise to assume that my ideas and beliefs are accurate, clear, and reasonable if I have not tested them?
- Do I ever enter sympathetically into points of view that are very different from my own, or do I just assume that I am right?
- Do I know how to question my own ideas and to test them?[13]

Projects

Project 1-1 *(Objective 1)*

Online Project

Browse the Web for the following information:

- Find articles on the changing office; at the IAAP website (www.iaap-hq.org), check the magazine *OfficePro.*
- Determine the diversity statistics in your province as reported in the most recent Statistics Canada documentation (www.statcan.ca). Prepare a short summary of the articles, giving the Web addresses; submit your summaries to your instructor.
- Review the brochure *Employability Skills 2000+* produced by the Conference Board of Canada

(www.conferenceboard.ca). List the skills you already possess and those you need to acquire. Compare the list of skills needed with this and/or other courses in your current program of study. Prepare a short summary of these needed skills and identify in which chapter and/or course you will acquire them.

- Find information on standard legal forms that might be used by an organization that requires employees to sign a confidentiality agreement.

Project 1-2 *(Objectives 2 and 3)*

Collaborative Project

In teams of two or three, interview two administrative professionals. You do not have to interview these people in person; you may choose to do it by e-mail. Ask them the following questions:

- What are your roles and responsibilities?
- What skills and qualities do you need in order to be successful?
- What types of technology changes have occurred in your organization in the past five years? Two years?
- Describe the diversity of personnel within your organization. Have there been any issues in dealing with this diversity? If so, what were those issues and how were they handled?

Report your findings verbally to the class.

Project 1-3 *(Objective 5)*

Begin the development of a Professional Growth Plan, which you will add to in each chapter. This plan should identify the periodicals you will read and/or the professional activities you will attend. For example, you might decide to attend two meetings of your local chapter of IAAP or some other professional organization. Prepare this plan and save it on disk as "Progro1-3." You will be adding to this disk throughout the course. This portion of your Professional Growth Plan is to be titled "Improving My Knowledge of Today's Business World." You will be asked at the end of the course whether you accomplished the items listed on your plan.

Project 1-4 *(Objective 4)*

Read the Critical-Thinking Activity at the end of this chapter, and respond to the items at the end of the activity. Submit your responses to your instructor.

Chapter 2

Telework

LEARNING OBJECTIVES

1. Define telework and explain the various terms used.
2. Identify the advantages and disadvantages of telework.
3. Describe the individual qualities and skills necessary for success in telework.
4. *Determine and practise the qualities and behaviours necessary in self-management.*
5. Describe the essentials of an ergonomically sound workspace.
6. Explain the organizational commitment and techniques required to manage and support teleworkers.

A continually growing segment of today's workforce is choosing to work in locations outside of the traditional office. As noted in Chapter 1, in 2003 there were 134 million teleworkers worldwide. Participants in a study conducted in 1999 indicated that of the Canadian employers included in the study, 6 percent offered some form of flexible work arrangements, which included telework, and that 4.6 percent of women and 5.3 percent of men took advantage of the opportunity.[1] Research in 2000 conducted in the United States by the International Telework Association & Council indicated that there were 2.8 million new teleworkers from 1999 to 2000, with a projection by 2004 of 30 million.[2] The growing number of people in telework is not limited to North America. In the United Kingdom, there are over 1 million employees teleworking, with the projection that by the year 2010, 52 percent of the population will be in some form of telework.[3] A survey of 15 member nations of the European Union showed that Finland, Netherlands, and Sweden lead the world in per capita telework participation.[4] Clearly, telework is an international phenomenon.

Teleworkers work from home, from telework centres, from satellite offices, from clients' offices, from airport lounges, from hotel rooms, from their cars, or even from the local Starbucks®. Many public places now accommodate this work style. For example, a number of airports have enclosed workspaces with desks, telephones, and plugs for notebook computers. Hotels often have desks built especially for computers in the guest rooms, and many have fax machines/printers/copiers as permanent equipment also. Even places we traditionally think of as vacation spots (such as ski lodges and cruise ships) now have workstations. Literally, our society understands, promotes, accepts, and even demands support for an "anyplace and anywhere" work style.

Photodisc Green/Photodisc Collection

In 2003 there were 134 million teleworkers worldwide.

Telework Defined

You learned some basic definitions of telework in Chapter 1. However, before studying this chapter further, you need to understand the terminology. Though *teleworking* and *telecommuting* have often been used interchangeably, there are differences between the two. In this text, we will use the traditional definition of **telecommuting** as the work style of salaried employees (those paid by organizations for either full- or part-time work) who work at home for part or all of the workweek rather than going to a business office. *Telecommuting* was the original term used when virtual work was first introduced. *Telework* is a broader term that means using telecommunications to work from a home office, a client's office, or a multitude of other locations. **Mobile telework** describes the arrangement of individuals who spend a great deal of time travelling and/or on customers' premises (for example, doing consulting or sales work). The **virtual office** for purposes of this text means the operational domain of any organization that includes remote workers. One of the later manifestations of telework is the **virtual company**, one in which all or most all of the staff work from home. This model is relatively common for small startup companies since it requires minimal expenditures for office space and equipment. Figure 2-1 gives several Web addresses that will help you learn more about telework.

■ **Figure 2-1**

RESOURCES FOR TELEWORKERS

- www.att.com/telework—AT&T's telework webguide website
- www.ccohs.ca—Canadian Centre on Occupational Health and Safety
- www.ecatt.com—The status of telework worldwide
- www.gilgordon.com—A variety of teleworking resources
- www.nepi.org—National Environmental Policy Institute, which is studying telework
- www.telecommute.org—International Telework Association & Council

- Home Commuting Magazine

Why telework? The advantages to the individual and to the organization are many. However, there are distinct disadvantages also. Before an organization decides to support telework, or before an individual decides to become a part of the rapidly growing teleworker group, a careful analysis should be made of the advantages and disadvantages.

Advantages to the Individual Worker

The Canadian Centre on Occupational Health and Safety lists the following advantages and disadvantages to telecommuting for individuals and companies:[5]

- Fewer distractions from co-workers—resulting in greater productivity and deliverance from office politics
- More flexibility with organization of daily tasks—flexibility of work times and work style
- Savings in time, commuting, and other costs—no long commute to the traditional office, and elimination of commuting aggravations such as rush-hour traffic and parking; financial savings from at-home versus restaurant lunches and business wardrobe costs
- Higher job satisfaction—a sense of autonomy and the freedom to make mistakes and correct them on your own
- Access to family when working at home and the flexibility for two-career couples to work for different employers many kilometres or even cities apart
- The opportunity to remain in work despite moving from one part of the country to another
- Personal income tax incentive—the ability to claim a portion of the costs of establishing and running a home office, and of necessary supplies, equipment, and/or furniture when working as a contracted employee

If you know someone who is a teleworker, or if you have done telework, you may add your own list of advantages to the ones listed. Everyone's particular set of values determines whether he or she finds telework attractive. For example, if you value flexibility, autonomy, and freedom, you may find telework to be right for you. Also, if you have small children and you value having greater accessibility to them during the day, telework may be what you decide to do.

Disadvantages to the Individual Worker

Some of the disadvantages for the teleworker are as follows:

- Isolation and lack of socialization—working apart from the office team can be a lonely environment
- Lack of separation between home and work
- More distractions from family (if in a home environment)
- Potential for excessive working hours—and, if you are a **self-employed teleworker** (an individual owner not employed by an organization), there could be a loss of fringe benefits, such as paid vacations and insurance coverage
- Less awareness of changes in company—lack of organizational identity from few or zero ties with an organization and fewer opportunities for development and promotion
- Fear of being under-managed or "out of sight, out of mind"—no support group means the teleworker is responsible for all aspects of his or her job; lack of access to necessary equipment and often little or no support for telecommunication problems
- Potential for additional costs in purchasing supplies and perhaps even some necessary equipment, when such are not supplied by the employer

As is apparent from the lists of advantages and disadvantages, the telework environment is not a perfect one. It has its downside, just as working in the traditional office does. Each individual considering telework must determine his or her goals, career directions, priorities, and needs. Also, consideration needs to be given to personality and work style. The Myers-Briggs Type Indicator, developed by Isabel Myers and Katharine Briggs from the work of noted psychologist Carl Jung, purports to classify individuals according to their preferences on how they come to know and understand the world. For example:

- An individual who prefers to be energized by the outside world is classified as an extrovert.
- An individual who prefers to focus attention on the inner world is classified as an introvert.

Additionally, the typology classifies people according to intuition/sensing, thinking/feeling, and judging/perceiving. As an example of how these personality classifications might be used in determining your interest in telework, a person high in extroversion is more likely to be successful in telework if there is a high degree of communication with outside individuals. For example, a consultant who works from his or her home but often visits the site of the customer probably enjoys the work more than a person who is high in introversion. A person high in introversion probably requires little communication with others. For example, he or she may enjoy telework that involves the production of documents, such as setting up Web pages, writing reports, and so on.

Although a detailed explanation of the Myers-Briggs Type Indicator is outside the scope of this textbook, if you are serious about telework you may want to consider your personality type as defined by the typology. Many colleges and universities offer the instrument to their students.

Advantages to the Organization

Advantages to organizations in pursuing telework options include

- Improved employee retention—flexible employment opportunities where work can be done at remote locations or outside traditional office hours can improve employee retention; for example, women in their childbearing years may be provided telework in order to retain their expertise for the organization
- Often higher productivity—for example, the use of teleworkers can increase employee retention and productivity by approximately 20 percent, as some types of work can be done better in isolation and when workers are freed from meetings and office socializing; also, there is improved accuracy in employee performance evaluations based on net productivity and quality of work[6]
- Fewer lost hours due to traffic problems
- Reduced absenteeism
- Savings in energy, office space requirements, maintenance, and housekeeping—greater flexibility in allocation of onsite facilities and greater flexibility in staff size changes since facilities are less sensitive to teleworker staff size
- Financial savings from reduced office space; some studies report a savings of between $5000 and $10 000 per year on real estate costs[7]

- Increased number of potential candidates for a job—access to highly skilled workers across the country means greater competitiveness in a global economy; for example, high-tech companies dependent on technological skills are less concerned about where individuals work than about finding individuals with the necessary skills

As unlikely as it may seem, a fire chief in Fairfax County, Virginia determined that teleworking on certain aspects of his job improved his productivity. Report writing, for example, was one of his main activities. Since it demanded concentration and accuracy, this task could clearly be done better in isolation than at the firehouse. When he began to telework from his home office for certain periods of the week, his productivity shot up 20 percent, because he produced reports sooner after the incident he was writing about and more accurately.[8]

Disadvantages to the Organization

Disadvantages to the organization may be as follows:

- Contacting the employee
- Developing policies for and managing teleworkers
- Determining performance/evaluation methods
- Potential for increased selection and training costs
- Maintaining adequate communication between other employees or with customers
- Providing technological support and assuring that teleworkers remain part of the total workforce team
- Possible delay in customer service

These are generic disadvantages that are particularly true for organizations in the infancy of their efforts in telework. If an organization is going to commit to long-term telework, planning must be done to avoid these disadvantages. The supervisors of teleworkers must manage these workers differently than traditional workers. Following are some suggestions concerning management techniques.

When providing telework opportunities, the organization must think differently about the management role. How can managers not only measure the productivity of the worker but also help him or her to feel like part of the total organization while working in isolated locations? Consideration must be given to employing the right people in telework situations and then giving them the proper support. There are no easy answers, but many organizations are making the arrangement work effectively. Organizations are using videoconferencing, telephone conferencing, and computer conferencing to link individuals from their remote locations to individuals in the traditional office setting. Also, a number of organizations include teleworkers in biweekly or monthly staff meetings onsite at the organization. **Virtual teams** are used as well—dispersed workers who come together through telecommunications technology to accomplish a task.

Before the teleworker begins any task, both the manager and the teleworker must be clear about project expectations and timelines. Since teleworkers receive less informal feedback than other employees, they must receive adequate information during formal evaluation sessions. The concerns and techniques mentioned here address only a few of the myriad management issues. An organization that supports teleworkers must continually study and improve its support structures to assure the productivity of its teleworkers.

Societal Advantages

Societal advantages include

- Increased entrepreneurial activity
- Increased community stability
- Less pollution

Telework encourages entrepreneurial activity. Individuals can set up and maintain home offices at relatively low cost. Technology and the Internet provide new business opportunities that were not available in the past. To understand the relevance of this statement, just browse the Web and note the number of entrepreneurs who have started ventures. Additionally, more opportunities are available for women, since telework allows them to maintain a successful business operation while juggling family and home responsibilities.

Telework also provides for increased community stability. Teleworkers are generally more satisfied with their jobs and personal/family lives than the traditional worker. This can result in lower turnover for the company and thus greater community stability, as employees tend to stay with a company rather than move to a new area.

Telework practices also produce a significant environmental quality contribution. Fewer cars on the road means less pollution.

Telework Success

As you have already learned, the benefits of telework are many. However, before an individual considers telework, he or she should carefully examine the qualities and skills needed to be a happy, productive teleworker. Ask yourself:

- Do you have the maturity, self-discipline, and ability to work with little supervision?
- Are you flexible?
- Do you have an appropriate level of knowledge of technology—computers, e-mail, faxes, etc?
- Are you consistent and productive?
- Do you possess organized work habits?

Following are several additional but necessary qualities and skills.

Strategic Thinking

Individual **strategic thinking** involves the application of your experience and your wants and needs to determine your future directions. It demands the ability to separate yourself from the day-to-day issues for a period of time and take a hard look at what you want to accomplish in the next five or ten years of your life. Take a few minutes and complete Self-Check A.

Stephen Covey, a well-known authority in the area of establishing goals, suggests asking these questions as you begin to think strategically about your directions:

- What do I feel are my greatest strengths?
- What strengths have others who know me well noticed in me?
- What have been my happiest moments in life? Why were they happy?
- When I daydream, what do I see myself doing?
- When I look at my work life, what activities do I consider of greatest worth?
- What quality-of-life results do I desire that are different from what I now have?[9]

SELF-CHECK A ✔

Take a few minutes now to answer these two questions. What are my greatest strengths? What quality-of-life results do I desire? Jot down your thoughts.

_____

_____

_____

_____

_____

_____

_____

Once you ask and answer these questions, Covey suggests that you write a **mission statement** (a statement that lists what an individual or organization values and the future direction intended) to clarify your goals. A thoughtful mission statement

- Fulfills your own unique capacity to contribute
- Includes fulfillment in physical, social, mental, and spiritual dimensions
- Is based on quality-of-life results
- Deals with both vision and values
- Deals with all the significant roles in your life—personal, family, work, community
- Inspires you to achieve[10]

To understand more about how a mission statement is written, look at Figure 2-2, which shows one person's mission statement. If you are self-employed and have established a company, you also may want to write a mission statement for your company. Such a statement helps you remain focused on the direction you have determined for the company. An organizational mission statement is shown in Figure 2-3 on page 30.

■ Figure 2-2

PERSONAL MISSION STATEMENT —AN EXAMPLE

My mission is to

- Discover and use all of my talents and abilities
- Treasure my family
- Live true to the principles I hold dear (self-sufficiency, honesty, integrity, and giving)
- Be an outstanding worker—one who contributes to my employers and clients
- Provide adequate income for my family

Productivity

To be an effective teleworker, you must be productive. You must accomplish the job tasks to the satisfaction of your employer if you are a telecommuter or to the satisfaction of your clients or customers if you are an entrepreneur. If you are a telecommuter, your supervisor needs to be very clear with you about what is expected on each job and when that job is to be completed. If he or she does not provide you with adequate instructions, ask for clarification. Know what is expected to avoid doing a job incorrectly or missing a deadline. If you are working with a client or customer, you need to be certain you understand that person's expectations for the completed job and the timeline for completion. Repeat what you believe the expectations are. Then if there is a misunderstanding, the client or customer can correct you.

> **Communication Tip**
>
> Check your e-mail at specific times during the day—once at midmorning and once at midafternoon.

Productivity demands discipline. Certainly a large part of your discipline is driven by external sources—that is, your paycheque depends on discipline. If you are an independent worker, you understand the relationship of discipline and productivity. Those who are not disciplined enough to deliver the

---

■ **Figure 2-3**

MISSION, VISION, AND VALUES STATEMENT, ROYAL CANADIAN MOUNTED POLICE

MISSION

The RCMP is Canada's national police service. Proud of our traditions and confident in meeting future challenges, we commit to preserve the peace, uphold the law and provide quality service in partnership with our communities.

VISION

We will:

- Be a progressive, proactive and innovative organization
- Provide the highest quality service through dynamic leadership, education and technology in partnership with the diverse communities we serve
- Be accountable and efficient through shared decision-making
- Ensure a healthy work environment that encourages team building, open communication and mutual respect
- Promote safe communities
- Demonstrate leadership in the pursuit of excellence

CORE VALUES OF THE ROYAL CANADIAN MOUNTED POLICE

Recognizing the dedication of all employees, we will create and maintain an environment of individual safety, well-being and development. We are guided by

Accountability. There are two components of accountability. The first is the process of *rendering*

an account to those from whom we derive our authority of what we did, why we did it, how we did it and what we are doing to improve performance or results. An important element of this component is accepting the personal consequences of our actions. The second component of accountability is one of answerability—the obligation to provide information to others in our communities of interest with respect to our decisions, actions and results in light of clear, previously agreed upon understandings and expectations. For example, we inform our communities about our actions, but we must render account of our actions to our direct supervisors. In this organization authorities can be delegated, but accountability cannot.

Respect. Is the objective, unbiased consideration and regard for the rights, values, beliefs and property of all people.

Professionalism. Is having a conscientious awareness of our role, image, skills and knowledge in our commitment to quality client oriented service.

Honesty. Is being truthful in character and behaviour.

Compassion. Is demonstrating care and sensitivity in word and action.

Integrity. Is acting consistently with our other core values

Source: "RCMP Mission, Vision and Values," Royal Canadian Mounted Police site, www.rcmp-grc.gc.ca/html/vision_e.htm, accessed June 15, 2004.

product the customer/client needs soon find themselves with no customers/clients. You may have a little more flexibility as a telecommuter, since a team of individuals is usually involved on a project. However, if you continue to fail to produce, you will eventually be unemployed.

Discipline involves knowing when to tell friends you cannot talk on the phone—you have work to get done. One concern of the home-based worker is that society does not understand the implications of working at home. Individuals often call and say such things as "Did I get you out of bed?" when it is 8:00 a.m. If you respond "Of course, I am up; I am working," many people still do not get the picture. Somehow it is more difficult for the general public to envision you as actually working if you are at home. Fortunately, that image is beginning to change. However, you must be clear with your friends and relatives when they call; tell them you are working. Additionally, be sensitive to the needs of callers; ask if you or they can call back at a better time. If you are pleasant but firm, they will soon understand the situation.

A way of ensuring more discipline and thus greater productivity is to set objectives for yourself every day—just as you would if you were working in the traditional office. In fact, before you quit work each afternoon, you might write down (on your computer or Palm Pilot) the objectives you need to accomplish the next day. Another key to helping you remain disciplined is to put timelines by each objective. Obviously, some projects are going to take more or less time than you had envisioned, but estimates help keep you focused the next day. When you turn on your computer in the morning, you are immediately reminded of your tasks.

Do not let distractions interfere with your focus. For the home-based worker, distractions are numerous—household chores, children, and errands, to name a few.

> ### Human Relations Tip
>
> When a personal call interrupts your work time, tell the caller politely but firmly "I am sorry, but I cannot talk now. I am working on an important project. I will be free at 8 this evening. Are you available then?"

Formulate a plan for dealing with them. For example, if you have small children, you may need to hire some help during the day. When your children are of school age, help them understand when you can and cannot be disturbed.

You also need to be disciplined about when to quit work. High achievers may be tempted to work 14 hours a day. You might be able to keep up that schedule for a few days, but burnout and **sleep deprivation** will eventually occur.

Self-management is no small task for any one. It requires constant attention and self-nurturing. Take a few minutes now to evaluate your self-management skills by completing Self-Check B.

SELF-CHECK B ✔

Answer these questions with a yes or no.

1. I know what my values are.
   Yes ☑   **No** ☐

2. I am able to articulate my goals.
   Yes ☑   **No** ☐

3. I know my strengths.
   Yes ☑   **No** ☐

4. I understand my weaknesses.
   Yes ☑   **No** ☐

5. I seek to minimize my weaknesses.
   Yes ☐   ✓**No** ☐

6. I maintain an appropriate balance between my work and my personal life.
   Yes ☐   **No** ☑

Soft Skills: Self-Management

Self-management is the Soft Skills objective for this chapter. What does self-management mean? It means that you

- Have self-knowledge—you know your personal and professional strengths and weaknesses

- Are able to manage your time effectively
- Are able to handle stress
- Are able to balance your work and your personal life
- Understand your values
- Are able to articulate your goals

Creativity

In the traditional office setting, you generally have someone you can go to for help in solving problems. You are part of a team that can help you, and you soon learn each team member's strengths and weaknesses. You know what individual to go to for help. Not so in most telework situations. You have to be a creative problem solver. You have to figure out how a report should be written, what format is most effective, and what graphs and charts to include. The old proverb "Necessity is the mother of invention" is particularly true for the teleworker. Whatever occurs, you must be creative enough to find a solution.

Technology Skills

Technology skills are essential in many jobs today, including that of an administrative professional. However, the role that technology plays in the life of a teleworker cannot be overstated. Remember what telework means: using telecommunications to work from a home office, a client's office, a car, a satellite centre, or a multitude of other locations. Much of the time, a teleworker performs his or her job in isolation, with no readily available help when a problem with technology occurs. The teleworker must figure out the problem or get some assistance from an outside source. Many sources are available today to help with telecommunications problems. Microsoft®, AOL®, and Xerox®, for example, have telephone help lines available much of the day. Some help services even offer assistance 24 hours a day. Many manufacturers of telecommunications equipment offer online services. But using these services demands more understanding of telecommunications on the part of the teleworker than is demanded of the worker in the traditional office. For example, many traditional offices have a telecommunications department that provides assistance when problems occur. The assistants from this department can generally correct the problem for you. As a teleworker, you have to be able to understand the problem well enough to describe it accurately and to follow instructions from the online or telephone assistant. Also, you have to be able to apply what you read in manuals in order to prevent problems from occurring. In other words, you have to be your own troubleshooter.

As telecommunications equipment becomes more sophisticated, you, as a teleworker, must continue to upgrade your knowledge and skills. You can do so by reading computer periodicals, checking upgrades on equipment through the Web, and talking with other teleworkers about what they are using. Chat rooms exist for teleworkers to communicate with each other on a variety of topics. You can find them by using a search engine such as Yahoo!® or Google™ and entering the keywords teleworker chat rooms. Another option for keeping up to date on equipment is to enrol in a distance education course. Many community colleges and universities offer these courses. They allow you the flexibility of learning from your own home.

Success Detractors

Being a successful teleworker demands that you conquer isolation, noise, and family concerns. You also have to develop an appropriate balance between home and work responsibilities.

Isolation

To a great degree, the environment of a teleworker is one of isolation. If you have been accustomed to working in a traditional environment, you understand the differences immediately. You are not able to get a cup of coffee with a co-worker and exchange small talk. You do not have access to someone with whom you can discuss a work problem. You miss little things, such as walking into work with someone from the parking lot. The degree to which isolation bothers you depends somewhat on your personality traits. Are you an introvert or an extrovert by nature? As you learned earlier, the Myers-Briggs typology can help you discover several of your personality traits, including introversion and extroversion. However, Self-Check C on page 33 will offer you some insight as to whether you are an introvert or an extrovert. Take that quiz now.

If you discover you are more extroverted, you can still enjoy telework and be successful at it. However, you will need to seek more contact with others than someone who is introverted. Here are suggestions for feeling less isolated:

- Join a health club; exercise with people; sign up for an aerobics class.
- Make arrangements to have lunch occasionally with someone in a similar business.
- Go to a deli or coffeehouse where you can chat with people.
- Exchange pleasantries with the merchants with whom you deal—for example, your mailing service, your office supply store, and your grocery store.

Are You an Introvert or Extrovert?

Both a strong introvert and a strong extrovert will have some difficulty adapting to telework. Answer each question by recording R for "rarely," S for "sometimes," F for "frequently," or A for "always." Score your responses using this rating: Rarely = 1, Sometimes = 2, Frequently = 3, Always = 4. When you finish the quiz, go to the end of the chapter and read the comments that pertain to the type you most closely resemble.

1. I turn on the TV as soon as I get home. _S_

2. I do my best work with others around. _R_

3. Time goes more quickly when I am with others. _S_

4. I would rather walk in the city than in the woods. _R_

5. On my own, I get bored easily. _R_

6. I would rather go to a party than stay at home. _R_

7. I feel restless after a day spent alone. _R_

8. I do not like to eat alone. _R_

9. I get a lot of energy from others. _S_

10. I need colleagues to problem-solve. _S_

11. Frequent feedback helps me enjoy a project. _S_

12. When things go wrong, I call a friend right away.[11] _R_

(17)

- If you are a telecommuter, take advantage of company-sponsored professional development activities and company social events.
- Turn on the TV to a news program during your lunch to get in touch with what is happening in the outside world.
- Schedule jogs or walks with a neighbour who also exercises.
- Go to an occasional movie in the afternoon.

If you are extremely introverted, you probably need to work on enjoying interactions with others. For example, if your business involves working with clients or on teams, you may need to work on communicating with your contacts and enjoying your interactions.

Noise

Noise around the home can be a problem due to
- Noisy neighbours
- Garbage trucks
- Car and ambulance alarms
- Incessant barking of dogs outside the home
- Pets within the home making noise—dogs, birds, and cats
- Airplanes
- Neighbours doing yard work or having pool parties

Since noise can be a distraction when you are trying to work, you should try to lower the noise level around the house. Some of these solutions are more costly than others. Adding more insulation to your home is one solution, although a costly one. You can install acoustic foam on your walls, put in double-pane glass windows, and add wall-to-wall carpeting. Here are some less costly ways to lessen the noise:

- Add noise-reducing ceiling tiles
- Seal electrical fixtures with electric switch sealers
- Install self-stick foam weatherstripping to windows

Family Issues

If you have decided to become a teleworker and you are married, have a family, or live with other family members, you must talk with your family members about this arrangement. First of all, many people have misconceptions about what working from home means. To some, it means you are not really working or you have time to take on additional responsibilities around the house. Of course, these are gross misconceptions. You need to talk with your family about what teleworking is. Explain that you are serious about your work and that you cannot be a full-time parent or housekeeper and maintain a full-time work schedule. Every member of the family needs to understand his or her role in the new arrangement. Determine a division of household tasks. What are the spouse's responsibilities? What are the children's responsibilities? Who does the cooking? Who does the cleaning? Who buys the groceries? Once the responsibilities have been determined, write them down and post them in a place that is readily accessible to all family members. Other suggestions for keeping family issues to a minimum include the following:

Communication Tip

Have a family meeting once each week to discuss how the division of home responsibilities is working. Reassign responsibilities if necessary.

- Find a housecleaning service or an individual who can come in when needed; hire someone full-time if the workload becomes overwhelming.
- Decide if you need someone to help with the children either full-time or after school. If you do, call a child-care referral service and/or ask friends for recommendations. You need to be assured that you have a competent, caring individual looking after your children.
- Keep the lines of communication open with your family. When you believe someone is not doing his or her fair share, communicate your feelings.
- Do not expect perfection from your family as they perform their tasks. Be grateful they are chipping in to do their share of the work.
- Try to keep your home a low-maintenance one. Do not buy furniture or carpet that requires constant cleaning—such as glass tables or white carpet.

With both family and friends, continue to communicate your needs and expectations. Be sure they know your working hours, just as if you were going to the traditional office each day. To help your family understand when you cannot be disturbed, you may

- Close your office door
- Put a "Do Not Disturb" sign on the door
- Put a sign on a bulletin board in a place the family uses frequently to indicate your working hours for the day or week

Refer to your home office as your workplace. Dress for the office each day as if you were working outside of your home. This will help you get in the "mood" for work. Do not let family and friends think you can take on extra community projects because you are a teleworker. Give a business reason for your refusal, for example "I am sorry but I have an important project to finish. I simply do not have the time." Answer your business phone professionally with your name and/or your company name.

Work/Life Balance

Just as you cannot let family and friends interrupt your work to the point that you get nothing done, you also cannot ignore family and friends to the point that all you do is work. There must be a balance between family and work. What is that balance? You must answer that question for yourself. What is important is that you understand what a healthy balance is and maintain that balance. You may have heard the old saying "All work and no play makes Jack [or Jill] a dull person." The statement has great validity. If you allow work to

become all-consuming, you can develop stress levels that make you physically and emotionally sick. If you never read a book, listen to a news program, read a magazine, or learn something new outside of your job, you may find that you have fewer good ideas and less creativity in your work projects. Several questions about balancing work and life are given in Figure 2-4; if you answer yes to four or more of them, your life may be out of balance.

Management of the Teleworker

With the number of teleworkers increasing and the expectation that the numbers will continue to increase, the experienced administrative professional may have the responsibility of supervising a teleworker. Although this chapter has focused on the role, responsibilities, and success factors necessary for being an effective teleworker, some consideration needs to be given to the

■ Figure 2-4

WORK/LIFE BALANCE

1. Have you stopped seeing friends because it seems like a waste of your time?
2. Are family members complaining that they see too little of you?
3. Have you missed important family occasions because of work?
4. Do you see fewer movies/concerts/plays/sporting events and so forth because of work?
5. Do you find yourself feeling bored or empty when you're not working?
6. Are you unsure of what to do with yourself when you're not busy?
7. Does relaxing make you feel guilty or nervous?
8. Do you have trouble making conversation that isn't about your job?
9. Do you work to the point where you are simply too tired to do anything else?
10. Do you have trouble saying no to work-related requests?
11. Do you evaluate your day strictly by the amount of work you accomplished?
12. Have you been wondering recently what the point of all this work is?

Source: Alice Bredin, *The Home Office Solution* (New York: John Wiley & Sons, 1998), p. 126.

management of teleworkers. You learned earlier in this chapter that disadvantages to an organization in managing teleworkers include developing policies for them and determining performance/evaluation methods. In addition, the management techniques used are, by necessity, somewhat different than the regular management ones. You will learn more about regular management responsibilities in Chapter 17. Although a detailed discussion of telework management is beyond the scope of this chapter, an overview is presented here for your understanding of some of the unique management responsibilities.

Some of the issues that must be managed with teleworkers are

- Socialization
- Communication
- Selection of teleworkers[12]

Socialization

Since the teleworker is not at the same location with the traditional worker, the socialization process is very different. However, the teleworker still must understand the values and directions of the company and meet individuals who are part of the company. The manager of a teleworker should

- Help the teleworker understand the values of the company and determine if there is a match between the individual's and the company's values
- Introduce a mentoring system that allows the teleworker a contact person to help him or her understand the organization and assist when a problem or an issue comes up; such a system helps the teleworker feel less remote
- Offer teleworkers opportunities that bring them into the organization to engage in team meetings, professional development, and socializing activities of the organization, such as company picnics

Communication

In managing the teleworker, the manager must determine the most appropriate communication styles, which may vary with the particular job assignment. For example, if the teleworker is beginning a new project with a team, it may be appropriate to have a team meeting at the organization's office to go over the objectives and expectations of the project and discuss assignments for each member of the team. As the team members begin to work in their home workspaces, they may communicate through e-mail, conference calls (teleconferences), discussion boards, or online real-time meetings. The manager of the project may choose to schedule monthly team meetings at the organization's office or participate with the team in e-mail/online discussions or conference calls. The manager must understand the various communication processes available and what will work best in each situation. Communication between the manager and the teleworker is important and should result in work that is produced effectively with little confusion.

Selection of Teleworkers

You have already learned that if teleworkers are to be successful, they must possess certain characteristics, such as motivation, persistence, and technological competencies. As organizations are expanding into telework situations, managers need to give consideration to the variables that impact teleworker selection. Omari and Standen[13] identify these variables:

- Organizational environment—business goals, corporate culture, management style, co-workers/clients
- Type of telework—knowledge intensity, internal contact, external contact
- Teleworker—work motivation, personality, telework competencies, performance record
- Remote environment—physical, social, psychological
- Task characteristics—autonomy, variety, social integration, sense of value, clarity of goals

If you manage teleworkers, understand that your management role is different and that you must give consideration to the unique variables of the teleworker's environment. The success of the organization's telecommuting efforts and the success of the individual teleworker depend on it.

Home Workspace

Deciding to become a telecommuter or teleworker means that you will need to create a space in your home where you can work—a place you can call your "office." Before considering what type and size of workspace you need, ask yourself these questions: What type of work will I be doing? How much space do I need to accomplish the work? What furniture and equipment do I need? What should I consider when selecting furniture and equipment so that I avoid ergonomic health-related problems? Will I be working on highly technical material that requires a distraction-free workspace? Will I be meeting clients or customers in my workspace? What environmental factors are important to me? For example, do I need to be close to a window?

Once you ask and answer these questions, you are ready to consider the location and size of your workspace.

Workspace Size and Location

If you need a distraction-free workspace, locate your office away from the family living area of your home. A spare bedroom or a basement room may be the answer. If clients, customers, and/or co-workers will be meeting with you occasionally, the space should be close to an outside entrance. If you have extremely noisy neighbours on one side of you, locate your workspace on the opposite side of the house or as far away from the noise as possible. Ask yourself this question: How large does my space need to be? If you are a telecommuter who is working at home only one or two days per week, you can be less concerned about workspace. Your space may be a small area you set up with a minimum amount of equipment in a corner of a room. If you are working at home full-time, consider what type and size of desk you need and the space required for a copier, a computer, a printer, and any other equipment. Also consider the number and size of filing cabinets needed and whether you need bookshelves.

The location you choose must have adequate lighting for your equipment. You do not want to locate your computer so close to a window that the outside light causes a glare on your computer screen. Your location also needs to have sufficient electrical outlets and telephone jacks to accommodate your equipment. The electrical outlets must be in proximity to your equipment. Stringing extension cords across a room can be dangerous.

You want to be able to control the heating and cooling in the room. Working in an environment that is too hot or too cold contributes to lessened productivity.

The colour of your office can make a big difference in your productivity, because you are going to spend a major portion of your time in the office. We know from research that colours affect our well-being. Tones of grey tend to put workers to sleep. Cool colours, such as light greens and light blues, produce a calm and tranquil atmosphere. Red is an aggressive colour and is not appropriate when you need to concentrate for long periods of time. Warm colours, such as yellow, are cheerful and inviting. Colour research shows that people have more clarity of thought when working in yellow environments. Yellow also stimulates creativity and mental activity.

Equipment

Your equipment purchases should include the basics— a computer, printer, fax, copier, and scanner. Multifunction machines (such as a fax, printer, copier, and scanner all in one machine) are also available. To help you determine what equipment will best meet your needs, do the following:

- Read computer periodicals such as *Home Office Computing*, *PC World*, and *PC Computing*.
- Conduct online research; many equipment and software manufacturers advertise their products on the Internet. Figure 2-5 provides several online resources.
- Shop your local computer stores.
- Talk with people who use the technology. For example, discuss the best buys with other teleworkers, computer technicians, or friends who are computer-literate.

Workplace Safety

Be conscious of the need for security. Since you are often working home alone using computer technology and other expensive hardware, you want to do what you can to maintain a theft-proof environment. Here are several suggestions for keeping your workplace safe:

■ **Figure 2-5**

ONLINE RESOURCES FOR EQUIPMENT

- www.ats-systems.com
- www.computerland.ca
- www.computers-canada.com
- www.dell.ca
- www.ebay.ca
- www.fujifilm.ca
- www.fujitsu.ca
- www.hp.ca
- www.ibm.ca
- www.kodak.ca
- www.lexmark.ca
- www.minolta.ca
- www.pc-canada.com
- www.qps.ca
- www.zdnet.ca

- Install simple locks on windows so they cannot be forced open from the outside.
- Install a security system that contacts the police if there is a break-in.
- Install a deadbolt on the office door.
- Draw the shades when you are working at night.
- When travelling for a few days, leave a few lights on and put other lights on automatic timers.
- Be certain your office furniture and equipment is insured for the proper amount.

Health, Life Insurance, and Retirement Benefits

If you are a self-employed teleworker, you need to purchase health and life insurance and set up a program for retirement. Talk with several health and life insurance companies, and research the benefits available. If you have a friend who has a trusted insurance agent, you might start with that person. You must be concerned about providing adequately for you and your family during your retirement years. Options include **RRSPs** (registered retirement savings plans) and investments in **mutual funds** (funds that include a combination of stocks and bonds purchased through a mutual fund company) or individual **stocks** (ownership in a company) and **bonds** (a debt owed by an organization). Consult with a certified financial planner about your long-term plans and needs.

Ergonomic Guidelines for the Workspace

Ergonomics is the term used to denote the fit between people, the tools they use, and the physical setting where they work. The word is derived from the Greek words **ergos** ("work") and **nomos** ("natural laws"). Ergonomics refers to furniture and equipment that is physiologically sound so you remain healthy as you use it. You can find more information on setting up an ergonomically sound workspace by visiting the site of the Canadian Centre on Occupational Health and Safety at ww.ccohs.ca.

Individuals who sit at a computer keyboard every day for more than two hours should take special care to ensure their workstation is user-friendly. If it is not, some of the following ergonomic health issues may arise.

Ergonomic Health Issues

Due to the amount of time individuals spend at computer keyboards, there is a risk of **RSI** (repetitive stress injury)—injury caused by repeated performance of certain physical actions over a period of time, also known as *overuse disorders*. RSIs impact workers' health and cost the teleworker and/or businesses many dollars in lost work and insurance claims.

Carpal tunnel syndrome is one type of RSI. This condition occurs due to the compression of a large nerve, the median nerve, as it passes through a tunnel composed of bone and ligaments in the wrist. Symptoms include a gradual onset of numbness and a tingling or burning in the thumb and fingers. Other types of overuse disorders, which occur as a result of sitting at the computer for long periods of time, are **computer vision syndrome** (from screen glare) and back problems (from chairs that are not the right height or configuration for the user).

Figure 2-6 on page 38 gives several tips for helping to avoid RSIs.

Computer Workstation

Whether you are creating a new home office workspace or considering changes to an existing workspace on your employer's premises, careful consideration should be given to eliminating potential ergonomics-related health problems. The following material will help you to establish an ergonomically sound workstation that minimizes the risk of injuries at work.

Furniture and Equipment

Much of the workplace furniture today is modular. Desktops, shelves, and cabinets attach to partitions or walls. These units can be adjusted for height, efficiency, and attractiveness. When determining the type of furniture and equipment you need, pay attention to the following ergonomic factors:

- *Ergonomic chairs* should be purchased that are fully adjustable for seat height and back height so that the correct height from the floor is achieved and your back is adequately supported. It is also important that the chair's seat and back move independently of each other so that necessary adjustments can be made; otherwise, the chair can

■ Figure 2-6

ERGONOMIC TIPS TO HELP AVOID RSIs

- Be certain the light on your computer screen is bright enough. Position monitors parallel to overhead lights and perpendicular to windows.
- Place your computer monitor directly in front of you, with the top of the screen at eye level.
- Position keyboards and mice low enough so your shoulders are relaxed.
- Get a desk light if you are squinting while reading at your desk.
- Take frequent breaks—a one-minute break every 20 minutes.
- Take a short rest period (10–15 minutes) every two or three hours.
- Stand up every 30 minutes.
- Take more frequent breaks to increase circulation if you are stiff when you get up from your chair.
- Be certain your chair is adjusted properly for you. Adjust the angle and height of the backrest of the chair so it supports the hollow in your lower back. Your chair should also have armrests adjusted to the same level of your desk to take the pressure off your neck and shoulders.
- Use the following proper keyboarding techniques:
  - Always sit up straight.
- Sit close enough to the keyboard so you do not have to stretch to reach it and close enough to the monitor so you do not have to stretch to see it.
- Your wrists should be in a straight line with your forearms.
- Your wrists should never be bent to the side or resting on anything.
- Organize your workstation.
- Be certain that your keyboard is at an appropriate height for you. For most adults, the keyboard should be 60–63 centimetres from the floor.
- Use good posture.
- Keep wrists relaxed and straight, using only finger movements to strike the keys.
- Look away from the screen for a short period of time every 30 minutes.
- Focus on distant objects occasionally as an exercise to relieve strain on eye muscles.
- Maintain a viewing distance of 55–60 centimetres from the eye to the computer.
- Use proper hand and wrist position when keyboarding.
- Place the mouse at the side of the keyboard and at the same level. Have it close enough so you do not have to reach a long distance; a mouse pad or rest may help. Choose a mouse that fits your hand.

cause you health problems. Chair arms should be height-adjustable.

- *Your desk* should also be ergonomically correct. Ideally, it should be height-adjustable and have an adjustable keyboard pad offering keyboard and mouse support.
- *The monitor* is an integral part of a computer workstation, which when incorrectly placed forces you to work in a variety of awkward positions potentially resulting in headaches, aches and pains in the neck and shoulders as well as eyestrain. Research in this area indicates that the eyes naturally assume a straightforward and slightly downward cast of between 10 and 30 degrees.[14] Ideally the monitor should be placed at the same height

as the keyboard. When the monitor is improperly situated, you are forced to work with your chin tilted upward, and the head and upper body bent forward or sideways. These forced working positions will contribute significantly to your personal discomfort, and can lead to work-related injury.

Computer Equipment

In making your decisions on computer equipment check out ergonomic keyboards, trackballs, and mice. Some of the features of ergonomic keyboards are

- Split keyboards
- Built-in wrist rest

- Detachable wrist rest
- Chair-mounted keyboards
- Foot-switch support
- Mouse functions through keys

When correctly positioned in your workspace, keyboards should be approximately five centimetres below the desk surface so that your arms naturally assume a 90 degree angle when bent at the elbow.

Trackballs are the device of choice for many people whose hands cramp when they use a conventional mouse device. Microsoft manufactures a trackball whose internal moving parts are replaced with an optical sensor that provides the user with a precise pointer that stays stationary on the desk. Also available is a mouse that vibrates, helping the user to find an exact location on cluttered Web pages and Windows screens with less hand motion.

Courtesy of Kinesis Corporation, www.kinesis.com

Ergonomic keyboards offer split keyboard designs and built-in wrist rests, along with other features.

Lighting

To process information efficiently, an adequate lighting system that contains both ambient and task lighting should be created. Working in an environment with improper lighting can cause headaches, eye fatigue, neck and shoulder strain, and irritability. An administrative professional spends a large amount of time looking at a screen, so glare from a computer screen can be a major problem. Glare is caused by a number of factors, including light bouncing off objects such as picture frames, mirrors, and even glossy periodicals. Techniques used to reduce glare include

- Relocating items on the wall or framing artwork with non-glare glass

- Reorienting workstations to ensure that light comes from the side rather than in front of or behind a workstation
- Replacing overhead ambient lighting with flexible systems so lights can be easily repositioned and brightened or dimmed
- Using screens and draperies that diffuse light and deflect glare

Although this chapter cannot provide an in-depth approach to ergonomics (entire books have been written on the subject), several areas are addressed here. *Office Ergonomics*, a pamphlet produced by the Canadian Centre for Occupational Health and Safety that can be viewed on their website at www.ccohs.ca, contains several illustrations of correct workstation design. Figure 2-7 provides a workstation checklist.

■ **Figure 2-7**

WORKSTATION CHECKLIST

- Eliminate glare from your computer and your workstation.
- Be certain you have adequate light for reading without squinting.
- Adjust your chair height so that your feet are flat on the floor.
- Be certain your chair is sturdy—a base with five rather than four legs is more stable.
- Place your computer keyboard five centimetres below your desk surface.
- Eliminate loud noises from your workstation environment.
- If the colour of your workstation is depressive, change it or ask your employer if it can be changed.

Survival Strategies for a Teleworker

Once you have created your office workspace and begin to work as a teleworker, you will find that the following skills are essential:

- Creativity
- Self-management
- Productivity
- Strategic thinking

- Technology
- Continual learning

Certainly these skills are many of the same ones the traditional workplace demands. However, in the traditional workforce, you have the luxury of receiving input from your co-workers about your strengths and weaknesses and taking advantage of organization-sponsored staff development events if needed. As a teleworker, these opportunities are not as easily available to you. Thus, it behooves you to take care of yourself. You cannot keep up a pace of constant, effective work production if you do not also give yourself the opportunity for renewal. You do not want to become **insular** (narrow or provincial in outlook). How do you provide that opportunity of renewal? Here are some suggestions.

Take a Break

Give yourself breaks—breaks of 30 minutes and breaks of an hour or two. These breaks do not reduce your productivity; they improve it by giving you a chance to renew and think more creatively. Leave your cell phone at home and get out in the fresh air. Take a walk for an hour; notice the beauty of nature wherever you find it around you. If possible, go to a park; observe the children playing and the dogs enjoying their walks. Find some place to walk where you can let your mind be free of the stresses of work for a period of time.

Reward yourself with longer breaks where you have the chance to enjoy a beautiful setting and also work. That setting may be a week at Long Beach on the west coast of Vancouver Island or two weeks at a cottage on the shores of Lake Ontario. Remember, the teleworker can work from almost any setting as long as he or she has access to telecommunications. You may be surprised at how much work you actually accomplish and how creative and refreshed you feel for allowing yourself the opportunity for renewal. Growth comes when we let ourselves thoroughly experience the world.

Schedule Relaxation

If you are not very good at taking that walk in the park—you never quite find the time or you just forget about it—schedule the walk on your calendar, along with other relaxation activities. Schedule 30 minutes to read or watch television every evening, or schedule an

hour at a local club every week to play tennis with a friend. Although "scheduled relaxation" appears to be an **oxymoron** (a combination of contradictory terms), many of us have become so conditioned to accomplishing what is on our calendars that the only way we take advantage of a relaxing activity is to schedule it.

Exercise

Numerous studies have shown the importance of regular exercise for our bodies and minds. Yet most North Americans ignore the studies and fail to exercise on a regular basis. Here is why exercise is so important. The task of the cardiopulmonary system is to pump oxygen into your blood and then to pump the blood to all parts of your body. When you are sitting and breathing quietly with your heart at rest, less oxygen and blood are flowing to your brain than when you exercise. Your brain activity naturally slows because blood and oxygen are in lower supply.

The exercise should be **aerobic**. Aerobic exercise means the body uses oxygen to produce the energy needed for the activity. In order for an activity to be aerobic, it must meet three criteria: it must be brisk, be sustained, and involve a repeated use of large muscles. Walking, jogging, swimming, stationary cycling, and jumping rope are examples of aerobic exercise.

Both starting and maintaining an effective exercise program are hard tasks but well worth the effort—the payoff not only being a healthier body but also a more creative, productive brain. Here are some tips to help you sustain an exercise program:

- Write on a calendar the days you plan to exercise each week.
- Mark off the days you exercise as the week goes by.
- At the end of the week, count up the number of times you exercised. Did you meet your goal?
- Make arrangements for family or friends to exercise with you.
- Find an indoor location where you can exercise in extreme weather conditions.

Eat Properly

Eating properly may be more of a challenge for the teleworker than the traditional office worker. Why? It is easy to take a break in the kitchen and reach for whatever snack is available. It is also easy to get involved in a project and reach for a snack to break the tension. Most of us use food in a variety of ways—to feel better, to be sociable, to reduce boredom. Although food cannot solve our emotional and mental issues, we attempt to fool ourselves that it can. Certainly a major part of the way we treat food has to do with what we learned about food growing up. Did our parents allow us candy if we cleaned our room? Were we rewarded with a special meal celebration if we brought home good grades? To get our eating under control, we may have to undo the patterns we learned as children.

One of the tricks to getting your eating under control is to refrain from buying candy, cookies, and other snacks at the grocery store. If the food is not in the house, you cannot eat it. As you or another family member prepares the weekly grocery list, make certain it is replete with fruits and vegetables. Learn to cut out a major part of the fat that is in your diet, and reduce sugar and caffeine consumption. Excessive intake of fat, sugar, salt, and caffeine contributes to poor health and to certain diseases, such as hypertension and heart disease. The average cup of regular coffee contains 100 to 150 milligrams of caffeine. Nervousness, insomnia, and headaches have been related to as little as 250 milligrams of caffeine. The average North American consumes more than 57 kilograms of sugar a year. Excessive sugar consumption can lead to an increase in triglyceride levels in the blood, which can lead to cardiovascular disease. Too much salt can lead to an increase in blood pressure and to the development of hypertension.

Sleep

The proper amount of sleep is essential to mental and physical health. Studies show that many people have sleep deprivation; they have denied their bodies the proper amount of sleep for so long that it is affecting their physical health. Although the amount of sleep needed varies among individuals, studies show that most people need from seven to nine hours of sleep per night.

A number of us have problems getting the proper amount of sleep due to our busy schedules and stressful lives. The teleworker may go back to the "office" at the end of the day for another three or four hours of work. Teleworkers may also go to bed thinking about the projects for the day or the projects planned for the next day and find that sleep does not come for an hour or so after hitting the pillow. Practising the following techniques will help you fall asleep easily:

- Set aside the hour before bed for quiet activities such as reading.
- Take a hot bath.
- Turn off the TV in the bedroom and/or turn down the TV in an adjoining room.
- Practise deep-breathing exercises.
- Create a relaxing scene in your head—waves rolling up on a beach or a mountain stream.
- Be certain your mattress and pillow are right for you—the proper firmness or softness.
- Pay attention to the amount of coffee, tea, cola, and chocolate you are consuming; these stimulants can lead to sleep deprivation.

Reward Yourself

In the traditional work setting, rewards can come from your supervisor or from your co-workers in the form of a smile and a thank-you or a pat on the back, with the statement "Good job," or from a promotion and/or increase in salary. When you are a teleworker, you must remember to give yourself rewards. That may not be easy for you to do. However, being successful in life demands that you not only recognize your strengths but also reward yourself for them. You need to feel good about your work and your accomplishments. How do you reward yourself? Try these techniques.

- Make a to-do list of what you plan to accomplish each day. Then mark off your accomplishments at the end of the day. Say a mental "thank you" for your ability to stick to the task.
- Share your accomplishments with others. Tell your spouse, your children, and your close friends about what you have achieved. For example, if you have completed a complicated Web page project and the public response has been favourable, brag about it a little. Your family and close friends can be proud of your accomplishments also and share your successes.
- Reward yourself. Give yourself a night out at the theatre or buy something for yourself you have been wanting. Take the time to read a novel, go to a concert, or enjoy a meal at a restaurant with family or friends.

Chapter Summary

The summary will help you remember the important points covered in the chapter.

- There were 134 million teleworkers worldwide in 2003. There is a growing number of people in telework and the United Kingdom projects that by 2010, 52 percent of its population will be involved in teleworking.
- Advantages of telework for the individual include greater productivity, greater flexibility of work times and work style, decreased driving, greater access to family, and more autonomy, freedom, and opportunity to remain in work.
- Disadvantages of telework for the individual are isolation, lack of organizational identity, no support group, lack of access to equipment, loss of fringe benefits, fewer opportunities for development and promotion, and conflict between work and home responsibilities.
- Advantages of telework for the organization include financial savings, access to highly skilled workers across the country, flexible employment opportunities, opportunity for work to be done outside traditional office hours, greater competitiveness in a global economy, and increased productivity.
- Disadvantages of telework for the organization are managing teleworkers, experiencing increased selection and training costs, developing policies for teleworkers, determining performance/evaluation methods, and providing technological support.
- Societal advantages of telework include increased entrepreneurial activity, increased community stability, and less pollution.
- To be successful in telework, the individual must be able to think strategically, be productive, manage her- or himself, be creative, and use technological skills.
- Things that undermine telework success include isolation, noise, family issues, and work/life balance.
- The teleworker must be managed differently from the traditional worker. Managers must consider socialization, communication, and selection of teleworkers.
- The teleworker must consider home workspace and equipment and furniture needs.
- The teleworker must also consider workplace safety and health, life insurance, and retirement benefits.
- The teleworker must follow ergonomic guidelines in selecting and setting up the furniture and equipment in a home workspace.
- Survival strategies include both short and long breaks, relaxation, exercise, proper nutrition, sleep, and self-rewards.

Key Terms

The following terms were introduced in this chapter. The page on which the term was introduced is provided to help you locate the new term. Definitions are compiled in the Glossary at the end of the text.

- **telecommuting** 26
- **mobile telework** 26
- **virtual office** 26
- **virtual company** 26
- **self-employed teleworker** 27
- **virtual teams** 28
- **strategic thinking** 29
- **mission statement** 29
- **sleep deprivation** 31
- **self-management** 31
- **RRSPs** 37
- **mutual funds** 37
- **stocks** 37
- **bonds** 37
- **ergonomics** 37
- **ergos** 37
- **nomos** 37
- **RSI** 37
- **carpal tunnel syndrome** 37
- **computer vision syndrome** 37
- **insular** 40
- **oxymoron** 40
- **aerobic** 40

Responses to Self-Check C

Explanation of Score

12–20 Strong Introvert. You may need to get out more than you are doing now. The critical aspects of working at home, such as communicating with customers or co-workers, may feel like chores to you.

21–30 Moderate Introvert. You probably do not have many problems coping with the relative isolation of working at home. However, make regular interaction breaks a priority.

31–35 Introvert/Extrovert. You enjoy solitary and social time in a balanced way. You have trouble with isolation when a deadline or major project keeps you from your usual regimen of socializing.

36–41 Moderate Extrovert. You often feel cooped up and lonely. The good news is that you are not likely to let that happen very often. As an extroverted person, you probably initiate contact whenever you feel you need it.

42–48 Strong Extrovert. You may have trouble handling the isolation that comes with working at home.

Discussion Items

These discussion items provide an opportunity to test your understanding of the chapter through written responses and/or discussion with your classmates and your instructor.

1. Define telework. List five advantages and five disadvantages of telework for the individual. List five advantages of telework for the organization.
2. List and explain five qualities and skills necessary for success in telework.
3. Explain what is meant by self-management.
4. List what to consider when setting up a home office.
5. What is meant by ergonomics? Give five ergonomic guidelines to follow when establishing a new or adapting an existing workstation.
6. List and explain five survival strategies for the teleworker.

Critical-Thinking Activity

Ryan Stapleton has been working for A&I Telecommunications as an administrative professional for five years. His work involves researching and preparing reports, managing a website, providing computer and software training, and working on TQM teams. Recently, he was offered the chance to telecommute two days per week, with the rationale that researching and preparing reports plus managing a website require a work environment free of interruptions.

The company believes he can be more productive by working on these projects from a home office. A&I will provide him with the computer equipment he needs.

Ryan is married and has two children—one ten years old and one two years old. Ryan's wife works full-time away from the home. Ryan has now finished his first two weeks of telecommuting. Although Ryan thought his wife understood that he has a full-time job the two days he is home, she begins making additional demands of him. She suggests that he keep the two-year-old on the two days he is home. She also expects him to cook on those two nights. He tries keeping the two-year-old, but he cannot get any of his work done. However, since his wife is insisting on the arrangement, he is going to give it more time.

Ryan considers himself an extrovert. Although he enjoys the freedom of working on his own the two days each week, he misses the hubbub of the workplace. He also is getting a lot of e-mail and telephone calls from his supervisor and co-workers about work issues. The report he prepared during his first two weeks took more of his time than usual. He had to work from 8 a.m. until 10 p.m. every day to finish the report; his child-care duties and meal preparation also interfered with his work time. He believes his productivity is decreasing rather than increasing. Ryan wants to continue with the telecommuting, but he is not sure the hassles he is facing are worth it.

What advice would you give Ryan? Using critical thinking, suggest how the issues Ryan is facing should be handled.

Projects

Project 2-1 (Objectives 1, 2, and 3)

Online Project

Find and study at least three articles on the Web to discover the advantages and disadvantages of telework, current telework directions, statistics, and qualities and skills needed by the teleworker. Use the Web addresses given in Figure 2-1 or additional resources that you discover. Write a short summary of your findings, listing your sources. Submit your keyed report to your instructor.

Project 2-2 (Objectives 3 and 4)

Using your answers to Self-Check B, write a plan for improving your self-management skills. This plan is part of your ongoing Professional Growth Plan that you began developing in Chapter 1. Concentrate on only one area of self-management. For example, if stress is a problem for you, concentrate on improving your ability to handle it. Identify the actions you will take. Also, briefly address how the weakness you have identified relates to your values and attitudes. Save your self-improvement plan on your Professional Growth Plan disk as "Progro2-2." Develop an appropriate title for this portion of your plan.

Project 2-3 *(Objective 5)*

Research two articles using periodicals such as *Home Office Computing* and *PC World* or the website of the Canadian Centre for Occupational Health and Safety (www.ccohs.ca) to determine how to properly configure a workspace and how furniture and equipment should be used. Submit a short, keyed summary of the articles to your instructor, listing the resources you used.

Project 2-4 *(Objective 6)*

Collaborative Project

With two or three of your classmates, interview a manager of teleworkers. You may do this interview in a conference call or e-mail the manager with your questions. It does not have to be a personal interview. Ask him or her the following questions:

- How do you select teleworkers?
- How many teleworkers does your organization have presently? Do you expect to have more teleworkers in the future?
- What characteristics and skills do you look for in teleworkers?
- How do you introduce teleworkers to the organization's goals?
- Are there special issues that you have with managing teleworkers? If so, what are they?

Present an oral report of your findings to the class.

Chapter 3

Time, Stress, and Anger Management

LEARNING OBJECTIVES

1. Identify time wasters.
2. Manage time.
3. Define the causes of stress.
4. *Develop conflict resolution skills.*
5. Identify stress reducers.
6. Control stress.
7. Manage anger.

The information age in which we live is producing more stress in individuals than ever before. The price of this increased level of stress is high for both the individual and the organization. In a 2001 survey conducted by Ipsos-Reid for Aventis Healthcare, 62 percent of the respondents indicated that they experienced a great deal of stress on the job.[1] Every week millions of people take medication for stress-related symptoms. Physical problems that may be the result of stress include ulcers, headaches, high blood pressure, and even heart disease. Additionally, many psychological disorders are related to stress. And rather than stress-related problems decreasing, they are increasing. In fact, job stress costs North American businesses billions of dollars every year in absenteeism, lost productivity, accidents, and medical insurance. Thirty-one percent of the respondents in the Aventis survey who indicated they were experiencing workplace stress said that they had taken six or more days off from work as a result.[2]

A major cause of stress is poor management of time. Some of the errors we make are

- Trying to do too much in too little time
- Wasting time and becoming frustrated due to lack of productivity
- Not establishing appropriate priorities

Also, closely related to stress management are conflict resolution and anger management. Anger, with resulting violent conflicts in the workplace, has become one of the biggest problems facing today's corporations Just as mismanagement of time produces stress, so too does unresolved conflict and mismanagement of anger. The results of this have become so serious in our world that each of us must give careful consideration to managing our anger as well as our time and thus controlling our stress. This chapter can be extremely beneficial in helping you understand how to manage your time, reduce your stress, control your anger, and resolve conflict.

Time Management

Time management is really a misnomer, since none of us can control the number of hours in a day. Time is finite; we cannot increase or decrease time by managing it. But we can learn to manage the details of the way we use our time. Thus, **time management** really refers to the way we manage ourselves and our tasks in relation to the time we have in a day, a week, or a year.

Time Defined

Time is a resource, but it is a unique resource. It cannot be bought, sold, borrowed, rented, saved, or manufactured. It can be spent, and it is the only resource that must be spent the minute it is received. Every one of us receives the same amount of time to spend each day; we all have 24 hours every day to manage in relation to our professional and personal goals. We cannot speed the clock up or slow it down. Time passes at the same rate every minute, every hour, and every day. The difficulty with time management occurs as we try to manage ourselves in relation to the finite time we have; many of us do not understand how we spend our time. We do not understand our time wasters, and we certainly are not taking steps to manage ourselves more effectively in relation to our time. Many of us do not realize that once we have wasted time, it is gone and it cannot be replaced.

> ### Communication Tip
>
> A short pencil is better than the longest memory. When in doubt, write things down.

Time Wasters

Before you begin to analyze how you might do a more effective job in managing yourself in relation to your time, look at some of the common time wasters that are detailed in the following paragraphs. You may find that you have been guilty of many of these behaviours.

Ineffective Communication

As an administrative professional, you will communicate both verbally and in writing with people in the workplace (your employer and co-workers) and outside the workplace (customers and clients). The lines of communication between you and others must be open and easily understood. Think of the time you will waste if you must rewrite a letter because you misunderstood the instructions from your employer; think of the profits the company may lose if you make a customer unhappy and lose an account as a result of misunderstood communication.

Poor Telephone Usage

The telephone becomes a time waster when it is not used properly. Here are some of the mistakes people make that cause the telephone to be a time waster.

- Being unprepared for placing outgoing telephone calls
- Failing to give the proper information to a co-worker, client, or customer
- Failing to get the proper information from a caller—that is, name, phone number, and reason for call
- Using the telephone when it would be more efficient to use e-mail or a fax
- Engaging in personal conversations during work hours

Inadequate Planning

Many individuals do not plan what they need to do on a particular day. Lack of planning can cause both you and your supervisor problems. Consider this situation.

Your supervisor gives you a report on Friday afternoon that must be completed by Monday afternoon. You understand that the job is a high priority. The report is not lengthy, but you do not analyze how long you will need to produce it. On Monday morning, you have numerous interruptions; you do not begin the report until 2 p.m. Monday. As you get into the report, you see that it is very involved and that you will not be able to finish it by 5 p.m. You are embarrassed and frustrated when you have to admit to your employer that the report is not completed, and your employer is unhappy. Your lack of planning resulted in an important report not being produced in a timely manner. If such planning lapses continue, you could lose your job.

Improper Handling of Visitors

As an administrative professional, your responsibility is to make visitors feel comfortable and welcome. However, that does not mean you must entertain the visitors while they are waiting to see your employer. Also, you should not spend long periods of time chatting with co-workers who stop by your workspace to visit. Certainly if a co-worker comes by on a work-related errand, you may engage in pleasantries such as "Good morning. How is your day going?" But you should not spend a lot of time in idle chitchat.

Disorganization

Does your desk have a pile of file folders on it, with their contents spilling out? Do you have half-finished projects, half-finished memorandums, and a stack of filing sitting around? Disorganized individuals are a serious liability to their organization. They cannot be depended upon to provide information in a timely manner because they forget where the information is. They cannot meet deadlines because they forget to write them down. They

When your desk is disorganized, it is difficult to get work done quickly and efficiently.

waste an enormous amount of their time and other people's time searching for files, phone numbers, reports, and other necessary information.

Procrastination

Procrastination is the postponement or needless delay of a project or task that must be done. Many of us are guilty of procrastination. We postpone a project because we are

- Worried about how large it is
- Afraid we will fail at it
- Not interested in the work
- Angry with the person who delegated it to us

Of course, we do not want to admit any of these reasons, so we make excuses. We make statements similar to the following:

- I have no time to get started.
- I have too many other projects.
- I don't have what I need to do the job.
- Before I can get started, I have to consult with my supervisor.
- There really is no rush to begin; it's not due for three weeks.

Procrastinators are late for meetings, put off handling projects, and do not return telephone calls. Procrastinators may be such relaxed, easygoing people that their procrastination does not bother them as much as it bothers others. However, they can create stress for themselves with their last-minute efforts, and the stress they put on other members of their work group can be significant. Refer to Self-Check A and consider your time-wasters.

Time Management Techniques

You have considered the importance of time management, and you understand that time is a resource that must be used well. You have looked at some of the time wasters that we all face. Now you must understand how to do a better job of managing yourself in relation to time. This area requires constant work. We never become such effective time managers that we can forget about the constraints of time. However, when we pay attention to effective management techniques, we find that not only do we seem to have more time to get our tasks done, but we also reduce the stress in our lives.

Set Goals

A **goal** is an objective, a purpose, or an end that is to be achieved. The idea of establishing goals makes many people feel uncomfortable—having to write them down and then being expected to achieve them. How many of us have set New Year's resolutions in good faith and then failed to reach any of them? Even thinking of these resolutions at a later date results in a vague sense of guilt about not having accomplished what we set out to do.

Goal setting can produce these same feelings of hesitancy and guilt. However, if we are to accomplish anything on our job and in our personal lives, we must set goals. An old Chinese proverb states "If you don't know where you are going, any road will take you there."

In other words, if you do not establish goals, you become undirected and may wind up someplace you did not intend to go.

Organizational Goals

Most organizations are involved in strategic and organizational planning. When these plans are written, they include definite goals to be accomplished and deadlines to meet these goals. Employees are usually brought into the planning process. In fact, companies often ask employees to write action plans that reflect what they will accomplish to meet the goals of the organization. Then during their performance evaluations, these employees are evaluated on how well they met their goals.

Personal Goals

Personal goal setting is also important. This goal setting can take the form of deciding

- What your career goals are—what you want to be doing and where you want to be in five or ten years
- When you want to purchase a house
- When or if you want to start a family
- Where you want to live

Goal Attributes

Effective goals must be achievable. They should also challenge you so you have the opportunity for growth. They should be specific and measurable. Goal attributes are explained here.

- *A goal should challenge you.* A goal should require you to do more than you have been doing. It should challenge you to reach a higher level of accomplishment.
- *A goal must be attainable.* Although goals should challenge you, they should not be unrealistically high. Goals should be achievable with hard work, appropriate skills, and dedication to the task.
- *A goal must be specific and measurable.* If your goal is too vague, you will not know when you have achieved it. For example, "to become a more effective communicator" is too vague. How can you become a more effective communicator? You should determine behaviours in which you are going to engage to accomplish your goal. Your goal might be stated as follows:

  I am going to become a more effective communicator by paraphrasing, using direct and simple language, and listening to others.

Your next step is to establish methods for measuring the accomplishment of your objective. In the communication situation, you might determine that you are going to measure the accomplishment in the following way:

In order to determine if I have accomplished my objective, I will ask three people within my work group to evaluate my communication skills.

- *A goal must have a deadline.* Deadlines allow us to see if the goal has been accomplished. In the communication example given above, you might set yourself this deadline:

  Evaluation of my communication goal will occur by December 19, 2005 [within three months after it was set].

- *A goal should be flexible.* Sometimes external conditions impact your goals to the point that you cannot accomplish them. When this occurs, do not cling stubbornly to something that is no longer possible but do not be too quick to eliminate the goal. By working smarter, you may be able to offset the external factors. Also, you may be able to revise your goal or establish a different time frame for completion.

Analyze Your Time

Although you might think you know exactly how you spend your time, actually most people do not. Check periodically how you are spending your time. You might be surprised at what is taking up your time, and you might discover some time wasters.

Log Your Time

One way to determine how you spend your time is to chart on a time log the amount of time you spend in various daily activities. Certainly you should not become a slave to the log, and you do not need to be accurate to the second or minute. However, you should be faithful to the process for a period of one or two weeks so you have a realistic picture of how you are spending your time. Figure 3-1 on page 49 shows a time log.

Analyze the Log

The next step is to analyze your time log to discover ways in which you can improve the management of your time. Ask yourself these questions.

- What was the most productive period of the day? Why?
- What was the least productive period of the day? Why?
- Who or what accounted for the interruptions?
- Can the interruptions be minimized or eliminated?
- What activities needed more time?
- On what activities could I spend less time and still get the desired results?

■ Figure 3-1

TIME LOG

DAILY TIME LOG

Name _____ Day _____ Date _____

Time	Activity	Priority	Nature of Interruptions
		1 2 3	

Prepare an Action Plan

After you analyze your log, the next step is to prepare an action plan. The purpose of the plan is to set goals for yourself as to how you will increase your time management efficiency.

Establish Effective Routines

Here are some techniques that will help you manage yourself in relation to your time. Obviously, there are numerous other effective time management techniques; only a sampling is provided here.

Set Priorities

Many times you will not be able to do everything you are asked to do in one day. Thus, you must be able to set priorities—to distinguish between the most important and least important jobs and determine the order in which they should be completed. If you are new to a job, you may need help from your supervisor to determine which tasks are the most important. When you learn more about your position and your supervisor, you should be able to establish priorities on your own.

Prepare Daily To-Do Lists

Before you leave work for the day, prepare a to-do list for the next day. List all the tasks, activities, and projects that you need to accomplish. Then review your list. Mark the most important items A, the less important items B, and those remaining C. Use your list, with priorities in place, to

- Arrange papers on your desk in priority order, with the A's in one pile, the B's in another pile, and the C's in still another pile
- Prioritize telephone messages, marking them A, B, or C
- Prioritize the papers in the A pile by determining which you will deal with 1st, 2nd, 3rd, etc. Do the same with the telephone messages
- Work through the tasks in order of priority, periodically reviewing the remaining items to see if they need to be moved up in order

As you complete the items on your to-do list, mark them off. This step gives you a sense of accomplishment and calls your attention to what you still need to accomplish. As you prepare your to-do list for the next day, use the present to-do list. If it still lists items you have not been able to accomplish, transfer these items to the to-do list for the next day. A sample to-do list is shown in Figure 3-2 on page 50.

Simplify Repetitive Tasks

If you find yourself keyboarding a form numerous times, simplify the process. Prepare a template on your computer. Do you find yourself looking up the same address or telephone number several times? Make yourself a list of frequently used addresses and telephone numbers. Store these on your computer or memory redial if available on your telephone. Simplifying a repetitive task takes time to organize initially, but in the long run, the savings in time can be significant.

> **Communication Tip**
>
> Vary your repetitive tasks to ease the boredom. For example, file for 20 minutes, sort mail for 10 minutes, and prepare mailing lists for 15 minutes.

Conquer Procrastination

Pick one area where procrastination plagues you and conquer it. For example, assume you always put off filing. You find yourself with two or three weeks of filing stacked on your desk, and you are constantly rummaging through papers for something your employer needs. In your list of priorities, set aside 20 or 30 minutes every day (or whatever time you need) for filing; put it on your to-do list. Check it off when you have accomplished it.

Here are some additional ways you can conquer procrastination:

- Focus on one task at a time.
- Give yourself deadlines and meet them.
- Tackle the most difficult tasks first.
- Break down large projects into smaller more manageable components.

■ Figure 3-2

TO-DO LIST

September						
Sunday	Monday	Tuesday	Wednesday	Thursday	Friday	Saturday
31	1	2	3	4	5	6
7	8 Labour Day	9	10	11 Prepare report	12	13
14	15 Send memo on TQM meeting	16	17 Make luncheon reservations for Mr. A	18	19	20
21	22	23 Begin presentation for community meeting	24			27
28	29	30	1			4

My To-Do List—Sept. 11

Task	Priority
Make phone calls	A
Prepare report	A
Write memo on TQM meeting	B
File	C

- Do not let perfectionism paralyze you; do not be afraid to make mistakes.
- Recognize that you have developed the habit of putting things off; then take steps to correct the habit. For example, create whatever visual reminders you need; you might make a sign for your desk reminding you not to procrastinate. Do not let yourself make exceptions by saying "It's okay to procrastinate on this task." A lapse is like a car skid; it takes much more effort to recover than to maintain control from the outset.

Handle Paper Once

Do you ever find yourself rereading a piece of paper or shuffling it from the top to the bottom of the stack several times? Most of us do. In fact, many time management experts claim that handling paper over and over is the biggest paperwork

> **Human Relations Tip**
>
> Your goal is to get control and then stay in control of your paperwork. Handle each piece of paper one time only.

> **Human Relations Tip**
>
> Spend a few minutes at the end of each day getting your desk organized. You will feel much better about coming to work the next day if your desk is well organized.

time waster. The basic rule is to handle every piece of paper just once. Read it, route it, file it, or answer it. Get it off your desk as quickly as possible.

Organize Your Work Area

When you are working on a project, clear your desk of materials that relate to other projects. Put these materials in a file folder, label the folder with the name of the project, and put the folder in your drawer.

Keep "in" and "out" trays on your desk, and label the trays for incoming and outgoing material. If space permits, you may wish to have a tray on your desk for material to be filed. Keep frequently used supplies (such as pencils, pens, and paper clips) in your centre desk drawer. Organize your paper into letterhead, plain bond, memorandum, and so on.

Reduce Interruptions

Interruptions can be frustrating time wasters. Controlling or minimizing interruptions is crucial to efficient time management. Here are some suggestions for reducing telephone and visitor interruptions.

Telephone

- Give and record correct information during telephone calls.
- When placing calls, identify yourself, your supervisor (if you are placing a call for her or him), and what you need.
- When placing long-distance calls, be aware of time zone differences and the implications on the cost of the call and/or the inability to contact the person called due to differences in the hours of business.
- If the person called is not in, find out when the person will return.
- When taking incoming calls, find out who is calling and the nature of the call.
- If you are taking a call for your supervisor who is not in, let the person know when your supervisor is expected.
- If you take a message, repeat the name, phone number, and message to the caller to confirm the accuracy.
- When you have several calls to make, group them and make the calls when people are likely to be in the office. Early morning is usually a good time to reach people.
- Be prepared to leave a concise voice mail message that identifies yourself or your supervisor and a brief summary of the reason for calling.
- Keep your personal calls to a minimum. Let your friends know they should not call you at the office.
- Use e-mail and faxes as an alternative to leaving and receiving phone messages.

Visitors

- Set up appointments for visitors. Discourage people from dropping by unexpectedly to see you or your supervisor.
- Make visitors welcome, but do not make small talk for extended periods. Continue with your work.
- Discourage co-workers from dropping by to socialize. You can socialize on breaks and at lunch. Make it clear that your responsibility during working hours is to work.

> **Communication Tip**
>
> Learn to say no when it is appropriate. Learn to delegate to others or to ask for help if you cannot complete the task in the time allotted.

Use Good Communication Techniques

If your supervisor asks you to do something, be sure you understand exactly what you are to do. Paraphrase what you believe he or she said if you are not clear. Do not be afraid to ask questions. Transmit ideas in simple, clear terms. Define terms if necessary.

Listen carefully when someone is talking. When you are communicating with an individual face to face, look at her or him. Be sensitive to the person's body language, and also to the words the person is saying. Keep your mind open to new ideas; refrain from passing judgment on what the speaker is saying.

Time Management Systems

A number of systems can help you use your time well. These systems may be manual or computer systems.

Manual Systems

One type of manual system is a calendar that allows you to record all appointments for the day, week, month, and year. If you use a manual calendar, keep all activities logged on the same calendar.

Planning systems are also available. These systems include calendars; but they also include places to record prioritized daily tasks and appointments, monthly planning calendars for future years, sheets for recording goals, telephone/address directories, and delegation sheets.

Another type of manual system is a **tickler file**, a chronological record of items to be completed. The system may be one you design yourself or one you purchase. If you are setting up the system, place a guide for the current month in the front of the file followed by a separate guide for each day of the month. Place guides for each month of the year at the back of the file. To use this file, write notes on index cards of tasks that need to be accomplished and file them behind the appropriate dates (see Figure 3-3 on page 52).

Computer Systems

PIM (personal information management) software is a popular type of software that allows you to manage a wide variety of information. For example, with PIM software, you can access the following:

■ Figure 3-3

TICKLER FILE

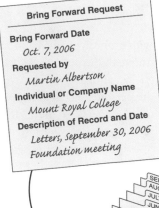

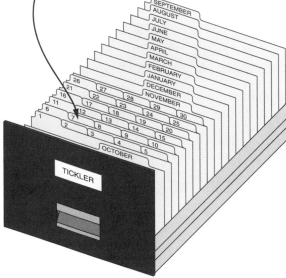

- Calendar software, which manages your schedule, address book, and to-do list
- Contact management software, which lets you track your contacts and keep detailed histories of your business contacts
- Information database software, which handles documents you have downloaded from the Internet or from another source

A number of companies produce PIM software:
- Microsoft Outlook®—calendar software. This software comes as part of Microsoft Office XP; it also may be purchased individually.
- Lotus Organizer—calendar software.
- Above & Beyond® 2000—calendar software. This is **shareware** or **trial software**, which means you

can download it from the Web for a trial period, in this case 21–30 days, to determine if the program meets your needs. Shareware PIMs are available at ZDNet® Software Library.
- Maximizer® and GoldMine®—contact management software. You may download both programs as trial versions.
- Info Select and Zoot™—database software. Zoot is available for a trial download from Zoot Software.

A calendar software page from a computer software package is shown in Figure 3-4 on page 53.

Time and stress management go hand in hand, each contributing to the other. If we do not manage our time well, we become stressed out; if we are stressed out, we cannot manage our time well. The next section of this chapter identifies some causes of stress and suggests some techniques you can implement to reduce them.

Stress—A Major Malady

As knowledge continues to expand rapidly and ever-changing technology becomes the rule rather than the exception, we must constantly learn new ways of performing our jobs. As businesses **downsize** (reduce the number of employees) and **rightsize** (determine the most efficient and effective number of employees and organizational structure), we may lose our jobs and even change our careers. As telework becomes a reality for more and more employees, we must adjust to working in very different conditions than in the past—often by ourselves. Such situations force us to deal with change as well as embrace it if we are going to be successful workers in the 21st century. All of these occurrences can and often do contribute to stress.

Stress is the body's response to a demand placed upon it. Our wants, needs, and desires are derived from stress of some kind. Stress cannot be avoided; in fact, we would not want to avoid all stress. If you never felt a need to achieve, you would not go to school. If you never felt a need to contribute, you would not accept a challenging job. Stress can and does have a positive impact on our lives. However, when stress becomes chronic, it is a negative health factor. **Chronic stress** occurs when a distressful situation is prolonged, allowing no rest or recuperation for the body; it can cause physical and emotional problems.

■ **Figure 3-4**

CALENDAR SOFTWARE

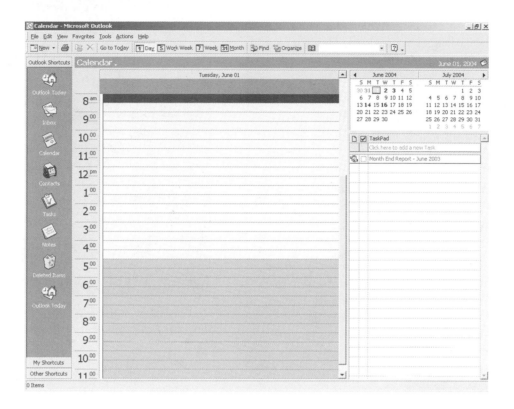

Causes of Stress

In addition to the change factors in our society that can cause stress, there are numerous other causes of negative stress. Some of the more common causes are discussed here.

Work Overload

Productivity is a key word in all organizations today. In order to compete in an international market, organizations are experiencing the need to be more productive; at the same time they are expected to reduce costs. Employees are often asked to produce more in less time with a greater degree of accuracy than ever before; thus, employees find themselves working long hours.

> **Communication Tip**
>
> Set up a job jar for each member of the family. On Sunday, determine tasks that must get done for the week and assign tasks to each family member. Or make the assignment of tasks a family activity in which each member volunteers for certain duties.

Dual-Career Families

In the majority of families today, both parents work. Parents must balance the pressures of the job with spending time with children and juggling the demands of grocery shopping, housework, and other responsibilities.

Single-Parent Families

The divorce rate in Canada continues to be high, and single-parent homes are not uncommon. The responsibility for raising children may fall on one parent. The responsibilities at home, along with the pressure of having to make enough money to meet the needs of the family, can cause stress.

Elderly Family Members

We are living longer than ever before. Many times this long life means that families include elderly family members who may require special care. Adult children may have to devote time and energy to assisting elderly parents in adapting to new living arrangements. Dealing with the challenges of the elderly family members can be difficult for everyone involved.

Economic Pressures

Even dual-career families may find it difficult to make ends meet. Individuals may work longer hours or take second jobs to bring in additional money for household needs. Single parents, too, may find themselves struggling to meet the financial needs of the family.

Distressing Work Conditions

Personality conflicts sometimes occur within the office. Co-workers can be unhappy in their personal lives, and this unhappiness may manifest itself on the job. You may be the innocent party who must face an unhappy individual at the office every day. You may also have to deal with a difficult supervisor—one who

Individuals sometimes take second jobs to help with the expenses at home.

Photodisc Green/Photodisc Collection

■ Figure 3-5

SUGGESTIONS FOR RESOLVING CONFLICT

- Identify what is causing the conflict. Is it power, resources, recognition, or acceptance? Many times our needs for these items are at the heart of the conflict.
- Determine what each person needs or wants. Ask questions to determine what the other person wants. Be willing to listen to the other person. Everyone feels a deep need to be understood. By satisfying that need in the other person, you may be able to lessen the conflict. If you do not understand what the other person is saying, paraphrase what you think you hear and ask for clarification. Be open to what the other person tells you.
- Identify points of agreement. Work from these points first. Then identify the points of disagreement.
- Create a safe environment. Establish a neutral location; establish a tone that is accepting of the other person's views and feelings. Acknowledge the other person's feelings. Behind anger may be fear. Let the

other person tell you how he or she is feeling. Watch how you position yourself physically in the room. Remember, you have a more difficult time competing with someone sitting next to you than with someone who is across the table or room. A circular seating arrangement may be appropriate if you have several individuals involved in a conflict.
- Do not react. Many times individuals act too quickly when a conflict occurs. Step back, collect your thoughts, and try to see the situation as objectively as possible.
- Do not seek to win during a confrontation. Negotiate the issues, and translate the negotiation into a lasting agreement.
- Actively listen. Watch the individual's eyes; notice his or her body language.
- Separate people from the issue. When the people and the problem are tangled together, the problem becomes difficult to solve. Talk in specific rather than general terms.

Soft Skills: Conflict Resolution

Conflict resolution skills, the soft skill for this chapter, are always important in workplace situations. Individuals and groups frequently face conflicts they must resolve. As an administrative professional, you should develop these important skills. When you are faced with conflict, address it. Suggestions for resolving conflict are given in Figure 3-5 on page 54. Read these suggestions carefully, and implement them as you work with others. Engage in **conflict resolution** (addressing and dealing with issues in a positive manner). Too many people try to avoid conflict. It usually does not go away; it merely gets worse. Here are some attitudes that help resolve conflict.

OPENNESS

Be open to what others think and feel. Also, state your feelings and thoughts openly without being negative. In other words, use "I" statements about how you feel and what you think should happen. For example, if you were planning a meeting and a conflict erupted about the type of meeting that should be held, you might say "I think the meeting should be a videoconference rather than a face-to-face meeting. It will save both money and time." You should not say, "You're not thinking! A face-to-face meeting would not be productive in this situation. Twenty people would have to travel from across Canada, costing both time and money."

Do you see the difference between these two statements? In the first one, you have used an "I" statement and you have stated your reason for why a videoconference is preferable. In the second statement, you began by accusing the others involved of not thinking. Such a statement immediately puts the individuals on the defensive. After all, you have suggested that they do not have the ability to think through a situation and come up with a logical conclusion.

EMPATHY

Listen with **empathy** (identification with and understanding of another's situation, feelings, and motives) to what others are saying. Express your concern and support for the other person's opinions. Be willing to change your position if others present appropriate reasons for doing so. In other words, do not be closed to the opinions of others.

EQUALITY

Give other people time to express their feelings. Evaluate all ideas equally. Do not base your opinion of an idea on whether the person is a friend of yours or whether you like or dislike the individual. Disagreements in which openness, empathy, and equality are present provide growth opportunities for all involved. We learn from hearing what others think and feel. We close ourselves to learning when we ignore the ideas of others.

---

is neither consistent nor considerate. These situations can cause stress.

Chronic Stress—Harmful to Your Health

Prolonged or chronic stress triggers the production of chemicals that cannot be broken down by our bodies. They remain in our system where they are capable of injuring our health. For example, chemicals produced by chronic stress can cause the following illnesses:

- High blood pressure
- Kidney damage
- Cardiovascular disease
- Migraine headaches
- Ulcers
- Elevated cholesterol
- Cancer

- Weakening of the immune system, which then leads to a number of illnesses

Chronic stress also can cause the following emotional problems:

- Depression
- Withdrawal
- Deep-seated anger
- Loss of self-esteem
- Self-rejection

Stress Reducers

Although we cannot avoid all negative stress, we must guard against its becoming a prevalent part of our lives. Healthy individuals find ways to get rid of negative stress so their bodies will not be damaged. Here are some stress reducers for you to practise.

Balance Work and Play

Many people comment that they work a 50- or 60-hour week, and the statement may be made with a sense of pride. Are these people producing a large amount of work? Maybe not. Do they have demanding and challenging jobs? Perhaps. Are they appreciated and respected for their work contributions? Not necessarily. We know there is a relationship between hours worked and productivity. Of course, individuals differ in the number of productive hours they can work. However, studies have shown that productivity decreases after extended periods of time. Most of us realize immediately when we are not being productive. When we become fatigued, the amount of work we produce goes down and our error rate goes up, signalling that it is time for us to slow down and take a break.

We can actually gain new energy by taking time to play. As adults we may have forgotten how to relax, and with complete abandon enjoy the world around us. Some experts writing in the field of creative energy urge us to take "joy breaks"—to stop for two to five minutes to play when we feel overtired or non-productive. We might even have toys at our desk—putty, a slinky, a kaleidoscope. These toys are small enough to keep in your desk. Just a few minutes of working the putty, moving the slinky back and forth, or looking at the various shapes in the kaleidoscope can release stress through relaxation, pleasant thoughts, and smiles.

Companies across the country are recognizing the importance of laughter for their employees. Major companies have used humour consultants to help create joy communities. Driving this move are the business issues that people face today (such as downsizing, international competition, increasing workloads, and technological change). Forward-thinking, progressive companies are realizing that if their employees are going to be productive and happy, they must help their employees use humour in the workplace. Studies have shown that humour can increase productivity, decrease absenteeism, and lead to better job satisfaction. Stanford University researcher William Fry has found that laughing 100 times a day is equivalent to ten minutes of exercise on a rowing machine. A good, hearty laugh pumps air into the lungs, increases oxygen intake, and causes muscles to relax. Laughter can even cause blood pressure to drop. After a hearty laugh, a person enters a deep state of relaxation that can last as long as 45 minutes.[3] A chuckle also helps. Take a few minutes

each day to read your favourite cartoon in the newspaper or to notice the funny antics of your co-workers. Laughter really is good medicine.

Another way to reduce tension quickly is to take a short exercise break. You might keep athletic shoes at your desk, and during a break spend five or ten minutes climbing stairs or walking briskly. Such physical activity allows you to release built-up tension, to open blocked thinking, and to trigger creative ideas.

SELF-CHECK B ✔

Take a few minutes now to write down several things that are fun for you and that you could do at the office during a two-to-five-minute break from your job.

— *read internet news.*

_____

_____

_____

_____

_____

Complete Self-Check B. How did you do? Were you able to come up with five or six items?

Distinguish Between Achievement and Perfection

Perfectionism is defined as "a propensity for setting extremely high standards and being displeased with anything else." Many of us believe we must do everything perfectly. Certainly, we must achieve and do things well; however, no human being can be perfect. To blame yourself continually for not doing everything perfectly is to engage in energy-draining behaviour. In fact, mistakes can be beneficial. Thomas Edison was asked how he came to hold so many patents. He answered that he dared to make more mistakes than ten other people and that he learned from each mistake. Edison knew that the creative process involved trial and error—failure and success. Unless we are willing to risk failure, we will never grow and learn.

Are you a perfectionist? Do you believe that everything you do must be done extremely well? Read and answer yes or no to the statements listed below.

1. If I do not do something well, I feel as though I am a failure.
   Yes ☑ **No** ☐

2. When I make a mistake, I spend many hours rethinking how I might have done it better.
   Yes ☑ **No** ☐

3. I have a reputation of being someone who is hard to please.
   Yes ☑ **No** ☐

4. When I am playing a sport (tennis, golf, baseball), I get angry with myself if I do not play my best game.
   Yes ☑ **No** ☐

5. I will not start a project unless I know everything I can about what I am to do.
   Yes ☐ ✓**No** ☐

6. I do not like to try new things.
   Yes ☐ ✓**No** ☐

7. I lose patience with others when they do not do things well. *depends*
   Yes ☐ ✓**No** ☐

8. I expect every piece of work I produce to be perfect.
   Yes ☐ ✓**No** ☐

Refer to Self-Check C. If you responded positively to all of the statements, you are probably caught up in a negative, perfectionist pattern of behaviour. Begin now to rethink how you view yourself and your work.

Recognize Your Limits

You must recognize when you are working too hard. Everyone has a different energy level. You may be able to work ten hours a day quite successfully; someone else may be able to work produc-tively eight hours a day. How do you know when you are working too hard? Become familiar with the symp-toms of stress, including the following:

- Anxiety
- Headaches
- Panic attacks
- Muscular neck pain
- Insomnia
- Jaw pain
- Phobias

If you develop these symptoms, seek help. Many companies have insurance programs that contain an Employee Assistance Plan (EAP) that provides for therapy sessions with psychologists or psychiatrists. These trained individuals can help you discover the causes of your stress and how you can alleviate it. If, however, this is not available at your place of work, check with your family physician; he or she can provide sources of assistance.

Exercise

Cardiovascular specialists have found that regular exer-cise can lower blood pressure, decrease fats in the blood, reduce joint stiffness, control appetite, and decrease fatigue. Exercise changes the body's chemistry, getting rid of toxins and producing endorphins and other hor-mones that increase creativity and silence negative self-talk. You will be more patient, calmer, and more receptive to others, as well as a better listener, after just 20 to 30 minutes of aerobic exercise.

What type of exercise should you do? Many exer-cises are good for your body—swimming, walking, and bicycling, to name a few. Participate in an exercise that you enjoy. What time of day should you exercise? It depends on you. You may prefer to exercise in the morning, while someone else may find the evening a better time to exercise. You may choose to exercise while following along with a video or a television program. You may join a health club or the local Y. Some clubs open as early as 5:30 a.m. and close as late as 11 p.m. or midnight. Most experts suggest exercising three to five times a week for a period of 30 minutes to an hour. When you begin exer-cising, go slowly. Train your body; do not strain it. If you

Communication Tip

Do not worry about things you cannot control. Remember what is important—family, friends, a place to live, and something to eat. Don't focus on things you can't change—learn the art of letting go.

have any medical problems or you are just beginning an exercise program, consult your doctor about the type of exercise that is best for you.

Eat Right

What you eat or do not eat affects your overall health. Excessive intake of fat, sugar, salt, and caffeine contributes to poor health and to diseases such as hypertension and heart disease. Remember that 0.2 litre of coffee contains about 180 milligrams of caffeine, 0.2 litre of tea about 70 milligrams, and 0.4 litre of cola about 45 milligrams.

Excessive amounts of caffeine can cause an individual to exhibit the same clinical symptoms as someone suffering from anxiety. Many people turn to junk food (candy, chips, and other munchies) to relieve stress. However, eating junk food increases stress. The high calorie and fat content of junk food also contributes to being overweight.

The average North American consumes about 60 kilograms of sugar a year. Excessive sugar consumption can lead to an increase in triglyceride levels in the blood, causing cardiovascular disease. Too much salt can lead to an increase in blood pressure and to the development of hypertension. The wisest course of action is to lower the intake of fat, sugar, salt, and caffeine in the diet.

Your diet should include plenty of fresh fruits and vegetables, and you should drink six to eight glasses of water a day. Whole-grain breads and high fibre are good for your body. Maintaining a balanced, healthy diet will help keep your energy level high and your stress level low.

Get Enough Sleep

Surveys have shown that approximately 40 percent of the adult population suffers from stress every day of their lives and find that they can sleep no more than six hours a night. What is enough sleep? It all depends on you; however, the general rule is at least seven hours, with many people needing eight or nine hours. You need to get enough sleep to function effectively.

> **Health Tip**
>
> Make time for yourself. Make taking care of yourself a No. 1 priority.

> **Health Tips**
>
> - Stop drinking caffeinated beverages at least six hours before retiring.
> - Drink a glass of milk before you retire to help you sleep.
> - Read about 30 minutes before you go to sleep to help you relax.

Manage Your Anger

Although we cannot always prevent ourselves from becoming angry, we can learn to recognize our anger and its causes and symptoms; we can also learn how to reduce that anger. As already discussed, we cannot add hours to our day to give us more time to do the many things we believe must be done. We can, however, learn to manage ourselves in relation to the time we have. As you have learned, stress is closely related to both anger and time management. When we are angry, we get stressed. When we do not have enough time to do what is important to us, we get stressed.

Having already learned some techniques to manage your time and deal with stress, the remainder of this chapter is devoted to helping you understand how to manage your anger more effectively whenever it occurs.

Anger Management

Anger—A Growing Corporate Problem

Over the past few years, incidences of violence in the workplace have increased. Shootings at a Kamloops office in the summer of 2002 is just one example of workplace violence that has received national news coverage. In fact, workplace violence has become such a large problem in North America that the Occupational Safety & Health Administration in the United States and the Canadian Centre for Occupational Health and Safety have both published specific guidelines on this issue and legislation exists in both countries. This legislation in Canada, known as "due diligence" legislation, when applied to occupational health and safety means that an employer shall take all reasonable precautions to prevent injuries or accidents in the workplace. Due diligence is defined as that level of judgment, care, prudence, determination and activity which a person would reasonably be expected to exercise under particular circumstances. This duty applies to all situations that are not covered by other, specific workplace legislation.[4]

Occupational health and safety legislation in Canada outlines the general rights and responsibilities of the employer, the supervisor, and the worker. In addition to there being federal legislation that applies to employees across the country employed by the federal government, each of the provinces and territories has its own legislation.[5] You can read more about the specific legislation in your province by going to the CanOSH (Canada's National Occupational Health and Safety) website at www.canoshweb.org.

Many organizations have started workplace violence prevention programs, which include helping individuals learn how to deal with and de-escalate conflict. Why is this happening? No one has all the answers to this question, but experts suggest that these issues may contribute to increased anger and violence:

- Ignorance of other cultures
- Belief that one is being treated unfairly
- Feeling hurt—often hurt feelings are manifested as anger
- Fear of losing a job or a promotional opportunity
- Feelings of inadequacy when faced with new procedures or technology
- Feeling out of control

Take a few minutes to answer the questions in Self-Check D.

Once you have established the fact that you are angry and that your anger has a specific focus, you are ready to put your anger into a more manageable perspective and take steps to reduce it. The following techniques will help you.

Relax

Deep-breathing exercises are one of the quickest ways to relax your body. Start by finding a comfortable position; sit in a comfortable chair or lie down. You may close your eyes if that makes you feel more at ease. Then slowly inhale through your nose until you feel your lungs fill up with air. Next, exhale slowly, through either your nose or mouth.

Use Positive Self-Talk

If you are angry, negative self-talk can escalate your anger; positive self-talk can de-escalate your anger. For example, assume you are playing a game of tennis with a friend who is extremely good. You miss a ball and say to yourself "I really am terrible!" You are engaging in negative self-talk, and negative self-talk on the tennis court causes you to miss more shots. In other words, your negative self-talk is a self-fulfilling prophecy. You decide you are terrible and you prove yourself right. Now consider a positive self-talk response. When you miss a ball, you say to yourself "No big deal; I'll get the next one." And you do! You hit a terrific ball. When you find yourself engaging in negative self-talk, turn it around by

---

SELF-CHECK D ✔

1. How are you feeling right now? Anxious? Hostile? Depressed? Numb? Frustrated? Sarcastic? Resentful? Paranoid? Victimized?

   Anxious
   _____
   _____
   _____

   Those words represent some of the names given to feelings of anger. The first step in resolving an anger problem is to identify the feeling as anger. The purpose of this step is to make the anger more specific. No one can manage anger that is vague and hidden by euphemisms.

2. If you selected any of the above words, what happened to make you angry? If you focus on the specific incident that triggered your anger, it becomes more understandable and easier to manage.

   _____
   _____
   _____
   _____

3. Who is the focus of your anger? Your spouse? Your partner? Your boss? The kids? All men? All women? Other races?[6]

   _____
   _____
   _____
   _____

- Recognizing the negative self-talk
- Stopping it immediately
- Beginning positive self-talk

Walk Away

Walk away physically if you can; if you cannot, walk away emotionally. When you were a child, did your mother ever say "Before you say or do anything when you are angry, count to ten"? Counting to ten allows you to interrupt your anger and cool off. It also allows you time to consider what other choices you might have. In your head, you are walking away from what is making you angry. Consider the following example, a common situation that often makes people angry.

You are waiting in line at the grocery store. The checker is slow, talking to customers as he scans their groceries. In addition, no grocery sackers are available, so the checker must sack the items. The person in front of you has forgotten two items and asks the checker if she can go get them; the checker agrees. You have an important appointment, and you have to be on time. You find yourself getting angrier and angrier, ready to scream at the person in front of you and at the checker.

What are your choices? You can walk away mentally—count to ten, sing a song to yourself, or envision yourself at one of your favourite places having a wonderful time. Or if you are going to be late for your appointment, you can physically walk away. Leave before you become angry and emotionally upset. You can always come back to the grocery store at another time.

Talk to a Friend

If a situation at work makes you angry, talk to a trusted friend or mentor about it. That person may be able to help you understand what is causing your anger and help you decide what you can do about the situation. For example, assume you have this situation at work.

You are chairing a team whose task is to recommend a new computer system. The team has met three times, and you believe progress is being made on the task. You believe the team has worked well together. Your supervisor calls you into her office, closes the door, and says she needs to talk with you about a serious matter. She tells you that two people on the team have complained you were not listening to what they were suggesting—that you had apparently already made up your mind about which computer system would be best and the team had almost no input. As she talks, you find yourself getting very angry. You believe that the accusations are totally false, and do not understand why anyone would make such statements.

To address the issue and avoid excessive anger, you might take these steps:

- Tell your supervisor that you have not made up your mind about the computer system and that you feel the team is working well together. However, tell her you want to think about the situation carefully and develop a plan to address it.
- Spend time talking with a trusted friend in the organization about the problem. Be open to the friend's comments. Then, develop a plan to address the situation.
- Talk with your supervisor about your plan.

Solve the Problem

Sometimes the same problem occurs frequently. For example, consider this situation.

You are the only woman in a department of men. Your job description is the same as the men's. Every time an important assignment comes up, the work is given to one of the men. You do a good job, and your supervisor (who is male) has given you excellent evaluations. However, you are beginning to think he does not value your work. You believe that as long as you are passed over in the assignment of more challenging work, you will not have a chance to learn and grow on your job. You also believe that without having the opportunity to do the challenging assignments, you will not have a chance for promotion. You wonder if your supervisor is guilty of gender bias. You are beginning to feel anger not only toward your supervisor but also toward the other men in the department.

What do you do? The problem is important enough that you should attempt to solve it. You can use a problem-solving approach, following the steps in Figure 3-6 on page 61.

Your Power and Your Potential

If you are to thrive in the business world today, you must master the multitude of changes that come your way in the form of technology, be productive and happy in your work, and be able to realize your full power and potential. When you are stressed to the point of being burned out on your job, angry a large part of the time, and finding too few hours in the day to accomplish what you must accomplish, you are not able to realize your full power and potential. By putting to use the techniques presented in this chapter, you have a chance to not only succeed in your job but also thrive in the world of change.

■ Figure 3-6

PROBLEM-SOLVING STEPS

1. Define the Problem or the Purpose

This first step may sound simple, but it is usually the most difficult of the steps. When attempting to define the purpose or problem, ask yourself:

- What problem am I trying to solve?
- Why is this decision necessary?
- What will be the outcome of this decision?

2. Establish the Criteria

The next step in the decision-making process is to determine the criteria you need to make a sound decision. When setting your criteria, ask yourself:

- What do I want to achieve?
- What do I want to preserve?
- What do I want to avoid?

3. Generate Alternatives or Possible Solutions

The next step in the decision-making process is to begin generating alternatives or possible solutions. What do you think you can do to solve the problem or make the decision? What alternatives are available to you?

4. Test the Alternatives and Make the Decision

The effective decision maker tests each alternative using this system:

- Eliminate alternatives that are unrealistic or incompatible with the needs of the organization.
- Select the alternative that appears to be the most realistic.

5. Evaluate the Decision

The last step in the decision-making process is evaluating the decision. In evaluating the decision, here are some questions to ask:

- What was right about the decision?
- What was wrong about the decision?
- How did the decision-making process work? What improvements are necessary? What changes need to be made for the future?

Chapter Summary

The summary will help you remember the important points covered in the chapter.

- Time is a unique resource; it cannot be bought, sold, borrowed, rented, saved, or manufactured. It is the only resource that must be spent the minute it is received.
- Time wasters include ineffective communication, poor telephone usage, inadequate planning, improper handling of visitors, disorganization, and procrastination.
- Good time management techniques include setting goals, analyzing our time, and establishing effective routines.
- Time management systems such as calendars, tickler files, and computer software can help us manage ourselves in relation to our time.
- Stress is the body's response to a demand placed upon it. Chronic stress occurs when a distressful situation is prolonged, allowing no rest or recuperation for the body. Chronic stress can cause physical and emotional problems.
- Factors in our society that contribute to stress are work overload, dual-career families, single-parent families, elderly family members, economic pressures, and distressing work conditions.
- Conflict resolution skills are always important in workplace situations. Attitudes that help resolve conflicts include openness, empathy, and equality.
- Anger is a growing corporate problem. Over the past few years, incidences of violence in the workplace have increased.
- Chronic stress is harmful to your health, causing illnesses such as high blood pressure, cardiovascular disease, migraine headaches, elevated cholesterol, and cancer. Chronic stress can also cause emotional problems such as depression, deepseated anger, and loss of self-esteem.
- Stress reducers include balancing work and play, knowing the difference between achievement and perfection, recognizing limits, exercising, eating right, getting enough sleep, and managing anger and time.
- These techniques can help you manage anger: relaxing, engaging in positive self-talk, walking away either physically or emotionally from an anger-provoking situation, talking to a friend about the situation, and solving the problem that is making you angry.
- The steps in problem solving are:

1. Define the problem or the purpose.
2. Establish the criteria.
3. Generate alternatives or possible solutions.
4. Test the alternatives and make the decision.
5. Evaluate the decision.

Key Terms

The following terms were introduced in this chapter. The page on which the term was introduced is provided to help you locate the new term. Definitions are compiled in the Glossary at the end of the text.

- **time management** 45
- **time** 46
- **procrastination** 47
- **goal** 47
- **tickler file** 51
- **shareware** or **trial software** 52
- **downsize** 52
- **rightsize** 52
- **stress** 52
- **chronic stress** 52
- **conflict resolution** 55
- **empathy** 55
- **perfectionism** 56

Discussion Items

These discussion items provide an opportunity to test your understanding of the chapter through written responses and/or discussion with your classmates and your instructor.

1. List and explain five time wasters.
2. What is PIM software, and how can it help you manage your time?
3. Is all stress unhealthy? Explain your answer.
4. List and explain five causes of stress.
5. List and explain five ways you can manage your anger.

Critical-Thinking Activity

Keri-An Mahar has worked in human resources at CanAsian for five years. She is in charge of employee benefits. Keri-An is an excellent employee—very competent, knowledgeable about human resources (holds an MBA, with a specialty in management), loyal, dependable, and respected by her colleagues. Two years ago, a new vice-president of human resources was hired. Keri-

An has tried to work with him, but the situation does not get better; in fact, it gets worse. He gives her inadequate information. He asks her at the last minute to prepare reports. He lies to her about company policies and directions. Then, he yells at her about violating the directions of the company. On several occasions, Keri-An has yelled back at him; she never felt good about the situation when she allowed this to happen. She has talked with him repeatedly about the issues from her perspective. He seems to listen but never responds. He has never complained about her performance; she believes he is satisfied with her work. Keri-An has considered leaving the job; however, she has two more years until she is vested in the retirement system. If she leaves now, she loses all of her retirement benefits. Recently, Keri-An began to have health problems. She went to her physician, who said her illness was the result of stress. He also recommended that she take at least three months off. Keri-An did so. The three months have passed, and Keri-An is ready to come back to work.

What suggestions would you make to Keri-An to decrease the stress on her job?

Projects

Project 3-1 *(Objectives 1 and 2)*

On the Student CD, file SCDP3-1a is a screen from your PIM software and file SCDP3-1b is an e-mail message from Martin Albertson. Considering both of these documents, put your to-do list in priority order, adding the necessary items from Mr. Albertson's memo. Assign an A to the items you must attend to immediately, a B to the items you should deal with this week, and a C to the items you should begin work on as soon as possible but that have no immediate deadlines. Then assign a 1, 2, 3, etc. to each item to put it in order within each category to indicate the order in which you will proceed with the items. Print out your new prioritized to-do list, and submit it to your instructor.

Project 3-2 *(Objectives 1 and 2)*

On the Student CD, file SCDP3-2a is a time log form. Print out five copies of it. For the next five days, use it to log the time you spend on various activities. If you are employed, log the time you spend at workday activities. If you are not employed, log the time you spend at personal activities.

After you finish that part of the project, analyze the way you spent your time during the five days. Student CD file SCDP3-2b contains questions to help you. Student CD file SCDP3-2c contains a Time

Effectiveness Questionnaire, which provides general questions concerning the use of time. Respond to these items. After you have analyzed the way you use your time and considered your answers to the Time Effectiveness Questionnaire, prepare an action plan using the form on the Student CD, file SCDP3-2d. Indicate what you will be doing to make more effective use of your time. Print out one copy of your action plan, and submit it to your instructor.

Project 3-3 *(Objectives 3, 5, and 6)*

Analyze the following case. Then respond to the questions following the case in a memorandum addressed to your instructor. Use the memorandum form on the Student CD file SCDP3-3.

A friend of yours, Indra, works in an office in your building. She is having problems. Her situation is described here.

Indra's Situation

Indra has worked for the company for three years. Recently, she was promoted to administrative assistant for the president of the company. The job is a demanding one. Her responsibilities include setting up meetings, making travel arrangements for the president and the board of trustees, arranging meals before the monthly board meetings, and responding to calls from the board members about various items. In addition, she supervises two office assistants and takes minutes at the board meetings and at the biweekly staff meetings called by the president. She is responsible for numerous other projects as well.

Indra is attempting to employ a new office assistant. This task is taking a long time. She is using a temporary employee until she can employ someone full time.

Indra has four children. She and her husband are in the process of getting a divorce, which has been a difficult, emotional process. The situation at home is very stressful.

Indra likes her job, but she is not being as effective as she usually is.

1. Are there stressors in Indra's work environment? If so, what are they?
2. What are the stressors in Indra's home environment?
3. What might Indra do to reduce some of the stress?

Project 3-4 *(Objectives 6 and 7)*

Ahmad, a friend of yours who has worked for CanAsian for two years, is extremely unhappy in his job. He has confided in you about the office situation and has asked for your analysis of what is happening. Respond to the questions at the end of this case by writing a memorandum to your instructor, giving your suggestions. Use the memorandum form on Student CD file SCDP3-4.

Ahmad's Situation

Recently, several personnel cutbacks have taken place in Ahmad's department. Now there are only two administrative assistants in the department; previously there were four. The other remaining administrative assistant has been with the company for only six months. Since Ahmad knows the operations well, having been with the company for two years, he has been asked to assume most of the responsibilities of the two assistants who left.

Ahmad has always felt good about his abilities. He is able to produce large amounts of work quickly. However, for the last two months, he has not been able to see the top of his desk. His supervisor has become irritated with him on several occasions when work was not completed on time. There never seems to be an end to the amount of work stacked on his desk; he cannot get caught up. Ahmad has not been feeling well or sleeping well lately. He wakes up two or three times a night, thinking about the office. He has resorted to taking sleeping pills in order to get some rest at night.

Additionally, Ahmad has been having trouble with the other administrative assistant, Maria D'Angelo. He has gotten very angry with her on several occasions. Ahmad's anger has demonstrated itself in the following ways:

- Ahmad yelled at Maria for not helping him with his workload. Maria has been doing her job, but she has not offered to help Ahmad. She does not believe she has the time; she can barely keep up with her own work.
- Ahmad called Maria incompetent when she asked for his help on an assignment. Ahmad has always been willing to help Maria in the past; she does not understand why he is not willing to help her now. She believes she deserves the help, since she has only been with the company for six months. The second time he called her incompetent, she became so upset that she screamed at him.

1. Identify the factors that have contributed to Ahmad's anger and stress.
2. What steps can Ahmad take to manage his anger?
3. What steps can Ahmad take to control his stress?

Project 3-5 *(Objectives 4, 6, and 7)*

Collaborative Project

Online Project

Work with three of your classmates on this project. Using the Web, search for three recent articles on the following:

- Conflict resolution
- Controlling stress
- Managing anger

Tip: You may want to use www.dogpile.com or www.google.com as your search engine.

Present your findings to the class. Turn in a written report of your findings to your instructor; cite all your references.

Project 3-6 *(Objectives 6 and 7)*

Share with your classmates some methods of relieving stress that you have found effective in your own life. Then add to the Professional Growth Plan that you began in Chapter 1 by describing how you can control your stress and manage your anger in the future. In preparing this plan, do the following:

- Identify the stressors that you have in your life at the present time. These stressors may be at home, at school, or at the office.
- Identify ways you can relieve these stressors.
- Identify situations that make you angry at the present time.
- Identify ways you can manage that anger.
- Identify ways you will seek to control stress and manage anger in the future.
- Identify some of the ideas that you have heard from your classmates that you will consider implementing.

Save your plan on your Professional Growth Plan disk under "Progro3-6."

Chapter 4

Ethical Behaviour and Workplace Standards

LEARNING OBJECTIVES

1. *Recognize the importance of ethical behaviour.*
2. Identify characteristics of an ethical organization.
3. Demonstrate awareness of basic workplace standards.
4. Identify traits of an ethical employee.
5. Define the steps necessary for ethical change.

The ethics of business enterprise, the dominant institution in North America and in the world, affects our society greatly. Highly successful business leaders are quoted in the news, and their behaviour is observed and often emulated by others, not only in the business world but also in the nation and the world at large.

However, the influence of business on society and the influence of corporate leaders on individuals are not always positive. Inferior products and services, environmental pollution, unsafe working conditions, unfair treatment of employees, and various other unethical behaviours are sometimes the outcomes of poorly run businesses and leaders who misuse their power and authority. When business leaders are irresponsible, our society and individuals within it are often the losers.

In this chapter, ethics is considered a **pragmatic** topic—one not only to be understood conceptually but also to be practised in the day-to-day operation of a business and in the lives of employees within the business.

Soft Skills: Business Ethics

Ethics is a systematic study of moral conduct, duty, and judgment. Certainly ethical behaviour has always been important for organizations and individuals. However, today more and more attention is being paid to ethical concerns. Why? Here are two answers to that question.

- Due to the coverage given to business through television, radio, and newspapers, we are more aware of unethical practices. For example, if an airline crash kills hundreds of people and the cause is faulty equipment due to improper maintenance by the airlines, the public knows that information quickly, due to extensive media coverage. If a company puts a food product on the market with an additive that may cause illness or even death, the public is informed through television, radio, and

newspapers. Few people around the world failed to hear about the Enron scandal. When the company filed for bankruptcy in 2001, secretive insider partnerships that had hidden millions of dollars in corporate debt were disclosed. Disclosure was due in part to ethical employees who "blew the whistle" on the illegal activities that were occurring. The result of instances such as these is public demand of improved safety and health regulations and management accountability. The term "whistleblower" now applies to ethical employees who bring to light the indiscretions of their organization.

- Technology has advanced so far today that horrendous uses of it are possible. For example, medical science has expanded to the point that ethics are of major consideration. Some of the questions we hear debated are these.

Soft Skills: Business Ethics (continued)

1. Does an individual have the right to determine when he or she dies and to seek assistance with death?

2. How long should a seriously ill patient be kept alive through artificial means?

3. Is it ethical to insert growth hormones into children who have no growth-hormone deficiency but who may be on growth curves shorter than their parents would like?

4. With the cloning of Dolly the sheep in 1997, the possibility of cloning humans is imminent. In fact, an article in *Time*, February 2001, reported that several scientists are forming a consortium to produce the first human clone.[1] Just because we have the ability to clone human beings, is it ethical? Here are several other questions that were asked in the *Time* article: What if cloning becomes popular and supplants natural selec-

tion? Will that skew the course of human evolution? What if a clone develops unforeseen abnormalities? Could the clone sue the parents for wrongful birth? All of these questions have implications not only for individuals but also for the various health professions and pharmaceutical businesses.

Obviously, these ethical questions are only a few of the issues we are facing. As technology opens new vistas for all of us, ethical questions will continue to occur. The point here is that wisdom on the part of business leaders and individuals who are employed by business is required now and in the future to face and solve the ethical issues that will confront us. An important aspect of this wisdom is **morality** (a set of ideas of right and wrong). All of us must strengthen our own ethical understandings and moral **integrity** (consistently adhering to a set of ideas of right and wrong), both within and outside the workplace.

The Ethical Organization

Ethics has become so important that it is the topic of numerous books, the subject of seminars, the basis for consulting businesses, and a concern of executives daily. A company can succeed or fail due to its ethical behaviour.

Every year *Fortune Magazine* prints a list of the "Global 500"—500 of the most admired companies around the world. The top Canadian company in 2003 was George Weston Limited. Some of the statements on their website that supported this recognition were ethical in nature; they were not about the size of the company or the amount of profit it makes. Here are some of the statements:

- The company is committed to employee growth and development
- The company is committed to improving the quality of life in the communities in which it serves and to participating with its employees in supporting community organizations.
- The company will contribute 1 percent of pre-tax profits to charitable organizations across Canada and will encourage employee volunteerism.[2]

Sun Life Financial Services, the next Canadian organization on the list, has a Code of Conduct that applies to all employees and directors. In part it aims "to

Human Relations Tip

It takes courage to live by a set of moral values; determine that you will do so.

promote principles of respect and fairness in the workplace and in dealings with the public and our stakeholders."[3]

These statements show a commitment to employees and community involvement, both characteristics of ethical organizations. Many organizations today are writing vision or mission statements that make clear the directions and values of the organization. Such statements let the employees know the directions of the organization, what it values, how it intends to live those values, and what is and what is not ethical behaviour within the organization. Although the scope of this book will not allow for an exhaustive treatment of all the characteristics of an ethical organization, a number of ethical characteristics are covered in the next section.

Is Socially and Environmentally Responsible

Certainly we have examples in our society where business has been socially and environmentally careless and irresponsible. Such is the case with the 1989 *Exxon Valdez* oil spill, which caused significant environmental damage. On March 24, 1989, the vessel grounded on Bligh Reef and spilled more than 40 million litres of oil into the biologically rich waters of Prince William Sound. The company Exxon was fined $150 million for this spill, the largest fine ever imposed for an environmental crime. As restitution for the injuries caused to the fish, wildlife, and lands of the spill region, Exxon agreed to pay $100 million. While this incident happened many years ago, it was as a result of this high-profile spill and the damage caused to the environment that the oil industry began to pay greater attention to the reduction of spills. In fact, only nine years later in 1997, the United States Coast Guard statistics reported that the volume of oil spilled in American waters had declined by two-thirds compared to the previous year, representing the lowest amount of spill recorded since the Coast Guard began publishing data in 1973. This case, including the reactions by citizens, the government, and the courts, reinforces international expectations of environmentally responsible businesses.

Business executives who are socially and environmentally responsible are constantly aware of the possible dangers in their businesses. Responsible executives take all necessary precautions to see that the environment is not polluted. They pay attention to government regulations regarding careful disposal of waste products. When building new buildings, they give top priority to cutting down as few trees as possible and protecting wetland areas and other areas that are environmentally important.

Is Internationally Aware

When opening businesses in other countries or buying or selling products in other countries, ethical business organizations understand the importance of learning and respecting the culture and business customs of the country. You will discover more about these cultural differences in the next chapter.

For the moment, however, consider the following. A basic precept of Japanese culture is to put the best face on even the worst situation. Consequently, a smile, a nod, even a spoken affirmative in business negotiations may merely mean a reluctance to disappoint. Business is also never conducted at the beginning of a meeting. There is a set ritual that includes introductions, the pouring of tea, and the exchange of business cards. In contrast, the French get right down to business matters quickly; but they may be slow in coming to decisions. However, whether the decision is good news or bad, they state their intentions unambiguously. In Latin America, you may behave as you like as long as you are comfortable with Latin ways. Eye contact must be unflinching; conversation must be nose to nose. Hugs and two-handed handshakes are common among mere acquaintances. Siesta is sacred, which means that almost all businesses, including stores and banks, close for two or three hours in early afternoon. Late arrival at meetings is customary, from a quarter of an hour to an hour or two.

Is Committed to Diversity

The ethical organization is committed to diversity in its hiring, promotion, and treatment of employees. The ethical organization

- Is intolerant of discrimination—racial/ethnic, gender, age and sexual orientation
- Maintains a policy against sexual harassment
- Provides for the physically challenged

Is Intolerant of Discrimination

Unfortunately, discrimination is ever-present in our society. Businesses are made up of people who bring their own particular prejudices to the workplace. **Prejudice** is defined as "a system of negative beliefs, feelings, and actions." These beliefs, feelings, and actions are based on *learned* categories of distinctions, *learned* evaluation of these categories, and *learned* tendencies to act according to the beliefs and feelings held. Prejudice can lead to acts of **discrimination** (treatment or consideration based on class or category rather than individual merit).

Discrimination may occur in many forms; race or ethnicity, gender, sexual orientation and age are some of the most likely forms. Discrimination may also involve sexual harassment. Discrimination has been so prevalent in our society that legislation has been enacted in an attempt to eliminate it. The Canadian Labour Code (CLC) and subsequent regulations form the primary source of federal employment and labour law. Additionally, at the provincial level, there are numerous statutory provisions that govern the employer/employee relationship. Human rights codes established at the provincial level state that every person has a right to equal treatment with respect to employment without discrimination based on race, ancestry, place of origin, colour, ethnic origin, citizenship, creed, sex, age, record of offences, marital status, family status, sexual orientation, or handicap. Figure 4-1 on page 68 lists areas of prohibited discriminatory practices identified in federal law.

Race/Ethnic Discrimination. Racial/ethnic tensions will always exist in a multicultural country like Canada. However, the existence of discrimination is no reason to accept it. Ethical businesses and individuals seek to eliminate discrimination. The ethical organization sets an example for its employees of non-discriminatory behaviours and demands that its employees behave in

■ Figure 4-1

PROHIBITED DISCRIMINATORY PRACTICES

- Discriminatory hiring, firing, or treatment in the course of employment
- Discriminatory employment applications, advertisements, or inquiries
- Discriminatory membership practices by employee organizations
- Discriminatory policies or agreements by employee or employer organizations
- Maintenance of gender-based wage differentials
- Freedom from sexual and other kinds of harassment in the workplace

non-discriminatory ways. The ethical organization has a procedure for handling discrimination and provides the information to its employees.

Gender Discrimination. The federal Employment Equity Act provides for employment equity for women, aboriginal peoples, disabled people, and visible minorities. Employers may not advertise a job specifically for a man or woman unless there are bona fide occupational requirements requiring a person of a specific gender—for example, if the position involves modelling men's clothing. We recognize in our society today that there are very few gender-specific occupations. A person may apply for any job, and the hiring decision must be based on whether the individual has the knowledge and skills needed for the job, not on whether the person is male or female.

Neither can employee pay be based on whether a person is male or female. Provincial employment standards legislation and the federal CLC prohibit pay discrimination because of gender. Men and women performing work in the same establishment under similar conditions must receive the same pay if their jobs require equal skill, effort, and responsibility.

As mentioned earlier, provincial human rights codes also prohibit discrimination based on sexual orientation. Gay and lesbian organizations have become active in helping to ensure that the rights of individuals are not violated on the basis of their sexual preference.

Age Discrimination. No distinction can be made in age, either in the advertising or hiring process or once an employee is on the job. For example, an organization cannot print a job vacancy notice that specifies a particular age or age range for applicants. Currently there is no legislation prohibiting organizations from establishing retirement age policies. A number of unions, however, have negotiated clauses that prevent an employer from forcing an employee to retire due to his or her age. Figure 4-2 lists steps for handling discrimination.

■ Figure 4-2

STEPS FOR HANDLING DISCRIMINATION

- Know your rights and know the laws. Know your organization's position on racial discrimination and sexual harassment, what is legal under your provincial human rights code, and what is the responsibility of your employer.
- Keep a record of all sexual harassment and racial discrimination infractions, noting the dates, incidents, and witnesses (if any).
- File a formal grievance with your company. Check your company policy and procedure manual or talk with the director of human resources concerning the grievance procedure. If no formal grievance procedures exist, file a formal complaint with your employer in the form of a memorandum describing the incidents, identifying the individuals involved in the sexual harassment or racial discrimination, and requesting that disciplinary action be taken.
- If your employer is not responsive to your complaint, your province may have human rights offices that can assist you. Check your local telephone directory for the address and telephone number of the Human Rights Commission office nearest you where you can file charges of discrimination.
- Talk to friends, co-workers, and relatives. Avoid isolation and self-blame. You are not alone; sexual harassment and racial discrimination do occur in the work sector.
- Consult a lawyer to investigate legal alternatives to discriminatory or sexual harassment behaviour.

Maintains a Policy Against Sexual Harassment

Sexual harassment has been defined in the Canada Labour Code as "any conduct, comment, gesture or contact of a sexual nature that is likely to cause offence or humiliation to any employee; or that might, on reasonable grounds, be perceived by that employee as placing a condition of a sexual nature on employment or on any opportunity for training or promotion." Three criteria that can be used to determine whether sexual harassment exists are:

- Submission to the sexual conduct is made either implicitly or explicitly as a condition of employment.
- Employment decisions affecting the recipient are made on the basis of the recipient's acceptance or rejection of the sexual conduct.
- The conduct has the intent or effect of substantially interfering with an individual's work performance or creates an intimidating, hostile, or offensive work environment.

Division 15 of Part III of the Canada Labour Code makes the organization responsible for preventing and eliminating sexual harassment. The organization is liable for the behaviour of its employees whether or not management is aware that sexual harassment has taken place.

The organization is also responsible for the actions of non-employees on the company's premises. Because of these liabilities, many organizations have published policy statements that make it clear to all employees that sexual harassment is a violation of the law and of company policy. These statements generally include a clearly defined grievance procedure so an employee has a course of action to take if sexual harassment does occur. Figure 4-3 lists the do's and dont's for supervisors to prevent sexual harassment in the workplace.

Provides for the Physically Challenged

Physically challenged individuals (persons with physical handicaps) could face biases based on their physical challenges. They may be treated differently due to their disabilities. The ethical organization abides by federal or provincial human rights statutes, acts, or policies in fulfilling their "duty to accommodate." The objective of the statute, act, or policy is to eliminate barriers that prevent full participation of existing and potentially new employees in the workforce. In addition to physical barriers, unnecessary job requirements and unequal access to training and development are also considered barriers to employment. The ethical organization

- Provides access for the physically challenged to all facilities

---

■ Figure 4-3

PREVENTING SEXUAL HARASSMENT IN THE WORKPLACE: DO'S AND DON'TS FOR SUPERVISORS

DO

- Educate management and employees as to what sexual harassment is; let everyone know that sexual harassment will not be tolerated.
- Designate a person or office where employees can bring concerns and complaints about sexual harassment.
- Publish options available to employees who feel they are victims of sexual harassment.
- Promptly and thoroughly investigate every complaint.
- Provide leadership by example in applying and promoting high standards of integrity, conduct, and concern for all employees.
- Be observant of language and behaviour of fellow supervisors and managers. Confront them on what may be perceived as sexual harassment.
- Maintain an environment free of retaliation or punitive actions against a complainant.

DON'T

- Permit sexual jokes, teasing, or innuendo to become a routine part of the work environment.
- Allow employment decisions to be made on the basis of any reasons other than merit.
- Allow social behaviour to become confused with behaviour in the workplace.

Source: "Sexual Harassment: An Employer's Guide for Supervisors," www.womenintrades.org/presexl.html.

- Provides proper equipment, and workspace, training and development
- Ensures that initial employment practices do not discriminate against the physically challenged

"Duty to accommodate" requires the employer to make every effort to accommodate employees with disabilities, unless to do so would create undue hardship on the employer. In determining undue hardship, an employer may take into consideration the health of the employee, safety, and costs.

In summary, the organization that values diversity

- Is intolerant of sexual harassment and any type of discrimination—racial/ethnic, gender, age, physically challenged
- Upholds its clearly stated policies and procedures that are committed to equal employment
- Has a human resources department with expertise in assisting minorities and women with special issues
- Publishes grievance policies that are clearly stated and distributed to all employees
- Provides diversity sensitivity training for its employees
- Holds managers accountable for consistently supporting and ensuring diversity within the environment

Is Involved in the Community

The ethical organization is cognizant of the needs of its community and assists with meeting these needs when possible. For example, the organization might

- Provide tutors for elementary and high school students
- Engage in mentoring programs for troubled youth
- Work with colleges and universities in providing intern experiences for students
- Provide computers (or other technology the business manufactures) to schools
- Serve on community boards and commissions
- Participate in the local chamber of commerce
- Contribute to community charities
- Provide leadership to solicit funds for worthy causes, such as disabled children, health care of the indigent, and shelters for the homeless
- Assist with arts programs by providing leadership and/or monies

Respects the Needs and Rights of Employees

Promoting employee productivity is important to the ethical organization. An ethical organization understands that employees have needs. They need to know the values and directions of the company, what is expected of them, and so on. Here are some ways the organization can meet the needs of employees:

- Provide employees with a copy of the values and goals of the organization; ask that managers go over these documents with the employees
- Encourage managers to consistently distribute important information about the organization
- Help employees set achievable goals that are consistent with the goals of the organization
- Administer employee performance evaluations fairly
- Support employees in learning new skills
- Reward employee creativity
- Challenge employees to generate new ideas
- Encourage collaboration and cooperation among employees
- Establish teams who work on significant organizational issues

An ethical organization also understands that employees have rights. Three such rights are a right to due process, a right to organize, and a right to privacy.

Right to Due Process

Generally, employees make a conscientious effort to contribute to an organization. In return, they expect to be treated fairly by an organization. People would not choose to work for an organization if they did not think they were going to be treated fairly. **Employment at will** (the doctrine that allows employees to be fired for good cause or for no cause) has been and still is an employment doctrine upheld by some organizations. In an unethical organization, adherence to such a doctrine can cause irreparable harm to employees. For example, companies have been known to call long-time employees into a supervisor's office, tell them they no longer have a job, and send them home immediately with no severance package and loss of all benefits. The doctrine of employment at will has come under considerable attack and is being replaced in most organizations by the right to due process. **Due process** means that managers impose sanctions on employees only after offering them a chance to correct the organizational grievance. An ideal system of due process is one in which employees are given

- A clearly written job description
- Organizational policies and procedures
- The assurance that all policies and procedures will be administered consistently and fairly without discrimination
- A commitment by top management that managers will be responsible for adhering to the values and morals of the organization
- A fair and impartial hearing if the rules are broken

Right to Organize

Approximately one-third of the Canadian labour force is represented by a trade union. Under federal or provincial labour relations legislation, every person is free to join a union of his or her own choice and to participate in its lawful activities. With more than half-a-million members, the Canadian Union of Public Employees (CUPE) is Canada's largest union.

Labour unions are instrumental in ensuring that the rights and benefits of their employees are upheld. Employees join unions in order to have stronger, collective voice in resolving the issues that arise in the workplace. They do this through negotiations and by creating collective agreements without which many employees could be at an economic disadvantage. These collective agreements enhance existing federal and provincial employment standards.

Right to Privacy

Canada's Personal Information Protection and Electronic Documents Act (PIPEDA) or similar legislation implemented provincially provides the ethical organization with guidelines regarding the individual employee's right to privacy. Certainly an organization has the right to information about an employee that affects the individual's performance. For example, if an individual has developed some type of physical illness that no longer allows the person to perform his or her job, the employer has a right to know about it. However, the employer does not have the right to know about illnesses that do not affect job performance. An employer does not have the right to know about a person's political or religious beliefs. In fact, in a job interview, the employer cannot ask questions about marital status, age, organizations to which the person belongs, where the person was born, what the spouse does, and so on. These questions are illegal. If

an organization acquires information about an employee's personal life while doing a legitimate investigation, the organization has an obligation to destroy the information, especially if the data would embarrass or in some way injure the employee. Also, an organization must give employees the right to give or withhold consent before any private aspects of their lives are investigated.

Adheres to Workplace Standards

An ethical organization abides by the Canada Labour Code and other statutory provisions at the provincial level that confer upon employees certain minimum standards of employment. Figure 4-4 on page 72 provides an overview of the topics covered by employment standards legislation. Specific requirements may vary by province.

Establishes and Lives Organizational Values

Many organizations today establish vision and value statements and make these statements available to their employees and to the public by posting them on websites and distributing them in organizational publications. Here are excerpts of mission/vision/value statements from two organizations—St. John Regional Hospital in New Brunswick and Sun Life Financial Services.

St. John Regional Hospital

As part of the Atlantic Health Sciences Corporation, our mission is to promote, protect, and improve the health and wellness of individuals, families and communities through quality care, education and research.

- *Our vision is to achieve the best possible health and wellness for our community.*

- *We value caring, respect, integrity and fairness while working together to achieve excellence.*

- *Our strategic directions are to improve workplace wellness; promote and improve the health of the population; improve access; deliver comprehensive health care services across the continuum of care; achieve excellence through research, education and innovation; and, demonstrate our accountability.[4]*

TOPICS COVERED BY EMPLOYMENT STANDARDS LEGISLATION

MINIMUM WAGES

Minimum wage rate payable to most workers varies from province to province. In 2002, the minimum wage rate in British Columbia was $8, in Quebec $7, and in Ontario $6.85.

HOURS OF WORK

While some provinces may authorize hours in excess, generally the legislation provides that no employee shall work more than 8 hours per day or 48 hours per week. In Quebec, the Act defined 40 hours per week to be a regular workweek for any employee.

OVERTIME

Overtime generally at a rate of one-and-a-half times the regular rate of pay is paid to employees who work in excess of approximately 40 hours per week. At the request of an employee, some employers may provide time off in lieu of overtime pay.

PUBLIC HOLIDAYS

Under federal and provincial law, employees are entitled to eight paid public holidays each year. They are: New Year's Day, Good Friday, Victoria Day, Canada Day, Labour Day, Thanksgiving Day, Christmas Day, and Boxing Day. Certain businesses also recognize Remembrance Day, and St. Jean Baptiste Day is in addition to these in Quebec.

VACATION PAY

After one year of service with an organization, an employee is entitled to two weeks' vacation with pay. At the employer's discretion this vacation may be taken at a time mutually convenient to the employee and employer and may occur within ten months of commencement of employment.

MATERNITY LEAVE

Provincial laws vary, but upon two weeks' written notice female employees are entitled to unpaid maternity leave provided the employee has been employed for a minimum number of weeks imme-diately preceding the estimated delivery date. Unemployment insurance benefits are available to employees on maternity leave and the employee is entitled to reinstatement in the same or equivalent job on her return.

PARENTAL LEAVE

Upon two weeks' notice an employee who has been employed a minimum number of weeks is entitled to parental leave. This leave is available to male and female employees and in the case of a female employee may immediately follow a maternity leave. At the end of the parental leave an employee is entitled to be reinstated to the same or comparable job at the same rate of pay, and with the same benefits and seniority accrued as of the date of the commencement of the leave.

COMPASSIONATE CARE LEAVE

In January 2004, the federal government introduced Compassionate Care Benefits. Benefits may be paid up to a maximum of six weeks to a person who needs to be absent from work in order to care for a family member who is gravely ill and at risk of dying.

EQUAL PAY FOR EQUAL WORK

Employees who perform substantially the same kind of work in the same establishment where the performance of duties requires the same skill, effort, and responsibility shall see no difference in their rate of pay. Difference in pay rates may exist where the differential is based on any factor other than sex such as seniority or meritocracy.

BENEFIT PLANS

When in place, they must be furnished to all employees with no differences based on age, sex, or marital status.

***

Source: "Employment & Labour Laws in Canada: Other Legislation Impacting the Employment Relationship," *Strategis Collection: Invest in Canada*, July 15, 2004, www.investincanada.gc.ca, accessed July 28, 2004.

Sun Life Financial Services

Our Mission: To Provide Lifetime Financial Security

We are in business to help people achieve and maintain the peace of mind that comes from having in place sound financial solutions that will evolve and adapt to their changing needs throughout their lifetimes. We accomplish this mission by providing innovative, customer-focused protection and wealth management products and services to individuals directly, or as members of the savings, pension and retirement plans we offer through their employers.[5]

Once you know the company mission/value statement, it is your responsibility to behave in ways that support the mission. If you find yourself in a company where you cannot support the mission/values, it is time for you to find another position.

Maintains a Safe and Healthy Environment

The ethical organization is committed to providing a safe and healthy organization for the community it serves. Johnson & Johnson exhibited commitment to a safe and healthy community environment in their handling of the Tylenol crises of 1982 and 1986. Someone from outside the company tampered with Tylenol bottles, lacing them with cyanide. Several deaths occurred as a result. Johnson & Johnson immediately removed all Tylenol capsules from the market (even though the deaths were confined to one area of the United States) at an estimated cost of over $100 million. They also mounted a massive communication effort to alert the public and deal with the problem. While this incident happened many years ago, it made all pharmaceutical companies aware of how vulnerable to potentially lethal tampering were their over-the-counter products. Efforts to implement anti-tampering seals were enacted by all pharmaceutical companies manufacturing and selling their drugs off the shelf.

Another company, Bridgestone/Firestone, faced enormous criticism over its failure to be forthcoming about dozens of fatal accidents that may have been linked to the company's tires. Firestone did go public on the situation, but documents obtained by Associated Press showed the company had data indicating safety problems years before the August 9, 2000

recall of 6.5 million tires. Firestone faced numerous lawsuits filed by individuals with family members who were killed or disabled as a result of the accidents allegedly caused by the tires. In the United States at separate House and Senate hearings in 2000, lawmakers admonished the tire maker—and Ford, which uses Firestone tires on its popular Explorer and other models—for not notifying the public about a problem even though complaints about the tires had been made worldwide for years.[6]

The public expects organizations to behave in ways that protect and maintain a safe and healthy environment for its customers. Additionally, the ethical organization is also committed to providing and maintaining a safe and healthy environment for its employees. For example, an ethical organization upholds the provincial regulations and/or acts that require employers to furnish a place of employment free from recognized hazards that can cause death, injury, or illness to its employees. Figure 4-5 gives a few of the guidelines that should be followed to keep the workplace safe.

Smoking

Smoking can be extremely dangerous to an individual's long-term health. Although the public is well aware of the dangers of smoking, some individuals within our environment continue to smoke. Non-smokers complain of eye, nose, and throat irritations resulting from second-hand smoke. Studies have shown that breathing second-hand smoke is unhealthy and can cause emphysema and lung disease. There is a growing trend in municipalities across the country to enact bylaws that prohibit smoking in public spaces, and many businesses have adopted smoking policies to protect the non-smokers. These policies prohibit employees from smoking inside the building; smoking may be allowed at a designated place (for example, a separate room for smokers).

Substance Abuse

Substance abuse is a huge problem in our society. **Substance abuse** refers to the use of alcohol or drugs to an extent that is debilitating for the individual using the substance. Drug and alcohol users are absent an average of two to three times more than other employees. Drug and alcohol users also perform at

■ Figure 4-5

SAFETY GUIDELINES

Ask these safety questions about your workspace:

- Is the space sufficient to perform tasks?
- Is the space sufficient for equipment?
- Can all items that are used frequently be easily reached?
- Does flexibility exist to rearrange the workstation if needed?
- Is the lighting sufficient?
- Is the height of the work surface appropriate?
- Is the height of the chair appropriate?
- Can the chair be adjusted easily?
- Does the chair feel sturdy?
- Can the work surface height be adjusted easily?
- Is the computer screen free of glare?
- Can the computer screen be tilted?
- Is the work surface depth adequate to allow the computer screen to be placed at an appropriate distance?
- Is the computer keyboard about five centimetres lower than the desk surface?
- Are document holders provided?
- Is the furniture light in colour?
- Is the equipment suitable for the work to be done?
- Is adequate storage space provided?

about two-thirds of their actual work potential. Thus, productivity in the workplace is lowered. Shoddy work and material waste are also evident with individuals who abuse substances. Mental and physical agility and concentration deteriorate with substance abuse. Chronic drug abuse creates wide mood swings, anxiety, depression, and anger. Employees who abuse drugs are more likely to steal equipment and materials to get money for their substance abuse habit. Substance abusers are also over three times more likely to cause accidents. Even small quantities of drugs in a person's system can cause deterioration of alertness, clear-headedness, and reaction speed.

Provides an Ergonomically Sound Environment

In Chapter 2 you learned about creating an ergonomically sound workspace for the teleworker. The same ergonomic considerations should also be implemented when establishing a workspace on your employer's property. Management of an organization has responsibilities in relation to ergonomics The responsibilities consist of providing an environment where factors such as lighting, acoustics, and other ergonomic factors that avoid RSIs are carefully considered.

Lighting

For employees to process information in an organization, an adequate lighting system must be maintained. Improper lighting can cause headaches, eye fatigue, neck and shoulder strain, and irritability. If improper lighting conditions continue over a period of time, productivity and morale are lowered, which in turn can cost a business considerable dollars.

Acoustics

Sound in the workplace can be good or bad. Soft background music and subdued conversations do not disrupt the workday; but street sounds and loud machines can, and may cause employees to become irritable. Also, an employee's efficiency and productivity may be decreased by offensive noise. For example, noise interferes with communication, makes concentration difficult, and causes fatigue. The long-term effect of offensive noise can be serious health problems for employees, including hearing impairment, sleep loss, and emotional damage.

These methods may be used to control noise:

- Install partitions with acoustical panels between workstations.
- Put noisy equipment in separate rooms.
- Provide conference rooms for small and large group meetings.
- Install carpet, draperies, and acoustical ceilings.

Colour

Colour can impact the productivity and morale of employees in the workplace just as it impacts the productivity of a teleworker. Attractive, cheerful, and efficient-looking workplaces tend to inspire confidence and trust. In contrast, drab or poorly painted workplaces can arouse doubt or mistrust. Tones of grey tend to put workers to sleep. Warm colours (such as yellow, red, and orange) create cheerful surroundings. Cool colours, such as green and blue, produce a calm and tranquil atmosphere. In celebrating its 100th anniversary, Crayola Canada asked Canadians to vote online for their eight favourite colours from among the crayon box's 120 shades. Of 51 000 votes cast the majority chose blue as their number one favourite, the colour red placing second.[7] Studies have shown that productivity increases and absenteeism decreases as a result of improved colour in the workplace.

Is Honest

An ethical organization is honest. It makes its policies and procedures clear to both its customers and its employees. For example, its pricing policies are made clear to buyers; its product warranty is upheld. Employees understand salary and promotion policies. Executives within the organization are honest. The ethical executive does not appropriate excessive and lavish perks to himself or herself. The ethical executive's word can be taken seriously; employees know and understand the direction of the company. Refer to Self-Check A.

Is Visionary

The visionary organization has the ability to look beyond the day-to-day activities of the organization. Executives within the ethical organization can help managers and employees understand where the company will be in 5, 10, or 15 years and assist others in formulating policies and objectives that will help the company achieve its goals. The organization, through its leadership, consistently articulates the vision of the company and constantly evaluates the daily operations of the company in relation to meeting the vision.

The Ethical Employee

Now that you have discovered some of the ethical characteristics of an organization, consider certain ethical characteristics of employees within the organization.

Respects the Organizational Structure

The organization today has fewer layers than in the past. Many organizations use teams to deliver products and/or services. However, there is still an organizational structure and a reporting line. Usually, an organization chart spells out the reporting structure. Being respectful

Photodisc Green/Photodisc Collection

Do not go over your supervisor's head; talk with him or her about issues.

of the organization means you do not go over your supervisor's head—that is, consult his or her superior—with issues or concerns. If you have an idea that you believe will help the productivity of the office, share it with your supervisor. If you cannot meet a deadline on a project, let your supervisor know. If you have problems with someone who reports to you, talk with your supervisor. Keep your supervisor informed on all significant items. The rule of no surprises between employee and employer is a good rule to follow.

Makes Ethical Decisions

Your own ethics are influenced by the following:

- Your religious beliefs
- Your philosophical beliefs
- The culture in which you grew up

The convergence of these factors plus the culture and expectations of the business organization where you are employed can make it difficult to determine what truly is right and wrong in a particular situation. Asking these questions can help you decide what is ethical.

- What are the facts in the situation?
- Who are the stakeholders, or who will be affected by my decision?
- What are the ethical issues involved?
- Are there different ways of looking at this problem? If so, what are they?
- What are the practical constraints?
- What actions should I take?
- Are these actions practical?

If you are still unclear about what you should do, ask yourself these questions.

- If my actions appeared in the newspaper, would I feel all right about everyone reading about what occurred?
- Is what I anticipate doing legal?
- Could I proudly tell my spouse, my parents, or my children about my actions?
- Will I be proud of my actions one day, one week, and one year from now?
- Do my actions fit with who I think I am?

Accepts Constructive Criticism

Your supervisor is just that—your supervisor. He or she has not only the right but also the responsibility to help you do your job well. You should be willing to accept constructive criticism; that is, criticism that can help you learn and grow. If your supervisor recommends that you do something differently, do not view his or her remarks personally. For example, assume you recently set up a meeting for your employer at a hotel where lunch was served. This was the first time you planned such a meeting, and you thought you did a good job. However, after the meeting, your employer told you the room arrangement was not satisfactory and the food was not good. How do you respond to such criticism? First of all, you deal with the issues at hand. You might say "Can we talk about it further? How should the room have been arranged? What type of meal would you suggest?" Keep an open mind; realize that you have much to learn and that everyone makes mistakes. You might also suggest reviewing the arrangements with your supervisor before the next meeting.

Always avoid an emotional response to criticism. Try to separate the issue from the critic; realize the critic is merely concerned with improving the situation. If you respond emotionally to the critic, you may succeed only in upsetting yourself (and possibly the person who is doing the criticizing). Do not dwell on criticism and carry it around with you. Learn what you can from the situation, determine never to make the mistake again, and then move on.

Respects Diversity

As the ethical organization is committed to diversity, so is the ethical employee. The ethical employee understands that the world is very diverse and that it will continue to become even more diverse in the future. The ethical employee accepts and respects the diversity of all people—whether that diversity is in ethnicity, race, gender, or age. The ethical employee understands that there is no place in the office for telling jokes that have racial, ethnic, or gender overtones.

Is Aware of Workplace Politics

Workplace politics are fed by networks of individuals where who you know can be more important than what you know. Favours may be handed out on the basis of the existing networks. In a truly ethical world, office politics would not exist. Unfortunately, we do not live in such a world and probably never will.

So what do you do about workplace politics? When you begin a new job, notice what is happening around you. Be aware of the power bases. Be aware of who knows whom and what the relationships are. Then hold on to your own value system. Do your job to the best of your ability. Do not gossip about office politics. Use your awareness of the power bases to get your job done. In other words, do not fight a power base when you know you cannot win. Spend your energies in doing what is right. Generally, if you hold on to your values and perform your job extremely well, you will be recognized and respected for who you are.

> **Human Relations Tip**
>
> Do not become involved in office politics; the time and energy it takes is not worth your effort.

- Take longer than the time allocated by the organization for lunch or breaks
- Spend an inordinate amount of time repairing makeup or eating breakfast upon arriving at work
- Use the copier for personal use

If someone confides a personal matter to you, do not spread the "juicy gossip."

Respects Others' Privacy

Respect the privacy of others within the office. If someone confides a personal matter to you, do not spread the "juicy gossip." If you have access to personnel files that contain confidential information about others, keep the information confidential. You may at times be given information that is not specifically labelled "confidential," yet should not be passed on to others. Also be sensitive to the handling of this information. Do not hide behind the rationale "But I was not told it was confidential." Use common sense here. Ethical conduct dictates that you are always discreet. Remember the Golden Rule: Treat others as you would want to be treated.

Is Honest

Being honest means the employee does not take anything that belongs to the company, is conscientious about using time wisely, and gives the company eight hours of productive work (or whatever the office hours may be) every day.

Honesty dictates that the employee *not*

> **Human Relations Tip**
>
> Deal honestly and directly with any mistakes you make. Inform the necessary people of the error, and state how you will correct the error.

- Send e-mail to family or friends on the office computer
- Take home office supplies such as paper, pens, and notepads
- Use the Internet for personal research or "chats"
- Use the telephone for personal calls
- Use the computer for preparing personal correspondence

Is Dependable

Do what you say you will do when you say you will do it. Do not make excuses for poor performance. Your employer or peers are not impressed with excuses. A survey done by Accountemps and reported in *From Nine to Five* polled 150 executives and asked them to list the most unusual excuses they had heard for someone being late to work or absent. The responses included the following:

- The wind was blowing against me.
- My favourite actress just got married. I needed time alone.
- I thought Monday was Sunday.
- I had to sort socks.
- I forgot to come to work.

In addition to providing a good laugh, these excuses point to the ridiculousness of trying to find a reason for irresponsible actions.

Is Cooperative

You may believe that when your particular job is finished, you need not worry about helping anyone else. However, you are an employee of the company. Just because you have completed your tasks does not mean you can sit and do nothing; there is still other work that must be done. Remember, the time may come when you have more work than you can do and need the help of a co-worker. When you help someone else, do not make that person feel obligated to you. Offer your help in the spirit of cooperation and with a desire to further the interests of the company.

To Assure Your Failure as a Professional and to Always Be Seen as Uncooperative

- Always have an excuse ready for why you cannot help someone else.
- Point out why the individual needs help. Obviously, the individual is incompetent or lazy.
- Forget about the importance of office productivity and customer satisfaction.
- Always look out for yourself. (You cannot possibly help because you have to go home early to take your sick pet to the veterinarian.)

Respects Clients and Customers

As an administrative professional, you must be respectful of your clients and customers. The adage "The customer is always right" is true. Stop and think about that statement for a moment. Literally a customer may be wrong; he or she is human and makes mistakes. However, what the statement means is that in the context of service to the customer, he or she is always right. As an administrative professional, you may need to listen to numerous unhappy clients and customers. Let the clients and customers get their anger out; then proceed to address the issue. At times, you will not be able to say yes to the customer; when that is the case, explain the rationale of the company. Always act as your client's advocate within the company, getting the information or providing the service (if at all possible) your client needs. Value the client's time. Do not waste the client's time by keeping him or her on the phone for too long or by being late for an appointment. Deal with irate clients calmly and professionally. Do not be defensive. Treat every client and customer as a

VIP (very important person). Without clients and customers, the company would not be in business and you would not have a job.

Keep the customer informed. If there are production problems, material shortages, or other problems that prevent the customer from getting an order on time, tell him or her. Keep a computer file on the clients and customers with whom you work. Record important information in your file, and review it if a client calls. Remember that all clients are important, whether you deal with them once a year or once a month.

You may have occasion to help entertain customers and clients. For example, you may be asked to take an out-of-town customer to dinner. If so, keep the situation on a purely professional basis. You also may occasionally receive gifts from clients and customers. Certainly a small gift may be appropriate, and you can accept it graciously. However, as a matter of ethics, you should not accept an extremely expensive gift, and some organizations have a policy prohibiting you from accepting *any* gifts.

Take a few minutes now to complete Self-Check B on page 79. When you finish, check your answers with those given at the end of the chapter.

Ethical Change

We do not live in a world in which all individuals and organizations are ethical. Such a statement is not meant to be negative. It merely suggests the inevitable—we do not live in a perfect world. We do live in a world in which employees make ethical mistakes but, in the majority of instances, consistently strive to improve themselves and the organizations in which they work. Ethical organizations require people within the organization to behave ethically, including top management as well as all individuals throughout the organization. The process of achieving ethical change requires understanding, a systematic approach, commitment, cooperation, and hard work. Consider the following factors that impede ethical change as well as certain pragmatic steps that produce ethical change.

Factors Impeding Ethical Change

Our backgrounds and beliefs often stand in the way of ethical change. As you read the statements in

Respond to the following statements with "Always," "Sometimes," or "Never."

1. I accept constructive criticism. _____

2. I respect the privacy of others. _____

3. I become involved in office politics. _____

4. I am dependable. _____

5. I make excuses when I cannot finish a job. _____

6. I help others with a task if my job permits. _____

7. I am honest with customers. _____

8. I use the telephone for personal conversations. _____

9. I believe it is all right to accept gifts from clients. _____

10. I talk with my employer first about any job-related issues. _____

Self-Check C, ask yourself if you believe these statements to be true or false. Now examine each of these statements individually.

Answer "True" or "False" to each of the following statements on the basis of your personal beliefs.

• Organizations are amoral. _____

• Organizational leadership is unethical. _____

• Values cannot be changed. _____

• Labels accurately describe individuals. _____

"Organizations Are Amoral"

Amoral is defined as "lacking moral judgment or sensibility, neither moral nor immoral." Generally, we readily accept that individuals should have ethics, but we are not so clear about what that means within the organizational framework. You may hear a statement such as "The organization has no right telling me how to behave." Yet if an organization is to be ethical, its employees must be ethical. The two are inexorably linked—the organization is the people who make up the organization, and the people within the organization are the organization. Managers have a right and an obligation to hold employees responsible for upholding the ethics of the organization and to hold them accountable for maintaining the skills required to produce the product or service of the organization.

"Organizational Leadership Is Unethical"

Certainly there are organizations in which the leadership does not behave ethically. However, to assume automatically that all management is bad is negatively stereotyping management. If we do not want to behave ethically, it is easy to shift the blame for our lack of ethical behaviour to management. Your first obligation is to uphold the organizational ethics yourself. Then if you find through repeated incidents that management does not uphold the organizational ethics, you may decide to leave. When management does not embrace organizational ethics, the organization may not be a good place to work.

"Values Cannot Be Changed"

Clearly, we have difficulty changing our values, since they are beliefs we have generally held from childhood. However, change is possible. Consider this example. Edgar learned at an early age that gender roles are fixed in our society—a female holds the more menial positions, a male the management positions. Edgar has a female supervisor and has discovered that women can indeed hold high-level positions and be extremely competent. He has altered his view of women as a result. Organizations, by upholding a set of values and giving support to changes a person makes, can help an individual change or redefine his or her values.

"Labels Accurately Describe Individuals"

When we attach a label to someone, we are usually not describing that individual accurately. For example, to describe a person as a "computer nerd" or a "party animal" is restrictive of the whole person's qualities and traits. Remember that labelling hinders rather than helps the change process. Labelling individuals often restricts our view of them. We begin to see them only as the label we have attached. We ignore their other qualities. If we are committed to ethical change within an organization, we must avoid the use of restrictive labels.

Supporting Behaviours

The organization and individuals committed to ethical change can take certain practical steps to produce the change. These steps include the following:

- Determine the ethical change needed.
- Determine steps required to achieve the objective.
- Practise the new behaviours.
- Seek feedback on the change.
- Reward the individual or group involved.
- Evaluate the effects of ethical change.

Determine the Ethical Change Needed

Consider this example of a setting in which ethical change is needed and is addressed within the organization.

As an administrative professional, you have two people reporting to you—Guy Beauchamp and Luyin Wu. You have been asked to lead a ten-person team who will be looking at hiring practices of administrative professionals. Presently CanAsian's number of minorities in this category is not consistent with the number of available minorities in the area. Of the administrative professionals presently working for CanAsian, 7 percent are Indo-Canadian, 3 percent are Latin-American, and 2 percent are Asian. The statistics for Calgary show that the availability of administrative professionals is Indo-Canadian, 25 percent; Latin-American, 10 percent; and Asian, 5 percent. The task of the team is to examine how CanAsian might change these statistics to be more representative of the area. You ask both Guy and Luyin to work with you on the team.

At the first meeting, Guy makes several statements that are interpreted by the team as being negative concerning the need for change. Luyin says nothing but exhibits body language that suggests she is upset with Guy. You believe you must try to help them modify their behaviours or the team will not be successful. You determine that the ethical changes needed are these:

- Guy—Demonstrate greater acceptance of all diversity.
- Luyin—State opinions in meetings in an open but non-confrontational manner.

Determine the Steps Required to Achieve the Objective

After thinking through the situation, you decide to approach each person individually and discuss the following:

- Guy—Discuss with Guy the importance of CanAsian improving the diversity statistics and ask his opinion of how this might be done. Ask him to prepare his ideas before the next team meeting and to go over his ideas with you. In this example, the team leader recognized that the approach to Guy must be positive, not negative. The team leader did not berate him for his behaviour, but asked for his help on the completion of the team report.
- Luyin—Discuss with Luyin the importance of stating her opinions in an open manner at the team meetings. Let her know you value her opinions and want to hear from her. Remember that Luyin is Chinese, and it may not be easy for her to state her opinions openly.

You also decide to clarify the objectives with the entire group at the next meeting, presenting the objectives positively.

Practise the New Behaviours

Give Guy and Luyin a chance to behave differently than they did in the last meeting by asking Guy to share his suggestions for improvement (that you have gone over with him before the meeting). If Luyin does not voice her opinions, ask for her response. Reward Guy and Luyin for doing a good job by publicly praising both of them.

After clarifying the objectives for the group, ask if anyone has questions and discuss whatever issues are raised.

Seek Feedback

Ask a trusted member of the committee to evaluate your behaviour and the behaviour of the team and to make suggestions for changes. If necessary, you might have a consultant observe the group and offer suggestions to team members for successfully completing their tasks. The team leader may also engage in team-building exercises with the group.

Reward the Individuals and the Group

Assuming Guy and Luyin show positive changes in their behaviour, reward them for their growth. Let them know you appreciate their work on the committee; that they did a good job; and that the results of their work will make CanAsian a better place to work. In addition, reward yourself for your work with the team. You deserve to be proud of your insights and willingness to work with the individuals. Mentally add this success to your list of strengths.

Evaluate the Effects of the Ethical Change

Observe whether the team's recommendations result in greater diversity in the numbers of administrative professionals who are employed. If not, you might want to discuss the problem with the human resources director.

Ethics—The Choice Is Yours

Although you cannot impact the ethics of an entire organization unless you are in upper management, you can carefully check out an organization's ethics before you accept a position. How do you check out an organization's ethics? Here are a few suggestions:

- Read the organization's Web page information. Are the ethics of the organization mentioned? Is a commitment to diversity mentioned? Is a commitment to the external community mentioned? What type of programs do they have for employees?
- Check the history of the organization. Have they ever made headlines for behaving unethically?

- Talk with acquaintances who work for the organization. Ask them to describe the ethical environment of the company.

As an individual employee, you can commit to behaving in an ethical manner. You can decide to follow the ethical stances mentioned in this chapter. You will

- Respect the organizational structure
- Make ethical decisions
- Accept constructive criticism
- Respect diversity
- Consider office politics
- Respect others' privacy
- Be honest
- Be dependable
- Be cooperative
- Respect clients and customers

You can also promise yourself that if for some reason (beyond your control) your organization begins engaging in grossly unethical behaviours, you will seek employment in another organization. Peter M. Senge, in his book *The Fifth Discipline,* tells the story of the frog: If you put a frog in a cup of tepid water, it will not jump out; the temperature is comfortable. If you continue to turn up the heat gradually over a period of time until the water is boiling hot, the frog will continue to stay in the water and die. The frog adjusts to the temperature as it is turned up and does not notice the difference in the environment or the threat to its safety. The moral of the story is this: Unless you are committed to observing the ethical behaviour of an organization and behaving in an ethical manner yourself, you may stay in an organization that becomes unethical and find yourself supporting those unethical behaviours to the detriment of your own value system and career growth. Commit now to "jumping out" of unethical waters before you "die" in them.

Chapter Summary

The summary will help you remember the important points covered in the chapter.

- The study of ethics and the ethical organization have been important to our society for a number of years. The lack of ethical behaviour by business can impact our society and the individuals within it.
- More and more attention is being paid to ethical concerns today due to the immediate coverage of business practices through television, radio, and newspapers and the advances in technology that have resulted in questions about ethical standards.
- The ethical organization is socially and environmentally responsible, internationally aware, committed to diversity, honest, and visionary. The ethical organization abides by provincial or federal employment standards, respects the needs and rights of employees, establishes and lives organizational values, maintains a safe and healthy environment, and provides an ergonomically sound environment.
- The ethical employee respects the organizational structure, makes ethical decisions, accepts constructive criticism, respects diversity, is aware of workplace politics, respects others' privacy, is honest, is dependable and cooperative, and respects clients and customers.
- Factors impeding ethical change include these mistaken perceptions: that organizations are amoral, that organizational leadership is unethical, that values cannot be changed, and that labels accurately describe individuals.
- Activities that help bring about ethical change include these: determining the ethical change needed, determining the steps required to achieve the objective, practising the new behaviours, seeking feedback on the change, rewarding the individual or group involved, and evaluating the effects of ethical change.
- Although an individual cannot impact the ethics of an organization unless he or she is in upper management, one can commit to behaving ethically and leaving an organization that is unethical.

Key Terms

The following terms were introduced in this chapter. The page on which the term was introduced is provided to help you locate the new term. Definitions are compiled in the Glossary at the end of the text.

- **pragmatic** 65
- **ethics** 65
- **morality** 66
- **integrity** 66
- **prejudice** 67
- **discrimination** 67
- **sexual harassment** 69
- **physically challenged** 69
- **employment at will** 70
- **due process** 70
- **substance abuse** 73
- **amoral** 79

Responses to Self-Check A

An ethical organization

- Is socially and environmentally responsible
- Is internationally aware
- Is committed to diversity
- Is involved in the community
- Respects the needs and rights of employees
- Establishes and lives organizational values
- Maintains a safe and healthy environment
- Provides an ergonomically sound environment
- Is honest
- Is visionary

Responses to Self-Check B

The most appropriate answers are as follows:

1. Always   3. Never   5. Never   7. Always
2. Always   4. Always   6. Always   8. Never
9. Sometimes (If the gift is small, it may be appropriate; each situation needs to be analyzed. Some organizations do not allow an employee to accept any gifts.)

10. Sometimes (On some issues, you may not need to involve your employer; but never go over his or her head.)

Discussion Items

These discussion items provide an opportunity to test your understanding of the chapter through written responses and/or discussion with your classmates and your instructor.

1. Why is ethical behaviour important for businesses?
2. List and explain six characteristics of the ethical business.
3. List and explain six characteristics of an ethical employee.
4. Can ethical change occur? If so, how?
5. What beliefs often impede ethical change?

Critical-Thinking Activity

Martin Albertson, your supervisor at CanAsian, gives his expense accounts to you each month. Your responsibility is to put the information on a form and return the form to him. Once he reviews and signs it, you send it to the president for signature. Last month you noticed Mr. Albertson included alcoholic beverages on the expense report (under the category of food and beverage). This month you noticed he did it again, and you remember the same thing occurring several months ago. Company policy specifically states that an employee cannot be reimbursed for alcohol. You believe it is merely carelessness on the part of your supervisor; you believe in his honesty. However, you are beginning to wonder if you are engaging in unethical behaviour by not calling his attention to these items. Mr. Albertson has always been clear about your responsibility for knowing and adhering to the policies and procedures of the company.

- What is the problem?
- What is your role in the issue?
- How should you handle the situation?
- Have you been behaving ethically by not calling it to his attention? If your answer is yes, explain your position.

Projects

Project 4-1 *(Objective 1)*

In this project, you are to examine your own ethics. Instructions are provided on the Student CD, file SCDP4-1. This project is a continuation of your Professional Growth Plan. Save your project on your Professional Growth Plan disk under "Progro4-1."

Project 4-2 *(Objectives 1, 2, and 4)*

Collaborative Project

Along with three of your classmates, interview two executives concerning the following:

- The importance of ethical behaviour
- The characteristics of an ethical organization
- The traits of ethical employees

As you are interviewing the executives, determine if their organizations have a vision or mission statement. If so, ask if you may have a copy of the statement. Present your findings to the class. Take notes during the interviews so you can report your findings accurately.

Project 4-3 *(Objective 5)*

Read the following case, and respond to the questions given. Submit your answers to your instructor in a short memorandum using the memorandum form provided on the Student CD, file SCDP4-3.

Case

Cindy Johal has been with CanAsian for eight months. She works in the human resources department as an assistant to the vice-president. During her eight months, she has demonstrated that she is an extremely capable individual and is committed to upholding the values of CanAsian. CanAsian has a non-discriminatory policy that it publishes for all of its employees. Included in this policy is a statement concerning sexual harassment, making it clear that there is no tolerance for any form of sexual harassment at CanAsian. Cindy is well aware of this policy; in fact, she assisted the director as he dealt with one case of sexual harassment. In this particular case, the employee accused of sexual harassment was terminated due to the seriousness of the charge and the finding that he was guilty of the charge.

Recently, CanAsian hired a new employee, Roy McEvoy, in the Accounting Department. One day in the break room, Cindy introduced herself to him. She knew he was a new employee, and she welcomed him to CanAsian. Since that time she has seen him three times in the halls. He made these remarks to her: "You look great today; you are certainly a beautiful girl." "Wow! That colour looks wonderful on you; you should wear blue more often." "How about coffee in the morning?" She merely smiled each time and said nothing.

She does not think he meant any harm by the remarks; she thinks he is merely trying to be friendly. However, she strongly believes that she should say something to him if he makes another remark.

1. Explain how Cindy should handle this situation. Should she report the incident to her supervisor? Why or why not?
2. Since Roy is a new employee, should he be helped to understand CanAsian's commitment to an environment that is free of sexual harassment? If so, who should help him?
3. What steps can be taken to assist Roy in assuring that his behaviours match the ethical standards of CanAsian? In answering this question, reread the section "Maintains a Policy Against Sexual Harassment" in this chapter. Then develop a plan to help Roy match his behaviours with the ethical commitment of CanAsian.

Submit your responses in writing to your instructor.

Case Solution for Part 1

Nerissa McNaughton's Case Solution

I chose to accept help, communicate clearly, pay attention to details, and strive for a mental and physical balance.

Part of being successful is realizing your limitations. While becoming Move Coordinator was an honour, I knew that I lacked some requisite skills. Fortunately, we had a skilled professional available. She drew up plans and educated executives on how to make the most efficient use of space. She showed me how to read plans, told me what to expect in people's reactions, and informed me of the details that needed to be considered. She stayed late on several occasions to supervise night moves, and to show me how to organize teams of workers efficiently. After learning from her, I felt capable of supervising moves on my own.

I learned that it takes many people to complete a project of this scale, and that good communication is key. The contractors, staff, and labourers need to clearly communicate their wishes. I could not expect a phone extension to be moved in time for the next workday if I forgot to inform the Information Services department of the move. The contractors could not knock out a wall if they didn't tell me to have everyone out of the area.

I learned that sometimes the smallest gestures make the biggest difference, and I consider this the most important lesson I have learned about success.

Emotions run high when work areas are torn down. It is very difficult to work from boxes, or move several times and discover there is less space than before. I became determined to do everything possible to make the staff comfortable. This meant listening to concerns and trying to find solutions, no matter how trivial they seemed. Sometimes this entailed grabbing a vacuum to clean out a dusty work area that was full of debris. When the new air-conditioning units malfunctioned and covered several offices with dirt, I took up a rag and made jokes with startled employees as I cleaned up the mess. Wielding a rag was not in my job description, but it helped improve the situation and that was what mattered. I have crawled under desks to hook up computers, helped with heavy lifting when items needed to be tweaked to make someone more comfortable, and made endless trips up and down stairs to sort out phones, cables, and wires. In return, my co-workers said and did little things to keep my spirits up. When I was feeling overwhelmed, someone would offer a pat on the back or tell me I was doing a fine job. One kind lady gave me a page out of her calendar that said something about success being disguised as hard work hiding behind overalls. Another laughed at the dirt covering her desk and said "Thank goodness it's not dust! I'm allergic to dust!" After one particularly difficult move, I found a stunning display of flowers on my desk from the department. It is indeed the little things that count—both given and received.

PART 2

COMMUNICATION: SKILLS FOR A DIVERSE WORKING ENVIRONMENT

A Success Profile

Charlene Charles
Management Assistant
The Children's Aid Society
Ontario, Canada

I enjoy my career! Two years ago, I decided to leave my full-time job and return to postsecondary studies in order to focus on the executive curriculum which would lead to the next phase of my professional career.

Seventeen years ago, I graduated from a medical secretary program. Upon returning to my hometown, I secured part-time employment with the local hospital as a secretary for the sports injury clinic. That contract position expired six months later, at which time I began working as the switchboard operator with the Health unit. Within two years, I became the secretary/statistical clerk, and then the program secretary for the Addictions department, a position I held for seven years. Following that tenure, I transferred to the Employment department, where I worked for five years. Each of these areas provided me with different opportunities to develop my secretarial skills. Professional development geared toward secretarial staff, however, was not as available as for other professional staff within the office. For personal interest, I continued to take continuing education courses from the local community college to keep up to date with the various software programs that I was currently using, that I would use in the future, or that might be beneficial to potential employers.

While working in the Employment department, I was introduced to an association designed for administrative professionals. I attended my first meeting of the International Association of Administrative Professionals, Quintus Chapter, in 1999, and became a member in 2000. This was one of the wisest decisions I have made. Becoming a member of the IAAP, networking with other administrative professionals, and doing some professional "soul searching" allowed me to realize I was heading into the next phase of growth in my professional career. I became interested in the role of executive assistants and the types of responsibilities and challenges that they encountered. I decided that I wanted to be an executive assistant to one or two individuals, and to be *the* person upon whom they would rely. To further my goal, I became actively involved with my IAAP chapter, accepting the role of Co-President for the 2001–2002 term. Eventually, I also returned to school on a full-time basis.

In 2003, I graduated with Honours from the Office Administration, Executive, program. What an amazing time! Not only was I heavily involved in my studies, but I was also a peer tutor, a member of the college's Office Administration Advisory Committee, and working on a part-time basis at the college. I had learned that there were many wonderful opportunities available to students if they made the effort to pursue them. I was one of two recipients of the 2003 Nicole Burgoin Memorial Bursary Award, as well as a recipient of the Keith McIntyre (Ontario Student Opportunity Trust Fund) Award, a tuition scholarship. The Ontario Student Opportunity Trust Fund (OSOTF) will award about 200 tuition scholarships of up to $1000. OSOTF is available to students who are Ontario residents, taking at least 60 percent of a full course load in a ministry-approved program, and not sponsored by an employer or agency. Applicants must also have good grades (80 percent average) and show financial need.

Returning to college to pursue the Executive program gave me the opportunity to become familiar with software commonly used in today's offices—Word, Excel, PowerPoint, Access, and Outlook. Further improving my already excellent typing speed and transcription skills was beneficial as well. I also completed courses in law, human relations, and communications. I found the study of human relations to be as important as my technical studies. Learning how people communicate, think, or work to accomplish a task helps prepare for personality conflicts and challenges that may be encountered in the workplace.

A month after completing my course of studies, I accepted my current position. I provide administrative support to a manager and a director. My duties include the scheduling of appointments, meetings, and interviews; preparing correspondence and reports; sorting mail; delegation of complaints to appropriate personnel; recording and transcription of various agency meeting minutes; and providing coverage for one other management assistant.

I continue to be involved with IAAP. For the 2003–2004 term, I again volunteered for the role of Co-President of my chapter, and have enjoyed another successful year of professional growth. I plan to write the exam to obtain my certification as a Certified Professional Secretary (CPS), and I have accepted a one-semester position teaching continuing education courses in keyboarding at a local community college.

Education (Medical Secretarial and Executive Assistant diplomas), experience (volunteer work or in-school opportunities), lifelong learning (completion of continuing education courses on an ongoing basis), and professional growth (membership in and involvement with the International Association of Administrative Professionals as Co-President of the local chapter) have been the key components in my successful professional career.

Charlene Charles' Case

I was a new employee still familiarizing myself with my job and other employees in the organization when I was asked by my supervisor to prepare an hour-long presentation with a colleague. The topic, which was to be offered to other assistants and frontline workers, was time management. It was to include manual and computerized tools that could be utilized by office assistants to assist them in performing administrative duties more efficiently. Sometimes we assume that everyone is comfortable using the same tools, but in many cases they are not. They may hesitate to ask for assistance, or just be unaware of tools that could make their jobs easier.

After being given the subject matter and the number of people that would be in attendance, we were told one last bit of information—we might be met with some resistance from those assistants who felt we were "telling them what to do" or "speaking down to them." With all the details in place, my colleague and I set off to prepare our presentation.

What steps would you take to pull this presentation together? Turn to the end of Chapter 8 to see my solution.

Chapter 5

The Communication Process

LEARNING OBJECTIVES

1. *Clarify your values.*
2. Develop skills needed in a culturally diverse workforce.
3. Explain the communication process.
4. Develop and use effective verbal and nonverbal communication skills.

You cannot be effective in the workplace without being an effective communicator. Your effectiveness as an administrative professional implies effective communication skills, since the majority of the administrative professional's day involves contact with people. Effective communication is the ability to process and exchange ideas and feelings so the person originating the communication and the person receiving the communication clearly understand what is being communicated. Building and maintaining effective communications are never easy. This statement is particularly true today in our complex, diverse world. People find it difficult enough to relate successfully to others who are like them. However, when people are from different cultures and backgrounds, of different ages, and even from different countries, the task becomes even more complex.

Since effective performance in the workplace depends greatly on the ability to communicate effectively, the question you must ask yourself is this:

How well do I communicate with others?

Take Self-Check A on page 90 now. Compare your answers with the suggested responses at the end of this chapter. Now ask yourself this question:

How do I become a more effective communicator?

Make up your mind to improve your communication skills throughout this course. Commit to carefully studying the concepts presented in this chapter and to using the effective communication techniques presented.

Communication—A Complex Issue

Forces that contribute to the complexity of communication today include the following:

- Our global world
- The increasing number of multinational organizations
- The greater diversity of the people who comprise the workplace
- The number of immigrants who are entering our country
- The technological workplace

Consider the Canadian population for a moment. According to the 2001 Canadian Census (a census done every ten years), the foreign-born population in 2001 was 5.4 million or 18.4 percent of the total population. This is the highest proportion since 1931. Between 1991 and 2000 alone, 2.2 million immigrants were admitted to Canada, the highest number for any decade in the

Respond to the following comments with a yes or no answer.

1. I am always aware of the nonverbal communication of others.
   Yes ☐ **No** ☐

2. I never allow my own biases to interfere with my communication.
   Yes ☐ **No** ☐

3. I pay attention to cultural differences that may be present in the communication process.
   Yes ☐ **No** ☐

4. I always listen well.
   Yes ☐ **No** ☐

5. I am non-judgmental of others.
   Yes ☐ **No** ☐

6. I use words precisely in my communication.
   Yes ☐ **No** ☐

7. I always seek to understand the other person's point of view.
   Yes ☐ **No** ☐

8. I offer advice only after understanding the situation presented.
   Yes ☐ **No** ☐

9. I allow myself to engage in critiquing the speaker.
   Yes ☐ **No** ☐

10. I use direct, simple language in my communication.
    Yes ☐ **No** ☐

■ Figure 5-1

HOW VALUES ARE LEARNED

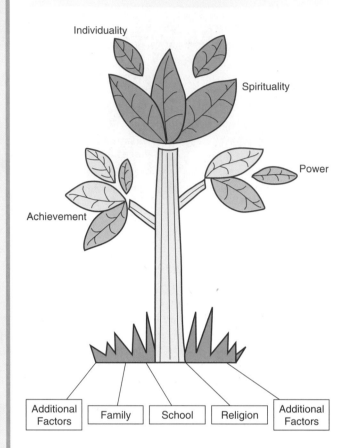

- 8 South Americans
- 6 North Americans[3]

This global world demands that we be globally literate—that we see, think, and act in ways that are culturally mindful of the vast differences in our world.

Our technology and the multinational nature of business add to the complexity of our communication. Our contacts with others may be through telecommunications—the Internet, fax, telephone, and virtual conferencing, for example—in addition to our face-to-face communication. Regardless of the form the interaction takes, you must practise effective communication techniques. Effectiveness assumes that you are

- Clear concerning your own values and attitudes
- Sensitive to cultural differences
- Aware of gender and age issues

past century. In 1996 census the proportion of foreign-born population was 17.4 percent.[1] It is predicted that by the year 2010 over 1.75 million immigrants will have arrived in Canada.[2] Already, many languages are spoken in the school systems of our large cities, such as Toronto, Vancouver, and Calgary. If we were a global village of 100 people, North Americans would be very much in the minority. That village would be composed of the following:

- 56 Asians
- 21 Europeans
- 9 Africans

Communication Tip

When you have a customer, caller, or business associate who does not speak fluent English, paraphrase what you believe the person has said. Then ask "Is that correct?"

Soft Skills: Value Clarification

The word **value** comes from the French verb *valoir*, meaning "to be worth." Values are our beliefs. They determine how we live on a day-to-day basis. For example, knowledge is a value. You probably would not be taking this course if you did not value knowledge. You want to learn. We may or may not spend much time thinking about what we value, but the decisions we make each day are influenced by the values we have.

Our early values are learned from significant people in our environment, such as our parents and other family members. In addition, values are learned from our educational, social, and religious structures, such as our schools and places of worship. However, our values are not static; that is, as we grow and change, our values may change. Figure 5-1 on page 90 graphically depicts a set of values that an individual may have. In this illustration, a tree is used to depict the growing and changing individual. The roots of the tree are the people and social and religious structures that have helped shaped the person's values. The branches of the tree contain the values by which the person operates. As the person continues to grow and change mentally, psychologically, and physically, an expanded root system may include other factors that shape the values of the individual, resulting in new values (branches) being added to the tree and even old values (branches) being chopped off. As you study the material in this course and perform the tasks given, you should come to understand your value system. Your value system shapes what you believe, how you live and work, and how you relate to others.

Values are not inherently good or bad. However, the way in which you live your values may involve behaviours that are either acceptable or unacceptable in our society. If we encounter someone who is not behaving appropriately for the values we hold, we sometimes say "That person has no values." Such a statement is incorrect; everyone has values. However, the values a person holds may not match our values or may not match those of the society in which we live. For example, one might say that Adolph Hitler was value-centred, one of his values being to build a superior race. In his attempt to do so, he engaged in one of the greatest atrocities of our history, killing over eight million Jews.

One of your values might be to become economically independent. To accomplish this value, you might decide to obtain an education and then seek a job in an organization that gives you the opportunity to move to higher levels of responsibility. Conversely, you might decide to rob a bank, get involved in drug trafficking, or engage in some other type of criminal behaviour to satisfy your need to become economically independent. In other words, the principles that you hold, the attitudes that you exhibit, and the behaviours that you demonstrate in living your values are legally and socially acceptable or unacceptable. Complete Self-Check B now.

SELF-CHECK B ✔

Stop for a moment and think about your values. List your top five values.

1. _Honesty_
2. _Independence_
3. _Ethics - work + personal_
4. _Punctuality_
5. _Trust_

Attitude Clarification

Generally, we do not give much thought to how our values may be different from other people's values. We sometimes assume that everyone has the same values and then operate from this assumption. Obviously, that assumption is not true, and it can cause communication difficulties if it is not understood. Also, we do not give much thought to the attitudes we demonstrate in pursuit of our values. **Attitude** is defined in the dictionary as "position, disposition, or manner with regard to a person or thing." Consider an example of a value you might have, recognizing differences. You value the importance of recognizing the differences of all individuals with whom you work. Yet recently, when one of your co-workers from Lebanon got "right in your face" when talking with you, you became irritated with her behaviour and asked her not to violate your space. She went away in puzzlement, not understanding that most North Americans do not stand extremely close to each other to talk unless they have an intimate relationship.

The attitude you demonstrated to this person did not reflect that you value recognizing the differences of all individuals. It reflected rudeness and even lack of consideration to the person from Lebanon. Just as you need to understand what you value, you also need to be clear about the attitudes you reflect to others. In the workplace, a great deal of attention is paid to the attitude of employees. In fact, during the formal evaluation process, an individual is often evaluated on his or her attitude. A positive attitude is always an asset, whereas a negative attitude is always a detractor.

Cultural Differences

With our population becoming more diverse and our organizations becoming more multinational, we must continue to be alert to the differences between the people with whom we work. We must be tolerant of these differences, not expecting that all people will react to situations the same way. We must understand and accept that diversity can mean that significant differences exist among our values, our assumptions, and our attitudes. Consider some of the cultural differences between people.

Trust is earned differently in various countries. For example, if an employee in Canada or in the United States performs well on his or her job, he or she earns trust quickly. Superior performance equates to trusting the individual to do the job well. In contrast, in Japan and Germany, trust is earned over a long period of time. For the Japanese and the Germans, trust may in fact be a result of family relationships or long-term knowledge of an individual.

Respect also is viewed differently in various cultures. For example, in Asian countries, great respect is given to the older generation. Respect is also given to people in authority, such as political officials. In Canada, we tend to believe that respect must be earned; it is not automatically given to specific people or groups of people.

Diversity can mean that significant differences exist in our values, our assumptions, and our attitudes.

> ## Communication Tip
> Treat every co-worker as a unique individual, recognizing that all people are different.

Nonverbal communication varies greatly across countries. A Japanese member of a work team may smile in a friendly but noncommittal manner. A North American usually takes the smile as an expression of agreement with what is being said. The German team member may interpret the smile as disagreement. An Italian may agree to a deadline without ever meaning to adhere to it. The Italian is merely being agreeable. When the Italian does not meet the deadline, the North American takes the behaviour as a sign of disrespect or lack of interest.

Canadian students learn from the time they enter school that class participation is important. We are taught to give our opinions. If students do not participate in class, they are considered to be uninterested or even unprepared for the class. In contrast, Asians regard teachers so highly they find it difficult to voice their own views in class. Doing so is almost a sign of disrespect to the teacher.

North Americans are considered demonstrative. Generally, we show our feelings easily. If we are happy, we smile a lot. If we are sad, we seldom smile. We are taught from an early age to make eye contact with people. To look down at the floor while someone is talking to you can mean disrespect for the individual or signify a lack of confidence on the part of the person looking down.

North Americans have certain concepts of time and space. For example, in Canada, it is important to be on time for business appointments. A certain amount of space distance is maintained when talking with people. When talking to an acquaintance, we generally maintain a distance of from 0.6 to 0.9 metres. Only when talking with someone with whom we have an intimate relationship do we get close. Figure 5-2 on page 93 highlights how these same behaviours are viewed very differently in certain other countries.

Due to a lack of understanding of our global cultural differences, we make mistakes. These mistakes are costly not only to our interactions with others but also to businesses. Here are some examples of cultural illiteracies that were costly to business.

- McDonald's took 13 months to realize that Hindus in India do not eat beef. When it started making hamburgers out of lamb, sales flourished.
- In Africa, companies show pictures of what is inside bottles so that illiterate customers know what they are getting. When a baby food

■ Figure 5-2

CULTURAL DIFFERENCES

- In Korean culture, smiling can signal shallowness and thoughtlessness.
- Asians, Latin Americans, and Caribbeans avoid eye contact as a sign of respect.
- Avoidance of eye contact in Japan means that the person is being polite and nonconfrontational. Mothers often scold their children for staring into people's eyes when they speak.
- In France and Mexico, being 30 minutes late to an appointment is perfectly acceptable.
- Latin Americans stand very close to each other when talking; the interaction distance is much less than in North America.
- Open criticism should be avoided when dealing with Asian employees, as this may lead to loss of face.
- In Japan and China, "yes" does not always mean "yes."
- Japanese are taught to withhold their personal opinions. An old Japanese proverb says "Silence is a virtue."

Source: Norine Dresser, *Multicultural Manners: New Rules of Etiquette for a Changing Society* (New York: John Wiley & Sons, 1996).

company showed a picture of a child on its label, the product did not sell very well.

- A U.S. television ad for deodorant depicted an octopus putting antiperspirant under each arm. When the ad flopped in Japan, the producers realized that octopuses do not have arms there; they have legs.
- A U.S. firm sent an elaborate business proposal to Saudi Arabia bound in pigskin. Since pigs are considered unclean by Muslims, the proposal was never opened.
- Kentucky Fried Chicken's "Finger-Lickin' Good" translated to "Eat Your Fingers Off" in Chinese.[4]

In the future, remind yourself not to expect people from different cultures to behave as you do. Educate yourself about other cultures. Here are some suggestions about how to do so:

- Read books on different cultures that are available in bookstores and/or your local library.
- Join a global chat group on the Internet.
- Talk with individuals from different cultures with whom you work about their life and the differences they see in various cultures.
- Set a goal to make it one of your top priorities to develop appropriate cultural expectations.

Gender Issues

The gender of an individual in all societies has significant importance in job roles, social responsibilities, family responsibilities, and even education and socialization. People are born female or male, but they learn to be girls and boys who grow up to be women and men. We are taught values, attitudes, behaviours, and roles on the basis of what our particular socialization group (parents, teachers, significant others) believes are right and appropriate for the male and the female. The appropriate roles and behaviours vary depending on what country we are born in and the position in society of the group teaching the behaviours (professional role or occupation, education attainment, and so on). The roles taught also may vary within a particular part of the country or within various communities in the same part of the country (ethnic communities). For example, with our diverse population, a city may have large numbers of various ethnic groups, with these groups having different cultures and backgrounds that socialize men and women in very different ways. Also, boys and girls who grow up in large cities as opposed to more rural environments may be socialized differently.

Gender roles are not static but change in response to events in our world. Very few women in Canada worked outside the home before World War II. Their role was one of wife, mother, and caretaker of the home and family. Since many men were in the armed services in World War II, women were needed to fill essential jobs in business and industry. That experience for women of working outside the home not only changed the way many of them viewed work roles but also changed the way many businesses and industries viewed the role of women in the workforce. Today, as you have already learned, we have greater numbers of women in the workforce than ever before in our history, and those numbers are expected to increase in the future.

An important concept that business and industry learned about more women being in the workforce is that different gender voices are needed. These different voices provide the opportunity for analyzing situations in various ways, often resulting in better decisions for the organization. For example, in producing and marketing products, different gender voices provide perspectives that can allow the organization to meet the needs of a greater number of people, with the likelihood of increasing the profit margin.

Before moving on, take a few minutes to reflect on gender roles in your own community. Using Self-Check C, respond to the items given.

Age Issues

With the Canadian population over 50 years of age increasing, it is expected that people will stay in the workforce beyond the traditional retirement age of 65. Thus, workforce teams will be made up of people with large variations in age. Just as people who grow up in different cultures and environments have different values and expectations, so do people who are of different ages. To help you think about the various generations and some of their characteristics, look at how various generations have been categorized by writers in the field:

Birth Dates	Generation Name
1930–1945	Silent Generation
1946–1964	Baby Boomers
1965–1980	Generation X
1981–2000	Net Generation or N-Geners

As writers have categorized these generations by age group, they have also studied how these generations behave and have assigned certain values/characteristics to each. For example, in his best-selling book *The Greatest Generation*, Tom Brokaw discusses the common values held by the men and women who came of age during the Great Depression and World War II, the Silent Generation. Some of the values he lists are duty, honour, courage, service, and responsibility for oneself.

Characteristics/values that have been identified for the generation of Baby Boomers include:

- They are committed to education.
- They are more individualistic than the Silent Generation—they always take care of themselves.
- They are skeptical about the status quo and politics.
- They believe in themselves.

SELF-CHECK C ✔

1. List the different professional roles carried out by men and women in your community.

   - political
   - Administration
   - Doctors/nurses
   - teachers

2. List the professional roles you identified in point 1 in order of status in your community.

   Doctors
   Political
   Nurses / teachers
   Admin

3. In your opinion, does one gender carry more status in professional roles than the other? If so, explain how.

   Men - tend to be trusted more in political roles with respect to their abilities

4. List the home activities carried out by men and women—for example, cooking, cleaning, or child care.
   auto repairs/maintenance
   - lawn maintenance
   - cooking cleaning
   - gardening
   - decorating

5. Is one gender responsible for more of the home activities than the other? If so, what are they?

   - women are still the majority → cooking, cleaning, childrearing
   - Men the majority - yard/auto's

6. If you could change the way gender in your community is viewed, what would you do?

   - Divide up tasks/chores/work differently roles.

In contrast, Generation X values/characteristics have been identified as follows:

- They have less belief in self.
- They are more tolerant than previous generations—accepting of most everything except narrow-mindedness.
- They are spiritual.
- They are not workaholics—a job is merely what one does to earn money.
- They are relational—they value good friends.

Don Tapscott in *Growing Up Digital* defines the Net Generation values in these terms.

> *They are the young navigators. They doubt that traditional institutions can provide them with the good life and take personal responsibility for their lives. They do value material goods but they are not self-absorbed. They are more knowledgeable than any previous generation and they care deeply about social issues. They believe strongly in individual rights such as privacy and rights to information. But they have no ethos of individualism, thriving, rather, from close interpersonal networks and displaying a strong sense of social responsibility.*
>
> *They appear very determined and even optimistic about the future, but are unsettled about the difficulties facing them including obstacles to a rewarding adult life. They are quite alienated from formal politics and depending on age, there are growing discussions about the need for fundamental social change.*[5]

As can be seen by analyzing these different generations, individuals who grow up in different times may have different values. However, recognizing these different values does not give one the right to characterize or make judgments about individuals on the basis of their ages. The information is given here to help you understand some of the differences in values that can occur due to the societal events that are happening during our lifetime. The importance of this information in the workforce is that people must recognize possible differences due to age and address the differences in positive ways.

An Action Agenda

Your task as you work in a diverse world in which value differences, cultural differences, and gender and age issues exist is to

- Recognize that these differences occur
- Constantly seek to understand these differences
- Understand their implications for communication

- Grow in your ability to communicate with all people

In order to grow in your ability to communicate, you must understand the communication process and the barriers to effective communication. Additionally, you must continually practise effective communication techniques. The next sections of this chapter will help you gain these skills.

The Communication Process

In understanding a culturally diverse workforce, you have already learned the importance of communication. Now consider the elements of the communication process—the originator, the message, the receiver, and the response.

The Originator

The **originator** is the sender of the original message. The originator transmits information, ideas, and feelings through speaking, writing, or gesturing. Although the originator is often a person, the originator may be a company, a committee, or even a nation. For example, in the advertisements you see on television about a particular product, the company is the originator of the communication.

The Message

The **message** is the idea being presented by the originator. Words are usually used in communicating the idea; but hand signals, gestures, or a combination of words and gestures may also be used. The transmission of these words or gestures usually takes the form of face-to-face exchanges, telephone conversations, voice mail, or written correspondence such as email, faxes, Web correspondence, and letters and memorandums. Other forms of transmission are radio, television, videocassette, audiocassette, CDs, and DVDs.

The Receiver

The person for whom the message is intended is the **receiver**. The receiver transfers the message into meaning. For example, if the message were "Please send this letter out immediately," the receiver would develop a meaning based on his or her understanding of the words and previous knowledge of the originator. The receiver may decide that the letter should be sent out in 30 minutes, for example; in another situation, the receiver might decide that two hours is the appropriate time frame.

The Response

The **response** (feedback) of the receiver lets the originator know whether the communication is understood. The response may be verbal or nonverbal (such as a nod of the head, a smile, or a shrug of the shoulders). If the response of the receiver indicates to the originator that the communication was misunderstood, the originator can send the message again, perhaps in a different manner. For example, in the situation of the letter to be sent out, assume the originator meant for the letter to go out within 10 minutes and the receiver did not send it out for 30 minutes; as a result, the letter missed the morning mail. In the future, the originator might frame the message in this manner: "Please see that the letter makes the morning mail." A communication model is shown in Figure 5-3.

Every element of the communication process is important. If the originator does not clearly state his or her message, problems can occur. If the receiver interprets the message incorrectly and responds inappropriately, there may be problems. Every person in the communication process has an obligation to communicate as clearly as possible, to frame his or her message well, and to ask questions if the message or response is unclear.

■ Figure 5-3

COMMUNICATION MODEL

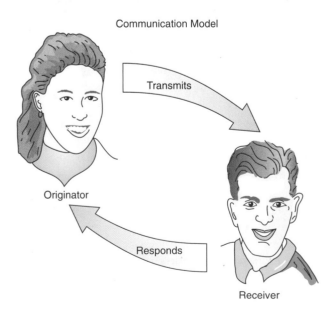

Communication Model

Transmits

Originator

Responds

Receiver

Verbal Communication

Verbal communication is the process of exchanging ideas and feelings through the use of words. Initially, the concept of verbal communication seems simple. We all understand words and know what they mean. In actuality, verbal communication is not simple at all. Words, although they may be spelled the same, have different meanings for different people. Add to this situation the complexity of a diverse workforce, and the relevance of words often having very different meanings becomes clear.

Verbal Barriers

Barriers do exist whether we are communicating with others of the same culture or of different cultures. Several of these barriers are given here.

Listening

Listening is the complete process by which verbal language, communicated by a source, is received, recognized, attended to, comprehended, and retained. The listener attends to the verbal language of the source with the intent of acquiring meaning. Thus, the main components of listening are not located in the ears, just as the main components of seeing are not located in the eyes. Our ears hear the sound vibrations to which we attend and comprehend; but our listening is based on our needs, desires, interests, previous experiences, and learning. As you can see, listening is a complex phenomenon involving the total individual. As we listen, our process of thought, which is composed of many separate and independent concepts, flows into ideas and emotions, and affects what we hear.

Studies show that the average person spends 70 percent of the day communicating with others, 45 percent of that communication time being spent listening to others. However, listening is considered one of the weakest links in the communication process. Research studies show that immediately following a conversation a listener retains approximately 50 percent of what was said. However, after 48 hours, the percentage drops to only 25 percent. In other words, 50–75 percent of what we hear is never processed.

Do you consider yourself a good listener? Complete Self-Check D on page 97 to determine your present listening effectiveness. Rate yourself by answering the statements with "Always," "Sometimes," or "Never."

Respond to the following comments with "Always," "Sometimes," or "Never" after the statement.

1. When people talk to me, I find it difficult to keep my mind on the subject. *Always*

2. I listen only for facts. *Sometimes*

3. Certain words and ideas can prejudice me against a speaker to the point that I cannot listen objectively to what is being said. *Sometimes*

4. I can tell by a person's appearance if that person will have something worthwhile to say. *Sometimes*

5. When someone is speaking to me, I am easily distracted by outside sights and sounds. *Always*

6. I interrupt the speaker to get my point across. *Sometimes*

7. When someone else is talking, I plan what I will say next. *sometimes*

8. I frequently criticize the speaker's delivery or mannerisms. *never*

9. I use the difference between the talking time of the speaker and my own comprehension time to analyze and relate to the speaker's points. *Sometimes*

10. I am aware of the nonverbal communication of others. *Always*

How did you do? Did you recognize yourself as an ineffective listener? If you are like most of us, your score can probably be improved. Improvement comes by understanding what causes poor listening and then working on effective listening techniques. Numerous characteristics produce poor listening behaviours. Consider the following ineffective listeners:

- *The* **talker**. Unfortunately, many of us are so intent on discussing what has happened to us that we have difficulty waiting for the other person to finish so we can begin talking. In fact, many times the eager talker will interrupt the speaker to get his or her point across. Such individuals absorb little of what the other person says. In addition, they are usually planning their story while the other person is talking.

- *The* **attention faker**. Have you ever talked with someone who seemed to listen to every word you said, but when it came time for the person to respond, you realized she or he had not heard a word? Have you ever sat in a classroom and intently watched the instructor during an entire lecture but were unable to answer any questions about what was said? Most of us are good at adopting an outward posture that leads the speaker to believe we are listening when actually we are thinking of something else.

- *The* **easily distracted**. Most people speak at approximately 135–175 words a minute, yet it is believed the brain can process information at about 500 words a minute. Listening allows plenty of time for the mind to wander. Unless the listener is committed to hearing the speaker, he or she can easily become distracted. Distraction can be in the form of **external noise** (physical sounds that hinder the listening process) or movement, either inside or outside the room. Distractions can also be in the form of **internal noise** (distractions that occur inside the listener), such as a problem that is bothering you. You may be thinking about your problem and miss the speaker's point totally.

- *The* **outguesser**. Have you ever known someone who would never let you finish a sentence but always finished it for you? That person may have assumed time was being saved when time was actually lost. Many times the outguesser makes an inaccurate assumption concerning your message. You therefore have to stop and explain to the outguesser that he or she has made a wrong assumption.

Language Usage

The language we use often prevents clear communication. Words in isolation have no meaning. They have meaning only because people have agreed upon a particular meaning. You might say "But what about the dictionary? Doesn't it contain the correct meanings of words?" Yes, it contains the correct meaning as agreed to by **etymologists** (specialists in the study of words). This meaning can be called the objective meaning of a word, and we use the dictionary to determine it. However, cultural differences impact the meaning of certain words. Although people in England speak the same language as people in Canada, they may use words in different ways. For example, when people in Canada have to wait in line, they refer to this behaviour as "standing in line"; the British refer to it as "queuing up." In England, an elevator is called a "lift." Napkins in England mean "diapers." The verb "scheme," for most North Americans, has a negative implication; in England, it is merely a synonym for "plan."

Meanings of words also change with time. New words come into existence, and others become obsolete because of lack of usage. The computer era has generated different applications for certain words. Remember when "bulletin board" meant only a board that was hung on a wall to which notes were attached? Now it can mean a public-access message system through computer linkage. "Chat room" in computer terminology does not mean a room at all in the standard definition of the word, but a location where people all over the world, connected by the Web, can "talk" with each other via computers.

Evaluation

One of the major barriers to communication is the tendency to judge the individual making a statement and then to accept or reject the statement on the basis of that **evaluation**. This evaluation is made from the listener's frame of reference and experience. If what is said agrees with the listener's experience, the listener tends to make a positive evaluation. If what is said does not agree with the listener's experience, he or she may make a negative evaluation.

Inference

Inference is the process of deriving logical conclusions from premises known or assumed to be true. The problem that can be caused from making inferences is that individuals may act upon what they believe to be true when it is in fact not true.

Consider Figure 5-4. What do you see in the illustration? Do you see a woman? Is she young or old? What is she wearing? You may have answered that she is a young woman with a small nose and a choker around her neck. What if I tell you that you are wrong? It is an old woman with a large nose and her head tucked down into a fur coat. Who is right? Look at the picture again. We are both right. Both a young woman and an old woman are in this picture.

Each of us thinks we see things exactly as they are; in other words, we are objective in our assessment of what we see. When other people disagree with us, we immediately think something is wrong with them. In actuality, we see the world through our own filter—a filter that has been established through our values, our culture, our background, and our teachings.

Figure 5-4

WHAT DO YOU SEE?

Noise

Noise in our environment creates distortion in the message being sent and prevents us from understanding the message as it was intended. Noise can come from any number of sources. It may be external noise, such as telephones ringing, a construction crew sawing and hammering, and traffic noise. It may be the internal noise of the receiver, such as having a sick child or anticipating a pending holiday; when we have numerous issues or problems on our mind, the internal noise blocks what the sender of the communication is attempting to say. The time of day the communication is delivered can also constitute noise. For example, if it is late on a Friday afternoon, we may not be able to hear a complex communication.

Cultural, Gender, and Age Differences

The cultural, gender, and age differences of our diverse workplace can and many times do make our communication even more complex. Due to the differences in values, backgrounds, and beliefs these differences often bring with them, major barriers can occur.

In addition to the verbal communication barriers that have been mentioned, there are numerous other barriers. Study Figure 5-5 to understand these barriers.

Effective Verbal Communication

In order to communicate effectively, we must learn to reduce communication barriers. Due to the number of people with whom we communicate each day and the different situations in which we find ourselves, it is impossible to reduce all barriers. However, we can make significant improvement in our verbal communication by using a variety of techniques. Study the ones presented in Figure 5-6 on page 101. Commit yourself to practising these techniques as you communicate each day. The improvement you see in your communication will be more than worth the effort you expend.

Understand the Other Person's View

In *The 7 Habits of Highly Effective People*,[6] Stephen R. Covey states that in all communication it is important to seek first to understand the individual, then to be understood. This approach is not consistent with what most of us do. Generally, we try to explain our position first. Often we do a sales job on it. Once we have finished, we then turn to the person for his or her response. The ability to listen first requires respect for the other individual and the ability to stop talking and truly listen. It requires active listening—the type of listening that is explained in the next section.

Listen Actively

Active listening requires that you listen for the meaning as well as the words of the speaker. Here are some suggestions for becoming an active listener:

- *Prepare to listen.* Drive distracting thoughts from your mind, and direct your full attention to the speaker.

■ **Figure 5-5**

COMMUNICATION BARRIERS

- *Hearing the expected.* We are often guilty of sizing up an individual and then only hearing what we think that individual should say.

- *Ignoring conflicting information.* If you have predetermined feelings about a subject, you tend to ignore new information on the subject. This new information may be valid, but you have made up your mind otherwise.

- *Evaluating the source.* It is difficult to separate what we hear from our feelings about the person speaking. If you like the person, you tend to accept what the person is saying. If you dislike the person, you tend to ignore what the person is saying.

- *Viewing things differently.* Individuals may view the same situation in different ways. For example, if one person sees people in an office laughing and telling jokes, the person may decide they are goofing off and no work

is being accomplished. Another person may interpret the office as a happy place and one where work is accomplished easily in teams.

- *Using word barriers.* Words have different meanings for different people. Even such simple words as "great," "small," "good," and "bad" are open to interpretation by the listener. Communication theorists say that a word in and of itself has no meaning. A word only has the meaning given to it by the communicator. To counter word barriers, communicators must always clarify the meaning attached to words.

- *Not noticing differences in position.* Breakdowns often occur because of differences in position. For example, your supervisor may tell you something you do not understand. Yet you do not ask for clarification because you fear he or she will think you are stupid.

- *Listen for facts.* Mentally register the key words the speaker is using, and repeat key ideas or related points. Relate what the speaker is saying to your experiences.

- *Minimize mental blocks and filters by being aware of them.* Know your biases and prejudices. Do not let them keep you from hearing what the speaker is saying.

- *Take notes.* When listening to a presentation or lecture, taking notes can be beneficial in jogging your memory later. Write only the main points of the message; do not attempt to record every word.

> **Communication Tip**
>
> Listen for feelings. Search beneath the surface. Listen to what is and what is not being said.

- *Question and paraphrase.* Ask questions when you do not understand what you have heard. Paraphrase by putting the speaker's communication in your own words and asking the speaker whether you have understood correctly.

Be Non-Judgmental

Try to understand the message as the speaker intends it. Be **non-judgmental**; do not attempt to judge the individual's culture, values, background, intelligence, appearance, or other characteristics. Listen to what the speaker is saying. In other words, give the person a chance to get his or her message across, without forming judgments.

> **Communication Tip**
>
> Pay careful attention to nonverbal communication; it helps you know whether your message is being received.

Avoid arguing with the speaker. If you are opposed to an idea, do not argue or become emotional. Control your reaction at least until you have heard everything the speaker has to say. Regardless of your acceptance or rejection of what a speaker says, your knowledge increases when you listen—even if you only learn another person's view.

Question

If you do not understand what someone is saying to you, one of the best things to do is **question** (a technique used to understand verbal communication through the use of questions) the individual. Questions can help us to

- Gain information
- Understand the other person's point of view
- Build trust
- Verify information

When asking questions, you should

- Know what you are trying to accomplish with the question
- Ask only one question at a time and keep the question easy to understand
- Try not to manipulate or trick with your questions

Give Feedback

When communicating with someone, listen to what that person is saying in its entirety, not only to the words. Remember that there are many ways to communicate, including the use of words, gestures, facial expressions, tone of voice, time, and space.

Seek **feedback** (clarifying statements and questions) from the individual with whom you are communicating. Use clarifying statements and questions such as:

- "Let me see if I can review the main points we have discussed." Then after you have reviewed the points, ask "Is that a correct summation? Have I left anything out?"
- "I understand your major concerns are … Did I hear you correctly?"
- "As I understand you, your major objections are … Have I stated them correctly? Do you have other objections?"

Nonverbal Communication

Nonverbal communication can be another barrier to effective communication. However, before you consider this area, keep two points in mind:

1. *People of different cultures give different meanings to gestures.* You learned about some of these differences in the first sections of this chapter. Here are some additional differences in the meanings given to gestures by people of different cultures:

   - The "OK" sign in Germany is a rude signal. The "OK" sign in Japan is used to signal the word money or change. It means you want your money in the form of change.
   - In the Middle East or Southeast Asia, never expose or point the sole of your shoe at

■ Figure 5-6

EFFECTIVE COMMUNICATION TECHNIQUES

Since communication is so important in effective human relations, how can you communicate better? Here are several techniques that will help you become a more effective communicator.

■ *Paraphrase if you do not understand.* To **paraphrase** means to restate the concept in your own terms. Then ask the speaker "Is this what you mean?"

■ *Get ready to listen.* Stop paying attention to the miscellaneous thoughts that constantly run through your mind. Direct all your attention to the speaker.

■ *Listen for facts.* Use the differential time between how long it takes the speaker to say the words (an average of 130 words a minute) and how long it takes you to comprehend them (approximately 500 words a minute) to review the key ideas presented. Raise questions in your mind about the material. Relate what the speaker is saying to your own experience. Mentally repeat key ideas, or associate key points with related ideas.

■ *Watch for nonverbal communication.* Observe the speaker's eyes, hands, and body movements. Do the nonverbal communications agree with what the speaker is saying?

■ *Use mnemonic devices to remember key ideas.* A **mnemonic device** is a formula, word association, or rhyme used to assist the memory. For example, if a person says that his objections to a jogging program include boredom with the activity, exhaustion in the process, and the time required, you might develop the mnemonic device of coining the acronym BET to remember these ideas.

■ *Minimize your mental blocks and filters.* All of us have certain biases and prejudices. However, if we are aware of these blocks, we can control them. You may have heard

people say, "You can't talk to CAs; they are only number crunchers" or "All athletes are stupid." In such statements, you can hear prejudices. An entire group of people or things is being **stereotyped** on the basis of a perception or an image held, which may be favourable or unfavourable. In this case, the image was unfavourable. Listening behaviours are improved if you become aware of your own blocks and filters, as well as the speaker's blocks and filters.

■ *Use direct, simple language.* Never attempt to use big words and long sentences to try to impress the listener or the reader.

■ *Utilize feedback.* When communicating with someone, listen to what that person is saying in its entirety, not only to the words. Remember, there are many ways to communicate, including the use of words, gestures, facial expressions, tone of voice, time, and space. If you believe the other person does not understand what you are saying, try to explain your point in a different manner.

■ *Time messages carefully.* You need to be aware of what is going on in the world of the receiver. We can cause problems for ourselves by trying to communicate with someone when that person is not ready to receive our communication. Stop, look, and observe what is going on in the world of the receiver before you attempt to communicate.

■ *Organize what you hear.* A listener who can identify the speaker's main points and the pattern of the speaker's remarks certainly has an advantage over the listener who simply listens to the words.

■ *Do not expect people from different cultures to behave the same way you do.*

■ *Commit to constantly improving your communication skills.*

another person. This is a grievous insult because the sole of your shoe is the lowest and dirtiest part of your body.

• In Thailand, never pat anyone on the top of the head. The Thai people believe that is where their spirits reside.

• In Russia, when entering a theatre or an auditorium and walking through the row to take your seat, always face the people already seated. If you face the stage, you are being impolite by passing your derriere directly in front of their bodies or faces.[7]

You must constantly keep in mind that how you interpret gestures may not be the same as how others do so.

2. *Conclusions cannot be drawn from only one element of nonverbal communication.* For example, a person may cross his or her arms because he or she is cold. You must take all elements of nonverbal communication as a whole, and you must be cautious about your interpretations.

Now consider four elements of nonverbal communication.

Body Language

Various body motions or gestures can have meaning; we refer to this as **body language**. Consider this situation. You are very intently talking with someone, and that person is leaning back in the chair with his or her arms crossed, frowning. Do you think the individual is interested in what you are saying? Believing what you are saying? Bored with the whole exchange? You probably answered yes to at least one of these questions, and perhaps to all of them. All of the nonverbal body language signs indicate that the message is not being received. Something about the message or the speaker is blocking the individual from truly listening to what is being said.

Although body language is extremely important, one gesture alone does not have significant meaning. One gesture merely gives you a clue that something may be wrong. When evaluating body language, consider all the gestures a person makes along with what the person says. For example, when you are communicating with someone, do not make the mistake of assuming that a frown indicates the person disagrees with what you are saying. If you are concerned about the body language, ask for an explanation. You might say "You are frowning. Is something wrong?" Such a question gives the person with whom you are talking a chance to explain his or her behaviour.

Voice Quality

A loud tone of voice is usually associated with anger; a soft tone of voice, with calmness and poise. Two people talking softly with each other usually indicates they are at ease. **Voice quality** (the loudness or softness of the voice, the pitch of the voice, and the enunciation of the words) is a nonverbal behaviour that reveals something about an individual. A person's voice is usually pitched higher when he or she is tense, anxious, or nervous.

Also, a person usually talks faster when angry or tense. If a person is nervous or upset, he or she may not enunciate clearly. In contrast, a low pitch and a slow pace usually indicate a relaxed tone. Other forms of nonverbal voice communication include the nervous giggle; a quivering, emotional voice; a breaking, stressful voice; and a whiny (upset) voice. Voice quality is so important that individuals whose voices are important to their success or failure on the job, such as TV and radio newscasters, spend time and effort to be certain their voices do not cause people to switch to another station. For example, a nasal voice or a very high-pitched voice is irritating to the listener.

Time

Another important nonverbal communicator is **time**. You have already learned in the first part of this chapter that not all cultures treat time in the same way. However, in Canada, we have learned to treat time in certain standard ways. For example, as a student, you have probably learned that turning in a paper or project late usually results in a grade penalty. In a business situation, people who are habitually late with reports or who are constantly late for work may find themselves fired. An applicant who is late for a job interview may forfeit the chance to get the job.

Space

Space is also treated differently in different cultures. However, in North America, we have defined space expectations. For example, at home, do you have a special chair that is considered yours or a special space that is considered yours? We tend to lay claim to a certain territory and defend it if someone else takes our space, a tendency known as **territoriality**. In the office, we also use space in special ways. In a traditional hierarchically organized firm, for example, people who have the same level of position may be allocated the same amount of space. In this scenario, it might mean that the president's office is larger than the vice-president's; the vice-president's is larger than a supervisor's; and an administrative assistant to the president might have a larger space than an administrative assistant to the vice-president. This type of space allocation is based on the perception that the president is more important than others in the hierarchy. There are firms, however, that base the allocation of space on the function of a person's job, and space is allocated on the basis of need and not a person's position within the firm.

Communication Improvement

If we are to develop effective relationships in the workplace, we must constantly work on communication in all forms. We must understand that our workforce is diverse; that different cultures exist; and that because of our cultures and backgrounds, we view situations differently. We must work to overcome the numerous communication barriers that exist, including discriminatory barriers. We must recognize that constant attention and effort to improving communication are essential. The process of improvement must be an ongoing, ever-present one. If we are diligent in our efforts, a fairer and more effective workplace will be the result.

Chapter Summary

The summary will help you remember the important points covered in the chapter.

- You cannot be effective in the workplace without being an effective communicator. Effective communication is the ability to process and exchange ideas and feelings so the person originating the communication and the person receiving the communication clearly understand what is being communicated.
- Forces that contribute to the complexity of communication in our world include globalization, multinational organizations, diversity of our population, the number of immigrants who are entering our country, and technology.
- All of us have values, which are not inherently good or bad. The way we set about to accomplish our values involve behaviours that are either acceptable or unacceptable in our society. An understanding of our own values and the recognition that others may not have our values are crucial in the communication process.
- The way we carry out our values often reflects the attitudes we have. A positive attitude is always an asset; a negative attitude is always a detractor.
- Understanding cultural differences demands that we understand that people from other cultures may have values different from our own.
- The gender of individuals in all societies has significant importance in job roles, social responsibilities, family responsibilities, and even education and socialization.
- As the traditional age of retirement extends beyond 65, it is important to understand that people of different ages often have different values.
- The elements of the communication process include the originator, the message, the receiver, and the response. Each element is important.
- Verbal communication is the process of exchanging ideas and feelings through the use of words.
- Verbal barriers to communication include listening; language usage; evaluation; inference; noise; and cultural, gender, and age differences.
- In order to be an effective verbal communicator, you should consider the other person's view, use active listening, resolve conflicts, be non-judgmental, question, and give feedback.
- Nonverbal communication can be a barrier to effective communication. The four elements of nonverbal communication are body language, voice quality, time, and space.
- Communication effectiveness is a process; improvement is ongoing and ever-present.

Key Terms

The following terms were introduced in this chapter. The page on which the term was introduced is provided to help you locate the new term. Definitions are compiled in the Glossary at the end of the text.

- **value** 91
- **attitude** 91
- **originator** 95
- **message** 95
- **receiver** 95
- **response** 96
- **verbal communication** 96
- **listening** 96
- **talker** 97
- **attention faker** 97
- **easily distracted** 97
- **external noise** 97
- **internal noise** 97
- **outguesser** 97
- **etymologists** 97
- **evaluation** 98
- **inference** 98
- **noise** 98
- **active listening** 99
- **non-judgmental** 100
- **question** 100
- **feedback** 100
- **paraphrase** 101
- **mnemonic device** 101
- **stereotype** 101
- **body language** 102
- **voice quality** 102
- **time** 102
- **space** 102
- **territoriality** 102

Responses to Self-Check A

The most appropriate answers are as follows:

1. Yes   3. Yes   5. Yes   7. Yes   9. No

2. Yes   4. Yes   6. Yes   8. Yes   10. Yes

Responses to Self-Check D

The most effective listeners would have responded with "Never" on the first eight items and "Always" on the last two items.

Discussion Items

These discussion items provide an opportunity to test your understanding of the chapter through written responses and/or discussion with your classmates and your instructor.

1. What is meant by value clarification? Do all individuals have values? Explain.
2. Identify and explain five verbal communication barriers.
3. Identify and explain five effective verbal communication techniques.
4. List and explain four elements of nonverbal communication.

Critical-Thinking Activity

Yuan Liang is a manager for CanAsian Airlines. He was transferred from China shortly after the merger of the two companies. He speaks English; however, he has never lived outside China although he had visited Canada several times before his transfer. He is having difficulty understanding the culture. Although you do not report to Mr. Liang, your employer, Mr. Albertson, has assigned you to work on a quality team chaired by Mr. Liang. In the first team meeting, you made several suggestions to Mr. Liang and the committee. Mr. Liang smiled and nodded in agreement with your suggestions; the team also voiced agreement. However, when the minutes from the meeting were sent out, you found no indication that your suggestions were going to be implemented. During the second meeting, Mr. Liang started the discussion with the same problem as was discussed at the last meeting—the one you thought had been resolved. After some discussion within the group (without your participation), you stated that you did not understand why the topic was being discussed again since you thought the group had agreed on a resolution at the last meeting. Mr. Liang only smiled and continued the discussion. However, after the meeting, he contacted your manager and told him you had embarrassed him before the group. Mr. Albertson called you in and asked you to explain the situation; he stated that you should have told him your concerns about the

meeting. You are angry and also defensive—angry with Mr. Liang because he did not talk with you and angry with your supervisor because he seems to be questioning your integrity.

Using several of the critical-thinking techniques presented in the last chapter, ask yourself these questions:

- Am I recognizing the cultural differences that are involved?
- Is my position on this issue reasonable and rational?
- Have I tried to understand the situation from Mr. Liang's point of view?

With those critical-thinking concepts in mind, answer these questions:

- How should I have handled the situation?
- What can I learn from this situation?
- Should I talk with Mr. Liang about my feelings?
- What should I say to Mr. Albertson?

Projects

Project 5-1 (Objective 2)

Online Project

Browse the Web for articles on the culture of Asians and Latin Americans. Summarize two articles, giving the Web addresses, and submit your summaries to your instructor. You might want to use the search engine www.google.com.

Project 5-2 (Objectives 2 and 3)

Collaborative Project

With a team of three or four of your classmates, discuss the case given here; then answer the questions given at the end of the case by writing a memorandum to your instructor, using the memo form on the Student CD, SCDP5-2. List the members of your team in the From section.

Case

In your position at CanAsian, you have two assistants who report to you, Guy Beauchamp and Luyin Wu. Luyin has been having some personal problems that she has talked with you about. She has come in late twice during the past month. Each time, Guy has made a remark (heard by the entire office) about Luyin coming in late. Luyin has not responded to Guy's remarks. Last week Luyin called in sick, but that evening Guy saw Luyin at the grocery store. The next morning (again while the entire office listened) Guy said "It's a shame you were sick yesterday; but you weren't so sick last night, were you?" Again Luyin said nothing; she merely lowered her head and kept walking to her desk. Today Luyin was late again. When she came in, Guy remarked "I wish I were the office pet." Luyin remained silent.

You think Luyin will soon solve her personal problems; she has been a good employee. You want to continue to give her a chance to work out her problems and get back on track at work. You know the situation cannot go on indefinitely, but she has indicated that the problem should be resolved within the next three weeks. You are very concerned about Guy's actions. Guy's work is also good, but he is out of line on this matter. Luyin does not want anyone to know about her personal problems. You are beginning to believe you cannot let Guy continue to disrupt the entire office with his remarks.

1. Who is the originator in this communication situation? Who is the receiver?
2. Explain the communication problem between Guy and Luyin.
3. Is there a communication problem between you and Guy? If so, what is it?
4. How should you handle the situation?

Project 5-3 *(Objective 4)*
Keep a five-day log of the time you spend speaking and listening. You cannot be accurate to the minute, but make a concentrated effort to record the amount of time spent on both speaking and listening. Also, record the effective and ineffective behaviours you engage in while listening and speaking. At the end of the five-day period, analyze your log. How much time did you spend speaking? How much time listening? What effective behaviours did you engage in? What ineffective behaviours occurred? Determine ways in which you can improve your communication. Write a report identifying improved communication techniques you plan to follow. Submit your report to your instructor.

Project 5-4 *(Objective 1)*
In this chapter, you were asked to list your five top values. Add to this list your next five values. You will have ten values when you finish, listed in order of importance to you. Next, list the attitudes you think you demonstrate to others. Once you have listed your attitudes as you understand them, check with a trusted friend or family member. Ask that person to tell you what attitudes he or she believes you demonstrate. Save a copy of your values and attitudes on the Professional Growth disk you began in Chapter 1. Title your list "Values and Attitudes." Save it under "Progro5-4." This project is a continuation of your Professional Growth Plan, which you will be adding to in each chapter.

Here is a list that may help you complete your top ten values.

- Knowledge
- Honesty
- Dependability
- Cooperation
- Tolerance
- Justice
- Honour
- Responsibility
- Peace
- Sharing
- Freedom

Chapter 6

Creating and Preparing Business Documents

LEARNING OBJECTIVES

1. Identify the characteristics of effective correspondence.
2. Compose letters and memos.
3. Use proper e-mail communication techniques.
4. Research and write a business report.
5. Identify skills and equipment required for dictation and transcription.
6. *Observe ethical and legal obligations in written correspondence.*

The importance of communication pervades not only our verbal communications but our written communications as well. In Chapter 5, you developed skills for communicating effectively in our multicultural workforce. You learned that if you are to be effective in your job, good verbal and non-verbal communication skills are essential. Letters, memos, and reports as well as e-mail are among the major communication documents in the workplace. Depending on the effectiveness of the writer of these documents, goodwill or ill will for the organization (and the writer) may be created. Thus, you need to add another communication skill to your list of qualifications if you are to be a truly effective administrative professional—the ability to compose effective business documents.

While transcription was once a widely used method of creating business documents, and it is still used regularly in medical or legal environments, it is less frequently used in today's offices. However, it is possible that as an administrative professional you may find yourself responsible for either transcribing notes made by your supervisor or dictating on behalf of your employer. This chapter will help you attain these necessary communication skills; practice will help you perfect them.

Types of Written Messages

The basic types of written messages that the administrative professional prepares are memorandums, e-mail, letters, and reports. As you begin your career, you may be asked to prepare routine correspondence, such as e-mail and interoffice memorandums. As you learn more about the organization and demonstrate to your employer your writing skills, the complexity and number of your writing assignments will probably increase. You should establish a goal now to become an excellent communicator through the written word. No matter what type of position you hold, written communication skills are invaluable to both you and the organization.

Memorandums

Due to its many advantages, e-mail has become the communication vehicle of choice for most interoffice correspondence. Memorandums, however, are still written particularly when the message is longer than a paragraph or two.

E-mails

The hard-copy memorandum is generally written when the message is a fairly long one and will not fit on one computer screen. Although an e-mail can be longer than one computer screen, the general rule is that an e-mail needs to be a very short communication. An e-mail several screens in length becomes cumbersome for the recipient who must go back and forth between screens to review the message.

Letters

One of the first letters you may be asked to write as a beginning administrative professional is a routine one, such as a letter requesting information. These letters are usually very direct,

> ### Communication Tip
>
> To add crispness to your business communications, avoid redundancies, such as *consensus of opinion*. The word *consensus* is all that is necessary.

with the first paragraph requesting the information, the second paragraph providing additional information needed, and the third paragraph specifying the action the writer wants and expressing appreciation to the reader for responding to the request. Once your employer is confident in your skills, he or she may ask you to compose letters in draft or final form for his or her signature. Whatever role you play in the composition of letters, the principles set forth in this chapter will help you be successful.

Reports

In addition to memorandums and letters, numerous reports are prepared in the workplace. These reports may be informal reports of two or three pages, or they may be formal reports containing a table of contents, the body of the report (with footnotes or endnotes), appendixes, and a bibliography. You will learn more about writing reports in a later section of this chapter.

Effective Correspondence

If any written communication—memorandum, e-mail, letter, or report—is to accomplish its goal, the writer must adhere to certain principles. The following principles will guide you when preparing any written communication.

Clear, Concise, and Simple

The reader should be able to determine without a doubt the purpose of the communication. Writing clearly requires good organization and simple expression. Conciseness in writing means that you express the necessary information in as few words as possible; say what you need to say without cluttering your correspondence with irrelevant information, needless words, or flowery phrases. Simplicity means that you use words that are easily understood; you do not try to impress the reader with your vocabulary. Principles to assist you in writing clearly, concisely, and simply are given in Figure 6-1.

■ Figure 6-1

WRITING PRINCIPLES

KEEP YOUR SENTENCES SHORT

Sentences should vary in structure and in length but on average should be no more than 15 to 20 words. Consider the following examples of a sentence that is too long and the shortened, more effective sentence.

Long sentence: In answer to your letter of June 12, I wish to tell you how pleased and happy I am with your asking me to speak at the meeting on July 12 and to tell you that it will give me great pleasure to speak to your group.

Short sentence: Thank you for the invitation to speak at your meeting on June 12. I will be delighted to do so.

USE THE SIMPLE RATHER THAN THE COMPLEX APPROACH

If a shorter word will suffice, use it. You should not use business communications to impress the

■ **Figure 6-1 (continued)**

WRITING PRINCIPLES

reader with the breadth of your vocabulary. The aim of business communication is to get your purpose across in a simple, concise manner. Write to express rather than impress. An effective writer can express complex ideas in clear, simple terms. For example, rather than writing *endeavour to ascertain*, use *try to find out*. Rather than writing *elucidate your meaning*, use *clarify your meaning*.

Write as You Speak

Ask yourself how you would say something if the reader were sitting next to you. A conversational tone is usually appropriate. (This tone may not be suitable for international correspondence. A section later in this chapter will present the principles of writing internationally.)

Edit Unnecessary Words

Verbosity (using too many words) weakens writing. Make sure every word is essential. Practise editing out unnecessary words. You might be able to cut as much as half of the length of your communication. Consider the following example containing unnecessary words and its concise rewrite:

> **Excessive:** At this point in time, I must tell you that our plant will be closed due to the remodelling of our facilities. We have wanted to remodel our facilities for the last five years but have been unable to do so due to the large demands of our customers for products. We have every confidence in our ability to complete the remodelling and get your order out by July 15.

> **Concise:** Since our plant will be closed for remodelling from June 1 to June 15, your order will be shipped on July 15.

USE ACTIVE VERBS

Active verbs can bring life to your sentences by emphasizing action. For example, say *We received your order for ten modular units today*, not *Your order for ten modular units was received today*.

VARY YOUR STYLE

Keep your writing interesting by varying your sentence structure, length, and vocabulary.

AVOID CLICHÉS

You have probably read such phrases as *according to our records, at your earliest convenience*, and *under separate cover*. These phrases are clichés; they are overused. Notice the following clichés and the improved wording.

> **Cliché:** according to our files
> **Improved:** our files indicate

> **Cliché:** at the present time
> **Improved:** now

> **Cliché:** in view of the fact that
> **Improved:** because

> **Cliché:** by return mail
> **Improved:** mail today

> **Cliché:** may I take the liberty
> **Improved:** (Omit the phrase entirely and make your statement.)

> **Cliché:** your kind letter
> **Improved:** (Omit *kind*—people, not letters, are kind.)

Complete

A business document is complete if it gives the reader all the information needed so the intended results are achieved. To help you achieve completeness in your writing, ask yourself these "W questions":

- Why is the correspondence being written?
- What is the goal of the correspondence?

- What information is needed before writing the correspondence?
- Who needs to receive the correspondence?
- What information needs to be included in the correspondence?

Refer to Figure 6-2 on page 110 for examples of ineffective writing when the W questions were not asked and corresponding examples of effective writing when the W questions were asked.

■ Figure 6-2

USE THE W QUESTIONS

Here are some examples of ineffective writing when the W questions were not asked, followed by effective writing when the W questions were asked.

Ineffective: Your order will be mailed soon. (When?)

Effective: Your order will be mailed October 9.

Ineffective: We will offer a seminar on May 12. (Where and what kind of seminar?)

Effective: We will offer an effective letter-writing seminar in the Executive Conference Room at 2 p.m. on May 31.

Considerate

Being considerate in written communication means that you use good human relations skills. Treat the reader with respect and friendliness, and write as if you care about the reader. When dealing with people face to face, courtesy and consideration are necessary in order to develop and maintain goodwill. The same or even greater concern must be evident in written correspondence since only the written word conveys the message; a smile, a nod, or a friendly gesture cannot be seen.

Never show your anger in business communication. You may be extremely unhappy about a situation, but to express your anger merely compounds the problem. Angry words make angry readers. Both parties may end up "yelling" at one another through the written word, and little is accomplished. Being considerate also means being believable. If a person asks you something, respond to the question. If you are unable to respond, explain why. If you must respond negatively, explain why. An explanation lets others know you are sincere.

Being considerate also means using please and thank you often. Do not be afraid to apologize when you make an error. We are all human; we all make mistakes. A courteous apology builds credibility and goodwill. Use these courteous phrases often:

We appreciate …

Thank you for …

Please let me know …

I apologize for …

You were very kind to …

You were very nice to …

Correct

Correctness in business writing means using correct grammar and mechanics, appropriate format, and careful proofreading. When you make errors in writing, you send a message to the reader that you are careless or, even worse, uneducated or lacking in intelligence.

Spelling, grammar, punctuation, capitalization, and sentence structure must be correct. To assist you in catching errors, use the grammar and spell check on your computer. However, remember that grammar and spell check features do not catch all errors. For example, if you use *your* rather than *you're*, the error will not be detected. Thus, you must have good grammar and spelling skills. In addition, you must be a good proofreader. Proofreading tips are given in Figure 6-3 on page 111.

Correctness means using the correct format. Readers expect business letters and reports to follow recommended styles and formats. If you use a non-standard format, you run the risk of detracting from the message by drawing the reader's attention to its layout rather than its contents. Standard formats for business letters and reports are given in the Business Document Formatting Guide on the Student CD.

> **Communication Tip**
>
> When you are in the "think" phase of writing a document, do not be concerned about formatting. It can interrupt your creative thought processes. Do your formatting when you are refining the document.

■ Figure 6-3

PROOFREADING TIPS

- Use your grammar and spell check features.
- Proofread your document on the screen before you print. Scroll to the beginning of the document, and use the top of the screen as a guide for your eye in reading each line.
- Proofread a document in three steps:
  a. General appearance and format
  b. Spelling and keyboarding errors
  c. Punctuation, word usage, and content
- Read from right to left for spelling and keyboarding errors.
- If possible, do not proofread a document right after keying it; let it sit while you perform some other task.
- Pay attention to dates. Do not assume that they are correct. Check to determine that Thursday, June 18, is actually a Thursday, for example. Check the spelling of months; check the correctness of the year.
- Do not overlook proofreading the date, the subject, the enclosure notation, and the names and addresses of the recipients.
- Use a thesaurus if you are not certain a word is appropriate.
- Watch closely for omissions of *-ed*, *-ing*, or *-s* at the end of words.
- Be consistent in the use of commas.
- Be consistent in the use of capital letters.
- Check numbers.
- Be consistent in format.
- Keep a good reference manual at your desk to look up any grammar or punctuation rules you question.

Correctness also includes accuracy. Although you cannot be perfect, you should do your best to be accurate. Get the facts before you begin the business doc-

ument. Check your information carefully. If you are quoting prices, be certain you have the latest price list. If you are presenting dates, confirm the dates. If you are giving sales figures, double-check the figures. Verify the correct spelling of any names used in the letter.

Prompt

The conscientious business correspondent is concerned about being on time. Prompt messages convey to the reader that the writer and organization care. Conversely, late messages convey several negative impressions, some of which are:

- The writer or organization does not care about maintaining a positive relationship with the reader or the organization.
- The writer or organization is grossly inefficient.
- The writer or organization is indifferent to the needs of the reader or the organization.

In general, replies to routine letters and memorandums should be sent within three to five days. Urgent messages (such as urgent e-mail or mail sent by overnight delivery) should be answered immediately (within 24 hours).

Positive

It is easier to hear the word *yes* than the word *no*. It is easier to accept a concern than a complaint. Positivism gives the reader a favourable impression of the person, service, or product. It helps the reader respond the way the writer intends. A positive tone is set by the words the writer chooses and how she or he uses those words. For example, some words possess positive qualities while other words possess negative qualities. Figure 6-4 on page 112   gives some positive and negative expressions. However, even a negative statement can be written in a positive tone. For example, *Do not litter* can be changed to *Please deposit all trash in the nearest receptacle*. To which statement would you be more likely to respond?

POSITIVE AND NEGATIVE WORDS

Positive	Negative
glad	sorry
immediately	whenever possible
pleasure	displeasure
satisfactory	unsatisfactory
Please let us know.	You failed to let us know.
Please send your cheque.	You neglected to send your cheque.
Your order will be shipped.	I hate to inform you that your order has not been shipped.

Appropriate in Tone

You set the entire **tone** (the manner of expression in writing) of the document, whether that tone is positive or negative, by considering your reader first and carefully choosing your words. You should establish a positive tone at the beginning of a letter and carry that positive tone throughout. In establishing a positive tone, you should adhere to the concepts spelled out in the previous sections. These concepts are as follows:

- Conciseness
- Completeness
- Consideration
- Correctness
- Promptness
- Positivism

In other words, as you have learned in these sections, you should write in a conversational tone—one that is appropriate for the reader. You should write to express your thoughts—not to impress the reader. You should treat the reader with respect and friendliness; you should never show anger. By saying *please* and *thank you* and referring to the reader by name, you tell the reader

that you care about him or her. Being prompt says to the reader that you care about the individual and the organization. By expressing statements in a positive rather than a negative manner, you help give the reader a favourable impression of you and your organization. If you carefully and consistently heed these guidelines, you will set a positive tone for the reader. In the process, you will have served your organization well.

Figure 6-5 on pages 113 and 114 illustrates the importance of tone. This figure shows a letter written in a positive tone (adhering to the concepts set forth) and a letter written in a negative tone. As a reader, to which letter would you respond favourably? Notice the first letter is written from the writer's point of view. There is no consideration of the reader; in fact, the writer is almost condescending to the reader. The overall tone of the letter is negative.

Effective in Paragraphing

Effective paragraphs possess unity, coherence, and parallel construction.

Unity

A paragraph has unity when all its sentences clarify or help support the main idea. All sentences in the paragraph must relate to the main idea. The sentence that contains the main idea of a paragraph is called the **topic sentence**. This sentence shapes the content of the paragraph. In the paragraph below, the topic sentence is the first sentence.

> *A management conference is being held on December 1 in Chicago. The major focus of the conference is on developing empowered teams in an organization. Please look over the information enclosed and give me a call by November 10 if you are interested in attending.*

The topic sentence is not always the first sentence. It may be at the beginning or end of the paragraph, or it may even be implied. The point to remember is that the topic sentence helps the writer stay focused on one main idea for the paragraph.

LETTERS WITH A POSITIVE AND A NEGATIVE TONE

McBEE CONSULTING
218–450 Gostick Place
North Vancouver, BC V7K 3A4
604-555-1515

November 19, 2005

Ms. Cordelia Ramsey
CanAsian Airlines
2300–888 3rd Street SW
Calgary, AB T2P 4C4

Dear Ms. Ramsey:

Since we at McBee Consulting know that most people have trouble writing letters, we are having a one-day seminar on letter writing that you must not miss. We have put together a program that will be beneficial for you. After our seminar, you will have no trouble explaining to your reader exactly what you expect of him or her and getting what you want.

Give my office a call at 604-555-1515 to register. We are looking forward to your positive response to this letter.

Sincerely,

Rhonda Edwards

Rhonda Edwards
Training Consultant

RE:dgb

LETTERS WITH A POSITIVE AND A NEGATIVE TONE

McBEE CONSULTING
218–450 Gostick Place
North Vancouver, BC V7K 3A4
604-555-1515

November 19, 2005

Ms. Cordelia Ramsey
CanAsian Airlines
2300–888 3rd Street SW
Calgary, AB T2P 4C4

Dear Ms. Ramsey:

Do you write letters frequently? If so, are you sometimes unable to find the right words to let the customer know you care about her or him?

If you answered yes to these questions, you are certainly among the majority of writers. As you know, writing can be a difficult process. All of us sometimes have writer's block. We can't decide how to say what we mean or say it effectively.

Join us and a number of individuals who work in positions similar to yours for a writing seminar on Tuesday, October 25, from 9 a.m. until 3 p.m. in the conference room of our office on 450 Gostick Place. The cost for the day is $150—a small price to pay for hearing a noted communication theorist, Abraham Gassell, and having a chance to learn from your colleagues about their writing techniques. Lunch is included in the price.

Just mail the enclosed card by October 1. I hope to see you soon.

Sincerely,

Marvin Hanley

Marvin Hanley
Communication Consultant

MH:km

Coherence

A paragraph has coherence when its sentences are related to each other in content, in grammatical construction, and in choice of words. Every sentence should be written so the paragraph flows from one thought to the next in a coherent fashion. The following sentences represent coherence in content and construction:

> *"There is only one social responsibility of business. That responsibility is for business to use its resources and engage in activities designed to increase its profits so long as it stays within the rules of the game." Those words are fighting words today even more than when they were written nearly 40 years ago by Nobel Prize–winning economist Milton Friedman. The great debate over business's responsibility to society, which bubbled in the '60s and '70s, is exploding now.[1]*

Repeating key words in a paragraph or using certain words for emphasis can achieve coherence. Consider the following use of repetitive words:

> *The anthropologist Elena Padilla describes life in a squalid district of New York by telling how much people know about each other—who is to be trusted and who not, who is defiant of the law and who upholds it, who is competent and well and informed, and who is inept and ignorant.*

In the following excerpt from an article in *Fortune* on multitasking, notice how the author uses "and" and "but," and contractions in the first paragraph. Notice also how he uses repetition in the last paragraph of the article:

> *Last night I was in a Chinese restaurant. At the next table there was a young woman with a fork in one hand and a cell phone in the other, using her mouth to chew and talk at the same time. … All of a sudden a goblet of water went flying off her table. Bang! Crash! And still she went on, multitasking. … That's the thing about multitasking. Some people can do it in such a way that each of their multiple tasks is accomplished as if it had been the subject of unique concentration. But not many. Most people are as lousy at multitasking as they are at everything else …*
>
> *I will spend time with my family when at home …*
>
> *I will not watch TV and go online at the same time.*
>
> *I will not watch TV, go online, and listen to MP3s at the same time.*
>
> *I will not watch TV, go online, listen to MP3s, check my stocks, talk on the phone, and toast an English muffin at the same time.[2]*

The writer used the conjunctions *and* and *but* to begin a sentence. At one point, we were taught not to use conjunctions to begin sentences. However, this rule no longer holds true. In fact, according to the *Harper Dictionary of Contemporary Usage*, it is perfectly acceptable to use *and* at the beginning of a sentence. Notice that the writer uses a contraction. We were taught in the past not to use contractions. However, contractions are perfectly acceptable today in all but the most formal writing.

Parallel Structure

Parallel structure helps you achieve coherence in a paragraph. **Parallelism** is created when grammatically equivalent forms are used within a sentence. Consider the parallel construction used in the following paragraph:

> *Superstitions are sometimes smiled at, sometimes frowned on, sometimes seen as old-fashioned, and sometimes seen as backwoods. Nevertheless, they give all of us ways of moving back and forth among our different worlds—the sacred, the secular, and the scientific.*

The following sentence illustrates nonparallel and parallel construction:

> ***Nonparallel:*** *The position is prestigious, challenging, and also the money isn't bad.*
>
> ***Parallel:*** *The position offers prestige, challenge, and money.*

Concerned with Readability Level

Readability is the degree of difficulty of the message. Items that contribute to a greater reading difficulty include long sentences and words with several syllables and/or very technical terms. Readability formulas such as the Gunning Fog Index and the Flesch-Kincaid Index provide readability indices. The higher the readability index is, the less readable the message. Business messages should be written to achieve a readability index between 7 and 11. This means that what you have already learned about short words and short sentences should be followed. You want the letter, memo, or report to be clearly understood by the reader. Obviously, if the document is not understood, the message is ineffective.

Formal reports that include technical or scientific terms may have a readability index of 14 or higher due to their complexity. However, these reports are not written for a general audience, but for an audience with the background and educational level to comprehend the report.

The Correspondence Plan

To be effective, written communications must be well planned and organized. For a formal report, you should make an outline before beginning. If you are a beginner at writing letters, you may find that making notes on a scratch pad will help you organize your thoughts. As you become more experienced in writing letters and informal reports, you may make only a mental outline of what you want to write. However, a formal report always requires an outline. Whatever the case, planning before writing saves you time and lessens any frustrations you may experience.

The steps in the planning process are as follows:

- Determine the objective
- Consider the reader
- Gather the facts

Determine the Objective

When writing letters or reports, determine what your objective is. Why are you writing the letter or report? What do you hope to accomplish? Business messages generally have one of three primary objectives: to inform the reader, to request an action or information, and to persuade the reader to take action or accept an idea. Some business messages have more than one objective. For example, the objectives may be to inform and persuade. What does the reader need to know about the subject? Will the reader want or need background information or support data? If your task is to persuade someone to accept an offer, consider what it would take to convince the person to say yes.

Consider the Reader

Who will receive your letter or report? How much does the person receiving the document know about the subject? Is the reader familiar with technical jargon that might be used? What is the educational level of the reader? What effect will the message have on the reader? Will the reader react favourably or unfavourably to the message? How much time does the reader have? Is the reader a busy executive who prefers short, concise memos, letters, and reports? Or does the reader need a great deal of supporting information and detail?

Gather the Facts

Before you begin to write a letter, memorandum, e-mail, or report, gather all the necessary facts. If you are writing a letter, memorandum or e-mail, ask yourself the W questions: Who? What? When? Where? Why? For example, assume your employer asks you to find an appropriate video on organizational ethics. You plan to write to several video companies to find out what videos are available. What do you need to tell the company so you get the most appropriate video for your organization's needs? Ask these questions before you begin:

- Who will be viewing the video?
- What type of knowledge do these people already have about ethics?
- What price range is appropriate?

If you are writing a report, here are some W questions to ask.

- Who is the audience? Who will read the report?
- What level of expertise about the subject do the readers have?
- Where can I obtain the information needed for the report? Do I need to research the subject? Is information available through library research, or must I do original research?
- What level of detail is important to the reader?
- What level of formality is important? In other words, should there be a title page? A table of contents? A reference section? Recommendations? An executive summary?
- Who should review the draft document of the report?

Communication Tip

If you are trying to avoid using certain words when you are writing, delete them from your spell checker's dictionary. Then if you mistakenly use them, the computer will flag them, giving you an opportunity to change the word.

- Who is responsible for making recommendations? Am I responsible or should I work with someone in developing the recommendations?
- Assuming an executive summary is needed, who is responsible for writing it?

Seek Help from Software Packages

You have learned that the readability level should be between 7 and 11. If you are a beginning writer, you may want to check the readability level of your writing. Grammar software packages contain a readability formula such as the Gunning Fog Index or the Flesch-Kincaid Index. Within a matter of seconds, you can obtain the readability of your material.

You have learned that you should use the grammar and spell check feature on your word processing software. You can quickly identify misspelled words by using the spell checker. You also know the spell checker will not detect all spelling errors. It will not detect such words as *to* for *too* and *here* for *hear*. If you are not a good speller, you may have someone who spells well proofread your material. Check your spelling expertise by responding to Self-Check A.

> ### Communication Tip
>
> Do not mix metaphors; e.g., *I got really steamed when he started buttering me up* is a mixed metaphor.

Grammar programs can help you find grammatical errors. They flag punctuation and capitalization errors. They also let you know when you have used the passive voice. A thesaurus helps you develop your vocabulary by suggesting alternatives for words you have used.

Memorandums

Characteristics of Effective Memorandums

In memorandums, as in letters or reports, it is essential that you adhere to the effective correspondence guidelines just presented. For example, memorandums must be clear, concise, simple, complete, considerate, correct, prompt, and positive. Additionally, certain guidelines are unique to memorandums, including the appropriate format addressed here.

Memorandums are usually prepared on a preprinted form or word processing template. This form or template generally contains the word *memorandum* and the following elements:

- Organizational logo
- *To* line
- *From* line
- *Date* line
- *Subject* line
- The notation *pc* (photocopy) or *cc* (courtesy copy) if copies are being sent to other individuals

When filling out the "To" portion of the memo, know what your company preferences are and follow them. For example, here are some general rules:

- Use the first name (or initial) and last name of the individual.
- Use the job title of the individual if it is company procedure to do so; many

organizations do not use titles in memorandums.

SELF-CHECK A ✔

Determine whether the following words are spelled correctly. If they are spelled incorrectly, what is the correct spelling? Check the correct responses at the end of this chapter.

accesible	harass
accurate	maintanence
appearence	milage
calender	ninty
changeable	occasionally
comittment	parallel
dilema	priviledge
embarrass	recieve
exhorbitant	succeed
fourty	superintendant

- Do not use personal titles such as *Ms.* or *Mr.*
- List the names in alphabetical order or by hierarchical order within the company.
- If you are addressing a memo to ten or more people, use a generic classification, such as "TQM Team." When sending memorandums, you may use specially designed envelopes. These envelopes are reusable and are generally large enough that standard-size stationery can be inserted without folding. An example of an interoffice envelope is shown in Figure 6-6.
- List *pc* or *cc* recipients alphabetically or hierarchically, whichever is company procedure.
- If the memorandum is more than one page long, key the additional pages on plain paper. A header, which includes the names of the individual(s) receiving the memo, date, and page number, should appear at the top of the second and all additional pages.

■ Figure 6-6

INTEROFFICE ENVELOPE

		INTER-DEPARTMENT DELIVERY		
Note—Cross Out Entire Line When Received and Re-use Until All Lines Are Full.				
Date	Deliver To:	Department	Sent By:	Department
		○		○
		○		○
		○		○

Figure 6-7 on page 119 illustrates a memorandum. Notice the memorandum uses side headings. This approach helps the reader scan the memo quickly and easily. Such an approach also helps the writer to focus on and clarify the message.

E-mails

When **e-mail** messages are sent in the workplace, e-mail guidelines and etiquette must be considered. If not, major mistakes can be made at great cost to the organization and the individual writing the e-mail.

E-mail Guidelines

When composing e-mail, adhere to these guidelines:

- Be certain you have thought through the purpose of your e-mail before you begin writing; in other words, know what you are trying to achieve with your e-mail.
- Be succinct. Before you send your e-mail, reread it. Delete unnecessary phrases, words, or sentences.
- Be polite. Think of your e-mail as a short letter and follow etiquette rules. Use *please* and *thank you.*
- Be appropriately formal when writing e-mail. The rule of thumb is to be almost as formal in e-mail as you are in standard memorandums to your employer and/or co-workers. The message below is too informal.

Inappropriate

jim, we need to have a meeting soon - can you arrange? I'm free next mon. thks.

Appropriate

Jim,

We need to meet soon to discuss our division's projected budget for the next six months. Are you available on Monday, November 14, from 9 a.m. until 10 a.m.? If so, let me know by this afternoon. We can meet in my office.

Ed

■ **Figure 6-7**

SAMPLE INTEROFFICE MEMORANDUM

CANASIAN AIRLINES

Memorandum

TO: Andrew Macino

FROM: R. T. Vanderveen   *rtv*

DATE: October 12, 2005

SUBJECT: Management Conference, December 1, Toronto

Purpose

Monaghan Consulting is holding a management conference on December 1 in Toronto. The main topic is developing empowered teams in an organization. I believe we can gain valuable information that will help us as we continue to build teams here.

Action

Please look over the information I am attaching to this memo and give me a call by November 1 if you and your staff are interested in attending.

Attachment

- Always capitalize the appropriate words, be specific about needs, and use a proper closing.
- Avoid using **emoticons** (faces produced at the keyboard by combining punctuation marks, an idea devised by the Internet counterculture to solve the problem of e-mail being devoid of body language). Figure 6-8 on page 120 illustrates a few emoticons. Save these for communications with your close friends or family.

■ **Figure 6-8**

EMOTICONS

G	"I'm grinning as I write this sentence."
LOL	"I'm laughing out loud."
:-)	"I'm smiling."
;-)	"I'm winking."
:-(	"I'm unhappy."
;->	Indicates that a comment is intended to be provocative.

- Fill out the *Subject* line provided on the e-mail form. Your description of the "subject" should be concise yet give enough information so the receiver knows at a glance what the message is about. For example, if you are sending an e-mail about a TQM meeting, the *Subject* should read "TQM Meeting, 2:30 p.m., November 1," rather than "Meeting."
- If you are replying to a message but are changing the subject of the conversation, change the *Subject* line also. Better yet, start a new message altogether.
- Organize the message and construct it tightly. E-mail should not be longer than one screen. If the length of your memo is longer than one screen, attach a separate document or send a hard-copy memorandum.
- Edit and proofread carefully. Do not send out an e-mail that contains inaccuracies or incorrect grammar.
- Use complete sentences.
- Capitalize and punctuate properly.
- Do not run sentences together; it is difficult to read e-mail constructed in this manner.
- Insert a blank line after each paragraph.
- Check your spelling.
- Always include your name and title in your signature (if appropriate) when replying to an e-mail.
- Assume that any message you send is permanent. The message can be sitting in someone's private file or in a tape archive.

E-mail Etiquette

- Do not use different fonts, colours, clip art, and other graphics in e-mail. Such an approach merely clutters your message and takes longer to send

and receive, particularly if you include numerous graphics.
- Do not key your message in ALL UPPERCASE as this connotes "shouting." It is okay now and then to emphasize a word or phrase in all capitals, but use the Caps Lock key sparingly.
- Avoid sending messages when you are angry. Give yourself time to settle down and think about the situation before you send or reply to an e-mail in anger. Take a walk around your office, drink a cup of hot tea to soothe your nerves, or wait 24 hours. Avoid expressions such as "You must be stupid if you do not understand that. ..." Such expressions constitute "flaming" and start "flame wars." In some cases, you may want to make a telephone call to or have a personal conversation with the person, rather than writing or responding to a flaming e-mail.
- Before you reply to an e-mail, ask yourself if you really need to reply. For example, a message to a list server that only says "I agree" should be sent only to the person who wrote the original e-mail or perhaps not sent at all. If the message was only for your information, no reply is needed.
- If another person needs to know about the information contained in an e-mail, send a copy of the e-mail to that person.
- If you send a message in haste and then immediately realize you should not have done so, use the "unsend" option if available.
- Answer your e-mail promptly. However, "promptly" does not generally mean you should respond within five or ten minutes. Your job involves more than answering your e-mail. The general rule is to read and respond to your e-mail once or twice a day (depending on volume).

See Figure 6-9 on page 121 for Netiquette tips.

Letters

Letters are more formal than e-mail or memorandums. A letter represents the company to the outside public—customers, clients, and prospective customers and clients. A well-written letter can win friends and customers. Conversely, a poorly written letter can lose customers and make enemies of prospective customers. One of your tasks as an administrative professional is assisting your employer with writing effective letters or writing letters yourself for her or his signature. Here are additional suggestions for writing effective letters.

Figure 6-9

NETIQUETTE

- Observe the Golden Rule in cyberspace; treat others as you would like to be treated.
- Act responsibly when sending e-mail or posting messages to a discussion group. Don't use language or photographs that are racist, sexist, or offensive. Be careful when using humour or sarcasm as they can be misunderstood.
- Use a style and tone that are appropriate to the intended recipient of your message. Observe proper spelling, punctuation, and grammar. Make sure the information you convey is accurate to the best of your knowledge.
- Conserve resources. Don't add to network congestion by downloading huge files, sending longwinded e-mail messages, or engaging in spamming.

Source: "Netiquette Tips," *Keying In* (Newsletter of the National Business Education Association) 11(2) (November 2000).

Classify and Organize the Type of Message

Letters can be classified into the following four categories according to the anticipated reader reaction:

Type of Message	Anticipated Reader Reaction
Favourable	Positive
Routine	Neutral
Unfavourable	Negative
Persuasive	Interested–Indifferent

- **Favourable messages** are those the reader will be pleased to receive. A favourable message might be a letter offering someone a job or a letter congratulating someone on a promotion.
- **Routine messages** have a neutral effect on the receiver. Many letters are routine messages, such as letters requesting information or letters relaying information.
- **Unfavourable messages** bring a negative reaction from the reader, such as a letter turning down a job applicant.

- **Persuasive messages** attempt to get the reader to take some action. For example, a letter to a busy executive trying to convince him or her to speak at a conference is a persuasive letter.

The type of message determines the organization of the letter or memorandum:

Type of Message	Organization
Favourable	Direct
Routine (neutral)	Direct
Unfavourable	Indirect
Persuasive	Indirect (persuasive approach)

Direct

If the reader's reaction to your message will be favourable or neutral, you should use the **direct approach**. Much of the routine correspondence you write falls into this category. Direct correspondence should have the following components:

- Begin with the reason for the correspondence. If you are making a request or an inquiry, state that request or inquiry:

  Do you sell a combination PDA and cellular phone?

- Continue with whatever explanation is necessary so the reader will understand the message:

  If so, please provide me with the capabilities of your product and the price. Send me any literature you have, including the price of your product.

- Close the letter with a thank-you for action that has been taken or with a request that action be taken by a specific date:

  I need the information by January 15; please respond using the address given in the letterhead. Thank you for your assistance.

The checklist presented in Figure 6-10 on page 122 will help you as you begin to write favourable and routine letters.

Indirect

When your message to the reader will cause an unfavourable reaction, your best approach is an **indirect approach**. At times, you must write correspondence refusing a request or an appointment or in some way saying no to a person. Even so, you want the person to accept the decision and to understand that you are

■ Figure 6-10

FAVOURABLE AND ROUTINE MESSAGE CHECKLIST

- Did you begin the first paragraph with the reason for the correspondence?
- Did you continue with whatever explanation was necessary?
- Did you close with a thank-you for action or with a request that action be taken by a particular date?
- Did you use the you approach?
- Is the correspondence clear, concise, and simple?
- Is the correspondence complete? Did you ask the W questions?
- Is the correspondence considerate?
- Is the correspondence timely?
- Is the correspondence positive?
- Do the paragraphs have unity, coherence, and parallel structure?
- Is the readability level appropriate for the intended audience?
- Is the format correct?
- Did you proofread carefully?

concerned. You want to leave the person with a positive impression. Follow these guidelines when writing indirect correspondence:

- Begin with an opening statement that is pleasant but neutral.

  Your plan to build a fund for a new arts centre in the community is commendable. I hope you are able to meet your goal.

- Review the circumstances and give the negative information.

  Every year CanAsian contributes several thousand dollars to important causes. However, even though your proposal is a worthy one, we have already expended this year's budget. If you are still in need of our help next year, please let me know. We will be happy to consider a proposal from you.

- Close the correspondence on a pleasant and positive note.

Good luck in your efforts. Our town needs more civic-minded groups such as yours.

An example of an indirect letter is given in Figure 6-11 on page 123. To help you in writing unfavourable messages, use the checklist presented in Figure 6-12 on page 124.

Persuasive

The **persuasive approach** is an indirect approach with special characteristics. Use the persuasive approach when you want to convince someone to do something or change an indifferent or negative reader reaction. By using this approach, you can, hopefully, change the reader's initial negative or indifferent attitude to a positive one. The persuasive correspondence should follow these guidelines:

- Begin with the *you* approach. This approach requires the writer to place the reader at the centre of the message. Rather than using *I* or *we*, the writer puts himself or herself in the shoes of the reader and uses *you* frequently. More information is given about the *you* approach in the next section of this chapter. Here is an example of an effective beginning for a persuasive approach.

  Your role as an administrative professional is often challenging. You deal with conflict, unhappy customers, changing technology, and numerous other challenges daily. Would you like to know how to handle these challenges effectively and keep your frustration level down?

- Continue by creating interest and desire.

  If you answered yes to the question, our monthly publication, The Effective Administrative Professional, will help you. It is packed with techniques and suggestions for handling office situations.

- Close by asking for the desired action.

  You can have this publication in your office every month for only $48 per year. That is a very small amount to pay for lowering your frustration level and making your job more fun. Fill in the information on the enclosed card, and return it by January. Your early return will guarantee you one free month of the subscription. We look forward to counting you as one of our many satisfied subscribers.

■ Figure 6-11

INDIRECT LETTER

CanAsian Airlines
2300–888 3rd Street SW
Calgary, AB T2P 4C4
1-403-555-2347

December 12, 2005

Mr. Steven Marceau
Higgins Association
19 Belmont Avenue
Toronto, ON M5E 5E2

Dear Steve:

Your invitation to speak at the conference on October 13 is an honour. Your group is a respected one, and I have enjoyed my association with it.

Unfortunately, the demands on my time at work now are extremely heavy. In addition to a new planning process that I must implement, we have recently employed two new managers who are looking to me for assistance in learning their jobs. As you might expect, I hardly have time to "look up." As I would not want to accept your invitation without having adequate time to prepare, I must say no this time. However, if you need a speaker in the future, please don't forget me. It is always a good experience for me to speak to your group.

Have you met Ramona Stanley, one of our marketing directors? She does an excellent presentation on listening, and she might be available to speak at your conference. Her number is 403-555-4378. Good luck with the program.

Sincerely,

Maria Martin

Maria Martin
Vice-President of Human Resources

MM:pjc

■ Figure 6-12

UNFAVOURABLE MESSAGE CHECKLIST

- Did you begin with a pleasant but neutral statement?
- Did you review the circumstances and give the negative information as positively as possible?
- Did you close on a pleasant note?
- If you had to say no to something, did you offer an alternative, if possible?
- Is the correspondence clear, concise, and simple?
- Is the correspondence complete, considerate, and correct?
- Is the correspondence prompt and positive?
- Do the paragraphs have unity, coherence, and parallel structure?
- Is the format correct?
- Did you proofread well?

Use the *You* Approach

With the *you* approach, the reader is uppermost in the mind of the writer. The *you* approach involves the use of **empathy** (mentally entering into the feeling or spirit of a person). If the writer is trying to sell a product or service, he or she must look at the benefits the product or service will offer to the reader, not the amount of sales commission. If the message involves something as routine as setting up a meeting, the writer must stress the benefits of the meeting to the reader. Such writing emphasizes *you* and *your* and deemphasizes the *I, we, mine,* and *ours.*

To carry out the *you* approach, adhere to two words of caution: Be sincere. Do not overuse the approach to the point of insincerity or even dishonesty. Your goal is not to flatter the reader, but rather to see the situation from his or her point of view and respond accordingly. Sincerity means being genuine, honest, and empathic with the reader.

Notice how the following examples of writing from what might be called the *I-we* viewpoint have been

changed to the you viewpoint. The changes are small, yet the meaning and tone are quite different:

> ***I-We Viewpoint:*** *We received your order for 100 seat belts today.*
>
> ***You Viewpoint:*** *Your order for 100 seat belts was received June 10.*
>
> ***I-We Viewpoint:*** *We sell the seat belts for $25 each.*
>
> ***You Viewpoint:*** *Your cost for the seat belts is $25.*
>
> ***I-We Viewpoint:*** *I will be glad to attend the conference.*
>
> ***You Viewpoint:*** *Thank you for asking me to attend the conference. I am delighted to accept your invitation.*

Take a few minutes now to check your understanding of what you have learned about writing. Rewrite the sentences in Self-Check B so they are effective. When you have finished, check your responses with those given at the end of the chapter.

SELF-CHECK B ✓

1. Your kind letter of October 8 was received today.
2. I wish to thank you for your recent order.
3. As per my letter of November 5, the modular furniture is unsatisfactory.
4. Please send us the information at your earliest convenience.
5. The error I made was unfortunate.
6. Your claim that we made an error in your bill is incorrect.
7. A preponderance of businesspeople was consulted on this esoteric matter.
8. People's propensity to consume goods is insatiable.
9. You will receive the merchandise without any more delay.
10. You will not be sorry if you buy one of our washing machines.

Ensure Mailability

Since letters represent your company to outside individuals, in addition to writing them well and using correct grammar, spelling, and punctuation, you must also format them correctly. If you need a quick review on letter styles and folding letters, refer to the Reference and Business Document Formatting Guides on the Student CD.

Your employer may on occasion return a piece of correspondence to you, informing you of an error that must be corrected before it can be mailed. Paying attention to all details will help ensure your effectiveness as an administrative professional.

Reports

The administrative professional's role in preparing reports varies. You may have the responsibility of keying the report, producing the final copies, and distributing the report to the appropriate individuals. Or your role may involve assisting with the creation of visuals for the report (charts, graphs, and so on), doing research for your employer, and even drafting some or all portions of the report.

The planning steps involved in the writing of a report include the following:

- Determining the purpose of the report
- Analyzing the audience who will receive the report

Once the initial planning has taken place, the writer begins to determine the content of the report by taking these steps:

- Prepare a summary of what should be included in the report.
- Gather information for the report.
- Prepare an outline of the report. The outline may be a detailed or informal one the writer prepares to get his or her thoughts organized.
- Draft the report. The body of the report should have (1) an introduction to help the reader understand the purpose of the report, (2) a main section that includes all the pertinent information, and (3) a conclusion or findings and recommen-

dations to help the reader understand what to do with the report.
- Prepare any necessary graphs, charts, and tables.
- Read and edit the report.
- Prepare the executive summary.
- Print and distribute the report.

Reference Sources

Most reports involve some type of research. The research may be **primary research**—the collecting of original data through surveys, observations, or experiments. The research also may be **secondary research**—data or material that other people have discovered and reported via the Internet, books, periodicals, and various other publications.

Primary Research

If you are conducting primary research, you must decide how to gather the information. You may decide to take these steps:

- Observe situations and individuals.
- Survey or interview groups of individuals.
- Perform an experiment.

Observational research involves collecting data through observations of an event or of actions. Survey research involves collecting data through some type of survey or interview. An interview is usually done in person; however, it may be done over the telephone. Sometimes **focus groups** are brought together to talk with an interviewer about their opinions of certain events or issues. In recent political campaigns, focus groups were used extensively to learn the opinions of people on various issues. A survey is generally done by mail; however, it also may be administered in person. For example, you may decide to assemble several people in your company and pass out a survey to be completed immediately. You generally get a better **response rate** (the number of people responding to a survey or questionnaire) on surveys administered in person than those done by mail.

Experimental research has generally been used in the sciences; however, it is becoming popular with businesses too. It may involve a researcher selecting two or more sample groups and exposing them to certain treatments. For example, a business may decide to test a marketing strategy before implementing a marketing campaign. Experimental groups may be selected and the marketing strategy implemented with the group. According to the outcome of the research, the business would proceed with the marketing strategy, modify it, or select another one.

Secondary Research

Until relatively recently, libraries were the major source for conducting secondary research. Although libraries are still a major source, the Internet has become another. In fact, most libraries today have become virtual ones, offering millions of pages of catalogued data on the Web. This approach allows several libraries to be connected to each other and eliminates the necessity for storing a large number of books and other documents on shelves.

With the huge amount of data now on the Web, the researcher's task of evaluating the data has become more important than ever. As you probably know, anyone can get on the Web and write almost anything he or she chooses. The information may or may not have any validity or reliability. If you are doing research on the Web, here are some questions you might ask:

- Is the information presented by a credible organization, company, or individual?
- If the information is presented solely by an individual, what are the individual's credentials?
- Is adequate support given for the points made?

When using secondary research in reports, that research must be documented. The Business Document Formatting Guide on the Student CD includes a section on documentation. Information is provided on **MLA** (Modern Language Association), **APA** (American Psychological Association), Web, and traditional documentation styles.

Parts of the Report

An informal report may have only one or two parts, with those parts being the body and an **executive summary** (a one- or two-page summary of the report). An informal report is written in a conversational style. Personal pronouns such as _I, you, me, we,_ and _us_ are used. Contractions are also acceptable.

The executive summary is written for the busy executive who

- Wishes to preview the report to determine if there is a portion he or she wants to read in its entirety
- Does not need a detailed understanding of all aspects of the report, but does need to know the major findings and recommendations

The executive summary

- Describes the background—why the report was necessary and what the problem or issue is
- Gives the major findings—what was discovered through the research
- Gives the recommendations that are being made as a result of the discoveries

The formal report normally deals with a more complex subject, is longer than the informal report, and requires more time and preparation. Formal reports are generally written in manuscript format and contain preliminary and supplementary parts. An explanation of each part is provided here.

Title Page

The title page contains the title of the report, the writer's name and title and the organization department or division name, and the date the report is being submitted.

Table of Contents

The table of contents lists each major section of the report and the page number of the first page of that section. A table of contents is not required; however, when a report is long, the table of contents helps the reader find particular parts of the report.

List of Tables and Illustrations

If numerous tables and illustrations are within a report, list the title of each one with the respective page number. This procedure helps the reader quickly locate and scan the data presented.

Body

The body is divided into the following major sections:

- Introduction
- Problem statement
- Research methods
- Findings and discussion
- Recommendations
- Conclusion

Footnotes/Endnotes/Internal Citations

Footnotes appear at the bottom of the page where the reference is made. Endnotes are grouped at the end of the document. Internal citations appear within the context of the document.

Bibliography or Reference Section

All references used in a report should be included in a bibliography or reference section. This section includes the complete name of the author(s), the title of the book or periodical, the date of publication, the publishing company, and the page numbers.

Appendix

A formal report may contain one or more appendixes containing supporting information such as tables, statistics, and other pertinent material. Multiple appendixes are labelled "Appendix A," "Appendix B," and so on. The appendixes are the last part of the report.

Collaborative Writing

You have learned throughout this text that teams are used extensively in organizations today. Teams may write reports or prepare presentations as a group. To be an effective member of any team, you need to use the skills presented in Chapter 5, such as listening actively and understanding and accepting cultural, gender, and age differences. Additionally, team writing or presentation assignments both require collaborative planning. **Brainstorming** will help to determine what the report or presentation should include and how it will be presented. (See Figure 6-13 for how to brainstorm.)

Additionally, if you are engaged in a team writing or presentation assignment, the collaborative writing guidelines presented in Figure 6-14 on page 128 will help you be successful.

Transcription

As a result of the increased user-friendliness of word processing software and e-mail, fewer executives today use transcription as an input method for document production. Many executives carry a notebook computer with them when they travel. These notebook computers can be connected to an office network making it just as efficient to send the documents through the network, as it would be to dictate them. The administrative professional is then responsible only for formatting the text of the documents.

For executives that do not possess keyboarding skills, however, dictating reports and other documents is often a preference, simply because they can speak more quickly than they can keyboard. This section identifies some of the special skills that are required whether you are dictating or transcribing business documents along with some tips for dictating and transcribing notes.

Transcription Skills

Transcription involves a variety of skills including the following:

* *Accurate keyboarding ability* saves time. Corrections are easily made and most word

■ **Figure 6-13**

BRAINSTORMING TECHNIQUES

- Say each idea aloud as it occurs to you.
- Have a recorder jot down each idea.
- Listen attentively to others' ideas.
- Piggyback on the ideas of others.
- Suspend judgment. Do not critique ideas as they are presented.
- Encourage an uninterrupted flow of ideas.
- Expect the outrageous to surface, which is perfectly okay in the brainstorming process; it encourages creativity.

Photodisc Blue/Photodisc Collecton

Effective team writing requires participants to listen actively and understand individual differences.

■ Figure 6-14

COLLABORATIVE WRITING GUIDELINES

- Determine the purpose of the writing assignment. What is the team to produce? What is the deadline? Must certain stipulations be met?
- Determine who the audience is. Who is to receive the final report? What is their background? How much do they know about the subject matter? In other words, determine what your style of writing should be and how much information to give the recipients.
- Select a team leader. The team leader is responsible for setting the procedures for the team writing meetings; facilitating the meetings; and helping the group meet deadlines, solve problems, and produce the document.
- Set a work schedule. Decide when and where you are going to meet. Set timelines and stick to them.
- Allocate the work. Define the tasks of each team member. Determine each team member's writing strengths, and use these strengths when assigning tasks.
- Monitor the progress. The group must stay focused and produce the written product by the deadline established.
- Reduce the chance of conflict by
  - Actively listening to each group member
  - Paying attention to cultural, age, and gender differences
  - Acknowledging the worth of the other group members and their points of view

processing software programs will automatically correct frequently misspelled words, but having to make corrections takes time. Make it a goal to produce mailable copies the first time.

- *Spelling, grammar, and punctuation* are easily checked by the word processing software; but remember, the software does not identify those words spelled correctly but used incorrectly, as may happen with *their* and *there*, for example.

- *Proofreading* for spelling errors should be done after running the program's spell checker. You should not only look for simple errors such as to, too, or two, but also consider the meaning of the content. Does it make sense? Are there any inconsistencies? The dictator might indicate a date as Tuesday, February 14 when it should actually be Wednesday, February 14 or Tuesday, February 13.
- *An extensive vocabulary* will prove beneficial when you have problems discerning what word or phrase has actually been dictated. Possessing a wide business vocabulary will enable you to insert a word or phrase that makes sense within the context of the document. You can then use the highlighting capability of your word processing software to highlight whatever is doubtful. This will make it clear to your supervisor that you need some clarification before proceeding to produce the final version of the document.
- *Standard formats for business documents* can usually be found in a procedures manual produced by your company. Be aware of the approved formats and apply them to the dictated material as you are transcribing.
- *Reference sources* such as a good dictionary, a word-division book, a thesaurus, and an office procedures handbook can be invaluable resources. Keep them close by, and use them in conjunction with the spelling and grammar checking features of your word processing software.

Transcription Techniques

A variety of dictation and transcription equipment is available on the market today. In all cases the administrative professional will require a headset and foot pedal in order to transcribe dictated material. In the physical process of transcribing dictation you will

1. Press the play forward section of a foot pedal to listen to the dictation
2. Listen and keyboard what you hear
3. Raise your foot from the pedal to stop the forward play of the dictation while you complete keyboarding the phrase
4. Press the foot pedal to continue, or press the reverse section of the foot pedal to listen to words or phrases you may have missed
5. Repeat steps 1–4 until the document is complete

Some tips to increase your productivity when transcribing dictation are presented in Table 6-1 on page 130.

Dictation Techniques

An originator who is aware of the skills required for efficient transcription creates the most successful dictation. Like the writing process, organizing your thoughts before beginning to dictate is the key to success. You learned in Chapter 3 the time management technique of batching your work—organizing and performing similar tasks at one time. Setting aside a specific time for dictation and assembling the necessary files before you begin contributes to efficiency on the job. Table 6-2 on page 131 presents some additional tips for effective dictation.

Equipment

From digital dictation systems to traditional cassette dictation/transcription units, there is a wide range of dictation and transcription equipment available. Executives who travel or whose job responsibilities are in the field commonly use portable dictation devices. Whether it is the digital portable pictured in Figure 6-15 or the microcassette portable seen in Figure 6-16 (see page 132 for both), these portable devices make recording reminders, documents, and instructions very convenient when one is not in the office.

Desktop equipment similar to the ones shown in Figures 6-17 and 6-18 (see page 132 for both) can be used for dictation and transcription. The unit with the microphone is used for dictation; the unit with the foot pedal and headset is used for transcription. These units contain adjustable volume, tone, and speed controls so that the playback can be modified for the individual transcriptionist. A digital display indicates the total dictation time and audio tones sound to indicate the location of dictated instructions.

Computer-based systems are another option for dictation and transcription. Once the appropriate dictation software is loaded onto the computer, the originator dictates using the computer or portable recorder and then transmits the recordings via e-mail, the Internet, or company intranet. Transcription software, which includes features such as variable-speed playback, foot-pedal operation, file management, and more, must be installed on the computer being used by a transcriptionist. This transcription software can be controlled using the keyboard (with **hot keys**—user-defined combinations of keystrokes that provide quick access to a command or menu) and/or a foot pedal.

To find out more about different dictation/transcription equipment and systems, check out the following websites.

- Dictaphone Corporation: www.dictaphone.com
- Start-Stop: www.startstop.com
- NextWave Solutions: www.next-wave-solutions.com
- Transcription Buddy: www.transcriptionbuddy.com

International Communications

Throughout this course, you have been reminded of the global nature of business and what that means for you as an administrative professional. Chances are great that, at some point in your career, you will be communicating in writing with individuals from various countries. The part of this chapter that focused on written communication dealt with the principles appropriate for North American firms. However, if you are writing to individuals outside of Canada, you must consider the differences in culture. You learned in Chapter 5 about various cultural differences. Although these differences vary from country to country, you need to be aware of them when communicating in writing. The result of such knowledge and understanding will be clear, concise, and appropriate communications with international businesses. Generally, communication must be more formal than what is used with Canadian businesses. To learn the particulars of a country, read about the country and its customs. General principles for international written correspondence are provided in Figure 6-19 on page 132.

Table 6-1 TIPS TO INCREASE YOUR PRODUCTIVITY WHEN TRANSCRIBING DICTATION

Plan transcription activities	■ Identify the number of items to be transcribed. ■ Determine the length of the items (how long will it take to transcribe each item). ■ Prioritize the order of transcription for all items.
Special instructions	■ At the beginning of each dictated item check for special instructions such as: 　■ Number of copies 　■ Enclosures, 　■ Special handling 　■ Distribution 　■ Draft or final form ■ Optional: Listen to the complete document if the dictator is new to you or has a heavy accent. This is not necessary when you are familiar with the originator's style of dictation and the vocabulary of the business.
Dating transcription	■ Date all documents. Documents may be revised several times. The date helps to identify the most current version. ■ The date of transcription or the date the document will be signed—not the date of dictation—should be used on all correspondence. ■ Adjust references to dates within the body of the document to conform with the date of transcription. For example, change "today" to "yesterday" when transcribing dictation created the previous day.
Listen actively	■ Concentrate while listening to the dictated material—eliminate as many distractions as possible. ■ Listen ahead to the next few words as you keyboard. Eventually you should be able to listen and keyboard continuously ■ Do not make changes to what has been dictated unless it is an obvious error such as an incorrect personal name or date. ■ Highlight words within the text that are unfamiliar to you or that you do not recognize.
Use precedents	■ Check your company procedures manual, reference book, or previous correspondence for formatting guidelines. ■ Check correspondence previously dictated by the same person for words or phrases frequently used by them.
Proofread	■ Proofread as you keyboard. ■ Run the spell checker when you have completed the transcription. ■ Proofread again for correctness of context and for incorrectly used words.

Table 6-2 TIPS FOR EFFECTIVE DICTATION

Preparation	■ Book time for dictation in your calendar.
	■ Assemble all necessary information—files, reports, calendar.
	■ Annotate—make notes in the margin of a letter or report or attached Post-It notes—to help guide you.
	■ Think about what you want to say—organize your thoughts before beginning to dictate.
	■ Avoid interruptions—close your door or put a "Do Not Disturb" sign on your door.
	■ Turn off the radio or CD player.
Instructions to the transcriptionist	■ Identify yourself—if necessary.
	■ Identify the type of message—e-mail, letter, report, etc.
	■ Indicate priority—rush, required immediately, due next week.
	■ Indicate number of copies (in addition to file copy) required and to whom they are to be sent.
	■ Provide special formatting instructions if any.
Dictation	■ Avoid moving around while using a recording device.
	■ Do not eat or chew gum or play with anything that could create a noise that would be picked up by the recording device.
	■ Avoid dictating while on a plane or in a car.
	■ Hold the microphone approximately 20 centimetres from your mouth.
	■ Use your natural, conversational speaking voice.
	■ Provide the correct name and if possible the address of the addressee.
	■ Spell out personal names and other proper names.
	■ Spell out technical terms not known to the transcriber.
	■ Provide punctuation and paragraphing instructions.
	■ Provide the transcriber with the original copies of the documents being responded to arranged in the same order as the dictated items.

■ Figure 6-15

WALKABOUT 5210 DIGITAL DICTATION KIT

Courtesy of Dictaphone Corporation

■ Figure 6-16

MICROCASSETTE PORTABLE DICTATION UNIT

Courtesy of Dictaphone Corporation

■ Figure 6-17

MICROCASSETTE DESKTOP DICTATION UNIT WITH MICROPHONE

Courtesy of Dictaphone Corporation

■ Figure 6-18

MICROCASSETTE EXPRESS WRITER WITH FOOT PEDAL AND HEADSET DESKTOP DICTATION UNIT

Courtesy of Dictaphone Corporation

■ Figure 6-19

GENERAL PRINCIPLES FOR INTERNATIONAL WRITTEN CORRESPONDENCE

- Use relatively formal language. Phrases such as *Very Honoured Professor Dr. Fruer* and *Your honoured servant* are used in some countries.
- Do not use expressions unique to North America; do not refer to events that are common only to Canada.
- Use the dictionary meanings of words; do not use slang.
- Always use the title of the individual with whom you are corresponding. First names should not be used.
- Be extremely courteous; use *thank you* and *please* often.
- Be complimentary when appropriate (but always sincere).
- Ask questions tactfully.
- Do not use humour; it may be misunderstood.
- Respect all customs of the country (social, religious, and so on).
- Learn all you can about particular countries; read extensively.
- Translate correspondence into the native language of the country.
- Send business cards that are printed in the native language of the country.

Soft Skills: Ethical and Legal Considerations

You were introduced to the importance of ethical behaviour in Chapter 4. Almost every day we hear on television or read in a newspaper about business ethics. In 2001, a United States lower court ordered Phillip Morris® to pay $3 billion to a man who had developed cancer. The man claimed he was not aware of the dangers of cigarettes. At the time of publication of this text, Phillip Morris was appealing the suit. Did Phillip Morris behave ethically? According to a jury, the company did not, even though it printed the hazards of smoking on its cigarette packages.

Ethical problems are difficult to resolve precisely because no rules exist to determine when something is ethical or unethical. Every organization and individual must make that determination independently.

In written correspondence, you, as an employee of an organization, must be honest, must maintain confidentiality (not divulge organizational business outside the organization), and must be loyal (act in the employer's interest). The organization must also act ethically in regard to its public responsibilities. Organizations must tell the truth about their products and services and not mislead the public. For example, airlines have an ethical obligation to the public to meet the scheduled flight times unless circumstances such as weather or mechanical problems arise. They also have an ethical obligation to be honest with the public as to why a flight is late. Automotive companies have an ethical obligation to the public to present correct written specifications of all vehicles. Not-for-profit organizations have an ethical obligation to present in writing to the public how their dollars are spent in meeting the needs of the underprivileged.

In written correspondence (newspaper ads, TV ads, marketing letters, brochures, and so on), organizations have legal obligations that are covered by various laws, including copyright, trademark, contract, and liability laws. These laws are also applicable to e-mail messages. For example, e-mail users must abide by the "fair use" rule of copyright law when forwarding copyrighted materials obtained from the Web. The fair use rule is very specific about when something can and cannot be used and provides guidelines about materials used in a commercial or not-for-profit nature, the length of the copied work in comparison to the entire document, and so on. In the Firestone Tire situation, Firestone had an obligation under liability law to inform the public of any defects in its tires that could cause personal injury, death, property damage, or financial loss. Tobacco companies today must print the health hazards of tobacco on all of their products. Unless the legal obligations of organizations are carefully observed in all written materials, the organization faces the consequences of costly lawsuits, loss of the public's goodwill, and loss of business.

Chapter Summary

The summary will help you remember the important points covered in the chapter.

- The basic business correspondence that the administrative professional prepares includes memorandums, e-mail, letters, and reports.
- Effective correspondence is clear, concise, and simple. This means the sentences are short and the vocabulary is easily understood, a conversational tone is used, unneeded words are deleted, active verbs are used, the writing style is varied, and clichés are avoided.
- Effective correspondence is complete, considerate, correct, prompt, and positive. The paragraphs have unity and coherence. The sentences are parallel in structure. The writer uses the appropriate readability level—usually between 7 and 11.
- When planning correspondence, the writer should determine the objective, consider the reader, and gather the facts.
- E-mail has revolutionized the way we communicate. E-mail is used extensively in businesses as well as homes. When e-mail messages are sent, e-mail guidelines, ethics, and etiquette must be considered.
- Etiquette is most important when sending e-mail. Never send an e-mail when you are angry, and answer your e-mail promptly.
- Letters and memorandums can be classified as favourable, routine (neutral), unfavourable, and persuasive. If the message is favourable or routine, the direct approach is used. If the message is unfavourable or persuasive, the indirect approach is used.
- The *you* approach should be used when writing letters. With this approach, the reader is uppermost in the mind of the writer. It involves the use of empathy.
- The planning steps involved in the writing of a report include determining the purpose of the report and analyzing the audience who will receive the report.
- Primary research may be essential for a business report. This research may include observational research, survey research, and/or experimental research.
- Secondary research, including sources from the Web and from libraries, is also used.
- The parts of a formal business report include the title page, table of contents, list of tables and illustrations, body, footnotes/endnotes/internal cita-

tions, bibliography or reference section, and appendix.

- Reports are often written through a collaborative process. This collaborative planning should include brainstorming.
- Dictation is often a preferred input method used by executives because they can speak more quickly than they can keyboard or handwrite.
- An effective transcriptionist possesses an extensive vocabulary and knowledge of business document formats, has the ability to keyboard accurately and to proofread for spelling, grammar, and punctuation errors, and makes use of appropriate reference sources.
- Transcription productivity is increased when you plan the activities, listen actively, follow any special instructions, use precedents, proofread, and date all transcriptions.
- Set aside specific time for dictation and assemble all necessary materials before you begin.
- Providing instructions to the transcriptionist, dictating in a quiet environment using your natural conversational speaking voice, spelling out proper names and technical terms, and including punctuation and paragraphing instructions will all contribute to efficiency during transcription.
- Dictation/transcription systems range from traditional cassette dictation/transcription units to computer-based systems.
- Dictation units have a microphone; transcription units have a foot pedal and headset.
- International correspondence is usually more formal than correspondence written to individuals within Canada. The writer must be aware of the customs and culture of the country to which he or she is writing.
- The writer and organization are responsible for ensuring that their written correspondence is both ethical and legal.

Key Terms

The following terms were introduced in this chapter. The page on which the term was introduced is provided to help you locate the new term. Definitions are compiled in the Glossary at the end of the text.

- **tone** 112
- **topic sentence** 112
- **parallelism** 115
- **readability** 115
- **cc** 117

Responses to Self-Check A

accessible
accurate (correct)
appearance
calendar
changeable (correct)
commitment
dilemma
embarrass (correct)
exorbitant
forty
harass (correct)
maintenance
mileage
ninety
occasionally (correct)
parallel (correct)
privilege
receive
succeed (correct)
superintendent

Responses to Self-Check B

1. Your October 8 letter was received today.
2. Thank you for your recent order.
3. The modular furniture we received on November 5 is unsatisfactory; the furniture does not match

what was ordered. A copy of our purchase order is enclosed.
4. Please send us the information by September 14.
5. You are correct.
6. Your bill has been reviewed carefully by our billing department. We can find no error in the computations. Please give me a call at 555-1500 if the bill is still unclear. I will be happy to discuss it with you.
7. A number of businesspeople were consulted on this matter.
8. People constantly consume goods.
9. You will receive the merchandise by January 10.
10. Our washing machine will be a good investment for your family.

Discussion Items

These discussion items provide an opportunity to test your understanding of the chapter through written responses and/or discussion with your classmates and your instructor.

1. Explain what is meant by clear, concise, and simple when referring to effective correspondence.
2. Explain the importance of Internet etiquette. Give five examples of good manners for the Internet.
3. How are letters classified?
4. Identify the parts of a formal business report.
5. Discuss the following items as they relate to the transcription of dictated material:
   a. Making changes to dictated material
   b. Dating transcribed material
   c. Using precedents
6. List ten principles you should adhere to when writing for an international audience.
7. Explain why legal and ethical considerations are important in writing.

Critical-Thinking Activity

One of the managers, Martin Helmholdt, asks the administrative assistant to write a letter to Judy Rogers congratulating her on becoming city manager of Vancouver. Judy worked for Mr. Helmholdt a number of years ago and moved to Vancouver five years ago. The assistant prepared a draft, but he is not pleased with the letter. He asks that you critique the letter before he gives it to Mr. Helmholdt. Here is the draft of the letter:

Dear Ms. Rogers:

I want to congratulate you on becoming city manager of Vancouver. I recognized your talent during the years you worked for me. I know you will do an excellent job for Vancouver.

Again, my congratulations on your success.

What suggestions would you make to the administrative assistant?

Projects

Project 6-1 *(Objective 1)*

Collaborative Project

Work with two of your classmates. Collect six business letters that you have received through the mail. Any type of business letter is acceptable. Using the characteristics of effective letters given in this text, critique the letters. Pick one letter to rewrite. Present your critique to the class along with your revised letter.

Project 6-2 *(Objective 1)*

Each sentence below is intended to be the beginning sentence of a letter. Rewrite the sentences so they will be effective.

1. I received your order today and wanted to thank you for it.
2. Enclosed please find my cheque in the amount of $510.36 in payment for your Order 34560.
3. I regret to inform you that the seatbelts you ordered are no longer being manufactured.
4. This cheque affirms my intent to subscribe to your weekly investment publication, *Financial News.*
5. I hope you will send us your subscription renewal today.

Project 6-3 *(Objective 2)*

Mr. Albertson has been asked by Dr. Greg Lee, president of Mount Royal College, to do a presentation on business ethics at a national conference for business executives scheduled on November 11 from 3 to 4 p.m. CanAsian is having a meeting of its executive management team (from Canada and its international locations) on November 8, 9, 10, and 11. The meeting will conclude at noon on the 11th. Mr. Albertson has decided to ask Yang Su from the China office to join him in the presentation. The presentation will be made by a panel with each participant allotted approximately 20 minutes to discuss international business ethics. A question-and-answer session will follow the presentations.

Write a memorandum to Mr. Su asking him to participate; the memorandum may go out with your name on it. Use the memorandum form on the Student CD, file SCDP6-3.

Project 6-4 *(Objective 2)*

Mr. Albertson has asked you to write a letter to Dr. Greg Lee, president of Mount Royal College (Lincoln Park Campus, 4825 Richard Road S.W., Calgary AB T3E 6K6), giving him the name of the individual who will be on the panel with him; Yang Su has agreed to be on the panel. Explain the presentation format and the time each individual will be given. Tell Dr. Lee you will be sending him a copy of the résumés of both Mr. Albertson and Mr. Su by November 8. Mr. Albertson does not know the room number for the presentation; he does know it will be at the Lincoln Park Campus. Ask Dr. Lee for this information. Mr. Albertson will sign the letter. Print out your letter on CanAsian letterhead. This letterhead is available on the Student CD, file SCDP6-4.

Project 6-5 *(Objective 2)*

Mr. Joey Premdas of of Floater Staffing Inc., 401—5920-1A Street SW, Calgary, AB T2H 0G3, asked you to participate in a panel discussion on the topic of effective communications in the workplace. You would like to do so, but your current workload is extremely heavy. Write a letter to Mr. Premdas saying no to his request. Print your letter on the letterhead stationery available on the Student CD, file SCDP6-5.

Project 6-6 *(Objective 2)*

One of your friends, Shanti Baboolal, has just received a promotion to office manager for A. B. Cushing Mills Limited, 7103—30th Street SE, Calgary, AB T2C 1N6. Write a letter of congratulations to her. Print your letter on the letterhead stationery available on the Student CD, file SCDP6-6.

Project 6-7 *(Objective 3)*

Three e-mails are on Student CD, SCDP6-7a, 6-7b, and 6-7c. Review these e-mails, determining what is wrong with each one. Then rewrite each e-mail as it should be written, using the e-mail forms on SCDP6-7d, 6-7e, and 6-7f. Make a copy of your e-mail, and submit to your instructor.

Project 6-8 *(Objective 4)*

Collaborative Project

Online Project

Team up with three members of your class. Mr. Albertson asks you to research articles on North American and international business ethics for the November 11 panel. He asks that you focus on the ethical responsibility of the company to society. You are to check the Web and your library for information. Once you have completed your research, prepare a detailed summary of your findings in informal report form. Include in the report an introduction (giving the research methods used), a body, and the findings. Also include a bibliography of your resources (use at least three).

Project 6-9 *(Objectives 4 and 5)*

Collaborative Project

Online Project

Team up with three of your classmates. Write a formal report about dictation/transcription, use, equipment, and technology. In addition to researching dictation and transcription equipment on the Web, you will need to do some original research. Survey local businesses to determine whether they use dictation and transcription, and, if so, what type of technology they use—computer-based, cassette, or something else. Develop a survey instrument that asks questions similar to these: Do you use dictation/transcription in your office? If so, for what and how often? What type of equipment do you use? Ask the approximate size of the business using these categories: small (1–10 employees), medium (1–50 employees), large (over 50 employees). Prepare the information obtained from the survey in graph form, categorizing usage by size of business. Include the survey form as an appendix to your report. Include a title page with the title and date of the report plus your name and the names of your team members.

Project 6-10 *(Objective 6)*

While doing research on the Web for Mr. Albertson on the ethics seminar, you discover a copyrighted article that you believe is very relevant. You mention it to one of your friends at CanAsian, and he asks you to forward copies via e-mail to his workgroup. What should you do? After you make your decision, write a memorandum to your friend telling him what you will do. Use the memorandum form on the Student CD, file SCDP6-10.

Project 6-11 *(Objective 6)*

Add to your Professional Growth Plan by determining how you will continue to observe ethical and legal obligations in your written correspondence. Save your plan on your Professional Growth Plan disk as "Progro6-11."

Chapter 7

Creating Effective Presentations

LEARNING OBJECTIVES

1. *Release your creativity.*
2. Deliver effective verbal and visual presentations.
3. Conquer presentation fears.

For years, research has shown that people retain more of what they hear when they see and hear the information at the same time. Good presenters have always understood the importance of appropriate visuals in getting their message across. Now with the advent of presentation tools such as Microsoft PowerPoint or Corel Presentations, we have the ability to easily produce a relatively sophisticated visual presentation.

This chapter is not designed to teach you how to use presentation software; you probably already know how to use it. However, it is designed to help you build effective visual presentations and deliver them successfully. Not only do you need to understand how to present, you also need to exercise creativity in making a presentation fit the intended audience. This chapter will help you attain these necessary skills and encourage you to use your own sense of creativity in the process; practice will help you perfect them.

Creativity

Creativity is important for producing effective presentations, but it is also important for dealing with the constant change that is occurring in offices today. In fact, creativity and change are closely linked. Creativity is needed to respond successfully to change, and creativity results in change. For example, in giving presentations, you probably have a goal of educating your audience about a certain concept or idea. Assume you are giving a presentation to your workgroup on developing empowered teams. You have two basic goals:

- Help the audience understand the importance of teamwork in today's workplace.
- Help the audience understand how to develop empowered teams.

In other words, through your presentation, you hope to effect change within the organization.

Definition

Creativity is defined as "having the ability or the power to cause to exist." Creativity is a process. It is a way of thinking and doing. It is a way of making new connections or new links. It is solving a problem in a new and different way. For example, assume you and your colleagues are going to give a presentation. You suggest that the presentation would be more effective if you used presentation software. Your colleagues think it would be too difficult. You know your idea will work, but it does not have a chance unless you are heard. You decide that rather than trying to talk with them, you will prepare one concept using presentation software and bring it to the next planning meeting. You do so and they agree that your idea is extremely effective and begin planning how software might be used throughout the presentation. You have used your creativity in changing individuals' minds. You did not just present your idea in one way; you thought of another way to present it, and you were successful. You brought about change. Do Self-Check A on page 139.

SELF-CHECK A ✔

Take a few minutes to get in touch with your creativity. Assume it is autumn and the leaves are falling. Using a computer, PDA, or piece of paper, key or write the following: *Ways that a falling leaf might be used.* Now let your creativity loose. Even if the idea seems a little crazy to you, do it. New, revolutionary ideas can occur by this very process.

How did you do? Did you come up with ideas you have never thought of before? Good for you! Compare your answers with a classmate's ideas. Did you have any of the same ideas? Did you get other ideas by seeing what your classmate had listed?

Soft Skills: How Creativity Works

Clearly, there are no rigid steps to becoming creative. Remember, it is a process—a process that can be different for each individual. However, here are some steps that can help release the creativity already existing within you.

HAVE FAITH IN YOUR CREATIVITY

First, have faith in the fact that you are creative. If you have an idea about something that is different from other ideas, do not immediately assume you are wrong. Try it out. Your idea may be the creative spark to solving a complex problem. Always maintain a spirit of inquiry. Ask questions. Do not assume that a question you have is too dumb to ask. Allow yourself the freedom to ask. Do not be uncomfortable when you do not know how something is going to turn out. By experimenting with the unknown, a wonderfully new and creative product can occur. For example, assume that Orville and Wilbur Wright had no faith in their dream of a flying machine. What if they had allowed their idea to die because of all the people who openly laughed and made jokes about their "craziness"?

DESTROY JUDGMENT

As you are thinking through a problem or an issue, do not be judgmental. Let your thoughts flow freely. Do not discard any of them. Do not let your mind tell you that an idea is "no good" or "ridiculous." To help you destroy judgment (which, by the way, is not easy to do), pay attention to every thought you have. Notice it; hear yourself think it. If you begin to be critical of your thought, attack the judgment. Say to yourself or out loud, "Judgment, get out!" Be firm. Do not let judgment have its say.

LOOK AND LISTEN

The story is told of a businessman who heard that a Zen master (who lived at the top of a mountain) knew the three basic secrets to life. Anyone who knew these secrets would live a happy, fulfilling life. The businessman climbed for two years to get to the top of the mountain. Once there he approached the old master and asked that he tell him the secrets. The master said, "Yes, I will tell you. The first secret is pay attention, the second secret is pay attention, and the third secret is pay attention."

You may be asking "Pay attention to what?" Pay attention to what you sense, what you think, what you hear, what you see. Pay attention to nature; pay attention to others.

ASK QUESTIONS

Michael Ray and Rochelle Myers, in their book *Creativity in Business*, report writing down the following questions that a four-and-a-half-year-old asked in less than an hour:

- What's behind a rainbow?
- What colour is the inside of my brain?
- What's inside of a rock? A tree? A sausage? Bones? My throat? A spider?
- Does the sky have an end to it?
- Why are my toes in front of my feet?

We smile when we read these questions. If you have children or younger siblings, they may have asked similar questions. As we grow up, somehow we do not allow ourselves to continue to ask questions. We think we should know all the answers; but obviously, we do not. Our continuing to ask questions (whatever they may be) helps us get in touch with our creativity. Do not frighten yourself at first by asking big questions, such as "What is the nature of humans?" Give yourself permission to ask small and even playful questions. Let yourself question things you have never questioned in your adult life. Complete Self-Check B on page 140.

SELF-CHECK B ✔

Now try one more exercise. Imagine you are on a roller-coaster ride. It is the tallest roller coaster in the world. Close your eyes and imagine the sensations. Feel the sense of anticipation as you travel the long distance up to the biggest drop-off you have ever seen. Feel the wind in your face as you start down the drop-off. Where's your stomach? Are you terrified? Exhilarated? Jot down your reactions.

_____

_____

_____

_____

_____

_____

Corbis/Magma Photo

Imagine the sensations you feel when you are on a roller coaster.

Lest you become too judgmental about the importance of creativity in business (and thus this whole section of the book), keep in mind that surveys show that one of the skills most wanted by organizations is creative thinking. Employers clearly understand that a successful employee is one who can creatively solve the problems he or she faces. John Kao, in a book entitled *Jamming: The Road to Creativity*, states that creativity is so necessary in the technology world that we either "create or fail."[1] According to Kao, we are going right through the Age of Information to the Age of Creativity. He suggests that companies should be auditing their staff to discover how many new ideas employees generate and who the most creative people are. An article in *Fortune*, June 11, 2001, discusses the creative surge at Microsoft: "Microsoft is getting more creative in large part because it has to." It is impossible to exaggerate the importance of creativity for all organizations and people in our fast-paced technological world.

Bring Your Personal Creativity to the Office

Begin to ask questions in your work environment. Realize that through your asking and finding answers, you may discover a more creative, more productive way to do the work of the organization. As you practise thinking creatively, you will find that you have not only successes but also huge frustrations. However, if you keep up the struggle, you will achieve a breakthrough. Often the breakthrough comes at a higher level of creativity than before. Do not lose your creativity when problems arise. You probably need it more then ever. **Aikido** (the Japanese soft martial art) teaches that you should never meet force with force. The person who breaks harmony by attacking or being aggressive in some way fails. Rather, you should move with the person rather than struggle against him or her. By moving in the same direction of the other person, you are able to effect more change than by attacking.

Now, let's look at how you can put creativity into action in developing and delivering presentations.

SELF-CHECK C ✔

Try another exercise. Select a photograph you have not looked at for a long time. Set it in good light, and get in a comfortable position. Look at the picture for five minutes. Keep your eyes on it; do not let your mind wander. After five minutes, turn away from the picture and record what you have seen.

_____

_____

_____

_____

_____

_____

_____

Do Self-Check C. Now try the same exercise with a friend. Ask your friend to look at the same photograph for five minutes and then record what he or she saw. Did your friend see exactly the same thing you saw? Probably not!

Planning a Presentation

With the team approach commonly being used in business today, an administrative professional is frequently expected to give presentations. These presentations may be informal ones to small group meetings or more formal ones to larger groups or conferences; they may also be group presentations. Presentation skills combine verbal and written communications. Developing verbal presentation skills, much like the written communication skills you covered in Chapter 6, is an ongoing process. You should strive to improve all your communication skills every day. Your understanding of and commitment to continual growth in all types of communications will increase your effectiveness in all areas of your life.

The Audience

As an administrative professional you may make presentations to three basic types of audiences.

- Co-workers in your organization
- Workplace teams containing a cross-section of people within your organization
- Colleagues within professional organizations to which you belong

The Plan

Planning means gathering and arranging your thoughts, developing your ideas, and finding unique ways to express them. Using your creativity in the process will help you put together a memorable presentation that holds the audience's attention and allows you to get your message across.

As soon as you know you are going to give a presentation, start a folder. Put whatever comes to your mind in the folder—ideas, quotations, and so on. You may even wake up in the middle of the night with an idea. Keep a pad and pencil by your bed to use in jotting down your thoughts. You do not want to forget them.

In the planning process, take the following steps.

Begin Early

A good presentation is not prepared just 30 minutes before it is given. You may get lucky and be able to deliver a presentation with little or no preparation, but that is a rarity. Do not tempt fate; begin early. You might say "I don't have time to prepare." If that is the case, then do not agree to give the presentation. Beginning preparation three weeks beforehand is not too soon. Also, by beginning early, you can spend a few minutes every day thinking about what you want to say and writing down your thoughts. Then you can come back to your ideas later and revise them or throw out material that no longer seems relevant. In other words, you have a chance to reflect on your thoughts.

Determine the Purpose

Is your purpose to inform your audience? To persuade? To inform and persuade? Spend some time determining the purpose. If you do not understand what the purpose of your presentation is, certainly no one else will. Once you have determined the purpose, write it down in one clear, concise statement. As you prepare your presentation, review the statement frequently to stay on track.

Visualize the Anticipated Audience

Who will the people be in the audience? Visualize your audience, as illustrated in Figure 7-1. For example, if your audience is a group of administrative professionals, you are familiar with their interests. You can use anecdotes or stories that will have meaning for them. Find out the age of your audience. A teenage audience will be very different from one made up of people in their fifties and sixties. Know something about the educational level and experiences of the audience. For example, if you are giving a presentation on software, you need to know what level of expertise the audience already has. You do not want to bore them by giving them information that is too elementary, nor do you want to confuse them by being too technical.

> **Communication Tip**
>
> When handouts are distributed at the beginning of a presentation, the audience can use them to make additional notes; when they are distributed at the end, the audience can comfortably focus on the presentation without feeling a need to take notes. Let your audience know.

■ Figure 7-1

VISUALIZE YOUR AUDIENCE

Find out how many people will be in the audience. Will there be 15 or 50? Numbers do make a difference. A small audience allows greater interaction; questions can be used effectively. With a large audience, there is little chance for interaction other than questions and answers at the end. If there is to be a question-and-answer period, make sure the audience has access to a microphone so everyone can hear the questions or comments. If that is not possible, repeat the question that has been asked to the audience prior to giving your response.

If you are providing handouts for the audience, you need to know the number of attendees so you have the appropriate number of handouts. Check the handouts beforehand to ensure that they do not contain errors. It would be embarrassing to discover just before the presentation that they have been incorrectly collated or that a page is missing. Decide at what point you would like your handout to be available for the audience—as they arrive or at the end of the presentation. If it will be at the end of the presentation, let the audience know so they are not distracted from your presentation by attempting to simultaneously make notes.

Also, it is a good idea to have the exact number of chairs needed for the audience. Having to add chairs after most of the audience has arrived makes you look as if you were not prepared; conversely, if you have too many chairs, it appears as though you did not have a good turnout for your presentation.

Determine the Length of the Presentation

Most presentations should be no longer than 20 minutes, with 30 to 40 minutes the maximum. Part of your task is to manage your topic; do not try to give the audience so much information that you drone on for an hour or more. People's attention spans are not that long; you will lose your audience.

Generally speaking, 175 words (or three-quarters of a keyed, double-spaced page) equals one minute of talking time. A 15- or 20-minute talk will be about 10 to 12 keyed pages.

Gather the Material

Research the topic if necessary in the library or on the Web. Do original research if needed. For example, you may want your audience to know how a certain group feels about a particular idea. If so, send a survey to a targeted group for their responses.

Construct an Outline

An outline should consist of an introduction, a body, and a conclusion. In the introduction, you tell your audience what you are going to say. In the body, you give them the information. In the closing, you remind them of what you said by giving a summary. In other words, you tell the audience the important points of your presentation three times. This repetition increases the chances that the audience will understand and remember what you said. Figure 7-2 illustrates a sample outline.

■ Figure 7-2

PRESENTATION OUTLINE

I. Introduction
   A. Opening statement to gain attention
      1. Development of opening statement
      2. Supporting material
   B. Second introductory point (if needed)

II. Body
   A. First main idea
      1. First supporting point
      2. Second supporting point
   B. Second main idea
      1. First supporting point
      2. Second supporting point
   C. Third main idea
      1. First supporting point
      2. Second supporting point

III. Conclusion
   A. Summary
   B. Application or challenge and final statement

Writing the Presentation

Once you have planned adequately, you are ready to begin the writing process. Your writing tasks include

- Developing an opening
- Using language well
- Developing an appropriate conclusion
- Preparing visual aids

Develop an Opening

The opening should immediately get the audience's attention. You might tell a story, use a quotation, ask a question, or refer to a current event. Begin with the unexpected and the unpredictable. Also, know what you do best. If you are a good joke teller, you might open with a joke. However, if you are not, avoid jokes like the plague. Nothing can be worse than starting a presentation with a joke that is in poor taste and offends someone in the audience or a joke that the audience does not think is funny. If you tell stories well, tell one. Not only should the opening get the audience's attention, it should also help you relax with your audience. Plan your opening well and open with something you do well. When you determine how you are going to open your presentation, ask yourself these questions:

- Is there a link between the story and the presentation?
- Is it a new story or joke? You do not want to relay one the audience has heard numerous times.
- Am I telling it as succinctly as possible? You do not want to spend one-third of your time on your opening story.
- If it is a joke, am I timing the punch line to elicit a laugh?

Then, as a transition from your opening into the presentation itself, outline the main points of your presentation—the audience needs to know what you are presenting.

Use Language Well

Nothing is more disconcerting than discovering that people are nodding off while you are talking. Obviously, you are not getting your message across in an interesting fashion. One technique that will help you get your message across is to involve the audience. People are always interested in their own concerns. When you know who the audience will be, think about how you can establish a link with them. For example, if the audience is a group of administrative professionals, what concerns does the audience have in common? Make your major points, relating those points to experiences both you and the audience have had.

Another technique that will help you is to refer to people, not to abstractions. Use interesting facts, figures, and quotations. For example, if you are giving a motivational talk on the importance of service, you might use the following quote from Mother Teresa: "Love cannot remain by itself—it has no meaning. Love has to be put into action and that action is service."

Use the active rather than the passive voice. Do not say "It is believed ..."; say "I believe. ..." Talk in a conversational tone. Talk *with*, not at the audience. Use the same tone you would use when trying to persuade someone who is sitting across the table from you at a dinner party. Be animated; if you do not appear to be interested in what you are saying, the audience certainly will not be. Never speak in a monotone; vary your tone of voice. Vary your expressions. A commanding speaker is

- Sincere
- Credible
- Concerned
- Enthusiastic
- Energetic
- Intense
- Knowledgeable

Develop an Appropriate Conclusion

Your conclusion should summarize the points made in your presentation and leave the audience feeling motivated to respond in the way you intended. Remember, your conclusion is the final impression you will make on the audience. Be forceful and positive. When summarizing, state the points in slightly different ways. You might also suggest a challenge to the audience, propose a solution to a situation, or use a compelling quote.

Prepare Visual Aids

Used properly, visual aids can greatly enhance the presentation. People remember 40 percent more when they hear and see something simultaneously. Many people today use presentation software, such as Microsoft

PowerPoint or Corel Presentations, to present visuals. Either of these software programs is easy to use and extremely effective. A section later in this chapter is devoted to the effective use of presentation software.

Once the presentation is written, put it aside for a day or two; then go back over it. Does the speech fit the anticipated audience? Does it meet the purpose? Is the opening creative? Will it get the audience's attention? Have you used stories and quotes appropriately and spaced them throughout the presentation? Remember, if you involve the audience, they will learn. A well-selected story or quote can involve the audience. Is the presentation the proper length? Remember, it is better to be too brief than too long. (The American president Abraham Lincoln delivered one of that nation's most celebrated addresses— the Gettysburg Address—in less than five minutes.) Are your visual aids effective? Are you using an appropriate number of visuals? Do you need to rewrite any parts?

Preparing to Give the Presentation

The Rehearsal

Rehearse the presentation just as you are going to give it. For example, if you will be standing at a lectern during the presentation, stand at a lectern during your rehearsal. If you are going to be using a microphone, use a microphone during your rehearsal. Ask a respected colleague to listen to your practice session and provide constructive criticism. If none of these options is practical, practise in front of a mirror. Go over your presentation completely three or four times. Speak slowly—you will speed up instinctively during the presentation itself. With repeated rehearsals, the text becomes part of your memory; you will be more at ease, since you are not likely to forget an important point during the presentation.

Appropriate Dress

The usual attire for a woman is a suit or dress; for a man, it is a suit and tie. Wear something you are comfortable in and that looks good on you. Bright colours are perfectly okay. Women should avoid necklaces and earrings that are too large and distracting. Rings and bracelets are appropriate, but women should not wear noisy bracelets, which distract audience members. Men

Photodisc Red/Photodisc Collection

Rehearse your presentation before a group of respected colleagues; ask for their constructive criticism.

may wear coloured shirts and bright ties. The colour of the suit should look good on the man. Men should not wear gold bracelets and a number of rings; they are distracting to the audience. Hair for both men and women should be well groomed and should not be in the eyes.

Presentation Room Check

If you have not visited the room where you will make your presentation, do so. Know how the room will be set up. Find out where the lectern is going to be if you are using one. Be certain you have the visuals in order; check them out on the actual equipment you will be using. Be sure you know how to use the equipment; if you are at all uncomfortable with it, ask a colleague to demonstrate. If you are giving a presentation with presentation visuals, be sure all the equipment is working properly and is placed so the audience can see your presentation.

Fear Control

First of all, realize that nervousness is normal. Even the professionals experience it. Kim Basinger is known for her stage fright; so is Barbra Streisand. In fact, one of the greatest fears individuals have (as shown in surveys) is the fear of speaking before an audience. Some of the things you have already learned to do will help you control nervousness—preparation and rehearsal. A well-prepared and well-rehearsed presentation can eliminate many of your fears. You know who your audience is, what you intend to say, and how you will say it.

The Day Before the Presentation

Remind yourself that you have prepared well. You have followed all of the steps mentioned previously; that is,

beginning early, determining the purpose of the presentation, rehearsing, and so on. Burn off some of your nervousness by exercising. Try not to push yourself to the limit with work responsibilities the few days before your presentation; when you are overly tired, you increase your chances of not doing a good job.

The Day of the Presentation

Arrive early enough to check out the microphone, the equipment, and the layout of the room. If changes need to be made, find someone who can assist you in making the changes.

In the 10 or 15 minutes before your presentation is to begin, find a private place (maybe a small room away from the gathering audience) and try these relaxation techniques:

- Say these four sentences several times to yourself:
  1. I'm glad I'm here.
  2. I'm glad you're here.
  3. I care about you.
  4. I know that I know.
- Sit in a straight chair, carry your ribcage high, and breathe deeply. As you exhale, push the air over your lower teeth in a ssss sound. Focus your efforts entirely on your breathing.
- Walk around. Take a brisk walk for a minute or two. Do some jumping jacks.
- Realize that some nervousness can help you. You can channel this nervousness into your talk, and it will become a positive energy source that adds to your effectiveness.
- Compose your thoughts.
- Right before you enter the room, swing your arms a few times.

As You Begin Your Presentation

- Walk slowly to the lectern. Arrange your note cards, look at the audience for a few seconds, and then begin.
- Realize that the audience is much less aware of your nervousness than you are. Also, realize that the audience is your friend; the audience wants you to succeed.
- Do not draw attention to your hands, which may be shaking as you begin. For example, instead of holding a hand microphone, leave the mike on a stand. Do not hold a glass of water. Leave your notes on the lectern; you do not want to call attention to shaking papers.

During the Presentation

During the presentation, observe the nonverbal feedback from the audience. Puzzled looks or blank stares are cues that the audience does not understand what you are saying. You may need to modify the rate of your voice or give another example or two to clarify what you mean. Smiles and nodding heads are positive reactions.

Maintain eye contact with the audience. If you are in a small group, look at each individual briefly. When you are in a large group, move your eyes from one side of the room to the other, concentrating for a period of time on each portion of the room. Use natural gestures. You may use your arms and hands to emphasize points. However, avoid too many arm and hand gestures; they can be distracting to the audience. Be natural; do not perform. Speak in a normal tone of voice; vary your tone; do not speak too fast. However, do not speak too slowly either; speaking too slowly can result in a bored listener. Articulate carefully. For example, do not drop your g's; say *learning*, not *learnin'*.

Presentation Critique

After you have finished delivering your presentation, critique what happened. Either evaluate yourself or have someone else evaluate you. You might want to videotape your presentation to help you in the critiquing process. You may also want to provide evaluation forms for the people in the audience. In critiquing yourself:

- Be kind. List the good along with the not-so-good.
- Do not try to solve too many problems at once. Pick one or two things to improve each time.
- Realize evaluation is an ongoing process.
- Build yourself up by thinking about how much you have improved.
- Get feedback from other people; really listen to the feedback. If someone compliments you, believe it.

Team Presentations

You have already learned that teams are being used extensively in businesses today and that team writing or presentation assignments require collaborative planning. The techniques presented for creating individual presentations in the previous section still apply, but in addition to knowing the purpose of your presentation, the people who will be in attendance, and how long the presentation should be, you need to take these steps:

- **Brainstorm** (that is, engage in problem solving) what the presentation should include and how it will be presented. (See Chapter 6, Figure 6-13 for brainstorming techniques.)
- Decide who will present which part of the presentation.
- Determine how you will make the transition from one speaker to another. It is usually a good idea for the speaker finishing to mention the next speaker's name.
- Practise your presentation as a group.
- If a PowerPoint presentation is going to be done, determine who will be in charge of it and who will actually key the presentation.
- Determine what the attire will be; each speaker should dress in a similar fashion.
- Determine how the group will be seated before the presentation begins and after each presentation is finished. For example, will there be a table with chairs for the speakers or will the speakers sit on a stage? In what order should the speakers sit? Generally the first speaker should be closest to the podium.

Electronic Presentations

You have already learned that individuals remember 40 percent more of a presentation when they both hear and see the information that is presented. Presentation software allows you to provide images for the audience.

PowerPoint is a widely used Microsoft software presentation package. Other software packages are available that assist you in creating visuals for your presentation, such as Photoshop, CorelDRAW™, Presentations®, or Acrobat®. Free presentation software is also available on the Web. However, since PowerPoint and Presentations are used so extensively and come bundled with Microsoft's Office Suite or Corel's WordPerfect Office package, either of which you may have on your computer, they are the packages referenced here. You can produce the following types of materials with PowerPoint or Presentations:

- Slides
- Handouts

- Speaker's notes
- Outlines
- Sounds and images
- Charts and spreadsheets

Your presentation materials are displayed to the audience on a computer screen or a projection system. Unless your audience is very small (three or four people who can gather around a computer), you should use a large projection screen.

You can also establish links to websites within your presentation. For example, assume you are doing a presentation on Chinese culture. You can use a weblink to show some of the historical sites in China. You can also use the presentation program to establish a virtual seminar by placing a number of Presentations or PowerPoint presentations from various presenters on the Web.

Here are some of the features these software programs offer in helping to make your presentation a powerful visual one:

> **Technology Tip**
>
> Apply special effects such as animation, transition, and sound in electronic presentations appropriately. Too many special effects can distract your audience.

- *Colour.* The use of colour adds interest to your presentation—hundreds of colour schemes are available for you to use to make professional-looking slides.
- *Clip art.* Clip-art collections are included with both PowerPoint and Presentations. However, if you do not find what you need there, you can purchase clip-art software or download clip art from the Web.
- *Movies and sound clips.* Through the use of multimedia technology, both Presentations and PowerPoint accept movies and sound clips, allowing you to see and hear a movie image on the screen.

Although preparing a visual presentation is more time-consuming than merely preparing a presentation without visuals, doing so is worth the effort if done well. Effective visuals will ensure that your audience learns and retains more from your presentation. Tips for preparing your presentation visuals are given in Figure 7-3.

■ Figure 7-3

TIPS FOR PREPARING PRESENTATION VISUALS

- Keep the text to a minimum on each slide. Make your points in as few words as possible. Do not put more than three or four points on each slide.
- Determine how many graphics you should have. You want to have enough graphics but not too many. Generally, you should not have more than one graphic for each slide.
- Use colour to enhance the slide; however, do not use a very dark colour. Dark colours make it more difficult to see the material.
- The visual presentation should be consistent. For example, typestyles should be the same for all major points; minor points may be in a different typestyle. However, do not use more than two different typestyles. (A slide looks cluttered when you use too many.)
- Make certain the visual can be seen and read

from all parts of the room. If your audience is large, you may need two screens, with one screen on one side of the room and the other screen on the other side of the room.
- Proofread the slide carefully. Errors are embarrassing, and they detract from your presentation, making the audience wonder about your attention to detail.
- Practise using the visual slides before the presentation.
- Make certain all equipment is in good working order.
- Make certain you know how to operate all equipment.
- Face the audience—talk to them not to the projected slide.
- Stand to the side of the slide when you are showing it.

Chapter Summary

The summary will help you remember the important points covered in the chapter.

- Develop and use your creativity when preparing presentations.
- To help you release your creativity, have faith in your creativity, destroy judgment, look and listen, and ask questions.
- Bring your personal creativity to the office.
- When planning presentations, begin early, determine the purpose, visualize the anticipated audience, determine the length of the presentation, gather the material, and construct an outline.
- When writing presentations, develop an opening, use language well, develop an appropriate conclusion, and prepare visual aids.
- Before giving the presentation, rehearse it several times.
- Conquer your fears. Nervousness is normal; however, you should always take steps to conquer your fears. Be well prepared and well rehearsed.
- During the presentation, watch for nonverbal feedback from the audience and maintain eye contact with the audience throughout.
- Use PowerPoint or some other presentation software to prepare a visual presentation. By providing the audience with images, you will help them remember 40 percent more of what you say.
- Once the presentation is over, do your own critique of it or have a trusted friend evaluate you.
- Team presentations require collaborative planning; this collaborative planning should include brainstorming to release the creativity of the group.

Key Terms

The following terms were introduced in this chapter. The page on which the term was introduced is provided to help you locate the new term. Definitions are compiled in the Glossary at the end of the text.

- **creativity** 138
- **aikido** 140
- **brainstorm** 146

Discussion Items

These discussion items provide an opportunity to test your understanding of the chapter through written responses and/or discussion with your classmates and your instructor:

1. Define creativity and give four steps for helping to release the creativity that exists within you.
2. List the planning steps involved in developing a presentation.
3. List some steps you might take to conquer your presentation fears.
4. Identify five techniques for preparing effective electronic presentations or slides that you consider most important. Explain why.

Critical-Thinking Activity

Your supervisor, Mr. Albertson, has become obsessed with acquiring the latest technology—whatever it may be. However, he never gets training for himself. He expects you to be able to solve the problem he is having with the technology he has acquired. If you cannot solve it, he gets angry. Applying the Aikido concept, what are some things you might do in this situation?

Projects

Project 7-1 *(Objective 1)*

Collaborative Project

Divide up into groups of four or five. Decide who will be the "starter" for the group. For example, the starter may be the person with the longest hair, the bluest eyes, or the youngest person. The purpose of this activity is to learn to release your creativity. Once the starter is determined, he or she begins a story. As a departure point, use this starter: "Everyone knows that Dorothy (in the Wizard of Oz) travelled down the Yellow Brick Road to the land of Oz. However, did you know that the land of Oz was actually on the moon and that the Yellow Brick Road was made of numerous moon crystals that glistened and even 'spoke' to Dorothy, giving her directions as she made her way to the land of Oz? In fact, these crystals sang a song in 'moon language' that went like this: 'Dorothy, Dorothy, follow this path. Run with us into the unknown. You can do it, you can, you can.'"

From this point, each person within the group is to add a little-known fact about Dorothy to the story. Tape your story if a recorder is available, and play it for the class.

Once you have finished the story, each person should discuss how he or she felt during this process. Was it difficult to be spontaneous? If so, why? Did you have trouble thinking of little-known facts? If so, why? Listen to each other carefully. Develop a list as a group of how creativity can be encouraged and released.

Project 7-2 *(Objectives 2 and 3)*

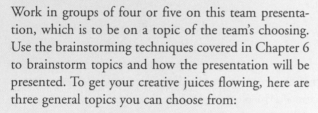

Collaborative Project

Work in groups of four or five on this team presentation, which is to be on a topic of the team's choosing. Use the brainstorming techniques covered in Chapter 6 to brainstorm topics and how the presentation will be presented. To get your creative juices flowing, here are three general topics you can choose from:

- Women in Management
- Diversity in Canada (or another area)
- The Future Workplace

The presentation is to be from 15 to 20 minutes in length; each team member is responsible for a portion of the presentation that is to be delivered verbally to the class. If you have the necessary software available to you, prepare a presentation using PowerPoint or some other presentation software. Your class members are to evaluate your presentation. An evaluation form appears on the Student CD, file SCDP7-2a. Run copies for your classmates, and distribute them before you begin your presentation. Your instructor will collect the evaluation forms at the end of your presentation and give them to you for review. What can you learn from the evaluation forms? Write a memorandum to your instructor, using the memorandum form on the Student CD, file SCDP7-2b. Detail the strengths and weaknesses of your presentation as revealed by the evaluation forms and as seen by your group. Use these headings in your memorandum: (1) Group Opinion of Strengths and Weaknesses of Presentation and (2) Class Members' Opinion of Strengths and Weaknesses of Presentation.

Chapter 8

Telecommunications

LEARNING OBJECTIVES

1. Discover how information is transmitted electronically.
2. *Recognize the importance of e-mail ethics.*
3. Develop and use proper telephone techniques.

Although the word is sometimes not understood, we actually use **telecommunications** daily. For example, you are using telecommunication technology not only when you access the Internet and send e-mail, but also when you use the fax and the telephone. Telecommunications is "the electronic transmission of text, data, voice, video, and image (graphics and pictures) from one location to another."

Today the telecommunication field is involved in a revolution that is rapidly changing the traditional ways we have employed these services. For example, systems are being developed that break down the barriers between the computer and the telephone, allowing us to communicate with anyone at any time by land lines or wirelessly—such as the integration of cell phones and PDAs (personal digital assistants), with wireless Internet access. The revolution promises to change and expand drastically our telecommunication capabilities.

This chapter is designed to help you understand the relationships between various telecommunication technologies, and envision what the future holds in store. For your day-to-day activities as an administrative professional in the workplace of the 21st century, an understanding of the human element of telecommunications is also important. We must never forget that a human being is on the receiving end of our communication. Additionally, there are ethical issues in telecommunications that demand our attention.

Telecommunications—The Revolution

Traditional telephone companies are in the process of transforming themselves from delivering a service that only connects people to people to one that connects *people to people and people to machines* through a wide range of telecommunication devices. Organizations that we never before thought of as providing telephone service are getting into the market. For example, computer companies such as Compaq®, Hewlett Packard®, and Dell™ are now providing telephone access through computers with the assistance of software. Additionally, telecommunication companies are merging with companies that are in a different business (for example, the merger between AOL and Time Warner) to garner more of the market and provide a variety of services. In other words, the market lines between companies have become blurred. Gone are the days when one super-monopoly owned the whole network support infrastructure. Couple these directions with the technology becoming available through **broadband** (short for "broad bandwidth") or fibre optics and there is indeed a revolution in the field. Broadband allows phenomenal changes in what can be sent to people from machines. Websites are available that move, talk, and sing. The information available from these sites can be sent to numerous machines—computers, cell phones, PDAs, televisions, and any combination of these. Consider what the following statements on the TELUS website tell us about its directions for the future:

We are not the same company we were a few years ago. We've made changes that will continue to transform us over the months ahead. These changes are focused on:

- *Our Customers—Faster, more efficient, customized and convergent solutions for our customers that integrate data, IP and wireless technologies.*
- *Our Strategic Intent—"Unleashing the power of Internet technologies to deliver the best solutions for Canadians at home, in the workplace and on the move."—Darren Entwistle, President and CEO*
- *Our Growth—Telus is focused on the high growth areas of wireless and data/IP.[1]*

To better understand some of the telecommunication terms, refer to Figure 8-1 on page 152.

In redefining themselves and providing a variety of new services, the traditional telephone companies, along with new service providers entering the market, are using a number of telecommunication pipelines—especially cable, DSL, fixed wireless, satellite, and ISDN. Analog dial-up (the traditional pipeline) is still with us, but the future is expected to bring a drastic decrease in its use. Broadband encompasses many different technologies—some mainstream, some **moribund** (dying), and some immature at the present time.

In addition to making more information available at faster speeds through pipelines, the broadband revolution is about making the information easier to retrieve when it gets to the other end. For example, **Bluetooth**™ (named for a 10th-century Danish king), a new technology standard for short-range wireless communication, uses microwave radio to transmit data over short distances. It thus can help laptops communicate with printers, cell phones with headsets, palms with vending machines, and each of these devices with the Internet. Bluetooth was developed by a consortium of companies including Ericsson®, IBM, Intel, Lucent®, Microsoft, Motorola®, Nokia®, 3Com®, Sharp, and Toshiba®. Presently, at least one company is working on a way to let people buy sodas from a vending machine simply by clicking on a PDA.

A discussion of broadband is given in the next section. Although you are not expected to have a detailed knowledge of the telecommunication pipelines, a general understanding will help you be conversant with the terminology and direction of telecommunications.

Analog Dial-Up

Modem technology that uses analog dial-up has been around for many years. The modem allows computers to communicate with each other by converting their

Dick Hemingway

The future will provide us with increased wireless communication possibilities.

digital communications into an analog format to travel through the public phone network. Then the information is changed back to a digital format that the computer can understand. The word *modem* is an acronym that stands for "modulate/demodulate." A computer modem "modulates" data so it can be transmitted on telephone lines in analog form, and it "demodulates" incoming signals so the computer's digital processor can understand them. Modems exist in the computer, and a regular telephone line connects the modem from the computer to the external telephone line.

While a modem technology represents the slowest of the technologies available today, in some areas of the country it is the only method of connecting to the Internet. Despite its slower speed, it has some advantages over the newer technologies:

- It is less expensive than other telecommunication pipelines.
- Dial-up is available everywhere phone lines are available.
- A modem is safer. It does not stay on 24 hours a day as other broadband connections do. Since your computer spends less time connected to the Internet, it is safer from computer hackers. Other broadband technologies discussed here are "always on," meaning the user does not have to dial in to the server and wait for a connection (as is presently the case with AOL). However, even though computer hackers are definite threats to "always on" pipelines, it is possible to protect companies and individuals by means of firewalls.

TELECOMMUNICATION TERMS

- **Backbone.** The part of the network used as the main path for carrying traffic between network endpoints.
- **Broadband.** Short for broad bandwidth. A high-speed network able to carry video as well as voice. Bandwidth describes the throughput of a network per unit of time, measured in kilobits, megabits, or gigabits per second.
- **Crosstalk.** Interference on analog lines created by cables that are too close together.
- **Firewall.** Software or hardware that filters or blocks traffic from a public or private network, preventing unauthorized or unrecognized access.
- **Packet-switched network.** One in which each signal, whether it carries music or video or e-mail, is chopped into tiny digital parcels that are commingled with hordes of other packets, routed to their destinations, and then reassembled. The Internet is a packet network. The phone system is a circuit network, in which each signal travels unbroken on its own end-to-end pipe.
- **Streaming media.** In theory, this means taking in information as it arrives, as opposed to waiting until all of it has reached your computer—like listening to radio or watching television but with a signal that travels over the Internet. The quality of streaming media is not excellent at present, but it is getting better as bandwidth increases.
- **VoIP (voice over Internet protocol).** Software and hardware that allow voice signals to be carried over an IP-based network, with "plain old telephone service" (POTS) quality and reliability.
- **VPN (virtual private network).** An authentication, encryption, and data-packaging technology that lets private network traffic travel over the public networks.
- **Walled garden.** The practice by which an Internet service giant such as AOL gives customers easier access to its own and its partners' content than to that of its competitors.
- **WLL (wireless local loop).** A broadband connection system that uses high-frequency radio links to deliver voice and data.

Cable

Cable is another way of accessing the Internet. A **cable modem** is an external device that connects to the computer and to a service provider's coaxial cable line. Although cable has been available for years as a modem for TV sets, these cable modems were not designed for data traffic, particularly high-speed data traffic. Also, they were designed only for one-way communications from television programmers to consumers; Internet communications require two-way service. Thus, the cable has required extensive upgrading. In Canada there has been strong growth in Internet connections by cable. In 2001 approximately 1.75 million or 30 per-cent of all households accessed the Internet regularly from home by means of a cable connection.[2] Industry experts forecast 1.5 million subscribers by 2007.[3] Many rural areas, however, may not have cable broadband for a long period of time, if ever.

Cable is fast. Figure 8-2 on page 153 shows a comparison of the download time and some of the pros and cons of the different broadband technologies. Notice that with cable, the time to download a 10 MB file is 1.4 minutes as against an analog time of 28.4 minutes. However, cable is not consistently fast. Because cable modems use shared connections, they are prone to slowdowns if too many users along a particular stretch happen to be online. Speedy access is never guaranteed at any given time.

DSL

DSL (digital subscriber line) superficially is much like cable. It is fast and it uses wires that run to the organization or home. However, these are the only similarities. DSL users report more consistent speed than cable users. Notice in Figure 8-2 that the download time for a 10 MB file is approximately the same as for cable—1.8 minutes as opposed to 1.4 minutes. DSL is available in **ADSL (asymmetric digital subscriber line)**, **SDSL (symmetric digital subscriber line)**, or **IDSL (Internet digital subscriber line)**. In most cases, ADSL and SDSL connections must be located within 18 000 feet of the service provider's central office. Consequently, they tend to be most widely available in urban and thickly populated suburban areas. ADSL download rates are higher than for the other two, but upload rates are capped at lower rates. The faster the rate desired, the more expensive the service. The majority of DSL users are businesses that already have telephone service in place. Most of the time DSL service can be purchased from the same company that provides telephone service to the business. However, the local telephone company does not have a monopoly on DSL service; it is available from multiple providers. Accord... Survey conducted in... nect to the Internet us... on page 154 illustrates h...

Fixed Wireless

Fixed wireless, or **WLL (wireless**
nology is making the transfer of data
available at relatively fast transfer spe...
Figure 8-2 that the download transfer t... ...ed
wireless is 2.7 minutes for a 10 MB file, slightly slower than cable and DSL but faster than satellite or analog. However, before presenting more information on fixed wireless, a distinction needs to be made between fixed and mobile wireless.

Mobile wireless service has been available for a period of time; it is the technology used for cell phones. **Cellular technology**, or **mobile wireless service**, breaks a large service area down into smaller areas called *cells*. When a customer places a call from a mobile unit, the nearest cell or transmitting station relays it to a central computer that in turn directs the call into the local telephone system.

■ Figure 8-2

PIPELINE COMPARISONS

Technology	Time to Download 10 MB File (minutes)	Pros	Cons
Analog dial-up	28.4 min	Cheapest Internet connection.	Provides a fraction of broadband speed.
Cable	1.4 min	Very quick downloads; comparatively quick installation.	Limited upload speed; bandwidth sharing can degrade performance.
DSL	1.8 min	Variable-bandwidth services can be tailored to your needs and budget.	Higher bandwidth tends to cost more; long waits for installation at present time.
Fixed wireless	2.7 min	Nice, if available.	Not yet widely available.
Satellite	3.4 min	New bidirectional services bring DSL-like speeds to rural users.	One-way service, though inexpensive, requires dial-up modem for uploads.

Source: Scott Spanbauer, "Cable vs. DSL vs. Everything Else," *PC World*, January 2001, 94–95.

DSL WORKS

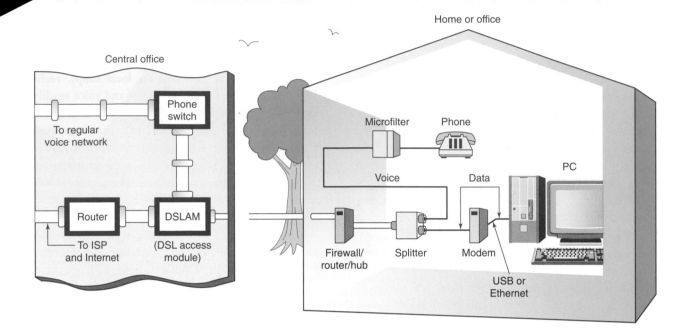

When a customer leaves one cell area and enters another, the computer automatically switches the transmission to the next nearest cell.

Today, voice communications and messaging are no longer sufficient for businesses and consumers. Access to the Internet, and through it to corporate networks, is now just as important. Although the speed of such data transfer is slow at present, new mobile wireless technology is being introduced that includes voice (with improved quality), messaging, location tracing, and data transmission. This technology may make mobile wireless a contender in the broadband market.

Fixed wireless technology is simpler than mobile wireless because it does not involve client devices moving in and out of coverage areas. WLL is offered primarily to businesses and homes in areas where the infrastructure is not in place to deliver broadband through cable or DSL. Data is converted to wireless signals and relayed to customers through a network of transceivers mounted on utility poles, street lights, and so on. Each subscriber has a small radio receiver and directional antenna oriented toward the nearest microcell. Fixed wireless offers a short installation time, greater installation flexibility, and performance equal to or greater than that of many wire line options. WLL costs more per month than cable or DSL; however, as more organizations and people subscribe, equipment prices should fall. Figure 8-4 on page 155 illustrates how fixed wireless works.

SELF-CHECK A ✓

1. How is the telecommunication revolution changing how we live and work?

_____

_____

_____

_____

2. Explain how traditional telephone providers are changing their services.

_____

_____

_____

3. Explain the differences between cable, DSL, and fixed wireless.

_____

_____

_____

_____

Figure 8-4

HOW FIXED WIRELESS (WLL) WORKS

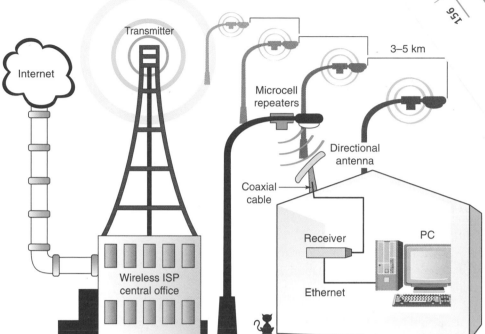

Source: Casimir Medford, "Pipe Dreams," *PC Magazine*, February 6, 2001, 156.

Satellite

Although satellite service has disadvantages over cable and DSL in its higher cost, the degrading of transmission due to heavy rain or high wind, and download time, it is the only broadband service presently available for a number of homes and businesses, particularly those in rural areas. In fact, it is projected that it will be almost ten years before the majority of homes and businesses will be wired for other broadband services. Since satellite is a shared service, as more people use the service, the speeds will inevitably be slower. However, companies are working to increase bandwidth and thus the upload and download times. Presently, satellite is slower than cable, DSL, and fixed wireless on download time at 3.4 minutes for a 10 MB file.

Before you move on to the next section, take a few minutes to reflect on your understanding of the telecommunication technology that has been described here and answer the questions in Self-Check A on the previous page. Check your answers with those at the end of this chapter.

Fax

One telecommunications device that has been in use for a period of time is the "facsimile" or **fax machine**, which electronically sends an image of a document from one location to another via communication networks. It has become a standard piece of office equipment. Of course, some documents that in the past would have been sent by fax are now being sent by e-mail at less cost; but if you are sending a document that is only available in hard copy, fax remains a viable option. Fax machines often include some combination of printing, copying, and scanning functions. The multifunction machines are inexpensive and particularly useful in teleworker environments where cost and space are considerations.

Confidential documents and documents that should be seen only by certain individuals within the organization should not be faxed—for example, ones that include sensitive personal information (social insurance numbers, evaluations, terminations, salaries) and financial statements, contracts, legal matters, etc.

...communications has revolutionized the way we communicate. Most correspondence to individuals within an organization today is written as **e-mail** (electronic mail). E-mail is also used extensively in the home. For many families it is the communication method of choice. It allows them immediate access, at a reasonable cost, to family members who may be scattered across the world. In fact, some e-mail services are free, and others have only a low monthly cost. Also, with the emergence of the digital camera, family photos can be sent electronically as attachments to e-mail messages. Additionally, students use e-mail as a communication tool with their peers and their instructors.

An elaboration of e-mail is IM (instant messaging), by which a line keyed on one computer is seen almost instantly in a window that appears in one corner of the screen of the recipient(s). IM avoids the delay of e-mail, which can stay unanswered for days if an individual does not check his or her inbox. AOL was the first to market

> ### Technology Tip
> Ethical practices must be followed when e-mail messages are sent.

> ### Technology Tip
> Do not use e-mail to send information that involves any type of legal action.

IM in the form of "buddy lists." Now other vendors have come into the market. In 2001, more than 60 million people worldwide were using IM regularly. It is projected that by 2004, approximately 7 billion people per day will use IM.

Concerns do exist in the workplace about IM. For example, it opens up potential security loopholes in office computer networks. Workers may tap IM for corporate business, chatting with a fellow employee about an issue and possibly sending company secrets across public networks.

You learned in Chapter 6 that when e-mail messages are sent in the workplace, e-mail guidelines and etiquette must be considered. In addition, e-mail ethics are also a very important consideration.

Telephones

As you have learned, the entire telecommunication field is changing quickly. Telephones in the past have used **POTS (plain old telephone service)** that carries signals

---

Soft Skills: E-mail Ethics

Throughout this course, there has been an emphasis on ethics, with the hope that you will understand its importance and accept the responsibility of behaving ethically. Although e-mail is fairly new, there is a growing body of ethical issues connected with the use of and responses to e-mail. Here are some suggestions for maintaining a solid ethical stance:

- Do not send personal e-mail from your office computer, as this takes time away from your work. Some companies have developed policies for e-mail usage—be aware of the policy at your firm.
- When people send you inappropriate e-mail, let them know politely that you cannot receive it. You might say, "I would enjoy hearing from you, but please send any personal e-mail to my home."
- Do not use e-mail to berate or reprimand an employee.
- Do not use e-mail to terminate someone.
- Do not use e-mail to send information that involves any type of legal action; third parties that should have no knowledge of the action may obtain the information.

- Do not forward junk mail or chain letters; both are inappropriate in an office.
- Do not forward unwanted or junk e-mail to a mailing list. This practice is known as **spamming**, and some organizations have established e-mail policies that result in loss of computer privileges for individuals who engage in spamming.
- Do not forward an e-mail unless you know it is true. For example, you may think you are being helpful forwarding a message about a computer virus. However, when you receive ten e-mail messages concerning misinformation about the viruses, you understand the importance of being certain that an e-mail is true before forwarding it.
- Do not include credit card numbers in e-mail messages. E-mail can be intercepted in transit; an unscrupulous individual can use a valid credit card number.
- Do not criticize or insult third parties.

Some organizations have even developed codes of ethics for using e-mail. Figure 8-5 on page 157 shows a portion of the code of ethics for Massey University.

■ **Figure 8-5**

CODE OF ETHICS FOR THE USE OF ELECTRONIC MAIL AT MASSEY UNIVERSITY

Forged e-mail. No electronic mail may be sent so as to appear to originate from another person, with the intention of thereby deceiving the recipient or recipients.

Menacing e-mail. No electronic mail may be sent that is abusive or threatens the safety of a person or persons.

Harassing e-mail. No electronic mail may be sent such that a person or persons thereby suffers sexual, ethnic, religious or other minority harassment or in contravention of the Human Rights Act 1993. The charge of harassment may be based on the content of the electronic mail sent or its volume or both.

Privacy of e-mail. No person may access or attempt to access electronic mail sent to another user, without the permission of that user, except when necessary as part of that person's duties in respect of the operation of the electronic mail system.

Privacy Act. No electronic mail may be sent that contravenes the rights of a person or persons under the Privacy Act 1993.

Source: "Code of Ethics for the Use of Electronic Mail," *Policy on the Use of Electronic Mail at Massey University,* its.massey.ac.nz/policies/email_policy.pdf, accessed July 14, 2004.

through standard line technology that has been in existence for years. Today, however, broadband technology, with its numerous pipelines for sending and receiving video, sound, text, and graphics, is providing options that have not been available in the past. One technology that promises to change telephone service drastically is *voice over Internet protocol (VoIP)*. By routing phone calls over the Internet, VoIP will be a focal point of the commingling of voice and data. It also has the capacity to change our notion of what a phone company is and how the Internet works. You learned earlier in this chapter that telephone service providers are changing drastically, with new players in the market that have never before been considered telephone providers. With IP, Internet service providers become telephone providers also. Here are some examples of this concept.

- With call waiting, a subscriber surfing the Web will see a small window pop up identifying callers and showing what they want.
- Cisco's® IP phone will include a virtual assistant who can screen calls and send them to you or to voice mail, depending on the caller.
- The Internet will be permeated by voice. Chat in chat rooms will gain new meaning when you can click on someone's Web or e-mail address and start talking instead of keying.

Additionally, software such as NetMeeting® or CUseeMe® and digital video cameras allow us to see each other over our PC monitors while we are talking.

Today many of the Internet-based telephone services offer free PC-to-phone or PC-to-PC calls from almost any place in the world. It is predicted that free service will soon be available all over the globe. In addition, for those individuals who do not want the potential inconvenience of being tethered to a computer, many vendors sell phone cards, which allow phone-to-phone traffic to be routed over the Internet. When using phone cards, however, you may incur additional connection fees and per-minute fees, in addition to possibly paying phone surcharges. Technological advances will continue to push this field, with new services available in the future. Internet-based telephone services also make it possible to enjoy video-phoning and videoconferencing options.

Multifunction units are beginning to be used that are a combination of cell-phone technology and data technology, available through a wireless pipeline. Disposable cell phones are being marketed, by which it is possible to make a few calls at a relatively low cost and throw away the cell phone after use.

Cell phones, combination cell phones and PDAs, videophoning and conferencing, and voice technology will be discussed in the next section. However, regardless of what happens with the technology, human beings must be able to use it well, and organizations must be better able to meet the needs of their clients and customers through the technology. Thus, good human relations remain crucial. If administrative professionals are to succeed in this world, they must constantly improve their communications and human relations skills.

Communication Tip

Good human relations remain extremely important as the needs of clients and customers are facilitated through the use of technology.

Cell Phones

Cell (cellular) phones, which use mobile wireless technology (discussed above), have become standard equipment for most people, in both their work life and their home life. Between 1995 and 2001 the number of cellular subscribers in Canada grew from 2.6 million to 10.9 million.[5] It is estimated that by 2005, more than 500 million people will be using cell phones internationally. As a population, we enjoy the ability to send and receive calls from any location at any time. In fact, cell phones are so popular that many people carry one with them constantly, whether for business or personal use. It is common to see people making calls from airplanes and theatres; so common, in fact, that many theatres now make an announcement asking people to turn off their cell phones before the show and restaurants and hospitals also post signs asking patrons and visitors to do so.

The popularity of "text messaging"—using your cell phone to send a text rather than a voice message—is growing rapidly. Once you have selected the "Message" item from the menu, the telephone keypad can be used to enter the letters of the words in your message. Press "Send" and enter the telephone number of the party to receive the message and it is like having e-mail wherever you happen to be. With these advances, your office can be anywhere you are—all you need is your cell phone and your laptop and you are ready for business. (If you are not familiar with this cell phone feature, check out the AT&T Wireless website at www.attwireless.com. Use the link to "Text Messaging" to view a demo.) As cell phone usage, and the features available for them, continues to grow, there will likely be more people using cell phones than use the standard telephone.

One technological change that has occurred with cell phones is the combination of cell phones with PDAs (personal digital assistants). Some of the capabilities available on these units are:

- Phone, fax, and e-mail messages delivered into a single mailbox reachable from the phone
- Corporate mail accounts and databases
- Weather forecasts
- Digital assistants to forward messages and manage how and when you can be reached
- Web browsing
- Audio services that enable you to play your favourite soundtracks
- **PIM (personal information management)**, including managing contacts
- Speakerphone for hands-free calls

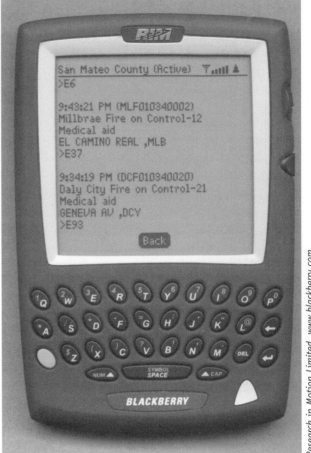

Cell phones are becoming PDAs.

- Speed-dial numbers
- Call waiting and call forwarding
- Complete transactions initiated from the desktop browser
- IM (instant messaging) e-mail
- Voice recording
- Text messaging (short messages—160 characters or so)
- Pictures and graphics
- Handwriting recognition systems

Videophoning and Videoconferencing

The videophone, its possibilities touted for decades, never really became widely used, nor was it perceived to have much benefit. Part of the problem was cost-effectiveness while getting it to work well enough to attract a broad audience. Today, with all businesses and many homes equipped with computers, videophoning and videoconferencing are more an issue of software and connection speed. In this increasingly global world, there is a need to network groups of people in real-time conferences. With a video camera and a connection to the Internet via broadband, videophoning and video-conferencing are available to both the business and home market at very reasonable cost.

Voice Technology

Voice messages used with our telephones have been commonplace since the 1980s. However, today we are seeing a phenomenal increase in the use of voice technology, with much wider application than voice mail. The future promises an even greater increase. You will be able to use voice commands to mine the Internet for just about any kind of information. Today, while standing in line at an airport, you can use your PDA to access

- Stock quotes
- Weather forecasts
- E-mail
- An electronic calendar
- A customer's order
- An Internet-based bookstore
- Directions to a meeting location

All of this can be done without touching a keypad—by voice command. Both wireless broadband and voice recognition technologies are fuelling this development.

Of relevance to you now in your day-to-day functioning in the workplace is the proper use of voice mail. Many times we dial a business, are asked to speak or key into the receiver our information or request, and are answered by a computerized voice. There is never any actual contact with a human being. In organizations, voice mail is used extensively. It has been estimated that only 25 percent of all calls placed reach the person for whom they are intended on the first try. Voice messaging has become an efficient way of answering the phone when an employee is unable to do so. It allows the caller to leave a message or be routed to someone else. If the caller leaves a message, the person receiving the message can then return the call as soon as possible. Some advantages of voice messaging include

- Greater productivity of workers by eliminating repeated telephone calls when the individual called is not available
- Less extraneous conversation (voice messages average 30 seconds; normal phone conversations average 4 or 5 minutes)
- Providing the frequent traveller with the ability to communicate with the office at any time

- Increasing delivery speed on communications by getting messages through even with time zone differences (even if the organization being called is closed for the day, a voice message can be left; the receiver can listen to it upon arriving at work the next morning or from the home office)

If voice messaging is to be effective, attention must be paid to the message content, length, and branching system. It is very disconcerting to be branched to several computerized voices and never get your question or issue resolved. If you, as an administrative professional, are involved in helping to design a voice message system, you must be certain that it is both effective and efficient. You must always consider first the ability of the system to respond to the needs of the clients or customers. Listed here are some of the disadvantages of voice messaging and suggestions for how to counter them:

- Voice messaging is often misused by the employee who consistently puts his or her phone on voice mail, even when in the workplace. Certainly there are times when it is essential to use voice messaging while in the office. For example, if work must be done with no interruptions and there is no one else to take the calls, voice messaging may be used. However, this situation should be rare. Do not hide behind a voice messaging system. An employee can save both parties time by answering the phone when in the office.
- A voice message may be poorly designed—too long and ineffective in routing the caller. The voice message needs to be succinct, clearly stated, and able to route quickly and efficiently. At every step, give callers no more than four options. Instructions should be short—under 15 seconds if possible. Give the most important information or answer the most frequently asked questions first. Tell the caller what you want him or her to do first, then the key to press; for example, "To transfer to our receptionist, press zero." If you give the number first, the caller may forget what number to press.
- A voice message may not allow the caller to talk with a person. Be certain your system allows the caller to talk with a person if necessary. No one likes to be lost in a voice message system that never allows the caller to be heard by a human being.
- The voice on a voice message may not sound pleasant. Remember, the sound and tone of your voice message greeting must create a favourable impression. On a voice message, vary your vocal

tone; do not talk in a monotone. Be careful, also, of background sound when recording a message.

Telephone Techniques

Telephone techniques remain extremely important in the effectiveness of all organizations. Attention must be paid to handling both outside and inside callers well. Business can be gained or lost due to effective or ineffective telephone procedures. You may be thinking "Why should I study effective telephone techniques? I already know how to use the telephone." But chances are, you do make errors when using the phone; we all do. You have probably also experienced ineffective telephone techniques used by others. Before you begin this section, take a few minutes to think through some of your own telephone behaviours, by completing Self-Check B.

SELF-CHECK B ✔

Answer each statement with a yes or no answer.

1. I am always pleasant with every telephone caller.
   Yes ☐   **No** ☐

2. I greet telephone callers with a friendly salutation.
   Yes ☐   **No** ☐

3. I give callers my full attention.
   Yes ☐   **No** ☐

4. I say "please" and "thank you" often.
   Yes ☐   **No** ☐

5. I keep a smile in my voice.
   Yes ☐   **No** ☐

6. I am attentive to the caller's needs.
   Yes ☐   **No** ☐

7. I avoid slang.
   Yes ☐   **No** ☐

8. I take messages accurately and completely.
   Yes ☐   **No** ☐

9. I use the caller's name frequently.
   Yes ☐   **No** ☐

10. I ask questions tactfully.
    Yes ☐   **No** ☐

Be Aware of Time Zone Differences

Due to the multinational nature of business today, calls are made frequently to places around the world, and obviously time zone differences must be taken into consideration when making calls. In Canada, the zones are called Newfoundland, Atlantic, Eastern, Central, Mountain, and Pacific time. A time zone map for Canada is shown in Figure 8-6 on page 161. Maps for other countries are shown on the Web at www.worldtimezone.com.

Keep a Smile in Your Voice

When you have customers or visitors in your office, a cheerful smile, a cup of coffee, and a magazine usually keeps the in-person callers happy, even when they have to wait. Since these services cannot be provided over the telephone, you must rely on your voice and your manner to make the voice-to-voice contact as pleasant as the face-to-face contact.

A winning voice makes the caller feel as if a smile is coming through the receiver. How do you develop such a voice? One way is to smile as you pick up the receiver. When you are actually smiling, it is much easier to project a smile in your voice. Treat the voice on the other end of the line as you would a person standing in front of you. Let the person know you are interested in him or her. Maintain a caring attitude. Never answer the phone curtly or rudely. Do not speak in a monotone; vary your voice modulation.

Be alert to what you are saying. Sometimes when we are tired or busy, we say things we do not intend or that can be misinterpreted. Here are some blunders that have been made on the telephone. Your experiences with the telephone will, no doubt, allow you to add to this list:

- *Good morning. Account Services. Lori screaming.*
- *You can go to any bank that is inconvenient for you.*
- *Thanks for holding me.*
- *We're open between 12 and noon.*
- *Ms. Brown is out to lunch.*

Good for a chuckle? Yes, but similar things can happen to any of us if we are not alert at all times.

Be Attentive and Discreet

Listen politely to what the other person says. Give the caller your undivided attention. Do not interrupt. Do not keyboard or flip through pages while talking—these sounds are picked up and can be heard by the caller. If the caller is unhappy about some situation, allow him or her to explain why. Most of a person's anger may be dissipated in telling the story. It is easier to handle an unhappy person after you have listened to the problem. Use good listening skills.

- Listen for facts and feelings.
- Search for hidden or subtle meanings.
- Be patient.
- Do not evaluate.
- Try to understand what the speaker is saying, both from the words and from the tone of voice.
- Help the caller; respond to what the caller wants or asks. Do not just try—do it! As a customer, which response would you prefer to hear—"I will see what I can do" or "I will get the document faxed to you immediately"?

- If you need to access information on the computer for the caller, inform the caller of this fact. Remember, the caller cannot see what you are doing. When you are not speaking to him or her, you need to let them know what you are doing.

Be discreet if your employer is unavailable. Carefully explain why your employer cannot answer the telephone. You may say "Mr. Albertson is away from the office now. I expect him back in approximately an hour. May I have him call you when he returns?" Never say "Mr. Albertson is not here yet" (at 10 a.m.), "He's gone for the day" (at 3 p.m.), or "He's playing tennis" (at any time of day). A good rule to remember is to be helpful about when your employer is returning but not specific about where he or she is.

■ Figure 8-6

CANADIAN TIME ZONE MAP

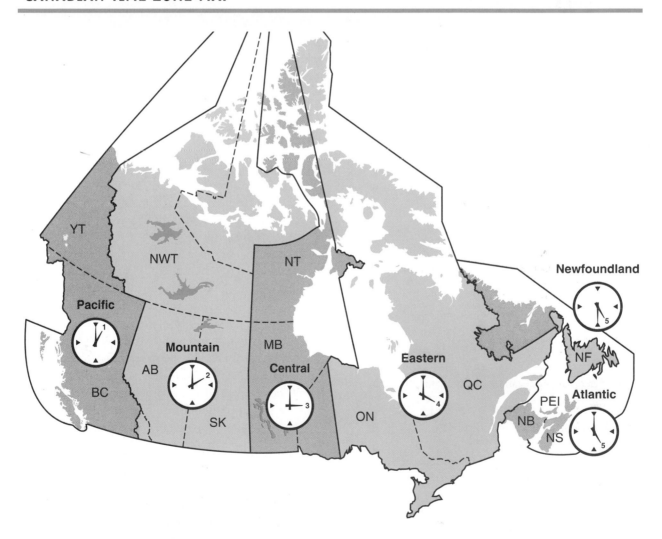

Use Correct English

Pay attention to your English and pronunciation. Anyone with a good grasp of the language would be uncomfortable to hear "This is her" or something similarly ungrammatical.

Avoid Slang

Slang is neither businesslike nor in good taste.

Avoid	Say
Yeah	Certainly
OK	Yes
Uh-huh	Of course
Bye-bye	Goodbye
Huh? I beg your pardon.	I did not understand *or* Would you please repeat that?

Take Messages Completely and Accurately

Incomplete messages are frustrating. Always get the necessary information. If you are not given all the information, ask the caller. Repeat the message to the caller so you can be certain it is accurate. You need the following information:

- The caller's name spelled correctly (Ask the caller to spell his or her name if you are not certain of how it is spelled.)
- The caller's company's name
- The telephone number (with area code if long-distance) - what # can you be reached
- The time of the call
- The message—exactly

Most organizations supply pads for taking phone messages. These may be in either single-sheet pads or duplicating sheets; the latter enable a copy to be kept of every message, which can be important in (for example) law offices.

Use the Caller's Name

It is flattering to the caller to be recognized and called by name. Frequent responses such as "Yes, Mr. Valentine. I will be happy to get the information" and "It was nice to talk with you, Ms. Keiba" indicate to callers that you know who they are and that you care about them as individuals.

Ask Questions Tactfully

Care should be used in asking questions. Ask only necessary questions, such as "May I tell Mr. Albertson who is calling?" or "When Mr. Albertson returns, may I tell him who called?" Never ask "Who's calling?" People are offended by such a blunt question. If your employer is not in or cannot take the call for some reason, ask about the nature of the call so you can handle the call or refer it to someone else. For example, you may say, "If you tell me the nature of your call, perhaps I can help you or refer you to someone who can."

Speak Distinctly and Clearly

Make sure the caller can understand what you say. You cannot speak distinctly with gum, candy, or a pencil in your mouth. Speak in a voice that can be heard. You do not want to shout or whisper. Also, speak at a speed similar to the caller's. This provides the caller with a conversation at his or her comfort level.

- Place the receiver firmly against your ear.
- Place the centre of the mouthpiece about 2.5 centimetres from the centre of your lips.
- Speak in a normal voice. Watch the speed of your voice. Do not talk too fast or too slow. Speak at a moderate rate.

Communication Tip

If you have regular callers with last names that are difficult to spell, store the names on your computer. When the person calls, you can look up the name quickly without having to ask for the spelling.

Handle Problem Calls

Most individuals are pleasant over the telephone, especially if you are courteous to them. Occasionally you may have a caller who has had a difficult day or for some other reason is unhappy. Many angry callers have been defused by an administrative professional taking the time to let them tell their story. Do not become emotionally involved in the situation. Remember that they are not angry at you, but rather at a situation or event.

Once you have listened, try to help the person get the problem solved. This may mean that you suggest a solution or that you tell the person you will have someone who can solve the problem call back. Do not put the person on hold or mishandle the call by transferring it to an individual who cannot help. Such approaches merely make the person angrier.

Sometimes callers refuse to give their name. You should have an understanding with your employer about what to do in such a situation. However, if you do not, put the person on hold while you tell your employer you are unable to get the caller's name. Your employer can then decide whether to speak to him or her.

Use Words to Identify Letters

Use words to identify letters in the spelling of names and places when necessary. Some spoken letter-names are hard to distinguish over the telephone. Figure 8-7 suggests some words to use for certain letters.

Photodisc Green/Photodisc Collection

■ Figure 8-7

WORDS TO USE TO IDENTIFY LETTERS

A as in **A**lice	**F** as in **F**rank
B as in **B**ertha	**G** as in **G**eorge
C as in **C**harles	**H** as in **H**enry
D as in **D**avid	**I** as in **I**da
E as in **E**dward	**J** as in **J**ohn

Do Not Discriminate

Have you ever found yourself being nicer over the telephone to the president of the company than to a client you do not know? If the answer is yes, make a point of being friendly before you know who is on the other end. Before answering the phone, try saying to yourself "A friend is calling."

Avoid Gender Bias

Some people still assume that all assistants are female and all executives are male. If you answer the telephone and the voice on the other end is female, do not assume she is an assistant and ask to speak to her employer. When addressing anyone, use terms that connote respect. Do not refer to a woman as a "girl," a "young lady," a "beautiful young thing," or a "gal," or use any other term that might be construed as gender-biased. Do not refer to a man as a "boy," a "hunk," or a "guy."

Keep a List of Frequently Called Numbers

A file of frequently called numbers is an excellent time saver. For quick reference, the numbers should be kept on your PIM software. You might also program the most frequently used numbers into your telephone.

Incoming Calls

The techniques you learned in the previous section apply to all calls. Here are some special techniques for handling incoming calls.

Adopt a friendly attitude before answering the phone.

Answer Promptly

When your telephone rings, answer promptly—on the first ring if possible and certainly by the third. You may lose a potential customer if you are slow in answering the telephone.

Identify Yourself and Your Organization

Your employer will usually instruct you on how to answer the telephone. If you work in a large organization, chances are you will not be the first person to answer any given call. The first person answering identifies the company; then the caller will ask for a specific person or department. As an administrative professional for Mr. Albertson, you might answer "Mr. Albertson's office, Rebecca Martin." If you need to identify the organization, you might say "Good morning. CanAsian Airlines."

Transfer Calls Carefully

Before you transfer a call, explain to the caller why you must do so. Make sure the caller is willing to be transferred. For example, you might say "Mr. Albertson is out, but Travis Figimara can give you the information. May I transfer you to Mr. Figimara?" You may also want to give the caller the extension number of the person to whom the caller is being transferred in case the transfer fails. The caller can then avoid having to call you again.

Be certain you know how to transfer calls. Callers dislike being told they are going to be transferred and then getting disconnected due to incorrect transferring procedures.

Put Calls on Hold Only After Requesting Permission

A caller may sometimes request information that you do not have at your fingertips. You may need to check with someone else or go to your files to get the information. When this happens, do not put the caller on hold without permission. You may say "I need to pull the information from my files. Would you like to hold for a moment while I get it, or shall I call you back?" If the caller agrees to hold, try to get back to the person as soon as possible. Nothing irritates a caller more than to be left on hold for a long time. When you return to the line, let the caller know you are back by saying "Thank you for waiting." If you are delayed in getting the information, go back to the person on hold and ask if she or he wants to continue to hold; apologize for the length of time it is taking.

Handle Multiple Calls

You might be responsible for answering more than one telephone line. If so, at times you will be answering a call on one line when another line rings. When this happens, you must remember that the caller on the second line does not know you are already on the phone. The caller is expecting to get an answer immediately. Excuse yourself politely by saying to the first caller "May I put you on hold for a moment? I must answer another phone." If the second call is going to take awhile, ask the caller for a number so you can call back as soon as you finish the first call. Then go back to the first caller with "Thank you for waiting." Your responsibility is to handle all calls as quickly and efficiently as possible.

Handle Cell-Phone Calls

If you are working offsite with a client or customer and you receive a cell-phone call, interrupting your work to answer may seem discourteous to the client or customer. Taking these outside calls conveys the impression that you have something more important to do than helping the client. Therefore, switch your cell phone to silent mode when assisting an in-person client. If you must keep your cell phone plugged in due to an urgent call you are expecting, be sure the client you are talking with knows about it. You might say "We may be interrupted by a call I must take, but I promise to be as brief as possible." If the call comes through, excuse yourself and do keep the conversation as brief as possible.

Screen Calls

Many executives have one telephone number that is published for callers and another, inside number that is not published. The executive uses the inside number to make outgoing calls; the number may also be given out to close friends or family members. The administrative professional is usually expected to screen calls that come from the published number. For example, when the executive receives a call, the administrative professional is expected to determine who is calling and why. The executive may refuse to take certain calls. If someone else in your company can handle the call, transfer it to that person after requesting permission from the caller to transfer. If no one is available to take the call, let the person know courteously that your employer is not interested. One response might be "I appreciate the information; however, Mr. Albertson is not interested in pursuing the matter at the present time."

Leave a Message When You Leave Your Desk

If you have to leave your desk, arrange for someone else to answer your telephone. You may forward it to a co-worker. Tell the co-worker where you can be reached and what time you will be back. If your employer is also gone, tell the co-worker in general terms where your employer is and when he or she will be back. You might say "Mr. Albertson is in a meeting and will be available around 3 p.m."

never say
"my boss will be back @ 2:00"
- say " " after 2:00"

Follow Through on Promises

If you make a promise to call back with information, do so. A broken promise can cause a cancelled order or a lost customer; a kept promise can enhance a reputation for reliability and trustworthiness. Help your employer remember promises made. If you know of information that your employer has promised a customer but has not followed through on, provide a tactful reminder of the need to follow through. Your employer will appreciate your assistance.

Outgoing Calls

As an administrative professional, you are often responsible for placing calls for your employer or for making business calls yourself. Just as incoming calls must be handled effectively, so must outgoing calls. Tips are provided in this section.

Place Calls Properly

Supervisors usually place their own calls to save time and to create a favourable impression. You may, however, work for someone who does not wish to place calls. If so, identify your supervisor before you transfer the call. For example, you might say "Mr. Albertson of CanAsian Airlines is calling." Then transfer the call to Mr. Albertson.

If your supervisor is not available or makes another call after you place one, make some subtle suggestions to her or him. For example, before you place the call, you might say "Mr. Albertson, are you going to be available for a few minutes? I want to place the call you requested to Mr. Chen." Your supervisor may merely be unaware that his or her habits are discourteous and irritating to the person being called.

Plan Your Call

Take a few minutes to plan your call. Keep in mind its purpose and what you intend to say. Avoid an unnecessary follow-up call by assembling any necessary files or reference documents that you might need during the call.

Once you get the person on the telephone, state your purpose clearly and concisely. For example, you might say "This is John Chin of CanAsian. I'm calling to verify your attendance at the sales meeting tomorrow at 3 p.m. in Conference Room A." You may want to

exchange pleasantries with the individual you are calling. However, the main purpose is to get your message across without wasting the other person's time. Complete Self-Check C.

The Future of Telecommunications

Twenty years from now, today's high-bandwidth solutions and scenarios will likely be irrelevant due to the dominance of fibre-optic networks. These networks promise to deliver bandwidth far greater than what cable, DSL, or satellite can offer. It is also predicted that fibre-optic connections, in addition to being the major network used by businesses, will also be widely used in homes. Eventually there will be fibre network interfaces in our homes that provide for virtual reality, DVD-quality streaming media, and almost anything else one can imagine—all over a fibre pipe. This will eventually result in ultrafast Internet connections that will be as common as telephone service today.

Broadband in public spaces, including airports and convention centres, is burgeoning. As broadband connectivity becomes widely used, providers will begin differentiating themselves by offering extra services. For example, some broadband companies now offer flexible subscription services for software and games.

SELF-CHECK C ✔

In Self-Check B on page 160, you considered some of your own telephone errors. Take a few minutes now to consider the mistakes others have made with you over the telephone. List those mistakes here, along with correction suggestions.

_____

_____

_____

_____

_____

Telecommunications will continue to affect our life outside the workforce. For example, wireless technology is transforming our automobiles into a multimedia data centre and productivity tool. With a connected car, you will be able to

- Receive data from roadside sensors that will alert you to traffic bottlenecks
- Be directed to empty parking spaces at the airport, where sensors and barcode readers will automatically produce a rental-car receipt
- Determine whether your flight is on time

- Access a virtual advisor that will allow you to access information, including your e-mail; this information may be delivered by a synthesized voice

The revolution of telecommunications promises to continue, with access to all types of data, video, audio, text, and graphics at faster speeds than we are presently experiencing. In addition, companies will continue to both merge and expand their services. They will not consider themselves merely providers of broadband pipelines, but also deliverers of telecommunication services that connect people to people and people to machines in a multitude of ways.

Chapter Summary

This summary will help you remember the important points covered in the chapter.

- The telecommunication field is involved in a revolution that is rapidly changing the traditional ways we have employed these services. Systems at various stages of development are breaking down the barriers between the computer and the telephone.
- Traditional telephone companies are in the process of transforming themselves from delivering a service that only connects people to people to one that connects people to people and people to machines through a wide range of telecommunication devices.
- Telecommunication companies are merging with companies in different businesses to garner more of the market and provide a variety of services. Gone are the days when a supermonopoly owned the whole network support infrastructure.
- The telecommunication field is undergoing a revolution, with numerous broadband pipelines available to organizations and individuals. These pipelines (in addition to standard analog dial-up) are cable, DSL, fixed wireless, and satellite. Information (including text, music, graphics, and pictures) can be retrieved from these pipelines at faster rates than in the past.
- Analog dial-up modem technology is the slowest technological pipeline. However, it is less expensive than others and is available everywhere phone lines are available.
- Cable is a means of accessing the Internet. Cable is fast and is becoming available to people in most areas of Canada.
- DSL is available in ADSL, SDSL, or IDSL. The majority of DSL users are businesses that already have telephone service in place.
- Fixed wireless technology is simpler than mobile wireless technology (the technology used by cell phones) because it does not utilize client devices moving in and out of coverage areas. Fixed wireless (WLL) is offered primarily to businesses and homes in areas where the infrastructure is not in place to deliver broadband through cable or DSL.
- Satellite has disadvantages over cable and DSL (higher cost, degrading of transmission in heavy rain or high wind, and download time); however, it is the only broadband service presently available for a number of businesses and homes, particularly those in rural areas.

- Fax is a telecommunication device that electronically sends an image of a document from one location to another via phone lines. It is an old technology, but the fax machine is still a standard piece of office equipment in businesses and homes.
- E-mail has revolutionized the way we communicate. It is used extensively in businesses as well as homes. When e-mail messages are sent, ethics must be considered. Do not send personal e-mail from your office computer. Do not use e-mail to berate or reprimand an employee. Do not use e-mail to terminate someone. Do not use e-mail to send information that involves any type of legal action.
- The broadband revolution promises to change telephone service drastically. For example, telephone calls can now be sent free from PC to phone or PC to PC to most global locations.
- Cell phones have become standard equipment for most people, in both their work life and their home life.
- Cell phones are now available as combination units with PDAs (personal digital assistants). PDAs are capable of sending phone, fax, and e-mail messages; retrieving corporate mail and databases, weather forecasts, and news headlines; and browsing the Web.
- With the ability to use computers to make telephone calls, videophoning and videoconferencing are now available. For example, by using a digital camera and an Internet connection that allows you to send a phone call through the Internet, videophoning and videoconferencing can be accomplished relatively easily.
- Voice technology is becoming widely available, and the future promises an even greater increase in voice technology.
- Voice mail should be used properly in the workplace. For example, a voice messaging system should be designed so the caller does not get lost in the system without ever being able to talk with a person. Also, the employee who is responsible for answering the phone should not misuse the system.
- Proper telephone techniques are important to the effectiveness of all organizations.
- The telecommunication revolution will continue. Twenty years from now, today's high-bandwidth solutions and scenarios will likely be irrelevant due to the dominance of fibre-optic networks, which networks promise to deliver bandwidth far

greater than what cable, DSL, or satellite can offer.

- As broadband connectivity becomes widely used, providers will begin differentiating themselves by offering extra services.

- Telecommunication companies will not consider themselves merely providers of broadband pipelines, but also deliverers of telecommunication services that connect people to people and people to machines in a multitude of ways.

Key Terms

The following terms were introduced in this chapter. The page on which the term was introduced is provided to help you locate the new term. Definitions are compiled in the Glossary at the end of the text.

- **telecommunications** 150
- **broadband** 150
- **moribund** 151
- **Bluetooth** 151
- **backbone** 152
- **crosstalk** 152
- **firewall** 152
- **packet-switched network** 152
- **streaming media** 152
- **VoIP (voice over Internet protocol)** 152
- **VPN (virtual private network)** 152
- **walled garden** 152
- **cable modem** 152
- **DSL (digital subscriber line)** 153
- **ADSL (asymmetric digital subscriber line)** 153
- **SDSL (symmetric digital subscriber line)** 153
- **IDSL (Internet digital subscriber line)** 153
- **fixed wireless** or **WLL (wireless local loop)** 153
- **cellular technology** or **mobile wireless service** 153
- **fax machine** 155
- **e-mail** 156
- **POTS (plain old telephone service)** 156
- **spamming** 156
- **PIM (personal information management)** 158

Responses to Self-Check A

1. The telecommunications revolution is changing the way we communicate, allowing us to
   - Make telephone calls from PC to PC or PC to telephone over the Internet
   - Send information through voice technology (speaking into the computer)
   - Hold computers in the palm of our hands, speak into them, and make phone calls; get data from our PCs; get stock quotes; and get newspaper headlines

   All of this can be done at faster and faster speeds over both wired and wireless pipelines.

2. Traditional telephone providers are changing their services by providing various broadband pipelines; providing voice and data services enhanced by real-time communications; and providing new services such as Web-based interfaces for billing and making payments, as well as customer care, and attendant functions realized using natural-language voice dialogues with machines.

3. The differences between cable, DSL, and fixed wireless are as follows:
   - Cable is a broadband pipeline that operates at very fast speeds in downloading information. A cable modem connects to the computer and to a service provider's coaxial cable line. It has limited upload speed, and bandwidth sharing can degrade performance. Because cable modems use shared connections, they are prone to slowdowns if too many users along a particular stretch of cable are online at one time.
   - DSL is also a broadband pipeline that operates at a fast speed, slightly slower than the cable pipeline for downloads. However, DSL users report more consistent speed than cable users. DSL stands for "digital service line." Most DSL service can be purchased from the same company that provides telephone service.
   - Fixed wireless (also referred to as wireless local loop) converts data to signals and relays it to customers through a network of transceivers

mounted on utility poles, street lights, and so on. Every WLL subscriber has a small radio receiver and directional antenna oriented toward the nearest microcell. Fixed wireless at this point is slower in receiving and sending data than cable and DSL.

Discussion Items

These discussion items provide an opportunity to test your understanding of the chapter through written responses and/or discussion with your classmates and your instructor.

1. Define telecommunications.
2. List and explain five telecommunication pipelines.
3. Explain the importance of Internet ethics. Give five examples of good ethical practices.
4. Explain the relevance of VoIP to the telephone.
5. List ten effective telephone techniques.

Critical-Thinking Activity

You have asked one of your assistants, Guy, to send an e-mail to a group of managers setting up a meeting with the superintendent of schools in Calgary to discuss a mentoring program CanAsian wants to begin with the public school system. The meeting is to be held on Monday, January 20, in Conference Room C, beginning at 8:30 a.m. and lasting approximately one hour. The managers are to forward written suggestions for a mentoring program to Mr. Albertson on Thursday, January 16. You did not review the e-mail Guy sent. His e-mail, a response from one of the managers, and Guy's response to the manager are on the Student CD, file SCDCTA8-1, SCDCTA8-2, and SCDCTA8-3.

Guy comes to you very upset. He says one of the managers is angry with him, and when he tried to handle the situation, it became worse. Review the e-mail exchanges. Has Guy made errors? If so, what are they? How should the present situation be handled? What advice would you give Guy on preventing such a situation in the future? (You may wish to use the e-mail section in Chapter 6 as a source of reference.)

Projects

Project 8-1 *(Objective 1)*

Online Project

Surf the Web for the following information:

- The status of cable, DSL, and fixed wireless broadband. Attempt to discover the capabilities of each of the telecommunication pipelines and the numbers of users of each service.
- The status of fibre-optic broadband. Attempt to discover projections of when this telecommunication pipeline will be available to large segments of the population.
- The features of cell phones. Attempt to discover the capabilities of features available and being developed and the projections for usage.

In searching the Web, you might want to use www.google.com or www.dogpile.com as your search engine.

Additionally, review periodicals such as *Fortune*, *PC World*, and *PC Magazine* in your search for information.

Present your findings orally to the class, or write a report of your findings, documenting your resources. Submit your report to your instructor.

Project 8-2 *(Objective 3)*

Four situations are provided on Student CD, SCDP8-2. Respond to each. Print a copy of your responses, and submit to your instructor.

Project 8-3 *(Objective 3)*

Collaborative Project

Choose a member of your class to work with on this project. Call each other, recreating situations 1, 2, 3, and 4 in Project 8-2, which are on Student CD, file SCDP8-2. Complete each of the situations twice. One of you should be the caller and the other the administrative assistant; then switch roles and replay the situations. Print out a copy of the Telephone Voice Rating Form (Student CD, file SCDP8-3). Complete the form and submit it to your instructor.

Project 8-4 *(Objective 2)*

Add to the Professional Growth Plan you began in Chapter 1 by developing your own behaviour guidelines for using e-mail ethically. Save your plan on your Professional Growth Plan disk as "Progro8-4." Develop an appropriate title for this portion of your plan. Before you begin your plan, review the e-mail ethics section in your text and Figure 8-7.

Case Solution for Part 2

Charlene Charles' Case Solution

First, my colleague and I listed various time management tools that we would cover in our presentation. Then we split them between us and researched them online or from various textbooks. We also consulted with our IT department for input on software tools that might be used to assist in managing time, and we pre-booked the multimedia equipment that we would need. After our research was complete, we compiled the information into a report to be distributed to the staff, since we intended the report to be used as a reference tool when they returned to their work areas. After a short rehearsal, we were prepared for our presentation.

On the day in question, we set up the multimedia equipment for our electronic demonstration, distributed our reports, and proceeded with our presentation. We approached the staff in a manner that allowed for a sharing of information, as opposed to dictating our thoughts. We also shared information about the tools that we were currently using to provide proficient assistance to our respective supervisors, and asked that the staff share any tips they had. We demonstrated the electronic tools available, and opened the floor to any questions or discussion. The presentation went well, and feedback was positive.

PART 3

OFFICE ADMINISTRATION: PROVIDING ADMINISTRATIVE SUPPORT

A Success Profile

Patsy Baader
Chief Negotiator's Office Assistant
Uchucklesaht Tribe
Community Researcher/Coordinator
Maa-Nulth Treaty Society
Port Alberni, British Columbia

I'm a mother of five rambunctious children. I was young when I had my babies, and even though I worked as a cosmetologist, and my husband had seasonal contract jobs with the Department of Fisheries and Oceans, we still couldn't make ends meet with our growing family. My parents advised me to leave hairdressing and go back to school. Cosmetology was not providing enough to support my children, so I followed their advice. It has been the best and most rewarding move of my life (besides the birth of my children, that is).

Now I have found happiness! I attended North Island College in British Columbia and met other women in situations similar to mine. They all wanted to find themselves, and/or a way to support their families. In that classroom, we became a family. I was told by a few of my classmates that a mature student with all the demands of a family would never be able to pass the Office Administration program. I set my mind to proving them wrong. With the support of my family, classmates, instructors, and friends I was able to graduate with straight A's. It was my determination to succeed in my goals that got me through the program. If you set your mind to anything you want to do, you will succeed. It's all up to you.

My first job after graduation was as a researcher for a new and growing company. Although it was a contract position, I was able to prove my organizational skills to the Chief Negotiator. Once that contract was completed, I was hired, not only by the Chief Negotiator, but also by the CEO of the company, as an assistant. Many doors have opened since I took on those responsibilities. Other companies have seen my capabilities as a very organized and strong representative. I now have two jobs, and more opportunities available. I am satisfied with the two that I have now, for they allow me the flexibility to spend time with my family. I must admit also that I love the travelling involved with both jobs.

I laugh when I remember how scared I was to go back to school and get my education. I now have many job opportunities open to me because of my computer skills and my comfort with public speaking. All of these skills I learned at college. I can't wait until fall when I return to school to continue my education in administrative skills. My only wish is that I had done so a long time ago.

Patsy Baader's Case

One of my coworkers was unable to come in to work due to a family crisis and there was no one to coordinate two upcoming meetings. Although I had never coordinated a large meeting before (for 40 to 60 people), my employer asked me to make the necessary arrangements. I was surprised that he had such confidence in me. I was not sure I could do the job, but whenever I am in a new and difficult situation, I take a deep breath, gather myself, and dive right in—just like you would do when you are about to dive into a cold lake on a hot summer day.

Read my case and consider the following questions. What would you do in this case? How would you begin to make arrangements? What would you need to consider in your planning? Turn to the end of Chapter 15 to see how I managed this challenge.

Chapter 9

Mastering Technology

LEARNING OBJECTIVES

1. Explain the functions of computer hardware components.
2. Utilize the Internet to research information on the Web.
3. Explain the difference between operating system software and application software.
4. Troubleshoot software problems.
5. Identify ethical computer behaviours.
6. *Demonstrate a commitment to continual learning in our technological age.*

The computer revolution has occurred. We live with the evidence of this statement daily as we work, shop, attend classes, and operate household appliances. Certainly computers will continue to get more powerful and less expensive, with new advances coming constantly. However, the revolution that promised computing power for everyone has already come to pass. It is the same with the Internet revolution. Today the **Internet** (the world's largest group of connected computers) and the **Web** (a huge collection of computer files scattered across the Internet) are a part of our daily lives. For example, as a society, we use the Internet and the Web to

- Send e-mail to our friends
- Buy numerous types of products—airline tickets, books, clothes, gifts, computer software and equipment, stocks, groceries, and prescription drugs, to name a few
- Research all types of information, from the latest in software to health issues to job information
- Take college classes online

At work, the Internet is invaluable in

- Sending e-mail
- Providing research information
- Allowing businesses to make information available to the public through Web pages
- Selling products
- Connecting businesses worldwide

Just as new advances will continue to occur with computers, so too will new advances with the Internet and the Web. The task today and for the future is to fully utilize the changes that will occur in computer and Internet technology to make work and home lives more productive and efficient—and that is no easy task. We must engage in **lifelong learning** (a commitment to continue to learn throughout life), realizing that as technology continues to become more powerful and to offer us more services, we must continue to learn how to utilize these changes effectively in our work and home lives.

The purpose of this chapter is not to teach you a software program or to make you an expert on the inner workings of a computer. No doubt you have already taken courses in which you learned various applications such as word processing, database, spreadsheet, and/or presentation graphics programs. The purpose of this chapter is to help you understand the basics of computer operations and be conversant with current computer and software terminology, along with computer ethics. You might want to review the objectives at the beginning of this chapter so you clearly understand the goals you are to accomplish.

Computer Classifications

The **microcomputer** (more commonly known as the PC) is the kind of computer you will be using in your work. However, you should also have a general understanding of the various other kinds. Computers are classified by their storage capacity and speed of operation. The classifications are as follows:

- Supercomputers
- Mainframes
- Minicomputers
- Workstation computers (supermicros)
- Microcomputers (PCs)

Supercomputers

The mightiest and most expensive computers are called **supercomputers**, which are a type of mainframe (see following). Although the prices of computers fluctuate, supercomputers sell for $27 million and up. They are used in organizations that process huge amounts of information. For example, biotech and high tech are teaming up today in projects involving the **genome** (determining the genetic blueprint of humanity) and **high-end protein analyzers** (identifying the sequence of the amino acids that make up proteins). Both of these projects require supercomputers. The convergence of medicine and computing is definitely here. Additionally, the federal government uses supercomputers for tasks that require mammoth data manipulation. Examples include national census data processing (for example, the 2001 Canada Census), worldwide weather forecasting, telephone network design, and medical imaging. Supercomputers now operate at a speed of over 12 **teraflops** (1 teraflop equals 1 trillion operations per second). With one 1 trillion bytes of memory and more than 160 **terabytes** (one 1 terabyte equals 1 trillion bytes) of disk storage, a supercomputer can hold many times more than the information contained in all the books in National Library of Canada. This capacity allows researchers to develop new

> **Technology Tip**
>
> If you misplace a document you have worked on recently, click the Start button and go to My Recent Documents in the pop-up menu. You will see a list of documents; click on the one you want to open.

drugs, improve airline safety, and continue to engage in human gene research. However, researchers are not satisfied with the speed and capacity of the present supercomputers. In fact, IBM is spending $100 million to design Blue Gene, a supercomputer 1000 times as powerful as Deep Blue, which defeated chess champion Gary Kasparov in 1997.[1]

Mainframes

Mainframes are large computers capable of processing great amounts of information very rapidly (although the speed is less than that of the supercomputer). Mainframes can support a number of auxiliary devices, such as terminals, printers, disk drives, and other input and output equipment. They are commonly found in large businesses and government agencies. The market for mainframes is not as great as in the past. Although these old computer giants helped put men on the moon, they have major competitors today—namely, the supercomputer and PC client-server networks. Even in the Internet business, where traditionally the mainframe has been used extensively, smaller, more flexible machines threaten to replace it. Although it is projected that the mainframe will continue to be used to a degree by large organizations, its use will be limited.

Minicomputers

The **minicomputer** (a midrange computer) was introduced in the 1960s and was generally used in midsize organizations. It is slower, has less storage capacity, and is less expensive than the mainframe. Most minicomputers became obsolete when the **microprocessor** (a single miniature chip that contains the circuitry and components for arithmetic, logic, and control operations) was introduced. Some minicomputers eventually grew to mainframe size and some became microcomputers.

Workstation Computers (Supermicros)

Workstation computers (supermicros) are the upper-end machines of the microcomputer (explained in the next section). They have processing power approaching that of a mainframe. They have a high-speed microprocessor, significantly increased memory, and hard disk storage capacity. Supermicros are **multiuser computers** (able to serve several users at the same time).

Microcomputers (PCs)

The microcomputer is the smallest of the computer systems. Microcomputers were made possible by the advances in technology in the 1970s that permitted the manufacture of electronic circuits on small silicon chips. In the work environment of today, administrative professionals, managers, and executives have PCs on their desks. PCs are very powerful, having more capabilities and storage capacity than the early mainframes, with the capacity of these machines continuing to grow as technological advances occur. One technological invention that has greatly increased the power of the PC is the **processor chip** (a type of microprocessor) that provides for increased speed and performance capability. Today's processor chips are known as the **Pentium® processor** (manufactured by Intel®), the Advanced Micro Devices **Athlon** for Windows®, and the **PowerPC** processors for the Mac™. Organizations use PCs to run basic applications such as word processing, spreadsheet, and e-mail programs and to connect employees internally to the company Intranet and externally to the Internet.

Due to the relative low cost of PCs, they are also purchased extensively for home use. PCs are used for balancing personal chequebooks, paying bills, planning investment strategies, doing homework, reviewing news articles on the Internet, talking with people all over the world, taking online courses, and even playing games. With the price of PCs decreasing, the home market is expected to continue to grow. Figure 9-1 on page 177 gives some tips on caring for your computer.

In addition to the desktop PC, portable computers—**notebooks** or **laptops**—are used extensively. Although notebooks and laptops are smaller than the traditional desktop PC, their power (which is continually increasing), capabilities, and portability make them very popular. For example, someone who travels frequently may use the notebook on a plane, in a hotel room, or in the car. The power of notebooks allows you to crunch data and handle graphics at speeds close to that of the low-end PCs. While on the road, you can also send and retrieve e-mail, check and record calendar events, and do research. You can transfer information from your desktop PC to your notebook. The administrative professional may use a notebook to take notes at a meeting and format the notes into minutes for later distribution in the organization.

The **PDA** (**personal digital assistant**) is a popular option in the portable PC market. At its most basic, the PDA serves as an appointment book, an address book, a to-do list, and a calculator, but you can also use it to

- Check your e-mail
- Retrieve telephone calls
- Transfer data from personal information managers such as Microsoft Outlook®
- Read newspaper headlines
- Check the financial markets
- Beam professional information that has traditionally been on business cards to clients or business contacts

Wireless PDAs, capable of accessing e-mail and the Internet without plugging in, are now available. **Wi-Fi** (short for "wireless fidelity") is the popular term for a high-frequency wireless local area network that connects users of PDAs and other portable computer devices to the Internet. This makes it possible to display Web pages from the wireless Internet to wireless PDAs. In addition, PDAs can become cellular phones and digital cameras. For personal use, we may soon be able to scan supermarket items with our PDAs and pick up the items at the checkout.

PDAs are also called **palms**, after Palm® Inc., the company that developed the original PDA. As the name suggests, palms can be held in the "palm" of your hand. These very small and powerful computers are inexpensive, costing from slightly over $100 to approximately

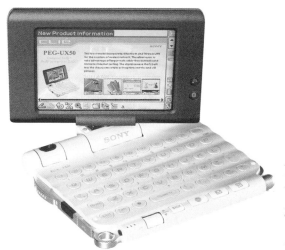

Sony of Canada Ltd., www.sony.ca

PDAs provide individuals with the flexibility of checking e-mail, maintaining calendars, and making phone calls on a computer that can be held in the palm of their hand.

■ Figure 9-1

COMPUTER CARE

- Keep your computer clean. Dust is a problem because it causes heat buildup in the components it covers. Vacuum every horizontal surface of your computer on a regular basis.
- Keep the keyboard clean. Purchase a can of compressed air to spray between the keys to remove dust. You also can purchase tiny computer vacuums specially designed for this task.
- Keep the mouse clean. Use alcohol on a cotton swab to wipe the rollers clean. Clean the ball inside the mouse with lukewarm soapy water and dry it thoroughly.
- Do not have food or drink near your computer. Spilling a soda or getting crumbs inside the keyboard may require a costly visit from a computer repairperson.
- Periodically turn off the monitor and wipe your screen clean with a static-free cleaner.
- Periodically delete files you no longer need from your hard drive. If you think you might need the files at a later time, save them to a CD or floppy disk.
- Back up your program and data files. A full backup of all program and data files with an incremental backup (a backup of only those files that have changed since the last incremental backup) performed at regularly scheduled intervals protects the integrity of your data.
- Periodically "defrag" your drive. The **defragmenter** feature of your operating system is a program that gathers the fragments of files that the operating system has scattered across the surface of your hard disk and reassembles them so each file's data is **continuous** (with no empty spaces between files). Defragging improves disk performance.
- Make certain you have a **surge suppressor** or a **UPS (uninterruptible power supply)** so that power fluctuations do not cripple your computer equipment.

$500. The number of PDAs in use has grown phenomenally, and continued growth and expanded applications are expected. For example, in 2001 more than 15 million PDAs were sold worldwide, and by 2008 sales are projected to reach nearly 61 million. Some experts in the field are projecting that we will eventually use PDAs to make purchases through infrared or other wireless technology. In other words, PDAs will take the place of cash, chequebooks, and credit cards. In the Scandinavian countries, for example, it is already commonplace to pay for candy and other small items with a cell phone.[2]

Information Input

Information for the computer is input in a variety of ways, including

- A keyboard
- Scanners
- Voice recognition technology
- Touch screens
- Digital cameras

Keyboard

You probably use a computer keyboard many hours every day. Obviously, it is the most frequently used input device and is expected to remain so indefinitely. Although voice recognition technology is growing and will continue to grow, the days of computers whose only input method is voice recognition are a long way off and such machines may never be commonplace.

Scanners

Scanners allow information to be input directly into a computer without the traditional keystrokes. They can scan text, drawings, graphics, and photos. They may also allow you to modify the copy by

- Adjusting the image size
- Retouching, cropping, and manipulating it in various ways
- Editing the scanned copy

For small offices and home use, there are multifunction scanners that can print, copy, fax, and scan.

Voice Recognition Systems

Although voice recognition technology has been used with mainframes and minicomputers for over 20 years, it has only become a real option for the PC user in the past few years. This is because of the development of **continuous speech recognition**, which allows you to speak almost naturally in complete phrases and sentences; the older technology, **discrete speech recognition**, required you to pause between words.

Even with continuous speech recognition systems, you need to modify your speech patterns to a certain degree. For example, you get the best results if you enunciate clearly and speak at a consistent rate and volume. With practice and by using proper speaking patterns, you can easily achieve an accuracy rate of more than 95 percent; some users report accuracy rates of 98 or 99 percent. In addition to accuracy, the systems are also fast, allowing you to talk at 160 plus words a minute. (In comparison, good keyboarders can key approximately only 80–100 words a minute; excellent keyboarders, 120.) In addition to speed and accuracy, other advantages of voice recognition are

- There are fewer problems with carpal tunnel syndrome because strain to your wrist is reduced
- It is an alternative for people who have difficulty using their hands to operate a keyboard
- It is an alternative for people who have difficulty spelling

The systems use headset microphones, which keep the recording element a fixed distance from your mouth and make it easy to change your bodily position without affecting the recording quality. Here are some of the voice recognition systems that are on the market:

- *Dragon NaturallySpeaking*®. Allows you to move the mouse by voice and correct a word by saying "Correct" followed by the correct word.
- *ViaVoice*® *Millennium.* Offers natural-language commands for Word, Excel, Outlook, and Internet Explorer®.
- *Philips FreeSpeech 2000*™. Offers language models for 13 other languages, including French, German, Spanish, and Dutch.
- *AOL's Point and Speak*®. Allows you to send e-mail without touching a single key. It also works with Windows-based word processing and spreadsheet programs to allow you to prepare reports and papers.
- *Microsoft Office XP Professional*® includes speech recognition.

Touch Screens

With a **touch screen**, the user touches the desired choice on the screen with his or her finger rather than using a mouse or trackball. Touch screens are used in a variety of settings, including the following:

- Hospitals, where the M.D. can use it to sign a virtual prescription for a patient
- Fast-food restaurants, where employees input food items ordered and compute the amount of the bill
- Gasoline stations, where customers start the pump by punching in the appropriate type of gasoline
- Office buildings, where visitors find the location of a particular office

Digital Cameras

Digital photography is evolving, but it already gives individuals more options than regular film. The **digital camera** becomes an input device when paired with a PC, allowing the user to print pictures in a variety of formats. Photographs may be inserted into e-mail documents, posted on a website, and used in other office applications (such as on letterhead and in reports). Digital cameras have quickly evolved from gadgets to serious photography tools designed for business users and professional photographers. You learned in Chapter 1 that the role of the administrative professional might now include designing and managing a Web page. The use of a digital camera provides a great amount of flexibility in designing the page. The quality of a camera depends mainly on the amount of information the camera's sensor can record. The number of **pixels** (picture elements) registered by the sensor measures **resolution** (the quality of the picture). One pixel is a spot in a grid of millions of spots that form the image. The current standard of image quality is the four-megapixel, or 4 MP, camera.

With the assistance of photo-editing software, such as Adobe's Photoshop®, photographs can be edited, altering colour and contrast, position, and features, for example. You can also add voice annotation to photos and enhance them with special effects. In addition, it is possible to convert already existing prints or transparencies to digital images by using scanners. Photographs may be stored on Zip drives or CDs. You will learn more about these storage devices in the next section of this chapter.

Since this chapter contains a lot of technical information, take a few minutes now to answer the questions in Self-Check A on page 179. Once you have completed

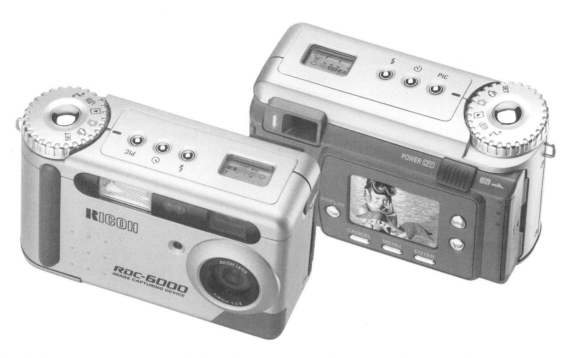

With a digital camera, the user can include photographs in various types of electronic documents.

Ricoh Co., www.ricoh.com

the Self-Check, refer to the answers at the end of this chapter. If you do not do very well, you might want to reread the first part of this chapter before proceeding to the next section.

SELF-CHECK A ✔

1. What are the five major computer classifications?

_____

_____

_____

2. What is a PDA and how is it used?

_____

_____

_____

3. How is information input into a computer?

_____

_____

_____

Storage Devices

Internal, online, and external storage are important when working with a computer. Memory capacities are expressed in million-byte units called **MB** (megabytes), billion-byte units called **GB** (gigabytes), and trillion-byte units called **TB** (terabytes). The internal storage capacity, or memory, of computers is referred to as **RAM** (random access memory).

RAM, which works very fast, is used to temporarily store and run software program instructions and store data currently in use. The sophisticated level of application programs in use today requires a minimum of 256 MB of RAM. If you try to run two or more programs with less than 256 MB, you might find that the computer runs out of memory and starts using your online hard disk space, which results in sluggish performance. Before you purchase a new computer, you need to know what type of work you will be doing and what type of software you will be using. Purchasing the highest RAM capacity you can afford ensures that, as new software comes on the market, your computer will be able to handle it.

A second type of storage on a computer is *online storage.* The access speed of such storage is slower than that of RAM. A hard disk drive is considered an online storage device. It is mounted into your computer console and cannot be removed. Your computer uses this storage memory the way you use a file cabinet—to organize, store, save, and retrieve software and data files. Before buying a new software package, you should consider how much hard disk storage you will need. People generally underestimate this. You will need enough to store the files for your operating system and application programs in addition to the data files you will create. Most computers today include at least an 80 GB hard drive; this is good enough for most users, but if you plan to work with memory-intensive media or graphics programs you will need more. Do Self-Check B.

Just as the internal or RAM storage capacity of computers has increased and will continue to do so in the years to come, so too will online storage capacity. However, online capacity is always finite. Thus, it is important to have secondary storage devices that allow you to remove data from the hard disk but still retain data files. Two secondary storage devices for the PC that you are probably most familiar with are floppy and compact disk drives.

Floppy drives, which use magnetic impulses to read from or write onto floppy disks, are standard equipment on almost all computers. Compact disk (CD) read/write technologies are also now widely available and offer a reasonably priced option for secondary data storage. Both provide an inexpensive method for taking data from the hard drive to save elsewhere, as a safeguard against a computer crash or destruction that would make the data inaccessible.

Other secondary storage devices are

- Zip and Jaz disks
- SuperDisks

SELF-CHECK B ✔

Stop! Take a few minutes to go to your computer and check out how much RAM and hard disk storage you have.

- To find out how much working memory you have, find the My Computer icon on your desktop. Right-click with the right mouse button and select Properties. The General tab in the top left-hand corner will show you how much RAM you have.

- To find out how much hard disk storage you have, find the My Computer icon on your desktop. Double-click with the left mouse button. Right-click on the C: drive icon; then left-click on Properties. You will see how much used and free space you have on your hard drive.

- DVDs
- Memory sticks

Floppy Disks

Floppy disks are indispensable storage mediums for the computer. The term *floppy* originated from the first size available in this apparatus (a 5.25-inch disk rarely used today), because it flopped when you waved it. The 3.5-inch disk used now consists of a flexible, magnetically sensitive wafer protected by a hard plastic case. "Floppy" is a misnomer for it, since it is housed in a rigid case, but the term continues to be used.

The amount of data that can be stored on such a disk is expressed in terms of **density**; disks can be *double-sided* and/or *high-density*. For example, a double-sided, high-density 3.5-inch disk may store 1.44 MB (megabytes). To give you an idea of what this means, a typical printed page, using single spacing, contains 2500 to 3000 characters. Thus, 1 MB holds 400 pages of single-spaced text.

Proper care must be taken when using and storing disks. The care of floppy disks is explained in Figure 9-2.

■ Figure 9-2

FLOPPY DISK CARE

- When labelling a floppy, write on the adhesive label *before* applying it to the case. Remove old labels before applying a new one.
- Store floppies in specially designed containers. This will keep them free of dust and smoke particles. Even a single smoke particle on the disk's magnetic surface can cause the drive to have problems reading it.
- Keep floppy disks away from water and other liquids. Dry them with a lint-free cloth if they get wet.
- Keep floppy disks out of direct sunlight and away from other sources of heat.
- *Write-protect* a disk if it contains data you do not want changed. To write-protect a 3.5-inch disk, turn it over and find the tiny latch in the lower left-hand corner. This latch is usually closed; slide it downward so that a small opening appears in the corner.

Zip, Jaz, and SuperDisk External Storage

Zip disks are available in 100 and 250 MB capacities (the equivalent of 70 to 175 floppy disks) and allow the user to

- Store large files with graphic images
- Archive old files that are not used anymore but must be maintained
- Exchange large files with other users

Removable **Zip drives** are also available that are reasonably inexpensive, portable, and easy to install. The capacity on a Zip drive is from 100 MB to 2 GB.

The **SuperDisk** holds 120 MB of data and solves one of the problems of the Zip format. Zip drives can read only Zip disks; the SuperDisk format can read floppies as well as SuperDisks. The **Jaz disk** provides the same portability as the Zip disk but holds more data than the Zip. The Jaz disk holds 1 GB (the equivalent of 850 floppy disks). All of these (Zip, Jaz, and SuperDisks) are used in portable drives.

CD-ROMs

Today all software packages come on a **CD-ROM** (compact disk read-only memory); to install them, you need a CD drive. Thus, most PCs include a CD-ROM drive in addition to a floppy drive, and many PCs now have internal CD-RW drives (see below) as standard equipment. CDs provide *optical* rather than *magnetic* storage, and the drive uses laser technology to read the data.

While such a laser drive can read the CD, it cannot write any data. CD-RW (read/write) drives, also known as *CD burners*, can. Two types of compact disks can be used by a CD burner:

- **CD-R** (compact disk, recordable) disks are *WORM* (write once, read many) media; the drive can write onto its surface only once. Moreover, the data cannot be erased. CD-Rs are commonly used for archiving large data files.
- **CD-RW** (compact disk, rewritable) media can be erased. A CD-RW drive can write, erase, and rewrite data to CD-RWs repeatedly. Such disks can hold 550 MB to 650 MB—more than a floppy—making them a good solution for sharing files. CD-RWs are quickly replacing floppy drives and disks.

> **Technology Tip**
>
> If you are printing several copies of a document, you can print the pages in order. Select Print in the File menu, and click Collate from the Print window. Enter the number of copies you want, and then click OK.

DVDs

DVD-ROM (digital versatile or digital video disk, read-only memory) is beginning to replace the CD-ROM. The DVD is the same diameter as a CD, but it has much more capacity. It can hold as much as 17 GB of data, 24.84 times what a CD can hold. DVD-ROMs are also faster than CD-ROMs, and they can take advantage of the high-quality video and multichannel audio capabilities being added to many DVD-ROM-equipped computers. All major PC manufacturers now have models that include DVD-ROM drives. The DVD technology is also capable of reading CD-ROMs.

A read/write version known as DVD-RAM (digital versatile disk, random access memory) drive is the DVD version of the CD burner. It has the capability of creating DVD-ROM disks containing nearly 5 GB of data.

The first DVD adopters were corporate users who used CD multimedia for training and sales presentations. The disks allowed organizations to make longer and higher-quality full-screen multimedia presentations. DVDs are used in airports and public places (kiosks in lobbies of hotels) where music and video are important parts of the presentation. Standards similar to those developed for CD technology are helping to bring down the cost of these drives as well as the media they use.

Information Output

The main two output devices are monitors and printers. If you want **soft copy** (copy shown on the monitor only; a printed copy is not necessary), the video display monitor or **CRT** (cathode ray tube) is appropriate. If you want **hard copy** (printed on paper), the printer is appropriate. A good example of soft copy is e-mail messages. Most of the time the receiver of the e-mail merely reads the message on the monitor and then saves it in the computer or destroys it. A printed copy may not be needed.

Monitors

Although computer technology advances quickly and major equipment changes are common, computer monitors have been the exception to the rule. Until recently, monitors have stayed basically the same, the changes being mainly in size, colour capability, and

Sylvania Displays, www.sylvania.com

Two of the major advantages of a LCD monitor are its slim profile and its colour accuracy.

image quality. The price of **LCD** (liquid crystal display) monitors is now little more than that of the traditional CRT (cathode ray tube) monitor. The major selling point of LCDs is their size. While traditional CRT monitors are 0.3 metres or more deep and take up a lot of space on a desktop, LCD displays are only a few centimetres deep. This makes them a practical alternative for normal desktops and for cramped quarters such as cubicles. Another advantage of the LCD is its colour accuracy. For example, if you send a digital signal for a certain shade of blue, the LCD will always produce that precise shade. CRTs are less accurate in comparison.

Printers

The most commonly used output device is the printer. The two types in use today are the inkjet printer and the laser printer. In the past, there was a vast difference in quality between the inkjet printer and the laser printer, the latter being far superior. However, inkjet printers have seen the most significant technological advancements of

the two, and now the differences are almost imperceptible. And while prices of both have decreased significantly, inkjet printers remain less expensive.

Inkjet Printers

Inkjet printers work by spraying ink onto the paper. For colour printing additional ink cartridges are used. Inkjet printers produce high-quality graphics and text, with quality and speed close to that of a laser printer. Their price has come down and now ranges from $75 to $150. However, other considerations are the cost of ink/toner products and the number of pages that can be printed with an ink/toner cartridge. Inkjet printers generally have operating costs of 5–10 cents per page for black and white and 10–20 cents per page for colour. Inkjet printers produce approximately six pages per minute and are capable of producing vivid colours and high-quality graphics.

Laser Printers

The **laser** printer uses a beam of light to form images on paper. *Laser* is actually an acronym for "light amplification by stimulated emission of radiation." Laser printers, in general, have faster printing speeds than inkjet printers, some being capable of printing 30 pages per minute, which is why most businesses use them. Although you may purchase a small model for approximately $250, most high-end lasers, particularly for networked printers, cost more. The operating costs are typically a few pennies per page, as opposed to 5–20 cents per page for the typical inkjet printer, making them a good alternative for very little extra cost in any business situation in which colour copies are not required.

Networked Printers

A number of businesses use **networked printers** (printers attached to a local area network). Depending on the needs of the business, networked printers can generate a cost savings to the business. For example, if colour or specialized functions are required in one department, but not for

> **Technology Tip**
>
> Use the personal organizer program on your PC to see at a glance what you have planned for a day, a week, a month, or even a year.

every worker there, the department might use a networked printer. This printer can provide the capabilities needed for a group of people.

Multifunction Peripherals

A multifunction peripheral is an output machine that can produce more than one type of output: generally, it can print, fax, copy, and scan. When purchasing a multifunction peripheral, consider these factors:

- *Space available.* One multifunction device takes up far less space than the machines it replaces and can be installed more easily, since a single hookup takes care of numerous functions.
- *Capability needed.* Multifunctions are available in various speeds, print resolutions, and capabilities.
- *Cost.* The cost can range from a low of several hundred dollars to a high of several thousand dollars, depending on capabilities and speed desired.
- *Downtime.* When a multifunction device goes down, you lose all functions—the copier, printer, scanner, and fax. This is an important factor to consider, especially in a small business or home office where there are no backup machines.

Take a few minutes now to respond to the items in Self-Check C. Once you have answered the questions, turn to the end of this chapter and check your answers.

SELF-CHECK C ✔

1. List the external computer storage devices.

   _____

   _____

2. What are the two major types of printers used today?

   _____

   _____

Computer Networks

Computers and other peripheral equipment, such as printers, can be linked through networks. These networks may be

- **LANs** (local area networks), which link technological equipment within an office or building
- **MANs** (metropolitan area networks), which link technological equipment over a distance equal to the size of a city and its surroundings
- **WANs** (wide area networks), which link technological equipment over an area of hundreds of thousands of kilometres
- **WLANs** (wireless local area networks), which wirelessly link various types of technological equipment within a building or several buildings within the same geographic area

The Internet

The growth of technology and the need for sharing information worldwide have spawned worldwide networks. The Internet is the world's largest group of connected computers, allowing people from all over the world to communicate. The Internet was created in the 1960s as a project of the U.S. Department of Defense. Since that time it has grown exponentially, with approximately 300 million Internet users worldwide. Internet capability has changed the way we live and work, and the number of users will continue to grow. Access to the Internet can be gained in the following ways:

- Cable
- **DSL (digital subscriber line)**
- Fixed wireless
- Satellite
- Analog dial-up

In the past, the only access to the Internet was through a modem attached to a telephone line (the analog dial-up option mentioned above), and this type of access is still used extensively around the world. However, telecommunications is moving rapidly; in addition to analog dial-up, the options mentioned above (cable, DSL, fixed wireless, and satellite) have become available. All of these options promise faster service than dial-up. However, where you live does affect the availability of various services. For example, while providers are working to widen **broadband** service (cable, DSL, wireless, and satellite), there are still areas of the country where dial-up is the only system available.

The Web

The World Wide Web, or simply "the Web," is a huge collection of computer files (more than 800 million websites and growing daily) scattered across the

■ Figure 9-3

WEB TERMINOLOGY

- *Browser.* A tool for retrieving information from the World Wide Web. Some common browsers available are Internet Explorer®, Netscape®, NeoPlanet®, and Opera®.
- *Home page.* The main entry or first page of a website.
- *HTML.* "Hypertext markup language"; the rules that govern the way we create documents so they can be read by a browser.
- *HTTP.* "Hypertext transfer protocol"; the protocol used by Web servers.
- *Hyperlink.* A (usually) underlined word or phrase in a document that, when clicked, displays another document or website.
- *Protocol.* A planned method of exchanging data over the Internet.

- *Server.* A computer that serves information and software to the Internet community.
- *URL.* "Uniform resource locator"; the address to a source of information.
- *Cookies.* Small files written to a computer's hard disk by some of the websites visited. They provide a method of recording information which is then available the next time you visit the site.
- *PDF (portable document format).* A file format into which documents of all types (word processing, spreadsheet, or graphic) can be converted so as to look the same as the original on any computer screen.

Internet. It is just one of many features of the Internet, which also comprises news articles, weather information, entertainment (games), e-mail messages, and encyclopedia information, to name a few. Helpful Web terminology is given in Figure 9-3.

The Web was created by Tim Berners-Lee, a consultant at the Swiss research laboratory CERN, as a tool for physicists to share research data. The general public did not use it until the creation of Mosaic™, a **Web browser** (an application program that provides a way to look at and interact with all the information on the World Wide Web). From this first browser, a number of other browsers have been developed, including Internet Explorer, Netscape, NeoPlanet, and Opera.

One of the biggest challenges, with the millions of pieces of information available on the Web, is finding data that meets your needs. *Search engines* have been developed to help with this process, and they are updated frequently to keep up with the new pages being submitted every minute. Figure 9-4 lists several search engines you might find helpful as you surf the Web.

Web Ethics

With the relative newness of the Web and the millions of people and organizations that use it daily, ethics has become an issue. Richard Spinello, author of *Cyberethics: Morality and Law in Cyberspace*, observes:

■ Figure 9-4

WEB SEARCH ENGINES

These search engines can help you find information quickly on the Web. Search engines are continually searching the Web for new pages.
- Google Canada (www.google.ca)
- HotBot® (www.hotbot.com)
- Ask Jeeves℠ (www.ask.com) (You can ask a question here in "natural language" and get a list of links to sites that may have the answer.)
- AllTheWeb (www.alltheweb.com)
- MetaCrawler® (www.metacrawler.com)
- AltaVista® (www.altavista.com)
- AltaVista® Canada (www.altavista.ca)
- Canadopedia (www.canadopedia.com) (Lists English- and French-Canadian sites.)
- Dogpile (www.dogpile.com) (Compiles search results from other search engines such as Ask Jeeves, Google, etc.)
- SearchEurope℠ (www.searcheurope.com) (For Europe.)
- Yahoo (www.yahoo.com)

If it is easier to publish and spread truthful and valuable information, it is also easier to spread libel, falsehoods, and pornographic material. If it is easier to reproduce and share digitized information instantly, it is also easier to violate copyright protection. And if it is easier to build personal relationships with consumers, it is also easier to monitor consumers' behaviour and invade their personal privacy.[3]

As an example, Bill C-6, the Personal Information Protection and Electronic Documents Act, makes it possible for people to sign legal agreements online using a "secure electronic signature," but it also presents the possibility of misuse and even fraud. Early adopters of electronic signature technology are expected to be banks and other financial institutions, and as the use of electronic signatures becomes widespread the risk of fraud is likely to increase.

Clearly, the power of the Internet can be abused. Here are more examples:

- **Proprietary data** (data owned/originated by people or organizations) is being sent and received at extremely fast speeds and in very high volumes.
- Customer information is easier to collect, analyze, and use for purposes not covered in typical privacy agreements.
- As health care goes digital, patient information can be inadvertently released; medical inquiries can be directed to the wrong people.
- Mailing lists may be sold, with the result being unsolicited advertisements from retailers.
- College and university students may purchase term papers over the Web to submit to instructors as their own.

Some work is now being done in Web ethics, with various organizations writing and posting their codes of ethics. However, the Web is the responsibility of all users, and everyone (both organizations and individuals) should commit to behaving ethically.

Intranet

The **intranet** is a private network that belongs to an organization and is accessible only by the organization's employees. To help you understand the relationship between the intranet and the Internet, think of the Internet as a worldwide network of computers and the intranet as an organization or business network of computers surrounded by a **firewall**—software that prevents unauthorized outside individuals from using the network. People inside the intranet can get out to the Internet, but those outside cannot get in. Intranets are used to share information that needs to be quickly and easily disseminated, such as company policies and in-house newsletters.

Wi-Fi technology is rapidly gaining acceptance in many companies as an alternative to a wired LAN. Companies that do have a wireless LAN should ensure that they have adequate security safeguards, because a Wi-Fi wireless LAN can be more susceptible to access from the outside by unauthorized users.

> ### Technology Tip
>
> Keeping current on technologies that impact your office means reading technology publications such as *Computing Canada* and *PC World*. Commit to reading at least one technology publication every month.

Extranet

An **extranet** also operates behind a firewall, but the firewall allows the inclusion of selected individuals, companies, and organizations outside the company. You can access an extranet if you have a valid username and password. Your identity determines which parts of the extranet you can view. An extranet, for example, may be used by

- Financial institutions to provide clients with account information and performance reports
- Health institutions to access medical records
- Businesses to allow stockholders to view their finances

Software

You have probably had fairly extensive experience using several software packages, including word processing, presentation, and spreadsheets. This portion of the chapter is not designed to teach you a software package. It is designed to help you

- Understand the difference between operating system software and application software
- Troubleshoot software problems
- Understand the importance of computer ethics in relation to software
- Learn how to avoid computer viruses

Operating System Software

An operating system is a program that enables your computer to read and write data to a disk, send pictures to your monitor, and accept keyboard commands. Without an operating system, you cannot perform any of the tasks required in your word processing program or in other application software programs. In understanding how an operating system works, consider this analogy. When you turn the key in your car, the motor starts. You merely perform the one function, without being aware of the various electronic parts and the interrelationship between them that it takes for the motor to start. Once the motor starts, you are ready to perform a whole series of other steps—putting the car in gear, stepping on the gas, turning on the heat or air conditioning, and so on. When you turn on your computer, the operating system begins working for you. It gets the computer ready to receive your additional commands, which generally come from application software programs, discussed in the next section.

> **Technology Tip**
>
> Think of your computer as a filing cabinet, and store your work items in folders (like you store paper records in folders).

A number of operating systems are available. The following list includes the major ones:

- Windows® XP
- Windows® Millennium
- Windows® 2000
- Windows® NT
- Linux®
- UNIX®

Operating systems are continually being modified and revised. Right now, as you are studying this text, newer operating systems are probably becoming available.

Application Software

Through application software programs, you tell the computer how to perform a specific task you need done. For example, you can produce a report with graphics by using a word processing program. You can add tables to the report by using a spreadsheet program. You can develop a presentation using graphics with presentation software. Numerous software programs are available; several of them are listed below.

- *Microsoft Office®*. Includes Word, Excel, PowerPoint, and Outlook

- *Microsoft Office® Professional*. Includes Word, Excel, PowerPoint, Access, Outlook, and Publisher
- *Microsoft Works® Suite 2004*. Integrated program
- *Money® 2004*. Personal financial management
- *FrontPage® 2003*. A package to help you develop a Web page
- *Publisher® 2003*. Desktop publishing
- *Lotus® 1-2-3*. A spreadsheet package
- *Lotus® Smart Suite Millennium Edition*. Includes word processing, spreadsheet, database, and presentation programs
- *Quicken 2004*. Personal financial management
- *Word Perfect Office 11*. Includes WordPerfect 11, Quattro Pro 11, and Presentations 11

Just as operating systems are continually revised and updated, so are application software programs. For example, both Microsoft and Corel have revised their office suite approximately every two years.

Free Software

Thousands of free software packages are available on the Web. Some of these packages, by categories, are shown in Figure 9-5 on page 187.

Troubleshooting

As you work with both computer hardware and software, problems are going to occur. One of your tasks as an administrative professional is to solve as many of your problems as possible. You need to become adept at **troubleshooting** (tracing and correcting problems). To be an effective computer troubleshooter, you should have the following general information:

- The operating system your computer uses
- The amount of RAM and hard disk space on your computer
- The functions of software packages you are using
- The assistance available to you within the organization in which you work (Is there a technician who can help you? If not, is there an administrative professional competent on the package you are using?)
- The services available from the software vendor

When you are working on a particular software program and encounter problems, you can take certain steps. As an example, the following troubleshooting assistance is available for most software programs:

- A Help feature allows you to ask questions and provides information on many topics.
- Online and telephone help from the software manufacturer is often available. Microsoft, Corel, Quicken, and AOL all have online and telephone help.
- Third-party manuals are available that help you learn new programs and/or answer many questions you might have. These manuals are available in most bookstores; for example, *WordPerfect for Dummies* is one source.

Computer Viruses

A **computer virus** is a program with unauthorized and often destructive programming code (instructions) that is introduced without the permission or knowledge of the computer user. It is called a virus because, like its biological counterpart, it is contagious. It can pass itself on to other programs with which it comes in contact. Computer viruses become active when the programming instructions that run operating system or application programs are opened. Once active, a virus can copy or reproduce itself and attempt to infect the computer's data files or the operating system or application files. For example, it may copy parts of itself to floppy disks, to the computer's hard drive, or into legitimate computer programs, or it may attach itself to e-mail messages where it can be easily spread to infect other computers. Viruses range from annoying but harmless, to destructive. They might cause messages to pop up on your screen, slow the computer's processing speed, delete all the data on your hard drive, or crash your computer completely. Viruses fall into one of the two following broad categories:

- File infectors attach themselves to the file that runs an application program (the ".exe" file). When the program is activated, the virus spreads to other programs on the hard disk.
- Boot sector viruses install themselves at the beginning of your hard drive where the computer stores the files it needs to start up. Unlike file infectors, these viruses become active every time you turn on your computer.

Early program viruses were usually contracted from floppy disks being used or shared by different computer users. More recently, viruses have been spread through an attachment to e-mail messages. Viruses attached to e-mail messages can very quickly spread an infection throughout a network. Figure 9-6 on page 188 illustrates how an infection from a computer virus can occur.

Those early viruses have since spawned other harmful programs that can be part of a virus but are not actually considered viruses themselves because they do not reproduce:

- *Logic* or *time bombs*, often set off by disgruntled ex-employees, exist harmlessly on a system until an event such as a specific date or time occurs, or when a certain combination of keystrokes is entered. They can completely erase a hard drive or target specific files.
- *Worms* resemble viruses, but rather than infecting files or operating systems they reproduce themselves from computer to computer by using the resources of affected computers to attack other

■ **Figure 9-5**

TYPES OF FREE SOFTWARE AVAILABLE ON THE WEB

Here are a few of the categories of free software available on the Web.

Business	Education
Accounting	Astronomy
Calculators	Chemistry
Databases	Teaching tools
Fax utilities	Graphics
Finance, investments	Clip art
Word processing	Animation video
Internet	Home/hobby
Web browsers	Genealogy
Web servers	Health and fitness
Message boards	Sports
Religion	

networked computers and spread copies of themselves.

- *Trojan horses* masquerade as useful programs. A Trojan horse pretends to be something interesting and harmless such as a game. However, it contains hidden instructions to perform a task that results in some harmful effect. (The term "Trojan horse" comes from the story in Homer's *Iliad* in which a huge wooden horse carried Greek soldiers through the gates of Troy.)
- *Malicious software* are programs that run within a Web browser. They are often hidden in the Java applet and ActiveX controls that improve the usefulness of Web sites.

Since the first computer viruses crept into the world of computing in the 1980s, they have become more and more sophisticated. In 1999 the Melissa virus, spread by e-mail, disabled e-mail servers around the world for several hours. While it was not intended to damage systems, the volume of messages produced slowed down Internet communications dramatically. Then there was the Love Bug virus in May 2002, which is said to have affected one in five PCs worldwide. The Sobig.F virus, by the time it peaked in the fall of 2003, infected one out of every seventeen e-mails. The subsequent Blaster worm infected at least 500 000 computers worldwide. Interestingly enough, a worm designed to protect computers against Blaster created sufficient havoc to bring down the entire check-in system of Air Canada worldwide.

It is important, therefore, to be aware of the need for security. Here are some suggestions on how to protect against viruses:

- Educate yourself about computer viruses.
- Make backups of your files regularly—before you have a virus.
- Download only from sources you trust. To **download** means to receive a file from another source and transfer the information to your hard drive or to receive a file via e-mail, a bulletin board, or an online service.
- Install and regularly update antiviral software. Installing such a program and maintaining current definitions is the single most important action you can take to protect against virus attack. Two widely used programs are offered by McAfee® and Norton™. Antiviral software is available as part of the package when you buy a computer. It is also free on the Internet, two packages being F-Prot® and Trend Micro™.
- Purchase new software programs in tamperproof packaging.
- Install a firewall.

■ Figure 9-6

VIRUS INFECTION CAN OCCUR WHEN A PROGRAM WITH UNAUTHORIZED INSTRUCTIONS IS INTRODUCED INTO A SYSTEM

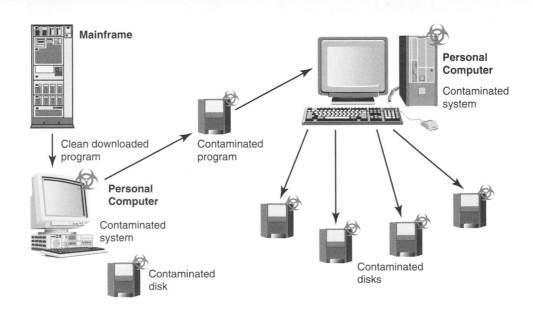

Computer Ethics

Computers have spawned behaviours by some individuals that are unethical or questionable. Just as we need to be ever-vigilant about behaving ethically within our work world, we need to be certain we are living the organization's values and our personal values as we perform computer work. One problem that has become pervasive with computers is the illegal copying of software. People often rationalize that computer software companies are getting rich anyway so it is okay to copy software for their personal use. According to the Canadian Alliance Against Software Theft (CAAST), as much as 40 percent of business software in Canada is obtained illegally. That means that one in every three businesses in Canada is running a program not purchased from a legal source. Compare this to 25 percent in the United States where organizations and individuals caught illegally copying software can be tried and fined. Penalties in the U.S. include imprisonment for up to five years and fines of up to $250 000 for the unauthorized reproduction or distribution of ten or more copies of software with a total retail value exceeding $2500.

In Canada, computer software is defined as a literary work, and is therefore covered by the Copyright Act that protects original literary, artistic, musical, and dramatic works. Recent penalties have included imprisonment and fines up to $20 000.

In addition to the copying of software being unethical and illegal, it can bring viruses into the system. Also, companies and individuals who copy software deprive themselves of the benefits of technical support and training provided by many software companies and the ability to buy upgrades at reduced rates. There is, however, one legal exception to copying—one backup copy of software may be made.

It is unethical to use a computer to gain entry into a company's databank; in fact, it is theft. You might ask "If I produced the data for the company, isn't it my property to do with as I please?" The answer is no; it is not your property unless you have specifically negotiated an arrangement with your company that allows you to retain the rights to the property. The property rights belong to the company that has used its resources to develop the product—in other words, paid you or others within the company a salary or a commission to develop the product. To usurp any property rights, including the right to use the property, is a form of property theft and is unethical.

It is also unethical to use workplace computers to send and receive personal e-mail, to take an Internet class unless the company authorizes the class, and to use the computer in any way for personal use. Employees sometimes believe it is acceptable to use a computer after the workday has ended for personal use or even to take a few minutes during the day to send an e-mail to a friend. It is not okay unless permission is granted by the organization. An employee should never assume that the absence of a policy regarding acceptable behaviour implicitly gives the employee the right to do as he or she pleases. Figure 9-7 lists a proposed "Ten Commandments" for computer ethics.

■ **Figure 9-7**

TEN COMMANDMENTS FOR COMPUTER ETHICS

1. Thou shalt not use a computer to harm other people.
2. Thou shalt not interfere with other people's computer work.
3. Thou shalt not snoop around in other people's files.
4. Thou shalt not use a computer to steal.
5. Thou shalt not use a computer to bear false witness.
6. Thou shalt not use or copy software for which you have not paid.
7. Thou shalt not use other people's computer resources without authorization.
8. Thou shalt not appropriate other people's intellectual output.
9. Thou shalt think about the social consequences of the program you write.
10. Thou shalt use a computer in ways that show consideration and respect.

Source: Ramon C. Barquin, "In Pursuit of a 'Ten Commandments' for Computer Ethics" (Washington: The Computer Ethics Institute, 1992).

Soft Skills: Continual Learning

This chapter reinforces the importance of continual learning in our technological age. Even though great care has been taken to include the latest information here, technology moves quickly. You can no longer assume that what you learn will be correct for a lifetime. All of us must be continual learners if we are to be productive workers and citizens in our society. Years ago, Alvin Toffler said in his book *Future Shock* that the educated person of tomorrow is the person who has learned how to learn. That statement is particularly relevant today and will continue to be. Here are some suggestions for you as you commit yourself to continual learning:

- Since none of us can keep all the newly emerging information in our heads, learn where to look for what you need. A number of sources have been discussed in this chapter, namely the Web, computer periodicals, and books.
- Develop an inquiring mind. Ask questions when you do not understand something. Do not be afraid to admit that you do not have all the answers. Part of ongoing learning is accepting what you do not know and being willing to do something about it.
- Commit to continuing your formal education. Take classes offered by your organization or classes offered at a college or university. Take a course though distance learning. Many colleges and universities now offer a wide variety of these courses that you can complete online in your home at a time that is convenient for you.
- Devote time to learning. Learning does take time, but the results are well worth it.

Chapter Summary

The summary will help you remember the important points covered in the chapter.

- Computers are classified as supercomputers, mainframes, minicomputers, workstation computers (supermicros), and microcomputers (PCs).
- Information is input to the computer by keyboards, scanners, voice recognition, touch screens, and digital cameras.
- Storage devices include floppy disks, Zip disks, Jaz disks, SuperDisks, CDs, and DVDs.
- Information is output from the computer by monitors, inkjet printers, laser printers, networked printers, and multifunction peripherals.
- Networks used within business organizations include local area networks, metropolitan area networks, and wide area networks.
- The Internet and the Web are computer networks used worldwide by organizations and individuals.
- The emergence of the Web nationally and internationally has brought with it the need to pay attention to ethical issues, such as maintaining confidentiality of individuals' financial and health records and not selling lists of names for marketing use.
- The intranet and the extranet are private networks used by organizations for internal uses and selected external uses.
- Operating system software enables a computer to read and write data to a disk and to accept commands from application software.
- Application software tells the computer how to perform a specific task, such as write a report, use graphics, and so on. Office suites are one example of application software.
- Numerous free software packages are available on the Web.
- Computer viruses can result in the deletion of all data on the hard drive and the crashing of your computer.
- Computers have spawned behaviours by some individuals that are unethical or questionable.
- Due to our fast-paced information age, it is important that we commit ourselves to continual learning of technological issues.

Key Terms

The following terms were introduced in this chapter. The page on which the term was introduced is provided to help you locate the new term. Definitions are compiled in the Glossary at the end of the text.

- **Internet** 174
- **Web** 174
- **lifelong learning** 174
- **microcomputer** 175
- **supercomputers** 175
- **genome** 175
- **high-end protein analyzers** 175
- **teraflop** 175
- **terabyte** 175
- **mainframes** 175
- **minicomputer** 175
- **microprocessor** 175
- **workstation computers (supermicros)** 175
- **multiuser computers** 176
- **processor chip** 176
- **Pentium processor** 176
- **Athlon** 176
- **PowerPC** 176
- **notebooks** or **laptops** 176
- **PDA (personal digital assistant)** 176
- **Wi-Fi** 176
- **palms** 176
- **defragmenter** 177
- **continuous** 177
- **surge suppressor** or **UPS (uninterruptible power supply)** 177
- **continuous speech recognition** 178
- **discrete speech recognition** 178
- **touch screen** 178
- **digital camera** 178
- **pixels** 178
- **resolution** 178
- **MB** 179
- **GB** 179
- **TB** 179
- **RAM** 179
- **floppy disks** 180
- **density** 180
- **Zip disks** 181
- **Zip drives** 181

- **SuperDisk** 181
- **Jaz disk** 181
- **CD-ROM** 181
- **CD-R** 181
- **CD-RW** 181
- **DVD-ROM** 181
- **soft copy** 181
- **CRT** 181
- **hard copy** 181
- **LCD** 182
- **inkjet** 182
- **laser** 182
- **networked printers** 182
- **LANs** 183
- **MANs** 183
- **WANs** 183
- **WLANs** 183
- **DSL (digital subscriber line)** 183
- **broadband** 183
- **Web browser** 184
- **proprietary data** 185
- **intranet** 185
- **firewall** 185
- **extranet** 185
- **troubleshooting** 186
- **computer virus** 187
- **download** 188

Responses to Self-Check A

1. Supercomputers; mainframes; minicomputer; workstation computers (supermicros); microcomputers (PCs)
2. A PDA is a personal digital assistant. At its most basic, it serves as an appointment book, an address book, a to-do list, and a calculator. You can also check your e-mail, stock quotes, newspaper headlines, and so on.
3. Computer keyboard; scanners; voice recognition technology; touch screens; digital cameras

Responses to Self-Check C

1. External computer storage devices include floppy disks, Zip disks, Jaz disks, SuperDisks, CDs, and DVDs.
2. The two major types of printers used today are inkjet and laser.

Discussion Items

These discussion items provide an opportunity to test your understanding of the chapter through written responses and/or discussion with your classmates and your instructor.

1. Explain the differences between the Internet, an intranet, and an extranet.
2. List and explain computer input devices.
3. Explain the difference between operating system software and application software.
4. Explain two ethical problems involving computers that may occur in organizations.

Critical-Thinking Activity

Guy has been working for CanAsian Airlines for slightly over a year as your assistant. When he started with the company, you gave him the Policy and Procedures Manual for CanAsian, which included a section on computer ethics. This section makes clear that all computers are the property of CanAsian and not to be used for the personal use of employees. Yesterday your supervisor, Martin Albertson, asked you why Guy was working overtime the evening before. Mr. Albertson said that he had worked until about 7 p.m. As he was leaving, he noticed that Guy was still at his desk. He walked over to say goodnight and noticed that Guy was writing some type of paper that did not appear to be related to CanAsian work. You had to answer that you knew nothing about it but that you would look into it. You asked Guy this afternoon why he was working late that evening. He stated he had a paper to do for a class he was taking but he did not have a computer at home. You thanked him for giving you the information and left to "mull over" what you should do. Guy has been an exceptional employee—he never misses work; he is always on time; his work is done promptly and accurately; he is polite and understands confidentiality. In fact, in his yearly review last month, you gave him an outstanding rating.

When you gave him the Policy and Procedures Manual, you did not go over it with him, but you did ask him to read it. After thinking about it overnight, you went back to Guy the next morning and asked him if he had read the Policy and Procedures Manual. When he answered yes, you asked him why he violated the company policy on using computers for personal business. Guy told you the manual did not discuss personal use of computers. He pulled it from his desk and showed you that there was no section on computer ethics. Now you are in a real quandary. Address the following items:

- Do you believe you made a mistake in giving Guy an incomplete Policy and Procedures Manual? Do you believe Guy is lying to you? Explain your answers.
- How should you handle the situation?
- How can you be certain in the future that employees understand and adhere to what is in the Policy and Procedures Manual?
- What will you report to Mr. Albertson after talking with Guy?

Projects

Project 9-1 *(Objectives 1 and 2)*

Online Project

Using one of the search engines listed in this chapter (such as www.ask.com, www.dogpile.com, or www.google.com) research the function of the microprocessor and the status of voice recognition systems. Write a short summary of your findings, identifying your sources. Submit your summary to your instructor.

Project 9-2 *(Objectives 2 and 3)*

Online Project

Search the Web for the following information:

- The newest office suite software available and the latest antiviral package available
- The most current operating systems in use
- The latest information on Wi-Fi technology

Write a summary of your findings, identifying your sources. Submit your summary to your instructor.

Project 9-3 *(Objective 4)*

Refer to the document on Student CD, SCDP9-3a. Numerous changes must be made. If you do not know how to make the changes, use the Help icon on your software package to troubleshoot. Print out a copy of the document with the changes you made. Using the memorandum form on Student CD, SCDP9-3b, write a memorandum to your instructor and provide the readability level.

Project 9-4 *(Objectives 2 and 5)*

Collaborative Project

Online Project

CanAsian plans to write a computer ethics policy to distribute to the staff. Working with two or three of your classmates, surf the Web for company policies that may be available and articles on ethics. From your research and information in the textbook, write a draft of an ethics policy for CanAsian. Submit your draft policy with a cover memorandum to Mr. Albertson. Use the memorandum form on Student CD, SCDP9-4. Additionally, you have been asked to research what other organizations are doing concerning policies on computer ethics for a section to be included in the Policy and Procedures Manual. Using the Web, see what you can find on the subject. Summarize your findings, citing your sources, and submit your findings to your instructor.

Project 9-5 *(Objective 6)*

Prepare another section of your Professional Growth Plan; describe how you will commit to continual learning throughout this course. Refer to the suggestions in your text on continual learning before you prepare your plan. Save your self-improvement plan on your Professional Growth Plan disk under "Progro9-5." Develop an appropriate title for this portion of your plan.

Chapter 10

Information Distribution and Reprographics

LEARNING OBJECTIVES

1. Explain how to process both incoming and outgoing mail.
2. Identify classes of mail and special services available through Canada Post Corporation.
3. Explain the types of copiers and their functions.
4. *Develop teamwork skills.*

For years mail could be defined with a fairly simple statement. Mail was written information sent via **Canada Post Corporation** to locations both within Canada and abroad. Then came electronic communications—fax, e-mail, intranets and extranets that allowed people within organizations to exchange data internally and externally, the Internet, and software packages that allowed the user to determine postage without ever entering a post office. Additionally, express services, such as Purolator Courier Ltd., FedEx® (Federal Express), UPS® (United Parcel Service), and DHL Worldwide Express™, have become big business as organizations expect their paper products to be delivered almost as quickly as electronic mail. Today the meaning of mail is much broader, with electronic mail (e-mail and fax) and mail delivery systems that include numerous private express companies in addition to Canada Post.

The result of the huge increase in electronic mail has been a significant drop in the volume of first-class mail coming into organizations and a resultant drop in revenue for Canada Post. In fact, Canada Post is now looking at its business differently. It has introduced a number of electronic options for customers, including *epost*™ and **PosteCS**™. *epost*™ is a secure and private Web-based service that allows consumers and businesses to view and pay bills over the Internet. PosteCS™ is a service that helps businesses communicate privately and confidentially over the Internet. In both cases an **electronic postmark**—a Canada Post digital date and time stamp, used to digitally "seal" the electronic package—is an option a user may select prior to sending a electronic "package." The electronic postmark verifies the existence of a document and that the document has not been opened by another party. You can learn more about these services through the Canada Post website at www.canadapost.ca.

Does this mean we are sending less mail than in the past? Absolutely not. In fact, we are sending more. What it does mean is that the way we communicate with each other and our expectations about effective communication have changed drastically. Electronic communication is here to stay and is a routine part of our everyday existence. Does this information mean that paper mail can now be ignored? Certainly not. Paper mail, though it may continue to drop in volume, is still extremely important to organizations.

This chapter will help you, an administrative professional, to understand your role and responsibilities in regard to traditional mail. Your mail duties may include anything from preparing incoming mail for your employer to reviewing and preparing outgoing correspondence to be mailed. After studying this chapter, you will be able to process mail more effectively. You will also become more knowledgeable about copiers and their functions. The soft skill you will focus on in this chapter is *teamwork*.

Incoming and Outgoing Mail

An administrative professional has numerous responsibilities regarding the handling of both incoming and outgoing mail. Unanswered or misplaced mail can be a significant cost to an organization in lost business. Your job as an administrative professional is to make certain that incoming mail is well organized and presented to the executive and that outgoing mail leaves the office in a timely manner by way of the most expeditious service.

Incoming Mail

In a large office, mail comes into a central mailroom where it is sorted according to the company's departments. In addition to sorting, the mailroom may offer additional services, such as opening the mail. If the mail is opened, correspondence is not taken from the envelope, since the envelope itself may have information the receiver needs to know. Mail opened in mailrooms is processed through automatic mail openers that also count the items, which helps a company analyze mail costs. Mail is generally delivered at set times twice a day (in the morning and the afternoon) so employees know when to expect it. Methods of delivery vary; mail may be

- Delivered by a mailroom attendant
- Picked up at the mailroom by the administrative professional
- Delivered by an electronic cart (That is, a self-powered, unattended robotlike cart uses a photo-electric guidance system to follow invisible chemical paths painted on carpeting, floor tile, or other surfaces. It is programmed to make stops at certain locations.)

In small offices, a Canada Post carrier may deliver the mail directly to the office, or the company may maintain a mailbox at the post office. If the organization maintains a post office box, you may have the responsibility for picking up the mail.

Sorting

Once you receive the mail in your office or department, you must do a preliminary mail sort. If several individuals work in the department, sort the mail according to the addressee. An alphabetical sorter is handy if you are sorting mail for a number of individuals. Once the mail is sorted, place the mail for each individual into separate stacks.

Electronic devices are used in large organizations to deliver mail.

Pitney Bowes Mailing Systems, www.pb.com

When this preliminary sort is completed, sort each person's mail in this order:

- *Personal and confidential.* The administrative professional should not open mail marked "Personal" or "Confidential." Place this mail to one side so you do not inadvertently open it.
- *Xpresspost, registered, or priority courier.* This mail is important and should be placed so the individual to whom it is addressed sees it first.
- *Regular business mail (Lettermail).* Mail from customers, clients, and suppliers is also considered important and should be sorted so it receives top priority.
- *Interoffice communications.* This mail generally is received in a distinctive interoffice envelope.
- *Advertisements and circulars.* Advertisements and circulars are considered relatively unimportant and can be handled after the other correspondence is answered.
- *Newspapers, magazines, and catalogues.* These materials should be placed at the bottom of the correspondence stack so they may be read at the executive's convenience.

Opening

Mail may be opened in the mailroom (as you have previously learned), or it may be opened in the individual's office. Mail opened in an individual's office is usually opened by hand, using an envelope opener. When opening mail, follow these procedures:

- Have necessary supplies readily available. These supplies include an envelope opener, a date and time stamp, routing and action slips, a stapler, paper clips, and a pen or pencil.
- Before opening an envelope, tap the lower edge of the envelope on the desk so the contents fall to the bottom and are not cut when the envelope is opened.
- After the correspondence is opened, check the envelope carefully to be certain all items have been removed.
- Fasten any enclosures to the correspondence. Attach small enclosures to the front of the correspondence. Attach enclosures larger than the correspondence to the back.
- Mend any torn paper with tape.
- If a personal or confidential letter is opened by mistake, do not remove it from the envelope. Write "Opened by Mistake" on the front of the envelope, add your initials, and reseal the envelope with tape.
- Stack the envelopes on the desk in the same order as the opened mail in case it becomes necessary to refer to the envelopes. A good practice is to save all envelopes for at least one day in case they are needed for reference. Then they may be thrown away.

Keeping Selected Envelopes

Certain envelopes should be retained. Keep the envelope when you notice one or more of the following things:

- *An incorrectly addressed envelope.* You or your supervisor may want to call attention to this fact when answering the correspondence.
- *A letter with no return address.* The envelope usually will have the return address.
- *A letter written on letterhead with a different return address from that on the envelope.* For example, a person may write a letter on hotel letterhead and write the business address on the envelope.
- *A letter without a signature.* The envelope may contain the writer's name.

- *An envelope that has a significantly different postmark from the date on the document.* The document date may be compared with the postmark date to determine the delay in receiving the document.
- *A letter specifying an enclosure that is not enclosed.* Write "No Enclosure" on the letter and attach the envelope.
- *A letter containing a bid, an offer, or an acceptance of a contract.* The postmark date may be needed as legal evidence.

Dating and Time Stamping

Although all organizations do not use date and time stamping procedures, it can be an important step. It furnishes a record of when the correspondence was received. For example, a letter may arrive too late to handle the matter mentioned in the letter; in this case the stamped date of receipt is a recorded confirmation of the day the letter was received and of the resultant inability to take care of the matter. Or perhaps the correspondence is not dated; in this case the date stamped on the letter shows approximately when the correspondence was written. Date and time stamping may be done with either a hand stamp or a small machine.

Reading and Annotating

A large amount of mail crosses the desk of a busy executive every day. As an administrative professional, you can help by scanning it and underlining the important words and phrases with a coloured pen or pencil. You should also check mathematical calculations and verify dates that appear in correspondence.

The next step is to **annotate** (to make notations about previous action taken or facts that will assist the reader). You can annotate by writing notes in the margin of the correspondence or by using sticky notes. The advantage of sticky notes is that they can be peeled off and destroyed when you and the executive are finished with them. Discuss with your supervisor which of these methods is preferred. If an enclosure is missing from the letter, make an annotation. If a bill is received, check the computations. Note any discrepancies by annotating. If the correspondence refers to a previous piece of correspondence written by the executive, pull that item and attach it to the new correspondence, noting the attachment. Annotations may also be used to remind the executive of a previous commitment. For example, he or she might have agreed to have lunch with the person writing. When answering the letter, the executive may want to refer to their lunch plans.

Organizing

After you have completed the preliminary mail sorts and have opened, date and time-stamped, read, and annotated, you are ready to do a final sort. Here is one arrangement that may be used:

- *Immediate action.* This mail must be handled on the day of receipt or shortly thereafter.
- *Routine correspondence.* Such mail would include memorandums and other types of non-urgent mail.
- *Informational mail.* Periodicals, newspapers, advertisements, and other types of mail that do not require answering but are for the executive's reading should be included here.

Notice another method of sorting mail provided in the Communication Tip here.

After you have organized the mail, you are ready to put it in folders with labels indicating the categories established. A good practice is to colour-code the folders. For example, the Immediate Action folder might be red, the Routine Correspondence folder blue, and the Informational Mail folder yellow. Colour coding helps the executive see at a glance what mail needs to be handled first. Folders also help maintain confidentiality; someone walking into the executive's office could not easily read the material. The folders should be put on the executive's desk in a predetermined area. He or she may have an inbox. Whatever the procedure, it should meet the executive's needs.

The executive may also ask that you bring the mail twice a day. For example, if outside mail is received in the morning and afternoon, the executive may ask that you organize and bring it approximately 30 minutes after you receive it each time.

You may handle a large portion of the mail yourself if the executive does not need to see it. This is especially true if you have been working for the company and the executive for a while and are familiar with the procedures and the executive's style. However, never destroy mail (even what you might consider junk mail) unless you have a clear agreement with the executive about making decisions in this regard.

Communication Tip

Incoming mail may be sorted into folders with these labels: Urgent Mail; Signature Needed; Read—Action Needed; and Read—Periodicals and Printed Matter.

Routing

At times, more than one person may need to read a piece of correspondence or a publication. In the case of correspondence, if you feel it is urgent that all individuals immediately receive the information, make photocopies of the correspondence and send a copy to each person on the list. If it is not urgent, route the correspondence, using a routing slip to save copying costs. A routing slip is also an effective method for circulating publications.

You can purchase routing slips or create your own (an example is shown in Figure 10-1). For example, if you route correspondence to the same individuals regularly, you can create a routing slip that already has the individuals' names printed on it. If you are circulating several publications to the same people at the same time, vary the order of the names on the list so that the documents do not always start their circulation with the same person, whoever is at the top of the list.

Handling During the Executive's Absence

In Chapter 15 you will be introduced to some of the responsibilities of an administrative assistant while an executive is out of the office and travelling on behalf of the company. One of your responsibilities while the executive is travelling is to handle the mail. In that case, here are guidelines:

■ Figure 10-1

A ROUTING SLIP

ROUTING SLIP			
Description of Document:	*Draft — Travel Policy and Procedures*		
Date:	*October 21, 2004*		
Please circulate to:			
Order	Name	Date	Initial
3	Guy Beauchamp		
2	Luyin Wu		
1	Keri-An Mahar		
4	Ryan Hughs		
	Return to:	*Guy Beauchamp*	

- Talk with the executive before he or she leaves about your mail-handling responsibilities. Be specific with any questions so you have a clear understanding. Mistakes in handling mail can be costly to the company.
- When urgent mail comes in, handle it immediately according to the executive's directions. For example, you may give it to the person in charge or you may fax it to the executive.
- Answer mail that falls within your area of responsibility promptly.
- Maintain mail that has been answered (with the answer attached) in a separate folder; the executive may want to review it when he or she returns.
- Maintain mail that can wait for the executive's return in a separate folder. Retrieve any previous correspondence that the executive will need when reviewing the mail. Place this correspondence in the folder also.

Mailrooms today use a wide variety of electronic equipment in processing the mail.

Thomas Michael Cochran/PhotoEdit

Outgoing Mail

An administrative professional's responsibilities for handling outgoing mail will vary. In a large company he or she is responsible for preparing the mail for processing by mailroom employees. Mailroom employees may pick up the mail at various times during the day, or the administrative professional may be responsible for taking the outgoing mail to the mailroom.

Mailrooms today are automated. In large companies, they may be **outsourced** (handled by an outside firm) as a cost-saving measure. Some firms that handle mail services for organizations are Kelly Management Services®, Pitney Bowes Management Services®, and Xerox® Business Systems. The Internet is used extensively to gather postal-related information, access postal-related associations, and keep track of delivery status (with express carriers such as Purolator and others providing online delivery information). Multifunctional equipment is used to fold, sort, label, and attach postage. Software is used in such functions as maintaining mailing lists. Incoming mail may also be processed via computer imaging and integrated into an electronic communication system. The photo here shows multifunctional equipment from Pitney-Bowes. More details can be found at

- www.neopost.ca
- www.francotyp.ca
- www.pitneybowes.ca

In the mailrooms of large companies, PC-based software allows staff to easily check in the **accountable items** (express items), including registered mail items or items sent via private courier. Using a wand, an attendant is able to scan a bar code on incoming items to establish their identity and enter the recipient's name. Mail can then be easily sorted by whatever delivery scheme is being used—floor, building, department, and so on. Mailrooms also use software to track mail expenditures by departments or divisions within the organization. Such tracking allows budget managers to control their postal budgets more effectively.

In a small company, the administrative professional usually has the responsibility of preparing and processing the mail, which may even include taking it to the local postal office or calling the mailing service to arrange pickup. Whether you work in a large or a small company, certain standard responsibilities are a part of the process. These are discussed next.

Preparing Correspondence for Mailing

By following these procedures consistently and carefully, you can save your organization both time and money.

- Address envelopes carefully. When using today's computer software packages, you need only key the address once; you may then either address an envelope or prepare a label without rekeying. Your task is to be certain the address is keyed correctly the first time. Check it carefully against your records. When an address of an organization changes, be sure to correct your mailing list.

- Check that every letter or memorandum is signed.
- Make sure special mailing notations are included and correctly positioned on the envelope.
- Make certain all enclosures are included.
- If enclosures are sent in a separate envelope (because they are too large to send with the letter), be sure the address on the second envelope is correct. Mark it with the appropriate class of mail.
- Put all interoffice correspondence in appropriate envelopes with the name and department of the addressee listed on the envelope.
- If a mailroom employee applies postage and seals your mail, neatly stack your correspondence for the employee who picks it up.

Technology Tip

Key addresses carefully; check the keyed address against your records to be certain it is correct.

Figure 10-2 on page 200 illustrates a correctly addressed envelope.

Adhering to Automation Requirements

As an administrative professional, you are responsible for seeing that outgoing mail is properly prepared for the automated sorting equipment that Canada Post and private services use. Envelopes that are not legible or that do not show a postal code are removed for hand sorting, which takes longer to process. In addition to being sorted by postal code, mail is also sorted by bar code. Check your next utilities statement. Many utility companies now have bar codes on their return envelopes, which allow fast sorting with a **BCS** (bar code sorter). Private mail services, such as FedEx and UPS, also use bar codes to sort their huge volumes of mail.

In Canada's six-character alphanumeric postal code system, the country is divided into 18 zones. Each code has the following pattern: letter-number-letter (space) number-letter-number. The first letter represents the regional zone, normally a province. In the case of Ontario, however, its population size necessitates several major sub-zones. The two characters that follow, a number and a letter, provide additional division of the region by city, town, or municipality. The second group of characters identifies more specifically the location within a city, town, or municipality—whether the item is to be delivered to one side or the other of a street, or perhaps a specific building on a street or even a specific floor of a large building. For example, in "T2P 5C5,"

T designates the province of Alberta, 2 designates the city of Calgary, and P designates an area within Calgary. The next three-character group identifies the west tower of a large building known as the Bankers Hall. See Figure 10-3 on page 201 for an illustration of Canadian geographic postal code regions.

The Canada Post website at www.canadapost.ca is an excellent resource when you need a postal code. Select "Find a Postal Code" on their home page and you are immediately provided with a form. Fill out the form and click "Submit." A national database is searched, and if the code is found it is displayed. While most of today's businesses will use the Internet to obtain a postal code, postal codes are also available from Canada Post by telephone (1-900-565-2633) or on CD-ROM (obtainable by calling 1-800-565-4362).

In the addressing of envelopes or packages, Canada Post requests that

- The address be keyed in *ALL CAPITALS* (though *Upper-and-Lowercase* is also acceptable)
- The attention line be keyed as the first line of the address
- No punctuation be used unless it is part of a name
- The CPC-approved two-letter provincial (or state) abbreviations be used; see the Reference Guide on the Student CD or the *Canadian Addressing Guide* on the CPC website for a complete listing of these
- The municipality (city), province, and postal code be keyed on the same line

More detailed information about addressing mailable items is available in the *Canadian Addressing Guide* provided by Canada Post Corporation; it can be downloaded from www.canadapost.ca/business/offerings/address_management/pdf/addressing_guide-e.pdf.

Here you will find examples for correctly addressing the following:

- Civic addresses
- Rural route and general delivery
- Post office box
- Bilingual addresses
- U.S.A. and international addresses

There is also other useful information, such as

- Correct abbreviations for street types, directions, and designators

■ Figure 10-2

A CORRECTLY ADDRESSED ENVELOPE

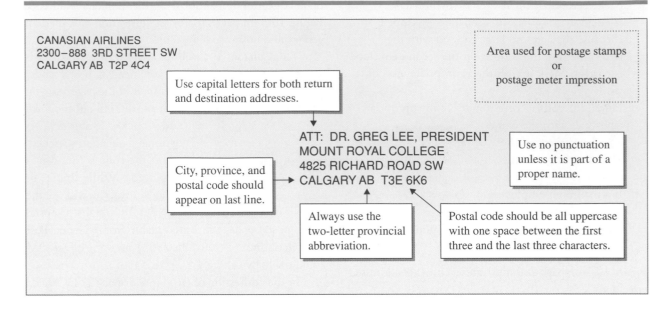

- Approved two-letter Canadian provincial and U.S. state abbreviations
- English and French versions of country names

Keeping a copy of this guide handy will ensure you are doing all you can to expedite your company's mail.

Sealing and Stamping

If you work in a medium-to-large office, you may not be responsible for sealing and stamping the mail; the outgoing mail is likely sent to a mailroom where these tasks are done with automated equipment. If you work in a small office, however, you may seal and stamp envelopes using a postage meter. Envelopes are fed into the meter and stacked, sealed, weighed, meter-stamped, and counted in one continuous operation. The metered mail imprint serves as postage payment, a postmark, and a cancellation mark all in one. A postage meter either prints directly on envelopes or on adhesive strips that are then affixed to packages.

Businesses rent or lease postage meters from a number of private companies. Only meters manufactured by Ascom, Neopost, Prancotyp-Postalia, or Pitney Bowes are approved by CPC for use in Canada.

Electronic Postage

In the United States **e-stamps** (electronic postage, also referred to as **PC postage**), is available through Stamps.com (www.stamps.com). This service allows postage to be generated via the Web to a PC. This type of postage is rapidly gaining users due to its convenience, particularly in small offices and home offices. Larger organizations will also be able to take advantage of electronic postage as PC postage vendors develop better ways to control postage expenditures. The first step to using PC postage is to apply for a postal licence, which can be obtained online in just a few hours. With e-stamps, postage can be printed on labels or on envelopes, packages, mailing tubes, or anything else that needs mailing. At the time of writing, Canada Post had no immediate plans to begin offering this service.

Maintaining Mailing Lists

Most companies have correspondence they send to certain groups of individuals. As an administrative professional, your responsibility is to maintain a current mailing list. You must periodically update addresses as well as occasionally add new names to the mailing list. By using the appropriate software you can maintain mailing lists on your computer, updating them quickly and easily. You can print address labels and envelopes from your mailing lists.

Services Through Canada Post

Even though the way we send and receive mail has changed drastically with the advent of electronic technology, the main provider of mail services in Canada

■ Figure 10-3

CANADIAN GEOGRAPHIC POSTAL CODE REGIONS

Courtesy of Canada Post Corporation

remains Canada Post (a Crown corporation). Regular and special mail services provided by Canada Post, private mail services, and international mail are presented in the next section. While the following information is current as of the time of writing, the services and charges change periodically. It is important for administrative professionals to keep current and check this site frequently.

Domestic Postal Service Classifications

Domestic mail (mail delivered within Canada) falls into several classifications. We will look at the major ones here.

Lettermail

Although we think of Lettermail as basically letters and other types of personal and/or business correspondence, the term refers to any type of mail that measures no more than 90 by 235 millimetres and weighs 50 grams or less. In addition to letters it includes cards, postcards, invoices, receipts, financial reports, and other promotional or non-promotional mailable items partly keyed or handwritten.

Incentive Lettermail™

Canadian businesses, government departments and organizations that deal in large volumes of Lettermail can obtain discounted prices by signing an Incentive Lettermail Agreement with Canada Post. To be eligible for the lower postage prices Incentive Lettermail provides, mailable items must all be the same size with machine-readable addresses. They must be presorted when delivered to a CPC outlet.

Admail™

There are two types of direct mail available from Canada Post—Addressed Admail™ and Unaddressed Admail™. Admail is a targeted mail service that enables

Macdonald-Cartier Academy
Private Junior High School
270 Crichton Street.,
Ottawa, Ontario
K1M 1W4

040609 18:42 KOA J0X 098
www.canadaPost.ca
www.Postescanada.ca

THOMSON NELSON
1120 BIRCHMOUNT ROAD
TORONTO ON M1K 5G4

Nelson
1120 Birchmount Road
Toronto, ON M1K 5G4

CANADA POSTES
POST CANADA
00.49
M1K 5G4 2004-06-11
NE 0103300015

SANJEV SINGH
156 RIVEREDGE ROAD WEST
HILL VALLEY NS B3P 1P4

An envelope with a cancelled stamp, and one with a metered postage mark.

businesses to promote their products and services by delivering their message directly to specific neighbourhoods.

Unaddressed Admail, often referred to as "householder mail" because it does not contain any specific delivery address, consists of items such as flyers, coupons, or product samples. It is and can be targeted on the basis of geographic location, demographic and consumer purchasing behaviour, or residential versus businesses locations.

Addressed Admail, on the other hand, enables businesses to promote their products and services on a more personalized basis.

Business Reply Mail™

Another form of direct mail service is Business Reply Mail. Communication between a business and its customers can be enhanced when businesses use either self-addressed postage prepaid business reply cards or envelopes to obtain information for a database, or to request information, initiate customer service, raise funds, or receive payments or subscription renewals.

Xpresspost™

Xpresspost offers next-business-day delivery to local or regional destinations and two-day service between most major Canadian destinations. Documents, packets, and parcels that do not exceed 30 kilograms in weight, or

3 metres in combined length and **girth** (a measurement around the thickest part) may be sent as Xpresspost. Xpresspost envelopes, labels, and boxes are available at Canada Post outlets. Pickup service is also available for a fee to Canada Post account customers only.

Priority Courier™

Priority Courier is the fastest mail service available from Canada Post, with overnight, guaranteed, on-time next-day delivery by noon to most destinations within Canada of documents, packets, and parcels. The service operates 365 days a year. Items must weigh 30 kilograms or less and measure 3 metres or less in combined length and girth. Prepaid envelopes, available in two different sizes, may be purchased in advance and used at any time.

Regular Parcel

Regular Parcel is the most economical shipping service offered by Canada Post for packets and parcels being shipped within Canada. Delivery within three business days to local destinations, four to six days regionally, and five to ten days between other Canadian destinations is standard. Regular Parcel is used for mailing items such as books, circulars, catalogues, and other printed or non-printed matter that weighs no more than 30 kilograms. Regular Parcel must measure 3 metres or less in combined length and girth. A surcharge applies if any one dimension exceeds a metre.

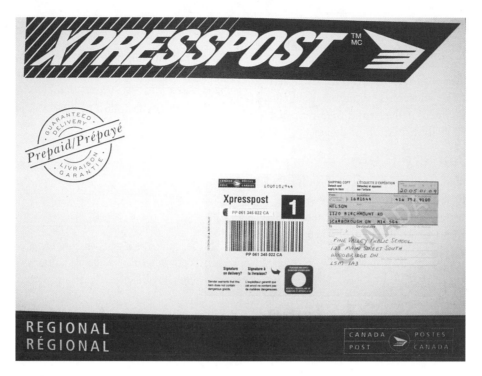

An Xpresspost envelope.

Expedited Parcel™

Account customers who regularly have a high-volume parcel shipment business to other businesses or consumers may find the Expedited Parcel service offered by Canada Post convenient. More information can be obtained at the Canada Post website at www.canadapost.ca.

Publications Mail™

Periodical publications produced in Canada may be eligible for distribution at the Publications Mail rate. The periodical must be published at least twice a year, be mailed in Canada for delivery in Canada, be individually addressed or bundled and unaddressed, and contain

less than 70 percent advertising in at least half the issues mailed in a year. The maximum allowable weight varies from 50 grams for individually addressed items to 25 kilograms for bundled unaddressed copies. Rates are based on the weight of the piece and the distance from origin to destination.

Other Products and Services

Canada Post offers several services that are beneficial in special situations: Advice of Receipt, Collect on Delivery, Insured Mail, and Registered Mail. Additional information can be found at the Canada Post website, www.canadapost.ca.

A Priority Courier label.

Advice of Receipt

An Advice of Receipt card is available only for Registered Mail items destined for United States or international delivery, and must be purchased at the time of mailing. The addressee's signature is obtained on the card at the time of delivery and then returned to the sender, providing confirmation of delivery.

Collect on Delivery (COD)

This service, available for parcel delivery only, allows mailers to collect the price of goods and/or postage on merchandise from the addressee when the item is delivered. The amount to be collected from the recipient may not exceed $1000.

Insured Mail

This service provides compensation to a mailer for loss or damage of mailable items. Coverage up to $1000 is available for Lettermail; up to $100 on Regular Parcel when Delivery Confirmation is purchased; and up to $5000 on Xpresspost. Items may not be insured for more than their value. A detailed list of items not eligible for Insured Mail can be found in the *Canada Postal Guide*, available at www.canadapost.ca.

Registered Mail

Registered mail provides proof of mailing and/or proof of delivery for valuable mailed items. The sender is given a receipt, and Canada Post obtains a signature and date of delivery along with the printed name of the individual who signed for the item. The name of the person who signed for the delivered item is available to the sender by noon the following business day. A secured image of that person's signature can be viewed on the Canada Post website at no charge. Hard copy of the signature may also be obtained for a fee or by calling the Customer Relationship Network.

Registered Mail may include Lettermail, non-document materials such as coins or jewellery, and literature for the visually impaired. There are some unacceptable items; a list may be found at www.canadapost.ca. Do the Self-Check to check your understanding of Canada Post's mail classifications.

U.S. and International Mail

With organizations continuing to expand into international markets, you may need to send paper mail to the United States or internationally. The principal categories of international mail provided by Canada Post Corporation are

SELF-CHECK

Take a few minutes now to check your understanding of what you have learned to this point about Canada Post mail classifications. Answer the following questions:

1. Describe the following types of mail: Lettermail and Xpresspost.

    _____

    _____

    _____

2. Describe these special services offered by Canada Post: Advice of Receipt, COD, Insured Mail, and Registered Mail.

    _____

    _____

    _____

How did you do? Check your answers with the ones provided at the end of this chapter.

- U.S.A. or International Letterpost
- Xpresspost U.S.A. or Xpresspost International
- International Incentive Letterpost

U.S.A. or International Letterpost

U.S.A. and International Letterpost items are shipped via "air mail" and can include letters, cards, postcards, and self-mailers (items without a cover) weighing no more than 50 grams and oversize items no more than 500 grams. Items must be posted in Canada and bear a Canadian return address if a return address is used.

Xpresspost U.S.A. or Xpresspost International

At a cost much less than a courier, Xpresspost U.S.A. or Xpresspost International provides fast, guaranteed on-time delivery, with confirmation, of documents, packets, and parcels to the United States and other participating countries. A list of participating countries can be found at www.canadapost.ca.

International Incentive Letterpost

If you are involved in sending a large amount of mail internationally, you may want to check out International Incentive Letterpost. This service offers large-volume Canadian businesses an incentive-based "air mail" or "surface mail" service for commercial mail addressed to the U.S.A. and/or other international destinations. More information on this service is available at www.canadapost.ca.

Private Mail Services

Several private companies in both the United States and Canada offer mail services. In addition to service within North America, many of these private companies offer international service. Four major companies are Purolator Courier Ltd., FedEx, United Parcel Service (UPS), and DHL Canada.

You can find information about each of these companies at their websites:

- www.purolator.com
- www.fedex.com
- www.ups.com
- www.dhl.com

Some of the services offered by UPS and by other companies are

Courtesy of Federal Express Canada

Private mail services such as FedEx offer fast service both within Canada and internationally.

- Document exchange, an electronic delivery service enabling customers to send time-sensitive documents, images, and software for immediate worldwide delivery via the Internet
- Same-day delivery service to virtually anywhere in Canada as well as from many international business centres 24 hours a day, 365 days a year
- Overnight delivery of letters, documents, and packages
- Daily pickup services
- Online tools that allow selection of services, calculation of rates, lookup of addresses, validation and printing of labels, and tracking of shipping history by user-defined criteria

Additional Delivery Services

Most large cities also have messenger or courier services available. For example, if you wish to have a document delivered to a customer across town, you can call the messenger service to pick it up.

The company Mail Boxes Etc.SM also provides packing and shipping services. They pack the material, ship it, insure it, and make certain it reaches its final destination anywhere in the world. They will also stuff envelopes, meter mail, accept CODs, and hold and forward your mail while you are away.

Some small rural communities in Canada may not have a postal outlet. In these instances bus, truck, or rail service where available can be used for parcel delivery. Most bus companies offer services every day of the week, and sometimes delivery might be made as soon as the day after shipping. Pickup service is also offered by some bus companies; check with their local offices for rates and delivery/pickup options.

Some of our most northern communities can only be accessed by air. The airlines that serve these locations have different rates depending on weight and the urgency of the delivery. Pickup and delivery options are also available with air services.

Reprographics

Reprographics refers not only to the process of making copies but also to any piece of equipment that makes copies of an original. The advent of copiers and multi-function units (combination copiers, scanners, fax, and printers) has made the job of the administrative professional much easier. Rather than having to rekey a document, he or she can simply save or scan it into the computer, make any needed changes, and print it out. Copiers are used constantly in offices.

However, their convenience has also brought abuses. Too many copies are made, and people end up throwing away a lot of paper. Conserving paper is **ecologically** important (important to the relationships between human groups and their physical and social environments). As an administrative professional, you will be using copiers daily; your task includes making ethical decisions when doing so.

This section will help you understand the types of copiers available and remind you of the importance of ethical copying.

Types of Copiers

Copiers are available in two types—analog and digital. Although digital technology is rapidly overtaking the copier market, analog copiers are still used and may be the best choice for small offices and teleworkers. Analog copiers, while making the first copy quickly, take longer to produce multiple copies than digital copiers. Since digital copiers have fewer moving parts than analog copiers, they are less likely to jam. Analog copiers are generally less expensive than digital machines, and the cost per copy is lower. However, digital copier prices are dropping, and many believe analog machines will be obsolete in the not-too-distant future. Digital copiers are becoming more intelligent and, when networked with fax machines and printers, they give users the ability to produce all types of output directly from their workstations.

Another way to categorize copiers is by the number of copies they make. **Low-volume copiers** typically produce from 12–30 **cpm** (**copies per minute**) and run from 500 to 4000 copies per month. **Mid-volume copiers** produce 20–49 cpm and run from 5000 to 85 000 copies per month, and **high-volume copiers** produce 50–135 cpm and run from 100 000 to 400 000 copies per month.

Copier Features

The features of copiers vary with their size and price. Some of the features are given here. If you are involved in helping select a copier for your organization, you need to carefully analyze the various features available and compare them with the needs of your organization. Figure 10-4 on page 207 lists a number of questions you should ask when selecting a copier.

Paper Capacity

Paper capacity is the number of sheets the paper tray can hold. Low-volume copiers hold from 100 to 999 sheets, medium-volume copiers from 1000 to 1999 sheets, and high-volume from 2000 to 5000 sheets.

Duplexing

Copying on both sides of a sheet of paper is known as **duplexing**. This feature saves paper and reduces the number of sheets to be filed away. An operator can duplex merely by pushing the proper buttons. Originals printed on only one side can easily be copied on both sides for a new copy. When necessary, it is just as simple to have duplexed originals copied on one side of the paper. Consider duplexing large documents intended for distribution through the mail, since mail costs are based on weight; less paper means a lighter package that results in lower postage costs.

Document or Digital Editing

Copiers that have an editing function scan the image and convert it to digital signals. Then using control keys or a wand (similar to the type used in retail stores to scan letters and numbers on price tags), the operator can *mask* (omit part by covering), move, and manipulate the image.

Collate and Staple

Collating means assembling, in chronological order, the pages in a multiple-page document. Depending on your needs and the equipment being used, you can program copiers to collate only or to collate and staple sets of materials.

Automatic Folding

Some copiers fold 11 × 17 inch (432 × 279 millimetre) copies to 8-1/2 × 11 inch (216 × 279 mm) size. This feature allows drawings and schematics to be kept in a convenient format for handling and distribution. The fold can also be **offset** (not folded to the edge of the paper) so that the folded materials can be placed in three-ring binders.

Environmentally Friendly Features

Many copiers incorporate organic photoconductors, recyclable materials, toner-save modes, and energy-save modes. Some vendors offer their own brands of recycled paper as well as programs that allow customers to recycle their toner cartridges.

Combination Copiers

For many years we have been hearing that increasing use of technology would eventually result in the "paper-

■ Figure 10-4

COPIER SELECTION QUESTIONS

QUESTIONS FOR THE ORGANIZATION

- How many people will be using the copier?
- How many copies will be made per month?
- Is there a projected increase or decrease in copy volume over the next three years?
- What features are needed? Is the ability to collate and/or staple multiple page documents required?
- Will colour copying be needed?
- What materials will be copied? What percentage of copying will be on letter-size paper? What percentage of copying will be on legal-size paper? What percentage of copying will be on 11 × 17 inch paper? What percentage of copying will be stapled?
- What space limitations exist for the copier? (If there are space limitations, the size of the copier becomes an issue.)
- Should a maintenance contract be purchased?

QUESTIONS TO BE ANSWERED DURING A DEMONSTRATION

- What is the quality of the copy?
- Are the copies clean and crisp?
- If it is a colour copier, are the colours clear?

- Is the machine easy to operate?
- Is the interior easily accessible for removing jammed paper and replacing toner?

QUESTIONS TO BE ANSWERED ABOUT THE DEALER/VENDOR'S BACKGROUND

- Is the vendor authorized to sell and service the model being considered?
- How long has the dealer/vendor been in business?
- Have any complaints been filed against the vendor with the Better Business Bureau?

QUESTIONS TO ASK OF THE DEALER/VENDOR

- What is the purchase price of the machine?
- What is the cost of supplies, especially toner?
- Do you carry parts for the brand?
- What is your response time on a typical service request?
- What is the cost of the service?
- Are maintenance contracts available? If so, what is the cost?
- Is key operator training available?
- How long have you been in business?

---

less office." While this has not turned out exactly as predicted—it seems we still need a hard copy of most communications—it is important for businesses to cut costs wherever possible. Limiting the amount of dedicated equipment—fax machines, printers, scanners, and copiers—can result in savings for an organization. All-in-one machines combine the functions of these four paper-handling devices. This type of equipment provides an economical alternative for smaller firms. Larger firms can analyze the needs of different departments in their organization and put combination copiers in areas where documents are being printed, scanned, copied, and faxed. Dedicated equipment can then go where only one function is required.

Control Systems

If you have ever worked in an office, you are probably aware of the copying abuses that persist. Employees often make ten copies of a document when only eight are actually needed. The extra copies are made "just in

case"; but, more often than not, they eventually get thrown away. Another widespread abuse, clearly an ethical violation, is copying for personal use.

To curb abuses, many organizations use copy control devices. Every system operates somewhat differently, but they all have the same basic features. For example, in one system the user might enter an account number onto a keypad to gain access to a copier; in another, the user might insert a card that is only good for a certain number of copies, and copying costs are automatically charged back to the appropriate department or division. Each department or division can then check copy costs against a specific account. If abuses are occurring, appropriate action can be taken.

Ethical Considerations and Etiquette

Every employee should be ethical in the use of copying machines. He or she should also be aware of the legal restrictions on the copying of certain documents.

Copyright is the exclusive right granted to the author or creator of an original body of work to reproduce or authorize someone else to reproduce the material. Behaving ethically when copying means that you *do not* engage in the following activities:

- Copying documents for your personal use.
- Copying cartoons, jokes, and similar types of information to be distributed to your friends and co-workers.
- Making copies of documents you need for an outside professional group, such as a service club—unless you have approval from your organization to do so.
- Copying materials restricted by the Copyright Act, such as published works (for example, textbooks), birth certificates, passports, driver's licences, and so on. Generally speaking, without the express, written consent of the author, the Act makes it illegal to reproduce copyright materials for commercial distribution. If you have questions about what is legal to copy, check with your organization's solicitor or check the Copyright Act.

In addition to ethics, etiquette is an issue whenever a number of individuals use the same copier. Figure 10-5 gives several etiquette considerations.

Shredders

For those times when a machine malfunctions and copies must be destroyed, businesses often install a **shredder**—a machine that cuts paper into strips or confetti-like material—near the copier. Today shredded paper is recycled by many businesses as packing material. Since mailrooms process a large amount of paper and often pack materials for shipping, they use shredders too.

The shredder market has increased over the past few years due primarily to the impact of technology. As we have mentioned, unnecessary copies are often made, and often these contain confidential or sensitive information. If these are tossed into wastebaskets, people with unethical motives can use this information to the detriment of the company. Consider:

- Social insurance numbers (SINs) and birth dates can be used to create false identity papers and open fake chequing accounts.
- Competitors can use information gathered from discarded papers to damage the company. For example, a company's bid on a project may get into the hands of a competitor who then underbids just enough to win the contract.

Figure 10-5

ETIQUETTE CONSIDERATIONS WHEN COPYING MATERIALS

When sharing a copier with several people, be considerate of their time. Observe the basic courtesies:

- If you are involved in an extensive copying job, let your colleagues interrupt when they have only a few pages to copy.
- If the machine malfunctions while you are copying, try to fix the problem. If you cannot do so, call the key operator in your company or a service repairperson. *Do not* walk away, leaving the problem for the next person to deal with.
- When toner runs out, refill it.
- When paper runs out, add more.
- When paper jams, clear it.
- If you are using additional supplies such as paper clips, scissors, and so on, return them to their location before leaving.
- If you have run copies that are not usable, destroy them. Put them in a shredder and/or a recycle bin. Do not leave a messy work area for the next person to clean up.
- Return the copier to its standard settings.

- Information about new technology being developed by the company may get into the hands of information criminals who use it to the detriment of society.

You have certain responsibilities as an administrative professional in shredding papers:

- Know the company policies on shredding.
- Know when a document is confidential or sensitive.
- Never toss unneeded copies in the trash without questioning whether they are confidential or sensitive.
- Shred all appropriate, unneeded copies.

Recycling

Our technological age is spawning the use of more paper rather than less, even considering the number of electronic messages sent and received. This has serious repercussions for our environment: we are losing valuable forests and land (in establishing landfills).

Because so much paper is being used, recycling programs are becoming common in businesses. Such programs can save millions of tonnes of paper every year. Organizations often provide recycling bins for paper and outsource the collection and shredding of paper to private vendors.

In addition to recycling paper, organizations need to use recycled paper products. Sixty-four percent less energy and 58 percent less water is used in the production of recycled paper than in the production of virgin papers. In addition, the manufacture of recycled paper produces 74 percent less air pollution and 35 percent less water pollution.

Additionally, organizations need to look at how they can reduce the use of paper in the office. Here are several suggestions:

- When appropriate, use both sides of the page (duplex your documents).
- Convert scratch paper into memo pads, telephone answering slips, and similar items.
- Print only the number of copies needed.
- Send interoffice mail via e-mail.
- Make hard copies of e-mails only when documentation of the communication is necessary.
- Shred used paper and use it to package materials instead of plastic pellets.

Soft Skills: Teamwork

You have been introduced to the importance of teamwork in collaborative writing in Chapter 6 and in presentations in Chapter 7. However, teamwork is vitally important to your success in almost all workplace situations. You learned in Chapter 1 that the word *team* can be traced back to the Indo-European word *deuk*, meaning "to pull." A truly effective team consists of two or more people who need each other to accomplish the best results possible.

In this chapter, you have learned the importance of working closely with your employer in processing incoming and outgoing mail. You must understand your employer's needs when processing mail—how it is to be sorted, organized, and routed. If the two of you fail to work together in setting parameters, the results may be angry clients or customers who have not received prompt responses to their requests or inquiries. Obviously, this example is merely one important team situation in the workplace. You work with a number of individuals—your workgroup, other administrative assistants, your employer, and your administrators—on a daily basis in various types of teams.

If you are to be an effective team member or leader, you must understand what it takes to make an effective team. Then you must work to build effective teams within the organization. Most of us understand teamwork in sports. We watch championship basketball and football, and we notice groups of specialists. However, these specialists do not act independently of each other. Their success depends not only on individual excellence but also on their ability to work together. Team members must complement each other's special-

ties. They must come together, concentrating on doing their best to win. This analogy holds true in the workplace. The effective workforce team is a group of people, each with his or her own special talents and skills, who come together to produce the best product or outcome.

Characteristics of an effective team include the following:

- Team members are skilful in discussion. They pay attention not only to the words said but also to the tone of voice and what is not said.
- Team members have excellent inquiry skills. They ask appropriate questions of each other.
- The team encourages an atmosphere of openness and trust.
- Team members encourage new ideas.
- The team creates a safe haven for all participants to be honest in their statements and actions pertaining to the goals of the team.
- Team members actively listen to each other. They do not interrupt.
- Team members resist the temptation to criticize each other or each other's ideas.
- Each team member builds his or her own self-awareness. When a team member is frustrated or confused, he or she silently asks: What am I thinking? What am I feeling? What do I want at this moment?
- Team members explore impasses. They ask these questions of each other: What exactly has happened? What is our objective? What does the data reveal? What do we need to do? What is the best decision consistent with organizational goals?

Chapter Summary

The summary will help you remember the important points covered in the chapter.

- The administrative professional's responsibilities for incoming mail include sorting, opening, keeping selected envelopes, date and time stamping, reading and annotating, organizing, routing, and handling during the executive's absence.
- The administrative professional's responsibilities for outgoing mail include preparing correspondence for mailing, adhering to automation requirements, sealing and stamping, using electronic postage, and maintaining mailing lists.
- Canada Post classifications of mail include Lettermail, Priority Courier, Xpresspost, Regular Parcel, Admail, and Business Reply Mail.
- Lettermail is any type of mail that measures no more than 90 by 235 millimetres and weighs 50 grams or less.
- Xpresspost offers next-business-day local and two-day national service.
- Priority Courier is the fastest mail service available from Canada Post, with next-day delivery by noon to most destinations.
- Special mail services include Advice of Receipt, Collect on Delivery, Insured Mail, and Registered Mail.
- The principal categories of international mail provided by Canada Post are U.S.A. or International Letterpost, Xpresspost U.S.A. or Xpresspost International, and International Incentive Letterpost.
- A number of private mail and courier services offer fast and efficient delivery of mail, including Purolator, FedEx, UPS, and DHL Canada.
- The administrative professional uses copiers daily and should be knowledgeable about the types of copiers and their basic features. Copiers are available in two types—analog and digital. Digital technology is rapidly overtaking the copier market; however, many analog copiers are still in operation. Combination copiers cut equipment costs as these all-in-one devices combine the capabilities of a fax, printer, scanner, and copier.
- When making copies, the administrative professional should be ethical—that is, not copy documents for personal use, not copy information such as cartoons and jokes to be distributed to friends and co-workers, and not copy materials restricted by the Copyright Act.
- Shredding a document is important when the information is confidential or might be used to harm the organization.
- In order to save costs and help protect the environment, businesses are instituting recycling programs.
- The effective administrative professional understands the importance of teamwork and is constantly developing team skills.

Key Terms

The following terms were introduced in this chapter. The page on which the term was introduced is provided to help you locate the new term. Definitions are compiled in the Glossary at the end of the text.

- **Canada Post Corporation** 194
- *epost* 194
- **PosteCS** 194
- **electronic postmark** 194
- **annotate** 196
- **outsourced** 198
- **accountable items** 198
- **BCS** 199
- **e-stamps** or **PC postage** 200
- **Xpresspost** 202
- **girth** 202
- **reprographics** 205
- **ecologically** 206
- **low-volume copiers** 206
- **cpm (copies per minute)** 206
- **mid-volume copiers** 206
- **high-volume copiers** 206
- **duplexing** 206
- **collating** 206
- **offset** 206
- **copyright** 208
- **shredder** 208

Responses to Self-Check

1. *Lettermail* is any type of letter and other types of personal and/or business correspondence which measures no more than 90 by 235 millimetres and weighs 50 grams or less. It includes cards, postcards, invoices, receipts, financial reports, and other promotional or non-promotional mailable items that are partly keyed or handwritten.

   Xpresspost™ is a next-business-day delivery to local or regional destinations and two-day service between most major Canadian destinations. Documents, packets, and parcels sent by Xpresspost cannot exceed 30 kilograms in weight, and cannot exceed a combined length and girth of 3 metres. Xpresspost envelopes, labels, and boxes are available at Canada Post outlets. Pickup service is also available for a fee to Canada Post account customers only.

2. In *Advice of Receipt* service, a card provides the mailer with confirmation of delivery of Registered Mail items destined for delivery in the United States or other international destinations. The card must be purchased at the time of mailing. When the item is delivered, the addressee's signature is obtained on the card, which is then returned to the sender.

COD service is available for parcel delivery only. The price of goods and/or postage on merchandise is collected from the addressee when the item is delivered and given to the mailer. The amount to be collected from the recipient may not exceed $1000.

Insured Mail service provides compensation to a mailer for loss or damage of mailable items. Items may not be insured for more than their value. Coverage up to $1000 is available for Lettermail; up to $100 for Regular Parcel when delivery confirmation is purchased; and up to $5000 for Xpresspost. Items not eligible for insurance coverage are listed in the *Canada Postal Guide*, available at www.canadapost.ca.

Registered Mail provides proof of mailing and/or proof of delivery for valuable mailed items. The sender is given a receipt for the item mailed. Canada Post obtains a signature and date of delivery along with the printed name of the individual who signed for the item. The name of the person who signed is available to the sender by noon the following business day. A secured signature image can be viewed on the Canada Post website at no charge. A hard copy of the signature may also be obtained for a fee or by calling the Customer Relationship Network. Registered Mail may include Lettermail and other non-document materials such as coins or jewellery and literature for the blind. A list of unacceptable items may be found at the Canada Post website.

Discussion Items

These discussion items provide an opportunity to test your understanding of the chapter through written responses and/or discussion with your classmates and your instructor.

1. What are the administrative professional's responsibilities in preparing incoming mail?
2. Identify the mail classifications used by Canada Post.
3. List and explain the types of special mail services offered by Canada Post.
4. List and explain the two major types of copiers. Explain the differences between low-volume, mid-volume, and high-volume copiers.
5. List six characteristics of an effective team.

Critical-Thinking Activity

Brendan Paul is a clerk in the mailroom. He has been with the company for six months. He seems like a nice young man who is eager to succeed in his job, but he has made several mistakes. You have also heard other employees complain about this. The mistakes you have noticed are as follows:

- You had an important item to mail, and had requested that it be insured for $500. Brendan failed to have the package insured.
- You had asked that an advice of receipt be provided for a mailable item. Brendan sent the item without requesting the advice of receipt.
- On several occasions, when picking up your mail, Brendan had inadvertently left your outgoing mail on other desks in the building. The employees at these desks had returned the mail to you.
- One afternoon this week Brendan had been an hour late picking up the mail. That meant you had had to take a piece of correspondence that Mr. Albertson wanted sent by Xpresspost to the post office yourself in order to get it out the same day. Mr. Albertson was not happy; he had needed you for some additional assignments.
- Two mornings this week (and on several previous occasions) Brendan had missed you on his mail run; he had neither picked up your outgoing mail nor brought you the incoming mail.

Each time Brendan had made a mistake, you had talked with him about the error. He had been very apologetic, giving the excuse that he still had a lot to learn. However, the last time you had called a mistake to his attention, he had become defensive.

What should you do?

Projects

Project 10-1 *(Objective 1)*

Here is a list of Mr. Albertson's incoming mail that you are to handle. Explain how you would sort and place items in folders. Prepare a list of the mail as it is to be arranged, listing the folder you would place each piece in. If there are problems, explain how you would handle them. Submit your work to your instructor.

1. A confidential letter to Mr. Albertson
2. A copy of the *National Post*, a newspaper
3. A new product advertisement
4. A letter with enclosures
5. A letter sent by Xpresspost
6. A letter from China sent by Priority Courier
7. A catalogue of computer supplies
8. A letter with no letterhead address
9. A letter stating a cheque is enclosed; no cheque is enclosed
10. A letter referring to a letter written two weeks ago by Mr. Albertson
11. A copy of *Canadian Business*, a magazine
12. A letter sent by FedEx for next-day delivery

Project 10-2 *(Objective 1)*

Student CD, file SCDP10-2a contains a form letter and SCDP10-2b a mailing list. There are two changes to be made to the letter:

(1) The session has been moved to March 21.
(2) The session will be held in the Galaxy Room of CanAsian.

Make the following three changes to addresses on the mailing list:

(1) Luther Maston of Vitale Furniture has moved to 1915—14 Avenue NE, Calgary, AB T2E 1G8.
(2) David Sam of VosDan Construction has moved to 39—22 Street NW, Calgary, AB T2N 4W7.
(3) Tien Wang of S & G Imported Car Parts has moved to 108 Prestwick Avenue SE, Calgary, AB T2Z 3S6.

Look up the postal codes for the other eight names given below, and add them to the mailing list.

Once you have made the changes to the letter and the mailing list, prepare letters and envelopes for only those individuals whose postal codes start with T2E. Use the letterhead from Student CD, file SCDP10-2. Sign the letters for Mr. Albertson with your initials under the signature, fold the letters, and place them in the envelopes. Bundle the envelopes in alphabetical order; putting one copy of the revised letter on top. Print out a copy of the revised mailing list, sorted alphabetically by company name. Submit the package to your instructor.

Mary Giovannetti, Hunt Manufacturing Corporation,
135 MacLaurin Drive, Calgary, AB

Allan Argent, Robinson Drugs,
3407—26 Avenue SW, Calgary, AB

Brendan Mahar, The Roof Shop,
6032—5th Street SE, Calgary, AB

Allan Argent, Kaczmarski Services, Inc.,
400—620 12th Avenue SW, Calgary, AB

Janet McDonald, Soft Warehouse,
310—605 1st Street SW, Calgary, AB

Bruce Milley, Western Business Systems,
3200 118th Avenue SE, Calgary, AB

Tony Kwok, Stampede Organic Foods,
221 18th Street SE, Calgary, AB

Addas Abbah, Computers Unlimited,
2807 36th Street SW, Calgary, AB

Project 10-3 *(Objective 2)*

Online Project

Using the Canada Post website, at www.canadapost.ca, determine what class of mail and what mail services you would use to send the following items:

1. A package weighing 3 kilograms that must be at its Canadian destination within two days. The package is valued at $3000.
2. A letter that must be to the addressee before noon on the date after it is written.
3. Three books that weigh a total of 3 kilograms.
4. A package that weighs 5 kilograms, is worth $400, and must be to the addressee in the United States by the next day.
5. A letter for which you need evidence of delivery and that must reach its Canadian destination the next day.
6. A package weighing 5 kilograms that must be received in Japan within two days.
7. Valuables that are worth $5000.
8. A letter that must reach China within three days.

Project 10-4 *(Objectives 3 and 4)*

Collaborative Project

Work with two of your classmates on this task. Search the Web for the types of copiers available from two manufacturers; for example, copiers made by Xerox and Canon™. You are working for CanAsian; the copier is for your work area. Approximately 300 copies are made every week. Recommend which copier the company should purchase and give your reasons. Submit your recommendations in memorandum form to your instructor, citing your Web references. Use the memorandum form file SCDP10-4 on the Student CD. As you work on this assignment, use the effective teamwork characteristics you learned in this chapter. In your memorandum to your instructor, include a statement describing how you worked together as an effective team.

Project 10-5 *(Objective 4)*

Recently, your two assistants, Guy Beauchamp and Luyin Wu, have not been getting along well. Almost every day one of them comes to you with a complaint about the other. You do not understand the problems; they seem to be petty and a waste of time. For example, Guy complained one day that Luyin was five minutes late getting back from lunch, which caused him to be five minutes late in taking his lunch. Luyin complained that Guy was pushing his work off on her. Your advice to both of them was to work together to handle the problem situations. However, the situation is getting worse, not better. You decide you need to help. You know they must work together as a team and with you as a team. What suggestions would you make to them? Submit your suggestions in a memorandum to your instructor. Use the memorandum form file SCDP10-5 on the Student CD.

Chapter 11

Financial Transactions and Recordkeeping

LEARNING OBJECTIVES

1. Demonstrate an understanding of basic business financial services, procedures, and software support.
2. Use and maintain various financial forms and documents.
3. Reconcile a bank statement.
4. Establish and maintain a petty cash fund and register.
5. Understand and interpret basic financial statements including income statements and balance sheets.
6. *Demonstrate a commitment to community involvement.*

While you are working as an administrative professional, the type and size of the organization you work for will determine how much responsibility you will have for financial recordkeeping. Every organization—no matter how large or small—must keep financial records. The time you spend on these activities each day will vary with the size of the organization and the degree of automation in place.

A large organization may have an accounting firm or department that handles the payment of all bills, reconciliation of statements, and payroll. The role played by an accounting department or firm in maintaining financial integrity is highly specialized.

In a smaller firm you may be expected to invoice clients, collect on accounts, handle purchasing, and maintain records of financial transactions. To do so, you need to know how to prepare a deposit slip, reconcile a bank statement, and maintain a petty cash fund. While this chapter is not intended to cover all aspects of accounting, you will become familiar with the type of basic financial information processed in the office and the processes and terms related to financial recordkeeping.

Banking Activities

Administrative professionals in smaller firms will often find that managing banking transactions is a responsibility of the job. Handling money on behalf of your organization is an important and exacting task. You will need to know how to

- Prepare currency and cheques for deposit
- Prepare cheques for payment of current accounts
- Keep a register of all deposits made and cheques written
- Understand a bank statement
- Reconcile the bank statement with the register

Depositing Funds

Funds should be deposited regularly. A current account (business chequing account) is the type of account generally used by business organizations. To make a deposit, you will need to prepare a **deposit slip** in duplicate listing all the items—endorsed **cheques** (a legal document authorizing the bank to pay a specific sum to a designated payee) and cash—that are to be deposited. Your financial institution will provide a book of multiple-copy deposit slips encoded with your account number and company name when a new account is opened.

When you present your deposit, the financial institution will remove and retain the original deposit slip and stamp the copy. The copy remains in the deposit book and serves as a record. Your organization may have a number of accounts, and for each there will be a separate deposit slip book. Figure 11-1 illustrates the most common elements of a deposit slip; the format will vary from one institution to another.

Preparing Cheques for Deposit

When preparing cheques for deposit, you should take care to ensure that the cheques are valid. The bank will refuse to accept a cheque if it is **postdated** (that is, the date on the cheque is still in the future) or **staledated** (the cheque was written more than six months ago). Figure 11-2 on page 216 offers some guidelines for including any cheque you have received in a deposit.

Endorsing a Cheque

Endorsing a cheque means signing it on the back. Endorsing is done by the **payee**, the organization or person to whom the cheque is written. Endorsement legally permits a financial institution to transfer monies to the payee; the institution is then able to collect the funds from the **drawer**, the organization or person who has written the cheque. Endorsements can be done in ink by hand. If, however, you were processing a significant number of cheques for deposit, it would be more efficient to use a rubber stamp. An endorsement stamp containing the company name and account number into which the cheque is to be deposited can be ordered from your bank or financial institution.

■ Figure 11-1

SAMPLE DEPOSIT SLIP

① The date of the deposit

② The name of the company making the deposit

③ The account that is to be credited

④ The amount of cash for deposit

⑤ A listing of cheques for deposit

⑥ The initials of the depositor and teller

⑦ The total of the deposit

First Settlers' Bank of Alberta
MAIN BRANCH
CALGARY, AB
T5H 1L9

DEPOSIT
CURRENT ACCOUNT

DATE:	①			
COMPANY NAME: ②		ENTRÉE EXPRESS		
ACCOUNT NUMBER: ③		4536 505 212		
CASH	④	CHEQUES	⑤	
×5		1.		
×10		2.		
×20		3.		
×50		4.		
×100		5.		
×		6.		
Coin		7.		
TOTAL CASH		→		
		VISA		
		US CHEQUES		
Initials		SUBTOTAL		
Depositor Teller		LESS US EXCHANGE		
⑥		NET DEPOSIT	⑦	

■ Figure 11-2

GUIDELINES FOR PREPARING CHEQUES FOR DEPOSIT

- Ensure consistency between the values expressed in words and figures.
- Ensure that the cheque has been signed.
- Ensure that the cheque is not postdated or staledated.
- Ensure that the cheque has been written in ink.
- Ensure that all cheques are appropriately endorsed.
- Group all cheques drawn on a given bank together.

There are three types of endorsements (see Figure 11-3):

- **Blank endorsement** is simply the signature of the payee. Once a blank endorsement is made, the cheque can be cashed. This type of endorsement should only be used when the payee is at the bank and immediately before the cheque is presented to the teller.
- **Full endorsement** permits a cheque to be transferred from the original payee to another payee. The words "Pay to the order of" followed by the name of the new payee are written on the back of the cheque preceding the signature of the endorser

(the original payee). Once endorsed in this way, only the second payee will be able to endorse it further for deposit or cash.

- **Restrictive endorsement** provides the highest level of protection and "restricts" what can be done with the cheque. The words "For Deposit Only To" followed by the full account number are written or stamped on the back of the cheque, transferring the cheque to the depositor's account. Such an endorsement specifies that the deposit must be placed in a designated account, and that it must be deposited in full—no cash can be paid out from the cheque. No signature is required. Restrictive endorsement is widely used in business, especially when deposits are made by mail, through a night depository, or an ATM.

Paying Invoices

Business organizations use cheques rather than cash to pay invoices received from other businesses. An **invoice** is a bill itemizing the goods or services bought and sold. The vendor or seller—the business organization that has supplied the service or product—presents the invoice to the purchaser. Figure 11-4 on page 217 illustrates a typical invoice with common information.

Before writing cheques in payment of invoices or monthly statements, it is important to ensure that the items listed in the invoice are legitimate and that the amounts and extensions are accurate. **Monthly statements**

■ Figure 11-3

BLANK, FULL, AND RESTRICTIVE ENDORSEMENTS

Diane Blaney	*Pay to the order of* *Roy Blaney* *Diane Blaney*	*For Deposit Only* *To the Account of* *Entrée Express* *245 987-2134*
Blank Endorsement	Full Endorsement	Restrictive Endorsement

■ **Figure 11-4**

COMPLETED INVOICE FOR COMPUTER COMPONENTS

FIRST CLASS COMPUTERS
210–605 1st Street SW
Calgary, AB   ①
T2P 3S9

INVOICE

INVOICE TO:	Rasmussen Realty Services	③	INVOICE DATE:	June 23, 2005
②	6030–5th Street SE	④	INVOICE NO.:	**1009932**
	Calgary, AB	⑤	TERMS:	Net 30 days
	T2H 1L4			

QTY	DESCRIPTION	UNIT PRICE	AMOUNT
2	19" TFT flat-panel monitor	325.00	750.00
2	Internal DVD CDRW combo drive	150.00	300.00
2	Optical cordless mouse ⑥	35.00	70.00
			$1120.00
	⑦	GST	78.40
		PST	84.00
		TOTAL	$1282.40

① The name and address of the vendor   ④ The invoice number

② The name and address of the purchaser   ⑤ The terms of the sale

③ The invoice date   ⑥ The details of what was sold

⑦ The total amount payable, including taxes

document activities on an account—purchases and payments made during the month—and are usually due at the beginning of each month.

Working as an administrative professional with responsibility for the accounts payable, you must verify the accuracy of these invoices and/or monthly statements prior to making payments. Check the invoice against prices quoted or against records detailing prices previously paid for similar items. To verify the accuracy of monthly statements, compare the items listed on the statement against invoices received, sales slips, and other records of account payments. Then, when you are satisfied that the invoice or statement is accurate, prepare the cheque.

You can write cheques for any amount up to the amount currently on deposit with your bank or financial institution. Your organization may use commercially available software such as Quicken or Simply Accounting to manage its accounting activities. These software programs include the capability of producing cheques. If you are not using a computer to prepare cheques, cheques can be written by hand or prepared by typewriter or a cheque-writing machine.

Whether the cheque is being prepared by hand, computer, typewriter, or cheque-writing machine, it will need the signature of someone authorized by the organization to sign on its behalf. Individuals authorized by the organization to sign cheques will have provided appropriate documentation and signature samples to the financial institution.

Writing Cheques

Your organization's financial institution will provide you with a supply of cheques. Cheques are available in the following formats:

- A chequebook with a stub attached on which you record the details of the cheque being written. (See Figure 11-5.)
- A book with an accompanying register in which you record the details of each cheque written and deposits made. (See Figure 11-6.)
- Voucher cheques, which contain a form directly below the cheque for recording the details of the payment, help both the company and the payee to identify the purpose of the cheque. (See Figure 11-7 on page 219.)

Writing a cheque out to "Cash" is risky. Such an instrument can be cashed by anyone into whose hands it falls. Cheques should always be written as payable to a specific payee. Figure 11-8 on page 220 offers some guidelines for the preparation of cheques. Answer the questions posed in Self-Check on page 223.

■ Figure 11-5

COMPLETED CHEQUE WITH STUB

No. 156	$1282.40
Date	June 30, 2005
To First Class Computers	
For Computer accessories	

Previous Balance	7856	00
Amt. Deposited	750	65
Total	8606	65
Amt. This Cheque	1282	40
Balance	6324	25

Rasmussen Realty Services
6030–5th Street SE
Calgary, AB T2H 1L4

No. 156

June 30, 2005

PAY TO THE ORDER OF   First Class Computers------ $1282.40

Twelve hundred eighty-two----------40/100 **DOLLARS**

First Settlers' Bank of Alberta
MAIN BRANCH
CALGARY, AB
T5H 1L9

Memo: Computer accessories

Mark Rasmussen

0004 123 456 987

■ Figure 11-6

CHEQUE REGISTER RECORDING DEPOSIT, CHEQUE, AND BALANCE

CHEQUE REGISTER								
Cheque No.	Date	Description	Amount of Cheque		Amount of Deposit		Balance	
							7856	00
	25/06	Deposit			750	65	8606	65
156	30/06	Computer accessories	1282	40			6324	25

■ **Figure 11-7**

COMPLETED VOUCHER CHEQUE

Rasmussen Realty Services	**156**
6030 – 5th Street SE	
Calgary, AB T2H 1L4	

July 1, 2005

PAY   Twelve hundred eighty-two-----40/100   **DOLLARS** $1282.40

TO
THE
ORDER
OF

FIRST CLASS COMPUTERS
210-605 1st Street SW
Calgary, AB T2P 3S9

Mark Rasmussen

0004 123 456 987   **AUTHORIZED SIGNATURE**

REMITTANCE ADVICE — PLEASE DETACH BEFORE DEPOSITING CHEQUE

DATE	DESCRIPTION	AMOUNT
June 23	Computer accessories as follows:	
	2 - 19" TFT flat-panel monitor	750.00
	2 - Internal DVD CDRW combo drive	300.00
	2 - Optical cordless mouse	70.00
	GST	78.40
	PST	84.00
		$1282.40

Reconciling the Bank Balance

You saw in the previous section on writing cheques how the cheque register is used to record and track the cheques written. It is also used to record deposits to the account as they are made. You can see in Figure 11-6 that entering both cheques and deposits and then calculating the current balance after each entry keeps your financial data and the information about the balance of your account current.

At the end of each month, your financial institution will provide you with a statement of all activities on your account for that one-month period. The balance in the cheque register will not be equal to the balance shown on the bank statement. There are a number of reasons why this difference exists. It may be that

- All deposits made may not yet have been recorded by the bank
- All cheques you have written may not have been cleared for payment
- Interest or other credits may have been added to your account by the bank
- Service charges may have been deducted from your account by the bank
- An entry or calculation error may exist

Accounting for the differences between the two figures is known as *reconciling the bank balance.*

Human Relations Tip

The Conference Board of Canada has identified numeracy skills as a fundamental requirement in the workplace. Commit now to continuing to improve your capability in this area.

■ Figure 11-8

CHEQUE-WRITING GUIDELINES AND TIPS

- Use ink to prepare all handwritten cheques.
- Write the amount in figures starting close to the preprinted dollar sign and write the figures close together to prevent additional figures being added.
- Date each cheque and stub.
- Using the fewest possible words, write out the amount starting at the extreme left of the line, putting an initial capital on the first word only.
- If cheques and stubs are not already numbered, number them consecutively.
- Ensure that the values expressed in words and in figures are identical.
- If using cheques with a stub, first complete the stub including details of all bills—if more than one—being covered by the cheque; then complete the cheque.
- Identify the purpose of the cheque in the bottom left corner. Some cheques include a line for this purpose (see Figure 11-5).

- If using a **cheque register**, enter the details of the transaction into it.
- Whenever space remains on a line, such as after the payee's name or in the words or figures area of cheque, fill the space up with a line so that nothing else can be added.
- Ensure the individual name of the payee is correctly spelled. Courtesy titles (*Mr.*, *Mrs.*, or *Dr.*) are unnecessary.
- Mistakes should not be erased or covered up with liquid paper. Write "VOID" in large letters across the face of the cheque and the stub and prepare a new cheque. Retain the cheque and stub in the files, or if using a register record the cheque as "VOID" in the register and retain the cheque in the files.
- Obtain a signature from an authorized signatory. Ensure the signature is completed in ink.

The Monthly Bank Statement

The **monthly bank statement** sent to you by your financial institution may also include your cancelled cheques. These are the cheques you have written that have been cleared by the bank; that is, the amount has been deducted from your account and given to the payee. Figure 11-9 on page 221 shows the front page of a statement. You can see how the bank itemizes deposits made, cheques that have cleared, interest payable if any, and any fees charged for the month.

On the back of the statement, most banks provide a form you can use to reconcile the final balance on the statement with the one in your records. An example of such a form is shown in Figure 11-10 on page 222; the four steps outlined in the figure will result in identical final balances recorded on both the cheque register and bank statement. Your bank balance will be reconciled.

> **Technology Tip**
>
> Software programs such as Quicken or Simply Accounting will reconcile the balance by prompting you to enter the amounts of the cancelled cheques, interest, and any fees that have been charged.

If your financial institution does not provide a reconciliation form, you can easily prepare one on your computer. Create a master as shown in Figure 11-11 on page 223.

Cancelled cheques provide a legal proof of payment and should be filed once you have completed the monthly reconciliation. Your company will likely have a policy governing the length of time that cancelled cheques are to be retained. Create a records management system for the cancelled cheques on the basis of how frequently you find it necessary to refer to them once they have been filed.

Electronic and Online Banking

In July 2002, the Canadian Bankers Association determined that 75 percent of the Canadian public felt the

■ Figure 11-9

SAMPLE MONTHLY BANK STATEMENT

First Settlers' Bank of Alberta
MAIN BRANCH
CALGARY, AB T5H 1L9

Rasmussen Realty Services
6030–5th Street SE
Calgary, AB T2H 1L4

STATEMENT OF ACCOUNT		ACCOUNT TYPE	STATEMENT FROM/TO	
Branch No.	**Account No.**	CURRENT CHEQUING	May 30, 2005	June 30, 2005
123	456 987		Page 1 of 1	

DESCRIPTION	WITHDRAWALS	DEPOSITS	DATE	BALANCE
BALANCE FORWARD				8821.88
PAYMENT TO 00864501355	486.29		June 01	
AVIVA/CGU INSURANCE	57.33		June 01	
CHQ 155	114.36		June 01	8163.90
TERASEN GAS	148.00		June 06	8015.90
ALBERTA HYDRO	68.00		June 15	7947.90
TELUS	91.25		June 23	
DEPOSIT		750.00	June 23	8606.65
INTEREST		11.28	June 30	
SERVICE FEE	9.95			8607.98
	975.18	761.28		

technology available to them from their financial institution made their personal banking more convenient. They also reported that 34 percent of Canadians do at least some of their banking online, 40 percent use ATMs and 16 percent use the Internet as a primary method of conducting personal financial transactions. Canadians are the highest users of debit cards in the world, with an average of 71.7 debit card transactions per person.[1]

ATMs (automated teller machines) (also known as **ABMs—automated banking machines**) are located throughout the world at banks and elsewhere. They enable you to obtain cash, make deposits (depositing can only be done at bank locations) and check your account balance at hours of the day when banks are not open for business. While ATMs are used widely for personal banking—1.2 billion ATM transactions were logged in 2002[2]—most companies will not make use of them, unless they are sole proprietorships or small partnerships.

EFT (Electronic funds transfer)—though not the ATM variety—is often used by business organizations to process payroll. Rather than having to write cheques for each employee, the organization provides the bank with a list of employees and the amount payable to each, and the bank transfers the funds from the organization's current account to the individual employee accounts. The employee receives only a statement showing gross pay, an itemized list of deductions, and the net amount deposited to their account. Financial institutions encourage businesses to use this transfer service, because it is so much more efficient than writing individual paycheques at the end of each pay period.

EFT is also a convenient method of bill payment. Canada Post's *epost*™ has a constantly growing list of companies from whom you may receive invoice statements online. With *epost*™, you can receive and pay bills, and manage accounts online. You can find out more about this service by visiting the Canada Post website at www.canadapost.ca.

■ Figure 11-10

SAMPLE RECONCILIATION FORM FOUND ON BACK OF MONTHLY STATEMENT

First Settlers' Bank of Alberta

Balancing Your Records

Follow the four steps listed below to balance your statement.

Step 1   Add to your cheque register, as a deposit, any interest paid. Subtract from your cheque register, as a withdrawal, service charges.

Step 2   Compare withdrawals and deposits on the statement with entries made in the cheque register.

Step 3   List in the columns below all withdrawals and deposits recorded in the cheque register that are not listed on this or previous statements.

DEPOSITS		
01/07	1151	25

OUTSTANDING CHEQUES		
01/07	1282	40
05/07	585	15
	1867	55

Step 4

The Ending Statement Balance for your current account is shown on the reverse of this monthly statement.

Enter Ending Statement Balance	8607.98
Add total of outstanding deposits recorded in register	1151.25
Subtotal	9759.23
Subtract total of outstanding withdrawals recorded in register	1867.55
Present account balance on your records should be	7891.68

The account is balanced when the amount above matches the last balance listed in the cheque register. If these two amounts do not agree:

- Review the above steps for entry or calculation errors.
- Check to ensure that all deposits and withdrawals shown on the statement are recorded in the cheque register.
- Check for calculation errors in the cheque register.

Notify the branch within 30 days regarding any errors or irregularities noted on this statement.

Preauthorized automated transfer is another method employed by both individuals and business organizations to make regular payments on accounts in cases where the amount invoiced every month is constant. One example might be the monthly utility account. Preauthorized automated transfer can also be used to transfer funds from one account to another within a financial institution.

Banks and other financial institutions are making it easier for companies to maintain their financial records. EFT and online banking access make the company's financial data instantly available. Canadians are enthusiastic adopters of electronic banking technology, using the Internet at an increasing rate to manage their personal financial records. Canadian Bankers Association statistics indicate that more than 85 percent of retail banking transactions in Canada in 2002 were conducted electronically.[3] Computer and Internet banking is likely to keep growing as banks devote significant resources to developing and refining technology and security.

The Petty Cash Fund

In this chapter you have learned that most business organizations commonly use cheques to pay accounts and control their financial records. All business organizations—large and small—will also occasionally need to

■ Figure 11-11

BANK RECONCILIATION FORM

BANK RECONCILIATION
Rasmussen Realty Services
As of September 30, 2005

Cheque Register Balance		15 400.23	Bank Statement Balance			15 300.12
ADD:			ADD:			
Interest earned		60.71	Deposit of 07/29			1 295.85
		15 460.94				16 595.97
DEDUCT:			DEDUCT:			
NSF cheque—J. Lee	1500.00		Outstanding cheques:			
New cheque order	25.00		No. 156	1282.40		
Service charges	15.95	1 540.95	No. 157	1393.58	2 675.98	
Reconciled balance		13 919.99	Reconciled balance			13 919.99

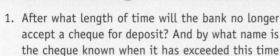

pay for small incidental items such as postage, taxi fares, specialty office supplies, or refreshments. Requisitioning a cheque for a small amount of money if you are working in a large organization, or writing one if you are working in a smaller business firm, is both time-consuming and inefficient. A **petty cash fund**—the name is derived from the French word *petit* for "small"—is usually established to handle the payment of purchases of small incidental items required by the office in the normal course of conducting business.

Establishing and Operating the Petty Cash Fund

Establishing a petty cash fund to cover these expenses is done by writing a cheque on the current account of the business. The cheque can be for any amount. Usually the amount is based on either an estimate of or an actual calculated value of previous incidental expenses over a specific period such as one month. A member of the department or office is designated to monitor the fund.

Responsibility for operating the fund is often delegated to the administrative professional. If you are given this responsibility, you should

- Keep on hand only sufficient funds to cover expenses for a specific period—two weeks, a month, or a quarter
- Complete or obtain a petty cash voucher (see Figure 11-12 on page 225) indicating the amount, date, and purpose of the expenditure
- Retain receipts for all expenditures (attached to petty cash voucher)
- Record all transactions using a petty cash register (see Figure 11-13 on page 225) or spreadsheet
- Ensure you can account for all monies—*cash on hand* plus *receipts and/or vouchers* should equal the full value of the fund
- Keep the cash and vouchers secure
- Prepare a petty cash fund summary on a regular basis (see Figure 11-14 on page 225)
- Replenish the fund before it gets too low by requesting a cheque for the amount needed to restore the total to its original value (usually the total of all vouchers and/or receipts)

Financial Statements

While no two business organizations are identical in their operations, there are two financial statements that managers, owners, creditors, or investors generally rely on as an accurate representation of the financial viability of the company: the balance sheet and the income statement.

A **balance sheet** is a combination of three things:

- A list of what the company owns—its *assets*
- A list of what the company owes—its *liabilities*
- The difference between the two—its *net worth*

While the balance sheet is important because it gives a picture of the financial state of the organization on a specific day, the **income statement** (also know as the profit and loss statement) is likely considered more important. It is a summary of an organization's income and expenses over a specific period of time—a month, a calendar quarter (three months), or a year. It shows the amount of money made (profit) or lost (loss) during that period. This information makes it possible to forecast future directions for the organization.

The Balance Sheet

A balance sheet provides information about an organization's **net worth** at a specific time of the year. The document itself has four main sections—the heading section, the assets section (current and fixed), the liabilities section (current and long-term), and the owner's equity section. The assets section of the balance sheet should equal ("balance" with) the liabilities and owner's equity.

The *heading section* identifies the who, what, and when of the statement. This information is displayed in three separate horizontally centred lines at the top of the page. The first line identifies the organization, the second line the type of statement, and the last line the period of time covered by the statement.

The *assets section* includes two types of **assets** of the organization—the **current assets** and **fixed assets**. Current assets are cash, or items such as accounts receivable or inventory that could readily be converted into cash on short notice. Fixed assets comprises land, buildings, or equipment that will be used over the length of the life of the organization and are virtually permanent. On a balance sheet, listing current assets before fixed assets is known as using the **liquidity order**.

Liabilities are the debts of the organization. The *liabilities section* follows the assets section, and, like it, is presented in two parts—current liabilities and long-term liabilities. Current liabilities will include items such as **accounts payable** or bank loans. They are identified as current because payment is expected to be made within the next 12 months or in the course of "current" operations. On the other hand, long-term or fixed liabilities usually include mortgages or other debts that will be paid over a period of time in excess of one year. While the format and content of a typical balance sheet will vary from firm to firm, it should remain the same from year to year. Figure 11-15 on page 226 provides a sample balance sheet for a firm called Rasmussen Realty Services.

The Income Statement

An income statement consists of two main sections—the heading and the body. The body of the income statement is divided into three subsections—the revenue section, the expenses section, and the profit or loss section.

As in the balance sheet, the *heading section* answers the question, *who, what,* and *when* by identifying the organization, the type of statement, and the period of time covered. The *when* is very important. It may be for a one-month period only or for a longer period such as a quarter or a year. The example shown in Figure 11-16

Figure 11-12

A COMPLETED PETTY CASH VOUCHER

No. 256	$50.75

PETTY CASH VOUCHER

DATE: May 30, 2005

PAID TO: First Class Computers

EXPLANATION: Graphics tablet

CHARGE ACCT.: Supplies

APPROVED BY:	RECEIVED BY:
M.A. Albertson	*Keri-An Mahar*
Authorized Signature	Recipient Signature

[handwritten margin note: owner's equity equals your net worth.]

■ Figure 11-13

PETTY CASH REGISTER PAGE

DATE	VOUCHER NO.	DETAILS	CREDITS	PAYMENTS
May 1			250.00	
May 5	250	Postage		15.75
May 9	251	Taxi to Spence and Associates		35.00
May 12	252	Toner		49.25
May 22	253	Cleaning supplies		8.56
May 24	254	Courier		10.45
May 29	255	Disk labels		7.95
May 30	256	Graphics tablet		50.75
Totals			250.00	177.71
June 1		Cash on hand	72.29	
		Cheque No. 135 to replenish fund	177.71	

PETTY CASH REGISTER

■ Figure 11-14

PETTY CASH REPLENISHMENT REQUEST FORM

RASMUSSEN REALTY SERVICES
Petty Cash Replenishment Request

Petty Cash Summary
May 1 – May 30, 2005

Postage and delivery	26.20
Miscellaneous office supplies	107.95
Travel	35.00
Cleaning supplies	8.56
Total payments	177.71
Cash on hand	72.29
Total petty cash fund	250.00
Submitted by:	*Kaili Tanner*

on page 227 identifies the type of financial statement—"Income Statement"; the name of the company—"Rasmussen Realty Services"; and the period of time—one month.

The *body* of the income statement is formatted in three vertical columns. The column at the extreme left, the widest, is used to describe listed revenue and expense items. The second or middle column (the first money column) is used when there is more than one item in a section. These detailed amounts are totalled, the total being placed in the third column (the second money column). The third column at the extreme right is the totals column. When there is only one item in the revenue or expense section, the middle column is not used and the amount is placed directly in the totals column.

The first section in the body itemizes all sources of revenue under the heading "Revenue" or "Income." The next section of the body details all expenses under the heading "Expenses." Last is the net profit or net loss section. This amount is calculated by deducting total expenses from total revenues. A positive result in this calculation corresponds to a net profit; a negative result, a net loss.

Whether or not you are routinely involved in financial recordkeeping, as an administrative profes-

■ Figure 11-15

EXAMPLE OF A BALANCE SHEET

Rasmussen Realty Services
BALANCE SHEET
December 31, 2005

ASSETS

Current Assets			
Cash		$60 500.00	
Accounts Receivable	$30 000.00		
Less: Allowance for Bad Debts	11 500.00	18 500.00	
Marketing Supplies		5 000.00	
Prepaid Taxes		7 450.00	
Total Current Assets			$91 450.00
Fixed Assets			
Furniture, Fixtures, and Equipment	15 000.00		
Less: Accumulated Depreciation	4 500.00	10 500.00	
Strata Unit	80 000.00		
Less: Accumulated Depreciation	16 000.00	64 000.00	
Total Fixed Assets			74 500.00
Total Assets			$165 950.00

LIABILITIES

Current Liabilities		
Accounts Payable	7 850.00	
Salaries and Wages Payable	23 600.00	
Provincial Taxes Payable	2 000.00	
GST Payable	4 500.00	
Total Current Liabilities	33 450.00	
Long-Term Liabilities		
First Mortgage Payable	75 000.00	
Total Liabilities		$108 450.00

OWNER'S EQUITY

Mark Rasmussen, Capital, January 1		50 000.00
December Net Income	15 000.00	
Less: Drawings	7 500.00	
Excess of Income over Withdrawals		7 500.00
M. Rasmussen, Capital, December 31		57 500.00
Total Liabilities and Owner's Equity		$165 950.00

sional you need to understand the role played by the company's accounting department and recognize the importance of current financial information, and you need to be able to interpret financial statements. Whatever role you play in maintaining financial records, remember that accuracy and confidentiality are critical.

Careers in Accounting

The field of accounting is highly respected, and as your business experience grows you may decide to develop accounting expertise. In addition to postsecondary education through local colleges, a number of Canadian accounting organizations also provide education and professional training. These include

- Canadian Institute of Chartered Accountants
- Certified General Accountants of Canada
- Certified Management Accountants of Canada
- The institutes of chartered accountants in each province

Successful completion of a series of required courses plus practical experience lead to the following certifications:

- Chartered Accountant (CA)
- Certified General Accountant (CGA)
- Certified Management Accountant (CMA)

You can learn more about the profession by visiting the following websites.
- www.cica.ca
- www.cga-canada.org
- www.cma-canada.org

■ **Figure 11-16**

SAMPLE INCOME STATEMENT FOR A ONE-MONTH PERIOD

Rasmussen Realty Services
INCOME STATEMENT
For Month Ending January 31, 2006

Revenue:		
Commissions Earned — Residential Properties	$25 000.00	
Commercial Properties	10 000.00	
Total Revenue		$35 000.00
Expenses:		
Salaries	10 000.00	
Computer Lease	2 000.00	
Utilities — Gas and Electric	250.00	
Telephone	125.00	
Advertising	4 500.00	
Total Expenses		16 875.00
Net Income		$18 125.00

Soft Skills: Committed to the Community

In Chapter 4 you learned about business ethics and the characteristics of the ethical organization. The 2001 Enron scandal in the United States and the 2004 sponsorship scandal in Canada serve to illustrate what can happen when procedures governing financial documentation are abused or ignored. In addition to ensuring that appropriate "checks and balances" are in place to protect financial integrity, the ethical organization understands that it has a social responsibility to the community. HSBC Canada is an example of one corporation that accepts that responsibility. The following statements are made on HSBC's Web page.

- HSBC has been part of the Canadian community for over two decades. By supporting local traditions and institutions, such as the Vancouver Sun Run or the University of Toronto, we help to build stronger communities.

- Sponsorships give HSBC an opportunity to support and participate in local events and uphold the values of the community.
- HSBC has been making financial donations to good causes throughout history. In recent years we have focused on two areas: education and the environment.[4]

The ethical organization is cognizant of the needs of its community and encourages its employees to participate in community activities. For example, you and other employees of your organization might

- Serve on community boards and commissions
- Participate in the local chamber of commerce
- Provide leadership to solicit funds for worthy causes

Participating in professional or community activities could give you the opportunity to practise the financial recordkeeping skills discussed in this chapter.

Chapter Summary

The summary will help you remember the important points covered in the chapter.

- Every organization, regardless of size, must keep financial records.
- Routine banking activities include:
  - Preparing currency and cheques for deposit
  - Preparing cheques for payment of current accounts
  - Maintaining a register of all deposits made and cheques written
  - Reconciling the bank statement with the register
- Depositing funds should be done on a regular basis.
- The bank will not accept postdated or staledated cheques.
- Endorsing a cheque means signing it on the back; endorsement is done by the payee.
- There are three types of endorsements: blank, full, and restrictive.
- An invoice is a bill prepared by a vendor or seller.
- A monthly statement documents activities such as purchases and payments made on an account.
- Quicken and Simply Accounting are commercially available software programs used to manage accounting activities.
- Cheques are available in three formats—a chequebook with stubs, a chequebook with register, or voucher cheques.
- Reconciling the bank balance will account for the differences between balances on the monthly statement and cheque register.
- A petty cash fund is established to handle purchases of incidental items.
- The petty cash voucher is a form used to record the amount, date, and purpose of incidental expenditures.
- A balance sheet is a list of the company's assets, liabilities, and net worth.
- An income statement is a summary of an organization's income and expenses over a specific period of time.
- Current assets include cash, or assets that can readily be converted into cash.
- Fixed assets are assets that will only be used up over the lifetime of an organization.
- Liquidity order is current assets appearing before fixed assets on a balance sheet.
- Current liabilities include items on which payment is expected to occur in the course of "current" operations.
- Long-term or fixed liabilities include items on which payment will be made over a period of time in excess of one year.
- Professional accounting certifications include
  - Chartered Accountant (CA)
  - Certified General Accountant (CGA)
  - Certified Management Accountant (CMA)

Key Terms

The following terms were introduced in this chapter. The page on which the term was introduced is provided to help you locate the new term. Definitions are compiled in the Glossary at the end of the text.

- **deposit slip** 214
- **cheque** 214
- **postdated** 215
- **staledated** 215
- **endorsing a cheque** 215
- **payee** 215
- **drawer** 215
- **blank endorsement** 216
- **full endorsement** 216
- **restrictive endorsement** 216
- **invoice** 216
- **monthly statement** 216
- **voucher cheque** 218
- **cheque register** 220
- **monthly bank statement** 220
- **cancelled cheques** 220
- **ATM (automated teller machines)** 221
- **ABM (automated banking machines)** 221
- **EFT (electronic funds transfer)** 221
- **preauthorized automated transfer** 222
- **petty cash fund** 223
- **balance sheet** 224
- **income statement** 224
- **net worth** 224
- **assets** 224
- **current assets** 224
- **fixed assets** 224
- **liquidity order** 224
- **liabilities** 224
- **accounts payable** 224

Responses to Self-Check

1. The bank will not accept a cheque that has been dated six months or more prior to the day it is presented to the financial institution. Such a

cheque is known as a staledated cheque.

2. Cancelled cheques are those that have been cleared by the bank and provide a legal proof of payment. They should be filed once the monthly reconciliation has been completed.

3. A cheque made out to "Cash" can be presented to a financial institution for payment by the bearer—that is, anyone holding it.

4. Restrictive endorsement provides the highest level of protection, as it restricts what can be done with the cheque. Putting the words "For Deposit Only To" followed by the full account number on the back specifies that the cheque may only be deposited, in full, into the designated account. No cash can be obtained on it.

Discussion Items

These discussion items provide an opportunity to test your understanding of the chapter through written responses and/or discussion with your classmates and your instructor.

1. Explain how the role of an administrative professional might vary depending on the organization.

2. List and explain the purpose of each of the three different types of cheque endorsements.

3. What steps would you take to reconcile a bank statement with the cheque register, and if the two are not equal how would you try to resolve the issue?

4. Identify the major components of a petty cash fund and explain the steps you would take to establish such a fund.

5. Identify and explain the differences between an income statement and a balance sheet.

Critical-Thinking Activity

Each department of CanAsian Airlines operates and manages its own petty cash fund to cover the cost of incidental office-related expenses. In your department, Guy has been delegated the responsibility of maintaining this fund. As his supervisor, you are authorized to sign the requisition to replenish the fund that is sent to the accounting department at the end of each month.

Over the past few months you have observed Guy opening the petty cash box and giving what appears to be small amounts to various individuals in the office. When you review the requests to replenish the fund,

however, you notice that no reference to these persons appears on the requisition; nor are petty cash vouchers signed by these individuals included with the requisition. The Policy and Procedures Manual, given to all new CanAsian employees, has a section on maintaining the fund. It states clearly that these monies are only to be used for office-related expenses.

While you have every confidence in Guy's ethics and integrity, and in his ability to maintain this fund, you suspect that Guy has been advancing monies to these individuals for personal use.

- How will you bring up this issue with Guy?
- What questions will you ask him?
- What directions could you provide to help him resolve this issue?

Projects

Project 11-1 *(Objective 1)*

Online Project

Using the Internet browser of your choice, search for information on computer accounting or money management software. Many vendors of software will include an online demo highlighting the best features of the software. Run the demos and compare the features of two software programs. Prepare a summary of your comparisons and submit it your instructor.

Project 11-2 *(Objective 1)*

Collaborative Project

Work with two of your classmates on this task. Choose from one of the following:

(a) Interview a bank manager to determine what type of automatic or electronic services it provides for its business clients. Prepare a presentation for your class.

(b) Interview an administrative professional about his or her responsibilities for financial recordkeeping in their business organization. Prepare a presentation for your class.

Background to Projects 11-3, 11-4, 11-5, and 11-7

CanAsian Airlines considers itself a good corporate citizen. The Mission and Values Statement of the company encourages and supports all company employees who wish to make a commitment to the community. CanAsian is a strong supporter of the United Way, which annually raises funds to support a variety of community health and social service providers. The annual United Way campaign is scheduled to begin soon, and you have decided to volunteer to serve on the local CanAsian fundraising committee. You know that at the first meeting, a chairperson, a recording secretary, and a treasurer will need to be selected. You have decided to put your financial recordkeeping skills to use and plan to volunteer for treasurer. At the meeting your offer is accepted, and you will now begin to keep track of all income and expenses during the three-month campaign.

Complete Projects 11-3, 11-4, and 11-5 before submitting them to your instructor.

Project 11-3 *(Objective 2)*

As a first step, you open a chequing account (215 331 789). You will deposit all funds received to this account and use it to make payments as necessary. The bank has provided you with a cheque register to document and record all transactions. The campaign officially begins the first week of October and in that week you receive a number of contributions. They included cheques as follows:

Martin Albertson	$1,500	Luyin Wu	$120
Guy Beauchamp	$75	Keri-An Mahar	$500
James Robertson	$600	Greg Lee	$250

Each department at Head Office has held a 50/50 draw where the proceeds of ticket sales are divided equally between the winner and the fundraising campaign. At the end of the week, in addition to the cheques you have received, you also have the following cash to be readied for deposit: fifty $1 coins, thirty-five $2 coins, ten $5 bills, three $10 bills, and two $20 bills.

A cheque register, a deposit slip, and six cheques are on your Student CD, file SCDP11-3a, 11-3b, and 11-3c. Use the information provided to complete the deposit slip. Be sure to put a restrictive endorsement on the cheques and record the deposit in the cheque register.

Throughout the month you continue to receive direct contributions and cash funds from raffles and 50/50 draws. The weekly deposit totals are as follows:

Week 2	$5346 (cash $346; cheques $5000)
Week 3	$2894 (cash $594; cheques $2300)
Week 4	$1785 (cash $285; cheques $1500)

Assume that you have made these deposits at the end of each week and that you have entered them into the cheque register. (In an actual situation, you would also issue individual receipts for each contribution.)

Project 11-4 *(Objective 2)*

The fundraising committee had some interesting ideas to encourage the widest possible involvement of the employees at Head Office. Implementing these ideas required the purchase of some items. You have received a number of invoices and, at the beginning of the last week of the month, have set aside time to pay them. As you are the person who opened the bank account, you are authorized to sign the cheques.

Cheque forms are on your Student CD, file SCDP11-4. Use the following information to prepare these cheques. Be sure to enter the amounts into the cheque register as well.

Lumiere Restaurant	$250	(raffle prize of a dinner for two)
Staples Office Supplies	$33.33	(raffle and 50/50 draw tickets)
The Casual Gourmet	$65.23	(fundraising committee lunch)
The Village Bouquet	$65.75	(floral arrangement— monthly raffle sales winner)
High River Rentals	$250	(rental of barbecue for luncheon)

Project 11-5 *(Objective 3)*

In the first week of November, you receive the first monthly statement from the bank (SCDP11-5a). The balance as of the end of October is $10 977.76, which includes interest of $20.84 and processing fees of $2.85. You notice that the last deposit you made was too late to have been captured in this statement, and that two of the cheques you had written do not appear on the list of cancelled cheques. They were for Staples and The Village Bouquet. Print out a copy of the reconciliation form SCDP11-5b from the Student CD. Reconcile the bank statement with the cheque register you have created on the basis of the transactions recorded in Projects 11-3 and 11-4.

Project 11-6 *(Objective 4)*

Guy is planning on taking an extended vacation and will be away from the office for the next month. Usually you would delegate the responsibility of maintaining the petty cash fund to another member of your staff, but because Luyin is still fairly new you have decided to add this to your other duties.

Guy has processed the replenishment request, so you will be starting a new petty cash register for this month. The balance is $150. Print out a copy of the petty cash register form SCDP11-6a from the Student CD. Record the amount of $150 on the first line of the "Credits" column. (Use the current month of the year in completing this exercise.)

The following were the cash payments you made from the petty cash fund during this month:

Day	Voucher No.	Description	Amount
1	115	Whiteboard pens	$7.34
5	116	BlueLine Taxi to airport	$15.00
8	117	Floral arrangement	$21.39
15	118	Coffee supplies	$18.48
25	119	Courier	$13.65
30	120	Plant fertilizer	$6.41

Total the cash payments and calculate the balance as of the end of the month. Forward the balance to the beginning of the next month, and using the petty cash replenishment form SCDP11-6b found on your Student CD summarize the month's expenses and prepare a request for funds.

Project 11-7 *(Objective 5)*

Fast-forward to the end of December and the conclusion of the United Way campaign at CanAsian's head office. It has been a very successful campaign, and employees at the head office location have been very generous in their direct contributions and participation in the various fundraising activities organized by the committee. It is now time to prepare a statement itemizing the revenues raised and the expenses incurred. As treasurer of the committee, this is your responsibility.

Combine the information in Projects 11-3 and 11-4 regarding revenues raised and expenses incurred in the first month of the campaign with the following data:

Month 2		Month 3	
Cheques from various individuals	1,500.00	Cheques from various individuals	2,210.00
Barbecue lunch ticket sales	900.00	Karaoke night— ticket sales	3,000.00
50/50 draw and raffle sales	1,500.00	50/50 draw and raffle sales	985.00
Purchase flowers— monthly prize winner	65.75	Purchase flowers— monthly prize winner	65.75
Paper napkins, etc.—barbecue	105.55	Printing charges	210.00

Refer to Figure 11-16 for an example of this document.

Project 11-8 (Objective 6)

Add to your Professional Growth Plan that you began in Chapter 1 by describing how you can demonstrate a commitment to community involvement. For example, if you have an interest in assisting with the education of young children, you might volunteer to help in an elementary school; or if you enjoy working with the sick, you might volunteer to work in a hospital. The purpose of this project is to encourage you to think about your strengths and interests so you can assist your community. Remember, the ethical organization and individual seek to give back to the community in whatever way possible. Think futuristically and commit to working in your community in the future. You will not be engaging in this activity this semester unless you decide you want to do so. Save your plan on your Professional Growth Plan disk under "Progro11-8."

Records Management

1. Define records management and explain how it is used within an organization.
2. Identify and use records storage systems.
3. Use the basic indexing rules.
4. *Increase decision-making skills.*

Technology has significantly impacted the manner in which records within an organization are handled. We now have the ability to create, use, maintain, and store records technologically without ever making paper copies. However, the paperless office that was touted as a possibility, even a probability, has not materialized. In fact, we are seeing an explosion in the amount of paper records as well as electronic records generated. We seem to want both. Think about this statement from your personal perspective for a moment. How many times have you read an e-mail and then printed out a paper copy even though your software allows you to maintain an electronic copy? According to studies done by Hewlett-Packard, workers who say they regularly print pages from the Internet print an average of 32 pages a day.[1] How many times have you transferred a piece of correspondence to a disk for electronic storage and also made a paper copy for a manual file? We seem to have difficulty giving up paper even when we have excellent technological records management capabilities.

What does this mean for the administrative professional in today's workplace? It means you have to be proficient in both electronic and manual (paper) records management systems. And that is not an easy task. A major complaint of executives is that it is often difficult and sometimes impossible to find essential information when it is needed. This inability to find a record or to find one quickly is not only a frustrating process but a costly one as well. It can

- Cost the organization hundreds or thousands of dollars
- Force the management of a company to make decisions on the basis of incomplete information
- Result in the loss of a valuable client
- Hinder a legal case due to lack of information

The administrative professional is the individual most often held responsible for finding a record and for finding it in a timely manner. An understanding of records management procedures and techniques can simplify the process for you and allow you to become known as the person who can locate needed materials instantly—a skill that can make you invaluable to your supervisor and the organization. This chapter will help you learn the basics of records management. Your ongoing task regarding records management is to keep current on new developments in the field.

Records Management Defined

A **record** is any type of recorded information, whether that information is an e-mail message, a letter, a report, a spreadsheet, a contract, a personnel record, or any other type of organizational record. **Records management** is the systematic control of records from the creation of the record to its final disposition. In order for a records management system to function, there must be information, equipment, and people. Information is generated by many sources and can appear in many forms—as a paper record or as an electronic record stored on disk, videotape, or microfilm, or on numerous other electronic media. Equipment in a records management system includes all the hardware used in processing documents. People include the necessary personnel to get the right documents to the right individuals at the lowest cost. *Since both electronic and paper systems are used in most organizations today, this chapter will emphasize both manual and electronic procedures.*

Records Management Components

If a records management system is to be effective, it must include these essential components:

- An organization-wide records structure
- A records storage system
- Rules for filing
- Appropriate filing supplies
- Necessary equipment and media
- Retention schedules
- Active-to-inactive file procedures
- Procedures for updating the management system
- Records management manuals and ongoing training for personnel

These components are necessary for an electronic system, a manual system, or a system that combines the two (prevalent in most organizations). The processes are shown graphically in Figure 12-1 on page 235. The components of the records management system are explained in detail in the next sections.

Organization-wide Records Management System

The records management department or the person in charge of records management must clearly state the organization's file structure. This structure should be comprehensive in approach; that is, it should include how records are to be filed, how long they are to be kept active, and how inactive records are to be stored. Without such clarity, personnel within each department may file records in very different ways, resulting in great confusion, mishandling of records, and loss of important records.

Records Storage Systems

An important consideration in any records management system, whether that system is electronic or manual, is how the records are stored. **Records storage systems** include alphabetic (alphabetical order) and numeric (numerical order). Both of these systems have several variations that are explained in the following paragraphs. Records in a manual or electronic system may be stored by either of these methods.

Alphabetic Storage Methods

The **alphabetic storage** method uses the letters of the alphabet to determine the order in which a record is filed. This is the most common method; it is found in one form or another in every organization. Figure 12-2 on page 235. illustrates a manual alphabetic file. An electronic alphabetic screen is shown in Figure 12-3 on page 236. Documents are filed according to the basic alphabetic filing rules, which are given in a later section of this chapter.

Advantages of an alphabetic system are that

- It is a **direct access** system. There is no need to refer to anything except the file to find the name.
- The dictionary arrangement is simple to understand.
- Misfiling is easily detected by alphabetic sequence.

Variations of the alphabetic storage method include **subject filing** (arranging records by their subject) and **geographic filing** (arranging records by geographic location).

SUBJECT FILING. Subject filing is used to some extent in most organizations. An illustration of a manual subject file is shown in Figure 12-4 on page 236.

Although subject order is useful and necessary in certain situations, it is the most difficult classification to maintain. Every record must be read completely to determine the subject—a time-consuming process. It is a difficult method to control, since one person may read a record and determine the subject to be one thing and another person may read the record and decide the subject is something entirely different. For example, one person classifying records concerning personnel grievances may decide that the subject is *Grievances* while another may decide that the subject is *Personnel—Grievances.*

You learned earlier that an alphabetic system is direct—a file can be found by going directly to the file's name. A subject system can be considered direct or indirect. When the system is direct, the subject file is a

■ Figure 12-1

RECORDS MANAGEMENT COMPONENTS

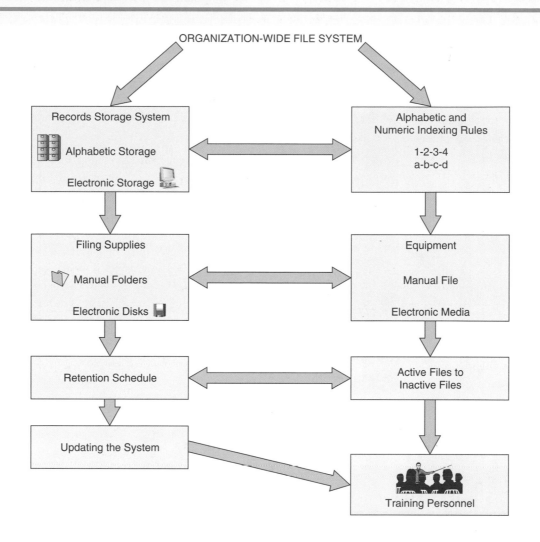

■ Figure 12-2

MANUAL ALPHABETIC FILE

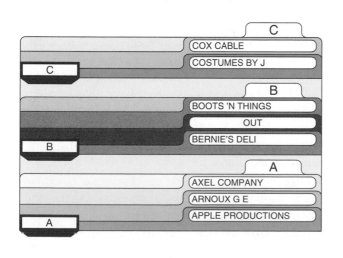

simple one (with few subjects consisting of only a single sheet of titles) and access can be obtained directly through its alphabetic title. However, most subject systems are more complex and demand some type of index. For electronic systems, cross-reference terms can be incorporated within the index. Without an index, it is almost impossible for the subject storage method to function satisfactorily. This index may include several levels or several cross-references. Figure 12-5 on page 237 illustrates two- and three-level subject indexes. The index should be kept up to date: as new subjects are added old ones should be eliminated. When new subjects are added, the index provides guidance, and helps to avoid the duplication of subjects.

A good example of a subject index is the index to your local Yellow Pages, which precedes the directory. Take a few minutes now to look at it. It gives you the subject areas. If this subject area is not where the information

■ Figure 12-3

ELECTRONIC ALPHABETIC SCREEN

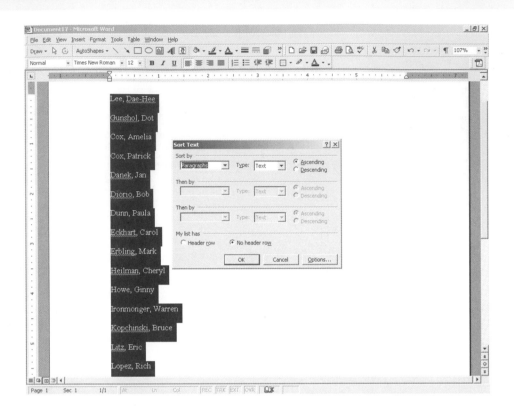

■ Figure 12-4

MANUAL SUBJECT FILE

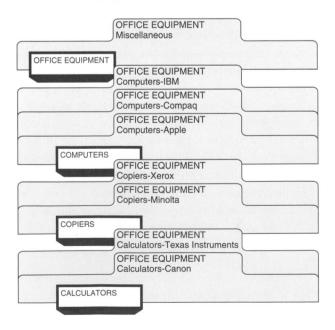

is located, the user is given the correct subject area. Here are some examples.

Advertising Art & Layout Service
See Artists—Commercial; Graphic Designers

Doctors
See Chiropractic Physicians; Clinics; Dentists; Hospitals; Optometry, Physicians & Surgeons—M.D.; Physicians & Surgeons—DO; Physicians & Surgeons—Podiatrists

One of the major advantages of the subject method is that all records about one subject are grouped together. For example, notice above that all dentists are grouped together; all hospitals are grouped together, and so on. If this information were filed using a straight alphabetic method, each dentist would be listed by name and each hospital would be listed by name. Obviously, such a system is not helpful in finding information if you do not know the name of a hospital or a dentist.

GEOGRAPHIC FILING. Another variation of an alphabetic system is the geographic method, with related records

■ Figure 12-5

THREE-LEVEL SUBJECT INDEX

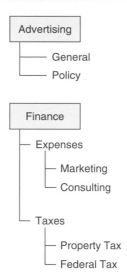

■ Figure 12-6

MANUAL GEOGRAPHIC FILE

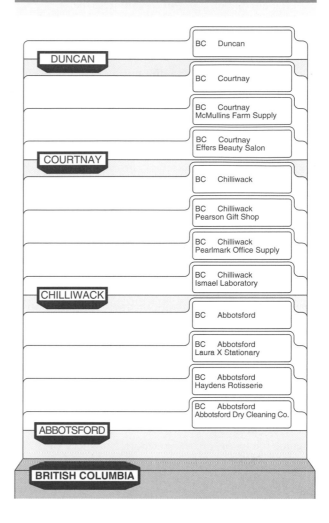

grouped by place or location. Geographic filing is considered a direct method if you know the location of the file needed. If you do not, it is an indirect system. It requires a separate geographic file in a manual system or the appropriate **keywords** (unique identifiers) set up for an electronic system so you can query the system in a variety of ways. Geographic filing is particularly useful for

- Utility companies—street names and numbers are of primary importance in troubleshooting
- Real estate firms—they have listings according to land areas
- Sales organizations—they are concerned with the geographic location of their customers
- Government agencies—they file records by province, municipality, or other geographic division

In a manual geographic file by province and city, file guides are used to indicate the province and city. File folders are arranged alphabetically behind the guides, with tabs indicating the company or individual. Figure 12-6 shows a manual geographic arrangement.

Numeric Storage Methods

Under the **numeric method**, records are given numbers that are arranged in a numeric sequence when stored. The numeric method is particularly useful to

- Insurance companies that keep records according to policy numbers
- Law firms that assign a case number to each client
- Real estate agencies that list properties by code numbers
  The manual numeric file has four basic parts:
- Numeric file
- Alphabetic general file
- A file containing the names of the clients, customers, and/or companies with the number assigned to the individual or company
- A file containing a list of the numbers that have been used

In practice, here is how the manual numeric method works:

1. When a document is ready to be filed, the file containing the names of the clients and customers

is consulted to get the number of the particular client or customer.

2. The number established is put on the document; the document is put in the numeric file.

3. If the client or customer is new and no number is established, the document may be put in the alphabetic file until the client or customer has enough documents (a minimum of five) to open an individual numeric file.

4. If it is necessary to establish a new numeric file, the file containing the list of numbers is consulted to determine the next number to be used.

Figure 12-7 illustrates the manual numeric method. Here are three variations of numeric filing:

- Chronological filing
- Terminal-digit filing
- Alphanumeric filing

CHRONOLOGICAL FILING. In **chronological filing**, records are arranged by date—usually by year, month, or day—in reverse order with the most recent on top/at the front of a folder. Additionally, other calendar divisions (such as weeks, months, or quarters) may be used as primary sort fields for document groupings. While the principle of chronological filing is applied to the storage of records in all filing systems, chronological filing as a system on its own is best suited for records that will later be referred to by date. Such records include daily or quarterly reports, invoices or statements, and follow-up systems.

■ Figure 12-7

MANUAL NUMERIC FILE

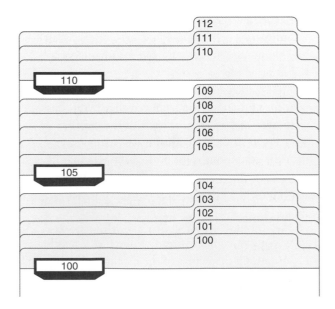

Many offices use chronological filing for follow-up systems. A follow-up system is also known as a **tickler file** or **BF/PA** (bring forward/put away) system. Most people use some form of tickler file in their personal lives. If you mark important dates such as birthdays and anniversaries of family and friends on a calendar, you are using a tickler file. This calendar note "tickles" your memory so that you don't forget these important times of the year.

In the office, a tickler file may be either manual or electronic. A **manual tickler file** in the office can take the form of

- A hard-copy calendar
- A card file; cards are stored in a drawer or box with two sets of tabbed guides:
  - 12 monthly tabbed guides
  - 31 daily numbered guides
  (See Figure 3-3 on page 52.)

The **electronic tickler file** in the office can take the form of a

- Computer calendar—for example, Microsoft Outlook®
- Computer database—for example, Corel Quattro Pro

The example of a tickler file illustrated in Chapter 3 is the computer calendar used by PIM software to organize to-do items by the date the task is due to be completed. Once the items have been keyed into the PIM system, you can readily call up what you are to accomplish each day. This is an efficient system for keeping yourself organized.

In relation to records management, however, it may not be the best one to use. The documents easiest to retrieve are those that have been stored. Often a deadline or other time-sensitive information is contained in a business document—information that requires action days or even weeks later. Rather than leaving such a document unfiled, putting a "BF" notation (which includes the date it should be "brought forward") on it releases it for filing and simultaneously flags it for attention at a later date. In this way the document is stored and easily accessible as a reference for others in the office but will be retrieved and distributed to the requisitioner on the follow-up (BF) date.

While it may seem most efficient to use an electronic tickler file for this task as well, it has one major disadvantage—the potential for lack of access by anyone other than the individual who maintains the system. For example, your computer calendar files are usually password-protected so that the information is available only to you; a manual tickler file system permits access to all staff, even when you are absent.

TERMINAL-DIGIT FILING. In the basic numeric method, as the files increase, the numbers, chronologically assigned to new files, become higher or longer. When they become several digits long, it becomes difficult to file items correctly and all new files tend to congregate in one drawer of the system. One remedy is to use **terminal-digit filing**.

In terminal-digit filing, the last two or three digits of a six- or nine-digit number are used to identify the primary division for storing the records. When indexing, the digits are usually separated into groups of two or three digits with a space in between. The numbers are then read from right to left rather than left to right. For example, assume that you are setting up a file, and the file number is 129845. That number would be indexed in two-digit groups (12-98-45) and read from right to left.

The document would be indexed first by the last two digits, 45. The next digits indexed would be 98, then 12. The document would be stored in a drawer labelled "45," behind a guide labelled "98," in a folder labelled "12" directly behind the one labelled "11." The next file opened in this series would be assigned the number 12-98-46. It would be placed in drawer "46" behind guide "12" and after file "11." In this system new files are evenly distributed throughout the filing system and do not accumulate in the same drawer.

ALPHANUMERIC FILING. Alphanumeric filing combines alphabetic and numeric characters. For example, RM-01 Records Management may be the main directory, with the subdirectories being RM-01-01 Manual Filing Methods and RM-01-02 Electronic Filing Methods.

Manual Filing Procedures

When filing manual records, certain procedures should be followed before placing the record in the file, including:

- **Inspecting**. Checking to see that the correspondence is ready to be filed. A release mark (such as the supervisor's initials, a file stamp, or some other agreed-upon designation such as PA [put away] or BF [bring forward]) lets you know the record is ready to be filed.
- When a BF notation is identified on a record, make a note in your follow-up system for the specified date that includes the name of the person and a description of the record to be retrieved.
- **Indexing**. Determining the way the record is to be filed—the name, the subject, the number, or the geographic location.

- **Coding**. Marking the record with the name, subject, location, or number that was determined in the indexing process.

When filing records electronically, you must also follow certain procedures. For example, if you are using a subject file, you must have the appropriate keywords so the system can display information in a variety of ways. Database software and document management software are particularly helpful in filing electronic records.

Database and Document Management Software

Database programs include dBase IV®, FoxPro®, Corel Quattro Pro®, and Microsoft Access®, among others. Free database programs are also available on the Web.

With **database software**, the user can organize, enter, process, index, sort, select, link related files, store, and retrieve information. Data can be shared within the organization, across the organization's intranet, and over the Internet. **Electronic indexing** sorts the records and stores the information on the basis of one or more key fields. The keyword is a unique identifier chosen by the user. For example, if you are working in a human resources department and entering employee information, the keyword might be the employee's social insurance number. In this case, you would be using a numeric filing system. You can **query** (ask) the database to display information in a variety of ways. For example, you might ask for employees who are making a certain salary level or employees who have been employed for a specified period of time. Information may be stored on a variety of media, including DVDs and CDs. **Integrated packages** combine database software with spreadsheet and word processing software so users can easily move stored information from one application to another.

Document management software is also available to assist you in managing electronic, microimage, and paper systems. For example, Dochive® is a document management program available from the Canadian company Skymark Group. Document management programs are helpful if an organization decides to move from a manual to an electronic system. For example, with document management software, paper documents can be digitized and stored on a variety of media, including CDs, optical media, and hard drives, or even online.

Some of the advantages of a document management system are:

- Retrieving documents faster
- Reducing labour costs involved in processing files

- Viewing, printing, faxing, e-mailing, or annotating any document from your PC
- Recovering manual filing and storage space for other business use
- Storing backup copies of all files in a safe location
- Generating activity reports by department and user
- Generating records retention and disposal guidelines

You have already learned that you must perform certain functions before filing a record manually, such as inspecting, indexing, and coding. So too must you perform certain functions before filing an electronic record. You must determine how you want the information sorted. For example, do you want to sort by name, by location, or by number? If you want to sort by location, will you sort by state, by city, and then by name? In other words, you have to pay careful attention to setting up your electronic file system in a manner that lets you retrieve the data quickly and accurately.

Rules for Filing

The rules for filing, which are an important component of any effective records management system, may vary slightly from organization to organization according to the needs of the entity. The organization must be clear about its indexing rules and make them clear to all administrative professionals in writing. ARMA International, the Association of Records Managers and Administrators, has suggested some standard rules, provided later in this chapter, with which you will want to become familiar. ARMA also provides additional services, including

- *The Information Management Journal* and *InfoPro*, published quarterly, offering assistance to professionals in the records management field; *InfoPro Online* is also available
- A bookstore offering recent publications on records management
- Information on how to obtain the CRM (Certified Records Manager) designation
- Career Placement Services, by which employers may post a position and applicants may search for one

For more information about ARMA go to www.arma.org.

Storage Supplies and Equipment

Storage supplies, equipment, and media are very different, depending on whether the document management system is manual or electronic. As you have learned earlier in this chapter, most organizations have both types of systems today, and you need to be knowledgeable about them.

Basic Manual Filing Supplies

Basic manual filing supplies include file guides, file folders, suspension folders, and labels.

FILE GUIDES. A file guide, usually made of heavy pressboard, is used to separate the file drawer into various sections. Each guide has a tab on which is printed a name, a number, or a letter representing a section of the file drawer in accordance with the filing system. Guides with hollow tabs in which labels are inserted are also available. The filing designation is keyed on the label and inserted in the table. Figure 12-8 illustrates one type of file guide. Guides are always placed in *front* of the folders.

FILE FOLDERS. A file folder is generally made of manila (strong paper or thin cardboard) in one of two sizes—either 8-1/2 × 11 inches (letter size, 216 × 279 mm) or 8-1/2 × 14 inches (legal size, 216 × 356 mm). Other colours of folders are available, including blue, yellow, green, red, and so on.

The filing designation for the correspondence placed in the folder is keyed on a label that is then affixed to the tab of the folder. The tab may be at the top of the folder for traditional drawer files or on the side of the folder for open-shelf filing. Folders are made with tabs of various widths, called **cuts**, designated straight cut, one-half cut, one-third cut, and one-fifth cut. File folders may be purchased with these cuts in various positions. For example, if you are buying folders of one-third cut, you may want to have all the tabs in first position

■ Figure 12-8

FILE GUIDE

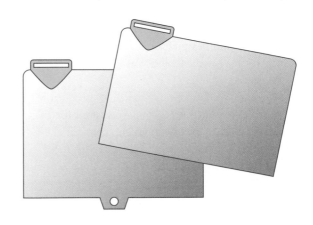

(on the left). Or you may want to have the tabs in first, second (in the centre), and third (on the right) positions. By choosing tabs in three positions, you are able to see the file captions on three folders at once. Figure 12-9 illustrates the cuts in various positions.

A file folder can store up to 100 sheets of paper. As the number of sheets in a folder increases, the records will tend to ride up in the folder and may begin to cover the label. To prevent this, score lines along the bottom edge of the folder allow you to refold it, giving it a flat base on which the documents can rest.

When placing documents into a file folder, the most recent document is put in front (on top of other documents) with the top of the document to the left. This way, when a folder is removed from the cabinet, placed on a table and opened, it is ready to read like the pages of a book.

SUSPENSION FOLDERS. In addition to standard file folders, suspension folders are available. These are sometimes called "hanging" folders, because small metal rods attached to them allow them to hang on the sides of the file drawer. Plastic tabs and insertable labels fit into pre-cut slots on the folder and may be moved into any position.

FILE FOLDER LABELS. File folder labels may be purchased in various configurations, including continuous

> ### Communication Tip
>
> To keep your desk clean and improve your organization, keep a small file beside your desk. Place all ongoing projects and pending files in order of importance in this file. You can quickly retrieve the important work without having to rummage through numerous papers on your desk.

folder strips, separate strips, rolls in boxes, or pressure-sensitive, adhesive labels. Different-coloured labels can speed up the process of filing and finding records and eliminate much misfiling. It is easy to spot a coloured label that has been misfiled, since that colour stands out from the other colours that surround it.

Some of the ways coloured labels may be used are to

- Designate a particular subject (for example, green labels may designate budget items; blue labels, personnel items)
- Indicate geographic divisions of the country
- Designate particular sections of the file

When preparing labels for files, consistency should be observed in keying them. Here are some suggestions for preparing labels:

- Key label captions in ALL CAPITAL letters with no punctuation.
- Key the label in a type size large enough to read easily but small enough that the complete caption will fit—a size of 12 to 14 points is recommended.
- Begin the caption two spaces from the left edge of the label; key any additional information five spaces to the right.
- Always key the name on the label in correct indexing order.
- Use the same style of labels on all folders. For example, if you decide to use labels with colour strips, be consistent. If you decide to use coloured labels, be consistent.
- Key wraparound side-tab labels for lateral file cabinets both above and below the colour bar separator so the information is readable from both sides.

Manual Equipment

Vertical drawers are typical of the traditional storage cabinet, the most common variety having four drawers. Lateral files are similar to vertical files except that the drawer rolls out sideways, exposing the entire contents of the drawer at once. Less aisle space is needed for a lateral file than for a vertical file.

Movable-aisle systems consist of modular units of open-shelf files mounted on tracks in the floor. Files are placed directly against each other. Wheels or rails permit the individual units to be moved apart for access. The movable racks are electrically powered. Because these movable systems take up less space than standard files, they are being used more and more

■ **Figure 12-9**

FOLDER CUTS

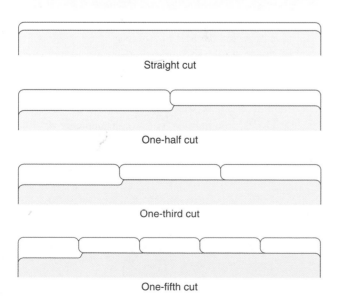

Straight cut

One-half cut

One-third cut

One-fifth cut

Lateral files use less space than vertical files.

today. Movable systems may be manual, mechanical, or electrical. Manual systems are small, with two to four carriages. They require no power; the user merely pushes the files apart. Mechanical systems operate by turning a crank. Electrical systems move carriages with motors.

Features that provide safety both for the administrative professional using the system and for the file contents are a top priority of companies. Protection devices are available for all systems. The most basic device is a key-operated carriage lock that prevents the system from rolling on the rails. Another safety device is a strip that runs the length of the file cabinet at floor level. Pressure of more than a few ounces stops cabinet movement. Still another safety device is an infrared photoelectric beam. If a person or an object breaks the beam, the system stops moving. When the person or object is no longer breaking the beam, the system resets itself. To ensure safety of materials, users may have a badge that is swiped through a reader to allow entrance to the system, or they may enter a password code. Also, some systems can be fitted with locking doors.

Electronic Equipment, Media, and File Management

Large computers, such as supercomputers and mainframes, have for some time now served as electronic filing equipment, and with the growth and widespread use of the personal computer it too has become a major component of such equipment. With database and document management software, about which you learned earlier, personal computers networked with other PCs can

- Provide electronic document storage
- Serve as an access device for scanned and electronically generated documents
- Maintain records inventories
- Retrieve paper and electronic documents based on the same file code
- Store records retention and destruction data

Electronic Media

In addition to electronic records being stored on the hard drive of a computer, they may be stored on a variety of external storage media. The major ones are as follows:

- Floppy disks, which come in double-sided and high-density 3.5-inch disks that store 1.44 MB.
- Zip disks, which can store 250 MB.
- Any type of **CD** (compact disk) technology, including **CD-R** (CD, recordable) and **CD-RW** (CD, rewritable). CD-R is **WORM** (write once, read many) technology. It has become popular in digital archiving, since the information cannot be modified or erased and can be read any number of times. If the information stored on the CD needs to be revised, CD-RW technology is used. CDs provide 650 MB of storage.
- Any type of **DVD** (digital versatile disk) technology, including **DVD-ROM** (read-only memory), **DVD-R** (write once), and **DVD-RAM** (random access memory, rewritable), and **DVD-RW** (rewritable). The storage capacity of DVDs is 17 GB. DVDs are more expensive than CDs, but the cost is dropping rapidly. It is expected that DVD storage will replace CD storage.

Note that storage capacities are constantly being increased, and the above figures may not be current by the time you read this.

Electronic File Management

Our dependence upon the computer and electronic storage of data has resulted in an increasing number of files being created and stored. You learned earlier in this chapter that it is important to develop a sound records management system for hard copy files. Likewise, it is just as important to do so for electronic files. As an administrative professional, you need to develop an effective and efficient method of storing and retrieving electronic documents, whether they are stored on your hard drive, the office network, or other media.

Files created with any application software cannot be saved unless you create a filename. Filenames must be unique—no other file in the folder can have an identical name. Filenames can include any of the letters of the alphabet, the digits 0 through 9, and any of a variety of special characters including but not limited to !, @, or . These files can be stored on a floppy disk in the "A:" drive, in the hard drive usually known as the "C:" drive, or in a network drive that might be designated by any letter of the alphabet from "G:" to "Z:."

The space available on the media being used can be quite large. Most computers have hard drives of 80 to 120 GB. But unless the files are organized in some way, it would soon be impossible to locate and retrieve anything—the files would be much like pieces of paper tossed randomly into a drawer. Organization is mostly achieved by creating electronic "folders," into which related files are inserted.

For example, while working for Martin Albertson in the Corporate Marketing and Communications division of CanAsian Airlines, you would likely create electronic documents related to Marketing and Communications as well as documents related to any external community activities to which Mr. Albertson is committed. These documents might include press releases, promotional materials for advertising, and documents dealing with his volunteer commitments as a member of the Board of Governors of Mount Royal College. To effectively manage these topics, you would create three folders named, for example, "Press Releases," "Advertising," and "College Board." With this organization in place, a letter that Mr. Albertson has created in response to a document received from Dr. Lee, President of Mount Royal College, would be saved in the folder "College Board."

To further organize your files, you can also create folders within these folders. While it is possible to create folders within folders within folders, it is best to keep the organization shallow (many folders at the same level) rather than deep (folders within folders within folders). Also, choose meaningful names for the files and folders you create. This will make retrieval of files quick and efficient. Many administrative professionals create a file-naming system for electronic files that parallels the hard copy system. It might be alphabetic, subjective, or numeric, or a combination of these systems. The most important aspect of electronic file management is to create a system that makes retrieval quick and easy and to be consistent in the naming of your files and folders. Figure 12-10 illustrates the file structure of the folders on the Student CD-ROM; Figure 12-11 illustrates the file structures in Chapter 1 of the same CD-ROM (see page 244 for both).

In a networked environment, storage media are divided into directories. You will be allocated a section of the network on which to store your files, similarly to having a file cabinet by your desk. Within the networked environment you will be granted access rights to this and certain other directories; in some of the directories you may only be able to read, and not to modify, the content of files. Often, master documents—documents that will be used by all employees of a department or organization—are placed in these restricted directories. They can be copied into your dedicated directory and from there they might be altered and saved within your own system, leaving the original unchanged. Figure 12-12 on page 245 illustrates the file structure of network drives.

The reason most people tend to print out hard copies is because they are worried something will happen to the computer and the files will be lost. However, in a large organization, computer services likely has a backup schedule in place. With *incremental backup*, new or changed documents are backed up daily. Also, complete network backups are usually scheduled at weekly, monthly, or quarterly intervals; this is known as *full backup*. However, this protection will not normally include your own hard drive; you will need to develop a similar backup schedule yourself if you are storing important files locally.

Establishing a retention schedule for hard copy documents is covered in the next section of this chapter. Here are some suggestions for how long to retain electronic files when hard copies of the documents are printed and stored in a manual system:

- *Daily correspondence.* Five to ten days. Create five or ten folders named Day 1 to Day 5, or to Day 10 for a two-week system. Store all correspondence in Day 1 on Monday of the first week, in

■ Figure 12-10

FILE STRUCTURE OF STUDENT CD-ROM

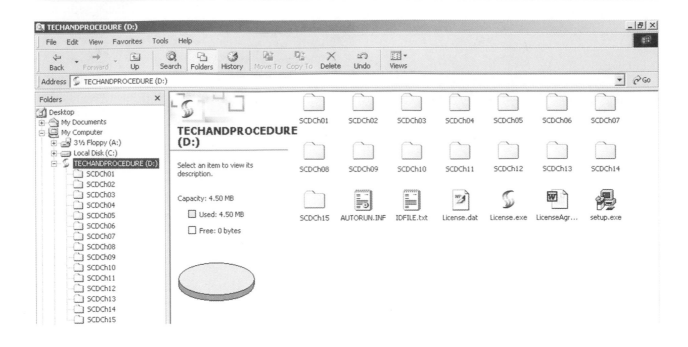

■ Figure 12-11

FILE STRUCTURE OF CHAPTER 1 OF STUDENT CD-ROM

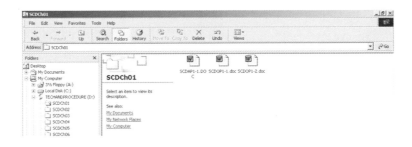

Day 2 on Tuesday of the first week, etc. Once the designated period is over, return to the Day 1 folder and delete the documents which were created and stored one or two weeks previously. You can then reuse the folder. This will help to keep your directory active.

• *Weekly, monthly, quarterly or annual reports.* Retain until the next report is created. You may be able to use the format or some text of the previous document in the preparation of the current report.

• *Agenda.* Use the previous agenda to create the current agenda for a meeting. Updating the previous document is quicker than beginning from scratch every time an agenda for a regularly scheduled meeting is required.

• *Proposals and special reports.* Use the "versions" capability of your word processing software so you

■ Figure 12-12

FILE STRUCTURE OF NETWORK DRIVES

can return to a previous version of a document if need be. Once the file is printed and distributed, delete it, or archive it to a floppy disk or a CD.

Keeping your file structure clean by regularly deleting unnecessary files will make your computer run faster, and make your file retrieval more effective.

Microform Storage

In addition to the storage of records in paper and electronic form, microforms have been used to store records. For example, personnel departments have stored personnel records of former employees on microforms and libraries have stored research information on microforms. There are two types of microforms—**microfilm** (a roll of film containing a series of frames or images) or **microfiche** (a sheet of film containing a series of images arranged in a grid). Today many organizations are moving to **COLD** (computer output to laser disk) technology to organize information that was historically stored on microforms. A COLD system indexes data and places it on an optical disk, making it much easier to find and display. The users define indexing fields, and searches may be done on the basis of single or multiple indexes. The software allows for a fast search and retrieval of files.

COLD technology includes these advantages:
- A dramatic reduction in cost associated with the creation of microforms and printed reports
- Instant access to information and the elimination of the cumbersome and time-consuming tasks associated with microform retrieval
- Reduction of repetitive and time-consuming tasks of administrative personnel
- Reduction in space required to store microforms
- Instant access in branch offices or remote sites to COLD data through network storage
- Confidentiality of information controlled through information security systems

New versions of COLD technology are constantly being released. The latest version as this book went to press was 4.20.

Retention Schedules

In both electronic and manual systems, it is important to know how long records should be retained by the organization. The cost of maintaining documents that are no longer of any use can be significant, particularly in manual systems, due to the floor space necessary for the file cabinets. Additionally, even though electronic storage is not nearly so space-intensive, there is some cost to maintaining unneeded documents.

The retention schedule should identify

- The period of time a record should be retained
- How long records are needed in the active area of the organization
- The length of time records should be retained in inactive storage

As an administrative professional, you generally will not make retention schedule decisions. The general approach is to consult with the legal counsel of the organization (or if it is a small organization, use an outside legal firm), then develop appropriate schedules for specific types of documents. A sample retention schedule is shown in Figure 12-13. If the company does not have a records retention schedule, the administrative professional should check with the supervisor before making any decisions about how, when, and if documents should be transferred or destroyed.

The Canadian government provides publications concerning records management that can be accessed from its website at www.archives.ca. Other records management sites are at

- www.cio-dpi.gc.ca/cio-dpi
- www.rmicanada.com

To understand more about retention control, consider the following categories into which records can be classified:

- **Vital records**. These are records that cannot be replaced and should never be destroyed. They are essential to the continued effective operation of the organization. Examples are corporate charters, deeds, tax returns, constitutions and bylaws, insurance policies, procedures manuals, audited financial statements, patents, and copyrights.

■ **Figure 12-13**

RETENTION SCHEDULE

RETENTION SCHEDULE			
Record Category	Retention Period	Retained in Active File	Retained in Inactive File
Personnel files (terminated)	6 years	2 years	4 years
Payroll records	8 years	3 years	5 years
Patents	Indefinitely	Indefinitely	—

- **Important records**. These are records necessary to orderly continuation of the business and are replaceable only with considerable expenditure of time and money. Such records may be transferred to inactive storage but are not destroyed. Examples are financial statements, operating and statistical records, physical inventories, bank statements, and board minutes.
- **Useful records**. These are those that are useful, though not necessary, for the smooth, effective operation of the organization. Such records are replaceable, but their loss involves delay or inconvenience. They may be transferred to inactive files or destroyed after a certain period of time. Examples are letters, memorandums, reports, and bank records.
- **Nonessential records**. These are records that have no future value to the organization. Once the purpose for which they were created has been fulfilled, they may be destroyed. For example, a memorandum written to arrange a meeting generally has no value once the meeting has occurred.

Active-to-Inactive File Procedures

At some point in the life of a record, on the basis of records retention information, you decide to either destroy it, retain it permanently, or transfer it to inactive storage. Two common methods of transfer are perpetual and periodic.

Perpetual Transfer

With the **perpetual transfer**, records are continuously transferred from the active to the inactive files. The advantage of this method is that all files are kept current, since any inactive material is immediately transferred to storage. The perpetual transfer method works well in offices where jobs are completed by units. For example, when a lawyer finishes a case, the file is complete and probably will not need to be referred to at all or certainly not frequently. Therefore, it can be transferred to the inactive files.

When distinguishing between active and inactive records, the following categories should be used:

- *Active records*. Used three or more times a month; should be kept in an accessible area.
- *Inactive records*. Used less than 15 times a year; may be stored in less accessible areas than active records.

- *Archive records.* Have historical value to the organization; are preserved permanently.

Periodic Transfer

With **periodic transfer**, active records are transferred to inactive status at the end of a stated period of time. For example, you may transfer records that are over six months old to the inactive file and maintain records that are less than six months old in the active file. You might carry out this procedure every six months.

Maintaining and Updating the File Management System

The records management needs of an organization change over time. Additionally, new manual and electronic systems, equipment, and storage possibilities become available. Organizations must keep current on what is available and change systems as appropriate. Although changing systems can be expensive in the short term, new systems often save money in the long term by offering improved speed and accuracy and requiring less staff time to operate. For example, with electronic filing of records, new software is available that offers more features for improving a records management system. New features can save the organization considerable money and provide for more efficient management of records. If the organization is large, generally at least one person in a management position is responsible for the ongoing maintenance and updating of the system.

Ongoing Training of Personnel

With changes in records management systems and new equipment, ongoing training should be provided to those involved in records management. The organizational person in charge of records management generally provides this training.

Indexing Rules

In order to store and retrieve records effectively, a set of rules must be followed. ARMA has published a standard set of rules covering alphabetic indexing and cross-referencing. The same rules are used whether you are working with an electronic or a manual system.

If you are presently working in an organization or when you begin your career, you may find that the indexing rules used are slightly different from those presented here. Sometimes, organizations deviate from the rules according to their own internal needs. At other times, deviations may merely mean the individuals setting up the system were not aware of the most recent indexing rules. You might want to call attention to the differences if they are significant; however, it is best to wait until your supervisor has come to respect your competence.

Alphabetic Indexing

The rules in this chapter are compatible with ARMA's Alphabetic Filing Rules. Some terms used in determining filing order are

- **Filing unit.** Each part of an individual or company name
- **Key unit.** Primary or first unit used in alphabetizing
- **Alphabetizing.** Comparison of units in a caption, unit by unit and letter by letter to determine a difference
- **Caption.** One or more filing units such as the entire name or a part of the name by which the record will be stored

Rule 1: Indexing Order of Units

A. *Personal names.* A personal name is indexed in this manner:
   - The surname (last name) is the key unit.
   - The given name (first name) or initial is the second unit.
   - The middle name or initial is the third unit. If determining the surname is difficult, consider the last name as the surname.

B. *Nothing comes before something.* A unit consisting of just an initial precedes a unit that consists of a complete name beginning with the same letter. Punctuation is not considered when indexing. See Table 12-1 (Rule 1A) on page 249 for examples of indexing personal names.

C. *Business names.* Business names are indexed as written, using letterheads or trademarks as guides. Each word in a business name is a separate unit. Business names containing personal names are indexed as written. See Table 12-1 (Rule 1B) on page 249 for examples of indexing business names.

Rule 2: Minor Words and Symbols in Business Names

Articles, prepositions, conjunctions, and symbols are considered separate indexing units. Symbols are considered as spelled in full. When the word *the* appears as the first word of a business name, it is considered the last indexing unit.

Examples of articles, prepositions, conjunctions, and symbols that are commonly found in business names are given here. See Table 12-1 (Rule 2) on page 249 for examples of indexing minor words and symbols in business names.

Articles	a, an, the
Prepositions	at, by, for, in, of, off, on, out, over, to, with
Conjunctions	and, but, or, nor
Symbol	&, #, $, %

Rule 3: Punctuation and Possessives

All punctuation is disregarded when indexing personal and business names. Commas, periods, hyphens, apostrophes, dashes, exclamation points, question marks, quotation marks, and slashes (/) are disregarded, and names are indexed as written. See Table 12-1 (Rule 3) on page 249 for examples of punctuation and possessives in indexing.

Rule 4: Single Letters and Abbreviations

A. *Personal names.* Initials in personal names are considered separate indexing units. Abbreviations of personal names (*Wm., Jos., Thos.*) and nicknames (*Liz, Bill*) are indexed as written.

B. *Business names.* Single letters in business and organization names are indexed as written. If there is a space between single letters, index each letter as a separate unit. An acronym (a word formed from the first letter, or first few letters, of several words) is indexed as one unit regardless of punctuation or spelling. Abbreviated words (*Mfg., Corp., Inc.*) and abbreviated names (*IBM, GM*) are indexed as one unit regardless of punctuation or spacing. Radio and television station call letters are indexed as one unit. See Table 12-1 (Rule 4) on page 249 for examples of single letters and abbreviations in indexing.

Rule 5: Titles and Suffixes

A. *Personal names.* A title before a name (*Dr., Miss, Mr., Mrs., Ms., Professor*), a seniority suffix (*II, III, Jr., Sr.*), or a professional suffix (*D.D.S., M.D., Ph.D.*) after a name is the last indexing unit. Numeric suffixes (*II, III*) are filed before alphabetic suffixes (*Jr., Sr.*). If a name contains both a title and a suffix, the title is the last unit. Royal and religious titles followed by either a given name or a surname only (*Father John*) are indexed and filed as written. See Table 12-1 (Rule 5A) on page 249 for examples of titles and suffixes in personal names.

B. *Business names.* Titles in business names are filed as written. See Table 12-1 (Rule 5B) on page 250 for examples of titles and suffixes in business names. Do Self-Check A.

SELF-CHECK A ✔

Complete the table below to determine if you understand the first five indexing rules. Determine the following: key unit, second unit, third unit, and fourth unit. Check your answers with those at the end of the chapter.

	Unit			
	Key	*2*	*3*	*4*
Henry Hubert Bowers, Jr.	____	____	____	____
Roger Alan Le Feve	____	____	____	____
500 Cafeteria	____	____	____	____
The 500, Inc.	____	____	____	____
Z. T. Glasier, III	____	____	____	____
U-R Rental Company	____	____	____	____
CBC Television	____	____	____	____
Sister Mary Vanetta	____	____	____	____
Physicians' Hospital	____	____	____	____

Rule 6: Prefixes—Articles and Particles

A foreign article or particle in a personal or business name is combined with the part of the name following it to form a single indexing unit. The indexing order is not affected by a space between a prefix and the rest of the name, and the space is disregarded when indexing.

Examples of articles and particles are *à la, D', Da, De, Del, De la, Des, El, Fitz, L', La, Las, Le, Lo, Los, Mac, Mc, Saint, San, Santa, St., Ste., Ten, Van, Van der, Von*, and *Von der*. See Table 12-1 (Rule 6) on page 250 for examples of prefixes in personal and business names.

Table 12-1 EXAMPLES OF INDEXING RULES 1–7

Examples of Rule 1A
Index Order of Units in Personal Names

Name	Key Unit	Unit 2	Unit 3
Carlos Almeida	ALMEIDA	CARLOS	
Carlos A. Almeida	ALMEIDA	CARLOS	A
Carlos Anthony Almeida	ALMEIDA	CARLOS	ANTHONY

Examples of Rule 1B
Index Order of Units in Business Names

Name	Key Unit	Unit 2	Unit 3	Unit 4
Beaumont Health Centre	BEAUMONT	HEALTH	CENTRE	
Beaver Creek Golf Club	BEAVER	CREEK	GOLF	CLUB
Chuck Beaver Pharmacy	CHUCK	BEAVER	PHARMACY	

Examples of Rule 2
Index Order of Units in Minor Words and Symbols in Business Names

Name	Key Unit	Unit 2	Unit 3	Unit 4	Unit 5
A Bit of Honey	A	BIT	OF	HONEY	
At Home Laundry	AT	HOME	LAUNDRY		
The $ and ¢ Shop	DOLLARS	AND	CENTS	SHOP	THE

Examples of Rule 3
Index Order of Units with Punctuation and Possessives in Personal and Business Names

Name	Key Unit	Unit 2	Unit 3	Unit 4
Ahmad's Grooming	AHMADS	GROOMING		
A-Z Video Company	AZ	VIDEO	COMPANY	
North/South Printing	NORTHSOUTH	PRINTING		

Examples of Rule 4
Index Order of Units for Single Letters and Abbreviations in Business and Personal Names

Name	Key Unit	Unit 2	Unit 3	Unit 4
CTV Television	CTV	TELEVISION		
G.M. MOTORS	GM	MOTORS		
J. V. Hildebrand	HILDEBRAND	J	V	
Jas. W. Hildebrand	HILDEBRAND	JAS	W	
Wm. R. Hildebrand	HILDEBRAND	WM	R	
J K of Toronto	J	K	OF	TORONTO

Examples of Rule 5A
Index Order of Units for Titles and Suffixes in Personal Names

Name	Key Unit	Unit 2	Unit 3	Unit 4
Father James	FATHER	JAMES		
S. R. Fitzgerald II	FITZGERALD	S	R	II
S. R. Fitzgerald III	FITZGERALD	S	R	III
S. R. Fitzgerald, Jr.	FITZGERALD	S	R	JR
S. R. Fitzgerald, Sr.	FITZGERALD	S	R	SR
Frederick Johns, MD	JOHNS	FREDERICK	MD	

Table 12-1 EXAMPLES OF INDEXING RULES 1–7 *(continued)*

Examples of Rule 5B

Index Order of Units for Titles and Suffixes in Business Names

Name	Key Unit	Unit 2	Unit 3
Doctors' Hospital	DOCTORS	HOSPITAL	
Dr. Atkins Bakery	DR	ATKINS	BAKERY

Examples of Rule 6

Index Order of Units for Prefixes in Personal and Business Names

Name	Key Unit	Unit 2	Unit 3	Unit 4
Paul Alan LaFaver	LAFAVER	PAUL	ALAN	
MacDugal's Meat Market	MACDUGALS	MEAT	MARKET	
McDouglas & Edwards	MCDOUGLAS	AND	EDWARDS	
Mary Lou St. Marie	STMARIE	MARY	LOU	

Examples of Rule 7

Index Order of Units for Numbers in Business Names

Name	Key Unit	Unit 2	Unit 3	Unit 4
4-Cent Copy Centre	4	CENT	COPY	CENTRE
4th Street Garage	4	STREET	GARAGE	
400–410 Daniels Court	400	DANIELS	COURT	
Four Seasons Health Spa	Four	SEASONS	HEALTH	SPA
Highway 30 Café	HIGHWAY	30	CAFÉ	
Highway Service Station	HIGHWAY	SERVICE	STATION	

Rule 7: Numbers in Business Names

Numbers spelled out in business names (for example, *Seven Seas Restaurant*) are filed alphabetically. Numbers written in digit form are filed before alphabetic letters or words (*B4 Photographers* comes before *Beleau Building Co.*). Names with numbers written in digits in the first units are filed in ascending order (lowest to highest) before alphabetic names (*229 Club, 534 Shop, Bank of Chicago*). Arabic numerals (*2, 3*) are filed before Roman numerals (*II, III*).

Names with inclusive numbers (*33–37*) are arranged by the first digit(s) only (*33*). Names with numbers appearing in other than the first position (*Pier 36 Café*) are filed alphabetically and immediately before a similar name without a number (*Pier and Port Café*).

When indexing numbers written in digit form that contain *st, d, nd, rd*, and *th* (*lst, 2d, 2nd, 3d, 3rd, 4th*), ignore the letter endings and consider only the digits (*1, 2, 3, 4*). See Table 12-1 (Rule 7) for examples of numbers in business names.

Rule 8: Organizations and Institutions

Banks and other financial institutions, clubs, colleges, hospitals, hotels, lodges, magazines, motels, museums, newspapers, religious institutions, schools, unions, universities, and other organizations and institutions are indexed and filed according to the names written on their letterheads. See Table 12-2 (Rule 8) (on page 252) for examples of organizations and institutions as indexing units.

Rule 9: Identical Names

When personal names and names of businesses, institutions, and organizations are identical (including titles as explained in Rule 5), filing order is determined by the addresses. Compare addresses in the following order:

- City names
- Province or state names (if city names are identical)
- Street names, including *Avenue, Boulevard, Drive, Street* (if city and state names are identical)
  a. When the first units of street names are written in digits (*18th Street*), the names are filed in ascending numeric order and placed together before alphabetic street names.
  b. Street names with compass directions are considered as written (*South Park Avenue*). Numbers after compass directions are considered before alphabetic names (*East 8th, East Main, SE Eighth, Southeast Eighth*).
- House and building numbers (if city, province or state, and street names are identical)
  a. House and building numbers written as figures (*912 Riverside Terrace*) are considered in ascending numeric order and placed together before alphabetic building names (*The Riverside Terrace*).
  b. If a street address and a building name are included in an address, disregard the building name.
  c. Postal codes are not considered in determining filing order. See Table 12-2 (Rule 9) on page 252 for examples of identical names.

Rule 10: Government Names

Government names are indexed first by the name of the governmental unit—federal, provincial or territorial, municipality, or city. Next, index the distinctive name of the department, bureau, office, or board. The words *Office of, Bureau of,* and so on, are separate indexing units if they are part of the official name. *Note:* If *of* is not part of the office name as written, it is not added.

A. *Federal.* The first two indexing units of a Canadian (federal) government agency name are *Canada Government.* See Table 12-2 (Rule 10A) on page 253 for examples of federal government names as indexing units.

B. *Provincial/territorial and local.* The first indexing units are the names of the province/territory,

municipality, or city/town. Next, index the most distinctive name of the department, board, bureau, office, or government/political division. The words *Province of* or *Territory of, City of, Department of, Board of,* and so on, are added only if needed for clarity and only if they are in the official name. They are considered separate indexing units. See Table 12-2 (Rule 10B) on page 253 for examples of province and local government names.

C. *Foreign.* The distinctive English name is the first indexing unit for foreign government names. The remainder of the formal name of the government, if necessary, follows this. Branches, departments, and divisions follow in order by their distinctive names. States, colonies, provinces, cities, and other divisions of foreign governments are followed by their distinctive or official names as spelled in English. See Table 12-2 (Rule 10C) on page 253 for examples of foreign government names. Do Self-Check B.

SELF-CHECK B ✔

Check your knowledge of Rules 6–10 by completing the table below. Determine the key, second, third, and fourth units. Check your answers with the correct ones given at the end of the chapter.

	Unit			
	Key	2	3	4
Moncton Cleaners	___	___	___	___
3rd Street Movie	___	___	___	___
43–47 Rogers Road Materials	___	___	___	___
7 Seas Restaurant	___	___	___	___
Etienne Laberge, 712 Royale, St. Augustine Quebec	___	___	___	___
Ministry of Health and Welfare	___	___	___	___
Department of Skills Training, Province of Saskatchewan	___	___	___	___

Cross-Referencing

Cross-referencing should be done when a record may be filed under more than one name. Here are some rules for cross-referencing personal and business names.

Table 12-2 Examples of Indexing Rules 8–10

Examples of Rule 8

Index Order of Units for Organizations and Institutions

Name	Key Unit	Unit 2	Unit 3	Unit 4
Bank of Montreal	BANK	OF	MONTREAL	
First United Church	FIRST	UNITED	CHURCH	
Winston Churchill Elementary School	WINSTON	CHURCHILL	ELEMENTARY	SCHOOL

Examples of Rule 9

Index Order of Units for Identical Names

Name	Key Unit	Unit 2	Unit 3	Unit 4	Unit 5	Unit 6	Unit 7
Liz Bowman 212 Luther St. John, New Brunswick	BOWMAN	LIZ	ST. JOHN	NEW BRUNSWICK			
Liz Bowman 818 Oak Vancouver, British Columbia	BOWMAN	LIZ	VANCOUVER	BRITISH COLUMBIA			
Brother's Pizza 11120—114 Street Edmonton, Alberta	BROTHERS	PIZZA	EDMONTON	ALBERTA	114		
Brother's Pizza 10510 Jasper Avenue Edmonton, Alberta	BROTHERS	PIZZA	EDMONTON	ALBERTA	JASPER		
Brown Computers 500 Columbia Building Edmonton, Alberta	BROWN	COMPUTERS	EDMONTON	ALBERTA	500	COLUMBIA	
Brown Computers Five Hundred Building Edmonton, Alberta	BROWN	COMPUTERS	EDMONTON	ALBERTA	FIVE	HUNDRED	
Elder Market 213 Clendenan Street Toronto, Ontario	ELDER	MARKET	TORONTO	ONTARIO	213	CLENDENAN	STREET
Elder Market 944 Clendenan Street Toronto, Ontario	ELDER	MARKET	TORONTO	ONTARIO	944	CLENDENAN	STREET

Table 12-2   EXAMPLES OF INDEXING RULES 8–10 *(continued)*

Examples of Rule 10A

Index Order of Units for Federal Government Names (Units 1 and 2 are Canada Government for each example)

Name	Unit 3	Unit 4	Unit 5	Unit 6	Unit 7	Unit 8	Unit 9	Unit 10
FISHERIES AND OCEANS								
Violation Reporting								
Recreational Fishing	FISHERIES	AND	OCEANS	VIOLATION	REPORTING	RECREATIONAL	FISHING	
ENVIRONMENT CANADA								
Pacific Environmental								
Science Centre								
General Inquiries	ENVIRONMENT	CANADA	PACIFIC	ENVIRONMENTAL	SCIENCE	CENTRE	GENERAL	INQUIRES
CUSTOMS AND REVENUE AGENCY								
Income Tax Department	CUSTOMS	AND	REVENUE	AGENCY	INCOME	TAX	DEPARTMENT	

Examples of Rule 10B

Index Order of Units for Local Government Names

Name	Key Unit	Unit 2	Unit 3	Unit 4	Unit 5	Unit 6	Unit 7
Ministry of Municipal Affairs							
Province of British Columbia							
Victoria, British Columbia	BRITISH	COLUMBIA	PROVINCE	OF	MUNICIPAL	AFFAIRS	MINISTRY
Kings County							
Department of Public Works							
Campbell's Cove,							
Prince Edward Island	KINGS	COUNTY	PUBLIC	WORKS	DEPARTMENT	OF	

Examples of Rule 10C

Index Order of Units for Foreign Government Names

Name	Key Unit	Unit 2	Unit 3	Unit 4
United States of America	UNITED	STATES	OF	AMERICA
Polska Rzecapospolita Ludowa	POLISH	PEOPLES	REPUBLIC	
Estados Unidos Mexicanos	UNITED	MEXICAN	STATES	

Cross-Referencing Personal Names

Cross-references should be prepared for the following types of personal names:

1. *Unusual names.* When it is difficult to determine which is the last name, index the name that *appears last on the original record* first. Then prepare a cross-reference with the *first-appearing* name indexed first.

Original	Cross-Reference
Tam Tran	Tran Tam
	See Tam Tran

2. *Hyphenated surnames.* Deal with these as shown below.

Original	Cross-Reference
Sue Loaring-Clark	Clark Sue Loaring
	See Loaringclark Sue

3. *Similar names.* "See also" cross-references are prepared for all possible spellings.

Baier	Bauer	Bayer
See also	*See also*	*See also*
Bauer, Bayer	Bayer, Baier	Baier, Bauer

Cross-Referencing Business Names

Cross-references should be prepared for the following types of business names:

1. *Compound names.* When a business name includes two or more individual surnames, prepare a cross-reference for each surname other than the first.

Original	Cross-Reference
Peat Marwick and Main	Marwick Main and Peat
	See Peat Marwick and Main
	Main Peat and Marwick
	See Peat Marwick and Main

2. *Abbreviations and acronyms.* When a business is commonly known by an abbreviation or an acronym, a cross-reference is prepared for the full name.

Original	Cross-Reference
IBM	International Business Machines
	See IBM

3. *Changed names.* When a business changes its name, a cross-reference is prepared for the old name and all records are filed under the new name.

Original	Cross-Reference
DaimlerChrysler	Chrysler
	See DaimlerChrysler

4. *Foreign business names.* The name of a foreign business is often spelled in the foreign language on the original. The English translation should be written on the document and the document stored *under the English spelling.* A cross-reference should be placed under the foreign spelling.

Original	Cross-Reference
French Republic	République Française
(tr. from *République Française*)	*See* French Republic

■ Figure 12-14

EFFECTIVE DECISION-MAKING STEPS

- Evaluate the Decision
- Test the Alternatives and Make the Decision
- Generate Alternatives or Possible Solutions
- Establish the Criteria
- Define the Problem or the Purpose

Soft Skills: Effective Decision Making

As you learned in Chapter 3, effective decision making is clearly important in all areas of your work as an administrative professional.

A **decision** is the outcome or product of a problem, a concern, or an issue that must be addressed and solved. The process by which a decision is reached includes five steps, which are shown in Figure 12-14 on page 254. You should systematically follow these steps in making a decision.

To help you improve your decision-making skills in records management, review the section on decision making in Chapter 3. Then assume you are the records management professional and apply the steps to the following records management situation.

You have recently been hired by a small company to assist in setting up a coordinated records management program. The company has been in existence only two years, but it is growing rapidly. A manual file system has been used in the past, with a few individuals filing information on their computers in certain situations. Each individual has decided how he or she would file the documents electronically. There is no overall records management strategy. In using the decision-making model, you make these decisions:

- The problem is to establish an *effective*, *coordinated* records management program.
- In establishing the criteria, you determine that you want to establish both a manual and an electronic filing system that can be used by all employees to store and find materials quickly and easily. You want to avoid a high-cost system, but you also

need to provide a system that can grow as the company grows.
- The alternatives you generate are as follows:
  (a) Establish a manual system with the assistance of internal staff.
  (b) Establish an electronic system with the assistance of internal staff.
  (c) Employ a firm to assist with both the manual and the electronic system.
  (d) Determine the type of database and document management software available and implement the system with limited internal support.

- After reviewing the alternatives, you decide to use database and document management software to implement the electronic system and provide detailed standards for manual filing. You have extensive experience in database and document management software; you have also identified two experienced individuals within the company who can assist you. Additionally, you have identified one individual who can assist with setting up the manual system.
- Once the records management system is designed and implemented, and has been used for six months, you evaluate its effectiveness and find that the system is working well. You feel the correct decision was made. However, you discover that you did not provide enough training on the electronic system for some individuals. You immediately implement an ongoing training program, and you begin writing a comprehensive document management manual.

Chapter Summary

The summary will help you remember the important points covered in the chapter.

- A *record* is any type of recorded information, whether that information be an e-mail, a letter, a report, a spreadsheet, a contract, a personnel record, or any other type of organizational record.
- Records management is the systematic control of records from the creation of the record to its final disposition.
- An effective records management system has these components:
  (a) An organization-wide records structure
  (b) A records storage system
  (c) Alphabetic and numeric indexing rules
  (d) Appropriate filing supplies
  (e) Necessary equipment and media (electronic and manual)
  (f) Retention schedules
  (g) Active to inactive file procedures
  (h) Procedures for updating the management system
  (i) Records management manuals and ongoing training for personnel
- Document management systems may be manual, electronic, or a combination of the two.
- There are two basic records storage systems, alphabetic and numeric.
- The alphabetic storage method uses letters of the alphabet to determine the order in which the record is filed. Variations of the alphabetic storage method include subject filing (arranging records by their subject) and geographic filing (arranging records by geographic location).
- Numeric records are given numbers that are arranged in sequence when stored. Variations of this system are chronological filing, terminal-digit filing, and alphanumeric filing.
- In the filing of manual records, the procedures to be followed include inspecting, indexing, and coding.
- In the filing of documents electronically, database and data management software are available to assist you.
- Consistent filing rules should be used. ARMA has developed indexing rules that are widely used.
- Basic manual filing supplies include file folders, suspension folders, file guides, and file folder labels.
- Manual equipment includes vertical drawer cabinets, lateral files, and movable-aisle systems.

- Electronic filing equipment includes PCs and larger computers such as supercomputers and mainframes.
- Electronic filing media include floppy disks, Zip and Jaz disks, CDs, and DVDs.
- Microform filing media include microfilm and microfiche.
- COLD technology allows the organization of information that was historically stored on microforms. A COLD system indexes data and places it on an optical disk, making it much easier to find and display.
- Retention schedules (providing the length of time a record should be maintained) are essential to effective records management systems.
- *Vital* records are those that cannot be replaced and should never be destroyed.
- *Important* records are those necessary to an orderly continuation of the business.
- *Useful* records are those useful for the smooth, effective operation of the organization.
- *Nonessential* records are those that have no future value to the organization once the purpose for which they were created has been fulfilled.
- Records may be transferred to inactive files through perpetual or periodic transfer.
- Cross-referencing is necessary when a record may be sought under more than one name.
- The steps in effective decision-making are:
  (a) Define the problem or the purpose.
  (b) Establish the criteria.
  (c) Generate alternatives or possible solutions.
  (d) Test the alternatives and make the decision.
  (e) Evaluate the decision.

Key Terms

The following terms were introduced in this chapter. The page on which the term was introduced is provided to help you locate the new term. Definitions are compiled in the Glossary at the end of the text.

- **record** 233
- **records management** 233
- **records storage systems** 234
- **alphabetic storage** 234
- **direct access** 234
- **subject filing** 234
- **geographic filing** 234
- **keywords** 237
- **numeric method** 237
- **chronological filing** 238

Responses to Self-Check A

Name	Key Unit	Second Unit	Third Unit	Fourth Unit
Henry Hubert Bowers, Jr.	Bowers	Henry	Hubert	Jr
Roger Alan Le Feve	LeFeve	Roger	Alan	
500 Cafeteria	500	Cafeteria		
The 500, Inc.	500	Inc	The	
Z. T. Glasier, III	Glasier	Z	T	III

Name	Key Unit	Second Unit	Third Unit	Fourth Unit
U-R Rental Company	UR	Rental	Company	
CBC Television	CBC	Television		
Sister Mary Vanetta	Sister	Mary	Vanetta	
Physicians' Hospital	Physicians	Hospital		

Responses to Self-Check B

Name	Key Unit	Second Unit	Third Unit	Fourth Unit
Moncton Cleaners	Moncton	Cleaners		
3rd Street Movie	3rd	Street	Movie	
43–47 Rogers Road Materials	43	Rogers	Road	Materials
7 Seas Restaurant	7	Seas	Restaurant	
Etienne Laberge, 712 Royale, St. Augustine, Quebec	Laberge	Etienne	Saint Augustine	Quebec
Ministry of Health and Welfare	Canada	Government		Health
Department of Skills Training, Province of Saskatchewan	SK	Province	Skills	Training

Discussion Items

These discussion items provide an opportunity to test your understanding of the chapter through written responses and/or discussion with your classmates and your instructor.

1. List the essential components of a records management system.
2. Identify and explain records storage methods.
3. Explain the features of database software and document management software.
4. What is COLD technology and how is it used?

Critical-Thinking Activity

CanAsian has a relatively good company-wide records management program. Both manual and electronic management systems are maintained, with individual offices filing their records manually as long as they are active and moving to electronic storage after the active period has passed. No company-wide records management manual has been produced. The records manager has encouraged individual offices to move to electronic filing for most active records; however, most offices have not followed the recommendation. You have moved to electronic filing for almost all records. A number of the administrative professionals have seen your system and have asked for help in transferring their files to an electronic system. Mr. Albertson has given his permission for you to work with them.

Using the decision-making model presented in this chapter, describe the problem and the steps you would take to assist them in filing and managing their records. What suggestions, if any, would you make to the records manager?

Projects

Project 12-1 *(Objective 1)*

Collaborative Project

Team up with three of your classmates on this task. Interview one administrative professional concerning records management; your interview may be done by e-mail. Ask the questions listed below. Report your findings orally to the class.

1. What records management system(s) do you use (manual, electronic, or a combination of these systems)?
2. What storage methods do you use (alphabetic, numeric, or alphanumeric)?
3. If you use alphabetic, do you use subject and/or geographic?
4. What is your role in document management?
5. Do you use document management software? If so, what packages?
6. Does your company have a records retention schedule? If so, may I have a copy?
7. What aspect of records management is the most difficult for you?
8. What suggestions do you have for the beginning administrative professional as to how to handle records management?

Project 12-2 *(Objectives 2 and 3)*

Load Student CD, file SCDP12-2. For each group of names, indicate the indexing units and put the names in correct alphabetical order. The correct response is given for the first group as an example. Using the form on the disk, key your responses, and submit your work to your instructor.

Project 12-3 *(Objectives 2 and 3)*

Load Student CD, file SCDP12-3a. Print out the document and cut on the cut lines to create index cards.

Index and code the units on each card. Arrange the cards in correct alphabetic sequence. Load Student CD, file SCDP12-3b. Use or print out the document to record the number printed in the top right corner of each card as they appear from top to bottom (front to back) when arranged in alphabetic order. Submit a copy of your work to your instructor.

Project 12-4 *(Objectives 2 and 3)*

Load Student CD, file SCDP12-4a. Print out the document and cut on the cut lines to create index cards. Index and code the units on each card for a geographic classification system. Arrange the cards in correct order for a geographic system. Load Student CD, file SCDP12-4b. Use or print out the document to record the number printed in the top right corner of each card as they appear from top to bottom (front to back) when arranged in geographic order. Submit a copy of your work to your instructor.

Project 12-5 *(Objectives 2 and 3)*

Load Student CD, file SCDP12-5. Indicate the subject you would use in storing the correspondence listed. Mark your answer to the right of each item. Print out and hand in your answers to your instructor.

Project 12-6 *(Objectives 2 and 3)*

Using the index cards from Project 12-4 create a database. Enter the customer information. Also add a field for the customer number. (The number is in the top left corner of the card.) Retrieve the list by province; print out a copy of the list. Next, retrieve the list by customer number; then print out a copy of the list. Turn in both printouts to your instructor.

Project 12-7 *(Objective 4)*

Online Project

Using the Web, find the latest database and document management software available. Determine which packages you would recommend if you were setting up an electronic storage system. Write a memorandum to your instructor using the form on the Student CD, file SCDP12-7. Explain what packages you would use and why. Identify the Web sources you used.

Project 12-8 *(Objective 4)*

Add to your Professional Growth Plan by determining how you will continue to increase your decision-making skills. File your plan on your Professional Growth Plan disk as "Progro12-8."

Chapter 13

Workplace Visitors and Scheduling Appointments

LEARNING OBJECTIVES

1. Develop effective techniques for receiving workplace visitors.
2. Describe electronic and manual methods used for calendaring and scheduling.
3. Apply guidelines for scheduling and cancelling appointments.
4. Maintain a record of appointments and coordinate with other scheduled activities.

Interaction with members of your own organization as well as with members of external or public groups is a significant part of the day-to-day activities of an administrative professional. Good verbal communication skills are critical, and as an administrative professional you play an important role projecting a positive image of your company. In Chapter 8 you learned how important it is to develop good verbal communication skills when using the telephone. In this chapter, you will increase your communication skills by learning how to receive workplace visitors. You may wish to review the section on telephone techniques in Chapter 8 before proceeding.

As an administrative professional, you will also be responsible for scheduling appointments for your supervisor and for maintaining a record of the appointments your supervisor has scheduled. In Chapter 3 you learned that there are software packages that include calendaring functions and that, in addition to manual calendars, administrative professionals and their supervisors use electronic calendars extensively. Also, in Chapters 8 and 9, you saw that many people now use PDAs or cell-phone-and-PDA combination units so they can add entries to their electronic calendar at any time and from any location. In this chapter, you will enhance your organizational ability by maintaining executive schedules in manual or electronic form.

Workplace Visitors

In many large organizations, a receptionist initially greets all visitors. Other than through telephone communication, this may be the first contact the visitor will have had with the company. It is important that it is a positive one. The receptionist may keep a register with the name of the visitor, company affiliation, nature of the visit, person the visitor wishes to see, and date of the visit recorded. After obtaining this information from the visitor, the receptionist notifies the administrative professional that the caller has arrived. If this is a first-time visit for the caller, your job may involve going to the receptionist area and escorting the visitor to your employer's office.

In small companies, you may also serve as the receptionist. In other words, you may have the responsibility of greeting all visitors to the organization and seeing that they are directed to the proper people. Regardless of whether you work in a large or small organization, you should use the techniques described below. In Chapter 8 we discussed being on the receiving end of ineffective telephone techniques. At some time in your life, you may also have experienced inappropriate reception techniques. Before beginning this section, take a few moments to think about those situations; then complete Self-Check on page 260.

Greet people you have not met with a smile and a handshake.

Photodisc Green/Photodisc Collection

Know Your Supervisor's Expectations

Generally your supervisor will have definite expectations with regard to handling certain visitors. For example, certain people usually have immediate access to your supervisor. The president of the organization, the chairperson of the board, a valuable client or customer, a distinguished civic official—these people are usually granted immediate access. Here are some questions you can ask your supervisor to learn his or her preferences concerning visitors:

- Will you see certain people immediately, regardless of how busy you are?
- Will you see friends or relatives immediately?
- Will you *not* see certain people under any circumstances? How are job applicants handled? Should they be referred to the human resources department? How are sales representatives handled? Should they be referred to the purchasing department?
- Do you want me to make introductions if you have not met the visitor?
- Do you set aside a particular time of day for seeing visitors?

Greet the Visitor

Even though the receptionist may already have greeted the visitor, your role as an administrative professional is to welcome him or her to the organization. Greet the person graciously with a simple "Good morning" or "Good afternoon." Use the visitor's name if you know

it. Everyone appreciates being called by name, and it lets the visitor know you care enough to make an effort to remember the name.

If you have never met the visitor, rise from your chair and say "Hello. I'm Eleanor Wilkerson, Mr. Albertson's administrative assistant," shake hands, and then ask the client to be seated. As you shake hands, look the person in the eye, smile, and say "I'm happy to meet you." Always extend your hand first to the visitor. However, if the person seems to back off, do not force a handshake. Simply drop your hand to your side, smile, and say "I'm happy to meet you." Do not be embarrassed that the person has not offered his or her hand.

Business greetings in North America have become relatively informal. This statement, however, is not true for international visitors. A later section of this chapter deals with greeting international visitors. Sometimes greetings for people in Canada begin with a hug if the person is a close friend or long-time acquaintance. You may find that your supervisor greets some individuals in this warm, informal manner. However, as an administrative professional, you do not initiate such an intimate greeting with someone entering your office. But if the caller initiates it, do not recoil in surprise or embarrassment; this response is awkward for both parties. If a frequent caller to your office insists on this greeting and you are uncomfortable, you might mention it to your employer. He or she can politely tell the caller that you are uncomfortable with such a greeting.

You might greet a co-worker who has been away from the workplace for a period of time with a more informal greeting such as a hug. However, always take into consideration the occasion and the setting. Never hug someone who is at a higher or lower rank in the company than you are. It can look as if you are currying favour or taking advantage of someone.

Always give a visitor your immediate attention. It is discourteous to leave someone standing at your desk while you finish filing papers, preparing a report, or talking on the phone. If you are on the phone when a visitor arrives, make eye contact and when appropriate ask the caller to hold while you greet the visitor. Tell the visitor you will assist him or her in just a moment. Return to your telephone call and finish as quickly as possible. If you must answer the telephone when a visitor is at your desk, excuse yourself.

Keep Confidential Information Confidential

If confidential information is on your desk or computer screen when a visitor arrives, be certain the visitor cannot read it. You might casually place the papers in a folder on your desk or remove the information from the screen. You can handle these situations nonchalantly while smiling and greeting the visitor appropriately.

Determine the Purpose of the Visit

When a scheduled visitor (one with an appointment) comes to the workplace, you probably already know the purpose of the visit. When you receive an unscheduled visitor, however, you must find out why the person is calling. Your initial greeting may be "Good morning (or afternoon). How may I help you?" Such a greeting gives the person a chance to respond with his or her name and the reason for the call. If the visitor does not volunteer the information you need, ask for it. *Avoid* blunt questions such as

- What is your name?
- What do you want?
- Where do you work?

Keeping a register of workplace visitors is a polite, proven way to get the information you need. Merely ask the visitor to record the necessary information on the register. The register should have a place for the date, time, visitor's name and affiliation, person visited, and purpose of the call, as shown in Figure 13-1. Most visitors regard registering as routine, and do not object to providing the information. In fact, some administrative

■ Figure 13-1

A REGISTER OF WORKPLACE VISITORS

REGISTER OFFICE VISITORS				
Date	Time	Name and Company	Person Visited	Purpose of Call
06/11/—	9:00	John Paterson, Apex Security	M.A.	Security system
06/11/—	9:45	Gabriel Sierra	K.M.	Interview
06/11/—	10:15	Don Heinrich, Crowfoot District News	D.B.	Sales rep

professionals have to keep a register of the time their employer spends with clients for billing purposes; for example, lawyers bill by the hour. If you use a register frequently, you may want to transfer the information to a computer file for ease of use.

Another way to get information about a visitor is to ask for the person's business card. The card will have the visitor's name, title, company name, address, and telephone number. If you proceed in this manner, you still need to determine the purpose of the visit. Once you have the visitor's card, you can say "May I tell Mr. Albertson the purpose of your visit?"

You will save the visitor and your supervisor time by finding out the purpose of the visit and referring the visitor to the appropriate person. Be considerate if you must refer the visitor to someone else. Call the office of that person to determine her or his availability. If the person can see the visitor immediately, escort the visitor to the other office if possible. If you are unable to leave your desk, give the visitor specific instructions on how to find the office. If an appointment must be made for another day, check with the visitor to set a mutually convenient time.

Remember Names and Faces

As you have already learned, you should use a visitor's name. The following pointers will help you learn names quickly:

- Listen carefully to the person's name when it is pronounced.
- If you do not understand a name, ask the person to repeat it.
- Write the name down phonetically if the pronunciation is difficult.
- Use the name when you first learn it. For example, you might say "I'm very happy to meet you, Ms. Woods."
- Use the name again before the person leaves. Practice helps you remember the name for future meetings.
- Ask the person for a business card. Attach the card to an index card with notations about the visitor. Place the index card in a card file, and refer to it often. Another possibility is to transfer the card information to your computer; include notations that will help you remember the person. For example, you might describe the person's appearance—tall, wears glasses, black hair, slight build.

If you receive a visitor who has been in the office before but whose name you have forgotten, be tactful and say "It's good to see you again." At least you will let the person know that you remember him or her. If the person has an appointment, however, forgetting the name is unforgivable. It is your responsibility to check all appointments every day on both your calendar and your supervisor's calendar. By doing so, you identify an appointment that has been scheduled without your awareness, assuring that you know the name of the person, the reason for the appointment, whether your supervisor needs an introduction, and so on.

Make the Wait Pleasant

If the visitor has to wait, your job is to make that wait as pleasant as possible. If coffee or tea is available, offer it to the person. Tell the visitor approximately how long the wait will be. If possible, explain the reason for the delay—particularly if the visitor had an appointment. For example, you might say "I'm sorry, but Mr. Albertson had an unexpected meeting; he will be available in about ten minutes." Such an approach lets the visitor know you are concerned but that the delay is unavoidable. Offer the visitor something to read so the wait does not seem so long. It is good to have copies of *Forbes*™, *Fortune*®, *Canadian Business*®, a local or national newspaper, or organizational publications on hand.

After the visitor is situated, you are free to go back to your work; you are not expected to chat. The visitor realizes you have other duties. However, if the wait is going to be longer than anticipated, tell the person. He or she may decide to come back later or see someone else in the organization if that can be arranged.

Make Introductions

Have you ever been in a business situation where you were the only person in the group who did not know everyone present and no one introduced you? If you have, you know how awkward it is. The most important rule concerning introductions is this: *Make them.* Do not let someone feel ignored or insignificant because he or she was not introduced. In making introductions, there is one basic rule: *The most important person is named first, regardless of gender.* To help you understand this rule, here are some examples.

- A customer/client is more important than your supervisor.
- A government official is more important than your supervisor.

- Your supervisor is more important than a new employee who is at a lower level on the organizational chart.

If the president of another company visits your supervisor, you would say "Mr. Paterson, this is Mr. Albertson." Or if your supervisor does not know the name of the visitor's company, you would say "Mr. Paterson, president of Apex Security, this is Mr. Albertson." If you have some information about the person you are introducing, mention that information when making introductions.

It may not be necessary to use the titles *Mr., Mrs., Miss,* or *Ms.* In other words, you may use the first and last names of the individuals when introducing them. However, be sure of your supervisor's preference. When in doubt, use titles. *Always* use the title *Dr.* and government titles such as *Senator.*

When introducing people of equal rank in business situations, the social rules for introductions apply. A man is introduced to a woman. You would say "Ms. Sierra, this is Mr. Lin." A younger person is introduced to an older person. You would say, "Father, this is my friend Gabriel."

Follow these steps when introducing people or when being introduced.

- Stand up. (Both men and women should stand.)
- Make eye contact with the person, and move toward the person.
- Use a firm but not crushing handshake.
- Repeat the person's name when you are introduced. For example, you might say "I'm very glad to meet you, Mr. Yarzab" in a formal situation or "Hello, Thomas" in a less formal situation.

Communication Tip

When introducing business associates, mention something about the other person. For example, you might say "Mr. Arar, I would like you to meet Mr. Albertson. He is the head of marketing at Phillips International and a Vancouver Canucks fan."

Handle Interruptions

You may need to interrupt your supervisor with a message when visitors are present. Do so as unobtrusively as possible. You can knock on the door or telephone your supervisor, whichever she or he prefers. If you knock on the door, hand your supervisor a note; never give the information verbally. The visitor should not be privy to the information. This approach can also be used if a visitor overstays the time allocated. It provides your supervisor with a convenient means of letting the visitor know other people are waiting or other responsibilities require his or her attention.

Handle the Difficult Visitor

It is not always easy to be pleasant to visitors, especially those who are ill-tempered and discourteous. At such times, however, you must keep foremost in your mind your role as an ambassador of goodwill.

Your job is to find out the name of the visitor and why that visitor wants to see your employer. Be wary of a visitor who tries to avoid your inquiries by using evasive answers such as the following:

- It's a personal matter.
- I have reason to believe Mr. Albertson will be interested in what I have to say.

To these, you may respond "I'm sorry, but Mr. Albertson sees callers only by appointment. If you tell me the purpose of your visit, I'll check to see if Mr. Albertson can see you at another time." If the visitor still refuses to reveal the purpose of the visit, you may offer him or her a sheet of paper and suggest that he or she write a note to the executive; then take the note to your supervisor. Your supervisor will let you know if he or she will see the visitor. If your supervisor is in a conference, you might suggest that the visitor write a letter requesting an appointment at a later date.

Sometimes a visitor is upset or angry for reasons that have nothing to do with you or the company. Something may have happened on the way to your office, and the person is venting his or her frustrations on you. If you are curt and further provoke the visitor, the situation is aggravated. Let the visitor talk. Listen. Try to understand the visitor's viewpoint. Most of the visitor's anger or frustration will be released through talking. Your role is to be even-tempered and tolerant.

Do not disclose specific information about the organization or your supervisor to unidentified visitors. If a person comes to your office and asks for specific information, your response should be "I'm sorry. I don't have that information."

Greet Government Officials

You should greet provincial or federal government officials using the title of whatever office they hold followed by their last name (for example, *Senator Marchand, Minister Laing,* or as is the case with the

Prime Minister or provincial premiers, *Mr. Prime Minister* or *Mr. Premier*). If you are introducing a government official, present the person within the organization to the government official; for example, say "Senator Marchand, this is Keri-An Mahar, our Director of Human Resources."

Greet Internal Visitors

Co-workers are in and out of each other's offices frequently. However, if you have not met a co-worker, stand and offer your hand when introducing yourself or being introduced. If a co-worker drops by your office for a quick question, you do not need to offer the person a seat unless he or she is your superior; doing so will probably prolong the visit. If you are visiting a co-worker who has a modular workspace (rather than a standard office), either knock or say the person's name from the entrance to the workspace.

Communicate Effectively with the International Visitor

You learned earlier that organizations are becoming increasingly international in scope. If you have frequent international guests, you need to become aware of their cultures and customs. You can make a poor impression and possibly lose business if you do not make a point of this. Do not assume any custom is good or bad just because it is different. For example, we might say that the Irish drive "on the wrong side of the road." But do they? No, they merely drive on the *other* side of the road. Here are some suggestions for communicating with the international visitor.

Greetings

Greetings differ depending on the country. Europeans and South Americans shake hands, although South Americans hug and kiss on the cheek (for both the same and opposite gender) when they know someone. However, women in many other countries do not enjoy the status or prestige of North American women. If you are greeting a woman from another country, wait for her to extend her hand. If she does not, you can assume that women do not shake hands in her country.

> **Communication Tip**
>
> In Europe, do not begin a conversation with "What do you do?" Also, do not ask questions about family and personal background. Europeans consider such approaches too personal.

When greeting people from Asian countries, you may bow. Many Asians have accommodated to the handshake greeting and do not expect you to bow. However, when an Asian is visiting you, a nice gesture is to bow in recognition of the culture. If you do bow, follow these guidelines:

- Your hands should remain at your sides.
- Your back and neck should be held in a rigid position, with eyes looking downward.
- The person in the inferior position always bows longer and lower.

When greeting people from India, Bangladesh, and Thailand, hold your hands together in front of your chin in a prayer-like position and nod your head.

In Latin America, people commonly greet each other with a full embrace and pats on the back. Other countries engaging in this custom are Greece and Italy. In Russia, it is common to be kissed and hugged. In Saudi Arabia, a male guest may be kissed on both cheeks after hands are shaken. Although handshaking is common in France, people also kiss each other on alternate cheeks as a greeting.

The general rule for all international callers is not to use first names. Use titles and last names. Remember that in China, the first name is the surname; thus, Zhao Xiyang is Mr. Zhao, not Mr. Xiyang.

During the greetings, your supervisor should offer a business card. You should do the same if you have one. A business card is important with all international visitors, but for Asians it is almost a ritual. The card is not merely handed over, it is presented. You should receive the card gracefully, using both hands.

Welcoming

You may have the responsibility of making arrangements for international visitors to visit your organization. You should read about your visitor's country before the visit. Numerous books are available in local libraries and bookstores. Information is also available on the Web. Additionally, you might talk with people within your organization who have travelled to the particular country of the visitor. Being knowledgeable is the best way to avoid showing any disrespect to the visitor.

Here are guidelines for making arrangements:

- Meet (or have someone meet) the guest at the airport and drive him or her to the company or hotel. Remember that language may be a problem. A common practice that works well is to carry a sign with the person's name on it.

- Provide a driver for the individual (if possible) while he or she is in the country.
- Arrange for complementary food and/or flowers to be delivered to the visitor's hotel. However, be certain that you choose the appropriate food and flowers. For example, Muslims and Hindus do not drink alcoholic beverages. Do not send a person from Iran yellow flowers; yellow means you wish the person dead. Do not send Chinese white flowers; white is the colour of mourning.
- When arranging for dinners, respect the dietary customs of your guests. Hindus do not eat beef; Muslims and Jews do not eat pork.
- If the international visitor brings family members, offer to arrange outings for the family.

Ongoing Conversations

When talking with international visitors, be sensitive to possible language difficulties. Do not talk in long sentences. Keep slang and **acronyms** (words formed from the initial letters of other words) out of your vocabulary. Make sure you are being understood. You might ask "Did I explain that clearly?" However, never talk down to the person; do not assume that the person knows little about Canada. Most people from other countries know more about North American culture than we know about other cultures. Language difficulties do not mean stupidity. In fact, the international visitor has probably prepared for the visit just as much or more than you have. He or she is concerned, just as you are, about making a favourable impression.

Maintaining Calendars

Working as an administrative professional, you may find yourself providing administrative support to more than one executive in the firm. It may be that, as a member of a team, you will be responsible for maintaining the calendars of several people in your group. When this is the case, you should consider yourself not a member of a group but rather a member of a "team of two"—you plus each individual supervisor. It is important to be aware of the personal preferences of each member. Your supervisor may have a preference for dealing with his or her daily routine. He or she may wish to maintain his or her own calendar and just let you know what they have

scheduled each day, or may wish you to maintain the schedule on his or her behalf. As an administrative professional, you may be responsible for scheduling appointments, maintaining a record of the appointments your supervisor has personally scheduled, and coordinating this with other scheduled activities.

Schedule Appointments

An **appointment** is a time set aside for people to discuss an issue. When it comes to scheduling appointments, understand your supervisor's preferences and know which appointments should be given preference and how much time should be allocated for each appointment. Enter regularly occurring appointments/meetings into the calendar once per year. When a new regular commitment is undertaken, enter that into the calendar for the balance of the year. This way, when a request for an appointment is received, you can be sure to avoid conflicts in the schedule. The guidelines in Figure 13-2 on page 266 will assist you in scheduling appointments for your supervisor.

Your most important responsibility as an administrative professional in maintaining your supervisor's calendar is to ensure that conflicts are avoided and that the calendar is constantly updated. Requests for appointments are usually received in one of three ways—by telephone, by mail/e-mail, or in person.

- *When appointments are requested by telephone,* determine the purpose of the appointment to ascertain whether your supervisor is the most appropriate person. To reduce any margin of error, confirm that you and the caller have identical information by repeating the time, date, and place of the appointment to the caller as you enter it into the calendar. Obtain and record the caller's telephone number and or e-mail address in the event you might need it later to change any of the details of the appointment. If required, provide them with directions to your office.
- *Appointments requested by mail or e-mail* will normally contain the requisite information of who, what, when, and where, and as a result you may be able to enter the specifics into the calendar and provide a confirmation to the sender that the appointment has been scheduled. Incoming mail or e-mail may contain announcements about meetings or conferences of interest to your supervisor. Make a note of these on the calendar and draw them to your supervisor's attention.

■ Figure 13-2

GUIDELINES FOR SCHEDULING APPOINTMENTS

- Know preferred times for scheduling appointments.
- Ensure that scheduled appointments do not overlap.
- Record the exact time (beginning and end), location, and purpose of the appointment.
- Allow for unstructured time (15 minutes) between appointments.
- Accurately record the name, company, and phone number/e-mail address of the visitor on the calendar.
- Provide a client or visitor with more than one option for an appointment with your supervisor so that she or he may choose a specific time.
- Avoid making appointments the day before your supervisor leaves on a business trip, before an important report is due, or too early or late in the workday.
- If you must allocate a short length of time to an appointment, specify the beginning and end times so that the person is aware of the time frame.
- Avoid scheduling appointments on Monday morning.
- If you must refuse a request for an appointment, provide an alternative as well as a legitimate reason for doing so.
- Schedule any away-from-the-office appointments either early or later in the day.

- *When an individual is in the office personally making the request*, you might provide them with a reminder of the date and time established as mutually convenient.

Confirming appointments is a regular activity for administrative professionals working in some types of offices such as medical or legal. Check the policy in your office or the preference of your supervisor to see whether you will be expected to perform this task.

Manual Calendars

Even though we live in an electronic age, the **manual calendar** (desk calendar) still appears on many desks. When this is the case, both you and your supervisor will have calendars. Whether you have decided to use a manual or an electronic calendar, it is important that you check your supervisor's calendar daily to verify that the two contain the same information and that there are no conflicts.

There are a variety of manual calendar styles available on the market that can meet the needs or preferences of your supervisor. They are available in a variety of sizes, from pocket to desktop, loose-leaf, or wirebound, and they can be customized to create a unique system for any individual.

For example, if your supervisor has a large number of appointments each day, he or she may prefer a style that displays one day on two facing pages as illustrated in Figure 13-3. This style also includes space for notes and reminders. Also available are styles that enable the user to view all appointments for a week or all days of the month on two facing pages as illustrated in Figure 13-4 on page 267. There are many products on the market that meet the same needs; the examples given here are from Day-Timers, an international company providing time management, calendaring, and organizational products throughout North America. You can find out more about the variety of manual and electronic products they market at www.daytimer.com.

■ Figure 13-3

DAYTIMER APPOINTMENT CALENDAR, TWO-PAGE-PER-DAY FORMAT

Courtesy of Day-Timers, Inc., www.daytimer.com

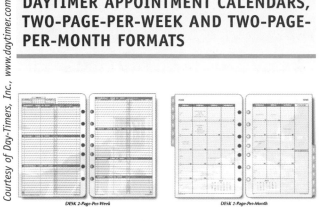

■ Figure 13-4

DAYTIMER APPOINTMENT CALENDARS, TWO-PAGE-PER-WEEK AND TWO-PAGE-PER-MONTH FORMATS

Courtesy of Day-Timers, Inc., www.daytimer.com

DESK 2-Page-Per-Week   DESK 2-Page-Per-Month

Commonly two types of information are recorded when maintaining calendars—appointment data and reminder information. Usually at the end of a year, when it is time to set up a calendar for the next year, the previous year's calendar serves as a source of information about regularly scheduled events. As an administrative professional managing your supervisor's calendar, you will enter not only business appointments and events, but other, more personal items such as birthdays, anniversaries, etc. It is a good idea to use a pencil to record these and other events so that it is easy to make adjustments if commitments suddenly need to be changed.

The calendar is also useful for identifying blocks of time dedicated to work on major projects or reports. Your supervisor may also ask you to schedule a daily or weekly planning session for the two of you to meet and organize upcoming activities. Spending time discussing these anticipated activities and updating the calendar with appointments your supervisor may have made while out of the office is a good way to avoid conflicts in the schedule.

Use the calendar as well for making reminders to yourself or your supervisor. Then check the reminders daily and again at a specific time each week to see that everything has been done. Never turn the page of the calendar over unless you are sure that nothing has been overlooked. If an item has not been attended to that day, transfer it to the reminder activities for the next day so that it does not get forgotten.

List of Appointments

Depending on the preference of your employer, you may be expected to prepare a list of appointments every day. This can be done either at the end of the previous day or first thing every morning. It serves as a quick reminder for your supervisor when he or she arrives at the office and should include the time, purpose of the appointment, name and affiliation of the caller, and any necessary reminders. It also reminds you that information or files that may need to be reviewed before an appointment or referenced during the appointment need to be retrieved and placed on your supervisor's desk along with the list of appointments.

If you are using an electronic system, the list of appointments can be quickly and easily printed out along with any recorded daily reminders. If you are using a manual system, you will need to refer to the calendar and transfer the events to a form similar to the one in Figure 13-5 on page 268.

Electronic Calendars

You learned about PIM (personal information management) software in Chapter 3. This software includes a database that allows you to manage your contacts as well as an **electronic calendar** to manage your appointments. A number of companies produce this type of software. If your office uses Microsoft Office, Outlook is the calendaring component; WordPerfect Office includes Calendar; and Lotus has Organizer. These calendaring components can also be purchased separately. Some advantages of electronic calendars are listed in Figure 13-6 on page 268. See Figure 13-7 on page 268 for an illustration of Outlook Calendar and an appointment recurrence dialogue box.

There are some potential disadvantages to electronic calendars. Access is always password-protected. If you or your supervisor is absent from the office, it will be impossible for anyone else to check your calendars. Make some provision to ensure that someone is aware of your scheduling procedures and has access to the information in the calendar.

Early electronic calendars were only available when a user was actually at his or her workstation. You learned in Chapters 4 and 5 that many people now use PDAs or cell-phone-and-PDA combinations to access calendars via the Web from any location. This capability has effectively eliminated this early disadvantage.

■ Figure 13-5

MANUAL LIST OF DAILY APPOINTMENTS

Appointments for June 8

Time	Appointment	Reminders
9:30	Luyin Wu—Performance Review	Review contents of evaluation file
10:30	Interview with Jan Argent (applicant for Regional Sales Representative position)	Résumé attached
11:00	Work on Quarterly Sales Report	Monthly reports supplied by Financial Services attached
12:30	Lunch with Sara and Ryan	
2:00	Meet with Executive Committee—Board Room	Copies of system purchase recommendation attached
4:30	Meet with Mayor—City Hall	
6:00	Speak at Chamber of Commerce dinner meeting. Turner Valley Room—Fairmont Palliser Hotel	Notes and agenda attached
		35th anniversary next week—confirm reservations

■ Figure 13-6

SOME ADVANTAGES OF USING ELECTRONIC CALENDARS

- Can display a visual or provide an audible reminder of an upcoming scheduled event.
- Can be easily edited—appointment details revised or cancelled.
- Can be minimized on the computer desktop so other software can be used and other activities undertaken.
- Unlimited additional details can be included—you are not restricted by space (as when using a manual calendar).
- Integrates with the mail program—notices and agendas can be automatically sent to meeting participants. Participant acceptance or rejection automatically generates a response to the sender.
- Automatically generates a list of appointments, tasks, and reminders that can also be printed out.
- Recurring events are entered more easily—one entry can be automatically copied throughout the calendar.
- Includes task list—incomplete tasks automatically are forwarded to next day.

■ Figure 13-7

OUTLOOK CALENDAR SHOWING APPOINTMENT RECURRENCE DIALOGUE BOX

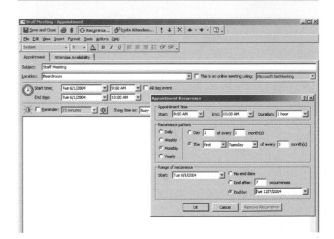

It is now very easy to upload and download information and keep an individual's schedule current. Figure 13-8 on page 269 illustrates Outlook Calendar in one-day view with previous/current month and task pad displayed.

Many larger offices today are networked. The **networking software** includes a flexible and powerful set of applications that provide the members of an organization with the tools to organize, schedule, and collabo-

■ Figure 13-8

OUTLOOK CALENDAR IN ONE-DAY VIEW WITH PREVIOUS/CURRENT MONTH AND TASK PAD DISPLAYED

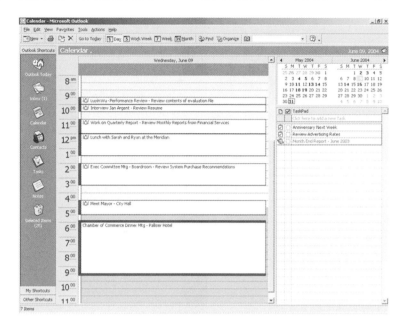

rate. It is possible in such a networked environment to link all calendars within the organization (or just a specific group within the organization, for example, the Executive Committee), giving each person access to multiple calendars. You will find the task of maintaining current schedules for your supervisor and yourself is much more efficiently accomplished using the networked calendar. It operates in the same manner as the single workstation electronic calendar in that you can enter appointments, tasks, and reminders, cancel appointments, and rearrange schedules as events change.

One of the advantages of networked, linked multiple calendars becomes evident when you, the administrative professional, are attempting to arrange a meeting with a larger group. Consider how long it can take to schedule a meeting of four or five people. You have to choose a time when all the required people will be available and when a meeting room is available. Doing this manually may require a phone call or e-mail to each person—just writing the note might take five minutes or longer. Then you need to read the replies and compare them to determine a time suitable for everyone. Using scheduling software in a networked environment, finding a meeting time is simple. You provide the software with the names of the participants, the tentative date, the time, and the length and location of the meeting. It can automatically review the calendar of each potential participant, whether there are two or twenty-two, as well as the required resource (the meeting room). If there are conflicts, you are notified. You can then decide whether to schedule the meeting as tentatively planned or direct the software to try and determine a time suitable to all.

When you are using networked calendaring software, you must be very careful how you enter the information. It is important that you select the correct date, time, and length of the event, and that you keep the calendar up to date.

There are a number of companies today who market Web-based scheduling software. Use your browser software to search for "Calendaring Software" and review some of the features available with products from ScheduleView and Office Talk.

Cancelling Appointments

If your employer cannot keep an appointment, your responsibility is to cancel it. Appointments may be cancelled by a telephone call or by an e-mail (if they are internal). Be sure to give a reason, and offer to reschedule. A detailed explanation is not necessary. You might say "Mr. Albertson has been called out of town unexpectedly, and he will be unable to keep the appointment. May I schedule another appointment for next week?"

Chapter Summary

The summary will help you remember the important points covered in the chapter.

- When receiving workplace callers, know your employer's expectations. Your employer will usually see certain people without an appointment. Your employer may also decide not to see certain people.
- Appropriate techniques for receiving office callers include the following:
  - Greet the visitor with a handshake if you have not met him or her previously.
  - Determine the purpose of the caller's visit.
  - Call the visitor by name.
  - Make the wait pleasant by offering the caller coffee or tea and reading material.
  - Introduce the caller to your supervisor if appropriate.
  - Do not be discourteous to callers—even the difficult ones.
- When dealing with international guests, know their cultures and customs. Use the appropriate greeting; be sensitive to language difficulties.
- As an administrative professional working for one or several supervisors, consider the personal preferences of each individual when maintaining calendars.
- Enter regularly occurring appointments and/or meetings into the calendar once per year.
- When making appointments over the telephone, confirm that you and the caller have identical information by repeating the time, date, and place of the appointment to the caller as you enter it into the calendar.
- Check your supervisor's calendar daily to verify that both of your calendars contain the same information and that there are no conflicts.
- At the end of a year when it is time to set up a calendar for the next year, the previous year's calendar serves as a source of information about regularly scheduled events.
- Use the calendar to schedule dedicated blocks of time to work on major projects or reports, or to allocate time for daily or weekly planning session between you and your supervisor.
- Access to the electronic calendar is always password-protected. Make provisions to ensure that someone is aware of your scheduling procedures and has access to the information in the calendar if you or your supervisor is absent from the office.

- Networking software includes a flexible and powerful set of applications that provide the members of an organization with the tools to organize, schedule and collaborate.
- When cancelling an appointment, provide a reason, and offer to reschedule.

Key Terms

The following terms were introduced in this chapter. The page on which the term was introduced is provided to help you locate the new term. Definitions are compiled in the Glossary at the end of the text.

- **acronym** 265
- **appointment** 265
- **manual calendar** 266
- **electronic calendar** 267
- **networking software** 268

Discussion Items

These discussion items provide an opportunity to test your understanding of the chapter through written responses and/or discussion with your classmates and your instructor.

1. List eight techniques for effectively handling the workplace visitor.
2. Explain how you would treat an international visitor.
3. List the advantages of using an electronic calendaring system over a manual calendaring system.
4. Describe how you would cancel an appointment with a client.

Critical-Thinking Activity

Guy Beauchamp, one of your two assistants, has been working for CanAsian for almost two years. Luyin Wu, your other assistant, has been working for CanAsian for almost a year. Although Guy is French, he was born in Quebec City and came to Calgary to go to college. He is fluent in both English and French. Guy is extremely outgoing and will kiss you on both cheeks when he greets you. Although Guy is proud of his heritage, he believes he is a blend of French and Canadian cultures. Luyin is from China and has been in Canada only two years. She learned English in school in China, but she does not always understand slang expressions. She is quiet and reserved. Both are good employees; both enjoy their jobs. Luyin lives with a married sister who came to Canada five years ago. Guy is married and has his own home.

When Mr. Albertson found out he would be travelling to China, he talked with Luyin on several occasions about the culture. She had never seemed willing to talk about her life before, but she seemed eager to share certain things with Mr. Albertson. She said that in her culture, older people are greatly respected. She said she was shocked when she came to Canada and heard young people talk disrespectfully to their elders. She also said that she did not like public displays of affection. When Guy heard about this, he became embarrassed. He decided he must have offended Luyin on numerous occasions without realizing that he was doing so. He did not say anything to her, but the next day he asked you how he should handle the situation. What advice would you give Guy?

Projects

Project 13-1 (Objective 1)

You receive the following visitors in your office today. How would you deal with each situation? Write a memorandum to your instructor, using the memorandum form on the Student CD, file SCDP13-1, and state what you would do.

1. A sales representative comes in and asks for an appointment to see your supervisor; your supervisor has told you he does not like to see sales representatives.
2. Your supervisor has been called out of town unexpectedly. He scheduled an appointment with Mr. Chlebovec for 11 a.m. but failed to tell you about this appointment. You forgot to check his calendar. Mr. Chlebovec comes in at 10:50 for his appointment.
3. A woman comes in to see your supervisor. She refuses to give her name or the purpose of her visit. However, she says the matter is urgent. She seems upset.
4. Ms. Nicole Botha comes in to see your supervisor. Ms. Botha has an appointment at 11 a.m., and it is now 10:55 a.m. Your supervisor has had an extremely busy morning, and he is now in a conference that will last until 11:20 a.m.
5. R. T. Yip is in your supervisor's office. He had an appointment at 2 p.m. It is now 3 p.m., and your supervisor has an appointment with Ms. Carol Haile. Ms. Haile has arrived.

6. George O'Casey arrives at 3 p.m. for his appointment with your supervisor. Upon checking your appointment book, you find that Mr. O'Casey's appointment is really for 3 p.m. tomorrow.

Project 13-2 (Objective 2)

Online Project

Browse the Web for information on various scheduling and calendaring software. Identify and compare the features offered by the various suppliers marketing this type of software. Prepare a short summary of your findings, giving the Web addresses; submit your summary to your instructor.

Project 13-3 (Objectives 3 and 4)

Your supervisor, Mr. Albertson, relies on you to keep his schedule up to date at all times. On the Student CD, file SCDP13-3, you will find a calendar. Monday is a statutory holiday, so the calendar pages are for the balance of the week from Tuesday to Friday. Today is Tuesday; the following activities occur on Tuesday. Make the appropriate adjustments to the calendar.

1. A letter arrives in the mail announcing the grand opening of a new location of the company that supplies your office with weekly floral arrangements. They invite Mr. Albertson to a wine-and-cheese celebration at 5:30 on Thursday the 8th.
2. Jim Rosza calls to say he will not be able to keep the luncheon appointment on Thursday. He asks if it could be changed to Friday. You check the calendar and see that Mr. Albertson is meeting his daughter and her fiancé for lunch. You let Mr. Rosza know about the conflict, and tell him you will check with Mr. Albertson and call Mr. Rosza back to confirm.

    Later in the day, you check with Mr. Albertson. He lets you know that he cannot cancel the luncheon with his daughter and suggests you find another time that is mutually convenient. You call Mr. Rosza to see if Wednesday is appropriate, and he agrees.
3. Judy Hafey, the secretary of the Board at Mount Royal College, calls to say the Board meeting has been cancelled for this week.
4. Mr. Albertson asks you to find an hour and a half in his schedule this week when he can get together with you to organize the materials he will need for the trip to China next week.
5. Keri-An Mahar calls to see if Mr. Albertson can see her today to review interview questions to be used when interviewing applicants on Thursday

for the sales representative position. You suggest 1 p.m. and she agrees. She feels one hour would be sufficient.

6. On Wednesday morning you receive a call from John Paterson. It is 8:15 a.m., and he tells you he is stuck in traffic because there has been an accident on the highway. He asks if Mr. Albertson will still be available to see him if he is 45 minutes late. After looking at the calendar, you confirm that this is fine.

7. At the end of the day on Wednesday, on his way out the door, Mr. Albertson asks you to remind him on Thursday that he needs to book reservations for dinner with his wife and to order flowers to celebrate their anniversary.

Submit the revised calendar to your instructor.

Project 13-4 *(Objective 1)*

Add to your Professional Growth Plan by describing some effective techniques for receiving workplace visitors. If you have had a negative experience when visiting an office describe how you would have acted in the same circumstances. Save a copy on your Professional Growth disk under "Progro13-4."

Chapter 14

Planning and Organizing Meetings and Conferences

LEARNING OBJECTIVES

1. Identify the responsibilities of the administrative professional for meetings and conferences.
2. Become familiar with the types of meetings—audio, online, and video.
3. Prepare meeting notices.
4. Prepare agendas and minutes.

Meetings are a way of life in the workplace. In a business environment that is downsized, multi-national, and driven by technology (with e-mail, faxes, and computers providing for quick communication throughout our world), you might expect fewer meetings. However, in reality, the opposite is true. As teams handle more work, the number of meetings is increasing rather than decreasing. Even estimating conservatively, administrative professionals could average four hours a week in meetings. This average generally increases the higher a person's position in the organization. Management could possibly spend as much as 50 percent or more of each week in meetings. Time is money. Obviously, these meetings are costly to business, so meeting time must be spent as productively as possible.

This chapter will help you develop the knowledge and skills needed to assist your supervisor in planning, organizing, and facilitating productive meetings.

Necessary Meetings

Meetings are a good means of generating ideas, sharing information, and making decisions. Calling a meeting can be appropriate in the following situations:

- Advice is needed from a group of people.
- A group needs to be involved in solving a problem or making a decision.
- An issue needs clarification.
- Information needs to be given to a group.
- A problem exists but it is not clear what the problem is or who is responsible for dealing with it.
- Quick communication is necessary with a large number of people.

Unnecessary Meetings

Unfortunately, unnecessary and unproductive meetings are held daily in organizations. These meetings generally occur when no clear purpose or agenda is defined or when no follow-up takes place. They are not only a waste of an individual's time but also a waste of the organization's time. Everyone has been to such meetings. Sometimes the major purpose of meetings seems to be one or more of these:

- To consume large quantities of coffee and dough-nuts at the company's expense
- To engage in small talk with co-workers
- To get away from work responsibilities for a while
- To ask others' opinions about a subject
- To avoid making a decision

These events often result in participants' wondering why a meeting was called in the first place. Clearly, if people give no thought to the purpose, agenda, or conduct of meetings, such inane gatherings will persist. Meetings are generally not a good idea in the following situations:

- Confidential or sensitive personnel matters must be addressed.
- There is inadequate data for the meeting.
- There is insufficient time to prepare for the meeting.
- The information might be better communicated by memo, fax, e-mail, or telephone.
- Group members feel considerable anger or hostility among themselves, and need time to calm down before coming together.

Types of Meetings

For years, meetings were traditional in nature; that is, the participants gathered face to face at a common location. Now, with the technology that is available, we can choose the type of meeting to have. The traditional and the electronic meeting both have certain advantages and disadvantages. By carefully analyzing the purpose and the outcomes expected, you can determine which type of meeting will be most appropriate.

Traditional Meetings

The traditional meeting where people gather for face-to-face discussion of an issue or a problem at one location has a number of advantages:

- All individuals have a chance to talk informally with other participants before, during, and after the meeting.
- The body language of the participants can be closely observed.

Human Relations Tip

Schedule meetings only when absolutely necessary. A poorly structured meeting with no apparent purpose results in a waste of employees' time, frustration for many, and unnecessary costs for the organization.

- People generally feel more relaxed with the informal setting.
- If the issue to be discussed is a difficult one, the atmosphere allows attendees to deal more effectively with the issue.
- A creative, interactive group discussion is more likely.
- Widespread participation among group members is more likely.

Clearly, there are also disadvantages to the traditional face-to-face meeting; some are listed in Figure 14-1 on page 275.

Electronic Meetings

Telecommunication technology provides alternatives to face-to-face meetings through several electronic options referred to as **teleconferencing**—a general term applied to a variety of technology-assisted two-way (interactive) communications via telephone lines, DSL, cable modems, and other high-bandwidth connections. You learned about these connections in Chapter 8. If you do not recall the specifics of bandwidth, you may want to review that chapter now. There are three main types of teleconferencing: audioconferencing, online conferencing, and videoconferencing.

Audioconferencing

Audioconferencing in its simplest form is a type of conferencing in which participants talk with each other using standard telephones or speakerphones. Most local telephone providers offer a service that allows you to add additional callers to your line by pressing the appropriate button (usually labelled "Conference") on your telephone. If your phone does not have this capability or you have not opted for this service, you can access a conference operator through your local telephone service provider, who will set up the call for you and make sure all callers are on the line at the appropriate time. Additionally, a number of communications companies (such as Tele-Conferences.net, MCI Canada, and Synamics) can assist you with audioconferencing. Additional services available from these companies include:

- On-demand conferencing from any touchtone phone with no reservation and no operator required
- Simplification of material distribution through faxes and voice mail

■ Figure 14-1

DISADVANTAGES OF FACE-TO-FACE MEETINGS

- Travel to and from a face-to-face meeting can be costly, particularly if the travel is from another city, province, or country. Cost includes not only transportation to and from the meeting and/or hotel rooms if the meeting requires an overnight stay, but also the time lost in travel. A study done by the U.S. firm InfoCom and sponsored by MCI WorldCom revealed that the typical executive flies to 4.6 meetings a month, taking at least a day of travel time for sessions that last an average of only 3.2 hours.
- The meeting room may be costly; or if the meeting is held within the company, finding a vacant room or tying up a room that is used for multiple purposes can be a problem.
- Coffee, lunches, and other refreshments for the participants are needed if the meeting is a fairly long one. Individuals need breaks in long meetings.
- The face-to-face meeting can be harder to control, since people are freer to interact with each other.
- If not controlled by the chairperson, socializing can consume a major part of the meeting time.
- Time can be lost waiting for people who are late.
- Individuals (particularly those who work together daily) may tend to rely on their colleagues' suggestions or solutions; thus, creativity can suffer.

- Phone-add capabilities for videoconferencing, enabling audio-only participation in a videoconference using a telephone
- The ability to take your audioconferences onto the Internet.

You can review the services provided by audioconferencing companies by accessing their websites. If you do not have a company name, use the keyword *audioconferencing* to locate companies who provide these services.

Audioconferencing allows several people at locations around the world to talk with each other at one time through telephone technology.

Advantages of audioconferencing include:

- Assembling individuals on short notice (assuming their schedules allow)
- Connecting individuals at any location
- Using familiar and readily available telephone technology
- Reducing travel time and expense
- Reducing the administrative overhead involved in meetings
- Broadening meeting participation
- Receiving digital recordings of meetings

One of the primary disadvantages of an audioconference is the lack of visual input. However, that can be minimized by use of an ordinary fax machine to transmit reports, spreadsheets, graphs, and so on. In addition, visual messages can be written on an **electronic whiteboard**, a display screen on which multiple users write or draw. Participants in the conference can see what is written on the whiteboard on a video screen and can add or make changes to it. In other words, whiteboards allow for **interactivity** (information transmitted from one location to another and acted on by participants at any location). They can also be used as **stand-alone conventional dry-erase boards** or **electronic dry-erase whiteboards**. In the first case the whiteboard is used without connection to a computer or a projector—like a standard classroom whiteboard. In the second case it is connected to a computer, but without a projector; all annotations to the board can be saved to the computer, printed out, and e-mailed or faxed to participants.

Online Conferencing

Online meetings link individual participants via a computer. A variety of terms are used to describe these meetings, including *computer conferencing, keyboard conferencing, Web conferencing,* and *data conferencing.* The term *online meeting* is used in this textbook, since it is exactly descriptive. Online meetings may have a video portion; however, currently most do not. Videoconferencing is dealt with in the next section.

Online meetings utilize techniques that allow groups of people anywhere in the world to exchange ideas via the computer. This technology allows people to work successfully and productively. For example, a group of people can work in **real time**, simultaneously creating electronically produced documents such as presentations, spreadsheets, reports, and proposals. An **outside** or **remote facilitator** (a person trained in facilitation techniques who is not part of the decision

making of a meeting and whose role is to keep the meetings productive, positive, and efficient) may be used. Online meetings, as explained earlier, may have a video portion. For example, if participants do not know each other, cameras used at the beginning of the meeting allow each person to introduce himself or herself and provide background information. Additionally, computers can be connected to the Internet.

In setting up online meetings, you have two basic options:

- Have your meetings fully hosted on a vendor's website and pay a per-use or monthly fee
- Purchase software for use on your own website; some companies who provide website service include the following:
  - Contigo™ i2I
  - MicroSoft Office Live Meeting
  - WebConference.com
  - Gentner
  - MCI Canada
  - Sprint Canada

Software packages available include NetMeeting® and HelpMeeting LLC™. With these and other similar software packages, you can:

- Share files
- Show presentations
- Conduct chats
- Utilize whiteboarding

Videoconferencing

Videoconferencing is a system of transmitting audio and video between individuals at distant locations. Individuals can see and hear each other. It is also referred to as **virtual conferencing**, since it allows participants to enter and move around rooms electronically. For example, virtual conferences can be set up that allow participants to enter a conference room and view the speaker, post questions for the speaker, and enter a chat room to talk with other conference participants.

One of the largest obstacles to videoconferencing in the past was the amount of bandwidth needed. However, the technology is steadily improving, especially for organizations that utilize DSL, cable modems, T1 lines, and other high-bandwidth connections. Videoconferencing also has limits as to picture quality. Vendors continue to work on ways to make videoconferencing more attractive. For example, Vianet Technologies® is using the company's Wavelet™ compression technology to eliminate portions of images, such as a background, that are not crucial. This procedure helps reduce the bulk of data needed for video frames, improves speed, and clarifies details in the parts of the image that remain. With advances in technology, expectations are that videoconferencing will become a more productive tool.

Videoconferencing may be accomplished through the use of Web conferencing software or through vendors who provide videoconferencing services. Video software includes Webcam32™, CuseeMe, and shareware Webcam32. Service providers include such organizations as TKO VideoConferencing and ADCOM.

Advantages and Disadvantages of Electronic Meetings

Just as face-to-face meetings have advantages and disadvantages, so do electronic meetings. Some of the advantages are:

- Simplicity—participants can join a meeting or conference anytime anywhere
- Savings in travel time, meals, and hotel rooms
- Ability to take care of the concerns of multinational organizations without expensive travel and resultant time commitments
- Ability to present a considerable amount of information concisely through sophisticated audio and video technology
- Ability to bring together people with expertise in different areas to discuss problems of mutual concern with a minimum of effort
- Availability of software packages and service providers

Some of the disadvantages are:

- Less spontaneity between individuals due to a fairly structured environment
- Inability to see body language of all participants at any one time
- Inability to pick up small nuances of body language over the monitor
- No or relatively little socialization between participants
- Less chance for effective brainstorming on issues

Organizing Meetings

Several types of meetings are held within an organization. Executives usually meet on a regular basis with the people who report to them. These meetings are generally

Steve Chenn/Corbis/Magma Photo

Electronic meetings allow for individuals at distant locations to discuss issues without having to spend time and money travelling.

referred to as *staff meetings*. Meetings are often held with customers and clients of the business, generally involving only two or three people. Other types of meetings, which may be more formal in nature, include board meetings, committee meetings, and meetings of special task forces or project teams. Everyone from the organizer to the participant has a role to play in ensuring successful meetings.

The Executive's Role

The executive has certain roles in planning meetings. He or she must determine the purpose of the meeting, who should attend, and the number of attendees. He or she may work closely with the administrative professional in accomplishing these tasks.

Determining the Purpose of the Meeting

Unless the administrative professional is calling the meeting, it is generally not his or her responsibility to determine the purpose of the meeting. However, he or she must understand the purpose of the meeting in order to make appropriate arrangements. If your supervisor does not tell you the purpose of the meeting, ask. Your asking may help your supervisor define the purpose; in other words, it may help crystallize his or her thinking regarding the meeting.

Determining Who Should Attend

The decision as to who will attend a meeting is generally not the prerogative of the administrative professional. However, you may be asked for input if you have worked for a company for a considerable amount of time. Also, you may, through total quality management initiatives, be calling a meeting yourself. In either situation, you can use the ideas presented here to help determine who should be at a meeting.

If it is a problem-solving meeting, individuals who have knowledge of the problem and who will be involved in implementation of the solution should attend. For example, if the issue is to establish a strategic plan for the business, the top-level executives of the business should be involved—the president, the vice-presidents, and possibly the board of trustees.

In determining who should attend, consider who is most affected by the problem or issue and who can contribute to the solution. Also, you need to think about the backgrounds of the people. For example a **heterogeneous group** (a group having dissimilar backgrounds and experiences) can often solve problems more satisfactorily than a **homogeneous group** (a group with similar backgrounds and experiences). A heterogeneous group can bring varying views to the problem and encourage creative thinking through the diversity that is present. However, a more heterogeneous group demands a skilled facilitator in order to make the meeting productive.

Determining the Number of Attendees

The ideal number of attendees is based on the purpose of the meeting and the number of people who can best achieve the purpose. The best size for a problem-solving and decision-making group is from 7 to 15 people. This size group allows for creative **synergy** (the ideas and products of a group of people developed through interaction with each other). There are enough people to generate divergent points of view and to challenge each other's thinking.

Small groups of seven people or less may be necessary at times. For example, if the purpose of the meeting is to discuss a personnel matter, only the human resources director and the supervisor may be in attendance. If the purpose of the meeting is to discuss a faulty product design, only the product engineer, the manager of the engineering department, and the line technician may be present. Advantages to having only a few people in a meeting are:

- Participants may be assembled more quickly since there are fewer.
- The meeting can be informal and thus provide for more spontaneity and creativity.
- Group dynamics are easier to manage.

The disadvantages of a small group include the following:

- Points of view are limited due to the size of the group.
- There may not be enough ideas to create the best solution to the problem.
- Participants may not be willing to challenge each other's point of view if they are a close-knit group.

> **Communication Tip**
>
> Set up a folder for each meeting you are planning; keep all materials about the meeting in the folder. Once the meeting is over, file the folder for a period of time for future reference.

The Administrative Professional's Responsibilities

In planning meetings (whether they are face to face or some type of electronic meeting), the administrative professional has a number of responsibilities. As you have just learned, you must work closely with your supervisor to determine the purpose of the meeting, who will attend, and the appropriate number of attendees. There are other responsibilities you can handle on your own; however, you must understand your supervisor's preferences in these areas. When you first join an organization or begin to work with a supervisor, take time before each meeting to learn his or her needs and preferences. Once you have spent time with a particular supervisor, you will have less need to discuss the details with him or her. However, you should always discuss the purpose of the meeting and general expectations with your supervisor. Otherwise, you may waste your time taking care of details only to find that your supervisor is not pleased with the direction you have taken.

Selecting and Preparing the Room

A room can impact what happens during a meeting. You have probably attended meetings where these problems occurred:

- The room was too large or too small for the group.
- The participants could not be heard.
- The room was too cold or too hot.
- The lighting in the room was not adequate.
- The ventilation was poor.

Room inadequacies can start a meeting off on the wrong foot. As you have learned already, meetings are expensive. The arrangements should allow for maximum effectiveness from the participants. If you carefully plan the room arrangements, you can help the meeting begin on a positive note.

When you know how many people are to attend, look for a room of the proper size. Most businesses will have several conference rooms of varying sizes available. If there is someone who normally schedules the conference rooms, contact this individual to reserve the room. If you have to choose between a room that is too large or too small, generally choose the smaller room. For example, 20 people in a room that accommodates 80 can intimidate the group, because of all the empty space. However, you do not want to attempt to put 40 people in a room that fits only 20. In addition to the room being too crowded, you may be violating local fire department restrictions. If you must take a room that is too large, there are ways of making the room seem smaller. For example, set up chairs or tables in one corner of the room. If movable partitions are available, arrange them around the actual space that will be used for the meeting.

Check the temperature controls before a meeting. Remember that bodies give off heat, so the room will be warmer with people in it. A standard rule is to aim for about 20 degrees Celsius. Be sure you know whom to call if it gets too hot or too cold during the meeting. You do not want a room that is hot and stuffy, nor one that is ice-cold, when you are trying to make important decisions.

Check the ventilation. Is the airflow adequate? Is the lighting bright enough? If visuals are going to be used, can they be seen? If you have any questions about the temperature, ventilation, or lighting, check with the building maintenance personnel well before the meeting begins. Give them a chance to correct the problem. Avoid calling at the last minute.

If you are selecting a room for an electronic meeting, be certain the room is large enough to accommodate the equipment needed. The seating arrangement must allow all individuals to see the monitors, electronic whiteboards, or whatever other is used. With a videoconference, the meeting is usually held in a permanently equipped room. Check the electrical outlets in the room. Are there enough? Are they positioned so you do not have to string extension cords across the room? (Doing so can be a hazardous.)

Determining the Seating Arrangement

The seating arrangement of a room depends on the objectives of the meeting. The four basic seating arrangements are rectangular, circular, semicircular, and U-shaped. Figure 14-2 on page 280 shows these arrangements.

The **rectangular arrangement** allows the chairperson to maintain control, since he or she sits at the head of the table. Conversation is usually directed to the chair. The rectangular arrangement is also appropriate if the purpose is to have individuals talk in groups of twos or threes. Individuals seated next to or opposite each other are able to talk among themselves. If discussion is important, the table should not be too long. A long table may make communication difficult due to the inability to see the nonverbal behaviour of all participants. A long table can also prevent the chairperson from taking part in discussions if he or she is at a distance from participants.

The **circular arrangement** is effective for minimizing status positions. In a circle, it is difficult to determine the chair, as no one sits in a position of control. The chairperson has less control in a circle than in any other arrangement. If the circular arrangement is used, communication channels should be fairly equal among all members. The arrangement encourages a sense of warmth and togetherness.

The **semicircular** and **U-shaped arrangements** work well for small groups of from six to eight people. The chair has moderate control, since he or she can sit in a fairly dominant position. These two arrangements work well for showing visuals because the visuals can be set up at the front. The U-shaped and semicircular arrangements are desirable for semiformal meetings.

The circular arrangement is most effective for informal meetings; the rectangular arrangement, formal meetings.

Sending Meeting Notices

The most effective way to notify participants within an organization of a meeting is by e-mail. Since many people now keep their calendars on the computer, you may be able to check when participants are available. Another way to inform internal participants is by interoffice memorandum. When notifying participants of a meeting, include the following information:

- Purpose of the meeting
- Topics to be considered at the meeting

FOUR BASIC SEATING ARRANGEMENTS

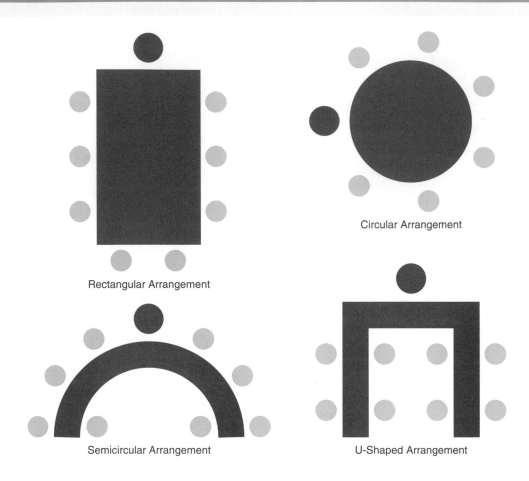

Rectangular Arrangement

Circular Arrangement

Semicircular Arrangement

U-Shaped Arrangement

- Materials that should be read before the meeting and brought to the meeting
- Date of the meeting
- Start and end times
- Location
- Name of the person to whom the addressee should respond and when the response should be made as to attendance

An example of a meeting notification is given in Figure 14-3 on page 281.

When considering the time of the meeting, generally avoid Monday mornings, meetings immediately after lunch, and meetings near the end of the day. Meetings should generally last no longer than two hours. When people have to sit for longer than two hours, they get restless and lose interest. Should a meeting run two hours or longer, short five-to-ten-minute breaks should be given every 40 or 45 minutes, depending on the participants. By being observant, you will know when it is

time for a break. Signals include lack of participation, individuals leaving the room, and individuals losing their focus. Breaks allow people to move around a little; generally, they will return to the meeting ready to concentrate and get back to the task at hand.

It is important to begin and end meetings on time. If the meeting notice states that the meeting will begin at 9 a.m., begin sharply at 9. Do not wait for stragglers. People will soon get the message that you start on time, and they will be there. The same holds true for ending meetings; end them on time. People will appreciate your being respectful of their time constraints. Also, by stating an end time, the chairperson of the meeting can help the group accomplish its objectives in the time allocated.

As an administrative professional, you may also have the responsibility of following up to determine if people are planning to attend the meeting. Even if you have asked people to let you know, some may not respond. The usual method of follow-up is a telephone

MEETING NOTIFICATION

CANASIAN AIRLINES

Memorandum

TO: All Managers

FROM: Martin Albertson   *ma*

DATE: November 12, 2005

SUBJECT: Meeting Notice

A meeting will be held on November 22 from 9 a.m. until 11 a.m. The meeting will be held in Conference Room A, with the purpose being to

- Discuss accomplishment of objectives for this year
- Review goals and budget for next year

Please send a summary of your accomplishments to the other managers by November 20 and bring a copy to the meeting.

It is important that everyone be in attendance. If you cannot attend, please let me know by November 16.

call or an e-mail reminder. A good idea is to contact the administrative professionals who work with the individuals invited; they can remind them of the meeting. Let your supervisor know who will be attending and who might be late. You can write this information directly on a copy of the memo or e-mail that announced the meeting and give it to your supervisor. Another alternative is to prepare a special form for noting attendees. If a number of people are unable to attend, let your supervisor know so he or she can decide whether to cancel. Although cancelling a meeting is not generally a good idea, it is best to do so if key individuals cannot make it.

Preparing the Agenda

Everyone should know what to expect before coming to a meeting. Participants should receive a detailed **agenda** at least a day (preferably a week) beforehand. It should include the following information:

- Name of the meeting or the group
- Date of the meeting
- Start and end times
- Location
- Order of topics and activities of the meeting
- Person responsible for presenting each topic or activity
- Action expected on each item
- Background materials (if needed)

You might also allocate a time period for the presentation of each agenda item. Although this process is not essential, it does remind people of the importance of time and adhering to a schedule. If time frames are not listed, the facilitator of the meeting may need to move things along. The order of the agenda items can vary. Some people think the most difficult items should be presented first so participants can deal with them while they are fresh. Others think the difficult items should be presented last. Check with your supervisor to find out which order he or she prefers. The format of an agenda varies from company to company and sometimes even within an organization from department to department. Most word processing programs include a template that simplifies the production of an agenda. One example of an agenda is shown in Figure 14-4.

Notice in this example how the word "Action" is listed after certain agenda items. This indicates that a decision should be made during this meeting. Such an approach helps participants know what is expected of them. If they are to make a decision, they can come pre-

pared to do so. If a decision is not going to be made on an item, the individual in charge of the meeting should let the group know what will happen with regard to the item. Will it be discussed again at a later date? Will it be referred to another group to deal with? When participants understand what is expected of them, they are better contributors.

When sending out materials prior to a meeting, keep them as concise as possible. Most people will not take the time to read verbose materials.

Determining the Procedures

Highly structured procedures generally are not appropriate for small committee meetings, departmental meetings, informational meetings, and other informal meetings. For a formal meeting, you may need to adhere to *Robert's Rules of Order* (first published 1876; now in tenth edition)—a set of guidelines for *parliamentary procedure* covering the conduct of participants. While such rules are not strictly adhered to at informal meetings, they are essential at meetings of the board of directors of a corporation or at annual business meetings of a professional organization. You should become familiar with them, and with the terminology given in Figure 14-5 on page 283.

Check your local bookstore or library for more information; you will find a number of books available. The following websites provide additional information on chairing successful meetings, meeting planning, and *Robert's Rules of Order*:

- www.robertsrules.com
- www.3m.com/meetingnetwork
- www.meetingwizard.org

Preparing Materials for Your Supervisor

You should prepare a folder for each meeting your supervisor will attend or lead. The folder should include the following:

- Meeting notice with a list of the people who will be in attendance
- Materials that have been sent out before the meeting
- Notes that are needed at the meeting
- Visuals or handouts

■ Figure 14-4

MEETING AGENDA

AGENDA
Planning Meeting
Conference Room A
October 22, 2005

I. Accomplishments on 2005 Plans		All Managers
II. Goals for 2006	ACTION	Martin Albertson
III. Projected Budget for 2006		Elias Tobin
IV. Planning Timelines	ACTION	

■ Figure 14-5

MEETING TERMINOLOGY

Ad hoc (special) committee. A committee created to deal with a specific task or issue. Dissolved once the task is complete.

Amendment. A change in the wording of a motion that has been made.

Bylaws. The rules and procedures that govern the operation of an organization.

Minutes. A written record of the meeting.

Motion. A formal expression of a proposal or an action to be undertaken. It must be recorded verbatim (that is, in the exact words spoken by the mover) in the minutes. It requires a mover (the presenter of the motion) and a seconder (a person who may or not support the motion but is in favour of the motion being discussed), and after being debated it is voted upon by the meeting participants.

Parliamentary procedures. The procedural rules that ensure all participants have an opportunity to participate in the decision-making process.

Quorum. The minimum number of participants required to be present at a meeting before decisions can officially be made.

Resolution. A formal expression of opinion or direction of an organization (similar to a motion).

Standing committee. A committee created to deal with ongoing matters.

If your supervisor is participating in an offsite meeting, you may also need to include directions to the meeting site. Through the use of such online sites as www.mapquest.ca, you can get maps, driving directions, and even traffic reports (see Figure 14-6 on page 284).

Preparing Materials for Attendees

If handouts are to be distributed during the meeting, prepare them well in advance of the meeting. If there are several pages, place the handouts in individual folders. Sometimes attendees are expected to take notes. If so, you might provide a pad of paper in the folder and make extra pens and/or pencils available.

Ordering Equipment

Determine what equipment, if any, is needed for the meeting. Then follow through to see that it is available. You might make a list of the equipment needed and note on the list what arrangements have been made. List the person responsible for obtaining each item. If something is your responsibility, note that. Before the meeting begins, take your list to the room and check that the needed items are all there.

Ordering Food and Beverages

For a morning meeting, coffee, tea, and juice can be provided. Water should also be available. For an afternoon meeting, you may want to provide coffee and/or soft drinks. Providing beverages is not mandatory, however. Check with your supervisor to see what he or she prefers to do.

For a luncheon meeting, you may have the responsibility of selecting the menu, calling the caterer, and arranging for the meal to be served. Avoid a heavy lunch if you are expecting people to work afterward. A salad or light entree is more appropriate for a working lunch.

For a dinner meeting, you may have the responsibility of working with an outside caterer. Sometimes there are health issues to consider. If you know the attendees, provide food that meets their needs. If you do not know the attendees, ask the caterer to recommend several meals to you. Be certain to ask your supervisor what the budget allocation is for the meal.

For a dinner meeting at a hotel, you can expect assistance from the hotel staff. You will usually be responsible for selecting the menu. If the event is formal, you might wish to have table decorations and place cards. You should know the group when selecting the seating arrangement; your supervisor can help you with this. You want to avoid seating two people next to each other who do not get along.

Handling Duties During the Meeting

The administrative professional's responsibilities during the meeting are varied. You may be expected to greet the participants and to introduce individuals if they do

■ Figure 14-6

ONLINE MAP SITES

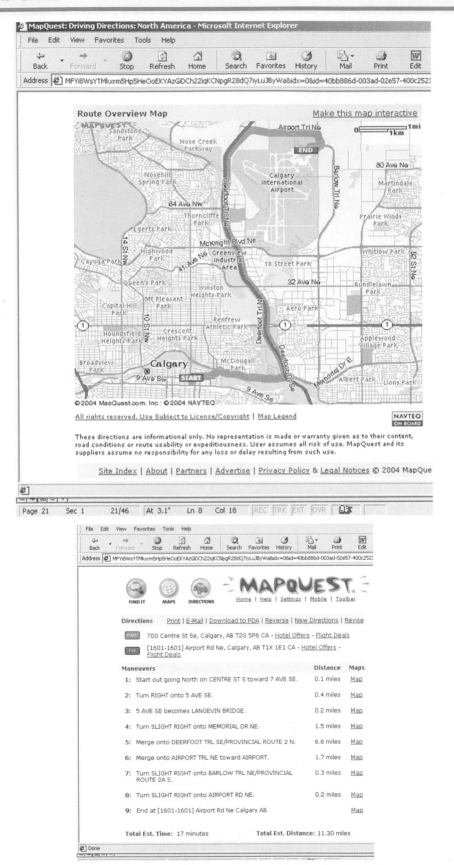

By using online sites such as www.mapquest.ca, you can obtain driving directions for your supervisor.

not know each other. Your courteousness, warmth, and friendliness can go a long way toward making people feel comfortable and getting the meeting off to a good start.

Your main responsibility during the meeting will probably be to take the minutes (a record of the meeting). Sit near the chair so you can clearly hear what he or she says. You may wish to use a laptop computer to take notes. The computer can save you time. After the meeting is over, all you have to do is read over your notes and make necessary changes to the file. Such an approach is faster than taking notes by hand or recording the meeting on tape and then having to key everything after the meeting.

Minutes should contain a record of the important matters presented in the meeting. You do not need to record minutes verbatim (with the exception of motions), but you do need to record all pertinent information. Items that should be included in the minutes are given in Figure 14-7.

Minutes are not necessary for all meetings; however, they do remind attendees of what happened and what responsibilities they might have after the meeting. Minutes are needed in the following situations:

- When decisions are made that affect a large number of people
- In formal meetings, such as board of directors' meetings
- When attendees act upon a list of different topics and a record is necessary to recall the events
- When the same type of meeting is held on a regular basis and a record is needed of the continual activities of the group
- When meeting results need to be reported to the president or other officers of the organization

Following Up After the Meeting

Your duties after the meeting include seeing that the meeting room is left in order, preparing the minutes, and handling other details.

ROUTINE TASKS. These routine tasks are essential after a meeting:

- Return all equipment. See that additional tables and chairs are removed from the room. Clean up any food or beverage leftovers, or notify the cleaning staff if the room needs a general cleaning.
- Write items on your calendar that require future attention by you or your employer.

■ Figure 14-7

ITEMS TO BE INCLUDED IN THE MINUTES OF A MEETING

- The date, time, and place of the meeting
- The type of meeting (regular, special, monthly, and so forth)
- The name of the group
- The name of the person presiding
- The members present and absent
- Approval or correction of the minutes from the previous meeting
- Reports of committees, officers, or individuals
- Actions taken and/or motions made
- Items on which action needs to be taken and the person responsible for taking the action
- The date and time of the next meeting (if there is one)
- Time of adjournment
- The signature of the chairperson of the meeting
- The signature of the secretary for the group

- Send out any necessary follow-up memos.
- Evaluate the meeting. Review what happened; consider how you might improve the arrangements for the next meeting. Make notes for your files to review before the next meeting. If you used a caterer, make notes about the quality of the food, the helpfulness of the staff, and so on.
- Keep files on meetings long enough to refer to them when planning the next similar meeting. Your notes will help ensure future success. You might also keep names and telephone numbers of contact people.

Communication Tip

After a meeting, review with your supervisor what did and did not go well. Such a review helps you plan more effectively for the next meeting.

PREPARATION OF MINUTES. If minutes are necessary, they should be prepared and distributed within 24–48 hours of a meeting. Prompt preparation and distribution of minutes reminds attendees of what they must do before the next meeting. Non-participants may also get copies of minutes from a meeting. For example, minutes from a company board meeting may be made available to all executives within a company.

Minutes from a meeting are shown in Figure 14-8 on page 287. Although there is no set format for writing minutes, you should check previous minutes to get a sense of the format followed in your organization. Additionally, templates may exist in your organization that include preferred formatting codes and standard information that is common to all minutes. Some general guidelines are:

- Minutes are single-spaced. Margins should be at least 1 inch (about 2.54 centimetres). If the minutes are to be placed in a bound book, the left margin should be 1-1/2 inches (about 3.81 centimetres).
- The heading should be keyed in all capital letters and centred.
- Subject captions should be used as paragraph headings; subject captions usually correspond to the agenda topics.
- Minutes may or may not be signed. Those of board meetings and professional organizations are generally signed. If minutes are to be signed, a signature line should be provided.
- Minutes should be stored for future reference. Minutes may be stored in hard-copy form, on a disk, or on a microrecord. In addition, the agenda and all pertinent materials presented in the meeting should be stored with the minutes.

Organizing—The Key

Regardless of what your responsibilities are, the key is organization. Know what you have to do, and stay organized in doing it. As you plan a meeting, continue through the process of the meeting, and oversee the follow-up activities, ask yourself these questions:

- How can I best organize my time and efforts?
- When should each task be completed?
- Who is responsible for each activity?
- What should I discuss with my supervisor? What can I do on my own?

Refer to the Self-Check on this page.

The Chair's Responsibilities

The leader of a meeting—commonly known as the "chairperson" or "chair"—at which you are assisting is generally your supervisor. However, as you work on teams within the company, you may occasionally be the meeting chairperson. If a meeting is to go well, the chair must fulfill certain responsibilities:

Take a few minutes to check your understanding of the administrative professional's role in planning meetings by responding to the questions below.

1. What should you consider when selecting a room for a meeting?

_____

_____

_____

_____

_____

2. Which seating arrangements are most effective for semiformal meetings?

_____

_____

_____

_____

_____

3. What should an agenda include?

_____

_____

_____

_____

_____

_____

4. What should minutes include?

_____

_____

_____

_____

_____

Check your answers against those provided at the end of the chapter. How did you do?

- Keep the participants focused on the agenda.
- Encourage participation from everyone in the meeting.

■ Figure 14-8

MEETING MINUTES

BOARD OF DIRECTORS MEETING
MANAGEMENT ASSOCIATION

Calgary Chapter
November 16, 2005

TIME AND PLACE OF MEETING

The regular monthly meeting of the Board of Directors of the Management
Association was held on November 16 at the Regent Hotel at 6:30 p.m.
The meeting was called to order by the President, Aretha Edwards. All twelve
Board members were present.

READING OF THE MINUTES

The minutes of the October meeting were approved without reading since
each member received a copy prior to the meeting.

TREASURER'S REPORT

Margaret Mustoe reported that she received acceptance from Harold McLean
to speak at the December meeting and that his picture and vita have been
turned over to the Publicity Committee.

NEW BUSINESS

Membership Committee: The application of Theresa Pulliams for
membership was unanimously approved.

Service Committee: It was suggested that the merit award qualifications be
included in the Chapter Bulletin for the first week of December.

Program Committee: William Farr, Chairperson of the Speakers Bureau,
reported that he and the committee are planning to increase the number of
programs at the winter seminar. He also reported that the committee agreed
on "Ethics in International Business" as the theme for the seminar.

ADJOURNMENT

The meeting was adjourned at 8:30 p.m.

Rebecca M. Wylie
Rebecca M. Wylie
Secretary, Calgary Chapter
Management Association

- Limit the domination of any one person in the meeting.
- Positively reinforce all individuals for their contributions.
- Keep the discussion moving toward the outcomes determined.

Discussion of some aspects of these responsibilities follows.

Adhering to the Agenda

As you have learned, the purpose of a meeting must be clearly established and that purpose made clear in writing to the participants when the meeting is announced. When the meeting begins, the chairperson should reiterate the purpose of the meeting. The chair should also let the participants know what outcomes are expected. For example, if the purpose of a meeting is to establish a direction for the department for the next two years, the expected outcomes of the meeting may be to determine at least two departmental objectives.

If participants stray from the agenda, the chairperson is responsible for sensitively but firmly bringing them back to the topic at hand. The chair might say "Thank you for your comments. We can put that issue on the agenda for a future meeting. Now let's continue discussing the departmental objectives we must set."

Managing Time

You already know that meetings should begin on time, even if several people are late in arriving. Waiting for others is not fair to those who have made the effort to be on time. The chairperson is responsible for beginning and ending meetings on time. The chair must be sensitive to other commitments participants may have made. Time frames (both beginning and ending) should be established when the meeting notice is sent out.

Encouraging Participation

Before participants are invited to a meeting, the chairperson should give considerable thought to who should be present. The people in attendance should be those best in a position to discuss the issues, determine the direction, or solve the problem. Once the meeting begins, the chair is responsible for seeing that all individuals participate. The chair should help individuals feel secure enough to say what they really think. If, as the meeting gets under way, several people have not spoken, the chairperson may make statements such as:

- "Glenda, what direction do you think we should take to satisfy our needs in the 21st century?"
- "Guy, we haven't heard from you on this issue. What is your opinion?"

Let each participant know that you and the group value his or her opinion. Encourage everyone to contribute. Respect participants and the comments they make. You might make statements such as:

- "Thank you for that contribution."
- "That's a great idea."
- "Thanks. Can you expand on your idea? It may have possibilities for us."

The chair is also responsible for seeing that no one dominates the conversation, even if their contributions are beneficial. The chairperson can use statements such as:

- "Azmeena, that is an excellent idea. Eduardo, how could it be implemented in your area?"
- "Thanks, Azmeena; Eduardo, what do you think about the direction?"

Reaching Decisions

The chairperson is responsible for helping the participants reach a decision about the issue, problem, or direction if a decision is needed. The chair must carefully assess if all alternatives have been discussed. Then the chairperson needs to push for a decision on the issue. For example, the chair might say "We seem to have identified each issue and the possible solutions. Does anyone else have anything to add?" Then the chair can move to resolution by saying "Now let's determine which solution will work best in our present situation."

Photodisc Red/Photodisc Collection

One of the chairperson's responsibilities in a meeting is to encourage participation by all those present.

Once a resolution is reached, the chair can check to see if all participants agree by asking "Now that we have reached a resolution, is everyone in the room comfortable with it? Are we overlooking anything? Are there problems we haven't seen?"

Evaluating the Meeting

Generally, with informal meetings within an organization, no formal evaluation is necessary. However, an informal evaluation by the chairperson (and possibly the participants) should be done. The attendees are usually very forthright. They may tell the chair they found the meeting to be a waste of time. When attendees make such a statement, the chair should seek clarification on exactly what they meant. The chairperson may also want to ask individual participants how the meeting went. In either case, the chair should ask these questions of herself or himself:

- Were the attendees participatory?
- Was the nonverbal behaviour positive?
- Were the participants creative problem solvers?
- Did the participants exhibit a high energy level?
- Was the purpose of the meeting satisfied?
- Were appropriate decisions made?
- Can I improve in how I handled the issues, the people, or the meeting in general?

If the meeting is a relatively formal one, the chairperson may ask participants to fill out an evaluation form. If so, the administrative professional's role may be to prepare and administer the evaluation. A meeting evaluation form is shown in Figure 14-9.

Participants' Responsibilities

Just as a chairperson has responsibilities, so do the participants. Their role is much broader than attending the meeting. Their responsibilities begin before the meeting and continue after the meeting.

Before the Meeting

Participants are responsible for reading the meeting notice, responding to it promptly, and reading any materials sent out before the meeting. Participants are also responsible for understanding the purpose of the meeting and analytically evaluating the materials in relation to the purpose of the meeting. Participants must understand that they have been asked to the

■ **Figure 14-9**

MEETING EVALUATION FORM

Place a check mark in the "Yes" or "No" column. Attach any additional comments you may have to this form.

1. Was the purpose of the meeting accomplished?
   Yes ☐ No ☐

2. Was the agenda received in time to prepare for the meeting?
   Yes ☐ No ☐

3. Was the room arrangement satisfactory?
   Yes ☐ No ☐

4. Did the chairperson help the group accomplish the goals of the meeting?
   Yes ☐ No ☐

5. Did the chair adhere to the agenda?
   Yes ☐ No ☐

6. Were the appropriate people included in the meeting?
   Yes ☐ No ☐

7. Did all attendees participate in the discussion?
   Yes ☐ No ☐

8. Did attendees listen to each other?
   Yes ☐ No ☐

9. Did the chairperson encourage participation?
   Yes ☐ No ☐

10. Did the meeting begin on time?
    Yes ☐ No ☐

11. Did the meeting end on time?
    Yes ☐ No ☐

12. Were decisions that were made consistent with the purpose of the meeting?
    Yes ☐ No ☐

meeting because the chairperson believes they have something to offer. Each participant must take seriously his or her responsibility to contribute to the success of the meeting, which means being prepared. No one appreciates the person who comes to a meeting late and opens up the pack of materials for the first time—clearly not having read the material beforehand.

During the Meeting

During the meeting, participants are responsible for:

- Being on time
- Adhering to the agenda
- Making contributions
- Listening thoughtfully to other participants' contributions and responding if they have something to add
- Respecting the chair's role
- Not dominating the discussion
- Not being judgmental of others' comments
- Being courteous to each individual in the meeting
- Taking notes, if necessary

It is not always easy to listen carefully to others, to be non-judgmental, and to make contributions. Your mind tends to wander, focusing on other work-related tasks you need to complete or on your plans after work. However, your contributions can be the very ones that get the meeting back on track if individuals stray or help the chair keep the meeting focused. Your obligation is to help the meeting get better.

After the Meeting

Once the meeting is over, a participant's responsibilities do not necessarily end. The participant may have been asked to do some research or take some action before the next meeting, or the participant may have been asked to work with one or two other people to bring back a recommendation to the next meeting. The participant must fulfill all obligations by the designated time; others are depending on him or her to do so.

International Meetings

Your supervisor, with your assistance, may be responsible for setting up an international meeting, either electronic or face to face. In international meetings, remember that cultural differences do exist and these differences must be understood and respected. Otherwise, you may be dealing with an international incident rather than getting a resolution on an important contract or issue. Do your homework before the meeting. Find out as much as you can about the culture or cultures that will be represented. Then be sensitive to the needs of the individuals in the meeting.

International meetings are always more formal in nature. You must understand hierarchical considerations and use proper greetings and amenities. Figure 14-10 gives several suggestions on what to do and not to do in international meetings.

■ **Figure 14-10**

APPROPRIATE AND INAPPROPRIATE BEHAVIOURS AT INTERNATIONAL MEETINGS

- Greet each person properly in all meetings. Do not let yourself ignore greetings in an electronic meeting; greetings become doubly important in such a situation.
- Do not use first names of participants. Even though using first names is common in North American meetings, rarely is it an appropriate practice in other countries.
- Recognize the leader of the other group(s). For example, if the presidents of companies are involved, they should be recognized first and speak first.
- Take time for amenities before beginning the meeting.
- Shake hands with the participants, or bow if met with a bow from the international visitor.
- Dress conservatively.
- Do not ask personal questions; keep the conversation general (even at more informal times such as lunch).
- Disagree agreeably; some cultures consider it offensive to be contradicting.
- Do not use slang.
- Avoid gesturing with your hands. Many people take offence at such gestures.
- Watch your body language; remember that body language has different meanings in different cultures. Make certain you do not communicate something you do not mean through your body language.
- Use an interpreter if necessary.
- Do not mistake a courteous answer for the truth. "Yes" does not always mean "yes," and "no" may not mean "no."
- Remember the hierarchical nature of many countries; respect the hierarchy.

Conferences

A conference is much larger in scope and has more participants than a meeting. Executives may belong to a professional organization in a particular field of expertise, such as accounting, engineering, or human resources. Many of these organizations hold at least one major conference each year. Most companies encourage their executives to participate in conferences as a means of broadening their knowledge. Your role as an administrative professional may be to assist your supervisor in planning a conference.

As an administrative professional, you may be a member of the International Association of Administrative Professionals (IAAP), ARMA International, the Canadian Information Processing Society (CIPS), or some local organization. As a member, you may attend or help to plan some of their conferences.

Before the Conference

Preparing for a regional or national conference takes months of work. Good planning ensures a smooth, successful conference. Poor planning can result in a disorganized, ineffective conference. One of the major responsibilities of planning is to determine the location and meeting facilities for the conference. Contact the chamber of commerce in the city being considered. Ask for information about the city and appropriate conference facilities. Request conference planning guides from the hotels and conference centres that give floor plans of the facilities, dining and catering services, price list of rooms, and layout of meeting rooms. Figure 14-11 shows a portion of a hotel floor plan. Once the city and hotel have been selected, detailed arrangements need to be made for meeting rooms, guest rooms, meal arrangements, and so on.

■ Figure 14-11

HOTEL FLOOR PLAN

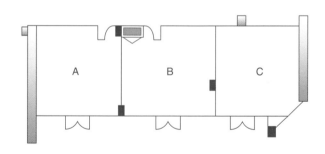
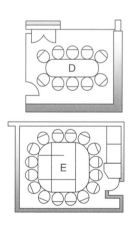
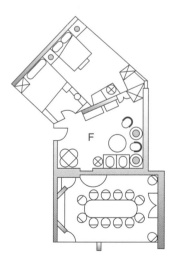

Meeting Room Specifications

		Theatre	Classroom	Banquet	Reception		Dimensions	Area
A	Bobbie Layne	45	35	46	60		24' × 24'	576
B	Billy Sims	50	35	46	60		24' × 24'	576
A&B	Combined	95	70	94	120		24' × 24'	1152
C	Joe Schmidt	45	32	40	50		23' × 24'	552
D	Pistons Boardroom		Conference seating for 14				20' × 17'	360
E	Lions Boardroom		Conference seating for 16				20' × 22'	430
F	Featherstone Suite		Conference seating for 14					

Statistics

You must contact presenters and make travel and lodging arrangements before the conference. If you are responsible for making arrangements for a presenter, you should determine the type of accommodations required—room (single or double, queen- or king-size bed), flight preferences, arrival and departure times, rental car needs, etc.

Some type of pre-registration is usually held before a conference with registration taking place during the conference. You may be responsible for mailing out and processing returned pre-registration forms. You also may be responsible for assisting with registration at the conference. If the conference is a large one, several people will be needed to staff the registration tables.

During the Conference

Your responsibilities during the conference may include running errands, delivering messages to participants, and solving problems that may occur. Other responsibilities may include checking room arrangements, equipment needs, meal arrangements, and so on. At a conference, you are a representative of the company for which you work or the organization of which you are a member. Therefore, you should present a positive image at all times. Keep a smile on your face, and handle even the most difficult situations with **aplomb** (self-assurance).

After the Conference

After the conference, your basic duties involve cleaning up and following up. These responsibilities include seeing that all equipment is returned, presenters are assisted with transportation to the airport, letters of appreciation are sent to presenters and others, expense reports are filled out, and bills are paid. You may also be responsible for seeing that the proceedings of the conference are published and mailed to participants. You may not be responsible for writing the report, but you may be responsible for working with the conference reporters in assembling and mailing the report. At some conferences, the sessions are recorded and attendees may purchase these audiotapes.

Those who have worked on a conference should have a meeting to evaluate the conference. They should ask these questions:

- What went right?
- What went wrong?
- Was the facility adequate?
- Was the registration process smooth?
- Were the meals good and served on time?
- Were the presenters effective?

Attendees usually fill out a formal evaluation of the conference. This evaluation may be of the conference as a whole and/or of individual sessions.

Keep a record of the evaluations to refer to before the next conference. These evaluations will remind you of what did and did not work at the previous conference. Also, keep all files containing information about the conference preparation. These files can be valuable in planning future conferences.

Chapter Summary

The summary will help you remember the important points covered in the chapter.

- Management spends as much as 50 percent or more of each week in meetings. Due to the frequency and cost of meetings, meeting time must be spent as productively as possible.
- Meetings are a good means of generating ideas; however, unnecessary and unproductive meetings are held daily in organizations. Meetings are not a good idea when there is inadequate data; when there is insufficient time to prepare for the meeting; when information could be better communicated by memo, fax, e-mail or telephone; or when there is a considerable amount of anger or hostility in the group.
- Meetings may be face to face or electronic, which includes audioconferencing, online conferencing, or videoconferencing.
- The executive's role in meeting preparation usually involves determining the purpose of the meeting, determining who should attend, and determining the number of attendees. The administrative professional may assist with these roles.
- The administrative professional's role, in consultation with the executive, includes selecting and preparing the room, determining the seating arrangement, sending meeting notices, preparing the agenda, determining the procedures, preparing materials for the supervisor, preparing materials for attendees, ordering equipment, ordering food and beverages, handling duties during the meeting, and following up after the meeting.
- The chairperson's responsibilities during the meeting include adhering to the agenda, managing time, encouraging participation, reaching decisions, and evaluating the meeting.
- The participant's responsibilities during the meeting include reading material before the meeting, being on time, adhering to the agenda, making contributions, listening thoughtfully to other participants, and carrying out any responsibilities assigned during the meeting.
- In planning and conducting international meetings, the chairperson and the administrative professional should become familiar with the customs and culture of the participants.
- Conferences are much larger in scope and have more participants than meetings. The administrative professional may be involved in planning a conference; carrying out duties during the conference, such as solving problems, running errands, and assisting with registration; and writing letters of appreciation, filling out expense reports, paying bills, and numerous other follow-up activities.

Key Terms

The following terms were introduced in this chapter. The page on which the term was introduced is provided to help you locate the new term. Definitions are compiled in the Glossary at the end of the text.

- **teleconferencing** 274
- **audioconferencing** 274
- **electronic whiteboard** 276
- **interactivity** 276 — *info transmitted from one location to another - acted upon by any prs @ any locaha* [handwritten annotation]
- **stand-alone conventional dry-erase boards** 276
- **electronic dry-erase whiteboards** 276
- **online meetings** 276
- **real time** 276
- **outside** or **remote facilitator** 276
- **videoconferencing** 276
- **virtual conferencing** 276
- **heterogeneous group** 278
- **homogeneous group** 278
- **synergy** 278
- **rectangular arrangement** 279
- **circular arrangement** 279
- **semicircular** or **U-shaped arrangement** 279
- **agenda** 281
- **ad hoc (special) committee** 283
- **amendment** 283
- **bylaws** 283
- **minutes** 283
- **motion** 283
- **parliamentary procedures** 283
- **quorum** 283
- **resolution** 283
- **standing committee** 283
- **aplomb** 292

Responses to Self-Check

1. Consider its size, arrangement, temperature, and ventilation and whether the room is large enough to accommodate the equipment needed.
2. U-shaped and semicircular are the most effective arrangements for semiformal meetings.
3. An agenda should include the name of the meeting or the group, date of the meeting, start and end times, location, order of agenda items, person responsible for presenting each agenda

item, action expected on each agenda item, and background materials (if necessary).

4. Minutes should include the date, time, and place of the meeting; the type of meeting; the name of the group; the name of the person presiding; the members present and absent; approval or correction of minutes from the previous meeting; reports of committees, officers, or individuals; actions taken and/or motions made; items on which action needs to be taken and the person responsible for taking the action; the date and time of the next meeting; time of adjournment; and the signature of the secretary for the group.

Discussion Items

These discussion items provide an opportunity to test your understanding of the chapter through written responses and/or discussion with your classmates and your instructor.

1. When is a meeting unnecessary?
2. List and define three types of electronic meetings.
3. List ten responsibilities that an administrative professional has when meetings are being held.
4. List ten appropriate behaviours when conducting an international meeting.

Critical-Thinking Activity

CanAsian Airlines is planning an online conference for its Calgary and Beijing executives. The meeting is being held to begin discussion of the strategic direction of the airlines for the next five years. You have been asked to coordinate with the various offices on agenda items. Once you receive the agenda items, you will be working with Mr. Albertson to send out the necessary materials and the agenda. You have contacted the appropriate administrative professional in each office to discuss these details. To date, you have received agenda items from two of the three executives in the Calgary office and one of the three executives in the Beijing office. You have e-mailed a reminder to the administrative professional in each office, asking for the executive's agenda; you have received no response. The meeting is only a month away, and you are becoming anxious. You know you must get the agenda out soon. You do not want to go to Mr. Albertson with the situation, but you do not know how to handle it. What should you do?

Projects

Project 14-1 *(Objectives 1, 2, 3, and 4)*

Collaborative Project

Mr. Albertson is planning a meeting with not-for-profit groups and several large businesses within the Calgary community to consider ways in which the organizations might work together on these major issues impacting the city: transportation, crime, inner-city housing, and public education. The not-for-profit groups involved in this meeting are the Department of Social Services, the Calgary Foundation, the Chamber of Commerce, the Asian-Pacific Coalition, the Junior League, and the First Nations Council. The businesses are Talisman International, MDS Health Care, Clark Associates, Inc., Godwin Tools, and Lowell Granite. The group's work will take approximately one year; recommendations from this group after one year of operation will go to the mayor for action.

The first meeting will be an organizational one to develop a mission statement and to establish goals for the group. Mr. Albertson has already contacted the community leaders, and they have agreed to serve on the task force. Mr. Albertson has asked you to handle several of the arrangements for him. Since this project is a fairly extensive one, you ask your two assistants to work with you. (Assemble a group of three for this project—you and two of your classmates.) Mr. Albertson is considering an electronic meeting. He asks you to use the Internet to research the advantages and disadvantages of audioconferencing and online meetings. Prepare a memorandum to Mr. Albertson, using the memorandum form on the Student CD, SCDP 14-1a, summarizing the results of your findings. Then draft a letter for Mr. Albertson, inviting participants to the first meeting; use the letterhead on the Student CD, SCDP14-1. The meeting will be held two days—Thursday, November 15, beginning with lunch at noon and ending at 4 p.m., and Friday, November 16, beginning with breakfast at 8:30 a.m. and ending at 11 a.m.

Prepare an agenda. The agenda on November 15 should include a welcome to the group from Mr. Albertson; lunch; an introduction of the participants; and a videoconference with Dr. Peter Sigman, who has been working with inner-city issues for over 15 years. Dr. Sigman will be in Toronto; the participants at the meeting will have a chance to interact with him after his presentation. The remainder of Thursday afternoon will be devoted to writing a mission statement for the group. On Friday morning, the group will begin to develop their goals. Mr. Albertson will facilitate both sessions.

Have a team meeting with your two classmates to determine who will be responsible for each task. Determine how you will work together as a team. Print out a copy of the team evaluation form from your Student CD, SCDP14-1c. Discuss it with your teammates so everyone understands what evaluation criteria are being used. Once you have completed the project, each member of your team should complete the evaluation form.

1. Refer back to the section in Chapter 14 that presents the administrative professional's responsibilities in assisting with meetings. Make a list of the things your group must do. Include menus for lunch and breakfast.
2. Write a memorandum to Mr. Albertson summarizing your research on the Internet; include copies of the articles you found.
3. Prepare a draft of a letter inviting the not-for-profit groups and the businesses to the meeting. Include an agenda. Give the draft to your supervisor for approval. The meeting will be held in the Board Room at CanAsian. (In this case, the supervisor will be your instructor.) Once your instructor has approved the letter and the agenda, prepare letters and envelopes for the invitees. Include the agenda for the two days. Addresses are given on the Student CD at SCDP14-1b.

4. Complete the team evaluation form separately, and then discuss your evaluation with your team members. Next, prepare a team evaluation that consolidates the opinions given by each team member. Turn it in to your instructor. Use the form given on the Student CD at SCDP14-1c. (Print four copies, one for each member of the team and one for your collective evaluation.)

Project 14-2 *(Objective 4)*

Attend a meeting of a professional organization—either a club you are a member of at school or another organization. Take notes at the meeting, and key your notes in the form of minutes. Turn the minutes in to your instructor.

Project 14-3 *(Objective 1)*

Conflict can occasionally arise between participants of a meeting. You are not generally responsible for solving the problem unless you are conducting the meeting; you can become one of those who helps resolve the conflict. You may wish to refer to the Soft Skills "Conflict Resolution" in Chapter 3 before beginning this project. Describe how you will continue to develop your conflict resolution skills. If you are presently employed, describe a conflict you may have participated in and how you might change your behaviour. This project is a continuation of your Professional Growth Plan. Save a copy on your Professional Growth disk under "Progro 14-3."

Chapter 15

Arranging for Business Travel

LEARNING OBJECTIVES

1. Make travel arrangements.
2. Prepare an itinerary.
3. Describe the responsibilities of administrative professionals regarding their executives' trips.
4. Complete an expense report.
5. *Maintain a positive attitude.*

Travel is a way of life for most business executives; and with our global economy, the amount of international travel has increased dramatically. Many North American businesses now are multinational, having locations both within Canada and abroad. Conversely, many companies abroad now have locations within Canada. Additionally, mergers between North American companies and companies abroad continue to occur. The car industry is a good example of international locations and mergers. For example, Honda®, Mazda®, Toyota®, Mitsibushi™, and Nissan® are some of the car manufacturers from abroad who have assembly plants in North America. The merger of Chrysler® with Daimler-Benz™ in 1998 was a megamerger of two large automobile makers into one company. The United States and other countries take advantage of land, labour, and technical expertise available in other parts of the world to decide where to produce and/or assemble a product.

Due to the global nature of our economy, executives often make trips abroad for businesses purposes. As an administrative professional, you also may travel occasionally. Or if you are working for a company who has subsidiaries abroad, you may have the opportunity to work in one of the international locations for a period of time.

In order to handle travel arrangements effectively, you must become familiar with the types of services available. This chapter will help you understand your options when making travel arrangements. It also will help you know how to handle other travel-related responsibilities.

Domestic Air Travel

Since time is an extremely important commodity for busy executives, almost all their travel is done by air. They usually do not have the time required to travel by car or rail. Thus, the emphasis in this section is on air travel.

An air traveller today can fly from Toronto to Vancouver in approximately five hours or from Winnipeg to Germany in approximately seven hours. During a flight, travellers can use their time productively by taking advantage of available technology. For example, executives can read and send e-mail, write letters and reports, and stay current on news or investments through the Internet. Computers and cell phones may not be used during takeoff or landing due to possible interference with the electronics of the airplane. (A flight attendant announces when they may and may not be used.) With our technological expertise, air travel has the potential of not only saving travel time but also allowing executives to continue to be productive.

PDAs and laptops allow us to continue to be productive as we travel regionally, nationally and internationally.

Flight Classifications

There are three classes of flight—first class, business class, and economy. Some flights offer all three classes, with business class being offered mainly on international flights. All large planes offer first class and economy. Today a number of airlines have added regional jets, smaller in size than the planes that fly longer routes within Canada or internationally. These regional jets also fly shorter distances (for example, from Calgary to Kelowna or from Calgary to Winnipeg). Regional jets generally have 30–100 seats and only one class of flight—economy. They may offer drinks and snacks or small boxed lunches.

At the opposite end of the spectrum from the regional jet is the luxury jet, which transports small groups of people (approximately 40–90) in "country club" style to almost all parts of the world. These luxury jets are very expensive and provide many amenities, including numerous attendants to handle the needs of the travellers, concierge service, spacious seating, and lavish food and beverages. Obviously, only a small portion of the population is able to utilize luxury jet transportation.

First-Class Accommodations

First-class accommodations are the most expensive of the three classes and the most luxurious. The seats are wider and farther apart and there is more legroom. The quantity and quality of food is better and more attention is paid to presentation of the meal. Cloth napkins, tablecloths, silverware, and china dinnerware are used. Alcoholic beverages are offered without additional cost.

Some airlines allow a traveller to eat at a time of their choosing. Headsets for listening to music or viewing movies are provided. Each passenger has his or her own video monitor and on some flights the traveller may make an individual choice from a selection of movies or DVDs. There are more flight attendants per customer than in economy or business, which means greater attention is given to each flyer. First-class customers have access to a private lounge in the terminal while waiting for their flight departure and are allowed to exit first and board at any time during the boarding process. Attendants take passengers' coats and hang them up; they also store passengers' parcels in overhead bins.

Business-Class Accommodations

Business-class accommodations are slightly more expensive than economy. The business-class section is located in front of the economy class—directly behind first class or at the front of the plane if first class is not offered. Accommodations may include more spacious seating than economy, complimentary alcoholic beverages, individual monitors and headsets for listening to music or watching movies, recliner seats, more legroom, and better food than economy class. Like first-class travellers, business-class travellers also have access to a lounge in the terminal while waiting for their flight departure and are allowed to exit first and board at any time during the boarding process.

Economy-Class Accommodations

Economy-class accommodations may provide complimentary snacks, soft drinks, fruit juice, tea or coffee, and meals. Seats are closer together; and fewer flight attendants are available to serve the needs of the customers. When available, food is served with plastic dinnerware and paper napkins. Since there are fewer flight attendants, service is slower than in first class. The events of 9/11 had a severe impact on airlines worldwide. Some airlines ceased operating. Of those airlines that continued to operate, many decided to cut back on costs by eliminating refreshment service altogether on short-haul or regional flights. Food providers in airports saw a business opportunity here and, in the Vancouver International Airport for example, began providing carry-on meals in specially designed bags.

Company-Owned Planes

Large companies may have their own plane or fleet of planes if the amount of travel within the company makes it advantageous to do so. Pilots employed by the company generally fly these planes, which are housed at local airports. Executives may be driven to the airport by company employees and picked up at the airport upon returning from a trip.

Special Services

Some airlines offer membership to frequent flyers in an airline club. These clubs offer a comfortable lounge for passengers who may have a layover between flights. The lounge area is equipped with computer workstations, telephones, reading material (newspapers and periodicals), comfortable chairs, drinks, snacks, and restrooms. First-class and business-class travellers automatically have access to these lounges.

Large airports generally provide free shuttle service from a parking or rental car location to the airport gate. However, you are charged for parking your car, with the fee based on how long your car is parked. Since parking at an airport for an extended period of time can become expensive, large cities generally provide private shuttle services to the airport from locations around the city.

Ticketing

Gone are the days of having only one type of airline ticket, the standard paper one that contains tickets for both your departure and your return. Although paper tickets are still available, the e-ticket is common. Some people prefer paper tickets in case they have to change airlines because of a strike or a missed connection. However, some airlines now charge an additional fee for issuing paper tickets.

Generally, you receive an e-ticket by e-mail or fax. It is a one-page document that gives only the basic information you need—your confirmation number and departure and arrival times. You present your e-ticket at the counter or gate of the airline, at which time you are issued a boarding pass.

Kiosks for quick check-in are available for the travelling public now in most airports. The traveller need only insert the credit card with which he or she has paid for the e-ticket; then the reservation information is retrieved from the airline database and a boarding pass printed. Travellers can then proceed directly to the departure gate with just a short stop to drop onto a conveyor belt any checked baggage they may have with them.

Changes or Cancellations

You may need to cancel or change a flight reservation. Generally, there is a charge for changing a flight, with most major airlines charging $100. Clearly, you should ask when making the original reservation if there is a charge for changes and, if so, how much it is. When you do cancel a flight, ask if you can use the ticket at a later time to either the same or a different location.

Ground Transportation

Once executives arrive at their destination, they may need some type of ground transportation to their hotel. That transportation may be a taxi or shuttle bus. When making arrangements, check taxi costs and the availability of shuttle services. Some hotels provide free shuttle service to and from the airport. Shuttle services are also available from private vendors, which may be less expensive than taxi service. Limousine service is also available at many airports, the cost being approximately the same as taxi service.

If executives must attend meetings at several locations during their stay, renting a car may be the most economical and convenient method of ground transportation. Toll-free numbers for car rental agencies are listed in the telephone directory. Cars may also be rented through airlines or travel agents or over the Internet. (More information on this topic is provided later in this chapter under "Online Reservations.") When renting a car, specify the make and model preferred and the date and time the car will be picked up and returned.

When arriving at the destination airport, executives pick up their cars from the rental location, which may be in the same building as the airport gates or in a separate building. If the car rental is in a separate location, a free shuttle service is available to take them to the checkout desk. The cost of a rental car is determined two ways—either by a daily rate plus an amount for each mile driven or by a daily rate with unlimited mileage. (The daily rate with unlimited mileage is the most common.) Company policy may dictate that executives rent a car no larger than midsize. Prices from rental agencies are determined by the size of the car, the classifications being full-size (the most expensive), midsize (moderately priced), and economy (the least expensive). Insurance is available upon rental of a car.

(Insurance is not mandatory if executives have their own coverage through a business or personal policy.) The executives are asked if they wish to purchase extended insurance coverage. Personnel at the rental agency fill out necessary authorization forms; the executives then sign the forms.

The car will have a full tank of gas when it is rented. The executive should fill the car up with gas before returning it, since the rental agency will charge for gas (generally at a higher price than can be obtained at a local gas station) if the tank is not full when the car is returned. The executive usually carries a company credit card, which can be used to purchase gas and rent a car. Some companies prefer to deal with only one car rental agency; you should know your organization's policy before reserving a car. Most car rental agencies provide maps and assist in planning the best route to the destination. They also supply information about hotels, restaurants, and tourist attractions. However, you can also use the Internet to find a map of the area the executive is visiting and information about hotels, restaurants, and tourist attractions.

Car Travel

If an executive is travelling only a few hundred kilometres, he or she may prefer to travel by car. Most top-level executives use cars furnished by the company; the company pays gasoline expenses. Other executives are reimbursed on a per-kilometre basis for any job-related travel. Your responsibilities for a trip by car may include determining the best route to follow, making hotel reservations, and identifying restaurants along the way. You may use the Internet to find this information. However, if your employer is a member of the local affiliate of the Canadian Automobile Association, you may choose to obtain map, hotel, and restaurant information from them rather than the Internet.

Rail Travel

Rail travel is also an option for the executive if the trip is a fairly short distance. Travel by train allows the executive the freedom to work during a trip. He or she can use a laptop computer, a PDA, and a cell phone on the train, just as can be done on a plane. Train stations are generally centrally located within a city, and their fares are usually less expensive than airfares. First-class and sleeping accommodations are available on trains, along with coach accommodations for more economical travel. Dining cars are also available; meals may be delivered in first-class accommodations. To find out about train travel in your area, look under "Railroads" in the Yellow Pages.

Office Services

Those executives who choose to take a computer along will find that hotel rooms are usually equipped with desks that, in some cases, will be wired for Internet connection. If, however, the executive chooses not to take a computer, a cell phone, and so on, on a trip, he or she may need office services while away. Most hotels in large cities will have these services available in a business centre. The services include access to computers, printers, office supplies, fax equipment, and even administrative assistance. When services are not available at the hotel, most concierges can find assistance for the traveller.

International Travel

As you learned earlier, many businesses now have international interests. Those interests may involve subsidiaries of the firm, separate firms, or partnerships with firms in other countries. Whatever the interests may be, travel abroad is quite common for executives in many companies.

Cultural Differences

Travellers need to be knowledgeable about and sensitive to the customs and culture of the country they are visiting. Information about other countries may be obtained from a variety of sources:

- *Consulates of the country to be visited.* (Look in the Yellow Pages under "Consulates.") These offices usually have printed materials available. They are also willing to answer questions about local customs and culture.
- *Travel books.* These books, available at libraries and bookstores, generally contain information about local customs and business practices.

- *Books about doing business with a particular country being visited.* These books are also available at libraries and bookstores.
- *Seminars and short courses.* The company may arrange for consultants to assist personnel in understanding the culture abroad. Additionally, local colleges and universities often provide short courses on doing business with particular countries.
- *The Web.* Numerous articles are available that review cultural differences internationally. Also, the Web is a good source for finding books concerning cultural differences.

Consider the following example of errors that are sometimes made when visiting China.

Roger Schmiedicke visited China for the first time to negotiate a contract for his company. He is 35 years old. The Chinese president with whom he was negotiating was much older. After a few amenities with the Chinese were taken care of, Roger submitted the contract. The contract was written in precise language with all contingencies covered. His presentation of the contract was extremely clear; he considered himself an effective communicator. After presenting the contract, he asked the Chinese official to sign it within 30 days. He then thanked the Chinese individuals in the meeting, shook hands with everyone, and left. After 30 days had passed, Roger called the president of the Chinese company and asked him if the contract was going to be signed. The president responded, through an interpreter, that they were considering the contract. Another 30 days passed, and there was still no signed contract.

What assumptions did Roger make about the Chinese? What should he have known about the Chinese culture that would have helped him in negotiating a contract?

Figure 15-1 lists several important societal and institutional differences between China and North America that Roger should have considered. Also, you may want to refer back to Chapter 5, which lists several cultural differences across nations.

Here are some general rules that apply to international travel:

- Learn the appropriate greeting for the country you will be visiting.

■ Figure 15-1

SOCIETAL AND INSTITUTIONAL DIFFERENCES BETWEEN CHINA AND NORTH AMERICA

- China is in transition from a planned economy to a market economy. North America has a market-driven economy.
- In China, the culture is centred on relationships; in North America, the culture is centred on individuals.
- In China, trust is placed in the people close to you; in North America, trust is placed in the written contract.
- The Chinese are quiet and reserved as a rule; the people of North America are more outspoken.
- In China, relationships come first; in North America, economics comes first.
- In China, respect comes from seniority, wisdom, and ability; in North America, respect comes from success, achievement, and wealth.
- Time has a much different connotation in China, accountability being marked by generations; in contrast, accountability in North America is often marked by weeks or months.

Communication Tip

When your supervisor brings back business cards from an international trip, file the cards according to the name of the trip. For example, if the trip was to Japan, set up a card file with the first card following the Japan tab including the date of the trip and the places visited. Place the business cards behind this card.

- Learn how to say "please" and "thank you" in the language of the country.
- Have business cards printed with your name and your company name in both English and the language of the country you are visiting.
- Do not criticize the people or customs of the country you are visiting. Show appreciation for the music, art, and culture of the country.
- Remember that business generally is more formal in other countries than it is in North America.
- Dress appropriately; this generally means business suits for men and conservative dresses or suits for women. Although dress in North America has

become more casual than in the past, you cannot assume that is true for international organizations. Casual business dress generally does not imply a professional image. It may be seen as sloppy dress. It is also important to be well groomed.

- Eat the food that is offered you; do not ask what you are being served; show appreciation to your host.
- Be courteous and respectful at all times.

Appointments

If you are involved in setting up appointments or meetings for the executive, remember time zone differences. **Jet lag** (the feeling of exhaustion following a flight through several time zones) can limit an executive's effectiveness. Since it takes the body about a day to adapt to the new environment for each time zone crossed, give the executive an extra day to recover from the trip before scheduling meetings.

If executives do not have the luxury of a full day before attending appointments, they can take advantage of certain techniques to help with jet lag. For example, if they are travelling west, they can postpone the time they usually go to bed by two or three hours for two days before the flight. If they are travelling east, they can retire a couple of hours earlier than usual. At the same time, they can also start shifting mealtimes to those of the destination city. Their body clock will not be fully adapted to the new time when they land, but they will have made a start in the right direction.

You should not schedule appointments for the day before the executive leaves on a trip, or for the day the executive returns. The day before a trip is usually busy in preparation for the trip, and when the executive returns from a trip, he or she must again contend with time zone changes.

Business Gifts

Generally, a gift is appropriate, particularly if the executive is meeting officials for the first time. The gift should be a small one, a nice pen or some memento representative of Canada. However, executives must be aware of customs and taboos when giving gifts to avoid offending someone without knowing it. Figure 15-2 lists some gift taboos.

■ Figure 15-2

UNDERSTANDING GIFT ETIQUETTE

- In English-speaking countries, including Britain, Ireland, and Australia, gifts are not expected and might even be considered inappropriate. Business gifts are also rarely exchanged in Spain and France.
- Gift giving is important in China, Japan, the Philippines, Russia, and Eastern European countries.
- When visiting China, present your gift to the Chinese official at your first meeting.
- In Korea, it is considered rude to open a gift in front of the donor.
- When giving gifts, be certain the gift is made in Canada. For example, it would be inappropriate to give a gift to an individual from China that was made in his or her country.
- Appropriate gifts include pens or pen-and-pencil sets. Items from your home province and books of historical areas of your province are also appropriate.
- Photo albums containing pictures of the people you met on your trip are appropriate gifts.
- Flowers are not a universally acceptable gift to take to someone's home as a gift to the host. If flowers are acceptable, the colour and type of flower are important. For example, in Italy, chrysanthemums are displayed mainly at funerals. In Brazil, purple flowers signify death.
- In France, it is appropriate to take flowers to a dinner host. However, chrysanthemums (primarily funeral flowers) or red roses (indicating romantic intent) should not be sent. Chocolates are also an acceptable gift for the French dinner host.

Flight Classifications

International flight classifications are the same as domestic air travel. Classes of flight are first class and economy, with business class available on most international flights. Weight and size restrictions for luggage may vary slightly from one airline to another. When travelling abroad, executives must arrive at the airport earlier than normal; most airlines suggest arriving two hours before the flight. This allows time for check-in, which is more involved than when travelling within Canada.

Passports

A **passport** is an official government document that certifies the identity and citizenship of an individual and grants the person permission to travel abroad. A passport is required in most countries outside Canada; check with a local travel agent to determine if the country being visited requires one. For many years the United States or Mexico did not require Canadians to present passports when entering or travelling within the country. Since the events of 9/11, however, border security has been tightened up. Passports are often being requested of citizens who are simply crossing the border for only a day or even a few hours. Even if a country does not explicitly require a passport, having one in your possession when you cross any border is a good idea, since it shows proof of citizenship.

Passport application forms can be obtained from a travel agency, a regional passport office, or any Canada Post outlet, or by downloading an online form from the Web. Since your local passport office is an agency of the Federal Department of Foreign Affairs and International Trade, you can find its telephone number by looking under "Passport Office" in the Blue Pages. While the Office prefers that you submit the application in person before an agent, applications may also be submitted by mail. In either case the items listed in Figure 15-3 must accompany the application.

Applications submitted in person will be processed within two weeks (ten working days); applications submitted by mail will be processed within four weeks (twenty working days). More information on the passport application process can be found at the Canadian Passport Office site, at www.ppt.gc.ca.

A passport is valid for five years from the date of issue. As soon the person to whom it is issued receives it, he or she should sign it to render it valid. Also, the information requested in the front pages, such as the address of the bearer and names to be contacted in case of an emergency, should be filled in. A traveller should always have the passport on his or her person while abroad; it should never, for example, be left in a hotel room.

■ Figure 15-3

INFORMATION NEEDED FOR OBTAINING A PASSPORT

- A completed application form signed by a **guarantor.**
- Proof of Canadian citizenship. For persons born in Canada this includes either a birth certificate (issued by the province or territory of birth) or a Certificate of Canadian Citizenship; for persons born outside Canada, either a Certificate of Canadian Citizenship, a Certificate of Naturalization, a Certificate of Retention of Canadian Citizenship, or a Certificate of Registration of Birth Abroad. Birth certificates are available from provin-

cial offices of the Registrar of Vital Statistics.
- Proof of identity through such documents as a provincial driver's licence or health care card, Old Age Certificate, or other federal identification card.
- Two identical passport photographs taken by a photographer within the past 12 months, signed on the back by the guarantor to signify that the photo is a true likeness of the applicant.
- Social insurance number.
- The applicable fee payment.

Visas

A **visa** is a document granted by a government abroad that permits a traveller to enter and travel within a particular country. It is usually in the form of a stamped notation on a passport indicating that the bearer may enter the country for a certain period. Some countries require the traveller to apply for and obtain a visa prior to the trip. Be sure to check with the consulate of the country in question sufficiently in advance of the executive's trip.

Currency

Before leaving Canada, the executive can exchange money from certain banks and currency exchange offices for the currency of the country being visited. The rate of exchange for various countries is published in the newspaper. If the executive prefers, he or she can exchange a small amount of money in Canada and exchange more money upon arrival at the country of destination. Any currency left over at the end of a trip can be exchanged back into Canadian currency. It is always a good idea to be aware of the exchange rates before travelling to another country and to pay attention to the rates once in the country. Exchange rates are not always the same; for example, the rate at a bank may be more favourable than at an airport.

The proliferation of **ATMs** (automatic teller machines) throughout the world has made the business of money exchange and obtaining funds while travelling much easier. Cash in the currency of the country is dispensed from the ATM. The exchange is automatically calculated and the traveller's account is debited in Canadian currency. Many companies establish accounts for travelling executives to utilize while travelling on business.

The **euro** became the standard currency of Belgium, Germany, Spain, France, Ireland, Italy, Luxembourg, the Netherlands, Austria, Portugal, and Finland on January 1, 1999. The seven notes and eight coins of this new currency have gradually displaced national currencies. A businessperson travelling between any of these countries will no longer have to worry about currency exchange.

Health Precautions

Before leaving for a country abroad, the executive should check with a physician concerning any medications or vaccinations needed. The environmental factors are usually different from those in Canada; and it is easy to develop some type of illness as a result of the food, water, or climate of the country. A physician can prescribe medications for stomach-related illnesses or colds. Also, vaccinations may be required before travelling to certain countries.

Travel agencies have information about possible health precautions. In some countries, you should not drink the water unless it has been boiled or purified. Another health precaution may be not to eat any type of raw fruit or vegetable unless it has been peeled.

Transportation Arrangements

Local arrangements within a country may include hotel, car, and rail accommodations. Hotel and rail arrangements should be made before arriving in a country. Car arrangements may be made after arriving.

Hotel Reservations

Hotel reservations can be made through travel agents or airlines at no additional cost. They may also be made online. The section "Online Reservations" later in this chapter gives additional information. Some hotels provide breakfast at no additional charge. If administrative assistance or a meeting room is needed at a hotel, a travel agent can arrange for these services; these arrangements can also be made directly with the hotel. However, making arrangements directly may be difficult, particularly if there is a language difference. When making hotel reservations, let the hotel reservations clerk know if the executive will arrive late. You simply ask the hotel to guarantee the room for late arrival; this procedure ensures that the hotel room is not released to someone else if the executive is arriving late in the evening.

Car Rental

Cars are readily available to rent. Travel agencies can arrange for car rentals before executives arrive in a country, or the executives can rent their cars after they have arrived. In most countries, a Canadian driver's licence is sufficient. You may obtain an International Driving Permit from a local CAA office. Travellers must have appropriate insurance. They should also familiarize themselves with the driving regulations of the country they are visiting. Conditions are often quite different from those in Canada. For example, the steering wheel may be mounted on a different side of the car or you may drive on the opposite side of the road.

Rail Transportation

Many countries have excellent rail service (particularly in Europe). Frequent service is relatively inexpensive. A traveller can get from one city in Europe to another in a relatively short period of time with a limited amount of inconvenience. The trains are generally clean, and the accommodations are comfortable. Underground rail and bus transportation is also convenient and an inexpensive way to travel. Answer the questions about international travel in Self-Check A.

Travel Arrangements

How travel arrangements are made depends on the company where you work. Many companies use one travel agency to schedule all travel. This agency becomes knowledgeable about the needs of the company, thereby providing the unique services the company requires. Other companies, particularly small ones, ask that individuals make their own travel arrangements. Whatever method the company uses, as an administrative professional, you will have a role in making travel arrangements.

Before an executive takes his or her first trip (whether that trip be by plane, car, or rail), talk with the person about travel preferences. If you are to be an effective agent, you must have the information listed in Figure 15-4 on page 305.

If an executive is travelling by air, you need to know

- The name of the preferred airline (if the executive has a preference) along with the frequent flyer number. A **frequent flyer program** is an incentive program offered by most airlines that provides a variety of awards after the accumulation of a certain number of mileage points. Awards may include upgrades from economy to first class and free airline tickets.
- Whether the flight is to be direct (if possible) or whether the executive is willing to change planes. Less expensive flights are sometime available if the executive is willing to change planes. The downside of changing planes is the hassle of getting from one flight to another and the increase in travel time.
- The class of flight—first class, business class, or economy. Company policy may dictate the class of flight that may be booked.
- Preference as to an aisle or window seat.

SELF-CHECK A ✔

Take a few minutes now to check your understanding of what you have learned about international travel. Respond to these questions.

1. What contributes to the increase in international travel?

_____

_____

_____

2. Where can you find information concerning customs and culture of a country an executive plans to visit?

_____

_____

_____

3. What are six general rules that apply to international travel?

_____

_____

_____

4. What is the relationship between jet lag and setting appointment times?

_____

_____

_____

5. How should business cards be handled when travelling abroad?

_____

_____

_____

Check your answers with those at the end of the chapter.

INFORMATION NEEDED FROM YOUR EMPLOYER ON TRIP PREFERENCES

- Dates and times of travel
- Cities to be visited
- Hotel preferences—price range, number of nights, single or double room, size of bed (full, queen, king), smoking or nonsmoking room
- Car rental preferences—type of car, size, make, model, number of days of usage, pickup and drop-off locations
- Reimbursement policies of the company— Is there a **per diem** rate (daily food allowance for which no receipts are required) or are receipts required for meals as well as other travel expenses?
- Arrangements for transportation to airport or train station
- Appointments to be made and where and when
- Materials—computer, business cards, and so on
- Who is in charge while the executive is away
- How correspondence and calls will be handled in the executive's absence
- The executive's credit card number or company account number for charging tickets, hotel, car rental, and so on

---

- Meal preferences. Low-calorie, low-cholesterol, salt-free, and other special meals are available upon request.
- The timeline for arriving at the airport. One hour prior to departure for domestic flights and two hours prior to departure for international flights was considered standard prior to the events of 9/11. The increased security at airports has resulted in an increased amount of time required for travellers to clear security prior to the departure of flights to all destinations, domestic or international.
- If you are making arrangements for more than one top-level executive to travel to the same location at the same time, company policy may

dictate that the executives fly on separate airlines. In case of a serious accident, both executives would not be lost to the company.

If an executive is travelling by rail, you need to have this information:

- Type of accommodations—coach or first-class
- Sleeping accommodations if the executive is going to be on the train for more than one day
- Ticket delivery (How will tickets be obtained? Are they to be picked up at the train station, mailed, or delivered?)

It is a good idea to set up a folder when the executive first tells you about an upcoming trip. Then you can put all notes and information relating to the trip in the folder. It is available for instant referral when needed.

Travel Agency Arrangements

Travel agencies perform complete travel services for a company; that is, they schedule flights, obtain tickets, make hotel reservations, arrange car rentals, and perform specialized services that the executives may need (such as obtaining workspace or meeting space at the destination). They also provide an itinerary, which lists flight numbers, departure and arrival times, hotel reservations, and car rentals. Figure 15-5 on page 306 shows an itinerary prepared by a travel agency. Also, travel agencies (through the use of computer software) can provide a list of all airlines leaving at the approximate time the executive wishes to travel and provide an analysis of fares. Travel agencies usually bill the company directly for tickets and other arrangements; travel agencies do not charge the business for their service. They receive commissions from airlines, hotels, and other service industries when services are sold.

Ask the travel agency to determine the least expensive flight available. Companies are cost-conscious; they want to keep travel costs as low as possible. Since airlines are so competitive today, reduced fares may be available on a particular airline. If that airline is not one the executive usually uses, ask if he or she is interested in getting a lower fare rate. Also, reduced rates are usually available for travelling over a weekend. However, the reduced rate has to be considered in light of the cost of additional hotel rooms and meals due to the longer stay. The reduced fare, considering other costs, may not prove to be cost-effective.

A TRAVEL AGENCY PREPARES AN ITINERARY

Prepared on 12/14/—11:20:26
Passenger: WOODS/PETER B 107548231 /WALLACE/DANIEL422825001

04 JAN SUN	12:15	**AIR** Air Canada flight no: AC144 class: Y no seat info. Calgary, AB(YYC) to Montreal Dorval, PQ(YUL) arrival: 18:12 Equipment: 320 flight duration: 3:57 NONSMOKING OPERATED BY AIR CANADA
	19:55	**AIR** Air Canada flight no: 7656 class: Y no seat info. Montreal Dorval, PQ(YUL) to Halifax, NS(YHZ) arrival: 22:25 Equipment: 142 flight duration: 2:30 NONSMOKING OPERATED BY AIR CANADA JAZZ
		CAR Pickup at Halifax International Airport drop off 06 JAN TUE National Car Rental type: LeSabre 4dr Car Auto A/C confirmation no: 96959103COUNT Rate guaranteed $38.80 per day, unlimited free miles
		HOTEL Cambridge Suites Hotel check out: 06 JAN TUE CAMBRIDGE SUITES HOTEL, NS 1583 BRUNSWICK ST. HALIFAX, NS B3J 3P5 Voice: 902 420 0555 Fax: 902 420 9379 or 1 800 565 1263 Confirmation no: 87312737 Room guaranteed to credit card Rate: $134.00 Rate guaranteed CHECK-OUT DATE: 06 JAN 1 ROOM(S) RESERVED—STUDIO—2 QUEENBEDS HOTEL GUARANTEED TO AMEX CANCEL BY 4PM TO AVOID BILLING NONSMOKING REQUESTED
05 JAN		**HOTEL** Cambridge Suites Hotel in MON Halifax, NS check out: 06 JAN TUE CAMBRIDGE SUITES HOTEL, NS 1583 BRUNSWICK ST. HALIFAX, NS B3J 3P5 Voice: 902 420 0555 Fax: 902 420 9379 or 1 800 565 1263 Confirmation no: 86002177 Room guaranteed to credit card Rate: $134.00 Rate guaranteed CHECK-OUT DATE: 06 JAN 1 ROOM(S) RESERVED—STUDIO 2 QUEEN BEDS HOTEL GUARANTEED TO AMEX CANCEL BY 4PM TO AVOID BILLING NONSMOKING REQUESTED
06 JAN		**AIR** Air Canada flight no: AC607 class: TUE 9:50 Y no seat info. Halifax, NS(YHZ) to Montreal Dorval, PQ(YUL) arrival: 11:10 Equipment: 319 flight duration: 2:30 NONSMOKING OPERATED BY AIR CANADA
	12:00	**AIR** Air Canada flight no: 107 class: Y no seat info. Montreal Dorval, PQ(YUL) to Calgary, AB(YYC) arrival: 14:13 Equipment: 320 flight duration: 4:13 NONSMOKING OPERATED BY AIR CANADA

Administrative Professional Arrangements

If you do not work with a travel agency, you have the responsibility of making the travel arrangements directly. You may choose to telephone the airlines, hotels, and car rental agencies. However, telephoning can be time consuming since airline and hotel lines are busy, and you often have to hold for an agent. Another method of making reservations is on the Web. Information is given about online reservations in the next section. Whatever method you use, you should compare prices. The travel industry is a competitive one. By taking the time to telephone several airlines and hotels or check several websites, you generally can save money.

Online Reservations

More and more people are using the Web to make airline reservations, book hotels, and reserve rental cars. Most airlines now state when you telephone to get reservation information that you may find a less expensive flight on their website. Some advantages of making travel arrangements online are listed in Figure 15-6.

Two major one-stop online travel-booking sites are www.expedia.ca and www.travelocity.ca. Both sites negotiate fares directly with major airlines and offer below-market deals to consumers. However, there are some disadvantages to special fares:

- They cannot be changed or upgraded.
- They are not valid for standby on other flights.
- No frequent flier miles are awarded.

Another one-stop site is www.flightcentre.ca, whose early success suggests it will do well in the travel market. All major airlines have a website as well. Web addresses for several one-stops and several airlines are given in Figure 15-7 on page 308.

Responsibilities Before the Trip

In addition to the duties in assisting the executive with travel arrangements, your responsibilities include:

- Preparing a complete itinerary
- Obtaining travel funds
- Preparing materials for the trip
- Checking the calendar
- Confirming appointments
- Understanding how matters are to be handled while the executive is away

Prepare the Itinerary

Once you have determined where and when the executive wants to travel and after you have made the appropriate travel arrangements, you need to prepare an itinerary. The **itinerary**, a detailed outline of the trip, is a record of all trip arrangements for you and the executive. An itinerary should include information on flight numbers, airports, departure and arrival times, hotel arrangements, car rental information, appointments, and any other pertinent information. You have already learned that a travel agency will provide an itinerary that includes flight, hotel, and car information. However, an agency does not have the information on

■ Figure 15-6

ADVANTAGES OF MAKING ONLINE TRAVEL ARRANGEMENTS

- Virtual travel agents are available any hour of the day or night and on weekends. There is no "holding" on the Internet.
- Fares of different airlines can be compared.
- Last-minute specials on airfare are given.
- Hotels and cars may be booked online.
- International travel advice and information is available on some sites, such as passport and visa information, political instability in foreign countries, health scares, and natural disasters.
- Frequent flyer bonus miles are available on some sites if tickets are purchased online.
- Weather information is given on some sites.

■ Figure 15-7

TRAVEL WEBSITE ADDRESSES

- www.travelocity.ca
- www.expedia.ca
- www.orbitz.com
- www.aircanada.ca
- www.airtransat.ca
- www.canadaairlines.ca
- www.westjet.ca
- www.alaskaair.com
- www.AA.com
- www.destina.ca

appointments and other special information. The executive needs an itinerary that reflects *all* the activities on the trip.

You will want to prepare multiple copies of the itinerary:

- One for the executive
- One for the executive's family
- One for the person who will be in charge while the executive is away
- One for your files

Figure 15-8 shows an itinerary prepared by the administrative professional. If the executive is travelling from one time zone to another, time zones should be included on it; otherwise, they are not necessary.

■ Figure 15-8

DETAILED ITINERARY PREPARED BY THE ADMINISTRATIVE PROFESSIONAL

Itinerary for Anthony Rezek

March 1–2, 2006

Trip to San Francisco

Monday, March 1 (Vancouver to San Francisco)

7:40 a.m.	Depart Vancouver—Vancouver International Airport.
	Air Canada Flight 531; tickets are in briefcase.
9:55 a.m.	Arrive San Francisco—San Francisco International Airport.
	Arrangements have been made for car at Hertz.
	Reservations guaranteed—Airport Hilton, telephone: 555-0145.
1:00 p.m.	Appointment with Colin Hlasny of Hlasny & Berkowitz in his office, 1214 Harwood Avenue, telephone: 555-0116.
	Correspondence file and driving instructions in briefcase.

Tuesday, March 2 (San Francisco)

10:00 a.m.	Appointment with Glenda Hall of San Francisco office.
	Reports in briefcase.
2:00 p.m.	Appointment with Joanne Sutherland of San Francisco office.
	Reports in briefcase.

Wednesday, March 3 (San Francisco to Vancouver)

10:55 a.m.	Depart San Francisco—San Francisco International Airport.
	Air Canada Flight 5111.
1:13 p.m.	Arrive Vancouver—Vancouver International Airport.

Obtain Travel Funds

Companies differ in how they handle funds for trips. Most of the time, airline tickets are charged directly to the company. Hotel, meals, and car rental may be charged on a credit card provided by the company. Another practice is for the individual to get a cash advance to cover all expenses of the trip. To do so, the individual fills out a travel form before leaving, indicating how much money he or she will need for lodging, meals, and so on. The company advances the money to the employee before he or she leaves on the trip. Another practice is for the executive to pay the expenses; he or she is then reimbursed by the company upon returning from the trip. Most company policies require employees to turn in a receipt for an expense above a certain amount.

If an executive is travelling abroad, he or she may wish to take a limited amount of money in traveller's cheques, which may be purchased from most local banks and travel agencies. Traveller's cheques come with two receipts, which serve as records of the cheques' serial numbers. One copy of the receipt should be kept in the files at the office and the other copy given to the executive. If cheques are lost, the individual gets reimbursed by producing the receipt. Therefore, the receipts should not be kept with the cheques. However, since credit cards are readily acceptable and ATMs are readily available in almost all international locations, it may be easier for the executive to use a credit card or, when he or she needs cash, an ATM.

Prepare and Organize Materials

Any number of items may be needed for a trip. If it is an international trip, items such as passports, medications, business cards, and small gifts may be necessary. Whether the trip is domestic or international, several items usually must be prepared, such as reports for meetings and presentation materials.

Here is a list of items that may be included in a briefcase:

- E-ticket or plane ticket
- Itinerary
- Credit cards, traveller's cheques
- Hotel confirmation
- Special materials, reports, or contracts for appointments
- Presentation notes
- Office equipment and supplies; for example, laptop and disks
- Reading materials
- Business cards
- Passport (for international trips)

Check the Calendar

Check your employer's electronic and desk calendars, along with your calendar, to see if any appointments have been scheduled for the period in which the executive will be gone. If so, find out if they are to be cancelled or if someone else in the company will handle them. Then notify the people involved. Also check other files, such as tickler files or pending files, to see if there are matters that should be handled before the executive leaves.

Confirm Trip Appointments

Write or call people the executive plans to see during the trip to confirm the appointments. It is wise to do this before preparing the itinerary. Get correct addresses and directions from the hotel to the location of all meetings. Make a note of these addresses and directions on the itinerary.

Know How Matters Are to Be Handled

Find out who will be in charge during your employer's absence. Check to see if your employer is expecting any important papers that should be forwarded. Be sure you understand how to handle all incoming mail. For example, your employer may want you to refer all mail that must be answered immediately to another executive within the office. Or your employer may ask that you answer the routine mail (signing the employer's name with your initials) and refer the non-routine mail to a designated executive.

Communication Tip

Prepare a folder for special materials that are to be taken on a trip. Label the folder appropriately, and place it in the executive's briefcase. Be certain you make copies of any information needed.

Your Role During the Executive's Absence

You may be tempted to tell yourself that you have worked hard in getting the executive ready for the trip so you deserve a little time off. However, such is not the case. There may be a more relaxed pace for you while the executive is away, but certain responsibilities are ongoing. Here are a few of them.

> **Communication Tip**
>
> Keep the person who is in charge while the executive is away apprised of all happenings. Just as you do not want your employer surprised, you also do not want the person in charge during your employer's absence to be surprised.

Handle Messages, Appointments, and Correspondence

Executives often call in to the office on a daily basis while they are away on trips. If possible, determine the time of day the executive may be calling so you can have all messages and items of importance ready to discuss with him or her. Always keep urgent messages and correspondence in a certain place on your desk so you can refer to them quickly.

While the executive is away, you may need to set up appointments for people who want to see him or her after the trip. Remember that the executive will probably already have a full day of work to handle on the first day back. Thus, it is not a good idea to schedule appointments for that day. If you must do so, however, remember to schedule as few appointments as possible and keep the timing convenient for the executive.

It is important that correspondence be handled. You may be responsible for seeing that all mail is given to the person in charge; you also may be required to assist the person in answering the mail. You may have the responsibility for answering routine correspondence. If so, keep a copy of the correspondence and response for your employer to review after she or he returns. So your employer will know of the visitors and telephone callers, you may wish to keep a log.

> **Communication Tip**
>
> Answer all correspondence and handle all visitors and telephone callers in a timely manner.

Make Decisions

You have the responsibility of making wise decisions within the scope of your responsibility during the executive's absence. You should know what matters to refer to someone else in the company and what matters to refer directly to the executive through an e-mail, a fax, or a telephone call. Certainly you do not want to put an excessive number of calls through to the executive while she or he is away, but there may be matters that the executive must be informed of immediately.

Use Time Wisely

The slower pace at the office while the executive is travelling gives you time to plan and organize your work. Perhaps you need to organize your desk, clean out the files, prepare new labels for folders, plan your work for the next two weeks, or catch up on your professional reading. While the executive is gone, you have the opportunity to do so. Use the time wisely.

Post-trip Activities

Briefing

When the executive returns, you must brief him or her on what occurred in the office during the trip, providing all necessary information. You should also inform the executive of the appointments you set up, the telephone calls and correspondence you received, and other items that require his or her attention.

Additionally, the executive may need to write several follow-up letters as a result of the trip. Thank-you letters are often sent. Information on products or services may need to be sent to customers. The executive may tell you what needs to be said and ask that you write or draft the correspondence. The executive may also need to answer correspondence that accumulated during his or her absence; he or she may ask that you do the answering.

Expense Reports

You may be handed several receipts (meals and incidental expenses) that need to be included on the expense report, in addition to flight and hotel expenses. The company provides expense forms, and, while the format of the forms will vary from company to company, they should be filled in correctly with the amounts totalled. Many organizations have a template created in a spreadsheet program. The form contains formulas that will automatically calculate the amount of money to be reimbursed to the traveller.

Figure 15-9 (on pages 312 and 313) illustrates the expense report used at CanAsian Airlines. It has been completed for Anthony Rezek's trip to San Francisco. The reverse side of the expense report provides those who travel on behalf of the company some guidelines for reimbursement of monies spent.

You should complete the report carefully, double-checking all figures and totals. You should also be sure that the necessary receipts are attached and that your figures match those on the receipts. Here are some tips for completing an expense report:

- Identify the employee, providing name, department, and address.
- Date the form.
- Enter expenses for each day, providing as much detail as possible:
  - Transportation costs
  - Meals with receipts
  - Per diem claim (no receipts required)
  - Charges for accommodation
  - Cost of company entertainment (lunch with a client)
- Total the column.
- Obtain signatures—the traveller and the authorized manager if necessary.
- Attach all relevant receipts. Double-check that the receipted values are correctly recorded on the form.
- Calculate the grand total.
- Deduct any monies advanced from the total.
- Calculate a net total.

■ Figure 15-9

EXPENSE REPORT

CanAsian Airlines
EXPENSE REPORT
(For reimbursement of employee expenditures)

Name:	Department:	Date:
Anthony Rezek	Marketing	5-Mar-06

Address:	2939 Dollarton Highway North Vancouver British Columbia	Postal Code: V7H 1B1

Purpose of Preapproved Travel (if applicable)

Meetings with architect regarding CanAsian space in San Francisco Airport

Date	Description*	Amount
Mon, Mar 1, 2004	Air fare	650.00
	Per diem	40.00
	Taxi to YVR	45.00
	Hotel	176.35
Tue, Mar 2, 2004	Breakfast	12.50
	Lunch — G. Hall	55.00
	Dinner	35.00
	Hotel	176.35
Wed, Mar 3, 2004	Car rental	92.30
	Taxi home	50.00
	Total	1332.50

Coding	Amount
	1332.50
Total	1332.50
Less: Advance	500.00
Balance	832.50

I certify the above is correct as detailed.

Anthony Rezek

Authorized Approval per Ref. Memo 1053

Admin. Approval per Ref. Memo 1053

M. Albertson

Date Received by Accounting

*Mileage (in km); Meals (B, L, or D); Hotel; Other.

■ Figure 15-9 *(continued)*

EXPENSE REPORT

Purpose of Preapproved Travel

Please state the purpose of the trip, and when and where the travel took place.

Mileage

For mileage claims the following standard distances are to be used (at the rate of $0.40/km):

Meals

For meals, either receipts must be provided, or the following per diem rates used when travelling:

Breakfast	$ 9.00
Lunch	$10.00
Dinner	$21.00
Total	$40.00

Hotel

Non-commercial lodging may be expensed without receipt at a rate of $50.00 per day. Commercial lodging expenses must have receipts attached.

Other Expenses

Receipts must be attached.

Soft Skills: Maintain a Positive Attitude

Sometimes when a manager is away and we are not sure how to handle something, we find ourselves thinking we cannot do the job. We may even become frustrated and negative about our abilities. Remember that soft skills have been stressed throughout this book. Why? From years of research, we know that people lose their jobs most often due to lack of "soft skills" rather than lack of knowledge or technological skills. We also know from research that one of the most significant differences between high and low achievers is their attitude. High achievers maintain a positive attitude. They believe they can perform their job well, make a difference on the job, and solve problems. Conversely, people with a negative attitude often believe they cannot perform their job well so they do not really try. Do not confuse a positive attitude with a **Pollyanna attitude** (a foolishly or blindly optimistic attitude). People who have a positive attitude do not see everything in life as wonderful. However, they do see ways to change a bad situation.

Think now about your attitude. Is it generally positive or generally negative? Answer the questions in Self-Check B on page 315.

Assuming you accept the importance of achieving and maintaining a positive attitude, answer the following questions:

- What is a positive attitude?
- How do you go about achieving and maintaining a positive attitude?

Attitude is defined as "a state of mind or feeling with regard to some matter or position." A positive attitude merely means that you believe in yourself; you believe that you have the power to make positive things happen in your life. Even though you might believe you have a positive attitude, consider these situations:

- Do you procrastinate in your coursework, putting off homework to the last minute and then doing a poor job?
- Do you engage in activities harmful to your health even though research shows the behaviour to be harmful?
- Are you extremely critical of everyone, including yourself?

If you answered yes to any of these questions, chances are your actions do not always reflect what you believe is a positive attitude. So how do you go about achieving and maintaining a positive attitude? Here are some suggestions:

- Practise visualization. Picture yourself in positive situations where you are achieving your goals and solving your problems.
- Listen to yourself talk. Do you often say "I don't think I can do that well" or "I know I won't be successful on that job"? Control your inner voice. Say to yourself silently or out loud "I didn't mean that. I know I can do the job well and be successful, and here is how I will be successful." Then think through the ways that will make you successful in the particular situation you are confronting.
- Remind yourself often of past successes.
- Surround yourself with positive people and ideas. Do not spend time with negative people. They can sap your energy and positive resolve.
- Keep trying to achieve whatever is important to you until you are successful.

SELF-CHECK B ✔

1. Do you think of yourself as successful in most situations?

   _____

   _____

   _____

   _____

2. Do you expect to do a good job?

   _____

   _____

   _____

   _____

3. Do you think about your failures often?

   _____

   _____

   _____

   _____

4. Are your best friends positive or negative people?

   _____

   _____

   _____

   _____

5. Now think of a time when you had a negative expectation of an action or event. Describe that expectation. Did it come true?

   _____

   _____

   _____

   _____

Chapter Summary

The summary will help you remember the important points covered in the chapter.

- There are three classes of flight—first class, business class, and economy.
- First-class accommodations are the most expensive and the most luxurious of the three classes, offering wider seats, more legroom, better food, better service, and complimentary alcoholic beverages.
- Business-class accommodations are slightly more expensive than economy and offer more spacious seating, complimentary alcoholic beverages, headsets, recliner seats, and more legroom.
- Economy-class accommodations provide complimentary soft drinks, fruit juice, tea, or coffee, and may provide snacks and meals. Seats are closer together and less service is provided. Economy class is least expensive.
- In addition to flying, the executive may travel by car or by rail. A local affiliate of the CAA can provide information for car travel, and the appropriate railroad can provide information about rail travel.
- When travelling internationally, the executive needs to be sensitive to different customs and cultures. The executive should take business cards printed with his or her name and the company name printed in both English and the language of the country being visited.
- Jet lag can be a factor in international travel; it should be considered when scheduling appointments.
- Small business gifts may be appropriate for business associates when travelling abroad.
- A passport is necessary when travelling internationally.
- A visa is a document granted by a government abroad that permits a traveller to enter and travel within a particular country.
- The euro has become the standard currency for Belgium, Germany, Spain, France, Ireland, Italy, Luxembourg, the Netherlands, Austria, Portugal, and Finland.
- Automatic teller machines dispense cash in the currency of the country being visited; exchange is calculated automatically and the account is debited in Canadian currency.

- Before leaving for an international trip, the executive should check with a physician or health authority about health problems that may occur due to the food, water, or climate of the country.
- Rail and bus transportation are other alternatives to renting a car.
- In helping the executive to schedule travel, the administrative professional must know the dates and times of travel, the cities to be visited, hotel preferences, car rental preferences, appointments to be scheduled, materials needed, and so on.
- If the executive is travelling by air, the administrative professional must know the name of the preferred airline, the class of flight, preferences as to an aisle or window seat, meal preferences, and so on.
- Arrangements for travel can be made through travel agencies or by the administrative professional using the Internet or calling the airline, hotel, and car rental agency directly.
- The administrative professional has several responsibilities before the trip, including purchasing the tickets, preparing an itinerary, obtaining travel funds, preparing materials for the trip, checking the calendar, confirming appointments, and understanding how matters are to be handled while the executive is away.
- While the executive is away, the administrative professional should handle messages, appointments, and correspondence; make the appropriate decisions; maintain a positive attitude; and use time wisely.
- When the executive returns, the administrative professional must bring the executive up to date on significant happenings while he or she was away and assist with any correspondence and reports that need to be prepared as a result of the trip.

Key Terms

The following terms were introduced in this chapter. The page on which the term was introduced is provided to help you locate the new term. Definitions are compiled in the Glossary at the end of the text.

- **first-class accommodations** 297
- **business-class accommodations** 297
- **economy-class accommodations** 297

- **jet lag** 301
- **passport** 302
- **guarantor** 302
- **visa** 303
- **ATMs** 303
- **euro** 303
- **frequent flyer program** 304
- **per diem** 305
- **itinerary** 307
- **Pollyanna attitude** 314
- **attitude** 314

Responses to Self-Check A

1. Contributions to the increase in international travel include the global economy; countries taking advantage of land, labour, and technical expertise available in all parts of the world; international markets; and technology.

2. You can find information concerning customs and cultures of other countries through consulates of the country to be visited, travel books, books about a particular country, the Web, and seminars and short courses offered at local colleges.

3. Six general rules that apply to international travel are (students may list any six of the following):
   - Learn the appropriate greeting for the country you will be visiting.
   - Learn how to say "please" and "thank you" in the language of the country.
   - Have business cards printed with your name and your company name in both English and the language of the country you are visiting.
   - Do not criticize the people or customs of the country. Show appreciation for the music, art, and culture of the country.
   - Remember that business generally is more formal in other countries than it is in Canada.
   - Dress appropriately; this generally means business suits for men and conservative dresses or suits for women. Also be well groomed.
   - Eat the food that is offered you; do not ask what you are being served; show appreciation to your host.
   - Be courteous and respectful at all times.

4. Since it generally takes the body about a day to adapt to the new environment for each time zone crossed, give the executive an extra day to recover from the trip before scheduling meetings.

5. Business cards should be given to all representatives of a company; the cards should be printed in English and in the language of the country being visited.

Discussion Items

These discussion items provide an opportunity to test your understanding of the chapter through written responses and/or discussion with your classmates and your instructor.

1. List and explain the three main classes of domestic flights.
2. List eight general rules that apply to travelling internationally.
3. What are some of the advantages of making travel arrangements online?
4. List four responsibilities of the administrative professional during trip preparation.
5. Explain why a positive attitude is important, and list five steps to achieving a positive attitude.

Critical-Thinking Activity

Numerous groups of Chinese administrators from the Beijing office of CanAsian visit the Calgary office. Mr. Albertson is often host for these groups. Mr. Albertson has asked you to visit China with Keri-An Mahar, who has recently been made vice-president of human resources, to learn more about the Chinese culture so you can be of greater assistance to him when he hosts these groups. You will be in the Beijing office for a week. In preparation for your trip, you do some reading about culture and talk with one of the administrative professionals (who was born in China) about the culture. You think you are fairly well prepared. However, during the trip, numerous situations occur that make you feel embarrassed about your lack of preparation. Here are a few of those situations:

- The Chinese officials always offer you their business cards. You notice immediately that the cards have their names, addresses, and so on, in Chinese on one side and English on the other. You do have business cards, but your name and pertinent information are only in English.
- Small gifts are given to you in each office but you have nothing to offer in return.

■ The Chinese officials take many photos of your visit; as you leave, they present both you and Ms. Mahar with photo albums.

■ Since the trip was a week in length, you took three bags with you. However, you were embarrassed as you went from the airport to the hotel because the Chinese host who met you insisted on carrying your bags.

■ In the first meeting that you had at the CanAsian office, you immediately extended your hand in greeting to each of the members of the Chinese group. Although they were very polite, you felt you had done something wrong.

■ In an effort to show your friendliness, you immediately made small talk with the Chinese. There was an interpreter present at all sessions. People were polite to you, but you knew you must have done something wrong.

■ The Chinese hosted you for all lunches and dinners. The tables were filled with food, but you were not familiar with many of the dishes; the food was very different from Chinese food you had eaten in Canada. You politely refused several of the dishes offered. You wonder whether you made an error.

Respond to the following questions. Before you do, read the information on the Student CD, SCDCTA-15. Additionally, discuss your answers with your classmates.

■ What errors did you make, and what should have been done?

■ What could you have done to prevent these errors?

Projects

Project 15-1 *(Objectives 1 and 2)*

Online Project

Mr. Albertson is visiting CanAsian's China office in Beijing from November 11 through November 16. Determine flight times and hotel arrangements by checking a website. The executive vice-president of the Beijing office, Pai Ying, will pick Mr. Albertson up at the airport. He will not need a car. He wants to leave the morning of Monday, November 11 and return the afternoon/evening of Saturday, November 16. He will fly first class and prefers low-calorie meals. He wants a nice hotel that includes a queen-size bed, a room for

nonsmokers, and exercise facilities. Mr. Albertson does not speak Chinese. His appointments while in China include the following:

November 14, 9 a.m., appointment with Chan Yi

November 14, 2 p.m., appointment with Sheng Mo

November 15, 10 a.m., appointment with Kuo Lu

November 15, 1 p.m., appointment with Niu Chih

You may want to use one of these Web addresses to determine the most appropriate flight times and hotel: www.travelocity.com, www.expedia.com, or www.orbitz. com. Prepare an itinerary, listing the appointments. Note the number of hours on the itinerary for travel time; also note the time difference from Calgary to China. Turn the itinerary in to your instructor.

Project 15-2 *(Objectives 3 and 5)*

While Mr. Albertson is in China, you ask one of your assistants, Luyin Wu, to sort the mail every day and the other assistant, Guy Beauchamp, to take care of telephone calls. You are devoting your time to a report that will take you several days to complete; you must have it finished by the time Mr. Albertson returns. Mr. Albertson calls in after being gone three days to see what important items may need his attention. You tell him there is nothing. However, after hanging up, you decide to check the mail and the telephone calls. You discover that he should have been informed of two calls and three letters. You thought you were clear in your instructions to both Luyin and Guy that they should call your attention to any important items. You are upset with them and call them in to voice your concerns. "I should have known you two would make a mess of the job." Both Luyin and Guy say they did not understand your instructions. You tell them you will take care of the mail and phone calls yourself. They are both concerned; Guy apologizes profusely and Luyin looks down and says nothing. The situation is tense in the office for the next few days.

Answer these questions:

■ How should you have handled the situation?

■ Did you demonstrate a positive attitude?

Once you have answered those questions, describe your role during Mr. Albertson's absence.

Project 15-3 *(Objective 4)*

On his return, Mr. Albertson gives you the receipts from his trip and asks you to complete the travel expense report for him. Use the expense form on the Student CD, file SCDP15-3, and enter the following data. You may print the form and fill in the items by hand or, if available, open the form in Excel and complete it on the computer.

- *Hotel rate (including continental breakfast).* $225.63 each night (November 12 to November 15)
- *Taxi charges.* To Calgary airport—$25.75; to hotel—$55; to appointments on November 14—$75.12; to appointments on November 15—$92.15; to Beijing Airport—$30.55; To home—$65
- *Meals.* November 13—lunch $25.25; dinner $65.84. November 14—lunch with Chan Yi $105.25; dinner $50.55. November 15—lunch $30.33; dinner with Niu Chih $225.66

Project 15-4 *(Objective 5)*
Add to your Professional Growth Plan by describing how you will continue to work on developing a positive attitude. File your plan on your Professional Growth Disk under "Progro15-4."

Case Solution for Part 3

Patsy Baader's Case Solution

Once I decided that I *could* arrange the plans for the meeting, I accepted the job and everything went smoothly. I booked a hall large enough for the group and arranged for catering. I organized a crew to set up the meeting place and to clean up after the event. A number of associates were travelling to the meeting from out of town, so I booked their accommodations and arranged transportation to and from the meeting location. For those associates travelling with small children, I organized child-minding services.

As a result of successfully organizing this meeting, I now have the responsibility of coordinating all company meetings. This experience also gave me the credentials to apply for a position as a meeting coordinator for another company. With my two jobs, I have never been happier. I am no longer under contract, since my employers have found me to be such a valuable employee; I have been made part of the full-time staff. I have found it challenging to keep two jobs and raise five children, but I have my goals, my ambitions, and a drive to succeed in office careers.

PART 4

YOUR CAREER: PLANNING FOR THE FUTURE

Chapter 16: Your Career Path

Chapter 17: Leadership

A Success Profile

Valerie Cochran, LLB
Vice-President, Human Resources
Capilano College
North Vancouver, British Columbia

When opportunity knocks, answer. This has been my motto since very young.

In high school I convinced the principal that I already knew how to cook and sew, being the oldest girl of five children, and managed to get excused from taking Home Economics in order to enrol in typing/shorthand and bookkeeping. When I graduated, I could type 100 words per minute, and had 140 words per minute in Pitman shorthand. My typing and shorthand skills allowed me to get a well-paying secretarial job at B.C. Hydro. I started in the typing pool, and was very quickly promoted to secretary in one of the divisions, with a substantial pay increase.

When I left Hydro, I travelled to London, England and started working with a temp agency. I was offered work with the director of personnel at a large conglomerate in Piccadilly Circus. I was to assist him in hiring and training clerical workers and junior managers. Although I had never done work like this before and was only 19 years old, I knew I was a quick study and accepted the position. I learned everything I could about best practices in personnel and training. I really loved the job and worked happily in London for seven years.

Once I returned to Canada, I registered at an employment agency. I was soon offered a position as a lawyer's assistant, and even though I had never worked in law before, I felt I could learn the job quickly. After working as a legal assistant for three years, I moved to another legal firm for a promotion to work as a paralegal. The keys to my success in the legal field were my ability to find answers to questions without having to delay the work or interrupt my boss, my anticipating the needs of the lawyers I was working with, and my sense of humour, which helped us through stressful days. Many times, I worked past midnight when my boss was immersed in a difficult trial. But I was learning so much that this did not bother me, and the overtime certainly helped with the mortgage!

There was very little in the way of training for legal support staff in those days, and so I began preparing precedent books and giving seminars for legal support staff. My first legal boss was appointed to a committee to design and implement a paralegal diploma program at a local community college. He asked that I join the committee, and the program was launched a year later. The college then asked me to teach some of the courses and, while I had never taught a college course before, I had done some training. Opportunity was knocking once again.

At the end of the first year, I was teaching full-time and had given up my paralegal position. As the program head I helped to design an expansion of the program and created continuing education courses for legal support staff in various areas of law. In order to keep up to date on legal matters, I went back to work in a law firm during vacation periods. It was at this time that one of the lawyers I worked with—who was also a friend, a professor of law at the university, and a wonderful mentor—convinced me to write the Law School Admission Test and go to law school. (She is now Chief Justice of the Supreme Court of Canada. Who could ask for a better mentor?)

I passed the LSAT and entered law school. After graduating, I did my articles, then worked with the Labour Relations Board for two years. I next practised labour law with a Vancouver law firm and continued to teach part-time at the college. When the college asked me to return full time, I agreed and taught law in the paralegal and business programs. I was eventually hired into my current position as vice-president of human resources.

The keys to my success have always been to work hard, recognize when opportunity was knocking, and know which opportunities would likely turn into personal successes. I don't ever think "This can't be done" but rather "In what ways *can* I get this done?" In addition, I never burn my bridges when moving from one job to the other. If I am not happy in my current job, I keep it to myself and concentrate on finding another position that will make me happier.

So always be aware of good opportunities, even if you are happy in your current job; and always leave a job with the employer feeling good about having had you and a bit sad that you are moving on.

Valerie Cochran's Case

I was working as a paralegal and assisting the senior litigation partner on an appeal to the Supreme Court of Canada. This was a difficult estate litigation case with little funding. When I mentioned that we needed to get 20 copies of the appeal books to our agent in Ottawa that week, the senior partner responded in frustration that he couldn't afford the copying charges for 20 copies, and that I should only send enough copies for the nine judges present. This breached the SCC rules, and I knew this would not be acceptable. I mentioned this, but he got very annoyed and yelled at me.

A few weeks later I got a call from our agent that we had been called upon for the next day. I contacted the senior partner to let him know, and he rushed into the office to ensure everything was ready for his court appearance. In reviewing our checklist, he noticed that we had only sent off nine copies of the appeal books to the Court. He became upset and said the Court would not be satisfied with so few copies, and that we needed to ask all the secretaries to start making the additional copies that were needed. He also insisted that I phone other law firms in the building and ask to use their photocopiers, since he had little time before he needed to leave for Ottawa.

What happened? How did this get resolved? Turn to the end of Chapter 17 to see how I managed this challenge.

Chapter 16

Your Career Path

LEARNING OBJECTIVES

1. Determine sources of job information.
2. Prepare a letter of application and a résumé.
3. Develop job interview skills.
4. Discover how to advance your professional career.
5. *Commit to living your values in the workplace.*

It is time to stop and reflect. You have almost completed this course. As you study the next two chapters, you need to think carefully about your skills and abilities, what you have learned in this course, and how you can most effectively use your knowledge and skills as you apply for a job and advance in your chosen profession.

First of all, consider the workplace you are entering or may already be in. It is probably not the workforce of your parents, and it is certainly not the workforce of your grandparents. In Chapter 1, you learned that the workforce is changing in these ways:

- More diverse than ever with more women, more older workers, and more cultural and ethnic diversity
- Increasing globalization of our economy, merger mania, downsizing, outsourcing, telework, and the constant growth of technology

You also learned that the Conference Board of Canada identified important skills that employers seek in new hires. The top ten skills listed by employers are as follows:

- Teamwork and interpersonal
- Information management
- Problem-solving/critical-thinking
- Time management
- Stress management
- Workload management
- Technology/computer
- Written and verbal communication
- Numeracy
- Leadership

Throughout this course, these and other soft skills have been identified as extremely important in the workplace: value clarification, self-management, ethical behaviours, decision making, positive attitudes, creativity, continual learning, conflict resolution, and anger and stress management.

As you reflect on both your hard skills (computer competency, English competency, and so on) and your soft skills, you need to analyze what all of this means for your career path. Where do you want your career path to go? What type of organization interests you? Where do you think your hard skills and soft skills will fit best? The days when an organization took care of its employees' career development are over. Your grandparents and possibly your parents may have worked for one organization all of their lives. However, it is highly unlikely you will work for one

As you reflect on your skills, ask yourself these questions.

- What are my strengths?
- What are my weaknesses?
- What have I achieved?
- What do I enjoy doing?
- Where do I want to be in five years? Ten years?
- Do I enjoy my work more when I am working with others?
- Do I enjoy working with people but also enjoy working independently?

organization your entire career. You will be responsible for your own growth and career path; sometimes changing jobs is a part of that growth. Ask yourself the questions posed in Self-Check A.

Now you are ready to begin thinking about what steps you must take to identify a job that fits your skills and interests, apply for that job, and succeed at that job.

Determine Sources of Job Information

One of the first things to do as you look for a job is to get all the information you can about available job opportunities. Information is available through:

- The Web
- Personal networks
- College placement offices
- Newspaper advertisements
- Public employment agencies
- Private employment agencies
- Temporary employment agencies
- Professional organizations
- Direct canvass

The Web

A variety of resources for job seekers are available on the Web, including tips for résumé and cover letter preparation and interviewing. You may also research companies in which you have an interest and actually post your résumé on the Web for employers' review. Here are several websites that provide helpful information:

- www.YourCareerWave.com. A self-assessment and personal growth program designed to help you identify and develop your employability skills
- www.jobbank.gc.ca. An electronic listing of jobs from across the country maintained by Human Resources and Development Canada
- www.monster.ca. Allows you to search for positions and post your résumé; also offers career advice and tips on preparing a résumé and interviewing
- www.careers.yahoo.ca. Allows you to post your résumé; recruiters can scan résumés without paying a fee
- www.yourmissinglink.com. Sends your résumé to human resources departments and provides a list of employers who receive it
- www.netjobs.com. Allows you to post your résumé and search for a job
- www.workopolis.ca. Allows you to post your résumé and search for positions in a variety of job categories; also offers advice on résumé writing, interviewing, and networking

You can also find sites aimed at a particular field by using a search engine such as www.google.com and keywords such as "jobs" and "administrative professional." By adding a geographic location to your keywords, you will limit the number of hits.

Personal Networks

Networking is defined as "the process of identifying and establishing a group of acquaintances, friends, and relatives who can assist you in the job search process." This approach is one of the best strategies for finding a job. In fact, some studies have shown that as many as 80 percent of jobs are obtained through some form of networking. Why? Consider this example. If someone in an organization tells you about a job vacancy, that person has some knowledge of your skills and abilities. Employing and training a new employee costs an organization a considerable amount of money, so the organization wants to hire the right person. When personnel directors hear about possible employees from respected employees, they are more confident of the applicants' abilities. Employers are not always able to tell from a résumé whether a person has the skills and abilities necessary for the job. Due to networking, an organization can hire an excellent employee with limited risk.

How do you go about networking? If you have a part-time job, let management know you are ready for a full-time position. If you take part in a co-op program, let the organization know you are interested in a

Corbis/Magma Photo

Networking is an excellent way to obtain job information. As many as 80 percent of jobs are obtained through some form of networking.

full-time job. Talk with friends in your community or church, or with associates in professional organizations to which you belong. You also might give them a copy of your résumé. A later section in this chapter deals with résumé preparation.

College Placement Offices

Many colleges maintain a placement office. Visit this office. Your school may not receive enough calls from employers to provide positions for all students, but counsellors are usually well informed about job opportunities in the community. They know the employers who need entry-level workers, and they can match a job to your qualifications and abilities.

Newspaper Advertisements

Employers and employment agencies list available positions in local newspapers. These ads describe the positions and the qualifications required and may provide information about the salaries offered.

Employment Agencies

There are two types of employment agencies: public and private. **Human Resources and Development Canada** is the national public employment agency. You can find their locations listed in the Blue Pages (the government section) of your telephone book. An advantage of using a public service is that it is free to the individual using the service. The federal government funds the agency.

Private employment agencies charge a fee for their services. Either you or the employing firm pay for these services. Most private agencies are paid by the organization hiring the employee. However, if you choose to use a private agency, you need to ask how the fee is paid. If you pay the fee, it is usually 5 to 10 percent of your first year's salary. Generally, you must sign a contract with private employment agencies. Information regarding how their fee is determined should be included in the contract. Read a contract carefully before signing it. When private employment agencies advertise jobs that are **fee-paid**, the employer pays the fee when the applicant is hired.

You should be prepared to take tests for private employment agencies. The types of tests include:

- Specific software packages, such as Microsoft Word, Excel, and PowerPoint
- Keyboarding speed and accuracy
- Grammar, punctuation, and proofreading skills
- Mathematical aptitude

Temporary Agencies

With the downsizing occurring today, many organizations hire temporary workers. These workers can be a cost-saving measure for a company, since fewer dollars are tied up in staffing and limited organizational perks are provided. Greater flexibility is another advantage for the organization, since there is no long-term commitment to the employees.

A **temporary agency** (one that offers temporary work) is not a source of job information in the usual sense. However, a temporary agency can help you know more about where you want to work. If you are not clear about the type or size of company you want to work for, you might try working for a temporary agency for a period of time. A temporary agency can place you in a number of different companies. Without any long-term commitment, you can gain an understanding of where you want to work as a full-time employee.

Some organizations also use temporary agencies to get first-hand knowledge of employees. For example, a business may hire an individual from a temporary agency, be extremely pleased with the employee's work, and offer the employee a full-time job.

Professional Organizations

If you are a member of a professional organization, check to see if it maintains a listing of jobs in your area. You should also ask individual members if they are aware of any openings.

Direct Canvass

If you are interested in obtaining a position with a certain company or in a particular type of business, the **direct canvass** or **cold canvass** (going directly to an organization without having an appointment or without knowing if a job is available) is sometimes successful. If you have a gift for selling yourself, you might find this approach beneficial. However, before you engage in the direct-canvass approach, find out as much as you can about the company. Never restrict your job search to walk-ins only. It can be time-consuming, and often has little likelihood of success.

Learn About the Organization

Once you have identified organizations with which you are interested in applying, spend time learning more about the organization—its mission and vision, its financial history, its reputation, the length of time it has been in business, and how it treats its employees. How do you do this? There are several ways:

- Ask friends, relatives, and acquaintances what they know about the organization.
- Check the organization's website for information. Many organizations have Web pages that provide the history of the organization, its philosophy, its strategic direction, and information about its products or services.
- Read periodicals, such as *Canadian Business*, which often profile some of the largest businesses in the country.
- Review an annual report of the company; most companies have their annual report available online.
- Consult your local chamber of commerce.
- Ask your college placement office for information.

When evaluating an organization, here are some questions to consider:

- What is the organization's service or product?
- Is the organization multinational? Does the organization have branches in other states?
- What has been the profit picture of the organization for the last several years?
- Is the organization financially secure?
- Is the organization growing?
- Does the organization have a good reputation in the community?

- Is there a good relationship between the employer and employees?
- Is the organization an equal opportunity employer?
- Are there opportunities for advancement?

Prepare a Résumé

The **résumé**, a concise statement of your background, education, skills, and experience, is an important part of your job application packet. Just as the letter of application is a sales letter, so is the résumé. It represents a very important product—you.

Chronological Résumé

A résumé may be **chronological** (listing the jobs you have had in reverse chronological order) or **functional** (highlighting and emphasizing skills) or a combination of the two. Figure 16-1 on page 327 illustrates the format and style of a typical résumé in chronological order. Notice that the education and experience are listed in date order, with the most recent education and experience first. Figure 16-2 on page 328 lists advantages and disadvantages of the chronological résumé.

Functional Résumé

The functional résumé allows you to concentrate on those skills and abilities that are more applicable to the job you are seeking. You cluster your education, experiences, and activities into categories that support your career goals. This type of approach is usually appropriate for the individual who has developed skills that are more relevant to the job than organizational names. It also works well if you have periods of time when you did not work; for example, you took a break from your career to have a child. It allows you to de-emphasize these gaps and emphasize your skill sets. A functional résumé is shown in Figure 16-3 on page 329. Other advantages and disadvantages of a functional résumé are shown in Figure 16-4 on page 330.

Combination-Style Résumé

The **combination-style** résumé allows you to present your experiences in reverse chronological skill set order. This style works best for the experienced worker who has held a number of different jobs. This style also works well when skills, titles, and organizational names

■ Figure 16-1

CHRONOLOGICAL RÉSUMÉ

COLETTE SOROS

2520 Boswell Avenue
North Vancouver, BC V7H 1L7

604-555-0113
e-mail: csoros@hotmail.com

CAREER OBJECTIVE
A position as an administrative assistant with the opportunity to use technology and human relations skills

COMPUTER SKILLS
Keyboarding at 90 wpm; proficient in Windows, Word, Excel, PowerPoint, Access, Internet research, and Web page design

EDUCATION
Capilano College, North Vancouver, BC, September 2003 to May 2005
Diploma in Administrative Systems

Courses studied: Business communications, organizational behaviour, management, accounting, English, psychology, administrative procedures, and computer software

EXPERIENCE
Intern, Admissions Department, Capilano College, September 2004 to May 2005
- Prepared spreadsheets using Excel
- Keyed correspondence using Word
- Prepared first draft of letters to students
- Filed correspondence on hard drive and disks
- Handled student inquiries
- Answered the telephone
- Assisted in designing schedule

Receptionist, Martin Paper Company, June 2003 to August 2004
- Greeted visitors
- Answered the telephone
- Keyed correspondence

HONOURS
- Dean's List
- Lieutenant Governor's Silver Medal

are equally impressive. It does not work well if you do not have numerous experiences that match a number of skills. Neither does it work well if you have multiple skills but a small number of different experiences (job titles or organizations for which you have worked).

ADVANTAGES AND DISADVANTAGES OF THE CHRONOLOGICAL RÉSUMÉ

ADVANTAGES

- Highlights titles and company names; advantageous when the names or titles are relevant or impressive
- Highlights consistent progress from one position to another
- Highlights length of time in each organization

DISADVANTAGES

- Readily shows gaps in work history
- Shows frequent changes of jobs
- Does not show most impressive or relevant work experience first if that is not the most recent

Résumé Sections

The sections of a résumé may vary; there is no one perfect model. How you set up your résumé depends on your situation and how you want to present your qualifications. However, certain parts are common to most résumés. The parts are discussed here.

Career Objective

This section lets the reader know what your present career goals are. For example:

Career Objective: A position as an administrative professional in a challenging business with opportunities to use my technology and human relations skills.

Notice that this objective did not specify a particular type of organization. If you are interested in a specialized field, you may note that in the objective. You also might list your long-term goal. In that case, your objective might be stated as follows:

Career Objective: A position as an administrative professional in a law firm, with a long-range goal of being a law office manager.

Relevant Skills

This section gives you a chance to identify your skill strengths. For example, you can list your computer skills, including the various software packages in which you are proficient and your keyboarding skill.

Education

In this section, list the schools you have attended and the qualifications you have obtained (if applicable). You might also list the courses or programs you have taken that pertain to the position.

Employment History

List the companies where you have worked, the dates of employment, and your duties. You may want to reverse the order of education and experience on your résumé. For example, if you have experience that directly relates to the job for which you are applying, you might list the experience first. Remember that the résumé is a sales piece. You want to call attention to your best selling features first.

Accomplishments

If you have participated in special activities, maintained memberships in professional organizations, or achieved honours, you may wish to list these. Such activities illustrate that you have many interests and leadership qualities. Employers are usually impressed with such characteristics. This involvement and recognition can provide an added advantage for you.

References

Do not list references on your résumé; the résumé is a place to highlight work experiences and skills. However,

FUNCTIONAL RÉSUMÉ

COLETTE SOROS

2520 Boswell Avenue
North Vancouver, BC V7H 1L7

604-555-0113
e-mail: csoros@hotmail.com

EDUCATION

Capilano College, Diploma in Administrative Systems, September 2003 to May 2005

SKILLS

- Computer—Windows, Word, Excel, PowerPoint, Access, Internet research, Web page design

- Keyboarding—90 wpm with high level of accuracy

- Human relations—handled student complaints, successfully worked in teams to produce products such as class schedules, answered the telephone

- Writing—drafted correspondence for supervisor's review; prepared final document

- Spreadsheet—prepared student enrolment numbers each semester; determined increases or decreases from previous semester

- Graphics—assisted in designing schedules, suggested graphics to be used

EXPERIENCE

- Intern, Admissions Department, Capilano College, September 2004 to May 2005

- Receptionist, Martin Paper Company, June 2003 to August 2004

HONOURS

- Dean's List
- Lieutenant Governor's Silver Medal

REFERENCES

Furnished upon request

■ Figure 16-4

ADVANTAGES AND DISADVANTAGES OF THE FUNCTIONAL RESUMÉ

ADVANTAGES

- Highlights skills
- De-emphasizes gaps between jobs
- Is more appropriate when changing career fields since skills are highlighted over positions held

DISADVANTAGES

- Is not a good style if skill areas are not relevant to targeted position
- Does not show advancement from one job to another
- Does not show organizations and titles held
- Is more difficult to review, since progression from one position to another is not apparent

you may choose to include a heading "References" under which appears the statement "References will be furnished on request." Both are acceptable choices; it is a matter of preference and style. On the résumé in Figure 16-1, notice that there is no reference section; in Figure 16-3 the section consists of the statement that they will be furnished upon request.

You need to think through your reference choices before sending out résumés or going on job interviews. Generally, if the employer is interested in hiring you, you will be asked to provide between three and five references. The most effective references are previous employers and instructors. Personal references are considered less effective. Do not use the names of close relatives or religious leaders (unless it is a church-related job).

Choose your references carefully. Select those individuals who know your qualifications well and will take the time to respond to a reference request. Before you list someone as a reference, obtain his or her permission. Once you have determined who your references will be, prepare a separate reference sheet, listing their names and professional titles, telephone numbers, and addresses. You then have your list of references available if you are asked for it during the job application process. It is important that you keep your list of references current. Contact them periodically, especially when changing jobs, your addresses, or your surname.

Personal Information

To a certain degree, a résumé reflects what is important in the changing business world. For example, prior to the antidiscrimination legislation of the 1960s and 1970s, almost all résumés included a section labelled "Personal Data." This section included such information as age, marital status, number of children, height, weight, and hobbies. Our laws now state that it is illegal to discriminate on the basis of national origin, ethnic group, sexual orientation, gender, creed, age, or race. Therefore, authorities recommend that personal items be left off the résumé. What the prospective employer needs to know is whether you have the qualifications for the job.

Résumé Length

If you are not an experienced job seeker, keep your résumé to one page. If you are an experienced job seeker, your résumé may be two pages due to your background and experience. However, generally a résumé should not be longer than two pages. Exceptions exist in certain fields, such as education, where research and publishing are important.

Electronic Résumé

Human resources departments and recruiters like job seekers are using technology extensively. A study done of 100 employers indicated that 85 percent of them accepted **electronic résumés** (statement of background and experiences submitted online via e-mail).[1] Other findings of this study reveal the following statistics:

- Seventy-seven percent of the employers accepted electronically submitted résumés for any position within their organization.
- Sixty-eight percent of the employers reported that they used an online résumé service to actively search for applicants.
- Seventy-eight percent of the employers indicated that electronically submitted thank-you and follow-up letters (to be discussed in a later section) were acceptable.

Many organizations have added sections to their home page that allow you to submit your résumé online. Computerized tracking systems are used to search for keywords in stored résumés. This helps to narrow the search to a few individuals. Not only do you need a traditional résumé with its bullets, bold headings, and different font styles, but you also need to prepare a version that can be submitted electronically to prospective employers.

There are two types of electronic résumés:

- Online via e-mail (the actual computer copy of your résumé in ASCII or .txt format)
- Converted hard copy (faxed or scanned documents)

When submitting your résumé and/or cover letter by e-mail, check with the employer to determine which format is preferred. You could submit your résumé as an attachment in Microsoft Word format or as text within the body of the e-mail. It is possible, however, that the employer will not open attachments due to the danger of a virus being present. If this is the case, use the job title in the subject line of the message and submit only one e-mail message that contains both your cover letter and résumé.

In the second method, your résumé is scanned into the computer as an image. OCR (optical character recognition) software reads the image and converts the contents to a text file (ASCII). If your résumé is not easy for the computer to scan, errors can be made at this stage. When preparing a résumé that is to be scanned into a computer or submitted online, follow these guidelines (remember, you are not creating a different résumé, merely altering the formatting):

- Use a basic, plain font (Times New Roman or Arial).
- Use a standard font size (12 points; avoid Times New Roman 10 points).
- Use all caps or bold for headings.
- Do not use italics, script, or underlining.
- Do not use abbreviations.
- Do not use bullets, as they may not translate properly when scanned.
- Do not use graphics, shading, boxes, lines, or columns.
- Make certain your name is the first item on your résumé. Put it at the top of each page on its own line.
- Use standard address format below your name on a separate line.
- List each telephone number on its own line. Include the area code if applicable.
- Use keywords. The computer is often programmed to pick up on certain words. Often these words will have been used in the advertisement. You should use them in your résumé. For example, an administrative assistant should list

specific software programs that he or she can use—Microsoft Word, Excel, PowerPoint, and so on. Since human relations skills are often part of the skills sought, use human relations as a keyword in your résumé.

- If printing, provide a high-quality laser printed original on standard-size paper—8-1/2 × 11 inches (216 × 279 mm), white only. Print on one side of the paper.
- Do not fold or staple.

All of these techniques will get your résumé into the company's system in the "cleanest" format possible. Then, artificial intelligence "reads" the text and extracts important information about you such as your name, address, phone number, work history, years of experience, education, and skills.

Write a Letter of Application

Once you are interested in an organization, your next step is to obtain an interview. The **letter of application** is the key to obtaining it. The letter is basically a sales letter, because it attempts to sell your abilities. Prepare it thoughtfully. Its appearance, format, arrangement, and content are extremely important in making a good impression.

The three basic goals of a letter of application are:

- To introduce yourself to the organization and arouse its interest in you.
- To present your most relevant selling points, including your skills and your background.
- To transmit your résumé and request an interview.

Introduce Yourself

In the opening, provide a brief statement of your qualifications. Let the person know you are interested in the organization and what you can do for them. Consider the following examples of effective beginnings:

Example 1

The position you have advertised sounds challenging. My diploma in Business Information Systems and my part-time experience as an administrative assistant while attending college have given me the skills necessary to perform the job well.

Example 2

Your employment announcement calls for an administrative assistant who is interested in learning the latest technology and has good computer skills. My training at Capilano College for the last two years has provided me with these skills.

In both cases, you let the prospective employer know you are interested in the position and you have the skills needed for the job.

Describe Your Abilities

The next paragraph of the letter should describe your abilities in more detail. It should also call attention to your enclosed résumé.

In May of this year, I will graduate from Capilano College. During my two years at Capilano, I have taken courses in administrative procedures, accounting, management, business communications, computer software, and organizational behaviour. I have strong computer skills and an excellent working knowledge of Microsoft Word, Excel, and PowerPoint. My résumé, detailing my school and work experience, is enclosed.

Request an Interview

Remember that the purpose of the letter is to get an interview. Therefore, you should ask directly for the interview.

Please give me an opportunity to discuss my qualifications with you. My telephone number is 416-555-0157.

A letter of application is shown in Figure 16-5 on page 333. Additional hints on writing a letter of application are given in Figure 16-6 on page 334. Carefully reading these hints will help you write effective application letters.

Fill Out the Employment Application

In some cases, you may be asked to fill out an **employment application** (a form used by organizations to obtain information about prospective employees). You may do this before or after being interviewed. In some organizations, all applicants fill out a form. Other firms ask only those people who are seriously

being considered for a position to fill out a form. Most organizations request that applicants print the information requested on the form.

If you are asked to do so, you should

- Read each question carefully before answering it.
- Avoid asking unnecessary questions of the individual who gave you the form.
- Take the time to print legibly.
- Spell correctly.
- Carry a pocket dictionary in case you need to look up a word.
- Fill in all blanks. If you have no response, print "NONE" or "NOT APPLICABLE."
- Have all the information with you that you need, such as your social insurance number, dates you attended schools, dates of employment, and complete addresses of previous employers and references.
- Be certain that the information you provide is consistent with what is in your résumé.
- Be careful not to spoil the form; you do not want to have to ask for another.
- A standard question included on the application is the reason for leaving your last position. State your reason in its most positive light. For example, if you were fired from your job, you might say, "My skills did not match those needed by the organization."
- Answer all questions truthfully. The final portion is usually a statement that the information you provided is accurate and that any misrepresentation is grounds for immediate dismissal. Some firms may discharge you, even after months of satisfactory work, if they discover you were untruthful on the application.
- Sign and date the form.

Human Relations Tip

Good human relations skills will help you get the job you want. Constantly practise these skills.

Prepare for the Interview

The interview will not be an ordeal if you adequately prepare for it. Knowing what to do and what to say helps eliminate a great deal of nervousness. In the interview, the employer will judge your appearance, personality, human relations skills, self-confidence, and other traits. The interviewer will question you about your experience and abilities, as identified in your letter of

LETTER OF APPLICATION

2520 Boswell Avenue
North Vancouver, BC V7H 1L7
May 21, 2005

Ms. Keri-An Mahar
Human Resources Department
CanAsian Airlines
2300–888 3rd Street SW
Calgary, AB T2P 4C4

Dear Ms. Mahar:

Your announcement for an administrative assistant posted on the Employment Opportunities
page of your website is most appealing to me. After reading the qualifications you are
seeking, I believe my skills and experience make me a strong candidate. My diploma
in Administrative Systems from Capilano College and my one year of work experience
have given me the skills and knowledge needed to perform the job well. I am interested
in working for CanAsian Airlines, and I am willing to work hard to demonstrate
my capabilities.

My courses included business communications, organizational behaviour, management,
accounting, English, psychology, administrative procedures, and computer software.
Additionally, I gained valuable, practical experience through an internship program where
I worked 20 hours a week in the Admissions Department of the college. I prepared spreadsheets
using Excel, keyed correspondence using Word, and handled student inquiries concerning
admission to the college. In addition to improving my computer skills, this experience also
helped me improve my communication skills. I learned how to deal with upset people, solving
their problems and calming them down. Prior to beginning college, I worked as a receptionist
for one year at Martin Paper Company.

My résumé, giving further details concerning my qualifications and experience, is enclosed.
May I have the opportunity to discuss my qualifications with you? I will call within a week
to check the status of my application. You may also reach me at 604-555-0113. Thank you for
your consideration.

Sincerely,

Colette Soros

Colette Soros

Enclosure

■ Figure 16-6

LETTER-WRITING HINTS

- Research the organization before writing your letter. One good source of information for most organizations is their Web page.
- Key the letter in proper form using an acceptable letter style.
- Print your letter on high-quality bond paper. Most office supply stores sell paper recommended for use in writing letters of application and résumés.
- Use correct spelling, punctuation, capitalization, and grammar. Always use the spell checker and grammar checker on your computer.
- Keep the letter short—one page. Put details in the résumé.
- Address the letter to a specific person. Never address an application letter "To Whom It May Concern." If you do not have a name, call the company or check with the place-

ment office, agency, or person who told you about the job.
- Send an original letter for each application. Do not send photocopies. Do not assume one letter will be appropriate for all organizations. Personalize each letter by reading and writing to the job notice published by the organization.
- Do not copy a letter of application from a book. Make your letter representative of your personality.
- Use three paragraphs—an opening paragraph in which you provide a brief statement of your interest and qualifications, a middle paragraph in which you describe your abilities in more detail, and a closing paragraph in which you request an interview.
- If you do not own a printer that produces quality work, have your cover letter and résumé professionally printed.

application and résumé. The interview is an opportunity for the prospective employer to get to know you and for you to get to know him or her. Although it may be a new experience for you, approach it with confidence.

If you have not had much experience in interviews, just for practice you might consider going to interviews for positions you do not think you are interested in. In fact, you may find you were wrong; the job may turn out to be of interest to you.

Portfolio Information

You may wish to prepare a portfolio of your work to take with you to the interview. A **portfolio** is a compilation of samples of your work. The work should be arranged attractively in a binder. Some possible items for inclusion are as follows:

- Letters you have written, which demonstrate your writing style and document formatting abilities
- Spreadsheets you have prepared
- Reports, including graphics
- PowerPoint slides

Preparing and presenting a portfolio during the job interview allows you to show what you can do rather than merely talk about it.

Location of Interview

Be sure you know the exact time and location of the interview. Do not rely on your memory. Write down the time, address, and person's name you are to see, and take it with you. When travelling to the interview location, allow time for unexpected delays. You do not want to be late. Excuses for being late will not change the poor impression it makes.

Number of Interviews

You may have more than one interview for a particular position. For example, a human resources professional may interview you first. Next, you may interview with your prospective supervisor. Finally, you may have a group interview with your prospective team members.

Team Interviews

A team interview may be with five or six people. Although this type of interview sounds intimidating, it need not be. Tips for a successful team interview are:

- Pay careful attention to the individuals' names as they are introduced.
- Remember to focus on each individual as the person asks a question.
- Listen carefully to the question, jot down a few notes to remind yourself of key points and answer it succinctly.
- When you ask a question, ask it of the group unless one person has said something about which you need more information.
- Make eye contact with all individuals if the question or statement is meant for the entire group.

The Virtual Interview

Occasionally organizations will conduct a **virtual interview** (an employee is interviewed via technology by an interviewer at a distant location). Here is how the virtual interview works.

Assume you are applying for a job in another city in Canada. Rather than flying to that city for the interview, you are interviewed in the city where you live. The company makes arrangements for you to go to a facility that has teleconferencing capabilities which links you electronically to a room in the other city.

If you are going to take part in a virtual interview, you need to be well prepared. When a camera is involved, most people get a little nervous. However,

your goal is to relax and treat the situation as if the person interviewing you were in the same room. Since the situation is unique, here are some suggestions:

- Greet the interviewer warmly and with a smile, just as you would in person. Repeat the interviewer's name. For example, say "I'm happy to meet you, Mr. VanDoss."
- Sit in the chair provided; sit back in the chair, not on the edge of your seat. Sitting on the edge of the chair can connote nervousness.
- Try to forget the camera is there; do not concentrate on it. Concentrate on the interviewer and the questions you are asked.
- Dress in colours that look good on you. Black or grey generally does not come across well on camera. Do not wear jewellery that jingles. The noise on camera is even more noticeable than in person.
- Pay attention to body language and small nuances of the interviewer. Do not spend an inordinate amount of time answering any one question. Be warm and informative but also be concise.
- Enunciate carefully. Poor enunciation is more pronounced on camera than in person.
- Once the interview is over, thank the person and leave the teleconferencing room.
- Keep in mind the hints for traditional interviews (given in the next section). Many of these also apply to the virtual interview.

Helpful Interview Hints

Observe these suggestions to help you make a good impression during the interview:

- Dress appropriately, which means dressing conservatively, even if you are applying for a position in a creative line of work, such as art and design. For both men and women, a suit is appropriate attire; wear a colour that looks good on you. Keep your jewellery to a minimum.
- If you wear an overcoat, hang it in the reception area. Do not take it into the office where you are being interviewed. You do not want to be burdened with numerous belongings.
- Be well groomed. Women may wish to have their hair done professionally the day before the interview; men should have an appropriate haircut.
- Get a good night's rest before the interview so you will be alert.
- Carry a briefcase. Women should try to do without a handbag—it's one less item to juggle.

You may be interviewed by a team.

Have an extra copy of your résumé in your briefcase in case the interviewer has misplaced the one you mailed. Have a pad and pen in your briefcase in case you need to take notes. Also have your list of references ready if you need to fill out an employment application.

- Greet the receptionist with a friendly smile, stating your name and the purpose of your visit.

> **Human Relations Tip**
>
> When you enter the office, do not forget to greet the receptionist or administrative professional with a smile and your name; thank the person as you leave. Such gestures indicate an interest in and a concern for others.

- Shake the interviewer's hand with a firm (but not tight) grip.
- Wait to sit down until invited to do so.
- Maintain appropriate eye contact.
- Try not to act nervous; avoid nervous gestures such as playing with your hair or jewellery.
- Display good humour and a ready smile.
- Show genuine interest in what the interviewer says, and be alert to all questions.
- Do not talk too much. Answer questions carefully.
- Be enthusiastic; demonstrate pride in your skills and abilities.
- Be positive. Do not criticize former employers, instructors, schools, or colleagues.
- Try to understand your prospective employer's needs, and describe how you can fill them.
- Be prepared to tell the interviewer something about yourself, a commonly asked question at the start of the interview.
- Express yourself clearly, with a well-modulated voice.
- Do not chew gum.
- Be prepared to ask questions. The interviewer will usually give you a chance at the end of the interview to do so. (Often-asked questions are given below.) Listen carefully to the answers to your questions.
- Be prepared to take tests. Expect to take tests pertaining to basic skills, such as keyboarding, spelling, math, proofreading, vocabulary, and reasoning ability. The law demands that any test given must relate to the job for which you are applying.
- At the close of the interview, attempt to determine what the next step will be. Will there be another interview? When can you expect to hear the results of the interview?
- Reiterate your interest in the job (that is, if you are still interested).
- Smile pleasantly and thank the interviewer for his or her time.
- Smile and thank the receptionist as you leave.

Questions the Interviewer Might Ask

Take a few minutes to read the questions in Figure 16-7 on page 337. Using Self-Check B on page 338, formulate answers to five of these questions. If you have concerns about the appropriateness of your answers, read the tips provided at the end of the chapter.

Questions You Might Ask

If given the opportunity by the interviewer, you might ask a couple of these questions:

- Could you describe the specific duties of the job?
- Could you tell me about the people with whom I will be working if I were accepted for the position?
- I read on your Web page that your organization has grown tremendously over the last few years. To what do you attribute this growth? Do you expect it to continue?
- Can you tell me about advancement opportunities in your organization?
- When will you make a decision about hiring?

What Not to Do in an Interview

Up to this point, you have been given suggestions about what to do during an interview. Here are some suggestions for what not to do:

- Avoid nervous gestures and movements, such as fidgeting, tugging at your clothes, and stroking your chin.
- Do not place personal belongings or your hands on the interviewer's desk.
- Do not argue. You are not participating in the interview to prove a point.
- Do not interrupt. Let the interviewer complete all questions or statements before you speak.
- Do not ask too many questions. Ask important questions only. If you ask when you can expect your first raise, when you might be promoted, or when you can expect a vacation, the interviewer may decide you are not interested in working.
- Do not tell jokes. Let the interviewer do that if he or she wishes.
- Do not comment on the furnishings of the interviewer's office.
- Do not brag. If the company hires you, you may have to live up to your boasts.

■ Figure 16-7

COMMONLY ASKED INTERVIEW QUESTIONS

QUESTIONS RELATING TO YOUR INTEREST IN THE COMPANY AND THE JOB

- How did you learn about this position?
- Are you familiar with our company?
- Why are you interested in our company?
- Why do you think you are qualified for the position?
- Why do you want this job?
- What is the ideal job for you?

QUESTIONS REGARDING YOUR ABILITY TO DO THE JOB

- What are your greatest strengths?
- What is your major weakness?
- Why should I hire you?
- If I talked to your former employer, what would the person say about you?
- What in your past job did you enjoy the most? Why?
- What in your last job did you enjoy the least? Why?
- If I talked with your former colleagues, what would they say about you?
- What can you tell me about yourself?

QUESTIONS REGARDING EDUCATION

- Why did you choose your major area of study?
- What was your academic average in school?
- What honours did you earn?
- In what extracurricular activities were you involved?
- Which courses did you like best? Least? Why?
- How have the classes you completed as part of your major helped you prepare for your career?

QUESTIONS REGARDING YOUR ABILITY TO FIT INTO THE ORGANIZATION

- If you disagreed with something your supervisor asked you to do, what would you do?

- What type of work atmosphere do you prefer?
- Is a sense of humour important at work? Why or why not?
- Tell me about a conflict you have had with someone. How did you handle that conflict?
- What is your definition of diversity?
- How do you handle pressure?
- How would your previous employers and co-workers describe you?

QUESTIONS REGARDING EXPERIENCE

- Have you ever been fired or asked to resign from a position?
- Why did you leave your previous job?
- Have you had any problems with previous supervisors?
- What are your greatest strengths?
- What do you not do well?
- Why should I hire you?
- What salary do you expect?

Note on salary: You should have an idea of an appropriate salary before going to an interview. You might check the job advertisements of your local newspaper for area salaries. Your placement office is another good source for local salary information.

You can ask the interviewer the starting rate for the company. If you are willing to accept that amount, merely respond that the rate is appropriate. If you think the starting salary is below average for that type of work, you can reply that you had hoped to start at a slightly higher salary but that you are interested in an opportunity to show what you can do and in taking advantage of opportunities for promotion (if this is true). If not, you can say you would not be interested given the salary offered. However, be certain before you respond that you are really not interested. Your chances of being offered a higher salary may not be good, and you may well lose out on a job offer.

Answer these frequently asked interview questions.

1. What can you tell me about yourself?

_____

_____

2. How would your previous employers and co-workers describe you?

_____

_____

3. How have the classes you completed as part of your major helped you prepare for your career?

_____

_____

_____

4. How would you describe your personality?

_____

_____

5. What skills do you possess that will help you excel in this position?

_____

_____

- Do not criticize. If you are hired, you will have ample time and opportunity to make constructive suggestions for improvement.
- Do not smoke. Most companies have no-smoking policies, and many people find smoking offensive.
- Do not chew gum.

Interview Follow-up

Promptly after the interview, write a **follow-up letter** thanking the employer for the interview and reviewing points of special interest. A sample follow-up letter is given in Figure 16-8 on page 339. Notice that it begins by thanking the interviewer.

> **Human Relations Tip**
>
> Know when to leave the interview. Take your cue from the interviewer. Do not take up his or her time with needless chatter once the interview is over.

A second follow-up letter may be advisable a week or two after the first one. Generally you should not risk annoying the employer; however, if you have heard nothing in regard to your application within a reasonable time, another, short letter is not out of place. The second letter should merely remind the employer of your having filed a letter of application and express a willingness to return for another interview if necessary.

Of course, after an interview, you may decide you are not interested in the position. In this case, you should promptly send a letter in which you express your appreciation for having been considered and explain why you do not want the position. Although you may not want the present position any longer, you might be interested in another position with the company later. If so, the courteous way you declined the first position may help you when being considered a second time. You want to keep all doors open if possible.

Succeed on the Job

Once you have successfully completed the interviewing process and have been hired, your task is to combine the skills and knowledge you have to perform the job well. Listen to what co-workers and supervisors tell you. Observe and learn what is expected and accepted in the office. Make sure you have a clear understanding of your job duties and how you will be evaluated. Most companies provide job descriptions that detail the responsibilities of particular jobs. If you are not given one, ask for it. If a job description does not exist, ask your supervisor to go over your duties with you.

Prepare Performance Appraisals

Usually, your job performance will be evaluated formally once or twice each year through **performance appraisals**. For the beginning employee, this appraisal may occur during the first three to six months and annually or semiannually thereafter. When you are first employed, you may be asked to establish short-range goals. If so, you will then be evaluated on whether you accomplished these goals. Your employer may also use a performance appraisal form, one that is the same for all employees in your classification within the company. Figure 16-9 on page 341 shows a portion of a performance appraisal form. Another method of

INTERVIEW THANK-YOU LETTER

2520 Boswell Avenue
North Vancouver, BC V7H 1L7
June 15, 2005

Ms. Keri-An Mahar
Human Resources Department
CanAsian Airlines
2300–888 3rd Street SW
Calgary, AB T2P 4C4

Dear Ms. Mahar:

Thank you for giving me the opportunity to interview for the administrative assistant
position that is open in the Human Resources Department. I appreciate the time you spent
with me, and I enjoyed learning more about CanAsian Airlines.

Because of my education and experience, I am confident I can be an asset to the
company. My skills in technology, communications, and human relations will help me
perform at a high level. The interview today reinforced my interest in joining your team;
I was extremely impressed with what I heard from you about CanAsian's philosophy
of management and the directions the company is taking. I welcome the chance to
become a part of the organization.

You may reach me at home by calling 604-555-0113 or by e-mail at csoros@hotmail.com.
Thank you again for your graciousness, and I look forward to hearing from you.

Sincerely,

Colette Soros

Colette Soros

Soft Skills: Live Your Values

In Chapter 5, you spent some time clarifying your values. Think back now to the values you identified as most important to you. In Project 5-4, you were asked to keep a list of your values. You may want to look back at that list now. Ask yourself this question: How can I live my values on the job I have now or on a future job? For example, assume you identified dependability as one of your values. How do you live that value on the job? You report to work on time. If your job requires eight hours of work each day, you work all of those eight hours. You do not spend an hour and a half for lunch every day when the organization allows an hour. You complete all projects in the time frame given you. If you know you will have

trouble completing a project on time, you immediately let your supervisor know your reservations. You establish a plan for getting the work done when it is needed.

Consider two more values you may have identified—cooperation and tolerance. How do you live cooperation at work? You cooperate with your supervisor and your co-workers. If an assignment requires overtime, you put in the hours graciously. You do not complain or look for excuses. How do you live tolerance at work? You do not judge other people. You listen openly to what they have to say. You do not evaluate people based on their gender, age, or ethnicity.

Think about your own values and how you will live them on the job by responding to Self-Check C.

SELF-CHECK C ✔

List three of your values. How will you daily live these values on a job? If you determine it is impossible to live your values, what steps will you take?

1. _____
   _____
   _____
   _____

2. _____
   _____
   _____

3. _____
   _____
   _____

evaluation may be a meeting with your supervisor in which your work performance is discussed and a formal written evaluation document is prepared, becoming part of your personnel file.

Whatever method of evaluation is used, you are usually evaluated on whether you

- Perform job assignments
- Maintain good working relationships with your employer and other employees

- Adhere to company policies regarding attendance, punctuality, sick leave, and so on
- Contribute to overall company goals

Remember, during your evaluation, your job performance is being evaluated. Be open to criticism and how you can perform better. Do not take the statements of the evaluator personally. Assume the evaluator is trying to help you improve, not hurt you. Figure 16-10 on page 342 offers some tips to help you during the evaluation process.

Advance on the Job

Advancing on the job may mean doing your present job more effectively and efficiently. Your first job, in all likelihood, will be at an entry level. You must learn your job well, work well with others, and learn new ways of doing your job better. Remain current on new equipment, software, and procedures related to your job. Increase your verbal, nonverbal, and written communication skills. Remember that you gain valuable work experience from whatever job you are assigned. Concentrate on doing each task of your job to the best of your ability.

Advancing on the job may also mean taking advantage of promotional opportunities that come your way. Remember that promotions usually come to those individuals who have performed well at their position in the company. Be ready for a promotion should the opportunity present itself. Learn as much as you can about other jobs in the company. Know how your present position fits into the organizational structure of the company. Stay informed about job openings in the company.

■ Figure 16-9

SAMPLE PERFORMANCE APPRAISAL FORM

CanAsian Airlines

PERFORMANCE APPRAISAL

Employee Name _____

Job Title _____

Supervisor _____

Assessment

4 Performance demonstrates consistent and important contributions that surpass defined expectations of the position.

3 Performance demonstrates attainment of the defined expectations of the position.

2 Performance has not reached a satisfactory level. Improvement is needed.

1 Performance demonstrates deficiencies that seriously interfere with the attainment of the defined expectations of the position.

Skills	Assessment
Organization	
Prioritizes tasks	
Plans steps to accomplish tasks	
Meets deadlines	
Attends to detail	
Communication	
Conveys ideas effectively	
Responds to ideas conveyed by others	
Demonstrates appropriate professional courtesy	
Demonstrates sensitivity to a diverse staff	
Problem-Solving Skills	
Demonstrates ability to identify problem	
Demonstrates ability to select best solution	
Follows through on chosen solution	
Takes action to prevent future problems	

■ **Figure 16-10**

EVALUATION TIPS

- Listen to what the evaluator is saying.
- Discuss the issues openly and honestly.
- Maintain a calm and professional demeanour.
- Provide the evaluator with important information relating to your performance, information the evaluator may not have.
- Maintain eye contact.
- Accept negative comments as a criticism of your performance, not of you as an individual.
- Resolve to correct your mistakes. Tell the evaluator you will do so.

- Discuss with your evaluator how you can improve your performance.
- If the evaluator is not clear about what direction you should take for the future, ask for clarification. You may want to write performance objectives.
- Accept praise with a smile and a thank-you. Let the evaluator know you will continue to work hard for the organization.

Leave a Job

You may decide to leave a job voluntarily, or you may be given no choice. Whatever your reasons for leaving (whether you are unhappy with a position and decide to leave on your own, you are looking for greater opportunities than you are being provided, or you are forced to leave for whatever reason), you must handle your departure professionally.

Human Relations Tip

Do not join the complainers in the organization. Remember that most complainers spend their time talking rather than doing. Be an action-oriented worker; do your job well and look for opportunities to grow and learn.

The Exit Interview

Most companies conduct an **exit interview** with the employee. A sample exit interview form is shown in Figure 16-11 on page 343. An impartial party (such as a staff member in the human resources department) generally conducts the interview. Your immediate supervisor is not involved.

This interview is not a time to get even, to make derogatory remarks about your supervisor, or to unduly criticize the company. Keep in mind the adage about not burning your bridges. If you are leaving on your own, you may wish to return some day. Regardless of your reason for leaving, you will probably need a reference from the company. Be honest but not vindictive in the exit interview. For example, if you are leaving for a

job that has greater opportunities for growth, say "I've decided to accept a position with greater responsibility."

You do not need to give all the reasons for your move.

A Layoff or Termination

You may have to face the situation of being laid off or fired. Assume first you are being laid off. The situation may be a downsizing of the company where other jobs are being eliminated in addition to your own. Keep in mind that you did not cause the situation. Even though the situation is difficult, the skills, abilities, and experience you gained from your job will help you to find another one. Remain positive and begin to think about what you want to do next.

Now assume you have been fired. Your feelings of fear, rejection, and insecurity are normal. However, it is no time to blame yourself. It is time to take a hard look at what skills you have. Listen to what your employer tells you about your performance. What can you learn for the future? What steps do you need to take to ensure that you do not find yourself in the same situation again? In what areas do you need to improve? Talk with family, friends, and your closest advisors. Realize that the job may not have been the best one for you. Commit to finding a job that will better match your skills and abilities.

■ **Figure 16-11**

EXIT INTERVIEW FORM

EXIT INTERVIEW/TERMINATION FORM

TO BE COMPLETED BY SUPERVISOR

Name _____   Social Insurance No. _____
         Last   First   M.

Job Title _____   Eligible for Rehire _____ Yes _____ No

Date of Hire _____ Termination Date _____   Comments _____

TO BE COMPLETED BY EMPLOYEE LEAVING				
	Satisfactory	Unsatisfactory	No Opinion	Comments
1. Workload/ responsibilities				
2. Working conditions				
3. Satisfaction received from work				
4. Attention to employee ideas				
5. Supervision				
6. Employer benefits				
7. Advancement opportunities				
8. Other				

Reason for Termination _____

Postemployment Plans _____

Additional Comments _____

_____ _____
Supervisor's Signature   Date

_____ _____
Employee's Signature   Date

Chapter Summary

The summary will help you remember the important points covered in the chapter.

- Sources of job information include the Internet, personal networks, college placement offices, newspaper advertisements, public employment agencies, private employment agencies, temporary employment agencies, professional organizations, and direct canvass.

- When you identify an organization with which you are interested in applying, learn as much as you can about the organization. Ask friends, relatives, and acquaintances about the organization, check out websites, read periodicals, obtain annual reports, consult the local chamber of commerce, and talk to college placement office personnel.

- The goals of a letter of application are to introduce you to the organization, describe your skills and background, and transmit your résumé and request an interview.

- The résumé is a concise statement of your background, education, skills, and experience. Résumé styles include chronological and functional or a combination of the two.

- You can post your résumé on the Web for review by prospective employers. You can also send your résumé over the Web directly to selected employers.

- Résumé sections include career objective, relevant skills, education, employment history, and accomplishments.

- Read an employment application form carefully before filling in each blank. Be truthful; state your background and experience accurately.

- The interview is extremely important. Most interviews are in person; however, you may be involved in a virtual interview. You must carefully prepare and present yourself to the best of your ability.

- Once the interview is over, send a follow-up letter thanking the employer for the interview and reviewing points of special interest.

- When you obtain a job, you must combine your skills and knowledge to perform well. You must listen to what co-workers and supervisors tell you, observe and learn what is expected and accepted in the office, and find out what your job duties are and how you will be evaluated.

- It is important that you live your values at work.

- Formal performance appraisals are usually done within three to six months after you begin work.

After that time, appraisals are done annually or semiannually. You are evaluated on whether you can perform job assignments; maintain good working relationships with your employer and other employees; adhere to company policies regarding attendance, punctuality, sick leave, and so on; and contribute to overall company goals.

- To advance on the job, you must do each task assigned to you extremely well; increase your verbal, nonverbal, and written communication skills; learn as much as you can about other jobs in the company; know how your present position fits into the organizational structure of the company; and stay informed about job openings in the company.

- If you decide to leave a job (either on your own or due to a layoff or termination), handle the situation professionally. Do not make negative comments about your supervisor, the job, or the company.

- If you are fired, remember that feelings of fear, rejection, and insecurity are normal. Take some time to analyze your skills. Listen to what your employer tells you about your performance. Learn from your mistakes.

Key Terms

The following terms were introduced in this chapter. The page on which the term was introduced is provided to help you locate the new term. Definitions are compiled in the Glossary at the end of the text.

Responses to Self-Check B

Here are suggested answers for Self-Check B.

1. Briefly talk about your education and job experiences. Do not spend more than a minute or two on your answer. Be concise; this question should not take up much time in the interview process.
2. Make several positive statements, such as "My previous employer would say I am a hard worker and I complete my tasks in a timely manner. My co-workers would say I am easy to work with and I care about them."
3. Briefly describe the computer courses you took and the software packages in which you are proficient. Talk about how your English and communication courses improved your writing skills and your ability to interact with others.
4. You might say you have an outgoing personality and you enjoy working with people.
5. You might mention your computer skills, writing skills, human relations skills, critical-thinking skills, and problem-solving skills.

Discussion Items

These discussion items provide an opportunity to test your understanding of the chapter through written responses and discussion with your classmates and your instructor.

1. List five sources of job information.
2. Explain what should be included in a résumé.
3. List ten helpful hints for making a good impression during the interview.
4. Explain the importance of living your values on a job.
5. What is the purpose of performance appraisals? What might you be evaluated on in a performance evaluation?

Critical-Thinking Activity

Arturo Herrera has just finished a two-year business course in college. He has done well in school. He is proficient in Microsoft Word, Excel, and PowerPoint. His math and English skills are good, and he works well with people. He has applied at five different companies for administrative assistant positions, but he has been turned down for all of them. Arturo knows he has the skills necessary to handle the jobs; he does not understand why he has not been hired. Here is what happened on his last job interview.

Arturo was ten minutes late for the interview. He left home in time to get to the interview, but he had trouble finding a parking place. When he went in, he told the receptionist he was sorry he was late but he could not find a parking place. Arturo was anxious over being ten minutes late, so he decided to have a cigarette while waiting for his interview. He did not see the no-smoking sign until after he had lit a cigarette. He did put out his cigarette immediately.

The first question the interviewer asked him was "Could you tell me a little about yourself?" Arturo thought he did a thorough job with the question. He spent ten minutes telling the interviewer about his life, starting from grade school. When the interviewer asked him if he had worked before, he said he had only had summer jobs. He told the interviewer he had recently been on four interviews and he believed the interviewers were unfair when they did not offer him the job.

What mistakes did Arturo make? How can he correct these mistakes in the future? How should he prepare for the next job interview?

Projects

Project 16-1 (Objective 1)

Online Project

Using the Web, identify three sources of job information; one site is to include jobs available for administrative assistants. Report your findings, including your sources, in a memorandum to your instructor. Include the information available on each website. List several administrative assistant job openings, including the city, province, company, and salary (if given). Use the memorandum form provided on the Student CD, file SCDP16-1 to report your findings to your instructor.

Project 16-2 (Objective 2)

Using one of the administrative assistant jobs you found in Project 16-1, apply for the position. Prepare a résumé and a letter of application. Use either a chronological or functional format, whichever best fits your background and experience. Save your résumé on a disk; label it RES16-2. Print out a copy. Then prepare that same résumé as an electronic résumé, making the necessary changes to fit the online format. Print out a copy of your electronic résumé. Submit your chronological or functional résumé, your electronic résumé, and your letter of application to your instructor.

Project 16-3 *(Objective 3)*

Collaborative Project

Work in teams of four on this project. Review the pages in your text on interviewing before beginning this task. Using the position you applied for in Project 16-2, assume you are going on an interview. Role-play that interview with your classmates with one of you being the employer, one being the interviewee, and the other two observing. When you have finished, the two observers are to critique your performance. Go through the steps again until each member of the team has played every role.

Project 16-4 *(Objective 4)*

Collaborative Project

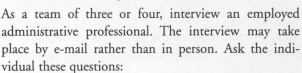

As a team of three or four, interview an employed administrative professional. The interview may take place by e-mail rather than in person. Ask the individual these questions:

- To what do you contribute your success in this position?
- What advancement opportunities are available in your company?
- What skills do you believe are necessary in order to be promoted?

Report your findings to the class.

Project 16-5 *(Objective 5)*

Before beginning this project, review the values you listed in Chapter 5 and saved on your Professional Growth Plan disk under "Progro5-4." Now list your major values and explain how you will commit to living those values in the workplace. Save the file as "Progro16-5."

Chapter 17

Leadership

LEARNING OBJECTIVES

1. Describe the characteristics of effective leaders.
2. Define the essential management responsibilities.
3. *Determine your own leadership values.*

As you assume positions of greater responsibility in the workplace, you may have one or more people reporting to you. Being an effective manager, one who is able to inspire people to produce at their maximum, means that you understand and apply basic leadership and management theory. Even if you do not become a manager or supervisor, you may have the opportunity to assume leadership roles in other areas. For example, you may assume these leadership roles:

- Leading teams within the workplace
- Serving as an officer in a professional organization
- Taking on responsible roles in civic and church organizations

Whatever form leadership takes, most of us find ourselves in leadership roles or have the opportunity to take on leadership roles at numerous times in our lives. By studying this chapter, you will understand some of the important aspects of leadership.

Leadership in the 21st Century

Throughout this course, you have learned that change will be constant in the 21st century due to technology, the multinational nature of organizations, a diverse population (with increased diversity expected in the future), and e-commerce. In addition, you have learned that we must consider ourselves part of a global community. Even if we wanted to think of North America in isolation, we cannot do so. Technology allows us to communicate on a worldwide basis, pulling together people of diverse backgrounds and cultures. Leadership in the 21st century demands two unique skills—skills that were not essential in the past but are imperative now. These skills are *change mastery* and an *international perspective*.

Change Mastery

The leader in the 21st century not only understands change but also embraces change, which is not easy. Change can be scary and even threatening to some people. The successful leader sees change as challenging but filled with opportunity. This kind of leader expects the future to be filled with shifting variables and understands that disruptions are an inevitable part of our changing world. The 21st-century leader is cognizant of these facts:

- Long-term results are more important than short-term results.
- Effectiveness, in addition to efficiency, is stressed.
- Strategic thinking is crucial.
- Actions to situations must be proactive rather than reactive.
- Organizations must be driven by plans rather than problems.

International Perspective

The organization of the 21st century will draw resources—financial, human, and technical—from all over the world. In order to be effective, the leader must understand and be able to function in an **interdependent** (mutually dependent on each other) world. This interdependent world is made possible by almost instantaneous communication available through e-mail, faxes, television, computers, the Web, and global transportation systems. The effective organization of the 21st century cannot think and act independently. Additionally, the effective organization not only is aware of the necessity of global interdependence but also cultivates that interdependency.

Characteristics of an Effective Leader

What are the characteristics of an effective leader in this global world of constant change? Here are a few important ones.

Understands Self

If leaders are to be effective, they must understand themselves (not just superficially, but deeply). We are all shaped by our background and experiences. Our families, our friends, the schools we attended, and society in general have told us how we should behave and what we should value. If we truly are to understand ourselves, however, we must at some point in our lives decide for ourselves what is important. How can we really know who we are? These ideas will help you:

- Understand that self-knowledge is a lifetime process. Just as the world changes, individuals change as a result of new experiences and new knowledge. If we are going to understand ourselves, we must commit to continuing the process through life. We must continue to explore our own potential, to reflect on our experiences, and to seek new challenges.
- Be willing to accept responsibility. Life is about accepting responsibility for our own actions. Have you ever known someone who never made a mistake, never made an error, never admitted to being wrong? Most

of us have had some experience with this type of individual. Unfortunately, this person usually has very little understanding of self. Knowing self means that we recognize our strengths and our weaknesses. We know what we can and cannot do. We know that all human beings make mistakes, and we are willing to admit when we make one. To make an error is not unique or even unforgivable. What is unforgivable, however, is to continue to make the same error and to refuse to learn from it. Knowing ourselves means that we accept our humanness, that we do make mistakes but we do not attempt to pass blame on to others.

Builds a Shared Vision

The ethical organization is visionary. The effective leader is able to build a shared vision of the organization with employees. Building this vision means employees at all levels of the organization must be involved. It means that leaders help employees consider these questions:

- What products or services does the organization produce? What should it produce?
- What values does the organization have? What values should it have?
- What contributions should the organization make to the community?
- What reputation does the organization have? What reputation should it have?
- Who are the clients and customers of the organization?
- How do people work together within the organization?
- Do the values of the individuals within the organization match the values of the organization?
- What contributions do individuals within the organization make to the community?

Effective leaders help employees understand the organization's vision and how their individual goals and objectives support that vision. Effective leaders publish the organization's vision statement so employees are aware of it. Additionally, a number of organizations today publish their value/vision statement on the Web to inform the general public about what is important to the organization.

> ### Communication Tip
>
> The time is always right to do what is right.— Martin Luther King.

Lives by a Set of Values

When we look back over history, we discover that values have been important topics of discussion among many leaders and philosophers. The writings and teachings of both Socrates and Plato asserted that virtue and ethical behaviour were associated with wisdom. After the rise of Christianity, Catholic theologians such as St. Augustine and St. Thomas Aquinas dominated ethical thinking. Correct behaviour in both personal and business dealings was necessary to achieve salvation and life after death.

Today ethical behaviour in business remains the accepted practice. The tough part becomes how that ethical behaviour is lived in the business organization. What practices are ethical? What practices are not ethical? Even though it can be difficult to determine what is and is not ethical in specific instances, few of us would disagree that our leaders must stand firmly on moral principles. Leaders must work within the organization to identify and define those principles and then ensure that they are carried out in the daily activities of the organization. When difficult decisions must be made, leaders must stand on their espoused values; they must *walk the talk*. Effective leaders understand this principle. They understand that establishing and living a set of values must begin with the top leaders and that living the organizational values must permeate every level of the organization.

Commits to Service

Effective leaders consider service to others as primary. In other words, effective leaders are not concerned first with building a career for themselves, but in understanding how they can serve the organization and its employees as well as the external community. For example, a leader's values may include a commitment to helping people grow, a commitment to diversity, and a commitment to helping the world become a better place. Figure 17-1 provides Home Depot's statement about its commitment to the community.

Empowers Others

Power is defined as "the ability or official capacity to exercise control; authority." Because the prefix *em* means "to put on to" or "to cover with," **empowering** means the passing on of authority or responsibility.

Leaders empower people when they

- Provide employees with access to information that will help them increase their productivity and effectiveness

The effective leader has a commitment to the community.

- Allow employees to take on more responsibility
- Allow employees a voice in decision making

Empowered employees feel a sense of ownership and control over their jobs. They understand they are responsible for getting their jobs done. Empowered employees usually are happier; they trust the organization, feel a part of it, and enjoy the rewards the job provides.

■ **Figure 17-1**

ABOUT HOME DEPOT CANADA

Home Depot, the world's largest home improvement retailer, currently operates in seven Canadian provinces (Alberta, British Columbia, Manitoba, Nova Scotia, Ontario, Québec, and Saskatchewan), 49 U.S. states, Puerto Rico and Mexico. Home Depot employs over 18,000 people in Canada.

Home Depot is a leader in employee development and volunteerism. The Retail Council of Canada recently recognized Home Depot's leadership in this area with an award for Excellence in Employee Development at the Retail Council of Canada's 2002 Excellence in Retailing Awards.

Home Depot's corporate culture believes in giving back to the communities it serves. Team Depot, an organized volunteer force, was developed in 1992 to allow associates to contribute to the communities where they work and live.

Source: "About Us," Home Depot site, www.homedepot.ca, accessed July 26, 2004.

The leader who empowers people has a core belief in people, believing that people are basically good, honest, and well intentioned. The leader believes that people will do the right thing when they have the resources available to accomplish a task. The leader understands that leadership is operating from a central core of values, even in the most difficult situations.

Rewards Risk-Taking

The organization of the 21st century, with change as a constant, will face risks daily. Ignoring the risks does not make them go away. The organization cannot take refuge in status quo, conformity to the norm, or security in the past. None of these stances make sense if the organization is to be successful. The organization must be willing to seek new answers to problems, try new approaches, and be flexible. If the organization is to be successful, it must have leaders who not only take risks themselves but also encourage others to take risks. Wise leaders who take risks demonstrate a number of characteristics, some of which are listed in Figure 17-2.

Here are some keys to successful risk-taking:

> **Communication Tip**
>
> Develop a risk-taker award to be given to employees who take risks.

■ Figure 17-2

CHARACTERISTICS OF LEADERS WHO TAKE RISKS

Wise leaders who take risks engage in the following behaviours:

- Gather information wisely
- Risk from strength
- Prepare thoroughly
- Display flexibility
- Envision what can be gained
- Understand what is at stake
- Stay on mission
- Possess the right motives
- Give their followers wins
- March forward with confidence

Source: John C. Maxwell, *The Right to Lead* (Nashville: Thomas Nelson, Inc., 2001), p. 66.

- *Trust your own abilities.* Do not put limits on your ability to learn and improve. As a small child you did not doubt yourself because you could not read, knowing you would soon learn that skill in school. Therefore, you should not doubt your ability to learn and try new things when you are 30, 50, or even 70.

- *Be open-minded.* Our assumptions can prevent us from seeing new possibilities. When analyzing situations that need solving, we need to discard our old assumptions. Where would we be today if Columbus and his colleagues had believed the world was flat, as did almost everyone in the world at that time? Where would we be today if Wilbur and Orville Wright had not believed they could build a flying machine?

- *Develop your intuitive powers.* Subconsciously we take note of many things our conscious mind does not realize. However, these subconscious thoughts can be brought to the surface of our consciousness if we listen carefully to ourselves (our intuition).

- *Overcome the fear of making mistakes.* Certainly when trying something new, you make mistakes. What you need to consider when taking risks is the likelihood of success. For example, you would not jump off a ten-storey building thinking you would live through it. That would be a foolish and senseless risk. Most people know intuitively when a risk makes sense and when it does not. Sam Walton, in building Wal-Mart, went through many failures and difficult times. Yet his vision was so clear and his understanding of what would yield success so deep that he endured the risks and temporary failures to achieve his dream.

- *Develop a support team.* Supportive colleagues can help you analyze a situation when you believe you have made a mistake. They can look at the situation more objectively than you can; they can help you determine what to do next. When your colleagues make mistakes, you can return that objectivity and support by helping them analyze their situations.

The task of the effective manager is to build an environment that supports risk-taking. Employees need to know they will not be punished for taking appropriate risks. They need to know that the organization will support their risk-taking ventures and reward their successes.

Moves Through Chaos

The effective leader learns from the chaos in the world and, in fact, is often shaped by the chaos. In this case, *shaping* means that the leader learns from both the good and bad experiences that happen during times of chaos. You have already learned that when you take risks, you often make mistakes. Mistakes are an inevitable outcome of continued risk-taking. The effective leader takes these mistakes, learns from them, and builds on the lessons learned from failure so success will be more likely the next time. For example, many highly successful people have been fired from jobs but they do not let that fact keep them from being successful in their next venture. They learn what they can from the experience, discard what is not meaningful, and continue to try to make a difference in the world. In other words, they are driven by their own inner beliefs.

Chaos is an inevitable part of being a leader in the 21st century. The successful leader accepts this inevitability. The successful leader practises the art of meeting individuals and situations where they are and moving them forward to bring about the desired outcomes.

Knows How to Follow

The effective leader knows the importance of stepping back and being a follower when the situation demands it. This person understands that leaders are sometimes followers and followers are sometimes leaders. A **bilateralness** (affecting two sides equally) exists, with the leader not only understanding the importance of following but also having the trust in others to know that they, given the proper opportunities and training, can be leaders too.

SELF-CHECK ✔

Stop for a few minutes, and consider the characteristics of an effective leader you believe you already possess. Now list the characteristics you would like to work on during the remainder of this course.

_____

_____

_____

_____

The men and women who lead at the highest level are extraordinary. They have many extraordinary characteristics, and they continue to develop these characteristics throughout their lives. Figure 17-3 lists some additional characteristics of these leaders. Refer to Self-Check on this page.

Leadership and Management Contrasted

Leadership is doing the right thing, while **management** is doing things right. The effective leader operates around a clearly defined set of values, with those values centring on what is right for an organization and its employees. Effective leadership relies on the leader bringing the appropriate set of values to the work environment. There is no real way to assess the values of the leader in isolation. They become apparent only as the leader guides an organization to accomplish its goals, which benefit not only the organization but also the external community and the individuals within the organization. The importance of leadership cannot be diminished, and the numerous books written on the subject attest to the fact that true leadership is to be valued and respected.

■ **Figure 17-3**

CHARACTERISTICS OF UNCOMMON LEADERS

The men and women who lead at the highest level have these traits.

- *Futurists.* Their dreams are bigger than their memories.
- *Catalysts.* They initiate movement and momentum for others.
- *Optimists.* They believe in their cause and their people beyond reason.
- *Activists.* They are doers and empower others by their actions.
- *Strategists.* They plan how to use every resource available to be successful.
- *Pragmatists.* Their legacy is that they solve the practical problems people face.

Source: John C. Maxwell, *The Right to Lead* (Nashville: Thomas Nelson, Inc., 2001), p. 22.

By contrast, management can be considered a subset of leadership. The functions of management include planning, organizing, recruiting, training, controlling, and evaluating. These activities are relatively concrete and can be quantified, measured, and assessed. If an organization is to be successful, these functions must be understood and carried out effectively. Although the characteristics of effective leaders and the responsibilities of effective managers are presented separately here, understand that the most effective managers are also effective leaders. Conversely, effective leaders are also effective managers.

Management Responsibilities

If you are to be successful in a supervisory role, you need to understand how to effectively perform the basic management responsibilities, including planning, organizing, recruiting and employing, training, motivating, delegating, and evaluating. These functions are presented here.

Plan

Planning is a crucial function of management. Without proper planning, an organization and its employees do not know where they are going. A major part of the planning process is setting goals and objectives. Although all organizations have goals and objectives, they may be very loosely defined or not defined at all. Defining them in writing and establishing measurable results is a process that was recommended by Peter F. Drucker in a seminal work entitled *The Practice of Management*. Drucker set forth the process that came to be known as **MBO** (management by objectives).[1] Although it has taken on numerous forms and variations, it is still used today; MBO is implemented through the planning process described here.

The planning process in which goals and objectives are set is usually done for a one-year period, which is called **tactical planning**, and for a three-to-five-year period, which is called **long-range planning**. Many times the overall goals of a company are set by top-level administrators—that is, the board of directors, the president, and the executive vice-presidents. Once these goals have been determined, they are distributed to the managers in the organization. Then the managers set objectives for their work units. In most organizations today, managers also involve their work groups in setting objectives. Managers are held responsible by upper administration for achieving the objectives defined. In some organizations, bonuses are awarded on the basis of the accomplishment of objectives.

Think about what your role in the planning process might be as an administrative professional supervising support staff. You may help set the objectives for your department or division. However, even if you do not, you will engage in planning the activities of your unit, which includes setting objectives. The employees who report to you must know what they are expected to produce. You should have a planning session at least once a year, preferably every six months, to look at what your unit should be accomplishing for the year. During this planning session, you and your employees determine what objectives should be accomplished, when they should be accomplished, the costs of accomplishing them, and how they will be measured. For example, assume that one of your objectives is to revise the document management system within your division. The objective might be written as follows:

> *Revise the document management system from a manual system to an electronic system by April 15. After two months of use, users will evaluate the system. The cost of the revision is in software, approximately $3000.*

Organize

Once the planning has been done, the work must be organized. Organization involves bringing together all resources—people, time, money, and equipment—in the most effective way to accomplish the goals. The three factors that affect how the work is organized are span of control, job analysis, and work periods.

Span of Control

Span of control refers to the number of employees directly supervised by one person. No formula rigidly defines the span of control; the number is determined more by the philosophy of management. Organizations are flatter today than in the past, with fewer levels of hierarchy. A flattened organizational structure usually means a greater span of control for supervisors. For example, rather than supervising five individuals, a manager may supervise as many as thirty. Here are some questions that need to be asked when considering span of control:

- Is the organization committed to a hierarchical or a flattened structure?
- Is the manager highly skilled and experienced? Does the manager have the skills needed to assume the responsibilities of an expanded reporting structure?

- Are the work-group members highly skilled and knowledgeable?
- Is the work the group is performing similar in nature?
- Is the work group given a great degree of autonomy? Is the work group allowed to make decisions without checking with the supervisor?

Job Analysis

A second factor in the organization of work is job analysis. To perform a job analysis, a supervisor must determine the requirements of a job and the qualifications needed by personnel to get the job done. Once this information is determined, it is usually compiled into a job description, such as the one in Figure 17-4. The job description includes skills, training, and education necessary for the job and a list of the job duties. Most companies have job descriptions for all employees, which are helpful not only in the hiring process but also in letting employees know what they are expected to do.

Work Periods

A third factor to consider in organizing work is the time in which the work is to be performed. The workweek is traditionally from 8 a.m. or 9 a.m. to 5 p.m., five days per week. However, factors such as flextime, nine-day fortnight, four-day weeks, job sharing, and telework make the workweek different from that of the past.

Recruit and Employ

Organizations usually establish procedures through their human resources departments that outline how they will recruit employees. There are certain legal considerations. For example, when placing advertisements, companies must ensure that the wording of the advertisement does not conflict with fair employment practices laws. Antidiscrimination legislation prohibits advertisements that show preferences in terms of race, religion, gender, age, or physical disabilities. An employer cannot advertise for a particular age group. Thus, expressions such as *young person* or *retired person*

■ Figure 17-4

JOB DESCRIPTION

Job Title: Administrative Assistant
Company: CanAsian Airlines
Reports to: Martin Albertson

SKILLS AND TRAINING

The position of Administrative Assistant requires excellent organizational and human relations skills. The ability to establish priorities on projects and to supervise administrative support staff is required. Excellent verbal and written communication skills are necessary.

Basic skills include computer (word processing, spreadsheet, and presentation software), document management, grammar and composition, and accurate keyboarding at 70 wpm.

EDUCATION AND EXPERIENCE

Four years of experience in an administrative professional role; a two-year postsecondary business studies diploma.

DUTIES

- Composing letters, e-mails, and reports
- Keying correspondence and reports
- Maintaining an electronic document management system
- Planning meetings and conferences
- Handling requests from the external community
- Supervising administrative support staff

cannot be used in advertisements. If you are recruiting employees, check with the appropriate individuals within your company to make sure you are observing the company rules and legal guidelines.

Once applicants are recruited, three major tools are used for screening and selection:

- Written applications
- Personal interviews
- Testing procedures

The manager or a team of people may review the applications. If you are part of that team, when reviewing the applications, you should be very clear about the knowledge, skills, abilities, education, and experience you are seeking. These questions will help:

- What type of person are we seeking?
- What qualifications does that person need to have?
- What education and experience does the person need?

With your criteria in mind, screen the applications and select the most qualified individuals to interview.

You may choose to conduct one-on-one interviews, team interviews, or a combination of the two. Before the interviewing process begins, compile a list of questions to ask of each candidate. Such a list keeps you and the team on target as you begin the interviewing process and helps you treat all interviewees with fairness and consistency. Additionally, the list helps remind you that certain questions are not legal. The following questions are unlawful to ask during the interview:

- Are you married? Single? Divorced? Separated?
- What is the date of your birth?
- Where were you born?
- Is your spouse a Canadian citizen?
- To what clubs do you belong?
- What are the ages of your children?
- What church do you attend?

You must keep up with the latest laws concerning discrimination and interviewing procedures. Otherwise, you may inadvertently put your company in jeopardy of a discrimination suit.

Set aside enough time for a thorough interview. You will probably need to spend an hour or more with each applicant. Do not consider this time wasted. Hiring the right person for a job is one of the most important things you will do as a manager.

The third screening tool is the test. Here, too, legal considerations are important. The use of tests in selecting administrative professionals is not prohibited, but testing practices that have discriminatory effects are. Keep in mind that the test must measure the person's qualifications for the job, not the person as an individual. If you are employing an administrative professional, for example, and a requirement of the job is that the person be able to key at a certain rate with an established degree of accuracy, you can give the person a keyboarding test. You can also give an administrative professional grammar and spelling tests since the individual will be required to produce documents free of grammatical and spelling errors. You cannot ask a person to take a math proficiency test unless the use of math is necessary in performing the job.

Train

The manager is responsible for two kinds of training— individual training and team training. Both types are discussed here.

Individual Training

Once a person is employed, the next step is to assist that person in gaining the knowledge necessary to be successful on the job. Certainly the individual comes in with a set of skills; however, remember that the person probably knows little or nothing about how your organization works. To be successful, that person must learn about proper company procedures. As a manager, you have an obligation in this area.

In addition to entry-level training, ongoing training for administrative professionals must also be provided as a result of the rapid changes in technology. The company, for example, may purchase a new software program. A new employee will also need training to become proficient on this software. Individuals within the organization or outside trainers may provide the training.

Another type of training for which a supervisor may be responsible is preparing employees for promotion. Company programs for promoting qualified workers can improve employee morale. Supervisors should watch for promising employees and use every opportunity to encourage and develop these employees. Additional training may be available through company-sponsored seminars, tuition-reimbursed courses at local colleges, or job internships in which an employee spends a period of time learning various jobs.

Team Training

The use of teams within the office demands that the manager be involved in team training. Teams often cannot function at their highest degree of productivity without acquiring some interpersonal skill development. These skills are generally necessary for all team members as they work together:

Ongoing training is essential.

- *Listening.* Summarizing, checking for understanding, and giving and receiving feedback
- *Resolving conflicts.* Identifying and resolving conflicts within the team or with individuals outside the team
- *Influencing others.* Gaining respect as a team and as individuals
- *Developing solutions.* Creatively generating and sorting through alternative solutions to issues
- *Ensuring ongoing quality.* Determining how results will be measured

In addition, a manager working with teams must take on the following responsibilities for the team to be successful:

- *Empower the team.* Give them the information needed to get the job done.
- *Trust the team.* Once the team has the information it needs, trust the team to produce the best possible solutions to problems.
- *Take a strong stand with the team when needed.* If the team is not accomplishing the task and is getting bogged down in personality issues, let them know that such behaviours are not acceptable.
- *Check on the team's development.* Are team members communicating with and trusting each other? Do they understand the goals of the team? Do they understand individual roles? Is every member involved in the process and product?

> ### Communication Tip
>
> Select an employee of the month. Honour that employee with a gift certificate, and place his or her picture in a prominent place for the month.

- *Do not micromanage.* To **micromanage** is to direct every small detail of another's work.

Motivate

Motivation comes from the Latin word meaning "to move." Motivation may be **extrinsic** (relying on factors such as salary increases or promotions) or **intrinsic** (coming from within the person—something gets done because it is right, fits the individual's values, and so on). Figure 17-5 on page 356 lists both intrinsic and extrinsic motivational factors that will help motivate others.

Delegate

Delegation means assigning tasks to others and then empowering them by providing the necessary information to get the job done. Delegation can be difficult for a manager, particularly one who has a need to control all aspects of a job. Yet no manager can possibly do it all. One widely accepted definition of management is "getting work done through others." Managers must delegate. Obviously, delegation means employees receive the proper information and training before being given a task. Once a task is delegated, employees should be trusted to perform.

Evaluate

Performance evaluation occurs whether or not there is a formal evaluation program. It is a consequence of the way jobs are designed and organizations are structured. Supervisors constantly observe the way people are performing. Most companies have formal evaluation periods in which personnel are evaluated every six months or every year. These evaluations may be individual evaluations, team evaluations, or work-group evaluations.

Individual Evaluation

Individual evaluations are essential even if team evaluations occur. Most companies use forms and processes developed for evaluations that come from the human resources department. This department may use a team within the company to develop the evaluation system. Once the evaluation process is developed, it should be followed consistently throughout the organization. Usually, the process involves an employee completing a self-evaluation and the supervisor preparing an evaluation. At the

■ Figure 17-5

MOTIVATIONAL TECHNIQUES

- *Set objectives.* Help the employees you supervise establish challenging, measurable objectives. Then help them commit themselves to achieving the objectives. This approach requires follow-through and planning on the part of the supervisor. You must not only know the objectives, but also follow up to see that the employee has achieved the objectives.
- *Give recognition.* As a supervisor, you need to become sensitive to the accomplishments of others. You can give recognition in a number of ways: verbal praise for a job well done, a thank-you letter written to an employee, and recognition in the organization's newsletter.

- *Develop a team.* Individuals need to be an accepted member of a group. As a supervisor, you can capitalize on this need by building a team of people who work together well. Productivity can be increased when every person in the group contributes to the overall effectiveness of the team.
- *Pay for the job.* As a supervisor, know what your employees do and then pay them fairly for their work. Reward employees who consistently give you outstanding performance with good salary increases.
- *Delegate work.* Employees enjoy doing meaningful and challenging work. Provide them this opportunity by delegating important projects to them.

---

evaluation conference, both evaluations are discussed and a final evaluation document is prepared. If the employee gives the supervisor new information that applies to the evaluation, the supervisor should accept that information and note it on the evaluation form. Read Figure 17-6 on page 357 carefully; the techniques provided will help you understand how to effectively evaluate employees.

Team Evaluation

Some companies use team evaluations in which employees who work together as a team are asked to evaluate each other. These may be given by the supervisors of the people involved in the team or discussed among the members only. If the members discuss the evaluation, the team leader needs to take a strong position in the process to ensure that the session does not become one of fault-finding or blaming others. Guidelines should be given to the team beforehand. The team leader should stress that the evaluation is meant to determine whether the team have completed their tasks successfully and what contributions were made by individual members.

Work-Group Evaluation

Work-group evaluations may also be a part of the evaluation process. Work groups should set measurable objectives that are related to the overall goals established by the organization. The manager and the work group might also evaluate what needs to be improved during the next six months or year by using a total quality approach. Here are some questions they might ask:

- *What needs to be improved?*
- *What actions should the work group take to improve the areas identified?*
- *Who does what and when is it done?* This stage is when the **action plan** is developed—it should list tasks to be achieved, including who is responsible for them and when each will be completed.
- *How do we know the action is working?* Once the action plan is implemented, it is monitored to determine if the desired results are achieved.
- *How can we ensure that the problem will not recur?* Once results are achieved, procedures, training, and other necessary measures are taken to ensure that the problem does not happen again.
- *What have we learned?* Areas where difficulties occurred should be reviewed so performance can improve.

■ Figure 17-6

EVALUATION TECHNIQUES

- *Evaluate performance on a day-to-day basis.* Employees should always know how they are doing. If a report or letter is not written or formatted correctly, let the employee know immediately. Praise a job well done. Give employees immediate feedback as to their performance. Do not save all criticism or all praise for a yearly evaluation session.
- *Allow adequate time for the evaluation.* The performance evaluation is important for both you and the employee. Set aside enough time on your calendar to do it well. You need to spend an hour or two with each employee. Hold the evaluation conference in an appropriate place. If you are using your office, ask that you not be interrupted and close the door to ensure privacy.
- *Give credit where credit is due.* Praise the employee for work well done. Too many managers consider an evaluation period a time for criticism only. It is not. It is a time to look at the total work of the employee. In what areas is the employee performing in an exemplary manner? In an average manner? Below expectations?
- *Be fair.* Analyze the employee's work on the basis of established criteria of performance, not of how well you like or dislike the employee. Stay away from personality traits. Stress job performance. When discussing

errors, suggest how the work could have been performed satisfactorily. Give the employee an opportunity to suggest possible alternatives. Word your comments as positively as possible. Do not say, for example, "Your performance is a problem." Instead, say "You are doing well in ... , but you need to improve in ... "

- *Listen to what the employee is saying.* Too often we listen to others with only half an ear. An employee may come to an evaluation session with a certain amount of anxiety and perhaps hostility. Let the person talk. By talking, the employee will release much of his or her anxiety and thus be more receptive to constructive criticism.
- *Avoid personal areas.* Sometimes a supervisor, with the best of intentions, will become too involved in the employee's personal life. Do not try to counsel an employee about problems that should be handled by a qualified professional.
- *Establish attainable objectives for improvement.* Help the employee set realistic objectives. A plan of action for improvement may be developed, including dates set for the accomplishment of each objective. Remember, this plan of action is a growth plan for improvement. Praise the employee for any resulting improvement.

Soft Skills: The Right to Lead

You have learned in this chapter that the effective leader has certain characteristics and is willing to follow a set of values to help the organization and its employees to learn and grow. You have learned that a number of management responsibilities are necessary in order for an organization to function efficiently. You have learned that there is a definite link between good leaders and good managers. Although management tasks are more concrete, each manager (in order to be the most effec-

tive) must have leadership characteristics—characteristics that keep the organization focused on doing what is right.

Needless to say, not all people have the characteristics mentioned in this chapter, and not all are interested in developing these traits. The process of learning how to lead is continual. No one is born with the right to lead; leadership is earned. It is individuals who consistently demonstrate a commitment to the skills defined in this chapter who earn that right.

Chapter Summary

The summary will help you remember the important points covered in the chapter.

- Leadership in the 21st century requires two unique skills—change mastery and an international perspective.
- An effective leader has these characteristics: understands self, builds a shared vision, lives by a set of values, commits to service, empowers others, rewards risk-taking, moves through chaos, and knows how to follow.
- Leadership is doing the right thing; management is doing things right.
- Although management responsibilities are more concrete and can be quantified, measured, and assessed, effective management and effective leadership are a blend. The effective manager is also an effective leader.
- Management responsibilities include planning, organizing, recruiting and employing, training, motivating, delegating, and evaluating.
- The process of learning how to lead is continual. No one is born with the right to lead. Only those who demonstrate a commitment to develop needed leadership characteristics earn that right.

Key Terms

The following terms were introduced in this chapter. The page on which the term was introduced is provided to help you locate the new term. Definitions are compiled in the Glossary at the end of the text.

- **interdependent** 348
- **power** 349
- **empowering** 349
- **bilateralness** 351
- **leadership** 351
- **management** 351
- **MBO** 352
- **tactical planning** 352
- **long-range planning** 352
- **span of control** 352
- **micromanage** 355
- **motivation** 355
- **extrinsic motivation** 355
- **intrinsic motivation** 355
- **delegation** 355
- **action plan** 356

Discussion Items

These discussion items provide an opportunity to test your understanding of the chapter through written responses and/or discussion with your classmates and your instructor.

1. List the characteristics of an effective leader.
2. Explain the difference between leadership and management.
3. Define the essential functions of management.
4. What is meant by MBO? Explain how it is used within an organization.
5. List five motivational factors.

Critical-Thinking Activity

Two months ago CanAsian offered you a position as records manager. You accepted the offer since the position matches your skills and career goals. Five individuals report to you. During the two months, two staff members have committed what you believe to be serious ethical violations. The situations are as follows.

Situation 1

One of your first responsibilities was to develop an electronic document system for personnel records. You asked two of your staff (Nazira and Theodore) to work with you on the project. As your team started to work, you reminded them of the confidential nature of the project, stating that no information could be shared with anyone. Two weeks into the project, Nazira reported she overheard Theodore discussing project details with two administrative professionals in the accounting department. He gave them details (including salaries, ages, and employment history) of three executives in the company.

Situation 2

Kami, one of the five members of your staff, worked overtime one evening on a project you assigned. You left the office at 5 p.m., but returned at 8 p.m. Kami was not working. She turned in the completed assignment the next morning. When Kami turned in her overtime for the week, she claimed overtime from 5 p.m. until 11 p.m. on that evening; overtime is paid at time-and-a-half.

How should you handle each situation? As you respond, ask yourself if you are living your values.

Projects

Project 17-1 *(Objectives 1 and 2)*

Collaborative Project

Work as a team with four of your classmates on this assignment. Interview two top-level executives (presidents or vice-presidents, if possible). Ask them the following questions:

- What are the characteristics of an effective leader?
- How did you develop your leadership skills?
- How is planning conducted in your organization?
- Do you provide ongoing training for your employees? If so, what types of opportunities do you provide?
- What process do you use to evaluate employees?

Summarize your findings and report them to the class.

Project 17-2 *(Objective 3)*

Assume you are in a leadership position, and identify the leadership values you would uphold and demonstrate to your employees. Add these values to your Professional Growth Plan disk, and save it under "Progro17-2."

Next, review all the Professional Growth Plans you developed during this course. Have you met your Plan objectives? Did you successfully complete all the items listed on your Plans? Write out a summary of what you intended to accomplish. Include an evaluation of your actual accomplishments and your future plans for professional growth. Submit this summary to your instructor.

Case Solution for Part 4

Valerie Cochran's Case Solution

When the senior partner first told me to send only nine copies of the appeal books to the Court, I knew this would not be sufficient. At that time I typed a memo of instruction to myself from him and had him sign that his instructions were for me to produce only nine copies of the books, rather than the required 20 copies. However, I disregarded his instructions and sent off the requisite 20 copies to our agent in Ottawa anyway.

When I informed the senior partner that I had already sent all 20 copies of the appeal books, he did realize that he had been rather unfair in his earlier instructions and appreciated the fact that I knew what to do and had done it, even though he had instructed otherwise. He left for Ottawa and won the case.

Glossary

ABM Automatic banking machine.

accountable items Express items; for example, items sent via FedEx, UPS, Purolator, and registered mail.

accounts payable The amount owed to a supplier or vendor for goods or services purchased on credit.

acronym A word formed from the initial letters of other words.

action plan A plan that includes specific tasks to be achieved, including who is responsible for each task identified and when the task will be completed.

active listening *Listening* for the meaning as well as to the words of the speaker.

ad hoc (special) committee A committee created to deal with a specific task or issue, which is dissolved once the task is complete.

adaptability The ability to adjust easily to change.

administrative professional Workplace support person. This occupation was formerly referred to as *secretary, receptionist*, and such specialized titles as *legal* and *medical secretaries*. Although these titles are still heard, due to shifting roles it is more common to use *administrative assistant, executive assistant, marketing assistant, payroll assistant, human resources assistant*, and *office manager*.

ADSL (asymmetric digital subscriber line) A form of DSL that supports peak downstream speeds of 144 Kbps to 2.2 Mbps and upstream rates from 90 Kbps to 640 Kbps.

aerobic Exercise that causes the body to use oxygen to produce the energy needed for the activity.

agenda An outline of what will occur at a meeting.

aikido The Japanese soft martial art.

alphabetic storage Uses letters of the alphabet to determine the order in which a *record* is filed.

alphabetizing Comparison of units in a *caption*, unit by unit and letter by letter, to determine a difference.

alphanumeric filing Using a combination of *alphabetic* and *numeric* characters in filing.

amendment Used to change the wording of a *motion* that has been made.

amoral Lacking moral judgment or sensibility; neither moral nor immoral.

annotate To make notations on a piece of mail concerning a previous action taken or facts that will assist the reader.

APA style Documentation guidelines established by the American Psychological Association.

aplomb Self-assurance.

appointment A time set aside for people to discuss an issue.

assets A list of what a company owns.

asymmetric digital subscriber line See *ADSL*.

Athlon A type of *processor chip* manufactured by Advanced Micro Devices.

ATM Automated teller machine.

attention faker A person who seems to listen to every word but actually does not hear much, if any, of what was said.

attitude Position, disposition, or manner with regard to a person or thing.

audioconferencing A type of conference in which participants talk with each other using standard telephones or speakerphones.

backbone The part of the network used as the main path for carrying traffic between network endpoints.

balance sheet A statement of a company's *assets*, *liabilities*, and *net worth*.

BCS Bar code sorter.

BF/PA "Bring forward/put away" system.

bilateralness Affecting two sides equally; two-sidedness.

blank endorsement The signature of the *payee* of a financial instrument.

Bluetooth A technology standard for short-range wireless communication.

body language Various meaningful body motions or gestures.

bonds Debt owed by an organization.

brainstorm To engage in problem solving.

broadband A *telecommunications* service that uses cable, DSL, wireless, and satellite connections. Short for "broad bandwidth," as in a high-speed network able to carry video as well as voice; *bandwidth* describes the throughput of a network per unit of *time*, and is measured in kilobits, megabits, or gigabits per second.

business-class accommodations A mode of air travel slightly more expensive than *economy class*, but less expensive than *first class*; located in front of economy class or directly behind first class.

bylaws The rules and procedures that govern the operation of an organization.

cable modem An external device that connects to a computer and to a service provider's coaxial cable line.

Canada Post Corporation Canada's postal service.

cancelled cheques Written cheques that have been cleared by the bank.

caption One or more *filing units* such as the entire name or a part of the name by which the *record* will be stored.

carpal tunnel syndrome A major occupational illness that occurs due to the compression of a large nerve, the median nerve, as it passes through a tunnel composed of bone and ligaments in the wrist.

cc Courtesy copy.

CD Compact disk.

CD-R Compact disk, recordable.

CD-ROM Compact disk, read-only memory.

CD-RW Compact disk, read and write.

cellular technology or **mobile wireless service** A technology that uses cells to relay information to a computer that in turn directs the call into the local telephone system; when a customer leaves one cell area and enters another, the computer automatically switches the transmission to the next-nearest cell.

cheque A legal document authorizing the bank to pay a specific sum to a designated *payee*.

cheque register A log used to record the details of each *cheque* written and deposit made.

chronic stress Occurs when a distressful situation is prolonged, allowing no rest or recuperation for the body; it can cause physical and emotional problems.

chronological filing The arrangement of *records* by date, usually by year, month, or day.

chronological résumé A *résumé* that lists a person's credentials in reverse chronological order.

circuit network A network in which each signal travels unbroken on its own end-to-end pipe. The phone system is a circuit network. See also *packet-switched network*.

circular arrangement An effective seating arrangement for minimizing status positions. Works well for small groups of from six to eight people.

coding Marking a *record* by the name, subject, location, or number determined in the *indexing* process.

cold canvass See *direct canvass*.

COLD Computer output to laser disk.

collating Assembling, in chronological order, the pages in a multiple page document.

combination-style résumé A *résumé* that presents experiences in reverse chronological skill set order.

compressed workweek A work arrangement in which employees work the usual number of hours (35 to 40), but the hours are compressed into four days. For example, a 35-hour week consists of three days of nine hours each and a fourth day of eight hours.

computer virus A program with unauthorized instructions that is introduced without permission or knowledge of the computer user.

computer vision syndrome A health problem that develops from screen glare.

confidentiality Secrecy of the information received or the confidences shared. Many firms require employees to sign a confidentiality agreement, to highlight the importance of this aspect to new employees.

conflict resolution Addressing and dealing with conflicts in a positive manner.

continuous Having no empty spaces between items.

continuous quality improvement (CQI) See *total quality management (TQM)*.

continuous speech recognition A computer voice recognition process that allows the user to speak in complete phrases and sentences to a computer.

copyright The exclusive right granted to the author or creator of an original body of work to reproduce or authorize someone else to reproduce the material.

cpm Copies per minute.

CQI or **continuous quality improvement** See *total quality management (TQM)*.

creativity Having the ability or the power to cause to exist.

critical thinking Conscious and deliberate inquiry. "Critical" comes from the Greek word *krinein*, which means "to separate, to choose."

crosstalk Interference on analog lines created by cables that are too close together.

CRT Cathode ray tube.

culture The ideas, customs, *values*, skills, and arts of a specific group of people.

current assets Cash, or *assets* such as accounts receivable or inventory, that can readily be converted into cash in a short period of time.

cuts Tabs on folders made in various widths.

database software Software that allows the user to organize, enter, process, index, sort, select, link to related files, store, and retrieve information.

decision The outcome or product of a problem, a concern, or an issue that must be addressed and solved.

defragmenter A utility that gathers the fragments of files scattered across the surface of the hard disk and reassembles them so that data is *continuous*.

delegation Assigning tasks to others and then *empowering* them by providing the necessary information to get the job done.

density The amount of data that can be stored on a disk; double-sided and high-density disks hold 1.44 *MB* of data.

dependability Trustworthiness. Examples are being at work on *time* if you are working at an established location; being productive when engaged in *telework*; willingness to put in additional time on important assignments; doing what you say you will do, and when you say you will do it.

deposit slip A form that accompanies a deposit and itemizes the amount of cash and/or value of *cheques* being deposited.

digital camera A camera that can become an input device with a PC, allowing the user to modify and print photographs in a variety of formats.

digital subscriber line (DSL) A technology that provides high-speed data communications over analog phone lines.

direct access A system that does not require referring to anything but the file to find the name.

direct approach Used when the *message* is favourable or neutral; it begins with the reason for the correspondence, continues with any needed explanation, and closes with a thank-you for the action that has been taken or with a request that action be taken by a specific date.

direct canvass or **cold canvass** Going directly to an organization without having an *appointment* or without knowing if a job is available.

discrete speech recognition A computer voice recognition process in which the user is required to pause between words.

discrimination Treatment or consideration based on class or category rather than individual merit.

document management software Assists in managing electronic, microimage, and paper filing *records*.

download To receive a file from another source and transfer the information to a hard drive or to receive a file via *e-mail*, a bulletin board, or an online service.

downsize To reduce the number of employees within a business.

downsizing Streamlining an organization so that it is more manageable and cutting *overhead costs*.

drawer The organization or person who has written a *cheque*.

DSL See *digital subscriber line*.

due process The requirement of managers to impose sanctions on employees only after offering them a chance to correct the organizational grievance.

duplexing In *reprographics*, copying on both sides of a sheet of paper.

DVD Digital versatile [or video] disk.

DVD-R Digital versatile [or video] disk, write once. A read/write version of DVD technology that can only be written to once.

DVD-RAM (digital versatile [or video] disk, random access memory) A read/write version of DVD technology that is also capable of reading *CD-ROMs*.

DVD-ROM Digital versatile [or video] disk, read-only memory.

DVD-RW Digital versatile [or video] disk, rewritable. A read/write version of DVD technology that can be written to more than once.

easily distracted Said of a person prone to be distracted by external or *internal noises* while another person is talking.

ecologically Pertaining to the relationship between human groups and their physical and social environment.

e-commerce Businesses that operate on the *Internet*.

economy-class accommodations The least expensive of the three classes of flight; seats are closer together, there is less legroom, and service is not as good as in *first class* or *business class*.

EFT See *electronic funds transfer*.

electronic calendar A computer program used for recording *appointments*, meetings, and other reminders. It includes a *database* feature that can be used to manage contacts in addition to a calendar.

electronic dry-erase whiteboard An *electronic whiteboard* connected to a computer but without a projector.

electronic funds transfer (EFT) A method whereby a bank uses computer technology to effect a transfer of funds.

electronic indexing Sorts the *records* and stores the information on the basis of one or more key fields.

electronic postmark A *Canada Post* digital date and time stamp, used to digitally "seal" an electronic package. It verifies the existence of a document and that it has not been opened by another party.

electronic résumé An online statement of one's background and experiences.

electronic tickler file A *tickler file* that can take the form of a computer calendar (for example, Microsoft Outlook) or a computer *database* (for example, Corel Quattro Pro).

electronic whiteboard A display screen connected to a computer on which multiple users write or draw; allows for visual and interactive input during a teleconference.

e-mail Electronic *message*, sent from one computer via a *broadband* pipeline to another computer.

emoticons Simulated faces produced by using the characters on the basic keyboard, used to communicate emotion, *tone*, or *attitude* in keyed text.

empathy Mentally entering into the feeling or spirit of a person.

employment application A form used by companies to obtain information about prospective employees' education, background, and experience.

employment at will The doctrine that allows employees to be fired for no valid cause, if the employer wishes to do so.

empowering The passing on of authority or responsibility.

endorsement See *endorsing a cheque*.

endorsing a cheque Signing a *cheque* on the reverse.

epost™ A secure and private Web-based service provided by *Canada Post Corporation* that allows consumers and businesses to view and pay bills over the *Internet*.

ergonomics The study of the fit between people, the tools they use, and the physical setting in which they work. For example, ergonomics can help in the design of office furniture and equipment that is physiologically sound so that the user remains healthy while using it. The Greek words *ergos* and *nomos* were combined to coin the word.

ergos A Greek word meaning "work"; *ergos* and *nomos* were combined to coin the word *ergonomics*.

e-stamps Postage via the Web to a PC. Also known as *PC postage*.

ethics The systematic study of moral conduct, duty, and judgment.

etymologists Specialists in the study of words.

euro The standard currency of Belgium, Germany, Spain, France, Ireland, Italy, Luxembourg, the Netherlands, Austria, Portugal, and Finland.

evaluation Careful judgment.

executive summary A one- or two-page summary of a report.

exit interview An interview done by the employer when an employee leaves the company.

external noise Physical sounds that hinder the *listening* process, such as traffic sounds.

extranet A private network that belongs to an organization such as a bank, and requires the authorization of selected external people for them to use it.

extrinsic motivation An impulse to action coming from outside the person, such as a possible salary increase or promotion.

favourable messages *Messages* the reader will be pleased to receive.

fax machine Short for *facsimile machine*, which electronically sends an image of an original document from one location to another via communication networks.

feedback *Responses* consisting of clarifying statements and questions.

fee-paid Jobs for which the employer pays a fee.

filing unit A part of an individual's or a company's name used for filing.

firewall Software that prevents unauthorized outside individuals from using an *intranet* or an *extranet*.

first-class accommodations The most expensive of the three classes of airline flights and the most luxurious.

fixed assets Land, buildings, or equipment that will only be used up over the length of the life of the organization.

fixed wireless or **WLL (wireless local loop)** A *broadband* connection system that uses high-frequency radio links to deliver voice and data.

flattened organizational structures A form of organization with fewer *management* levels than the traditional structures of the past.

flexibility Being responsive to change.

flextime approach The staggering of working hours to enable an employee to work the full quota of time but at periods defined by the company and the individual. Flextime helps to reduce traffic congestion at the traditional peak hours and allows employees needed *flexibility* in their schedules.

floppy disks Small external storage mediums for a PC.

focus groups People brought together to talk with an interviewer about their opinions of certain events or issues.

follow-up letter A letter thanking the prospective employer for an interview and reviewing points of special interest.

frequent flyer program An incentive program offered by most airlines that provides a variety of awards after the accumulation of a certain number of mileage points.

full endorsement Permits a *cheque* to be transferred from the original *payee* to another payee.

functional résumé A *résumé* that highlights and emphasizes skills; chronological order is not a consideration.

GB Gigabytes; billion-byte units.

genome The genetic blueprint of humanity.

geographic filing Arranging *records* by geographic location.

girth A measurement of the thickest part of a parcel.

goal An objective, a purpose, or an end to be achieved.

guarantor A person who can confirm the identity of an applicant.

hard copy Copy printed on paper.

heterogeneous group A group having dissimilar backgrounds and experiences.

high-end protein analyzers The sequence of the amino acids that make up proteins.

high-volume copiers Copiers that produce from 100 000 to 400 000 copies per month.

homogeneous group A group of people with similar backgrounds and experiences.

hot keys User-defined combinations of keystrokes that provide quick access to computer commands or menus.

Human Resources and Development Canada A federal public employment agency whose services are provided to customers free of charge.

IDSL See *Internet digital subscriber line*.

important records *Records* that are necessary to an orderly continuation of a business and are replaceable only with considerable expenditure of *time* and money.

income statement A summary of an organization's income, expenses, and profit or loss over a specified period of *time*.

indexing Determining how a *record* is to be filed: by name, subject, number, or *geographic* location.

indirect approach Used when one is delivering a *message* that is unfavourable. One begins with an opening statement that is pleasant but neutral, reviews the circumstances, gives the information, and then closes on a pleasant and positive note.

inference The process of deriving logical conclusions from premises known or assumed to be true.

information age A term that characterizes the present day, which is a time of tremendous explosion of knowledge.

initiative The ability to, on your own, start a plan or task and ensure its completion. It means having the ability to set your own work *goals*.

inkjet A type of computer printer that works by spraying ink onto the paper.

inspecting Checking to see that correspondence is ready to be filed.

insular Narrow or provincial in outlook.

integrated packages All-in-one software that combines *database* with spreadsheet and word-processing programs so users can easily move stored information from one application to another.

integrity Adherence to a code of behaviour.

interactivity Information transmitted from one location to another and acted on by participants at any location.

interdependent Dependent on each other.

internal noise Distractions that occur inside a listener as a result of his or her background, experiences, perceptions, problems, or issues, and that cause misinterpretation of communications.

Internet digital subscriber line A form of *DSL* that transfers data upstream and downstream at rates of 144 Kbps and does not have the strict distance limitations of *ADSL* and SDSL.

Internet The world's largest group of connected computers, allowing people from all over the world to communicate.

intranet A private network that belongs to an organization and is accessible only by the organization's employees.

intrinsic motivation An impulse to action coming from within the person, such as a desire to excel.

invoice A notice prepared by a vendor or seller of money the recipient owes to it in exchange for goods or services.

itinerary A detailed outline of a trip showing all the arrangements, including flight numbers, airports, departure and arrival times, hotels, car rental information, *appointments*, and so on.

Jaz disk External storage for a PC that holds 1 *GB* of data.

jet lag The feeling of exhaustion following a flight through several time zones.

job sharing A work arrangement in which two part-time employees perform a job that otherwise would be held by one full-time employee.

key unit The primary or first unit used in *alphabetizing*.

keywords Words that uniquely identify a file in an electronic system so one can find it by *querying* the system in a variety of ways.

krinein. The Greek word from which the "critical" in *critical thinking* is derived; it means "to separate, to choose."

LANs Local area networks. LANs link various types of technological equipment within a building or several buildings within the same geographic area.

laptops Portable computers.

laser A type of computer printer that uses a beam of light to form images on paper.

LCD Liquid crystal display; used in a certain type of computer monitor.

leadership skills Leadership is the ability to guide, direct, or influence people. An effective leader must unite followers to a shared vision. According to W. Edwards Deming, the aim of leadership should be to help people and machines and gadgets to do a better job. Leadership skills are developed over *time.*

letter of application Letter applying for a job, with the *goal* of arousing the prospective employer's interest, describing the abilities of the person writing the letter, and requesting an interview.

liabilities A list of what a company owes.

lifelong learning A commitment to continue to learn throughout one's life.

liquidity order The order of listing *current assets* before *fixed assets.*

listening The complete process by which verbal language, communicated by a source, is received, recognized, attended to, comprehended, and retained.

local area networks See *LANs.*

long-range planning Setting *goals* and objectives for a three-to-five-year period.

low-volume copiers Copiers that typically produce from 12 to 30 copies per minute.

mainframes Large computers capable of processing great amounts of information at high speed (although the speed is less than that of *supercomputers*).

management Leading and directing an organization or department, by means of human, financial, material, and/or other resources.

MANs Metropolitan area networks; link technological equipment over a distance equal to the size of a city and its surroundings.

manual calendar Loose-leaf or wire-bound pocket or desktop calendar used for handwritten entries of *appointments*, meetings, and other reminders. They are available in a variety of sizes and can be customized to create a unique system.

manual tickler file A *tickler file* that in the office can take the form of a hard-copy calendar or a card file.

MB Megabytes; million-byte units.

MBO *Management* by objectives.

merger mania Mergers occurring nationally and internationally at rates never heard of previously.

message The idea being presented by the *originator* of a communication.

metropolitan area networks See *MANs.*

microcomputer The smallest of the computer systems, commonly called a PC (personal computer).

microfiche A sheet of film containing a series of images arranged in grid patterns.

microfilm A roll of film containing a series of frames or images.

micromanage To direct every small detail of another's work.

microprocessor A single miniature chip that contains the circuitry and components for arithmetic, logic, and control operations.

mid-volume copiers Copiers that run from 5000 to 85 000 copies per month.

minicomputer A midrange computer.

minutes A written *record* of a meeting.

mission statement A statement that lists what an individual or organization *values* and the future direction intended.

MLA style Documentation guidelines established by the Modern Language Association.

mnemonic device A formula, word association, or rhyme used to assist the memory.

mobile telework A term used to describe the arrangement of individuals who spend a great deal of *time* travelling and/or on customers' premises.

mobile wireless service See *cellular technology.*

monthly bank statement A document provided by financial institutions detailing deductions and deposits on one's bank account. It may also be accompanied by all *cancelled cheques.*

monthly statement A document prepared by a vendor or seller listing purchases and payments made during the month.

morality A set of ideas of right and wrong.

moribund In a state of dying.

motion A formal expression during a meeting of a proposal or an action to be undertaken. It requires a mover (someone who makes the motion) and a seconder (someone who is in favour of discussing the motion). After debate, a motion is voted upon by the meeting participants. It must be recorded verbatim in the *minutes* of the meeting.

motivation What causes individuals to want to accomplish a task.

multiculturalism Being aware of and sensitive to the various cultural differences and backgrounds.

multinational corporations Corporations that operate both within and outside Canada.

multiuser computers Computers able to serve several users at the same *time*.

mutual funds Funds that include a combination of *stocks* and *bonds* purchased through a mutual fund company.

net worth The difference between *assets* and *liabilities*.

networked printers Printers attached to a *LAN*.

networking software A powerful set of applications that operates on a company's network. It includes *e-mail*, calendaring, and contact management, and provides the members of an organization with the tools to organize, schedule, and collaborate.

networking The process of identifying and maintaining contact with acquaintances, friends, and relatives who can assist you in the job search process.

noise Anything that creates distortion in a *message* and prevents the *receiver* from properly understanding it. See also *external noise* and *internal noise*.

nomos A Greek word meaning "natural laws"; *ergos* and *nomos* were combined to coin the word *ergonomics*.

nonessential records *Records* that have no future value to an organization.

non-judgmental Tending not to judge an individual on the basis of *culture*, *values*, background, intelligence, appearance, or other characteristics.

notebooks Portable computers.

numeracy skills Skill in the use of numbers and mathematics. In the office, it can be defined as the ability to decide what needs to be measured or calculated, to observe and record data using appropriate methods, tools, and technology, and to make estimates and verify calculations.

numeric method A method of filing *records* by assigning numbers to them.

offset Not folded to the edge of the paper.

online meetings Meetings that link participants by computer; also referred to as *computer conferencing*, *keyboard conferencing*, *Web conferencing*, and *data conferencing*.

originator The original sender of a *message*.

outguesser Someone who always tries to finish the statement or thought of the individual communicating.

outside facilitator or **remote facilitator** A person trained in facilitation techniques who is not part of the *decision* making of a meeting and whose role is to keep the meetings productive, positive, and efficient.

outsourced See *outsourcing*.

outsourcing The cost-cutting measure of getting an outside company or a consultant to take over the performance of a part of an organization's business or to complete a project. Used extensively today.

overhead costs Salary and benefit costs.

oxymoron A combination of contradictory terms.

packet-switched network A network in which each signal (whether it carries music or video or *e-mail*) is chopped into tiny digital parcels that are commingled with other packets and routed to their destinations. The *Internet* is a packet-switched network. See also *circuit network*.

Palm One of the leading manufacturers of PDAs.

palms Another name for PDAs.

parallelism A good practice in writing: making sure grammatically equivalent forms are used consistently.

paraphrase To restate a *message* in different words.

parliamentary procedures The procedural rules that ensure all participants have a voice and vote in the *decision*-making process.

passport An official government document that certifies the identity and citizenship of an individual and grants the person permission to travel abroad.

payee The organization or person to whom a *cheque* is written.

pc Photocopy.

PC Personal computer.

PC postage Postage via the *Web* to a PC. Also known as *e-stamps*.

PDA See *personal digital assistant*.

Pentium processor A type of *processor chip* manufactured by Intel.

per diem Latin for "per day"; the expression is used in conjunction with how much a company is willing to reimburse an individual for travel.

perfectionism A propensity for setting extremely high standards and being displeased with anything else.

performance appraisals *Evaluations* of employees done by the employer.

periodic transfer The transfer of active *records* to inactive status at the end of a stated period of time. See also *perpetual transfer*.

perpetual transfer The *continuous* transfer of active *records* to inactive status. See also *periodic transfer*.

personal digital assistant A small *PC* that can be held in the palm of your hand.

personal information management (PIM) A type of software that allows you to manage a wide variety of information:

manage your schedule, address book, and to-do list; track your contacts and keep detailed histories of your business contacts; and handle documents you have downloaded from the Internet or from another source.

persuasive approach An *indirect approach* used in a communication. It begins with the *you approach*, continues by creating an interest and desire, and closes by asking for the desired action.

persuasive messages *Messages* that attempt to get the reader to take some action.

petty cash fund A fund established to handle the payment of purchases of small incidental business office items.

physically challenged Having a physical handicap.

PIM See *personal information management.*

pixels The smallest visible element of a picture on a computer screen; usually a coloured dot.

Pollyanna attitude A foolishly or blindly optimistic *attitude.*

portfolio A compilation of samples of an individual's work.

postdated Dated for some time in the future, not today. Said of *cheques.*

PosteCS™ A service provided by *Canada Post Corporation* that helps businesses communicate privately and confidentially over the *Internet.*

POTS (plain old telephone service) Carries signals through standard telephone-line technology from one telephone unit to another.

power The ability or official capacity to exercise control.

PowerPC A type of *processor chip* manufactured by Apple.

pragmatic Relating to actual practice in day-to-day activities, as opposed to theory.

preauthorized automated transfer A transfer method used to make regular payments on accounts where the amount *invoiced* each month is constant.

prejudice A system of negative beliefs, feelings, and actions.

primary research The collecting of original data through surveys, observations, or experiments.

primary storage See *RAM.*

private employment agencies Privately owned employment agencies that charge a fee (either of the employer or the client) when providing services.

processor chip A type of *microprocessor* that provides for increased speed and performance capability of a *PC.*

procrastination The postponement or needless delay of a project or task that must be done.

proprietary data Data owned/originated by people or organizations.

query To ask an electronic filing system to display certain information.

question A technique used to understand *verbal communication.* In questioning, you: gain information; understand the other person's point of view; build trust; verify information.

quorum The minimum number of participants required to be present at a meeting before *decisions* can officially be made.

RAM Random access memory; also known as *primary storage.*

readability The degree of ease of comprehension of a *message.*

real time A way of collaborating online, by which individuals can simultaneously work on electronically produced documents such as presentations, spreadsheets, reports, and proposals.

receiver The person for whom a *message* is intended.

record Any type of recorded information.

records management The systematic control of *records* from their creation to their final disposition.

records storage systems A method of filing *records* that includes *alphabetic*, *numeric*, and *alphanumeric* systems.

rectangular arrangement A seating arrangement that allows the leader to maintain control.

remote employment Any working arrangement in which the worker performs a significant portion of work at some fixed location other than the traditional workplace.

remote facilitator See *outside facilitator.*

reprographics An inclusive term used to refer to the copying process.

resolution (1) A formal expression of opinion or direction of an organization. (2) The quality of a digital picture. (3) The act of addressing and dealing with a problem.

response *Feedback*; lets the *originator* know whether the communication is understood. May be verbal or nonverbal.

response rate The percentage of people responding to a survey or questionnaire.

restrictive endorsement The highest level of protection and "restricts" what can be done with the *cheque.*

résumé A concise statement of a person's background, education, skills, and experience that is sent with his or her *letter of application* when seeking a job.

rightsize To determine the most efficient and effective number of employees and organizational structure.

routine messages *Messages* that have a neutral effect on the *receiver.* See also *favourable messages* and *unfavourable messages.*

RRSPs Registered retirement savings plans.

RSI Repetitive *stress* injury, a generic name given to injuries that occur over a period of time. Also known as *overuse disorders.*

SDSL See *symmetric digital subscriber line.*

secondary research Data or material other people have discovered and reported via the *Internet*, books, periodicals, and various other publications.

self-employed teleworker Individual owner not employed by an organization.

self-management Having self-knowledge, managing *time* and *stress*, balancing work and personal life, understanding *values*, and articulating *goals.*

semicircular or **U-shaped arrangement** A seating arrangement that works well for small groups of from six to eight people.

sexual harassment Persistent torment arising from sexual conduct that is unwelcome by the recipient. May be either physical or verbal.

shareware or **trial software** Software that can be *downloaded* from the Web for a set trial period to determine if the program meets your needs.

shredder A machine that cuts paper into strips or confetti-like material.

sleep deprivation Denying the physical body the proper amount of sleep for a long period of time. Results in deterioration of physical health.

soft copy Copy shown on the monitor only; used when a printed copy is not necessary.

soft skill A business-related nontechnical skill. *Critical thinking* is considered a soft skill. Others are *verbal communication*, human relations, and *time*, *stress*, and organizational *management* skills.

space A nonverbal communicator indicating a person's status, function, or need. In a traditional hierarchically organized firm, for example, people who have the same level of position may be allocated the same amount of space. See also *territoriality*.

spamming Forwarding unwanted or junk *e-mail* to someone who has not requested it.

span of control The number of employees directly supervised by one person.

staledated Said of a *cheque* written more than six months ago. Such a cheque is not honoured by the bank.

stand-alone conventional dry-erase boards Whiteboards used without connection to a computer or a projector; similar to a standard classroom whiteboard.

standing committee An ongoing committee created to deal with a longstanding matter.

state-of-the-art technology The latest technology available—for example, wireless communications and voice-activated technology.

stereotype To evaluate an entire group of people or things according to a perception or an image held, which may be favourable or unfavourable.

stocks Certificates or book entries representing ownership in a company.

strategic thinking The application of experience and wants and needs to determine a future direction.

streaming media Media that enable you to process information as it arrives, as opposed to waiting until all of it has reached your computer—like listening to *Internet* radio or watching online television as the signal comes in.

stress The body's response to a demand placed upon it.

subject filing Arranging *records* by their subject.

substance abuse The use of alcohol or drugs to an extent that is debilitating.

supercomputers The most powerful and expensive of the *mainframes*.

SuperDisk External storage for a PC that holds 120 *MB* of data.

supermicro See *workstation computers*.

surge suppressor A device that keeps power fluctuations from crippling computer equipment.

symmetric digital subscriber line (SDSL) A form of *DSL* that transfers data upstream and downstream at symmetric rates of up to 2.3 Mbps over a single copper twisted-pair line.

synergy The ideas and products of a group of people developed through interaction with each other.

tactical planning Setting *goals* and objectives for a one-year period.

talker A person who in communicating has difficulty waiting for the other person to finish so he or she can begin talking.

TB *Terabytes*; trillion-byte units.

team A group of people working together. The word can be traced back to the Indo-European word *deuk*, meaning "to pull"; and obviously, if teams are to be successful, individual team members must "pull together."

telecommunications The electronic transmission of text, data, voice, video, and images (graphics and pictures) from one location to another.

telecommuting The work style of salaried employees (employees paid by organizations for either full- or part-time work) who work at home for part or all of the workweek rather than going to a business office.

teleconferencing A general term applied to a variety of technology-assisted two-way (interactive) communications via telephone lines, DSL, *cable modems*, and other high-bandwidth connections.

telework The use of *telecommunications* to work from a home office, a client's office, or a multitude of other locations. A broader term than *telecommuting*.

temporary agency A company that makes temporary workers available to employers.

terabyte (TB) One trillion bytes.

teraflop One trillion operations per second.

terminal-digit filing A *numeric* filing order in which the final digits of a number are used as the first *filing unit*.

territoriality Laying claim to a certain *space* and defending that claim.

tickler file A chronological *record* of items to be completed; used to "tickle" your memory and remind you to take certain actions.

time A resource that cannot be bought, sold, borrowed, rented, saved, or manufactured; it is the only resource that must be spent the minute it is received.

time management Directing ourselves and our tasks in relation to the *time* we have available in a day, a week, or a year.

tone The manner of expression in writing, which communicates the writer's *attitude* toward the subject matter.

topic sentence The sentence that contains the main idea of a paragraph; it is often the first sentence.

total quality management (TQM) The principle of continued improvement in an organization. Developed by Dr. W. Edwards Deming, an American statistician.

touch screen A computer screen that allows the user to input data by touching the screen with a finger or a pointer.

TQM team See *team*; *TQM*.

trial software See *shareware*.

troubleshooting Tracing and correcting computer or software problems.

unfavourable messages *Messages* that bring a negative reaction from the reader.

uninterruptible power supply (UPS) A device that keeps power fluctuations from crippling computer equipment.

unit See *filing unit*.

UPS See *uninterruptible power supply*.

useful records *Records* that are useful for the smooth, effective operation of an organization.

U-shaped arrangement See *semicircular arrangement*.

values Our beliefs that determine how we live on a day-to-day basis.

verbal communication The process of exchanging ideas and feelings through the use of words.

videoconferencing A system of transmitting audio and video between individuals at distant locations.

virtual company A company in which all or most all of the staff members work from home.

virtual conferencing Another term for *videoconferencing* since it allows participants to enter and move around rooms electronically.

virtual interview An interview via technology with an interviewer at a distant location.

virtual office The operational domain of any organization that includes remote workers.

virtual private network (VPN) An authentication, encryption, and data-packaging technology that lets private network traffic travel over the public networks.

virtual teams Dispersed workers who come together through *telecommunications* technology to accomplish a task.

virus See *computer virus*.

visa A document granted by a government abroad that permits a traveller to enter and travel within a country.

vital records *Records* that cannot be replaced and should never be destroyed.

voice over Internet protocol (VoIP) Software and hardware that allow voice signals to be carried over an IP-based network, with *POTS* quality and reliability.

voice quality The loudness or softness of the voice, the pitch of the voice, and the enunciation of the words.

VoIP See *voice over Internet protocol*.

voucher cheque A *cheque* that includes a form for recording the details of the payment.

VPN See *virtual private network*.

walled garden The practice by which an *Internet* service giant such as AOL gives customers easier access to its own and its partners' content than to that of its competitors.

WANs Wide area networks; link technological equipment over an area of hundreds of thousands of kilometres.

Web browser Software that provides a way to look at and interact with all the information on the *World Wide Web* in a single unified interface.

Web See *World Wide Web*.

Wi-Fi Abbreviation for *wireless fidelity*, the popular term for a high-frequency *LAN* that connects users of portable computer devices to the *Internet*.

wireless local area network (WLAN) A *LAN* that wirelessly connects various types of technological equipment within a building or several buildings within the same geographic area.

WLAN See *wireless local area network*.

WLL (wireless local loop) See *fixed wireless*.

workstation computers (supermicros) The upper-end machines of the *microcomputer*.

World Wide Web A huge collection of computer files scattered across the *Internet* (by some estimates there are now more than a billion websites).

WORM Write once, read many. Describes a medium, such as a *CD-R*, that can write data onto its the surface only once.

Xpresspost A postal service for which items cannot exceed 30 kilograms in weight and the maximum size for any item is 3 metres in combined length and *girth*.

you approach A communication method that requires the communicator to put the recipient at the centre of the *message*; *you* and *your* are used rather than *I* or *we*.

Zip disk External storage for a PC; holds 100 and 250 *MB* of data.

Zip drive Removable drive for *Zip disk*.

Endnotes

Chapter 1

1. Susan Crowley, "Hello to Our Future," *AARP Bulletin*, 3 (January 2000): 14–15.
2. Anne D'Innocenzio, "Financial Powerhouses Pushing Smart Cards," *The Grand Rapids Press*, December 25, 2000, p. A9.
3. Census 2001, www.statcan.ca, accessed April 2004.
4. Conference Board of Canada, "Performance and Potential 2002–2003," *Canada 2010: Challenges and Choices at Home and Abroad* (series) (Ottawa: Conference Board of Canada, 2002), available www.hrpartnership.adians.ca/default.asp?mn=1.8.18, accessed July 26, 2004.
5. "Performance and Potential 2002–2003."
6. "Performance and Potential 2002–2003."
7. "Office of the Future: 2005," International Association of Administrative Professionals (IAAP) site, www.iaap-hq.org, accessed January 15, 2001.
8. Census 2001, www.statcan.ca, accessed April 2004.
9. Laurier Institution, "Youth 2010: The BC Labour Market in the Future" (Vancouver: The Laurier Institution, 2000), www.rkunin.com/y2010, accessed July 26, 2004.
10. Christopher Conte, "New Focus on Older Workers," *AARP Bulletin*, January 2000, p. 2611.
11. Census 2001, www.statcan.ca, accessed April 2004.
12. Statistics Canada and Human Resources Development Canada, "The Evolving Workplace Series: Part-Time Work and Family Friendly Practices in Canadian Workplaces," Catalogue No. 71-581-MIE, 2003.
13. Richard Paul, *Critical Thinking: How to Prepare Students for a Rapidly Changing World* (Dillon Beach, CA: Foundation for Critical Thinking, 1993), pp. 17–36.

Chapter 2

1. Statistics Canada and Human Resources Development Canada, "The Evolving Workplace Series: Part-Time Work and Family Friendly Practices in Canadian Workplaces," Catalogue No. 71-581-MIE, 2003.
2. Ginger Kaderabek, "Office Sweet Office," *Computer Buyer's Guide and Handbook*, January 2001, p. 80.
3. "Office Sweet Office," p. 80.
4. "Telework America (TWA) 2000—Research Results," International Telework Association & Council site, www.telecommute.org/twa2000/research_results_summary.shtml, accessed March 3, 2001.
5. "OSH Answers: Telework/Telecommuting," Canadian Centre for Occupational Health and Safety site, www.ccohs.ca/oshanswers/hsprograms/telework.html, accessed July 26, 2004.
6. "AREVO (Advocates for Remote Employment and the Virtual Office)," 1996, www.globaldialog.com/~morse/arevo/index.htm, accessed March 3, 2001.
7. "Office Sweet Office," p. 81.
8. "Telecommuting (or Telework): Alive and Well or Fading Away?" International Telework Association & Council site, www.telecommute.org/aboutitac/alive.shtm, accessed March 6, 2001.
9. Stephen R. Covey, Roger Merrill, and Rebecca R. Merrill, *First Things First* (New York: Simon & Schuster, 1994) pp. 307–314.
10. *First Things First*, pp. 307–314.
11. Alice Bredin, *The Home Office Solution* (New York: John Wiley & Sons, 1998), pp. 38–42.
12. Kevin Daniels, David A. Lamond, and Peter Standen, eds., *Managing Telework* (London: Thomson International, 2000).
13. *Managing Telework*.
14. "OSH Answers: Office Ergonomics," Canadian Centre for Occupational Health and Safety site, www.ccohs.ca/oshanswers/ergonomics/office, accessed July 26, 2004.

Chapter 3

1. "The Aventis Healthcare Survey," May 2, 2001, available www.ipsos-reid.com, accessed July 2003.
2. "The Aventis Healthcare Survey."
3. Andrea Atkins, "Laughing Matters," *World Traveler*, November 1997, pp. 53–56.
4. "OSH Answers: OH&S Legislation in Canada—Due Diligence," Canadian Centre for Occupational Health and Safety site, www.ccohs.ca/oshanswers/legisl/diligence.html, accessed July 26, 2004.
5. CanOSH (Canada's National Occupational Health and Safety) site, www.canoshweb.org/en/legislation.html, accessed July 26, 2004.
6. "Anger Management Toolkit," AngerMgmt.com, www.angermgmt.com/measure.html, accessed July 26, 2004.

Chapter 4

1. Nancy Gibbs, "Baby, It's You! And You, And You …," *Time*, February 19, 2001, pp. 47–57, available www.time.com/time/europe/eu/article/0,13716,99079,00.html, accessed July 26, 2004.
2. "Company Profile," George Weston Limited site, www.weston.ca/en/abt_corprof.html, accessed July 26, 2004.

3. "Company Overview," Sun Life Assurance Company of Canada site, www.sunlife.com, accessed July 2003.
4. "Strategic Directions 2003–2006," Atlantic Health Sciences Corporation site, www.ahsc.health.nb.ca/strategicdirections03-06.pdf, accessed July 26, 2004.
5. "Mission Statement," Sun Life Financial Services site, www.sunlife.com, accessed July 2003.
6. Nedra Pickler, "Firestone Knew About Tire Problems," *King County Journal*, September 7, 2000, www.kingcountyjournal.com/sited/story/html/28445, accessed July 26, 2004.
7. Crayola Canada, www.crayola.com/canada, accessed July 2003.

Chapter 5

1. Census 2001, "Analysis Series—Canada's Ethnocultural Portrait: The Changing Mosaic," www12.statcan.ca/english/census01/products/analytic/companion/etoimm/contents.cfm, accessed July 26, 2004.
2. Conference Board of Canada, "Performance and Potential 2002–2003," *Canada 2010: Challenges and Choices at Home and Abroad* (series) (Ottawa: Conference Board of Canada, 2002), available www.hrpartnership.adians.ca/default.asp?mn=1.8.18, accessed July 26, 2004.
3. Robert Rosen and others, *Cultural Literacy* (New York: Simon & Schuster, 2000), p. 175.
4. Robert Rosen, Patricia Digh, Marshall Singer, and Carl Phillips, *Global Literacies: Lessons on Business Leadership and National Cultures* (New York: Simon & Schuster, 2000), p. 174.
5. Don Tapscott, *Growing Up Digital: The Rise of the Net Generation* (New York: McGraw-Hill, 1998), p. 9.
6. Stephen R. Covey, *Principle-Centered Leadership* (New York: Summit Books, 1990), pp. 45–46.
7. Roger E. Axtell, *Dos and Taboos of Humor Around the World* (New York: John Wiley & Sons, Inc. 1999), pp. 99–100.

Chapter 6

1. Geoffrey Colvin, "Should Companies Care?" *Fortune*, June 11, 2001, p. 60.
2. Stanley Bing, "Walk Now, Chew Gum Later," *Fortune*, September 17, 2001, pp. 61–62.

Chapter 7

1. John Kao, *Jamming: The Road to Creativity* (New York: Harper Business, 1996).

Chapter 8

1. "Corporate Profile," TELUS site, www.telus.com, accessed July 2003.

2. "Household Internet Use Survey," *The Daily*, July 25, 2002, www.statcan.ca, accessed July 2003.
3. D. April, "Internet by Cable," *The Connectedness Series* (Ottawa: Statistics Canada, 2000), available www.e-com.ic.gc.ca/epic/internet/inecic-ceac.nsf/en/gv00172e.html, accessed July 26, 2004.
4. "Internet by Cable."
5. H. Ertl and H. McCarrell, "The State of Telecommunications Services," *The Connectedness Series* (Ottawa: Statistics Canada, 2002), available www.e-com.ic.gc.ca/epic/internet/inecic-ceac.nsf/en/gv00172e.html, accessed July 26, 2004.

Chapter 9

1. Pamela Sherrid, "Bytes and Bits Meet Biotech," *U.S. News & World Report*, April 16, 2001, p. 33.
2. "Worldwide PDA Forecast 1998–2008," *eTForecasts*, September 2002, www.etforecasts.com/products/ES_pdas.htm, accessed July 26, 2004.
3. Richard A. Spinello, *Cyberethics: Morality and Law in Cyberspace* (Massachusetts: Jones and Bartlett Publishers, 2000), p. 120.

Chapter 11

1. "Technology and Banking: A Survey of Consumer Attitudes," Canadian Bankers Association site, www.cba.ca/en/viewdocument.asp?fl=3&sl=142&docid=408&pg=1, accessed July 26, 2004.
2. "Technology and Banking: A Survey of Consumer Attitudes."
3. "Technology and Banking: A Survey of Consumer Attitudes."
4. "HSBC in the Community," HSBC Bank Canada site, www.hsbc.ca/hsbc/business_en/in-the-community, accessed July 26, 2004.

Chapter 12

1. Dianna Booher, *E-WRITING: 21st-Century Tools for Effective Communication* (New York: Simon & Schuster, Inc., 2001), p. 51.

Chapter 16

1. Myrena S. Jennings, Lana W. Carnes, and Vicki K. Whitaker, "Online Employment Applications: Employer Preferences and Instructional Implications," *Business Education Forum*, February 2001, pp. 34–35.

Chapter 17

1. Peter F. Drucker, *The Practice of Management* (New York: HarperBusiness, 1993).

Index